CUP FINAL EXTRA!

CUP FINAL EXTRA!

by Martin Tyler

HAMLYN
London·New York·Sydney·Toronto

The photographs on the cover, endpapers and preliminary pages of this book are as follows
Cover: The Arsenal and West Ham United teams being led out on to the arena for the Cup final of 1980
Front endpapers: The first Wembley final in 1923, with the crowds covering the pitch before the game
Half-title page: The Huddersfield Town and Preston North End captains shaking hands before the final of 1922
Title page: Fifty years ago: Arsenal being presented to His Majesty King George V before the 1930 final
Back endpaper: The Arsenal team posing with the Football Association Challenge Cup, after winning in 1979

ACKNOWLEDGEMENTS

The Publishers would like to thank all those newspapers whose stories and photographs have been reproduced in this book for their kind permission to reprint this material.

Whilst every effort has been made by The Publishers to contact the owners of photographs reprinted, in some cases they have been unsuccessful and copyright holders are invited to contact the Publishers direct.

The Publishers would also like to thank the following individuals for their valuable assistance:
Frank Campbell, Secretary of Queen's Park Football Club
Stephen G. Wilkinson

Most of the newspapers were photographed at the British Library for the Hamlyn Group by Graham Portlock. Special colour photography was by Peter Loughran

Photographic Acknowledgements

Associated Newspapers Ltd, BBC Hulton Picture Library, British Library, Central Press Photos, Colorsport, Martin Corrie, Fox Photos Ltd, Keystone Press Agency, London Weekend Television, Mary Evans Picture Library, Popperfoto, Portsmouth and Sunderland Newspapers Ltd, Royal School of Military Engineering Photographic Section, Syndication International, Wembley Stadium Ltd. The colour photograph on the front cover was supplied by Sporting Pictures (UK) Ltd

Published by
The Hamlyn Publishing Group Limited
London · New York · Sydney · Toronto
Astronaut House, Feltham, Middlesex, England

© Copyright The Hamlyn Publishing Group Limited 1981
ISBN 0 600 34661 7

Filmset in England by
Photocomp Limited, Birmingham
Printed in England

CONTENTS

FOREWORD

BY IAN ST JOHN

At the time of the 100th Cup final, I am reminded again what a privilege it is to be on the list of players who have scored a winning goal at Wembley. And in 1965 I was very much aware at the time that my goal helped Liverpool make history.

Until we beat Leeds United, Liverpool had never won an FA Cup. Winning was one achievement that Evertonians could still boast about at our expense, because at that time they had already chalked up two victories in the competitions. They used to say we'd never win the FA Cup until the Liver Birds flew off the Liver building.

The details of the goal will always remain printed in my memory: Ian Callaghan's cross; the ball just clearing Willie Stevenson; Gary Sprake committing himself. I had to twist into a header to turn it into the net. But my clearest recollection is of the remainder of the game, the longest nine minutes of my life. It ended when Ron Yeats whacked an enormous clearance into touch. The final whistle went and I had become one of the fortunate few to sample the ultimate experience in football.

This book will bring back many memories for many fans. It also gives us all fascinating glimpses of what Cup finals were like before we were born. I wish it every success.

Opposite: The Sunderland players being introduced to His Majesty King George VI before the Cup final of 1937

Sports Argus.

BIRMINGHAM, SATURDAY, 26 APRIL, 1924.   ONE PENNY.

NO. 1,365.

WHO'S WHO IN THE GREAT F.A. CUP FINAL AT WEMBLEY TO-DAY.

ASTON VILLA CAMEOS.

Interesting Stories of the Rise and Merits of Eleven Young Athletes.

By "ARGUS JUNIOR."

THOMAS JACKSON.
(Goalkeeper.)

WILLIAM KIRTON.
(Inside Right.)

LEONARD CAPEWELL.
(Centre-forward.)

THE RIVAL SECRETARIES.

MR. G. B. RAMSAY (Aston Villa).   MR. F. J. WATT (Newcastle U.)

WILLIAM WALKER.
(Inside Left.)

ARTHUR DORRELL.
(Outside Left.)

THOMAS SMART.
(Right Back.)

THOMAS MORT.
(Left Back.)

FRANK MOSS.
(Right Half.)

VICTOR EDMUND MILNE.
(Centre-half.)

GEORGE BLACKBURN.
(Left Half.)

RICHARD YORK.
(Outside Right.)

HEIGHTS AND WEIGHTS.

ASTON VILLA.

THE WAY TO WEMBLEY.

NEWCASTLE SNAPSHOTS.

All About the Men Who Went to Wembley to Avenge 1905.

By "ARGUS JUNIOR."

"SANDY" MUTCH.
(Goalkeeper.)

THE CUP GOES EAST

FINAL EXTRA—PAGES 22-23

COCKNEY KINGS

THE YOUNG ONES—Pike, Allen and Stewart lead the lap of honour round Wembley with the FA Cup held proudly aloft at the end of their shock win over the Gunners.
Pictures by BRIAN RADFORD and DAVID HOOLEY

'ANDSOME!
—that's Brooking

By Frank Butler

BROOKING—best man

FINAL VERDICT

Arsenal 0
West Ham 1

Brooking (13)

Attendance 100,000   HT 0-1
Receipts £790,000

Tartan terrors in riot as Celtic triumph

By MARTIN FRIZELL

Celtic 1 Rangers 0

It'll be tough —Neill

By REG DRURY

OH BOY!
Trev's a superdad

By TERRY McNEILL

News of the World, May 11, 1980

THE ILLUSTRATED SPORTING AND DRAMATIC NEWS

THE F.A. CUP FINAL AT WEMBLEY

Sheffield Wednesday beat West Bromwich Albion after a Remarkable Match

WEST BROMWICH ALBION'S FIRST GOAL

BROWN SAVES : Sheffield Wednesday's goalkeeper clears effectively.

THE PRINCE AT WEMBLEY

INTRODUCTION

On 16 March 1872 The Wanderers and the Royal Engineers, winning their way through from an entry of 15 clubs, contested the first FA Cup final; the venue was Kennington Oval and The Wanderers won 1–0, an unexpected victory in front of a crowd of 2,000 followers, all doubtless totally unaware that they were witnessing the start of a story rich in sporting drama.

On 10 May 1980, Second Division West Ham United overcame Arsenal, also 1–0, in the 99th final. Though the scene was painted in more contemporary colours – one hundred thousand afficianados encased in Wembley's Empire Stadium, contributing more than £7 per head on average for the privilege of watching at first hand, rather than through the extensive television coverage, the most celebrated event in the British football calender – the context remained unaltered. West Ham and Arsenal, the final pairing from an entry of more than 450 clubs, faced a showdown totally different from the more form-orientated League competitions. West Ham's victory affirmed that the FA Cup had lost none of the glorious unpredictability which has set it on a pedestal above other tournaments.

Cup Final Extra commemorates the reaching of the one hundredth final in 1981 (not to be confused with the Centenary Final nine years earlier which celebrated one hundred years since the playing of the first final). Since there have been several excellent histories of the competition, *Cup Final Extra* represents a new approach, a study of the finals through the eyes of those who witnessed the epic and the not-so-epic from the press facilities of the time. Today these are the warm, comfortable seats in the Press Box at Wembley which affords such an excellent view – a sharp contrast to the plight of the predecessors of today's scribes, some of whom interrupted the flow of their report of the football to lament that a downpour, falling heavily on their unprotected vantage point, disturbed their concentration.

Our researches were concentrated not just on producing straight match reports from the newspaper cuttings of the day, though these are clearly a central theme. Our brief was also to investigate the growth of the interest in the competition from its first roots to the full bloom of nowadays, when the Cup final touches the lives of not just the committed football fans but millions for whom the final is *the one* football match of the year. That growth is reflected in the change of status of the match-report within a newspaper, from a column inch buried beneath the likes of pigeon racing in the nineteenth century to blanket coverage, which now finds the actual details of the match a relatively small filling in a sandwich between the fanatical build-up and heavily analytical post-mortems.

A third factor for consideration was the placing of the final in the context of the important world events that took place at Cup final time. The 1932 final provided a case in point. There have been few more controversial goals than the first scored by Newcastle United's Allen in their 2–1 win over Arsenal that year. A still picture from the British Movietone News film of the match was made available to Fleet Street and indicated that the ball had crossed the goal line before Richardson centred to provide Allen with his opening. The *Daily Herald*'s sense of priorities was, however, representative of the reaction the Monday following the match. CUP FINAL GOAL WAS NOT A GOAL proclaimed a headline that was nevertheless subordinate to HITLER SWEEPS AHEAD IN PRUSSIA, an account of the Nazi leader's increasing influence throughout the states that then comprised Germany. The San Francisco Earthquake and the sinking of the *Titanic* were among other historic happenings around Cup final time which helped reporters in their search for colourful imagery with which to describe the football.

At times less dramatic episodes have been retained in a further attempt to capture the distinctive flavour of each year, for example the clear national importance of the Oxford–Cambridge boat race in the late nineteenth century or the use of sport in the advertisements of the day. At times the right has been exercised of altering the original lay-out of a paper to incorporate into the available space other items of interest.

The detailed investigation itself produced some findings which standard works on football history may wish to incorporate. Many reference books give the result of the 1877 final as The Wanderers 2 Oxford University 0, but our investigations produced several references to an own goal from the Hon. A. F. Kinnaird, which credited Oxford University with a goal. Similarly the drawn match in 1876 was 1–1, not 0–0 as usually reported. The 1875 draw went to extra time (in those days it was optional). It seems certain too that the winner for Aston Villa against West Bromwich Albion in the 1895 final came from Devey, not Chatt. Similarly the Bradford local newspaper reporting the replayed final of 1911 cleared up another mystery. Some sources still name O'Rourke as the match-winner but quotes from O'Rourke himself admit that he did not touch the original effort at goal from Speirs.

Such confusion is not only confined to the distant past. The famous Stanley Matthews final of 1953 is often quoted as the match in which that other Stanley, Mortensen, became the first and only player to date to grab a hat-trick in a Wembley FA Cup final. One would not be churlish enough to attempt to rub out the

Above left: *C. W. Alcock, secretary of the Football Association, who first thought of an FA Cup*

Above centre: *Fans leaving Kingsway, in London, for the Crystal Palace in 1906*

Above right: *The Crystal Palace, with the 1914 final in progress*

Below: *All but one of the first 21 finals were at Kennington Oval. This is 1891*

achievement of that whole-hearted player who in truth should have taken the real credit for Blackpool's remarkable comeback to beat Bolton Wanderers. Yet respected reporters of the day recorded Mortensen's first goal as an own goal by Harold Hassall. One suspects it would have stayed that way had Mortensen not scored his two later goals, and thus needed the credit for the first for his hat-trick.

Though the Football Association was born out of a meeting in the Freemason's Tavern, Great Queen Street, Holborn on 26 October 1863, it was eight years before the Football Association Challenge Cup was instituted. In July 1871, the decision was taken by a committee including C. W. Alcock, Captain Francis Marindin, A. Stair, the FA treasurer and M. P. Betts. In the following October their resolution was ratified, and the affiliated clubs were asked to contribute to the buying of a suitable trophy. Towards the £20 needed to provide the original FA Cup – which was only eighteen inches high and made of silver – Queens Park from Glasgow contributed one guinea.

Queens Park took their place as one of 15 initial entrants. Eight others came from the central London area: the Wanderers, Barnes, Civil Service, Harrow Chequers, Upton Park, Crystal Palace, Hampstead Heathens and Clapham Rovers. Maidenhead, Marlow, Reigate Priory, Hitchin, Royal Engineers and Donington Grammar School made up the numbers. Subsequently Harrow Chequers, Reigate Priory and Donington Grammar School scratched from their Cup ties, so in essence twelve teams took the first tentative steps into Cup football.

When Wanderers and Royal Engineers qualified for the first final, several of the FA committee enjoyed some immediate reward for their foresight. Charles Alcock became the first captain to collect the FA Cup. M. P. Betts scored the first goal in a final, and it was sufficient to decide the tie, though he sought anonymity by playing under the pseudonym of A. H. Chequer – a reference to the football he had played for another club, Harrow Chequers. Captain Marindin began a long personal association with the Cup final by representing Royal Engineers in the match, which was refereed by another FA committeeman, A. Stair.

The Wanderers retained the trophy in 1873, the priorities of the day indicated by an eleven o'clock kick-off so that the crowd could also attend the more important

event of the Boat Race. But the era of the upper-class amateurs, predominantly from the south, was not to last long. Blackburn Rovers lost to Old Etonians in 1882, but the Lancashire mill town was to epitomise the growth of professionalism, at first an under-the-counter operation to buy success as the prestige of doing well in competitive football increased. The payment of players was finally legalised in 1885. The FA Cup thus included a new regulation: "Professionals shall be allowed to compete in all Cups provided they are qualified as follows: in Cup matches, by birth or residence for two years past within six miles of the ground or headquarters of the club for which they play. No professional shall be allowed to play for more than one club in any one season without the permission of the Committee of the Football Association. All professionals shall be annually registered in a book to be kept by the committee of the Football Association, and no professional shall be allowed to play unless he has been so registered."

By this time Blackburn Rovers, much suspected of attracting players by financial inducements, were on the way to completing a hat-trick of FA Cup wins, following on the victory of Blackburn Olympic over Old Etonians in 1883.

Hard on the heels of Blackburn Rovers came the growth of Preston North End, built up at great expense by Major Sudell to challenge Blackburn's successes. Preston duly became known as the "Invincibles" though they survived a shock defeat in the 1888 final before truly earning their nickname. Legend has it that Preston were so confident that they would beat West Bromwich Albion that Marindin, now risen to the rank of Major, was asked whether the team could be photographed with the Cup *before* the match. Marindin is purported to have replied: "Had you not better win it first?"

That final obtained all the now traditional elements of the FA Cup, including a full house at The Oval, with the

The 1921 Cup final at Stamford Bridge, and the Spurs leaving with the trophy

gates for the first time having to be locked and of course a complete upset in the result. West Bromwich Albion were inspired by Billy Bassett, and the hot favourites were beaten 2–1. Preston's response to the set-back could hardly have been more emphatic. The following season, 1888–89, they completed the first, and statistically most complete of the four league and Cup doubles; the league was won without a single defeat, the Cup without the conceding of a solitary goal.

In 1897 Aston Villa emulated the achievement, if not the statistics, completing the double with a 3–2 victory over Everton in a thrilling final at Crystal Palace. It would be 64 years before the feat would be accomplished again, and long before Tottenham's marvellous 1960–61 season wise voices were being raised throughout the land to say that it was an impossible task.

Tottenham Hotspur at least had history on their side when they met Leicester City in the 1961 final . . . the '1' at the end of the date had regularly been an omen for success. In 1901 Spurs had become the only non-league side to win the FA Cup, Sheffield United falling to the Southern League opposition in a replay at Bolton. In 1921 Tottenham had won the FA Cup again. Now a First Division side, Jimmy Dimmock's goal beat Wolverhampton Wanderers at Stamford Bridge. In 1951, Tottenham won the league championship in their first season back in the First Division. In 1961 they had already won the title by eight points by the time they beat Leicester City 2–0 at Wembley. Ten years later Arsenal re-emphasised the feasibility of a double in the fiercely competitive context of the modern game when their 2–1 win over Liverpool after extra-time took both trophies to Highbury.

The great charm of the FA Cup, its genuine unpredictability, does have a remarkable record of appearing in the finals. Tottenham Hotspur's 1901 victory was very much a case in point. Such uncertainty led to the aura of jinx and superstition which has surrounded the competition.

Newcastle United certainly felt they were cursed in the early years of the twentieth century. Between 1905 and 1911 United reached five finals, all staged at Crystal Palace. They won only one, and that in 1910 was well away from South London, when they took Barnsley to a

replay at Goodison Park. Yet in the 1950s Newcastle enjoyed a completely opposite relationship with Wembley Stadium; in 1951, 1952 and 1955 they lifted the FA Cup in style.

It is the unpredictability of the FA Cup that provoked the rituals such as Major Buckley's monkey-gland treatment for his Wolverhampton Wanderers team of 1939; and were Wolves, overwhelming favourites in that last final before the Second World War, beaten because the Portsmouth manager Jack Tinn wore his lucky spats? Yet Tinn himself had been a Wembley loser five years earlier despite the gambit of taking comedian Bud Flanagan into the Portsmouth dressing-room to ease the tension before the final against Manchester.

Don Revie, that most superstitious of managers, produced his "lucky" suit for the 1973 final, but Revie's Leeds United, a team crammed full of internationals, came second best to Sunderland, who earlier in the season had been floundering at the bottom of the Second Division. Revie's ill-fortune included his side being thwarted by surely one of the greatest saves in the history of the Cup finals, Jim Montgomery's remarkable reaction to Peter Lorimer's close-range shot.

Sunderland became the first Second Division winners for 42 years, but only three years later Southampton repeated the feat with Manchester United cast in the role of fallen favourites. West Ham United gloriously carried the cause of the underdog into the 99th final with another Second Division success.

Mention of Manchester United recalls another unusual superstition. Travelling on their coach from the Selsdon Park Hotel to Wembley for their 1979 final against Arsenal, I was aware that the music being played on the cassette deck was hardly that associated with the trendy habits of professional footballers. "We play Max Bygraves," I was told, "on the way to the matches as an incentive. If we lose we have to listen to it on the way back!" On that day it was an unsuccessful incentive. In one of the most dramatic of recent finals United scored twice in the last four minutes to wipe out Arsenal's lead only to see Alan Sunderland stretch the incredulity of the competition almost to breaking point by scoring the winner in injury time.

Many of the post-war finals were marred by what became known as the Wembley injury jinx, though the handicapping of a side through losing a player was nothing new to an FA Cup final. Bury's 6–0 win in 1903, which remains the record margin of victory in a final, was in no small measure helped by Fryer, in the Derby goal, being hurt. Yet in the 1950s those mishaps occurred with such alarming regularity that the clinging quality of the much-admired Wembley turf was regularly blamed. In 1952, for example, Wally Barnes twisted a knee and became a handicap that Arsenal could not overcome. A year later Bolton finally collapsed to Blackpool's pressure because left-half Eric Bell became a passenger, though he still contributed the goal that put Bolton 3–1 up in the second half. In 1955 Manchester City's Jimmy Meadows was so badly injured that he never played again, and a year later City's win over Birmingham City was marred by the incident in which that heroic goalkeeper Bert Trautmann broke his neck. The following season Manchester United's hopes of the league and Cup double disappeared when their goalkeeper Ray Wood was carried off after a violent charge by Aston Villa's Peter McParland; Jackie Blanch-flower took over in goal and was beaten twice by McParland, with Wood later returning to play on the field.

In 1959 Roy Dwight opened the scoring for Nottingham Forest against Luton Town, then broke a leg and watched the rest of the match on a hospital television. In 1960 Dave Whelan, the Blackburn Rovers defender, was another broken leg victim, while injury to Len Chalmers ruined Leicester City's attempt to overcome Tottenham Hotspur's double aspirations in 1961. After much campaigning substitutes were finally introduced into the FA Cup in the 1966–67 season.

In retracing the history of the FA Cup finals it has been remarkable how many present day problems are in fact old chestnuts. In the late nineteenth century there were complaints about the behaviour of supporters of northern clubs marauding through London during their visit south for the Cup final. We came across early complaints too that the ticket allocation for Cup final teams was not enough to satisfy the demand from the followers of the finalists. One would have thought, also, that the present system of the players organising a "pool" to gather the commercial advantages of reaching Wembley was a recent phenomenon. But as long ago as 1933, the players of Manchester City and Everton refused to allow one national newspaper to take pre-match photographs when the team visited the Empire Stadium. No explanation was recorded but the implication is clearly that an exclusive deal had been set up with a rival concern at some financial benefit to the participants.

Tradition from those earlier times also lives on in the present. Arsenal, for example, will always wash a new goalkeeper's jersey before it is used in a match. The habit comes from the unhappy experience of Dan Lewis who let a shot from Ferguson of Cardiff City squirm out of his hands and over the line in the 1927 final. Cardiff thus became the only non-English team to win the competition, and the sheen on Lewis's brand new jersey was given part of the blame.

John Radford, the Arsenal striker with a dry sense of humour, certainly knew of the story when he had to take over in goal from the injured Bob Wilson in the 1972 semifinal against Stoke City at Villa Park. Before putting on the jersey he wanted to know whether it had been washed!

The 99 years of competition have produced 40 winners, which surely empasises the democracy of the competition. Aston Villa now head this roll of honour:

7 wins: Aston Villa
6 wins: Blackburn Rovers, Newcastle United
5 wins: Arsenal, The Wanderers, Tottenham Hotspur, West Bromwich Albion
4 wins: Sheffield United, Bolton Wanderers, Wolverhampton Wanderers, Manchester City, Manchester United
3 wins: Sheffield Wednesday, Everton, West Ham United
2 wins: Bury, Old Etonians, Preston North End, Nottingham Forest, Sunderland, Liverpool
1 win: Barnsley, Blackburn Olympic, Blackpool, Bradford City, Burnley, Cardiff City, Charlton Athletic, Chelsea, Clapham Rovers, Derby County, Huddersfield Town, Notts County, Old Carthusians, Oxford University, Portsmouth, Royal Engineers, Leeds United, Southampton and Ipswich Town

I would like to record my appreciation of the considerable efforts in the compilation of this book of Simon Moore, whose baptism in journalism was most diligent. That the project was completed at all was totally due to the support and encouragement of Peter Arnold.

Wembley Stadium, the current Cup final venue. Denis Law and Gordan Banks, 1963

THE CUP FINALS

The Football Association Challenge Cup finals from
1872 to 1980, containing reports from contemporary
newspapers, fact boxes and, where appropriate,
current comment

THE ASSOCIATION CHALLENGE CUP.
THE FINAL TIE.

ON Saturday the last of the matches which have taken place in the competition for the possession of the Challenge Cup, presented by the committee of the Football Association, took place at Kennington Oval. The two clubs left in to contend for the honour of holding the trophy for the first year were the Wanderers and the Royal Engineers, and as the rivals on this occasion were certainly the two most powerful organisations supporting Association Rules, the excitement, not only among the partisans of the respective sides, but among the lovers of football generally, was intense. It may here be as well to state that during the earlier heats the Royal Engineers had defeated the Hitchin Club, the Hampstead Heathens, and the Crystal Palace, all without difficulty; while on the other hand the Wanderers had only defeated the Clapham Rovers by one goal, having drawn with the Crystal Palace, and enjoyed a walk over in their tie with the Harrow Chequers. Mainly in consequence of their easy triumph over the Crystal Palace Club on the previous Saturday, the Engineers were great favourites with the public, and that the estimation in which they were held was not unjustifiable may be gathered from the fact that for a period of two years they had never been vanquished. Moreover, the clever and effective manner in which they have always played, and still play, together, tended to produce a belief that they would be able, by better organisation and concentration, to defeat their opponents, despite the acknowledged superiority of the latter in point of individual excellence and skill. No pains, however, were spared by the Wanderers to collect their best representative eleven, and in this they succeeded admirably, as without doubt they mustered on this occasion the very best forces at their disposal, having both weight and speed forward, and certainly the two best backs in England to support the efforts of the ups. Within a few minutes of three o'clock the ball was set in motion by the Engineers, the assemblage of spectators being very fashionable, though the numbers were hardly so large as might have been expected, owing, possibly, in some measure to an advance in the price charged for admission. The captain of the Wanderers won the toss, and thus at the outset his side gained not only the aid of the wind, but a considerable advantage in addition in having a very powerful sun at their backs. At once the Wanderers set to work with the greatest determination, and at the outset their play forward displayed more co-operation than is their custom, the backing-up being vastly superior to anything they have shown during the present season. By this means, and with the aid of faultless kicking on the part of their backs, they were able during the first quarter of an hour to besiege the Sappers closely, to the surprise of many of the spectators. Thus consistently they maintained the attack, till at length, after some judicious " middling" by R. W. S. Vidal, the goal of the Engineers fell to a well-directed kick by A. H. Chequer. Ends were now changed, but any expectations of an alteration in the state of affairs were unfulfilled, as without any diminution of energy the Wanderers, although now faced by wind and sun, continued to besiege the lines of the Engineers without allowing any opportunities to the forwards on the latter side of effecting the rushes for which they are noted. Not long after the above goal the ball was again driven through the posts of the military goal by C. W. Alcock, but owing to a previous breach of the handling rule by another Wanderer, the claim was rightly disallowed. Still the game was maintained with the most remarkable animation on both sides, Renny-Tailyour, Mitchell, and Rich striving hard to pass the backs of the enemy. Once Muirhead, by an excellent run, did succeed in guiding the ball into the vicinity of the Wanderers' fortress, but A. C. Thompson interposed at the right moment, and the leather was safely removed. After this one or two chances were offered to the Wanderers, but none were realised, although more than one would doubtless have been successful but for the extremely efficient goal-keeping of Capt. Merriman. On one occasion a protracted bully raged on the very edge of the Engineers' lines, and once during its course the ball was absolutely driven against one of the posts; but here, too, the Wan-

derers failed to score. During the latter part of the game it was generally imagined that the Engineers would outstay their opponents, but until the finish the play continued as fast as ever, and soon after half-past four o'clock time was called, the Wanderers thus gaining the privilege of holding the cup for a year by one goal. It was generally admitted that the play all round was superior to anything that has been seen at the Oval. The Wanderers unquestionably surprised the spectators by the effectiveness of their play collectively, and certainly they have never shown to such advantage as in this contest. The Engineers played hard and well throughout, but they were outmatched in this instance, as they only on two occasions endangered the enemy's goal. It was in some measure the superiority of the backs on the side of the Wanderers that tended to produce the defeat of the Sappers, as the certainty of kicking displayed by Lubbock and Thompson throughout enabled the forwards of the victors to attack without fear. In extenuation of the reverse suffered by the Engineers, it should be stated that one of their best players, Lieutenant Creswell, broke his collar-bone about ten minutes after the start, and too much praise cannot be accorded to him for the pluck he showed in maintaining his post, although completely disabled and in severe pain, until the finish. Thus ended one of the most pleasant contests in which the Wanderers have ever been engaged, the posts of umpires and referee being absolutely sinecures. On behalf of the Wanderers, though all played up throughout in fine form, R. W. S. Vidal and T. C. Hooman attracted notice by their skilful dribbling. The umpires were J. H. Giffard (Civil Service) for the Engineers, and J. Kirkpatrick (Civil Service) for the Wanderers, A. Stair (Upton Park) acting as referee.

The first FA Cup

Sides :
Wanderers: C. W. Alcock, E. E. Bowen, A. G. Bonsor, A. H. Chequer, W. P. Crake, T. C. Hooman, E. Lubbock (back), A. C. Thompson (half-back), R. C. Welch (goal), R. W. S. Vidal, and C. H. Wollaston.
Royal Engineers: Capt. Marindin, Capt. Merriman, Addison, Mitchell, Cresswell, Renny-Tailyour, Rich, Goodwyn, Muirhead, Cotter, and Bogle.
We understand that the cup will be presented to the victors at the annual dinner of the Wanderers' Club, to be held early next month.

ASSOCIATION CHALLENGE CUP.
The presentation of the above cup will take place at the annual dinner of the Wanderers' Club, to be held at the Pall Mall Restaurant, Charing Cross, on Thursday evening, April 11, at seven o'clock. The transfer of the trophy to the Wanderers will be made by Mr. E. C. Morley, the President of the Football Association.

● The first FA Cup final gave immediate birth to some of its lasting traditions. The favourites, for example, did not win. Royal Engineers, their team composed entirely of officers, losing to a goal scored by M. P. Betts, who strangely played under the pseudonym of A. H. Chequer, a loose reference to him representing another club "a Harrow Chequer". Also the contest, as many in the 1950s, was marred by an injury, Lieutenant Cresswell suffering a broken collarbone after only ten minutes. Charles Alcock, whose forethought had established the competition, had a second goal ruled out for handball by a colleague.

The Wanderers, thus, won the first of their five finals, even though they had only drawn with Crystal Palace in an earlier round, both teams progressing under the prevailing rule, and drawn with Queens Park in the semi-final, the Scottish club without sufficient funds to stay in London for a replay.

The first final was watched by a crowd of 2,000, a substantial attendance when the admission price was one shilling, a high figure at a time when the average weekly wage was less than a pound.

Date 16 March 1872
Place The Kennington Oval
Score WANDERERS 1
ROYAL ENGINEERS 0
Teams WANDERERS R. de C. Welch, C. W. Alcock, M. P. Betts, A. G. Bonsor, E. E. Bowen, W. P. Crake, T. C. Hooman, E. Lubbock, A. C. Thompson, R. W. S. Vidal, C. H. R. Wollaston. ROYAL ENGINEERS Capt. Merriman, Capt. Marindin, Lt. Addison, Lt. Bogle, Lt. Cotter, Lt. Cresswell, Lt. Goodwyn, Lt. Mitchell, Lt. Muirhead, Lt. Renny-Tailyour, Lt. Rich.
Team Colours ROYAL ENGINEERS Red and blue
Officials Referee A. Stair (Upton Park). Umpires H. Giffard (Civil Service), J. Kirkpatrick (Civil Service)
Goal Scorer Betts
Attendance 2000
Guest of Honour Trophy presented by E. C. Morley, President of the FA
Copy *The Sporting Life* 23 March 1872

The Royal Engineers, Captain Marindin centre back

and, although we admit that Saturday's tide and weather were all in favour of making "fast" time, it must be taken into consideration that the steering of the boats was seriously interfered with several times by small craft drifting in their way at two or three critical periods. This would make several seconds difference, and we are quite content to accept the result as a proof of the superiority of the sliding seats over the fixed ones. We append the names and weights of the two crews:

Cambridge.	st	lb
J. B. Close, First Trinity (bow)	11	3
E. Hoskyns, Jesus	11	2
J. E. Peabody, 1st Trinity	11	7
C. W. Lecky-Brown, Jesus	12	1½
J. S. Turnbull, Trinity Hall	12	12½
C. S. Read, First Trinity	12	13
C. W. Benson, Third Trinity	11	5½
H. E. Rhodes, Jesus (stroke)	11	1½
C. H. Candy, Caius (cox.)	7	5

Oxford.	st	lb
C. C. Knollys, Magdalen (bow)	10	11
J. B. Little, Christ Church	10	11
M. G. Farrer, Brasenose	11	13½
A. W. Nicholson, Magdalen	12	5
R. S. Mitchison, Pembroke	12	2
W. E. Sherwood, Christ Church	11	1
J. A. Ornsby, Lincoln	11	3
F. T. Dowding, St. John's (stroke)	11	0
G. E. Frewer, St. John's (cox)	7	10

The following is a table of winners since the first race in 1829:

Year	Course.	Winner.	Time.	Won by
1829	Henley, 2m 2f	Oxford	14m 30s	Many lengths
1836	Westminster to Putney	Cambridge	36m	1min
1839	Westminster to Putney	Cambridge	31m	1min 45sec
1840	Westminster to Putney	Cambridge	29m 30s	¾ of a length
1841	Westminster to Putney	Cambridge	32m 30s	1min 4sec
1842	Westminster to Putney	Oxford	30m 45s	13sec
1845	Putney to Mortlake	Cambridge	23m 30s	30sec
1846*	Mortlake to Putney	Cambridge	21m 5s	Two lengths
1849	Putney to Mortlake	Cambridge	22m	Many lengths
1849	Putney to Mortlake	Oxford	Foul ...	Foul
1852	Putney to Mortlake	Oxford	21m 36s	27sec
1854	Putney to Mortlake	Oxford	25m 29s	11 strokes
1856	Mortlake to Putney	Cambridge	25m 50s	Half a length
1857	Putney to Mortlake	Oxford	22m 50s	35sec
1858	Putney to Mortlake	Cambridge	21m 23s	22sec
1859	Putney to Mortlake	Oxford	24m 30s	Camb. sank
1860	Putney to Mortlake	Cambridge	26m	One length
1861	Putney to Mortlake	Oxford	23m 27s	48sec
1862	Putney to Mortlake	Oxford	24m 40s	30sec
1863	Mortlake to Putney	Oxford	23m 5s	42sec
1864	Putney to Mortlake	Oxford	21m 48s	23sec
1865	Putney to Mortlake	Oxford	21m 23s	13sec
1866	Putney to Mortlake	Oxford	25m 48s	15sec
1867	Putney to Mortlake	Oxford	23m 22s	Half a length
1868	Putney to Mortlake	Oxford	21m	Six lengths
1869	Putney to Mortlake	Oxford	20m 5s	Three lengths
1870	Putney to Mortlake	Cambridge	22m 4s	1¼ lengths
1871	Putney to Mortlake	Cambridge	23m 5s	¾ of a length
1872	Putney to Mortlake	Cambridge	21m 16s	Two lengths
1873	Putney to Mortlake	Cambridge	19m 35s	Three lengths

* The first race in outrigged eights.

ROWING ON THE TYNE.

ARMSTRONG AND FORSTER.—A match in heavy ballast keel boats, for 15*l.* a-side, was brought off on the Tyne on Saturday, over a course the length of Howdon Dock, between Armstrong, of Willington Quay, and Forster, of Howdon. The weather was fine and favourable, and there was a numerous attendance of spectators, but no steamer was provided, and Robert Henderson, of Jarrow, the referee, had to accompany the race in a four-oared boat. Betting was brisk at 5 to 4 and 6 to 4 on Armstrong, who won the north side station on a toss. The start was a good one, but the favourite bored his man over to such an extent that Forster, to avoid a foul, stopped altogether for a moment. This slight stoppage enabled Armstrong to get away half a length in advance, and keeping in front throughout the remainder of the distance, he won easily by three lengths.

RILEY AND BAKER.—A small, unimportant open boat match, for 5*l.* a-side, was decided on the Tyne on Saturday afternoon, from the High Level-bridge to Waterston's Gates, between John Riley and W. Baker, both of Gateshead, the former receiving two lengths start. Christopher Peterson, of the Ouseburn, was referee, and a limited amount was invested at 5 to 4 on Riley. After the first dozen strokes, Baker's stretcher slipped out, and he was not able to bring all his power to bear upon the boat; Riley was therefore in front all the way, and won easily by five lengths.

RACQUETS.

THE INTER-UNIVERSITY MATCHES.

THESE annual matches will take place to-day and to-morrow (Wednesday), at Prince's Club, Hans-place, Sloane-square. The double match takes place to-day, Mr C. J. Ottaway and Mr E. O. Milne, both of Brasenose, playing for Oxford; Mr Sanders and Mr J. H. Gurney, both of Trinity, representing Cambridge. The single match to-morrow (Wednesday) will be between Ottaway and Sanders. The play each day will commence at two o'clock.

THE GUN CLUB, NOTTING HILL.

THE opening day of the season of this club was held in most beautiful weather on Saturday, and, notwithstanding the counter attraction of the boat race, a large muster of well-known sportsmen assembled. Proceedings were confined to 1*l.* handicap sweepstakes, at three birds each, and so large was the field of shooters that only five could be brought to issue. The first pool, amounting to 10*l.*, was divided between Mr G. Marshall (25½ yards rise) and Mr T. R. Peareth (25½), the former gentleman dividing the second with Mr S. Shirley, M.P. (26½), each taking 8*l.* The third, amounting to 20*l.*, was divided between Mr Carrington (27) and Mr Harrington Hudson. The fourth sweep, worth 20*l.*, was secured by Mr J. Davies (25), who also took 5*l.*, the fifth and last, dividing with Mr T. Lant (27).

J. Offer supplied the birds.

DOVER.

A COMMITTEE consisting of the officers and gentlemen connected with the First Battalion Rifle Brigade, stationed at Dover, organized a day's shooting which was most successfully brought off on Friday last. The weather was all that could be desired, and there was a large and aristocratic assembly. The programme consisted of 1*l.* sweepstakes at three and five birds each, the winners being Mr Campbell, Mr Bathurst, and Mr Hartopp. Score:

SWEEPSTAKES of 1 sov, three and five birds each.

Mr Hartopp	100—111-11—111-11—110 —11111-10
H.R.H. Prince Arthur	000—10 — — —11111-10
Capt. Bunbury	011
Mr Bowles	110—10 —01 —0 —000
Mr Lindsay	001—10 —01 —111-0—0110
Mr Bennett	101—00 —110
Capt. Grant	011—111-0 —110
Mr Prittie	110—10 —10 —0
Mr Stanhope	010—10 —10
Mr Campbell	111—110 —10 —0 —11111-11
Mr Fitzgerald	01
Mr Bathurst	01 —111-10—110 —111-1—11111-10
Mr Bannard	10 —111-10—111-10
Mr Lane	— —111-10— —0111
Mr Tufnell	— —111-0 — —1010
Mr Gough	— —0
Mr Burnell	— — —10

S. Hammond supplied the birds.

THE RAILWAY TAVERN, NUNHEAD, PECKHAM.

OWING no doubt to the counter attractions there was but a moderate muster at the above popular resort on Saturday last. During the afternoon a couple of matches were decided, one at seven birds each, 25 yards rise, between Mr Fowler and Mr C. Brown, and another at five birds, between Mr Fowler and Mr T. Brown, in both of which Mr Fowler was successful. The remainder of the afternoon was occupied in sweepstakes shooting.

MATCH, seven birds each, 25 yards rise.

Mr Fowler	0 1 0 0 0 1 1—3
Mr C. Brown	0 0 0 1 1 0 0—2

MATCH, five birds each, 25 yards rise.

Mr Fowler	0 0 0 1 0—1
Mr T. Brown	0 0 0 1 1—2

SWEEPSTAKES at three birds each, 25 yards rise.

Mr T. Brown	0 —111—000—011—00 —11—111—101
Mr Fowler	111—10 —011— —011—00— 01—010
Mr C. Brown	10 —1
Mr Harvey	10
Mr Mist	— — —100

S. Hammond supplied the birds.

THE WELSH HARP, HENDON.

THE usual Saturday afternoon's meet at the above well-known rendezvous was but thinly attended, and the whole afternoon was occupied in shooting sweeps, at three birds each.

SWEEPSTAKES at three birds each, 28 yards rise.

Mr Fox	10 —10 —010—111—0 —111—0 —110
Mr Franks	10 —111—011—0 —111—10 —0 —00
Mr Barns	111—0 —00 —10 —110—0 —111—010
Mr Fox	0 —001—011-0—011—000—100—0 —00
Mr Barns	0 —100—100 —00 —000—110—0 —00 —0
Mr Franks	111—001—101-1—101—010—101—111—110—10

S. Hammond supplied the birds.

A. LANCASTER, Gun and Rifle Manufacturer, 27, South Audley-street, Grosvenor-square.—Speciality for pigeon guns, used by the most celebrated trap shots of the day. Several good second-hand guns and rifles by the best makers, for sale.—ADVT.

WRESTLING.

FUNERAL OF JIM SCOTT, EX-CHAMPION WRESTLER.—On Sunday afternoon, the remains of Jim Scott, the great 11st wrestler, who died last Tuesday morning, were interred at Carlisle Cemetery, and the funeral was the largest ever witnessed in Carlisle. In his time Scott won upwards of 100 prizes in the wrestling rings of England and Scotland. He commenced his public career in the Newcastle ring in 1848, when he wrestled second for 9½st prize. Strange to say, his last appearance in public was also in the Newcastle ring, when in 1868 he was fourth for the all-weight prize. He won the 11st Wrestling at Newcastle two years. He was carried to the grave by the great champions of the day, the carriers including W. Jameson, of Penrith; R. Wright, Longtown; J. Edgar, Carlisle; T. Davidson, Castleside; Ben Cooper, Carlisle; J. Tiffin, of Dearham; J. Ivison, Carlisle; J. Snowdon, of Cockermouth, &c. Scott was 43 years of age.

FOOTBALL.

THE ASSOCIATION CHALLENGE CUP.

THE FINAL TIE.

ON Saturday last the final match to decide the right of holding the silver cup presented by the committee of the Football Association took place at Lillie-bridge. The struggle for supremacy rested between the Wanderers, who were the holders during the previous year, and Oxford University, the latter club having defeated early in the season the Royal Engineers, who were the runners-up in the spring of 1872. Owing to the difficulty of arranging suitable dates, the match had to be fixed for the day of the boat race, and in order to prevent the players from missing the sight, it was agreed to commence play at eleven o'clock in the morning. The day itself was not favourable for either side, as the Oxonians lost the valuable aid of C. E. B. Nepean, while on the other hand the Wanderers were not only unable to get the assistance of their half-back, A. C. Thompson, but were further prevented from securing F. H. Wilson in his place, and they also were crippled by the absence of W. P. Crake and T. C. Hooman. Owing to late arrivals the play did not commence until half-past eleven o'clock, the Wanderers, though they had won the toss for choice of positions, deriving no advantage from this success. Owing to the laws framed for the competition preventing the appointment of umpires connected with either of the clubs interested, some difficulty was experienced in the selection, though eventually Messrs J. R. Dasent (Gitanos) and J. H. Clark (Maidenhead) were found to officiate, the former for Oxford and the latter for the Wanderers, Mr A. Stair (Upton Park), assistant hon. sec. of the Football Association, acting as referee. The Oxonians followed their kick-off with great resolution, and at first they held a decided advantage, keeping their opponents strictly on the defensive, the Wanderers even at this early stage of the game feeling the want of a qualified half-back. Indeed, at the outset it seemed as if the Wanderers would have all the worst of it, and but for the unwearied defence showed by L. S. Howell (their back) without doubt some of the constant attacks made by the Oxford forwards would have been successful. For twenty minutes the game thus proceeded with a visible superiority to Oxford, the whole eleven working well together and with great energy. Gradually, though, the Wanderers aroused, and almost half an hour had passed when A. F. Kinnaird took advantage of a favourable opportunity, and by a splendid run outpacing the opposite backs, he placed a very well obtained goal to the credit of the Wanderers, to the intense delight of their eleven. Ends were changed, and the play showed a fresh infusion of vigour, J. R. Sturgis and A. Kinnaird making some fine runs on behalf of the Wanderers, and A. Kirke-Smith and W. R. Sumner on the side of Oxford. Again, though, a good piece of individual play crowned the Wanderers with success, as W. S. Kenyon-Slaney, by a well-executed run, once more helped to carry the ball between the Oxford posts, but both umpires allowed the claim of "off side," and so this success was not allowed. The Oxonians now tried every plan to retrieve their ground, and in the hopes of strengthening their attack, with questionable judgment determined on the removal of their goal-keeper. For a short time no disaster followed this *ruse*, but at length C. H. Wollaston, after a speedy run, reduced the Oxford goal by means of a neat kick with the left foot, thus placing the second goal to the credit of the Wanderers, entirely owing to the absence of the man between the posts. Again positions were reversed, and still, as before, the Oxonians had more than one chance, as they drove the ball almost into the very centre of the Wanderers' posts. Instead of "middling" the ball through from the side of the ground, they seemed anxious to force it through the goal, and in this they were unsuccessful, as when time was called at one o'clock the Wanderers were in the possession of two goals without any score to the credit of their opponents. Collectively the Oxford eleven played exceedingly well, and they were certainly most formidable antagonists. In point of individual skill, on the other hand, the Wanderers were superior, as A. F. Kinnaird, C. H. Wollaston, and J. R. Sturgis on several occasions easily eluded the Oxford backs, even with the help of the very persistent charges of F. C. Maddison. The success of the Wanderers was in a great measure due to the extremely brilliant play of their captain forward, as well as to the unvarying precision of their back (L. S. Howell). Among the Oxonians, A. Kirke Smith, C. J. Longman, W. E. Sumner, and F. C. Maddison played up well, and both the backs showed excellent form. Sides:

Wanderers: A. F. Kinnaird (captain), E. E. Bowen (half-back), C. H. Wollaston, R. K. Kingsford, A. G. Bonsor, W. S. Kenyon-Slaney, C. M. Thompson, L. S. Howell (back), R. C. Welch (goal), J. R. Sturgis, and Rev. H. H. Stewart.

Oxford University: A. Kirke-Smith, University (captain); F. H. Birley, University (half-back); G. H. Longman, University; R. W. S. Vidal, Christ Church; F. C. Maddison, Brasenose; A. J. Leach, St. John's (goal); H. B. Dixon, Christ Church; W. B. Paton, University; and C. C. Mackarness, Exeter (back).

The "Wanderers" have thus won the cup two years in succession:

1872—Wanderers beat Royal Engineers by one goal to none.
1873—Wanderers beat Oxford University by two goals to none.

Next season the holders will have to go through all the ties the same as the other competing clubs.

ASSOCIATION CHALLENGE CUP.

WANDERERS v. OXFORD UNIVERSITY.

The final match for the possession of the cup given by the committee of the Football Association will be played on the Amateur Athletic Ground, Lillie Bridge, West Brompton, this (Saturday) morning, commencing at eleven o'clock sharp. This arrangement will give those anxious to see the boat race ample time to reach Putney, Hammersmith, or any of the other places on the line of the race.

Date 29 March 1873
Place Amateur Athletic Club, Lillie Bridge
Score WANDERERS 2 OXFORD UNIVERSITY 0
Teams WANDERERS E. E. Bowen, C. M. Thompson, R. de C. Welch, Hon. A. F. Kinnaird (capt.), L. S. Howell, C. H. R. Wollaston, J. R. Sturgiss, Rev. H. H. Stewart, W. S. Kenyon-Slaney, R. K. Kingsford, A. G. Bonsor.
OXFORD UNIVERSITY A. Kirke-Smith, A. J. Leach, C. C. Mackarness, F. H. Birley, R. W. S. Vidal, C. J. Ottaway, W. B. Paton, F. B. Chappell-Maddison, C. J. Longman, H. B. Dixon, W. E. Sumner
Officials Referee A. Stair. Linesmen J. H. Clarke, J. R. Dasent
Goal Scorers Wollaston, Kinnaird
Attendance 3000
Copy *The Sporting Life* 29 March 1873

THE SPORTSMAN, TUESDAY, MARCH 17, 1874.

FOOTBALL.

OXFORD UNIVERSITY v. ROYAL ENGINEERS.

FINAL TIE FOR THE ASSOCIATION CHALLENGE CUP.

FAVOURED with fine weather and with the prospect of a grand contest, upwards of 2000 people visited the Surrey cricket ground on Saturday afternoon last, in order to witness the last tie for the possession (annual) of the Association Cup. In 1872 and 1873 the Cup was held by the Wanderers, and would have become their absolute property had they succeeded in winning again this year. Unfortunately for them they had to meet the dark blues on their own ground at Oxford, and took down such a miserably weak team that they were forced to submit to a most decisive defeat, only, however, as it transpires, at the hands of the new holders of the cup, as in the match on Saturday the University, after a magnificent contest, were declared the victors by two goals to love. The Engineers began badly by losing the toss, and were compelled to kick off from the Gasometer end against a somewhat strong wind. Both teams soon gave evidence of their excellence, and the ball vacillated between the goals, being first at one end and then the other Van Donop distinguished himself greatly by means of a very fine piece of dribbling play, but was eventually stopped by Ottaway, who forced the ball well back into the opposition territory again. Shortly after this a claim of "hands" was allowed against the Sappers, and almost immediately afterwards the Engineers sent the ball behind their own line, and as a consequence a corner kick was allowed to the Oxonians, which resulted in a loose scrimmage directly in the jaws of the R.E. fortress, and it was not long before the ball was well kicked through the posts by Mackarness, who thus was credited with the first goal for his university. Ends were changed, and the game became more than ever spirited, the Engineers, seemingly aroused to fresh efforts, strongly attacking the Oxford goal, and almost overthrowing the same. The 'Varsity men, however, were much elated with their primary success, and determined not to let slip a chance, they—chiefly by the aid of Ottaway, Maddison, and Vidal—again overcame all opposition, and rapidly carried the ball back into the Engineers' quarters, and finally Patton shot it between the posts, and thus obtained the second goal for the University. The all-round play which followed was very brilliant, but although both goals were imminently threatened on more than one occasion, no further advantage accrued to either side previous to the call of "no side" by the referee. When we remember how well all played, it seems almost invidious to make special mention of individual play, but, nevertheless, we cannot close without a word of extra praise for Ottaway, Birley, Rawson, Patton, and Vidal for the 'Varsity, and Renny-Tailyour, Digby, and Van Donop for the Engineers.

CRICKET.

THE final match between the English Eleven and Eighteen of Victoria took place to-day. The latter scored in their first innings 150, and the Eleven 166 runs, of which Mr W. G. Grace made sixty-four. Rain prevented the match being continued. The English Eleven have sailed for Adelaide.

THE English cricketers have had rather a busy time of it. A few days after the termination of their first match—that with the Victorian eighteen, in which they were beaten in one innings—they went to Ballarat to play against the district twenty-two, the local men having the valuable aid of Allan and Cosstick as bowlers. There was a splendid turf to play on, and the ground being unusually small, the batsmen had much the best of it. The largest scores ever made in the colony were got on this occasion. The Eleven made the enormous total of 470 runs. W. G. Grace contributed one hundred and twenty-six and his brother one hundred and twelve; but both batsmen gave several chances, which were missed by the field. Oscroft (run out) was next with sixty-five, and Greenwood was credited with sixty-two. The local players also made an unusually high score—276. W. H. Figgis got fifty-three and Watson thirty-three. The match was a draw, as the players had only time for an innings each. The Ballarat men are not satisfied with the result, and are endeavouring to arrange for another match. The Eleven next went to the mining township of Stawell, where they were treated to a ground which no batsman could approve. The Eleven went in with the foregone conclusion that they could do nothing on the bumpy wicket. They were disposed of in their first innings for 43, and only made 91 in their second, enabling the Twenty-two, assisted by Cosstick, B. B. Cooper, Conway, and Wills, to win, with ten wickets to spare. W. G. Grace's scores were fourteen and sixteen. A good deal of coaching adventure over bad roads brought the Eleven to Warrnambool, where they scored their first victory, the Twenty-two being beaten with nine wickets to fall, though assisted by Allan, Conway, and Wills. W. G. Grace made eighteen on this occasion. The first innings score of this team was 104, of which Jupp contributed fifty-eight and not out. The Englishmen are now in Sydney, where they have again been overmatched. The New South Wales Eighteen beat them, with eight wickets to spare. There is a very pronounced tail to the English team, and it is considered that it will be easily vanquished in the return match with the Victorian Eighteen. The English cricketers have not made themselves as popular as the members of H. H. Stephenson's and George Parr's teams, and many stories of internal dissensions, &c., have been circulated to account for their defeats. The explanation should rather be looked for in the improved colonial cricket, and the presence of at least three players in Mr Grace's team who are not up to All England Eleven form.—*Melbourne Argus*, Jan. 28.

Date 14 March 1874
Place The Kennington Oval
Score OXFORD UNIVERSITY 2
ROYAL ENGINEERS 0
Teams OXFORD UNIVERSITY C. B. B. Nepean, R. H. Benson, P. H. Birley, F. T. Green, Rev. A. H. Johnson, C. C. Mackarness, F. B. Chappell-Maddison, C. J. Ottaway (capt.), F. J. Patton, W. S. Rawson, R. W. S. Vidal. ROYAL ENGINEERS Capt. Merriman, Major Marindin (capt.), Lt. Addison, Lt. Blackburn, Lt. Digby, Lt. Olliver, Lt. Onslow, Lt. Rawson, Lt. Renny-Tailyour, Lt. Von Donop, Lt. Wood
Official Referee A. Stair
Goal Scorers Mackarness, Patton
Attendance 2000
Copy *The Sportsman* 17 March 1874

The Great Eastern Railway Cricket Club will be glad to arrange a match for Easter-Monday. Several Saturday afternoons also vacant. Address, W. B. Widdup, Superintendent's Office, Bishopsgate.

CRICKET.—Just published, John Lillywhite's Guide to Cricketers for 1874, post free, 1s. 1d. 10, Seymour-street, Euston-square, N.W. —ADVT.

TO CRICKET CLUBS, &c., SOUTH NORWOOD.—A large private ground, situated in close proximity to the South Norwood Station, and which in a short time will be properly inclosed, can be let for cricketing, &c., during the summer months. It is in every way adapted for this pastime, and matches and practice can take place any day in the week, with the exception of Monday. For full particulars and terms, address, Mr A. Holledge, the Jolly Sailor, South Norwood.—ADVT.

STANLEY v. TIMBRELL.

THIS match of 1000 up, even, between these celebrated players, will take place at Liverpool on Thursday, March 26 (the Grand National Day), for 1000*l*., and the Concert Hall, Lord Nelson-street, has been selected as the most convenient place for a match of such importance. The match will be played on a new table by Burroughes and Watts, and the price of admission will be 1*l*., 10*s*., and 5*s*., and tickets can be obtained from W Timbrell, Adelphi Hotel, Liverpool; or of S. W. Stanley, 303 Strand.—ADVT.

JOSEPH BENNETT'S BILLIARD ROOM.

MR JOSEPH BENNETT (ex-champion), late of St. James's Hall, has opened splendid rooms at 315, Oxford-street, known as the Oxford Billiard Gallery. Ten tables by Burroughes and Watts, five public and five private, 1*s*. 6*d*. per hour. One of the private rooms is fitted with a championship table. The best tables, the best room, the best light in the world. J. B. is in daily attendance to give private lessons and play with gentlemen. J. B. is open to play entertainment matches.—ADVT.

Wanted by W. Cook (champion) a room or rooms wherein to place two billiard tables. One of them the table won by Cook in Roberts's handicap at Manchester. Apply to 99, Regent-street, W.—ADVT.

● Probably the strongest team of the first five years of the FA Cup was the Royal Engineers of Chatham, but they were not to win until 1875, the fourth year of its existence. In those four years Royal Engineers lost only three matches, and two of these were the Cup finals of 1872 and 1874.

Modern soccer was largely a product of the public schools and universities, and the main FA Cup rivals of Royal Engineers were Old Etonians, Oxford University and The Wanderers, who were a side formed of old public school boys. One or two players played for more than one of these sides in FA Cup finals, for instance C. J. Ottaway, who was in the winning Oxford University side of 1874 also played for Old Etonians in 1875, his team mate R. W. S. Vidal, known as "The Prince of Dribblers", had been in the winning Wanderers side of 1872 and the Hon. A. F. (later Lord) Kinnaird played for Old Etonians and Wanderers. The four sides mentioned fought out every Cup final until 1879, when Clapham Rovers reached the final.

In 1873, the first winners, The Wanderers, were automatically into the final, being challenged by the winners of a knock-out competition to find a challenger. This was the only year in which this principle operated, and in 1874 all sides had to fight through the early rounds.

Royal Engineers, led by the redoubtable Major Marindin, reached the final, where they were expected to beat Oxford University. However the Royal Engineers were below form and were well-beaten on the day. One report read: "The final tie for the Challenge Cup was played on Saturday at Kennington Oval in the presence of upwards of 2,000 spectators. The well-known ability of both teams and the fact of its being the last tie caused the match to be looked forward to with great interest. The Wanderers held the Cup for two years, but were defeated this season in the third round by Oxford. The ground was in good condition and the weather fine. At 3.15 the Engineers having lost the toss kicked off from the Gasometer end against a fair wind. The Sappers at first carried the ball into the Oxonian territory, but Birley kicked it to Ottaway who, with Vidal, made an attempt to reach their opponents' goal, but were well crossed by Van Donop, who effected a fine run along the side of the ground, but Ottaway again made away with the ball. The Engineers were now unfortunate in twice violating the rule as to "hands" and very soon after kicked the ball behind which gave the Dark Blues the advantage of a corner-kick and, after a loose bully in front of the Engineer's goal, Mackarness sent the ball under the tape. Ends being changed the Engineers again threatened the Oxonian goal, but it was not long ere Ottaway, Maddison, and Vidal rushed away with the ball and Patton kicked the second goal for the Varsity. Ends were again reversed and Digby once or twice conducted the ball nearly the whole length of the ground, but was well received by Mackarness and Birley and the Engineers were compelled to act on the defensive for some time; they made one or two good attempts to score, however, the ball going a very little over the tape and Renny-Tailyour made a shot at the goal the ball rebounding off one of the posts. Towards the end some very determined play was shown by both sides, but neither was able to effect a goal. At 4.45 time was called, Oxonians being victorious by two goals to nothing. Oxford brought a very strong team – Birley, Vidal, Rawson, Patton and Ottaway especially distinguishing themselves. The Engineers scarcely played up to their usual form."

It is interesting to compare this report with that of *The Sportsman* reproduced. There is a remarkable agreement about the players who performed well.

The report in *The Sportsman* is still at the bottom of the newspaper's page, taking a minor place in comparison with articles about the following week's boat race. We include among other reports an item from Melbourne, where W. G. Grace's English cricketers were not doing too well in their matches against sides of 18 and 22 opponents. This was still three years before the first official Test match.

THE SPORTING LIFE, WEDNESDAY, MARCH 17, 1875.

LATE FOOTBALL.

ASSOCIATION CHALLENGE CUP.

ROYAL ENGINEERS v. OLD ETONIANS.

These teams met at Kennington Oval on Saturday last to play off the final tie, and the weather being fine, a large company assembled to witness the play, which was of a most exciting character. The Etonians won the toss, and selected the upper goal, with a strong wind at their backs, through the agency of which they kept the ball mostly in the Sappers' territory, making one or two shots at goal, and after thirty minutes' play, from an excellent corner-kick by Bonsor, a goal was secured. Ten minutes after change of ends, however, Von Donop made a fine run, and out of a bully in front of goal, the ball glanced off Renny-Tailyour's knee through the posts, thus matters were equalised. Reversing positions gave the Etonians the benefit of the wind again, and some determined attacks followed on each side, but, unfortunately, at this critical moment Ottaway came in violent collision with one of the Engineers, and sprained his ankle, which compelled him to retire; nevertheless, the Engineers were unable to lower their citadel before time was called. Afterwards, in order, if possible to avoid another meeting, it was agreed to play for an extra half hour, ends being changed at the expiration of the first quarter, but, nevertheless, neither gained any definite advantage up to the end, and the match therefore ended in a draw, each side having scored a goal. The Engineers' colours were scarlet and blue; those of the Old Etonians, light blue and white. J. H. Giffard (Civil Service) was umpire for the Engineers, and J. P. Dasent (Gitanos) for the Old Etonians; C. W. Alcock referee. The following were the players:—

ROYAL ENGINEERS.—Major Merriman (captain and goal-keeper), Lieutenants T. H. Sim (three-quarter-back), G. Onslow and T. H. Ruck (half-backs), P. Von Donop and A. Wood (right wing), A. T. Mein and Cecil Wingfield-Stratford (left wing), F. W. Rawson, W. H. Stafford, and W. H. Renny-Tailyour (centres).

OLD ETONIANS.—A. F. Kinnaird (captain) and J. H. Stronge (left side), W. S. Kenyon-Slaney and R. H. Benson (right side), F. J. Patton, C. J. Ottaway, and A. G. Bonsor (centres), A. C. Thompson and E. Lubbock (half-backs), F. H. Wilson (back), and C. K. Farmer (goal-keeper).

Yesterday (Tuesday) the Royal Engineers and Old Etonians again met at Kennington Oval, when the ground was in fine condition, and the weather all that could be desired. The Etonians, unfortunately, were only able to muster a poor eleven—Kenyon-Slaney, Ottaway, Thompson, and Benson being unable to play—nevertheless they made a good fight of it. Play did not begin until five minutes past three o'clock, when the Etonians kicked off from the upper end. The Engineers had a trifle the best of the play at starting, and after about fifteen minutes Patton unfortunately handled the ball right in front of the Eton goal, when it was carried through. An appeal on the ground of off-side, however, being made, the goal was disallowed, and the ball replaced in its old position, but the Engineers, after a sharp bully, forced it through the posts again, thus gaining the first goal. After change of ends, the game was most evenly contested, each team in turn holding the advantage, and several shots were made at both goals; the fine back play, however, on each side prevented any serious results until within a quarter of an hour of time, when the Engineers completely penned their opponents, and after several spirited bullies in front of goal, forced it through. The play during the last ten minutes was rather tame, nothing being scored by either side, consequently the Royal Engineers were hailed the victors by two goals to nothing. The Sappers all round performed well, and of the Etonians, Edgar Lubbock and Kinnaird played in grand form throughout. Bonsor unfortunately injured his knee early in the game, but although lame he played pluckily right up to the finish. The Engineers' team was the same that played on Saturday last, and the four substitutes in the Eton ranks were Drummond-Murray (goal-keeper), T. Hammond, Alfred Lubbock, and M. Farrer. C. W. Alcock officiated as referee. The Royal Engineers have always held a prominent position in the competitions for the Challenge Cup since it was first instituted in 1872, and thrice out of four years have played in the final games, being defeated by the Wanderers in 1872 and Oxford University in 1874, therefore their victory has been well earned.

LATE ATHLETICS.

BOXING AND WRESTLING CHAMPIONSHIP.

The following are the entries for these events received up to last (Tuesday) evening:—

Boxing Championship.—Heavy Weights: A. L. Highton, Queen's College, Oxford; B. J. Angle, Thames Rowing Club; W. Winthrop, Cambridge University Athletic Club; R. F. Smith, West London Boxing Club. Light Weights: L. Hasluck, German Gymnasium; L. Denereaz, City Gymnastic Club; H. J. Pitt, Manchester Athenæum Gymnastic Club; A. Aitchison; E. L. Hein, Somerset Football Club; H. Stapleton, German Gymnasium Club; H. S. Giles, London Rifle Brigade; D. Landell, German Gymnastic Society; Lord James Douglas; T. A. Skeate, West London B.C.

Middle Weights: H. Kiddell, Thames Rowing Club; J. Howell, Thames Rowing Club; J. H. Douglas, Broxbourne Cricket Club; A. S. Hunt, West London B.C.

Wrestling.—W. Winthrop, Cambridge University Athletic Club.

THE OXFORD AND CAMBRIDGE BOAT RACE.

Since our last there has not been any material alteration in the relative positions of the two crews in public favour; Oxford still rules the roast, and, if anything, the faith in them has become greater. Their good performance last Friday has not been affected by anything that has taken place since, and unless something very remarkable occurs we quite anticipate that the Dark Blue will start as warm favourites as their opponents did last year. For once in a way the weather has not to any appreciable extent interfered with their practice, and it is worth remarking that not one man has been absent from either of the eights from indisposition or any other cause since their arrival at Putney. Consequently the comments of persons on the banks with regard to the rowing of individuals in the boats have run less risk of being outrageously wrong, and the merciless attacks on the style of one man have not been utterly misplaced through a substitute having been found for him. Besides, the weather and the early practice of the crews have acted against the attendance of the ordinary Boathouse mob, and the forenoon practice and chill north-easters have had a great effect in keeping away the holiday crowd we have been accustomed to see when the eights were doing their principal work during the latter half of the day. On Saturday, for instance, both crews, as we stated they would do, did their principal work during the morning. Oxford were out about eleven, and were evidently determined on doing strong work, for they started from the Aqueduct at Putney right against the last of the ebb with a strong wind blowing. Rowing at from 34 to 35 they went right up to Chiswick church, going very cleverly through a rather awkward swell above Hammersmith Bridge, their boat carrying them very well indeed. They returned at a racing pace to Putney, and created a decidedly favourable impression. Cambridge followed, and paddled up to Chiswick, whence they had a sharp burst to Putney.

On Monday again the practice was done principally during the morning when there was a very small number of spectators, the weather being decidedly cold and uninviting. Oxford went out in their new Clasper at eleven o'clock, and rowed with several easies from Putney to Barnes—an experiment made with altered slides having in the meantime proved to be a failure, and caused their performance to be viewed rather unfavourably by those unaware of the change made in the boat. Turning at Barnes, they had a good hard, steady row from the Railway Bridge to Hammersmith Bridge, keeping very good time and swing throughout, and accomplishing the distance in 9 min. 7 sec.—not so fast as might have been expected, but not so bad considering that the steering was rather wide of the mark. After passing the Soap Works, going easily, the crew started for a hard row home, and finished in good style, and apparently very strong.

Cambridge went out between twenty and thirty minutes later, and after going a steady paddle to the Soap Works they eased. Afterwards they had a lively row to Chiswick Eyot, where there was a slight degree of unsteadiness manifested. After turning, they rowed from the Oil Mills to Putney at a practice stroke until near the finish, where they quickened, the time between Hammersmith Bridge and the Aqueduct being 8 min. 27 sec. They went below bridge and then returned to their boathouse.

Yesterday (Tuesday) morning, just before eleven, Oxford paddled up to the Point, and thence started for a row over the course from the Ship at Mortlake. Here they turned, and came back at a stroke varying from 36 to 37 to the minute for the greater part of the distance, when they quickened up to 39, the time for the whole distance being 20 min. 22 sec., and from Hammersmith to Putney 8 min. 22 sec.

Cambridge got afloat about twenty minutes to twelve, in their last year's Clasper, and rowed to the top of Chiswick Eyot, where they turned, rowing from 36 to 37, and finishing in 13 min. 25 sec.

● After losing in 1872 and 1874, the Royal Engineers finally lifted the FA Cup, though they needed a replay to overcome Old Etonians. As the cuttings (left) illustrate, the final still did not carry the weight of interest to take space from the Boat Race, which was regarded as one of the top contests of the sporting calendar. Indeed the report on the final in the *Sporting Life* does not record the names of the scorers of the two goals in the replay. The Royal Engineers were able to field an unchanged team, but Old Etonians had to make four changes and were the weaker for them. Charles Alcock's name reappears in the history of the competition by refereeing both matches.

Date 13 March 1875
Place The Kennington Oval
Score ROYAL ENGINEERS 1
OLD ETONIANS 1 (after extra time)
Teams ROYAL ENGINEERS Major Merriman (capt.), Lt. Sim, Lt. Onslow, Lt. Ruck, Lt. Von Donop, Lt. Wood, Lt. Rawson, Lt. Wingfield-Stratford, Lt. Stafford, Lt. Renny-Tailyour, Lt. Mein. OLD ETONIANS C. K. Farmer, Hon. A. H. Kinnaird (capt.), J. H. Stronge, W. S. Kenyon-Slaney, R. H. Benson, F. J. Patton, C. J. Ottaway, A. G. Bonsor, A. C. Thompson, E. Lubbock, F. H. Wilson
Team Colours ROYAL ENGINEERS Scarlet and blue; OLD ETONIANS Light blue and white
Officials Referee C. W. Alcock. Umpires J. H. Giffard (Civil Service), J. P. Dasent
Goal Scorers ROYAL ENGINEERS Renny-Tailyour; OLD ETONIANS Bonsor
Copy *The Sporting Life* 17 March 1875

Replay
Date 16 March 1875
Place The Kennington Oval
Score ROYAL ENGINEERS 2
OLD ETONIANS 0
Teams ROYAL ENGINEERS Unchanged. OLD ETONIANS Capt. E. H. Drummond-Murray, Hon. A. F. Kinnaird (capt.), J. H. Stronge, T. Hammond, A. Lubbock, F. J. Patton, M. Farrer, A. G. Bonsor, E. Lubbock, F. H. Wilson, C. K. Farmer
Team Colours Unchanged
Official Referee C. W. Alcock
Attendance 3000
Copy *The Sporting Life* 17 March 1875

Royal Engineers Chatham FA Cup winning team 1875.
Lieut H. L. Mulholland (12th man) Lieut G. C. P. Onslow Lieut H. E. Rawson Lieut A. L. Mein Lieut C. V. Wingfield-Stafford
Lieut R. M. Ruck Major W. Merriman (Capt and goalkeeper) Lieut H. W. Renny-Tailyour Lieut P. G. Von Donop
Lieut G. H. Sim Lieut G. T. Jones

* Rugby Rules. † Association Rules.

FOOTBALL.

MATCHES FOR THIS WEEK.

THIS DAY (WEDNESDAY, MARCH 15).

*At Blackheath, Hornsey Rovers v. Blackheath School.

THURSDAY, MARCH 16.

†At Borstal, Rochester v. The Reserve Yeoman.

[Saturday's fixtures will appear in our next.]

ASSOCIATION CHALLENGE CUP.

OLD ETONIANS v. WANDERERS.

The final match in the competition for the Football Association Challenge Cup was played at Kennington Oval on Saturday afternoon last, in the presence of a very large company of spectators, many of whom were ladies. The afternoon was fine, but a very strong south-westerly wind blew three-parts across the ground during the first half of the play, greatly assisting the Wanderers, who had won the toss, and of course elected to commence the match with the wind at their backs in case it might shift, or become less violent—as indeed it did—later in the day. The Etonians did not play by any means well together, so that despite their apparent individual superiority to their antagonists, the latter had decidedly the better of the game throughout, as they backed up well, whilst the play of their behinds was in every respect equal to that of the Etonians, Birley's kicking being especially accurate and well timed. Play commenced at twenty minutes after three o'clock, Meysey-Thompson kicking off for the Etonians, who had first to defend the Gasometer goal. The ball was at once carried down into the Eton portion of the ground, where for some minutes the chief part of the play was carried on until Kinnaird made a good run, but could not get by Stratford, who made a good kick, which, aided by the wind, sent the ball flying down to the Light Blue goal. Desultory kicking now followed for some time, until Maddison secured a corner-kick, from which, however, the ball was taken behind the line by the wind. Several times "hands" were called by either side, on the most frivolous pretexts, but no advantage accrued therefrom. Repeated attacks were now made upon the Etonian goal, but Quentin Hogg proved a capital custodian, and in every case failure resulted until a general advance on the part of the Wanderers enabled Wollaston and Hawley-Edwards to obtain the first goal in the match after about thirty-five minutes' play. The remaining ten minutes before half time were fully occupied by the Etonians in defending their goal from the further assaults of the Wanderers, who, however, had not succeeded in adding to their score ere ends had to be changed. Not many minutes then had elapsed before a general attack was made upon the Wanderers' goal, which fell in more senses than one, as owing to the wind and its defenders being forced back upon the posts, they were knocked down, and ball, Wanderers, and Etonians in a body went through the space between them which the tape should have covered. Thus both sides were equal. The remainder of the match calls for little comment. The Wanderers played the best, but with the wind against them the excellent back-play of Thompson and Edgar Lyttelton, and superior weight in the bully to contend with, they could never get the ball at any time, except once, behind the Eton goal, where Kinnaird, having hurt himself, was now in charge in place of Quentin Hogg, who went up to Welldon's place, the latter going short-behind in lieu of E. Lyttleton. The latter portion of the match, with this exception, was mainly in the centre and Wanderers' portion of the ground. Thus the match ended in a draw, and the two elevens have to meet again on Saturday next to decide the struggle for the possession of the Cup. The umpires were Messrs. W. H. White (South Norwood) and R. A. Ogilvie (Clapham Rovers), whilst Mr. W. S. Buchanan (Clapham Rovers) officiated as referee. The players were:—

OLD ETONIANS.—H. Alleyne, A. G. Bonsor, Quentin Hogg (goal-keeper), Captain W. S. Kenyon-Slaney, A. F. Kinnaird (captain), Hons. Alfred and Edgar Lyttelton (half-backs), C. Maisey, A. C. Meysey-Thompson (half-back), J. R. Sturgis, and J. E. C. Welldon (back).

WANDERERS.—F. H. Birley (captain) and F. B. Maddison (half-backs), W. Lindsay and A. H. Stratford (backs), W. D. Greig (goal), Hubert and Frank Heron, C. H. Wollaston, J. Kenrick, J. Hawley-Edwards, and T. B. Hughes.

SHEFFIELD ASSOCIATION.

The Sheffield Association, bent on retrieving their lost laurels during the last two years, decided on playing several test matches with a view of selecting the best available talent for their next encounter, v. London, at Bramall-lane, on the 25th inst. It has long been apparent that the Sheffield team has become very selfish, and each one stuck to the ball as if success depended on individual instead of combined efforts of the whole team. To put a stop to this malpractice, it was decided to play two matches—Eleven v. Next Thirteen—and anyone still persisting in sticking to the ball instead of crossing it, was to forfeit his chance of selection. The first match, played last Saturday, was a most even one. The Eleven were captained by Mr. J. C. Clegg, his side being distinguished by red, and the Thirteen by blue ringlets. Each side obtained two goals, so that the match ended in a tie. The players were as follows:—

REDS.—J. C. Clegg (captain), W. E. Clegg, W. Wilkinson, R. Gregory, W. Mosforth, C. Hudson, J. Housley, J. Hunter, W. Orton, G. Anthony, and W. Platts (goal).

BLUES.—W. H. Stacey (captain), A. B. Slowe, F. M. Butler, W. Oates, A. Woodcock, H. Sorby, T. Banks, G. Pinder, W. F. Bradshaw, J. Byrd, J. Bailey, S. Charles, and E. Bowling (goal).

On Monday a second match was played, when the Blues had another man added to their team, so that they mustered fourteen to eleven. The play was again excellent, and although the Reds had slightly the best of the play, they were ultimately defeated by two goals to *nil*.

The only change in the team on Monday was J. Henning in place of S. Charles on the "Blues" side, and the substitution of W. A. Matthews as fourteenth man. Mr. Whelan acted as umpire for the Reds *vice* Mr. R. W. Dickinson.

NOTTINGHAM FOREST v. BIRMINGHAM.

The first match ever played between these clubs at Nottingham took place on the Forest Ground, on the borders of that town, last Saturday afternoon. The weather, albeit a strong wind prevailed, was all that could be desired, and a very large number of persons assembled to witness the contest. The ball was set in motion at three o'clock, when Birmingham, who won the toss, were favoured with the wind. At first the home team appeared likely to score a goal through the efforts of their forwards, who very quickly carried the ball to the immediate front of the Birmingham citadel, which, for a minute or two, was in imminent danger of succumbing. Presently, in the heat of a hot scrummage, the ball was got away, and up to half-time matters remained pretty equal. After the change of ends Nottingham forced the pace, but their opponents still held their ground, especially for the next half-hour. At a quarter-past four o'clock Revis had a shy at the Birmingham fortress, the ball passing over the crossbar, and before play ceased two other smart kicks by Goodyer and Whyatt were all but successful, C. Quilter (goal-keeper) straining every nerve to avert defeat. The match, though no goals transpired, was splendidly contested throughout, and it is sure to become an annual affair. Players:—

FOREST.—S. W. Widdowson (captain), C. Rastall (goal-keeper), E. H. Greenhalgh, A. H. Smith, J. B. Carter, A. Castings, J. Whyatt, A. C. Goodyer, A. B. Baillon, H. Rothera, T. Oliver, and W. H. Revis.

BIRMINGHAM.—H. H. Webster (captain), Captain Brindley, T. Bryan, G. Pears, F. Baines, J. R. Riddell, J. H. Cofield, W. J. Nicholls, J. T. Eldridge, G. R. Quilter, G. F. Walker, and C. H. Quilter (goal-keeper).

RUGBY FOOTBALL UNION.

The second general meeting for the season 1875-76 will be held at the Westminster Palace Hotel, Victoria-street, on Wednesday, March 29, at eight p.m., when the following amendments to the laws will be brought forward:—Proposed by F. Luscombe (Gipsies), seconded by C. D. Heatley (Richmond).—Law 38. To add at the end, "If the ball pitch in touch, it shall be brought back and kicked off again." Law 37. To add at the end (3), "After change of goals at half-time." Law 38. To substitute, "Each side shall play from either goal for an equal time." Law 40. To add at the end, "When goals have been changed at half-time, the side which did not kick off at the commencement of the game shall then kick off."

Date 11 March 1876
Place The Kennington Oval
Score WANDERERS 1 OLD ETONIANS 1
Teams WANDERERS W. D. O. Greig, A. Stratford, W. Lindsay, F. B. C. Maddison, F. H. Birley (capt.), C. H. R. Wollaston, H. Heron, F. Heron, J. H. Edwards, J. Kenrick, T. Hughes. OLD ETONIANS Q. Hogg, J. E. C. Welldon, Hon. E. Lyttleton, A. C. Thompson, Hon. A. F. Kinnaird (capt.), C. Meysey, W. S. Kenyon-Slaney, Hon. A. Lyttleton, J. R. Sturgis, A. G. Bonsor, H. P. Allene
Official Referee W. S. Buchanan (Clapham Rovers)
Attendance 3500
Copy *The Sporting Life* 15 March 1876

Replay
Date 18 March 1876
Place The Kennington Oval
Score WANDERERS 3 OLD ETONIANS 0
Team Changes OLD ETONIANS Q. Hogg, E. Lubbock, Hon. E. Lyttleton, M. G. Faner, Hon. A. F. Kinnaird, J. H. Stronge, W. S. Kenyon-Slaney, Hon. A. Lyttleton, J. R. Sturgis, A. G. Bonsor, H. P. Allene. WANDERERS Unchanged
Officials Referee W. S. Rawson (Cambridge). Linesmen A. H. Savage (Crystal Palace), R. A. Ogilvie (Clapham Rovers)
Goal Scorers WANDERERS Wollaston, Hughes (2)
Attendance 1500
Copy *The Sporting Life* 22 March 1876

*** Reports of several matches unavoidably stand over until Saturday.

TWICKENHAM (SCRATCH) v. BUTE HOUSE.—Played at Petersham on Saturday last, and resulted in an easy victory for the visitors by five goals and seven tries to *nil*. The goals were kicked respectively by C. Plowman, Stainton, Hatton, and Donnan. Messrs. Twiss, Hall, and Bradshaw were conspicuous among the forwards.

RING.

JEM MACE AND JOE GOSS.

These champions leave England for America by the steamer sailing from Liverpool on Saturday, March 25, 1876. Their backers desire to give them a testimonial previous to their departure, and they beg to inform their patrons and friends of the West and East-Ends that they will be glad to see them all on Thursday, March 23, being the occasion of their Presentation and Farewell Benefit at the Royal Foresters' Music Hall, Cambridge-road, Mile-End, where, in addition to the array of talent engaged, all the champions have kindly consented to appear, including E. P. Weston, American walker, J. Sadler, champion sculler, Captain Webb, and a host of other champions. For full particulars, see bills.—[ADVT.]

DEATH OF "OLD" ALEC REED ("CHELSEA SNOB").—This celebrated pugilist died on Friday last in St. James's Union, simply from exhaustion of nature, at the ripe age of seventy-six. Through the kindness of Mr. George Langham, of the Cambrian Stores, who has on many occasions sympathised with him, he will be buried to-morrow (Thursday), at Brompton, at three o'clock. It is also intended, as a mark of respect, in consideration of his courage (especially with "Bishop" Sharpe), to erect a tombstone to his memory. Mr. W. Parker, well known to the P.R. fraternity, in conjunction with Mr. George Langham, &c., will superintend the funeral *cortége*.

ATHLETIC SPORTS.

BIRMINGHAM ATHLETIC CLUB.—The annual meeting of this club will take place on Saturday, July 29, at Portland-road Grounds.

AMATEUR ATHLETIC SPORTS AND BICYCLING.—Great improvements are being made at the Lillie Bridge Grounds. In addition to the present running track (one-third of a mile), a new one (quarter-mile) will be opened, so as to enable practice in all kinds of sport at any time of the day throughout the year when the ground is not otherwise engaged. Practice tickets for bona fide amateurs will be issued for the year at £1 1s., which will also admit to all sports, fetes, matches, &c., to be held on the ground. Weight-putting, hammer-throwing, high and long jumping, parallel and horizontal bars available, lawn tennis courts, skittles, bowling, and badminton. Bicycling will be taught under the superintendence of Keen (Champion), and bicycles repaired and housed on the grounds. The new open air skating rink, the largest in the world, a quarter of a mile in circuit, will shortly be open for skating and racing.—Apply, for full particulars, to Mr. J. H. Jewell, Secretary A.A.C., Lillie Bridge, Fulham, S.W.—[ADVERTISEMENT.]

FOOTBALL.

ASSOCIATION CHALLENGE CUP.

WANDERERS v. OLD ETONIANS.

On Saturday afternoon last, in bright but bitterly cold weather, quite 1,500 spectators assembled at Kennington Oval to witness the final match for the Association Challenge Cup. The original match was fixed for and was played on Saturday, the 11th inst., but at the call of "time" each eleven had scored one goal, and the match had to be left drawn. This time, however, the Old Etonians had an inferior team, as Meysey-Thompson, Welldon, and Quentin-Hogg were unable to play, and in their places Farrer, Edgar Lubbock, and Stronge were to be found. These did their duty well, but were not in the same practice as those whom they represented. Eton this time won the toss, and selected the Gasometer goal, and at half-past three Birley kicked off for the Wanderers from the Harleyford-road end, a cold north-easterly wind blowing at the time. For about half an hour the play was of a very even character, whilst "free" kicks abounded through the same vexatious and unmeaning calls of "hands" which had been so frequent during the last match. A general charge on the part of the Wanderers then enabled them to score a goal, Wollaston being the player credited with the final kick, and this was almost directly afterwards followed by a second, kicked by Hughes. Half-time was now called, but still the Wanderers held their own, and pressing down on their antagonists quickly added a third to their previous successes. During the remainder of the play, perhaps the Old Etonians had slightly the better of the contest, though they could not succeed in reducing the long score against them, so that at the finish the Wanderers were left victorious by three goals to love. The umpires were Messrs. A. H. Savage (Crystal Palace) and R. A. Ogilvie (Clapham Rovers), whilst Mr. W. S. Rawson (captain of the Oxford University team) officiated as referee. This is the fifth occasion on which the Challenge Cup has been competed for, and the victors have been as follows:—1872, Wanderers; 1873, Wanderers; 1874, Oxford University; 1875, Royal Engineers; 1876, Wanderers. The players were:—

OLD ETONIANS.—H. Alleyne, A. G. Bonsor, M. G. Farrer (half-back), Captain W. S. Kenyon-Slaney, A. F. Kinnaird (captain), Edgar Lubbock (back), Hons. Alfred and Edgar Lyttelton (half-back), J. H. Stronge (half-back), J. R. Sturgis, and F. H. Wilson (goal-keeper).

WANDERERS.—F. H. Birley (captain) and F. B. Maddison (half-backs), W. Lindsay and A. H. Stratford (backs), W. D. Greig (goal), Hubert and Frank Heron, C. H. Wollaston, J. Kenrick, J. Hawley-Edwards, and T. B. Hughes.

THE SCOTTISH ASSOCIATION CUP.

QUEEN'S PARK v. 3RD L.R.V.

The undecided tie-match for this challenge cup, presented by the Scottish Football Association for annual competition amongst the Association clubs of Scotland, was again played on Saturday last, on the ground of the West of Scotland at Partick, and after a spirited game Queen's Park won by two goals to nothing. The Queen's Park won the toss, and played downhill, and in about fifteen minutes succeeded in scoring the first goal, through the instrumentality of Highet, whilst after ends were changed they put another goal to their credit, Highet again giving the final kick. Several plucky runs were made by the Volunteers, particularly towards the close, but they were unable to score. The game finished in a most exciting manner, the Volunteers clustering around the Queen's Park goal in fine style, and Hunter nearly lowering their colours by a pretty shot, which went over the bar a few inches. The Queen's Park have thus won the cup for the third year. About 7,000 or 8,000 spectators witnessed the game. The sides were as follows:—

QUEEN'S PARK.—Dickson (goal), Taylor and Neill (backs), Campbell and Phillips (half-backs), Lawrie, W. M'Kinnon, M'Gill, Angus M'Kinnon, Highet, and H. M'Neill.

3RD L.R.V.—Wallace (goal), Hunter and Wallace (backs), White and D. Davidson (half-backs), Crichton, Drinnan, Scoular, Walker, W. Miller, and J. M'Donald.

CRICKLEWOOD v. HERTS RANGERS.

This match was played at Watford on Saturday, March 18. Cricklewood won the toss and chose the goal nearest the road, with a strong wind in their favour. It was obvious from the first that the Cricklewood were superior to their opponents, as they penned the home team close to their goal, and before long Fison obtained for them the first goal. At half-time the home team had the wind with them, but the Cricklewood backs, viz., Micklam and Redford, proved too strong, and only once was their goal in danger; whilst after a good run from Ince, Fison obtained a second goal for Cricklewood. For the Rangers, W. Gilbert played up very well indeed, and made some good runs. Sides:—

CRICKLEWOOD.—F. A. Thompson (captain), R. Redford, Micklam, and A. Fison (half-backs), T. and J. O'Connor, Hill (back), W. Sewell, Ince, Hart, Buck, and Ratcliff (goal).

HERTS RANGERS.—Edgar (captain) and C. J. Field (half-backs), A. R. Shum, W. Gilbert, C. Gearey, S. Holland, A. Bentley, M. Bevan, J. Macfarlane, R. Smith, and R. Lyster.

RICHMOND FOOTBALL CLUB.—The closing match of the season between members will take place at Richmond on the 25th inst. The teams will be photographed previous, and the annual dinner will be held at the Greyhound at seven p.m. after the match, when it is intended to present Mr. E. H. Ash with a testimonial in recognition of his great services to the club.

JOHN LILLYWHITE'S Football and British Sports Warehouse, 10, Seymour-street, Euston-square, London, NW.—[ADVT.]

CRICKET.

WOOLWICH v. SANDHURST.—The match between the Royal Military Academy, Woolwich, and the Royal Military College, Sandhurst, will be played at Lord's on Thursday and Friday, May 25 and 26.

NORFOLK ALLIANCE CLUB.—At the annual meeting of this club the following officers were elected for the ensuing year:—President, Frank Newling; treasurer, B. Farmer; captain, J. Ingarfield; deputy-captain, William Giller; committee: J. Ingarfield, W. Giller, J. Barrett, J. Bradford, H. Tattersfield, and C. Booty; honorary secretary, William Cole. The club is open for a few mid-week matches with clubs of medium strength on following dates:—May 31, June 7 and 28, July 12, August 2, 9, and 23, and September 13.—Address, William Cole, Rosa Cottage, Albert-road, Mile End, E.

THE Junior Marylebone Club will be glad to arrange Saturday afternoon home-and-home matches with clubs of equal strength; also a few day matches.—Address, J. Targett, 3, Hill-street, Dorset-square, N.W.—[ADVERTISEMENT.]

THE Christ Church United Club are open for home-and-home afternoon matches on June 24 (out) and July 22 (home).—Address, Mr. Baylis, 135, Junction-road, Upper Holloway, N.—[ADVT.]

LATE BICYCLING.

CANN AND THORPE.—We received last night (Tuesday) a telegram from Cann, stating that he would accept Thorpe's terms and take £5 for expenses, and postpone the match for two months. The two had originally agreed to ride ten miles at the Queen's Grounds, Sheffield, on March 13, for £25 a-side, and fresh articles had better be sent to us for signature, so that the fresh date may be definitely arranged. Thorpe should also forward the balance of £10 due from him, and the £5 for Cann.

RABBIT COURSING.

T. BANNISTER'S Bloomer, of Hazel Grove, will run Castle's Fred, the best of thirty-one courses, for £25 or £30 a-side. To run at Royal Oak Park in three weeks, and any fair man to be referee.

MR. GEORGE STOCKDILL, of Wardle, will match his bitch Bute to run Mr. Thomas Stott's Fly, of Rochdale, the best of twenty-one courses, for £20 a-side. The match can be made either at St. James's Tavern, Wardle, or King's Arms, Church-lane, Rochdale, any time to the 18th inst. To run in a fortnight or three weeks following.

OXFORD AND CAMBRIDGE RACKET MATCHES.

On the last two days the single and double-handed racket matches have been decided at Prince's Club, Han's place, Chelsea. The double-handed game was the first played on Tuesday, when the Hon. A. Lyttelton and E. P. Bouverie, both Trinity College, represented Cambridge, and A. J. Webbe, Trinity and H. J. Hollings, New College, Oxford. As in previous years, the rubber was the best of seven games. Cambridge were the favourites, and the result fully justified their being so. They won the first three games, then Oxford obtained the fourth, and, Cambridge being successful in the fifth, won the match by four games to one. The following were the scores:—First game, Cambridge won at 15 aces to 6; second, Cambridge won at 15 to 12; third, Cambridge won at 15 to 7; fourth, Oxford won—14 sett 3 to 14 sett 0; fifth, Cambridge won at 15 to 5. The single-handed match was played between A. J. Webbe, Oxford, and the Hon. A. Lyttelton, Cambridge. The rubber was the best of five games. The light blue again enjoyed the distinction of being the favourite, but the match was most stubbornly contested throughout, and to the surprise of most Webbe proved the winner. He began well by placing the two opening games to his credit, the first at 10 to 8, and the second at 15 to 9. Lyttelton, who had not, up to this time, played at all in his usual form, now freshened up, and won the third game at 15 to 7, and the fourth at 15 to 5. The next was the exciting and decisive game of the match. Lyttelton took the lead, and the score soon stood 7 to 4, and subsequently 13 to 9. It now looked a likely thing for Cambridge, but Webbe made four aces, which brought the score to 13 all. On the sette of 5, each got an ace, when Webbe added three others, but was then put out by Lyttelton, who scored a second ace. Webbe, by a fine volley, however, in turn, put his opponent out, and scored the fifth and decisive ace, thus winning the match by three games to two.

OXFORD AND CAMBRIDGE CHESS MATCH.—This match took place in London on Thursday, under the auspices of the St. George's Club. Oxford won eight games to two (one finished and the other unfinished, but adjudicated in their favour), one game being drawn.

FOOTBALL.—OXFORD UNIVERSITY v. WANDERERS.—On Saturday last there was a very large attendance of spectators at Kennington Oval to witness the final match for the possession of the Challenge Cup presented by the Committee of the Football Association in 1871. The Wanderers who won it the first two years of its institution were the holders, and opinions were divided on their chances of securing it again though their victory over Cambridge on the previous Tuesday had impressed a large majority in their favour. Each club was well represented and the ground was in excellent condition at the outset, the only drawback at the start being a rather high wind blowing directly down the ground from the Harleyford road. Play was announced to begin at half past two o'clock but it was past three before Birley kicked off for the Wanderers against the wind. The Wanderers as usual were by no means well together at the outset and the Oxford forwards tried hard to profit by their opponents' want of energy. Bain and Fernandez made some excellent runs along the upper touch line and Todd and Otter also worked hard. For a few minutes nothing fell to them though at length a long kick by Waddington drove the ball sharply into the centre of the posts and Kinnaird inadvertently stepped back between the posts with the ball in his hands. An immediate appeal was made to the umpires and after some consultation the verdict was given in favour of Oxford—a decision that seemed to be quite correct and fully confirmed by the spectators in the immediate vicinity of the Wanderers' goal. This reverse stimulated the Wanderers and they made a vigorous incursion into Oxford territory. Ultimately a corner kick fell to them but the ball was kicked behind and when it was brought out Bain took it down to the Wanderers' goal. Otter's dribbling was very clever and Todd, Hills, and Bain made some brilliant runs for Oxford, while all round the back play was the best that we have ever seen. The Oxonians pressed their opponents with the wind to help them but the Wanderers' backs prevented any further score before the call of half time. Ends were changed but the wind had dropped a little and the ground was getting greasy from a heavy shower. The Wanderers steadily began to improve their position and though Wollaston had to retire into goal the forwards played in splendid style, Kenrick showing well during the second half, while Heron, Hughes and Wace worked with unremitting energy. More than once they seemed to have an excellent chance of a score and one shot by Heron went just over the bar of the Oxford goal. Neither were the Oxonian forwards idle as Bain, Parry, and Todd made several splendid runs and one corner kick placed the Wanderers' goal in serious jeopardy. When only a few minutes remained of time the Oxford score had not been reduced, but here a fine run by Heron along the upper side followed by a good kick placed the ball neatly to Kenrick and the latter got it securely through the Oxford posts. When time was called each side had scored one goal and the captains tossed for choice of ends for the extra half hour that had been agreed upon in the event of a drawn game. The Wanderers winning, retained their positions at the Harleyford road end and before long a corner kick fell to them. Lindsay planted the ball well in the centre and when it was headed out by Oxford he had a second kick again directing it into the centre of the Oxford posts, this time so cleverly that the goal keeper could not save his charge. Soon after this Heron made a brilliant run and middled the ball in splendid form, but nothing resulted nor did any other score fall to either in the first quarter of an hour. After the change of ends the Wanderers never relaxed their efforts for a moment while Oxford got slack and the game was chiefly in University territory. During the last ten minutes the Oxford forwards played with more energy, but the Wanderers retained their advantage to the finish and won a hardly contested and well played match of two hours by two goals to one, making their fourth victory in this competition. Sides: *Oxford University*: E. H. Parry (captain), A. H. Todd, H. S. Otter, W. S. Rawson, and O. R. Dunell (backs), J. H. Savory and E. W. Waddington (half backs), J. Bain, A. F. Hills, P. Fernandez, and E. Allington (goal) *Wanderers*: F. Birley (captain), and F. T. Green (half backs), T. B. Hughes, J. Kenrick, C. Wollaston, A. Stratford and W. Lindsay (backs), C. A. Denton, Hubert Heron, H. Wace, and A. F. Kinnaird (goal) The Cup has been won as under:—1872 Wanderers, 1873 Wanderers, 1874 Oxford University, 1875 Royal Engineers, 1876 Wanderers, 1877 Wanderers.

Date 24 March 1877
Place The Kennington Oval
Score WANDERERS 2
OXFORD UNIVERSITY 1 (after extra time)
Teams WANDERERS Hon. A. F. Kinnaird, F. H. Burley (capt.), C. A. Denton, F. T. Green, H. Heron, T. B. Hughes, J. Kenrick, W. Lindsay, A. H. Stratford, H. Wace, C. H. R. Wollaston. OXFORD UNIVERSITY E. H. Allington, J. Bain, O. R. Dunnell, J. H. Savory, A. H. Todd, E. W. Waddington, P. H. Fernandez, A. F. Hills, H. S. Otter, E. H. Parry, W. S. Rawson
Official Referee S. H. Wright
Goal Scorers WANDERERS Kenrick, Lindsay; OXFORD UNIVERSITY Kinnaird (own goal)
Attendance 3000
Copy *Oxford University Herald* 31 March 1877

CITY AND COUNTY INTELLIGENCE.

PREACHERS AT CARFAX.

GOOD FRIDAY.

The Rev. the Rector, Morning.
The Rev. H. J. Turrell, Hertford College, Evening.

EASTER DAY.

The Rev. the Rector, Morning.
The Rev. W. B. Keer, Evening.

DEATH.

March 28, at 11, Beaumont Street, William Brunner, Esq., Solicitor and Coroner, in his 81st year, after a long illness.

HOURS OF SERVICE AT THE OXFORD CHURCHES.

THE CATHEDRAL.—Sundays, Holy Communion at 8, except on first Sunday in the month when it is celebrated after Morning Prayer. Morning Prayer at 10, Evening Prayer at 5. On Weekdays, Morning Prayer at 10 Evening Prayer at 5. On Holy Days the services are the same as on Sundays.

ALL SAINTS'.—Sundays, Morning Prayer, 11, Evening Prayer, 7. No week day service.

HOLY TRINITY.—Sunday, Holy Communion at 8 Morning Prayer, at 11; Evening Prayer at 8 and 6.30 On Wednesday, Evening Prayer at 7.

ST. ALDATES',—Sundays, Morning Prayer at 11, Evening Prayer at 7. On Wednesdays, Evening Prayer at 8. The Holy Communion is cetebrated on the 2nd Sunday in the month at 8.30 a.m., on the 3rd Sunday after Evening Prayer, on the last Sunday after Morning Prayer, on the 1st Sunday after Evening Prayer, and at 3.30 p.m.

ST. BARNABAS.—Sundays, Holy Communion at 8 and 11. Morning Prayer at 10.15. Litany and Catechising, 3 p.m. Evening Prayer at 7. Weekdays, Holy Communion daily at 8, Morning Prayer at 10, Evening Prayer at 8. On Holydays, Holy Communion at 8, Morning Prayer at 10.15, Evening Prayer at 8. On the first Sunday in the month the Eucharest is also celebrated at 7 a.m., and on the Chief Festivals also at 6 a.m., and on Ascension Day also at 5 a.m.

ST. CLEMENT.—Sundays, Morning Prayer at 11, Evening Prayer at 6.30. On the first Sunday in the month the Holy Communion is celebrated after Morning Prayer and on the third Sunday at 8 a.m.

ST. EBBE.—Sundays, Morning Prayer at 11, Evening Prayer at 7. On Tuesdays, Evening Prayer at 8 and on Thursday at 7.30. On the Chief Festivals, Morning Prayer is said at 11, and Evening Prayer at 7. The Holy Communion is celebrated on the first Sunday in the Month after Morning Prayer, on the fourth Sunday at 8.30 a.m. and on the third Sunday after Evening Prayer.

ST. PAUL'S.—Sundays, Holy Communion at 7 and 8 a.m., Morning Prayer at 11, Evening Prayer at 3 and 6.30. Weekdays, Thursday Morning Prayer at 7.30 Holy Communion at 8, Evening Prayer at 8. Other days, Morning Prayer at 8, Evening Prayer at 8. Holydays, Holy Communion at 8 a.m., Evening Prayer at 8 p.m.

ST. PETER-LE-BAILEY.—Sundays, Morning Prayer at 11, Evening Prayer at 3.30 and 7. On Wednesdays, Evening Prayer at 7. On the second Sunday in the month Holy Communion is celebrated at 8 a.m., and on the last Sunday after Morning Prayer.

ST. PETER IN THE EAST.—Holy Communion at 8 a.m Morning Prayer at 11, Evening Prayer at 7. On Wednesdays and Fridays, Morning Prayer at 11. On Holy days, Morning Prayer at 11.15.

SS. PHILIP AND JAMES.—Sundays, Holy Commuuion 8 and 11.30. Morning Prayer at 10.30., Evening Prayer at 3 and 7. Litany at 3.45. On Weekdays, Holy Communion at 7 45, Morning Prayer at 8.30., Evening Prayer at 8.30. On Fridays also the Litany at 12, noon.

ST. THOMAS THE MARTYR.—Sundays, Holy Communion at 8 a.m., Morning Prayer at 11, Evening Prayer at 3 and 7 p.m. Weekdays, on Wednesdays and Fridays, Holy Communion at 8 a.m., Morning Prayer at 8.30., Litany at 12, Evening Prayer at 7.30. On other days, Morning Prayer at 11.15.

It is with great regret that we this week have to record the death of our old and respected Coroner, W. Brunner Esq., who died on Wednesday, at his residence, 11 Beaumont Street. Mr. Brunner, who had attained the great age of 81 years, has been ailing for some time past, although he retained the perfect possession of his faculties to the last, except for a slight deafness. The news of his demise was received with much regret at the usual weekly meeting of the Druids on Wednesday evening, Mr. Brunner being one of the oldest Past-Archs of the Order, and the usual mark of respect was paid, namely, that no singing was allowed in Lodge. The respect thus shown by the Druids is also, we feel assured, shared by the whole of the citizens, as Mr. Brunner during the many years that he has held the important office of Coroner has always acted in the most conscientious manner, for while endeavouring to carry out the law to the fullest extent, he at the same time was always particularly careful of the memory of the dead and the feelings of sorrowing relatives and friends. Apart from his office the deceased had acquired the warmest feelings of respect and regard from a large circle of friends and acquaintances, and the intelligence of his death will be received by the citizens generally with great regret, as Mr. Brunner belonged to that class of public men whose loss one and all, without distinction of party, must sincerely deplore.

THE EDUCATION LEAGUE.—At a final meeting of the members of the League, held on Wednesday at Birmingham, a resolution was passed approving the recommendation of the Executive Committee to dissolve the League.

THE BICESTER HUNT.—Lord Valentia, the master of the Bicester and Warden Hill hounds, was on Monday evening entertained by the farmers of the hundred at a complimentary dinner at the King's Arms Hotel, Bicester. The Earl of Jersey presided, and there were upwards of 150 of the subscribers and farmers of the hundred present.

CHURCHMEN'S UNION SPORTS.—These Sports will be held on Monday next, on the Iffley Running Ground, which has been kindly lent for the purpose by the O.U.A.C. There are a large number of entries, and an excellent day's sport is anticipated. The prizee will be delivered in the evening, when the proceedings will be brought to a closs with the usual dance.

EMIGRATION TO QUEENSLAND.—The new iron barque, "Southesk," Captain Gray, R.N.R., sailed from Gravesend yesterday, bound for Brisbane, Queensland, having on board the following number of emigrants, viz., 62 married people, 158 single men, 82 single women, 35 children between the ages of 12 and 1, and 14 infants, making a total of 351 souls, equal to 319½ statute adults. The single women are under the charge of Mrs. Cochot, Dr. Garde acting as Surgeon-Superintendent.

PARLIAMENTARY PETITIONS.—The following petitions have been presented to the House of Commons:—By Mr. Mowbray from the principal and scholars of Brasenose College, Oxford, in favour of the Universities Bill. By Mr. Holt, in favour of the Cruelty to Animals Bill. By Col. North, from the Primitive Methodists of Minster Lovell and Eysham, in favour of closing Public-houses in England and Ireland on Sundays.

THE LATE CANON JENKINS' MEMORIAL.—Mr. Robert Thompson, secretary of the Locomotive Servants' Friendly Society (Oxford Branch), the appointed collector in this district for the subscriptions to the fund for raising a monument to the late respected Canon Jenkins, has been very successful in obtaining responses to his appeal, and has forwarded the money to the treasurer of the fund.

OXFORD COUNTY COURT.—The usual monthly sitting of this Court took place on the 20th inst., before W. H. Cooke, Esq., Q.C., Judge. There were 162 new plaints, 7 adjourned cases, and 15 judgment summones. The only case of public interest was the following:—Towle *v.* Gale.—This was an action brought by Mr. Towle, J.P., for £7 10., against Mr. Thomas Gale, of the Seven Stars public house, for the use and occupation of premises at Grandpont Mill, from February 1 to November 4, 1876. Mr. Gregson appeared for the defendent. The plaintif stated that he found the defendent occupying his premises from the time named, and he considered him a tenant. The defendant said he borrowed the premises to put a horse in for the races, and he then agreed to give Mrs. Talboys, who was in possession of the mill, 1s. 6d. a week as rent for the place. It was an engine house. This arrangement was made with Mrs. Talboys, Mr. Towle saw him three or four

THE FOOTBALL ASSOCIATION CHALLENGE CUP.
THE FINAL TIE.

WANDERERS V. ROYAL ENGINEERS.—On Saturday last the possession of the Challenge Cup presented in 1872 by the committee of the Football Association was finally decided. The Wanderers, who had won it in 1872 and 1873, were also the holders in 1876 and 1877, and hence victory on Saturday for them meant a permanent hold on the cup, which becomes, according to the rules, the property of any club holding it for three successive years. The weather, though cold, was gloriously fine, and the prospect of a hard fight attracted the largest gathering that has been seen at the Oval this year, over 3000 spectators being present during the game. To judge by the opinions of some the result was a moral for the Wanderers, and though on public form they were certainly the better eleven, there was nothing to justify the long odds that were talked about. Both clubs were well represented, and as the ground was in excellent condition, there was everything in favour of a fast game. The Engineers lost the toss, and at twenty minutes to four o'clock Hedley kicked off from the eastern end, with the sun in his face, and the wind, though blowing across the ground, slightly against him. The Wanderers were quickly at work, and Kinnaird had an unsuccessful shot at the opposite goal. Immediately afterwards Wace at the end of a short run crossed the ball, and Kenrick directed it safely into the centre of the Engineers' posts, this first score being obtained within five minutes of the start. Nettled at this early reverse, the Engineers made some vigorous attacks, the forwards being evidently bent on worrying the Wanderer half-backs and backs. At first the Sappers profited a little by this style of play, and for a few minutes the Wanderers were pressed. In one of these onslaughts Kirkpatrick fractured his arm, but with great pluck he kept his place in charge of goal to the end, and, indeed, it was not until the match was finished that the accident was known. The Sapper forwards gave the Wanderers little chance of rallying, and at last a good throw in by Morris enabled them to carry the Wanderers' goal with a determined rush. On the renewal of hostilities the Engineers held a momentary advantage, but the Wanderers were not to be settled, and at length they carried the ball down the ground in fine style, just missing another score. Shortly after the Wanderers again made a sharp attack, and after a free kick by Kinnaird the ball was a second time driven between the Engineers' posts. After the kick off the play became faster than ever, and some fine runs were made by Denton and Kenrick on the one side, by Heron and Wollaston on the other, while Hedley, Ruck, Bond, and Barnet were untiring for the Engineers. At half-time ends were changed, and not long after the resumption Hedley got the ball through the Wanderers' goal, but as he was given off-side, no score resulted. After this the game became more interesting, as the Engineer forwards grew less demonstrative to the Wanderer backs, and all round the play was excellent. The Wanderers, as they have always done on previous occasions, improved as time advanced, and after a very fine run by Heron, Kenrick landed the third goal for them. This third score was obtained about twenty-five minutes before the finish, and there was plenty of time left for the Engineers to recover their losses. The Wanderers, however, were not to be overcome, and ... Towards the last their play ... was excellent, Heron's dribbling being very fine, while Wace was usually on the ball, and the forwards generally were well together. More than once the Engineers looked dangerous, but the play during the second half was certainly in favour of the Wanderers, and finally at the end of an hour and a half they were left the winners by three goals to one. Sides:

Wanderers: Hon. A. F. Kinnaird (captain) and F. J. Green (half-backs), A. H. Stratford and W. Lindsay (backs), J. G. Wylie and H. Wace (centres), C. H. Wollaston and Hubert Heron (right side), J. Kenrick and C. A. Denton (left side), and J. Kirkpatrick (goal). C. Warner (Upton Park), umpire.

Royal Engineers: Lieuts R. S. Hedley (captain) and C. E. Haynes (centres), M. Lindsay and H. H. Barnett (right side), F. G. Bond and O. E. Ruck (left side), F. Heath and C. B. Mayne (half-backs), J. H. Cowan and W. G. Morris (backs), and L. B. Friend (goal). B. G. Jarrett (Old Harrovians), umpire; and S. R. Bastard (Upton Park), referee.

THE chief event in the football way in London was the final tie for the Association Challenge Cup, which took place at Kennington on Saturday afternoon, the Wanderers and the Royal Engineers being the last clubs left in to do battle for the cup. There was a very large attendance of visitors and capital football was played, the match ending in favour of the Wanderers by three goals to one. The cup had to be won three years in succession to become the property of any one club, and as the Wanderers had held it since 1876 they became the final possessors. They offered the cup back, but the committee refused to take it, having made up their minds to offer a new cup next year. The Sheffield and Birmingham Association played at Witton the same day, and Sheffield were the winners. Scotland and Wales played at Hampden Park, Glasgow, on Saturday. The weather was fine, and there was an attendance of over 12,000 spectators. The game resulted in the defeat of the Cambrians by nine goals to none. The Welshmen, who lost the toss, had immediately to defend their goal, and four minutes after the ball was set in motion Scotland obtained the first goal, while before the lapse of fifteen minutes their second goal was won. In rapid succession the Scotchmen gained the third, fourth, fifth, and sixth goals. After half time,

---

Date 23 March 1878
Place The Kennington Oval
Score WANDERERS 3
ROYAL ENGINEERS 1
Teams WANDERERS J. Kirkpatrick, A. Stratford, W. Lindsay, Hon. A. F. Kinnaird (capt.), F. T. Green, C. H. R. Wollaston, H. Heron, J. G. Wylie, H. Wace, C. A. Denton, J. Kenrick. ROYAL ENGINEERS L. B. Friend, H. H. Barnet, F. G. Bond, J. H. Cowan, C. E. Haynes, F. C. Heath, R. B. Hedley (capt.), M. Lindsay, C. B. Mayne, W. J. Morris, O. E. Ruck. **Official** Referee S. R. Bastard **Goal Scorers** WANDERERS Kenrick 2, Kinnaird; ROYAL ENGINEERS Not recorded **Attendance** 4500 **Copy** *The Sportsman* 25 March 1878; *The Sporting Clipper* 30 March 1878

---

despite every exertion of the Welshmen, their fortress was again and again assailed, the goal-keeper and backs being kept in active employment averting the attacks on their posts. But notwithstanding all their efforts their goal fell for the seventh, eighth, and ninth time, the game thus resulting as above—nine to none. The Welshmen played a very plucky game, but were deficient in the passing and dodging tactics observed by the Scotchmen. The season is now nearly over, and shortly we shall have the cricket fixtures before us, which bid fair to be unusually heavy this year, the Australian team's matches adding something like twenty first-class events to the list.

BICYCLING.

To make up for his loss when he rode 1000 miles in six days, Stanton's friends got him up a benefit at the Agricultural Hall on Monday night, but I am afraid when all expenses are paid the affair will turn out to have been no great catch. The opening of the bicycle season of 1878 was celebrated at the Queen's Grounds, Sheffield, on Saturday, with some sports under the direction of Mr H. Wilson, said to be for various prizes valued at £25. The day was bitterly cold, but notwithstanding this fact the affair was moderately well patronised. On the programme were three events, a Two-mile Bicycle Race (open to all who have never won a money prize), a Three-mile Open Race, and a One Mile Open Race. Only the two first named, however, were gone into, the one mile being reserved for Monday, the winners being—Two Miles: T. Egginton (160 yards start); Three Miles, F. Leeds (50 yards start); One Mile, W. Shaw (220).

WRESTLING.

A WRESTLING MATCH which excited a considerable amount of interest was brought off at the Higginshaw Grounds, Oldham, on Saturday afternoon. The athletes engaged were J. Butterworth, alias Dockum, of Oldham, and J. Schofield, of Hollinwood, and the conditions were to wrestle the best of three back falls in the Lancashire style, catch as catch can, at catch weight, for £25 a-side. The weather was exceedingly favourable and there was an immense attendance, between 3000 and 4000 persons being present. Schofield was self-trained, but Dockum very wisely selected a mentor, and was prepared by W. Petty, another well-known wrestler, from the Miners' Arms, George-street, Oldham. They were in excellent condition, but Dockum, who has been the hero of many a hard-fought bout, was at once installed the favourite, the betting, which opened at 22 to 20, closing at 6 to 4 on him. He was attended in the ring by his trainer, whilst Schofield was esquired by J. Coyle, alias Gall, of Wigan, and shortly after the hour announced every preparation was made. They commenced to work in the most determined fashion, and at first Schofield had rather the best of it, using his superior weight and strength to some advantage. When about ten minutes had expired the crowd broke into the inclosure, a portion of the paling having given way, and several who fell had a very narrow escape of being trampled to death. Thanks, however, to the supervision of the police who were in attendance, nothing serious occurred, and the men were only momentarily disengaged. Dockum now took the uppermost position, and working with great determination gained the first fall, the bout having occupied altogether 17min 30sec. After an interval of ten

---

minutes hostilities were renewed, and Dockum very quickly getting his opponent in such an awkward position that escape was totally impossible secured the second thrut in 2min 30sec. He was nearly 12lb lighter than his opponent.

PEDESTRIANISM, &c.

THE great pedestrian match which commenced on Monday week at the Agricultural Hall, Islington, was brought to a conclusion on Saturday, the termination being somewhat abrupt, as the crowd broke into the arena soon after eight o'clock, and it was found impracticable for any of the competitors to resume. As was clearly seen for the greater part of the week, O'Leary, from the long lead he had taken, was most likely to win unless some unforseen accident should happen, and it was also pretty clear that Vaughan, of Chester, would be second man, the latter having "Blower" Brown and Ide, of North Woolwich, as his nearest opponents. Throughout the week the attendance had been much larger than has been seen at any of these "shows" on previous occasions, and those who promoted the affair must have reaped a pretty considerable reward for their generosity on behalf of pedestrianism. On Saturday night at eight o'clock there could not have been less than 20,000 persons in the hall, and long after the contest was over the cry was "still they come." During the last day O'Leary was twenty-four miles in front of Vaughan, and he had only to keep on a slow pace to win, but several besides those I have mentioned above were kept on the track, on promise of extra payment, in order that the affair should not be quite so monotonous as it would have been if only one or two of the jaded walkers had been seen at intervals on the track. As the evening approached Vaughan began to go very queerly, "Blower" Brown was incapable of further effort, and they only kept on to secure their positions. O'Leary was pronounced the winner by 20 miles and 2 laps, having completed in the six days 520 miles and the odd distance. Vaughan turned it up at 500 miles, and Brown at 477, while Ide stopped at 406. The first prize is £500 and a belt worth £100, which will pay the Yankee well for his journey to this country, and the second prize is £100, while £50 goes to the third man. These were to be considerably increased if the "gate" turned out well, and as it did I presume more prize money will be received; but as I hear the judges were paid £1 less than was promised them it does not seem feasible that the competitors will get any further augmentation of their prizes out of the immense sum that must have been taken at the doors. Looking upon the affair as a whole I cannot see that it has been productive of any advantage to pedestrianism beyond proving the stamina of man, and I am sure it was a most pitiable spectacle when some of them became so footsore and leg-weary during the latter part of the contest. As I stated last week O'Leary was allowed a track to himself, and he had a wholesome tent wherein to take his rest, but the "common herd," as the Englishmen were called, had their rabbit hutches pitched in a part of the hall where the drainage was in a most defective state, so it is no wonder some of them were ill. O'Leary is not to be allowed to rest long on his laurels, for Howes and Weston have challenged him for the belt and £500 a-side, and the former's backer has staked £100 as an earnest of his intention. O'Leary does not, however, seem in a hurry to make a fresh match.

There was little else doing in the metropolis in this way on Saturday, the chief events being left over until Monday, when, at Lillie Bridge, A. Clark, of Bethnal Green, undertook to walk eight miles within the hour. He had been well-trained for the event, and although he "mixed" considerably, the "scythe-bearer" defeated him by 20 4-5th sec. At the Sportsman Ground, Plumstead, F. Anderson (54) won a 440 Yards Handicap, and at the St. Helena Gardens, Rotherhithe, A. Williamson (8) carried off the 130 Yards £25 Handicap.

At the St. Thomas's Recreation Grounds, Stanningley, on Saturday, T. Brady, of Hunslet, and J. Simmons, of York-road, Leeds, contested the best at run, hop, two strides, and jump, for £25 a-side, Simmons being allowed twenty-four inches start inside. Brady having won the toss went on first and covered about sixteen yards and a half, which Simmons followed and cut by one inch and a half. Brady then followed, but owing to his having sprained his ankle during his training he broke down in both his trials to cut, and was therefore defeated by one inch and a half.

The business at Hendon Recreation Grounds, Sunderland, on Saturday, opened with a 120 yards race between Maffin, of Cornhill, and G. Thompson, of Ayre's Quay, for £10 a-side. Maffin won easily by three yards. The next event was a foot-race between J. Mann and M. Henderson, both of Southwick, 100 yards, for £20, the latter receiving seven yards start. Henderson was declared the winner by three yards. The 440 yards race for £50 between M. Richardson, of the Felling, and J. Coulthard, of Gateshead, fell through. The concluding item was a race against time by A. Carter, of Sunderland, 11 years of age, to run two miles within 14min for a bet of £10. Carter accomplished the task with 1min 30sec to spare.

1879

THE FOOTBALL ASSOCIATION CHALLENGE CUP.

THE FINAL TIE.—Saturday last witnessed the settlement of the question which has been vexing Association players in England for the last six months as to which club was to be the fortunate one able to claim the honour of holding the challenge cup of the Football Association for the next twelve months. The Wanderers last spring, it may be remembered, won the cup outright by three successive victories, but they decided to offer it again to the Association. In the first round the holders were knocked out of the competition, and the decisive victory gained by the Old Etonians on this occasion caused them to be regarded as the most dangerous competitors for the cup, though as the affair advanced the victories of the Nottingham Foresters over prominent clubs, and the hard struggles between the Old Etonians and Darwen, left the final apparently much more open than had at first been believed. The Clapham Rovers having drawn the bye in the fifth ties were thus left in for the deciding struggle, and that they were expected to make a good bid for victory was proved by the attendance of spectators, who numbered between 2500 and 3000. A heavy shower about three o'clock was somewhat unfortunate, but when play began shortly before half-past three the sky had cleared again, and the wind, though blowing stiffly from the west, was not so violent as on the two previous Saturdays. The ground was in excellent condition, and when Ogilvie started the ball at 3.25 for the Clapham Rovers, with both wind and sun at his back, there was every prospect of a fast game. Major Marindin, to whose energy the resuscitation of the Old Etonian Club is mainly due, was unable, owing to illness, to occupy his place between the posts in the last two matches of the competition, and the team suffered also in the final by the absence of R. D. Anderson. The Clapham Rovers were the first to obtain any marked advantage, and a corner-kick from the lower flag by Bailey was so skilfully aimed that the Etonians were unable to get the ball away, and twice more Bailey made fine shots from the corner, though in each case, by desperate efforts, the defending side averted a score. Whitfeld made some good runs on the left wing for the Etonians, and Growse was particularly busy in the centre for the Rovers, but otherwise the forward play was by no means brilliant on either side, and hardly up to the standard of a final tie, while on the other hand the backs were admirable, Bailey and Prinsep never missing a chance for the Rovers, nor Christian for the opposite team. Some vigorous attacks were made by the Etonians, and three corner kicks were essayed without success, though on the second occasion Birkett just managed to prevent a goal by putting the ball on to the cross-bar. Not long before half-time Bevington missed an easy shot at the Eton goal, and neither eleven had gained any point when ends were changed. During the second half the weather was threatening, but with the exception of a slight fall of hail no damage was done, and the game was kept up briskly until the last. The Rovers' backs never relaxed their efforts for a moment, but as the game advanced the forwards flagged. The Etonians gradually took the lead, and twenty five minutes before the finish, after a good run along the centre, Goodhart crossed nearly to Clerke, and the latter with a clever shot landed the ball just within the Rovers' posts, this score forming the signal for enthusiastic applause from the partisans of Eton. On the resumption the Etonians had slightly the advantage until the end, and the expiration of the prescribed period left them the winners by one goal to none. Whitfeld's play was far and away the best on the Eton side, while Christian's accurate kicking helped materially to give them the victory. For the Rovers Bailey and Prinsep were throughout brilliant, and their back play all round was the best we have seen in this season's Cup competitions, but with the exception of Growse, who did a lot of work during the first half, the forwards were not up to the mark.

Date 29 March 1879
Place Kennington Oval
Score OLD ETONIANS 1 CLAPHAM ROVERS 0
Teams OLD ETONIANS J. P. Hawtrey, E. Christian, L. Bury, Hon. A. F. Kinnaird (capt.), E. Lubbock, C. J. Clerke, N. Pares, H. C. Goodhart, H. Whitfeld, J. B. T. Chevallier, H. Beaufoy. CLAPHAM ROVERS R. H. Birkett, R. A. Ogilvie (capt.), E. Field, N. C. Bailey, J. F. M. Prinsep, F. L. Rawson, A. J. Stanley, S. W. Scott, H. S. Bevington, E. F. Growse, C. Keith-Falconer
Official Referee C. W. Alcock
Goal Scorer Clerke
Attendance 5000
Copy *The Eton College Chronicle* 15 May 1879; *The Sportsman* 31 March 1879

FIRST TIES.

Forest School beat Rochester by four goals to two.
Sheffield beat Grantham by three goals to one, after drawn game.
Unity scratched to Remnants.
Upton Park beat Saffron Walden by five goals to none.
Leyton scratched to South Norwood.
Swifts beat Hawkhurst by two goals to one.
Reading beat Hendon by one goal to none.
Romford beat Ramblers by three goals to one.
Birch (Manchester) scratched to Darwen.
Old Etonians beat Wanderers by seven goals to two.
Royal Engineers beat Old Foresters by three goals to none.
Cambridge University beat Herts Rangers by two goals to none.
Grey Friars beat Great Marlow by two goals to one.
105th Regiment scratched to Minerva.
Barnes beat Maidenhead by four goals to none, after drawn game.
Runnymede scratched to Panthers after a draw.
Notts Forest beat Nottingham by three goals to one.
Pilgrims beat Brentwood by three goals to one.
Old Harrovians beat Southill Park by eight goals to none.
Finchley scratched to Clapham Rovers.
Oxford University beat Wednesday Strollers by seven goals to none.
Eagley (Bolton) (a bye).

SECOND TIES.

Oxford University beat Royal Engineers by four goals to none.
Clapham Rovers beat Forest School by ten goals to one.
Cambridge University beat South Norwood by three goals to none.
Minerva beat Grey Friars by three goals to none.
Darwen beat Eagley by four goals and a disputed goal to one goal.
Old Harrovians beat Panthers by three goals to none.
Old Etonians beat Reading by one goal to none.
Barnes beat Upton Park.
Swifts beat Romford by three goals to one.
Remnants beat Pilgrims by six goals to two.
Nottingham Forest beat Sheffield Club by two goals to none.

THIRD TIES.

Old Etonians beat Minerva by five goals to two.
Nottingham Forest beat Old Harrovians by two goals to none.
Darwen beat Remnants by three goals to two.
Clapham Rovers beat Cambridge University by one goal to none.
Oxford University beat Barnes by two goals to one.
Swifts (a bye).

FOURTH TIES.

Old Etonians beat Darwen (after two drawn games) by six goals to two.
Nottingham Forest beat Oxford University by two goals to one.
Clapham Rovers beat Swifts by eight goals to one.

FIFTH TIES.

Old Etonians beat Notts Forest by two goals to one.
Clapham Rovers (a bye).

FINAL TIE.

Old Etonians beat Clapham Rovers by one goal to none.

SHEFFIELD ASSOCIATION CUP.—FINAL TIE.

THURSDAY WANDERERS V. HEELEY.—The final match for the possession of this trophy was played between the above teams at Bramall-lane Grounds, Sheffield, on Saturday last. For once in a way the weather was on its best behaviour, and as football each succeeding season seems to become more popular in Sheffield a large attendance of quite 5000 spectators was hardly a surprise. Both elevens were known to possess some smart performers, but the Wanderers with their Nottingham contingent were decidedly favourites. The Wanderers won the toss, and at three o'clock the leather was set rolling by Hunter, the Heeley captain. The ground was in a very slippery condition, and, contrary to expectation, the Wanderers kicked against the wind with the sun right in their faces. From the very outset the play became tremendously fast, and spills were most frequent. At first Heeley showed to great advantage, and but for the excellent goal-keeping of W. Ellison, must have unquestionably scored. As it was, the Wanderers' fortress was kept intact until just before the call of half-time, when the oft-repeated efforts of their opponents were at length rewarded with a goal, Andrews, with a screw-kick, aided by the wind, being the lucky performer. Ends were changed, and immediately on a resumption the Wanderers went at it with determination, and finally equalised matters, amidst the greatest excitement. After this, although the Heeleyites tried all they knew to hold their own, they gradually had to give way, their opponents now profiting considerably by the aid of the wind. From a scrimmage in front of the Heeley citadel, a second goal was registered to the Wanderers, Ellison, regardless of consequences, rushing in and carrying the leather, together with several of the players, through the posts. Exceedingly fast play marked the recommencement of hostilities, which in other respects was virtually noted for the decided advantage of the Wanderers. A quarter of an hour before the call of time T. H. Sorby was entrusted with a kick from the corner. The ball was cleverly forwarded to A. W. Cursham, who, directing in his customary clever style, sent it into goal. Here the custodian interfered, but before he could get it safely away Wood interposed and succeeded in lowering the Heeley stronghold for the third time. No further score occurred, and when time was called the Wanderers were declared the victors by three goals to one. For the victors Greenhalgh, the Curshams, and Sorby played best, while Hunter and the Tomlinson deserve a word of praise for their plucky efforts in trying to avert defeat.

On Monday, March 31st, the House met to discuss the question "Is there any danger of the over education of women?" Various causes combined to make the House very thinly attended and the debate short and deficient in interest. Mumm opened, advocating the cause of the fair sex. He thought that everyone would own that knowledge in itself was a good thing, and that therefore the increase of knowledge among women was desirable and likely to improve them. The reasons on the other side were mostly fallacious and traceable to deeply-rooted prejudice. Men thought women unfit to be highly educated, partly because they took a natural pleasure in forbidding to others, as their inferiors, what they thought they might use themselves with advantage; partly because they believed that knowledge was likely to destroy those qualities in women which are most highly esteemed. This was a mistake arising from the consideration of special cases. That knowledge implanted in a mind not ready to receive is bad was indisputable, but this applied as much to men as women: at present, when women were still in the position of looking upon all knowledge as a kind of forbidden fruit, they were perhaps likely to attach an undue importance to the possession of it, but if their "free admission" into all branches of it were made a matter of course, they would soon reach the desirable condition of the other sex; those who were capable of being improved by knowledge would so improve themselves,—those who were not, instead of wanting to learn and not being allowed to, would find themselves made to learn without wanting to.

Chitty followed on the other side, thinking that much learning of any kind in women would be likely to produce the same undesirable results which are sometimes caused by too entire devotion to mathematics in men. He thought that the function of women was not the acquisition of knowledge, and that it would be likely to rob them of their special graces and virtues: it was good in moderation, but where was the line to be drawn? Lord Eskdaill thought there was not much danger of the over-education of women, but drew a terrible picture of the results of such over education if it should ever come to pass, describing the perils of a man married to a wife devoted to learning—the evening's rest destroyed, the dinner unordered—with great force and vividness. He confined learning apparently to Euclid and Thucydides. De Paravicini objected to young ladies' colleges, and Byass to learning on general grounds. The few succeeding speakers disagreed with the Opener.

—o—

OLD ETONIAN FOOTBALL CLUB, 1878—9.

It may be remembered that in October last a notice appeared in our columns, stating that this club, which seemed to have died a natural death, was to be revived on a somewhat new basis, and that a Committee had been appointed to manage its affairs. The re-organised club was entered for the Association Challenge Cup, and the venture was warmly taken up by Old Etonians in London and at the two Universities. There are now about 70 members, and there is every reason to hope that the club will each year be recruited with the best football talent which Eton can produce. Now that the coveted trophy is actually in the possession of the Old Etonian Football Club, a result for which the most sanguine scarcely ventured to hope, in this the first year of the Club's reorgansation, it may perhaps interest some of our readers to give a brief *resumé* of the principal matches played in the season of 1878—9.

In the 1st ties for the Cup the Wanderers were drawn the winners of the Cup for the three previous years. The Etonians were fortunate in being able to play their full strength, and the result of the match which had been looked forward to with great interest by lovers of the game, completely upset all calculations, resulting as it did in the defeat of the Wanderers, by 7 goals to 2. In the 3rd and 4th ties Reading and the Minerva Club respectively were met. The former match was won only by one goal to nothing, but it was played at a time when the frost rendered real football almost out of the question, as the ground was far more fit for skating than for running. The Minerva men played a very plucky game, but were overmatched. With the 4th ties came Darwen and endless trouble; nor was it until the third match that the Etonians succeeded in beating their North Country opponents, who played with a pluck and determination which could not but compel admiration. The Clapham Rovers drew blank in the 5th round, leaving the Old Etonians to contend with the Notts Foresters for the honour of playing in the final match. This match was perhaps the best in the whole competition, the play exhibited on both sides was excellent. Both teams played up as if they meant to win, but Eton had the luck, and just before call of time managed to secure the winning goal. The Clapham Rovers were not supposed to be so good as the Notts Foresters, but the Etonians were deprived of the services of two of their team, and the match was an even one, chiefly remarkable for the fine play of the backs on both sides, but resulting eventually in a win for Eton. The Cup now in the hands of the Old Etonians ought not to be allowed for many years at least to change its present owners, and indeed we feel no doubt that we shall in future seasons be able to repeat the success of 1878—9. In conclusion we would say that in our opinion that success has been due in no small measure to the energy and good management of the Captain, Major Marindin, R.E., and the Secretary, R. D. Anderson.

● A goal 25 minutes from time by C. J. Clerke brought Old Etonians their first FA Cup success, and completed a significant revival in the fortunes of the club, described in the cutting (column one).

The victory was achieved despite the absence of Major Maradin, the inspiration of the renaissance of the Old Etonians, who missed the final through illness. The chauvinism of the times is beautifully illustrated in the accompanying report from the Eton debating society and their discussion of the question: "Is there any danger of the over education of women?" One of the speakers, de Paravicini, may well be the same who represented Old Etonians in the 1882 FA Cup final.

THE SPORTING LIFE, WEDNESDAY, APRIL 14, 1880.

ASSOCIATION CHALLENGE CUP.
CLAPHAM ROVERS v. OXFORD UNIVERSITY.

The ninth competition for the challenge cup, instituted by the Football Association Committee in 1871, was concluded on Saturday last in presence of several thousand spectators. The Rovers won the toss, and Ogilvie having first elected to defend the goal nearest the gasometer, at a quarter past three the Oxonians kicked off against a strong breeze. Following up well, the University men quickly carried down the ball, and within a few minutes a kick by Phillips just sent the ball outside the Rovers' goal posts. The Rovers now played up well, Sparks, Lloyd-Jones, and Ram making capital runs, the last-named at the finish making a splendid kick, which sent the ball against one of the posts. For some time now the play was continued in the centre of the ground, the backs on both sides playing exceedingly well, until a combined rush down by the Clapham forwards resulted in a bully just in front of the Oxford goal, which was neatly saved by Parry. The next event was the Oxonians endangering the Rovers' goal, the excellent keeping of Birkett alone saving it from being reduced. A capital middle by Lloyd-Jones now threatened the University goal, but the final kick by Brougham was too hard and sent the ball over the cross-bar. Once again the play was very even, and when "half-time" was called ends were changed without either side having gained any advantage. The Oxonians now had the assistance of the wind, and after the Rovers' kick-off, they penned their opponents, and in quick succession gained two corner kicks, which proved unproductive. The Rovers, however, played the better together, and headed by Ram, Bailey, Lloyd-Jones, Stanley, and Sparks, carried down the ball in face of the wind, and more than once Parr had to use his hands to save his charge. Heygate, Phillips, Wilson, and Childs headed the Oxford attacks, and by dint of great exertions secured a couple of corner kicks, from which, however, nothing resulted. The game was now carried on so evenly that a draw appeared imminent, but about ten minutes before "time" a splendid run by Sparks enabled Lloyd-Jones to kick a goal for the Rovers, amid tremendous enthusiasm and excitement. The University made strenuous efforts to retrieve the day, but although several times within an ace of scoring, failed to do so, and the Clapham Rovers won a well-earned victory by one goal to none. Umpires, Messrs. C. W. Alcock and R. Barker; referee, Major Marindin, R.E. Sides:—

CLAPHAM ROVERS.—R. A. Ogilvie (captain) and E. Field (backs), V. Weston and N. C. Bailey (half backs), R. Birkett (goal keeper), A. J. Stanley, H. Brougham, F. J. Sparkes, F. Barry, E. A. Ram, and C. Lloyd-Jones.

OXFORD.—C. W. Wilson and C. J. S. King (backs), F. A. T. Phillips and B. Rogers (half-backs), P. C. Parr (goal-keeper), G. B. Childs, F. D. Crowdy, R. T. Heygate (captain), J. B. Lubbock, J. Eyre, and E. H. Hill.

Results of final Cup competitions:—1872, Wanderers; 1873, Wanderers; 1874, Oxford University; 1875, Royal Engineers; 1876, Wanderers; 1877, Wanderers; 1878, Wanderers; 1879, Old Etonians; 1880, Clapham Rovers.

ALEXANDRA PARK RECREATION GROUNDS, ROOD END, NEAR OLDBURY.

MONDAY.—The final heats in Mr. G. Felton's £8 Dog Handicap drew a tolerably good company here to-day, and after a couple of rounds had been got through the concluding struggle resulted as follows:—Smith's Hermit, 15lb, 27 yards' start, first; Crump's Pansy, 18¾lb, 23, second; Johnson's Rose, 12lb, 30½, third. Won by half a yard; two yards dividing second and third.

ROYAL OAK RECREATION GROUNDS, BURNT TREE, NEAR DUDLEY.

These old grounds, which have for a long time been lying idle, were the scene on Monday last of a very important dog race, the contestants being Bissell's Judy, the champion at her weight, and Wright's Charlotte, both of Hill Top, who were matched to run

Date 10 April 1880
Place The Kennington Oval
Score CLAPHAM ROVERS 1
OXFORD UNIVERSITY 0
Teams CLAPHAM ROVERS R. H. Birkett, R. A. Ogilvie (capt.), E. Field, V. Weston, N. C. Bailey, A. J. Stanley, H. Brougham, F. J. Sparkes, F. Barry, E. A. Ram, C. Lloyd-Jones. OXFORD UNIVERSITY P. C. Parr, C. W. Wilson, C. J. S. King, F. A. T. Phillips, B. Rogers, G. B. Childs, F. D. Crowdy, R. T. Heygate (capt.), J. B. Lubbock, J. Eyre, E. H. Hill
Officials Referee Major Marindin. Umpires C. W. Alcock, R. Barker
Goal Scorer Lloyd-Jones 80
Attendance 6000
Copy *The Sporting Life* 14 April 1880

MOSTON PARK GROUNDS, CHADDERTON, NEAR MANCHESTER.

SATURDAY, APRIL 10.—Another of Mr. Thomas Hayes's 300 Yards Handicaps was brought to a satisfactory conclusion this afternoon, in the presence of some 300 persons. Prizes amounting in the aggregate to £6 10s. were offered for competition, and the six heats into which the fifty-two pedestrians were classed produced some capital racing and a fair amount of speculation. The first and third heats were each won by half a yard by Whittaker and Lawson respectively, and in the sixth Tetlow, of Hulme, defeated Buckley, of Taunton, on the post. For the deciding contest Shaw, of Hulme, who had won his preliminary trial rather easily, was installed a warm favourite, and he won very cleverly, Richards finishing second, and Lindsey, who has been very unlucky of late, third. Messrs. Walter Hayes and J. Scholefield officiated as referee and pistol-firer respectively, and appended will be found a return:—Heat 1: J. Whittaker, Manchester, 33 yards' start, first; J. Sheldon, Hulme, 30, second; J. E. Hulme, Lees, 22, third; T. Royle, Manchester, 36, 0; R. Buttery, Sheffield, 8, 0. Won by half a yard. Heat 2: D. Shaw, Hulme, 26, first; A. Cooke, Hightown,

● Clapham Rovers, the beaten finalists of the previous year, gained a narrow victory over Oxford University in the 1880 final. According to *The Sporting Life* the game's only goal arrived "about ten minutes before 'time'." F. J. Sparks made the kind of solo dribble which still characterised the style of play of the day, and C. Lloyd-Jones "kicked" the winner. Only five of the Clapham side remained from the 1879 final, but two of them were numbered amongst the best sportsmen in the land. R.H. Birkett's handling skills in goal, which brought him an England cap against Scotland in 1879, also made him one of a rare band to represent England at rugby as well. N. C. Bailey's talent brought him 21 England appearances, and he was still playing for his country seven years after winning this Cup final. For Oxford University it was their fourth final – and their third defeat.

The choice of officials emphasised what a small family football still was at this time. Major Marindin was now the referee with Charles Alcock still involved in the final as one of the two umpires. A year later Alcock received a testimonial from the FA (see below left) in recognition of his 18 years service to the organisation he fostered.

THE SPORTING LIFE, WEDNESDAY, APRIL 13, 1881.

THE FOOTBALL ASSOCIATION CUP.
OLD CARTHUSIANS v. OLD ETONIANS.

At Kennington Oval on Saturday last the destination of the Association Cup was decided for the season by the Old Carthusians handsomely defeating the Old Etonians. The weather was fine, and the ground in capital condition, being all in favour of fast play. Some three thousand people mustered to witness the game, and the keenest interest was taken in the contest throughout. The Carthusians won the toss, and at twenty minutes to four Macaulay started the play for the Etonians, who began from the Gasometer goal. From the outset the Carthusians pressed their opponents, and the Light Blues' goal was repeatedly threatened. After several narrow escapes the Etonians looked like having a goal scored against them, Parry getting a fairly safe shot, which, however, failed. When the game had lasted half an hour, from a corner kick by Prinsep the ball was sent through out of a general bully in front of the Etonians' goal. Nothing further was done before half-time. On ends being changed Parry quickly gained a goal for his side, but the score was disallowed on the plea of off-side. Parry, however, shortly was the means of adding another goal to the Carthusians' account, and a third was scored, the ball going between the posts off the body of one of the Etonians. At time the Light Blues had no item as a set-off against their opponents' score, and were defeated by three goals to none. The cup was won by probably the best team that took part in the competition. Umpires, Messrs. E. H. Bambridge and C. H. Wollaston; referee, Mr. W. Pierce-Dix. Sides:—

OLD CARTHUSIANS.—L. F. Gillett (goal), E. G. Colvin and W. H. Norris (backs), J. F. M. Prinsep and J. Vintcent (half-backs), W. R. Page, E. G. Wynyard, J. A. H. Todd, E. H. Parry (captain), L. M. Richards, and W. E. Hensell.

OLD ETONIANS.—J. P. Rawlinson (goal), C. W. Foley and T. H. Trench (backs), Hon. A. F. Kinnaird (captain) and B. Farrer (half-backs), R. H. Macaulay, H. E. Goodhart, H. E. Whitfeld, P. C. Novelli, W. J. Anderson, and J. B. T. Chevallier.

Results of past matches: 1872, Wanderers beat Royal Engineers by one goal to *nil*; 1873, Wanderers beat Oxford University by two goals to *nil*; 1874, Oxford University beat Royal Engineers by two goals to *nil*; 1875, Royal Engineers beat Oxford University by one goal to *nil*; 1876, Wanderers beat Old Etonians by three goals to one; 1877, Wanderers beat Oxford University by two goals to *nil*. 1878, Wanderers beat Royal Engineers by three goals to one; 1879, Old Etonians beat Clapham Rovers by one goal to *nil*; 1880, Clapham Rovers beat Oxford University by one goal to *nil*; 1881, Old Carthusians beat Old Etonians by three goals to *nil*.

SCOTTISH ASSOCIATION CUP.
QUEEN'S PARK, GLASGOW, v. DUMBARTON.

More than usual interest was centred in this match, from the fact that both teams met on March 26, in the final tie, when the Queen's Park gained a victory by two goals to one, but upon an appeal by the Dumbarton men, the committee of the Scottish Association declared the match null and void, on the ground that the men had been interfered with by the crowd encroaching upon the space allotted for play. Consequently, the match was played over again on Saturday, at Kinning Park, Glasgow, where more than 12,000 spectators had assembled to witness the struggle, which proved very exciting. During the first portion of the game the Queen's Park scored three goals (two kicked by Smith and one by Kerr) to *nil*. After half-time, however, the Dumbarton team were seen to better advantage, and Brown scored in their behalf. This proved the only goal kicked during the second half, so that the result was a victory for the Queen's Park by three goals to one. Umpires, Messrs. J. Devlin and W. Broadfoot; referee, Captain Hamilton. Sides:—

QUEEN'S PARK.—R. M'Callum (goal), A. Watson and A. Holmes (backs), D. Davidson and C. Campbell (half-backs), Harry M'Neil, J. L. Kay, G. Ker, J. Smith, E. Fraser, and W. Anderson.

DUMBARTON.—J. Kennedy (goal), J. Hutcheson and J. Paton (backs), P. Miller, J. M'Kinlay, and J. Anderson (half-backs), D. M'Kinnon, A. Kennedy, J. Lindsay, R. Brown, and J. Meikleham.

THE YORKSHIRE CHALLENGE CUP.
DEWSBURY v. WAKEFIELD TRINITY.

On Saturday last the final tie in the fourth annual contest for this challenge cup was played on Cardigan Fields, Kirkstall-road, Leeds, where a very large company assembled. The weather was fine, and the ground in the best possible condition. For the first half of the game no score resulted, but subsequently A. Newsome dropped the only goal of the afternoon for the Dewsbury men, who thus won the cup by one goal to *nil*. Umpires, Rev. E. H. Dykes and Mr. J. B. Ogden; referee, Mr. P. B. Junor.

BIRMINGHAM ASSOCIATION CUP.
WALSALL SWIFTS v. ASTON VILLA.

The concluding match in this competition was decided on Saturday last at the Aston Lower Grounds, Birmingham, in the presence of about 8,000 spectators. The ground was in capital condition, and a fast game ensued. The Villa having won the toss, Yates kicked off for the Swifts, and the play throughout was of the most even description. Previous to half-time the Swifts scored one goal, but after change of ends neither side was able to score, the splendid goal keeping of Hobson for the Swifts saving his charge on several occasions. Thus the Swifts won by one goal to "love." Umpires, Messrs. J. Bryan and J. Adams; referee, Mr. Crump. Sides:—

WALSALL SWIFTS.—Hobson (goal), Jones and Sheldon (backs), Dyoss, Baker, and Ashwell (half-backs), Stokes, Meek, Yates, Tapper, and Lunn.

ASTON VILLA.—G. Copley (goal), H. Simmonds (back), E. Lee, T. Pank, and S. Law (half-backs), Andy and Archie Hunter, A. Brown, W. Crossland, Eli Davis, and H. Vaughton.

PRESENTATION TO MR. ALCOCK.

At the late general meeting it was intended to have handed to Mr. Charles W. Alcock, who for eighteen years has acted as secretary to the Football Association, the testimonial subscribed in recognition of his many and valuable services. Unfortunately, a family bereavement prevented the arrangement being carried out, and the presentation was deferred until Monday evening last, when a representative meeting was held at the Freemasons' Tavern, Great Queen-street, Long Acre. The testimonial consisted of a silver inkstand, a pair of silver candlesticks, a purse of £330, and a copy of the following resolution engraved on vellum:—"That the committee of the Football Association, on behalf of the subscribers to the Alcock Testimonial Fund, do present to Mr. C. W. Alcock, hon. sec. of the Football Association, a silver inkstand and candlesticks, with a purse of £330, in recognition of all that he has done during the past eighteen years to establish and further the Association game, and that the committee, in their name and in the name of all players scattered throughout the kingdom, tender to Mr. Alcock the expression of their sincere thanks for the zeal and energy with which, since its foundation in 1863, he has discharged his duties as hon. sec. to the Association, and further record their unanimous conviction that the success which has attended the Association in all its undertakings, and the established position the game now occupies among the winter sports, are due in no ordinary degree to the loyal and untiring devotion with which he has ever sought to promote its interest and prosperity." Major Marindin was repeatedly cheered as, in making the presentation, he alluded to the good work done by the recipient of the testimonial. Mr. Alcock had made the game, and from its institution, in 1863, had nursed it until, in 1881, in almost every village there was a club playing the rules of football introduced by him. After alluding to the undoubtedly healthful effects of the game and its general advance, the president formally went through the ceremony of the presentation. Mr. Alcock, in returning thanks, said that the rules which he had advocated were originated in 1859 by his eldest brother, but that the Association was not started till 1863. After speaking of the steady growth of what has proved to be a great institution from a very small beginning, and on the subject of the semi-professional players of football, Mr. Alcock again thanked the subscribers for the marks of their esteem. The proceedings closed with a vote of thanks to Mr. Ogilvie, who had acted as secretary of the testimonial fund

SPORTSMAN RUNNING GROUNDS, PLUMSTEAD.

Owing to the cold weather on Saturday last, there was but a moderate attendance at these grounds to witness the handicaps promoted for the benefit of Thomas Sullivan, when two handsome prizes were given for a 120 yards and a 440 yards handicap, with money prizes for second and third. A. Bullen was starter, and Mr. J. Bryant judge. Results:—

120 Yards Handicap.—The following won their heats:—J. Riddles, 14 yards' start; J. Best, 14; W. Baker, 12½; H. Sargent, 8; R. Ruff, 7; J. Boyd, 5; J. Dixon, 9; J. M'Guigan, 4½; G. Triggs, 9; P. M'Guire, 8½; E. J. Ryan, 17½. Second Round.—Heat 1: Best, first; Baker, second; Riddles, third. Won by half a yard. Heat 2: Sargent, first; Ruff, second. Won by a foot. Heat 3: M'Guigan, first; Dixon, second; Boyd, third. Won by a yard. Heat 4: Triggs, first; M'Guire, second; Ryan, third. Won by a yard and a half. Final Heat: Triggs, first; Best, second; Sargent, third; M'Guigan, 0. Won, after a splendid race all the way, by a foot; half a yard between second and third.

The 440 Yards Handicap will be run off next Saturday. Entrance, 6d., closes on Friday. Same day, half-mile handicap, for a handsome cup; entrance free, on the grounds.

Date 9 April 1881
Place Kennington Oval
Score OLD CARTHUSIANS 3
OLD ETONIANS 0
Teams OLD CARTHUSIANS L. F. Gillett, E. G. Colvin, W. H. Norris, J. F. M. Prinsep, A. J. Vintcent, W. R. Page, E. G. Wynyard, A. H. Todd, E. H. Parry (capt.), L. M. Richards, W. E. Hensell. OLD OLD ETONIANS J. F. P. Rawlinson, C. W. Foley, C. H. French, Hon. A. F. Kinnaird (capt.), R. B. Farrer, R. H. Macaulay, H. C. Goodhart, H. Whitfield, P. C. Novelli, W. J. Anderson, J. B. T. Chevallier
Officials Referee W. Pierce-Dix. Linesmen G. H. Wollaston, E. H. Bambridge
Attendance 4500
Copy *The Sporting Life* 13 April 1881

THE GREAT FOOTBALL MATCH.

BLACKBURN ROVERS v. OLD ETONIANS.

The anxiously looked for event, in which so intense an interest was manifested not only in Blackburn and East Lancashire, but throughout all the football circles in the United Kingdom, took place on Kennington Oval on Saturday last, when the Blackburn Rovers competed with the famous Old Etonians in the final tie for the English Association Challenge Cup. Although defeated the Rovers are not disheartened, and the form they displayed during the play on Saturday thoroughly justified their reputation and the interest they have evoked. Up to Saturday last the Rovers held an unbeaten card for the season, having by their splendid play defeated or drawn with the best clubs in England and Scotland. Their fine run of successes was the cause of all the excitement exhibited and the ovation which they were received at the Blackburn railway station on Friday morning by the large crowd that cheered them on their departure for the metropolis. The occasion was, indeed, an important one in football annals, and that large section of the public of Blackburn who take so lively an interest in the game recognised this, and sent away their favourites with a ringing cheer in true Lancashire fashion. The Blackburn Rovers as a club has been in existence upwards of four years, and although the composition of the club has been changed considerably since the commencement of their career, there were early indications manifested of those qualities which are the harbingers of success. It was during the present season more particularly that the Rovers have distinguished themselves, but they played up well for the cup during the two previous seasons in which they competed for it. In connection with the English challenge cup competition in 1880 they defeated Darwen by three goals to one, and were subsequently thrown out by Notts Forest, when the game stood six to nothing against the Rovers. In their second year they were considered a strong club, and were great favourites in connection with the cup competition. They were, however, thrown out during that season on a very memorable occasion—when they contested with the Sheffield Wednesday Club on the Alexandra Meadows under adverse circumstances, and were defeated by four goals to one. During the present season the Rovers defeated all comers up to Saturday last in the cup contest. They have, during the season scored the following victories:—November 26, Clitheroe, Lancashire cup tie, ten goals to one; January 7, Accrington Wanderers, Lancashire cup tie, seven to none; January 28, Church, Lancashire cup tie, six to none; January 30, Darwen, English cup tie, five to one; February 11, Wednesbury Old Athletic, English cup tie, three to one; February 25, Hole-i'th'-Wall Olympic, Lancashire cup tie, six goals to one; March 4, Rovers v. Witton, six to one; March 6, at Huddersfield, Rovers v. Sheffield Wednesday, draw, neither club scoring; March 15, at Manchester, Rovers v. Sheffield Wednesday, five to one; March 18, Rovers v. Darwen, at Darwen, five goals to one. The Rovers have also played during the present season with Nottingham County, when they were victors by ten goals to one. They have also beaten Aston Villa, Birmingham, by seven goals to two, and four goals to one in the return match; Beith by six goals to nothing; Jamestown by four goals to three, after a very hard and tight game; Dumbarton, five goals to one; 3rd Lanark, six goals to one. The Rovers had decidedly the best of the game in their competition with Queen's Park, Glasgow, when there was a draw, both teams making two goals. They have also defeated Notts Forest at Nottingham by two goals to none at Nottingham; and Walsall Swifts three goals to one on two occasions. Such splendid victories as the Rovers have achieved almost justified the confident predictions that they would become the possessors of the great trophy—the English Challenge Cup. They had certainly a good club to compete with in the Old Etonians, a club, too, that they had not met before, and on a comparatively strange ground, after travelling upwards of 200 miles. The Old Etonians have competed in the final tie English Association Challenge Cup during the last four seasons, and in 1879 they won the cup, throwing Darwen and Notts Forest out, and beating the Clapham Rovers in the final tie. In 1880 the Clapham Rovers wrested the cup from the present holders, and in 1881 the Old Carthusians defeated the Old Etonians. The Old Etonians had, however, for three consecutive years previous to 1879 won the cup, and they then became absolute owners of it. We award the Etonians the credit of playing a good game on Saturday last; they displayed really grand form, and we have reason to believe that they never executed better passing, although the Rovers had decidedly the advantage of them in that respect. J. Hargreaves, Douglas, Duckworth, and Brown played a splendid game, and Howarth proved himself, as usual, a most accomplished goal-keeper, while for the Etonians Rawlinson prevented several goals being scored by the excellent defence of his charge. For the Etonians the Hon. A. F. Kinnaird played a truly fine game, his speed and tackling being superb, while Macauley played a very fast game, and Anderson, Dunn, French, and Paravicini were always in it. The Etonians, although generally big men, lack the compactness and the physical endurance of the Rovers, who had on many occasions "hard lines." They, however, played a good game, and showed the Londoners what stuff they were made of. The Rovers had not the advantage of the assistance of Greenwood, who was prevented from playing in consequence of the injuries he sustained on the 11th of March at Glasgow, in the international match "England v. Scotland." The weather on Saturday was beautifully fine, and the ground in good condition. Some 6,000 people assembled on the Oval to witness the match, a large contingent being visitors from Blackburn. We may mention that for the first time in the history of the Kennington Oval the football match was played across the cricket crease. As the players made their appearance on the ground they were loudly cheered by the spectators, the varying stature and physique of the Rovers being greatly remarked upon by the metropolitan onlookers. During the first half the Old Etonians had the best of the game, but in the second, when the wind was in their favour, the Rovers pressed their opponents severely. During the afternoon Major-General Feilden, M.P., Mr. Coddington, M.P., and Mr. Briggs, M.P., made their appearance on the ground, and they were respectively loudly applauded. It is for us now to show in detail

HOW THE GAME WAS CONTESTED.

The Rovers lost the toss for choice of ends, and had to face the wind and sun in the first half. Strachan kicked off at three o'clock. The ball was passed to Brown who ran slightly forward, but as the latter was attempting to recross the leather, Kinnaird by a fine kick sent it well down his right. Suter met the aggressive Etonians, and admirably frustrated all endeavours to score, but a moment later a corner was obtained by the southerners, which passed away without effect. J. Hargreaves now became very noticeable for a fine run on the Rovers' left; passing Kinnaird, he was intercepted by French and a return visit was paid the Rovers' quarters. Sharples made a magnificent kick, which was replied to by Foley, and Dunn came down the field at a rattling pace. He and Macauley put in a fine amount of work at this juncture, and had it not been for the brilliant defence of Suter they would have scored. McIntyre also displayed great energy. Again the Eton boys came to the attack, which was kept up for a few minutes, Sharples at last relieving his side by a beautiful kick. Douglas and Duckworth got fairly away, and so neatly and effectively did they pass that a goal seemed certain. Paravicini and Foley were greatly exercised, and one of them kicked behind. Nothing, however, came of the corner. Suter earned the plaudits of the onlookers by magnificently tackling Novelli, who was racing towards the Lancashire goal at train speed nearly. Good play was now shown by Brown and Strachan, when Dunn receiving possession, apparently in an off-side position (against whom no claim was made), cantered briskly down the green, then passed to Macauley, who, with a long side shot, effected the downfall of the Rovers' fortress eight minutes from the start. Nothing dismayed, the northerners again put motion to the ball in the middle, but McIntyre was immediately called upon to display fine defensive powers in order to avert fresh disasters. Suter also a few moments later was busy with his head, after which J. Hargreaves sped away up the left, accompanied by Avery. This couple got very dangerous, and a splendid centre by Hargreaves nearly brought about the collapse of the Eton goal. Indeed, a point ought to have been scored, but instead of blocking the ball and then shooting with his right foot Strachan made use of his head, and the ball passed over the bar. After the goal kick F. Hargreaves again gave his brother and Avery the leather. Another splendid run transpired, but fate was against Blackburn, and danger once more began to threaten Howorth's position. Nothing could have been more brilliant than the fine dashing runs of Novelli, Macauley, and Dunn, who, together with their other comrades, fairly beat down upon the Rovers' defences. Here, however, a mighty barrier of brave backs obstructed their career. Suter was extremely clever, and as the others were very strong, the great pressure which bothered the Blackburn contingent was relieved. Douglas, after that ordeal was over, got grandly away on the right. A beautiful chance seemed in store for his side, but he put too much force to the leather when passing to centre, and French had a clear opening before him, when by a huge kick he undid the previous good run by Douglas. Time crept on, and still no further point was registered, which was to the credit of the Rovers, as they were greatly pressed; and if they could reach half time with only one goal against them it was thought a certainty that victory would smile upon them. An unfortunate mishap now occurred which, if the truth could be accurately ascertained, cost the Rovers a defeat. Avery had the ball near the centre, and was fast becoming dangerous, when he was badly charged, and for a few moments it was thought that some fracture had been sustained. Dr. Morley quickly relieved the fears of the Rovers' supporters on this point, but the injury was sufficiently serious as to render Avery's services during the rest of the match of comparatively little avail. Some more trying moments were passed over successfully by Blackburn, and after a most determined and grand struggle half-time was announced with the game in favour of the Collegians by one goal to nil. The wind now aided the Rovers, and hope beamed brightly among their friends that the tables would be quickly turned on their opponents. Brown early took matters in hand, then Douglas made a fine shot at goal, which Rawlinson just saved. J. Hargreaves also came in for attention, and it was quite apparent that the Blackburn forwards would keep up a lot of pressure. The southern backs, however, were perfect in every respect, either when in the scrimmages or when a flying kick was required. On the Rovers came time after time, Douglas sending in from the right, and J. Hargreaves from the left; but so powerful was the defence of the Etonians, and so dashing were they, that the northern forwards almost became weary of attacking, or if not weary were without the usual boldness possessed by them. It frequently happened during the earlier stages of the first half that when the ball was centred from either wing the forwards were seen lagging behind; this, coupled with the fact that French, Foley, Kinnaird, and Paravicini were playing a capitally defensive game, a long spell of time glided away. The home forwards whenever they got away, which was seldom the case, were ever frustrated by the Rovers' backs, who, to their credit be it said never wavered in their play at any moment of the game. Strachan now seemed as if he would break through all the spells which had kept them from scoring. A bold dash marked his career, but his final shot was parried by Rawlinson. From a smart canter up the Eton right danger really menaced Howarth's charge, but one of his best fisters landed the ball away. The Rovers assumed the attack once more, and spurred on by their eager supporters at last began to make use of their old dash. Half an hour had, however, passed by, the knowledge of which militated against the accuracy of their shots, for, fearful of defeat, the Lancashire forwards became unduly excited. Before impetuosity had been wanting, now it was too overcharged. The amount of dash now displayed by the Rovers is almost indescribable, and torrents of assaults were aimed at the goal defended by Rawlinson. Several corner kicks and throws-in ensued, shot were made at goal, but cruel fate thwarted every attempt at scoring. A splendid corner kick by Douglas at last seemed inevitably fruitful, the ball dropped grandly in front of the post. Breathless excitement pervaded during the brief *melée* which followed, the ball, however, was forced over the line only about an inch on the wrong side of the posts. Coming again to the attack hope was more brilliant than ever, for Strachan placed the leather at the foot of Duckworth, who had only the custodian to face, but he was evidently overcome with excitement, and the result was but a feeble straight shot in the hand of Rawlinson. Suter, nerved by desperation, rushed in from his position on the backs, and was near dribbling the ball between. The last minute had now arrived, and when, by a fine long kick Kinnaird planted the ball in mid-field, the matter was settled, and, with McIntyre and Suter struggling vainly to bring the ball again in front, time was called, Eton being victorious by one goal to nil.

THE DINNER.

After the match the players, members of the club, and the press dined at St. James's Restaurant, at the joint invitation of Mr. W. Coddington, M.P., and Mr. W. E. Briggs, M.P. A dinner of a most *recherche* description was provided. Mr. Briggs presided, and Mr. Coddington occupied the vice-chair at the post-prandial proceedings.

Mr. BRIGGS proposed the health of the Queen, and said that he had great pleasure in doing so, especially at this time, when she had had a miraculous escape from such a diabolical attempt upon her life—(hear, hear). No one knew what importance to attach to the life of her Majesty except those who had to do with public affairs, and who came into contact with those who ruled the destiny of this great empire. He was sure that, speaking from a social point of view, the example her Majesty had set to those who were the mothers of England was one which ought to command our affectionate love and respect—(hear, hear).

The toast was heartily endorsed.

Mr. CODDINGTON proposed the health of the Prince and Princess of Wales and the rest of the Royal Family. The Prince of Wales had taken a prominent position as a leading member of the Royal Family, and fulfilled those duties in a manner deserving of his ancestry. He had invariably sought and gained the estimation of the English people. He felt sure that when, in the course of events, the Prince succeeded to the throne he would be a worthy successor of a worthy mother. The Princess of Wales had endeared herself to the hearts of every English person. The Prince of Wales had taken a prominent part in promoting an institution which would be of great advantage to the country, namely, the promotion of a college of music—(hear, hear). He felt certain that, from the energetic way in which the Prince of Wales had taken up that matter, it would produce eventually a very great improvement in the musical feeling of the country, and it would, without doubt, assist in promoting good feeling amongst all classes of the country.

The toast was unanimously endorsed.

Mr. BRIGGS said that he rose to propose a toast, in a certain sense the celebrated toast of "Our noble selves." He was going to propose to them the toast of "The Rovers—(hear, hear)—their past and future success." As they knew he was their president, but owing to his Parliamentary duties and various other matters he had not been able to attend their matches as he should like to have done, yet he had been in possession on more than one occasion of the information of the manner in which they had been showing their prowess, and he would say—and this was by way of parenthesis—that he did not think that men could have done more and worked better than they did that day—(hear, hear). It was true they had not won, but what of that? They could not expect always to win if they had sun, wind, and tide against them, as they had had that day. Such a defeat was no defeat. It was equivalent to victory. It was what they called in the House of Commons a moral victory—(laughter). It would be for them the next time they met to turn that moral victory into a real one. Then look at the facts of the case, and see

PRESTON HERALD, MARCH 29, 1882.

whether there was any real reason for discouragement. Their captain, who had led them so many times and so nobly to victory, was unfortunate, like many celebrated generals in history, who was led to disaster by the loss of his baggage—(laughter)—and Carlyle or Thackeray or someone else had put it interrogatively, and had asked, "What is a hero without his baggage?" Their captain was on the war track, but he was not in his full and complete costume. They had to face both wind and sun in the first half, and he believed they knew as Rovers what that meant. It meant that the odds were considerably against them. He would not like to say that that goal was in the nature of a fluke, far from it, but it was a happy accident, and it happened at an unfortunate part of the game—(hear, hear). When they went back to Blackburn they need not hold their heads down in the least, or be discouraged in the least. They had fought a good game; they had played as Englishmen should do, in good humour, and at a crisis which would try that humour to the utmost. Their opponents, as far as he could judge—and their president knew something about those matters, for although he buckled himself in a somewhat larger belt than he used to do, and weighed eighteen stone eleven, yet there was a time when he used to play a very heavy forward—(laughter)—so he could appreciate their play that day. They had to meet a team that was, if not their equal, almost their equal, men who played straightforwardly, men amongst whom there were no petty jealousies, no watching one another's play to see whether they might possibly devote more attention to their neighbours than they did to themselves. And allow him to tell them this, that they had that day been simply beaten from this cause, that being equal as regarded other things, they were unlucky as regarded the position they were obliged to take at the beginning of the game. They lost the choice of goals, and, watching as narrowly as anybody could do and straining his eyes when watching their play, he could assure them that it was his firm belief that had they won the toss in the beginning they would now be victors instead of vanquished. When he was at Rugby they used to play a very good game at football, although he was not so sure that their rules were not better than the Rugby ones. He had had a good long time to think over matters—it was a good long time since he was at school—and he had come to the conclusion that the Association rules were really a better game to his mind—("Hurrah" and cheers). Dr. Arnold—now he was going to tell a story for the sake of illustration—once went into one of the class-rooms and examined the pupils. There was one boy who made some very foolish answers, and the doctor, who seldom lost his temper, after listening for several moments, gave that boy a good smack on the side of the head. The boy said, "I did my best." The doctor stopped, his whole demeanour changed, and he said, "Well, my boy, if you have done your best I beg your pardon." Now they could not do more than do their best. He believed that if they did their best, being neighbours of his, and Blackburn born and bred—(hear, hear)—if they held together, looking for the common good of all, listening to no outside whispering which might be poured into their ears, they did not know for what reason, they would yet be successful in carrying off the trophy. Let not outsiders influence them in the least. If they wanted advice from anybody, where should they seek it but from their captain. If anyone of them thought another did not play his game as well as he should do, go boldly to the captain and say so, and stand face to face with him. They had no need to whisper in corners, and allow that to sap the vitality of the club to which they all belonged. If they did this, and worked together, and if they did their best, believe him, when the day of trial came, and they were brought face to face with an antagonist who was equal to themselves, they would be able to devote the whole of their attention to the game. If they considered that a piece of unnecessary advice, pray forgive him, though he really did wish that club to prosper and do well—(hear, hear). The fame of the Rovers was not now confined to Blackburn. The proceedings of the Rovers were matters that commanded the attention of Lancashire men, and commanded the attention of the whole of England, and, he might say, the whole athletic world. They were chronicled in all the sporting papers. Now, he would urge them not to be discouraged by that defeat, but to be determined that henceforth nothing should stand in their way, but that acting loyally together, with their grand captain to lead them, they would stand finally on the pinnacle which he hoped they would reach, and which he was sure was the desire of them all, namely, that of the foremost football club in the whole of the United Kingdom—(applause). Before he called upon his colleague to second this motion he would ask him to couple the response with the name of their captain. He thought that one word or two ought to be said with regard to those who had taken that club in hand from the very beginning, and were now, he trusted, reaping at the hands of them all the reward which was their due. There were some, like his noble friend on his left (Mr. Boothman), who had seen from small beginnings that grand ending, and he was sorry to say that they were all to lose him, that he was going abroad, as they said in Blackburn, to foreign parts—(applause). Unless he mistook him very much he would not be "off side" when he was there, and he was sure to come home at last. He wished them in the future—and that was wishing himself, too, for he was bound up with them—prosperity. He wished them no disasters in the future, and he wished they might attain that goal—to use football language—which they hoped to reach—he meant to say the championship of England—(cheers).

Mr. CODDINGTON, M.P., said that he had great pleasure in seconding the toast of the evening, that of the Rovers' club. He should have been pleased with their success that day, and he could assure them that no man on that ground felt greater disappointment than he did when the victory was against them. It was some years since he was able to play football, but still he had always retained his interest in it, and he was highly gratified that the Blackburn Rovers had succeeded in making Blackburn notable as a town connected with one of the most celebrated clubs in England, and that club which he had hoped would have attained to the position of the premier club. His brother had on various occasions spoken to him about the achievements of the Rovers' club, and he had no doubt that that day they would have beaten the Old Etonians, because he understood that the Rovers had beaten one or two other clubs that had defeated the Old Etonians, and he naturally concluded that the Blackburn Rovers would beat the Old Etonians—("Quite true" and "Bravo"). Unfortunately that had not turned out to be the result. He (Mr. Coddington) quite believed, as Mr. Briggs had said, that it was due to a certain extent to accident—(hear, hear). The Old Etonians had the wind in their favour, and the sun in their favour, and the ball slipped under the goal by one of those mysterious flukes that he could not describe in football language, but in a game at billiards a man who scored 99, though beaten by a man who scored 100 might play as good a game as the man who scored 100. As it was, the Rovers had lost by one goal in a very peculiar manner in the course of the first eight minutes. During the remainder of the game they succeeded in preventing their opponents getting another goal, and it was quite clear that the Rovers played on equal terms with the Old Etonians. They had also to take into consideration that the Rovers had travelled 210 the previous day. He hoped that if they should play in the final at any future time the luck would be in their favour instead of against them. In coupling that toast with the name of Mr. Hargreaves he might say that he was a representative of one of the oldest families in Blackburn. He (Mr. Coddington) had the honour of knowing his father and grandfather, and never a finer man walked the streets than Colonel Hargreaves. The present Mr. Hargreaves was perhaps not exactly taking the same profession as his father and grandfather, but he was taking a leading part in athletic sports, and he had so far distinguished himself as to be the captain of one of the foremost clubs in England. He congratulated Mr. Hargreaves upon the prestige of his club. He hoped he would take care of himself, and continue not only to play football but as time went on he would follow some occupation or profession which would make him as distinguished as his father and his grandfather before him—(hear, hear). Before he concluded he wished to say that Major-General Feilden, the representative of the northern division of Lancashire, regretted that he could not accept the invitation to be present that evening, inasmuch as he had made a previous engagement elsewhere, but he came there that evening to be introduced to the captain and various members of the Rovers Club. He was very much interested in the whole of the play that afternoon. Mr. Coddington then submitted the toast, and resumed his seat amid applause.

The toast was enthusiastically drunk.

Mr. HARGREAVES, in reply, said that he thought he was never brought back to his school days more closely than he was that day, for he felt when he was at school that he was sent by his father, and he felt when he went to London that he was sent by Blackburn. When the ball made its mysterious disappearance out of the field and through the posts they were not disheartened. They thought at the time that it was nothing, but they had experienced these little things before, and no doubt they would do so again—("Very seldom"). Although they had not won this year, he did not think that the cup was lost altogether. They would, however, leave that to destiny. They had proved themselves for a length of time to be unsurpassed by any team in the world, or at least in England and Scotland. The Etonians were the first club they had met which had defeated them. They had some very formidable foes to meet yet, and they hoped to be successful. They had been taught a lesson that day which he did not expect to have been taught, namely, that they could be defeated by the Old Etonians ("Nil desperandum"). Speaking of school life again, as they were leaving the field he felt very much like he did when the early morning bell tolled him out of bed—he felt about as much inclined to leave the field as he did his bed, because he really believed that as their London friends called them porridge eaters, they would have shown the strength of porridge if not heavy food. If it had gone on there would been a hard contest, and by long endurance they might have been able to tell against their opponents. He thought they would almost have run them to ground if they had played another half hour—(hear, hear.) The Etonians had certainly the advantage of the Rovers in their speed. He would give way to that. It told upon them, and they would get credit for it all through England. But that speed could not last for ever against the Rovers' endurance, and he thought that they would have come out of the match with a good certificate had they had a little more time to play in. He concluded by thanking the gentlemen present for taking such a great interest in so very little a thing—("No, no") and their thanks were especially due to Mr. Briggs and Mr. Coddington—(applause.)

Dr. MORLEY proposed the health of the hosts in complimentary terms. It was gratifying, not only to those present, but to their constituents. He was sure that their social capacity was equal in every respect to their political capacity.

The toast was cordially drunk.

Mr. McIntyre then gave a song.

Mr. BRIGGS, in reply, expressed the pleasure he had in meeting friends in London from Blackburn.

Mr. CODDINGTON, responding, said that being the occasion of the final tie, they thought it was only fitting that they should invite them to dinner. He was pleased to meet so many of his Blackburn friends. They were all aware that Mr. Briggs and himself were opposed to each other politically, still that evening they were glad to meet on a social occasion—(applause). Whether they were Conservatives or Liberals, it was their duty to join together to promote the good of the town of Blackburn, and Mr. Briggs and himself had always worked most amicably together. It was suggested that whatever might be the result of the game, Mr. Briggs and he should finish it by playing a single-handed match—(laughter and applause). He concluded by thanking them for the drinking of the toast.

Mr. LLOYNDS proposed "The referee" and "The Press," which was seconded by Dr. PORTEUS, and responded to by Mr. Clegg, Mr. Livesey, and Mr. Lever.

The proceedings then terminated.

● The Old Etonians' victory in the 1882 final represented the last glorious page in the history of the amateur in the FA Cup. The accompanying account of the final implies that the Old Boys needed a certain amount of good fortune to beat the new challengers from the north in whose ranks was Fergus Suter, subsequently a key figure in the legalisation of professionalism which was just three years away.

The Hon. A. F. Kinnaird, celebrating his fifth victory in the eighth of his record nine appearances in the final, symbolised the passing of an era with his post-match head-stand in front of the Oval pavilion. Blackburn Rovers, who were missing D. H. Greenwood, injured playing for England against Scotland in Glasgow two weeks earlier, were to become more fearsome adversaries as the decade progressed. The Southern domination of the FA Cup was over.

Date 25 March 1882
Place The Kennington Oval
Score OLD ETONIANS 1
BLACKBURN ROVERS 0
Teams OLD ETONIANS J. F. P. Rawlinson, T. H. French, P. J. de Paravicini, Hon. A. F. Kinnaird (capt.), C. W. Foley, P. C. Novelli, A. T. R. Dunn, R. H. Macaulay, H. C. Goodhart, J. B. T. Chevallier, W. J. Anderson.
BLACKBURN ROVERS R. Howarth, H. McIntyre, F. Suter, F. Hargreaves (capt.), H. Sharples, J. Hargreaves, G. Avery, J. Brown, T. Strachan, J. Douglas, J. Duckworth
Officials Referee J. C. Clegg. Linesmen C. Crump, C. H. R. Wollaston
Goal Scorer Macaulay 8
Attendance 6500
Guest of Honour Major General Feildon
Copy *The Preston Herald* 29 March 1882

FOOTBALL.

* Played under. Rugby. † Association Rules

FOOTBALL ASSOCIATION CHALLENGE CUP.

FINAL TIE.—OLD ETONIANS (Holders) v. BLACKBURN OLYMPIC.

VICTORY OF THE NORTHERNERS.

LITTLE did the Football Association imagine, in offering the trophy for competition some dozen seasons back, that the affair would generate into the importance which it has of late assumed. The removal of various restrictions has caused the provincials to enter in far greater numbers, and to extend the contest from a coterie of metropolitan and public school teams to one in which the leading clubs throughout the length and breadth of England are engaged. With the exception of the recent "International" at Sheffield and the semi-final between Notts County and the Etonians a fortnight since, no such amount of interest has been excited this season as was evinced over the final on Saturday last on the ground of the Surrey County Cricket Club, familiarly known as "the Oval." Harking back awhile, we find that in the year of its institution the Wanderers, then the leading dribbling club in the kingdom, proved victorious over the Royal Engineers in the final by one goal to none, defeating Oxford University the succeeding spring by two goals to none. The dark blues attained the honour of holding the trophy in 1874-5, their opponents in the final being the Royal Engineers, the Sappers reversing the state of affairs the following year. By consecutive victories over the Old Etonians (1876), Oxford University (1877), and Royal Engineers (1878), the Wanderers obtained absolute possession of the Cup, but generously waived their right, and returned it to the committee. Since that time the "cracks" have gradually retrograded until at the present time they are morally, though not actually, extinct. In 1878-9 the Clapham Rovers and Old Etonians did battle for the supremacy, the "Old Boys" winning by one goal to none, the Clapham Rovers next year obtaining a similar verdict in their contest with Oxford University. This brings us to 1880-1, when the Old Carthusians beat the Old Etonians by three goals to none, whilst last year the memorable struggle between the Old Etonians and Blackburn Rovers took place, in which the latter—the first strictly provincial club that had the honour of contesting in the final—suffered defeat by one goal to none. It is somewhat singular that Blackburn should again furnish one of the last couple, especially when there were several considered superior to the Olympians, Notts County, Aston Villa, and Blackburn Rovers each apparently standing a better chance. Out of the eighty-four originally entered, the Old Etonians, Old Carthusians, Notts County, and Blackburn Olympic were left in for the semi-finals, and the holders defeating the "lambs," and the Carthusians suffering an unexpectedly severe reverse at the hands of the Blackburnites,

it was left for the last named and the Etonians to fight out the question of supremacy. Either side appeared sanguine of success, the visitors having gone in for a week's strict training at Blackpool, and journeying to Richmond on Thursday in order to obviate the weariness of a long railway journey. On the other hand, many stood by the proverbial luck of the public school men to again pull them safely through, as, in spite of assertions to the contrary, they had an undoubted advantage in playing on a ground with which they are so familiar. Into the equity of the final being decided at the Oval we do not wish to enter, especially when it is considered that if it had not been for the support accorded by the metropolitan clubs the competition would not probably be in existence; but we may venture thus far, and assert that if it was irrevocably settled by the powers that be that the contest should be played in London the Kennington ground was the only one they could feel justified in selecting. Olympic won by two goals to one, after two hours' play.

The morning opened fine and spring-like, and for once in a way the elements proved inmutable, and instead of a changeable series of "samples" a really favourable afternoon was experienced. The attendance, as anticipated, was far above that on the occasion of the contest between the Etonians and Notts County a fortnight back; indeed, it was the largest that has been seen there for several years, and from a rough estimate there could not have been fewer than 7000 assembled round the ropes or perched on every coign of vantage from which a glimpse of the game could be obtained. Play was announced for half-past three, and with commendable punctuality the elevens, which were exactly the same as announced, turned out to do battle. The Olympians had the gasometer end, and Kinnaird having ranged his followers in front of the Crown Baths goal, Hunter set the leather in motion at twenty-six minutes to four. French and Foley were the first to distinguish themselves for the metropolitans, and through their instrumentality the ball was promptly returned. Dewhurst then made a good run on the left, Chevallier, Kinnaird, and Macaulay repelling the attack, the ball going behind. Ward was next applauded for some fine defence, Bainbridge and Goodhart running the leather down, the latter having the misfortune to shoot over. The sphere still continued in the Blackburn quarters, Foley making several good throws in, but on each occasion the visitors managed to ward off danger. At first the play was a bit loose, each side in turn obtaining the advantage, and Dunn, Anderson, and Yates in turn making good dribbles. An allowance of "hands" proved fruitless, and after some good play by Warburton, Anderson and M'Aulay took the leather over and sent it behind, Kinnaird doing similar a few minutes later. A second free kick on the score of "hands" was accorded to the visitors, but the Etonians managed to ward off the danger, though an attack on the part of Dewhurst and Yates resulted in the latter just heading the ball over. The Etonians then made a determined attack, Macaulay and Anderson figuring prominently, but Dunn made a bad shot, and sent it over. Bully after bully in front of the visitors' goal resulted, but it was not until just half an hour after the start that Chevallier and Macaulay ran the leather down and passed to Goodhart, who shot it under the tape amid a scene of wild applause. Nettled by this reverse, the Lancashire lads, who were in splendid

fettle, played up with renewed vigour. "Hands" was given against Macaulay, followed by a dashing attack by the visitors' lefts. Goodhart next was within an ace of scoring, but Blackburn took the ball away, and it ultimately went over the goal-line. On kicking off the visiting forwards ran it smartly down, and Dewhurst was about to take his shot at goal when Foley averted the danger by kicking it behind. Gibson took the corner, but Anderson took the object of contention away, and from now till half-time the fight was carried on with varying fortune, though no further item was obtained. On change of ends Blackburn commenced to play up much better, and the advantage of their having gone in for strict training now became patent. Dunn and Bainbridge made a couple of fine dribbles on the left wing, but success did not attend their efforts. Warburton had a free kick for "hands," but Foley returned the leather. Shortly after Kinnaird had a place kick on a foul, and sent the ball between the posts, but the shot was disallowed, not having touched one of the opposing side in its course. An attack by Yates was warded off by Rawlinson using his hands in defence of his charge. A minute or two later Matthews dribbled down, and taking a good shot from the wing equalised the score, Rawlinson being unable to prevent the leather from going through. The next noteworthy item was the retirement of Dunn (hurt), this being a severe blow to the Etonians, who were tiring fast. With only ten men the old boys began to be severely pressed, Kinnaird, who was playing in magnificent style, and Paravicini several times warding off likely scores. A shot by Goodhart passed just outside the post, Macaulay also making a dashing attempt to score, Hacking averting danger. As time slipped away it became evident that the Olympians would win if only the contest were prolonged, and although the Etonians strove to score a goal, but, as was their luck on the 17th ult., no such advantage fell to them, and at the expiration of the ninety minutes the result was a draw, one goal to either side. It was then resolved to play on for an additional half-hour, though the Etonians were a man short. Little description is necessary, the Blackburnites, who were in the very pink of condition, being more than a match for their opponents, who were, with the exception, perhaps, of the captain, completely knocked out of time. During the first half (quarter of an hour) the old boys kept their goal intact, but shortly after changing ends Dewhurst ran down and passed to Crossley, who scored the winning point, as, although the Etonians rallied somewhat towards the close, they eventually retired defeated by two goals to one, after a couple of hours' play. The following were the sides:

Old Etonians (holders): J. F. P. Rawlinson (goal), P. J. de Paravicini and T. H. French (backs), Hon. A. F. Kinnaird (captain) and C. W. Foley (half-backs), A. T. B. Dunn and H. W. Bainbridge (left wing), J. B. T. Chevallier and W. J. Anderson (right wing), H. C. Goodhart and R. H. Macaulay (centre forwards).

Blackburn Olympic: T. Hacking (goal), S. A. Warburton (captain) and J. T. Ward (backs), W. Astley, J. Hunter, and T. G. Gibson (half-backs), T. Dewhurst and A. Matthews (right wing), J. Yates and W. Crossley (left wing), G. Wilson (centre forwards).

Umpires: Messrs M. P. Betts (Old Harrovians) and W. Pierce-Dix (hon. treasurer Sheffield Football Association). Referee: Mr C. Crump (president Birmingham and District Association).

THE HON. A. F. KINNAIRD

CAPTAIN OF THE "OLD ETONIANS"

THE ENCLOSURE

S. A. WARBURTON.

CAPTAIN OF THE BLACKBURN OLYMPIC

CROSSLEY KICKING THE DECISIVE GOAL.

THE PRESIDENT PRESENTING THE CUP

REMARKS.—During the regulation ninety minutes there was little to choose between the two elevens, the Etonians having slightly the best in the first half, whilst towards the close Dunn's retirement, and the fact of the old boys tiring fast, gave the northerners the upper hand. On continuing with only ten men, and these fairly done for, it was evident that through their training the provincials would eventually secure victory, and although for the first quarter nothing further was added, the Olympic had matters afterwards pretty nearly their own way, their opponents being terribly distressed. For the winners the back play was remarkably good, Hacking, as usual, being very smart in goal. At first the forwards seemed scarcely at home on the ground, which was too fast for their liking, but, quickly recovering themselves, showed to greater advantage till the finish, their weak point being their neglect to keep the ball down in shooting for goal. For the losers Kinnaird for the first few minutes was in rare form, and certainly seemed to possess the greatest stamina on his side. Paravicini, Rawlinson, Goodhart, Anderson, and Foley also deserve a word of praise, several of the forwards, however, being too wild, Macaulay perhaps being the leading offender in this respect.

The handsome trophy was afterwards publicly presented to the winners on the stand adjoining the pavilion, for the first time since the institution of the competition. Major Marindin, the president, in making the presentation, informed the victors that they should be proud of having secured the cup, as its holders were fairly entitled to the honour of being Champion club for the season. He spoke of the indomitable pluck of their antagonists, who had never been beaten except by the final holders of the trophy. Hearty cheers were then given for the rival elevens and the "Major," who also presented medals to the members of the Olympic team. In the evening a dinner was given at the St. James's Restaurant.

†LANCASHIRE CUP COMPETITION.
FINAL TIE.

DARWEN v. BLACKBURN ROVERS.—This most exciting match was played at Darwen on Saturday in the presence of an immense number of spectators. There was a strong wind blowing, and the toss having been won by M'Intyre, he chose to play with the wind in his favour. Punctually at three o'clock Ashton kicked off, but the ball was prevented from travelling far, being kept well in the centre of the field, until the Rovers got a throw in, but the play was soon at the visitors' goal, and Darwen made a very good attempt at scoring, but Woolfall was all there. The Rovers now retaliated, and began to shake off their indifference by making it hot for Broughton, who saved his charge well. Not to be said nay the visitors secured the leather, and made tracks for Darwen ground, where it was passed to J. Brown, who scored the first goal, twenty-five minutes having elapsed. On the ball being restarted, a run was made towards the Blackburn Rovers' goal, and Maguire equalised matters by putting it through. The visitors were next to appear conspicuous, one shot by Hargreaves hitting the cross-bar. "Hands" was claimed by the Rovers, and a free kick ensued in the mouth of the goal, and during the scrimmage Douglas gave it the final kick. Some give-and-take play ensued after this, but nothing of interest resulted until half-time. From the kick off the Blackburn team began by pressing Darwen, and had some narrow shaves at goal, and finally Avery shot it through the posts for the third time. Both sidesmen played up well, but could not break through, until Darwen made a run and Ashton scored goal number two when fourteen minutes of the game had to be played. This was the last item of interest, and the contest ended in favour of the Rovers by three goals to two.

†NORTHERN WELSH CUP.

BANGOR v. RHYL WANDERERS.—The final tie for the Challenge Cup of the Northern Welsh Football Association was played between the above clubs on Saturday, on the ground of the former society. There was a large gate. Rhyl worked hard, but unsuccessfully, and Bangor became the holders of the Cup for the second time, winning by three goals to two. The teams were:
Rhyl Wanderers : C. Jones (goal), C. Wright and J. Roberts (backs), W. H. Thompson (captain), R. C. Thompson, and J. Vaughan (half-backs), W. H. Roberts and D. Williams (right wing), J. Piercy and R. Hughes (left wing), and W. Roberts (centre).
Bangor : E. Lewis (goal), Vincent and F. R. Jones (backs), Humphrey Jones and J. Williams (half-backs), Hay and T. M. Jones (centres), D. Jones and R. J. Roberts (right wing), W. Lewis and J. Smith (captain) (left wing).
Umpires : T. B. Farrington (Conway F.C.) and W. Morgan (Carnarvon College F.C.). Referee : Robert Newton, Carnarvon Athletic F.C.

†MANCHESTER FREE WANDERERS v. BRADFORD.

THE Bradford club having been beaten by Dewsbury in the Yorkshire Challenge Cup competition, they were enabled to bring off their fixture with the Manchester

Date 31 March 1883
Place The Kennington Oval
Score BLACKBURN OLYMPIC 2
OLD ETONIANS 1 (after extra time)
Teams BLACKBURN OLYMPIC Hacking, Warburton (capt.), Ward, Astley, Hunter, Gibson, Dewhurst, Matthews, Yates, Crossley, Wilson. OLD ETONIANS J. F. P. Rawlinson, P. J. de Paravicini, T. H. French, Hon. A. F. Kinnaird (capt.), C. W. Foley, A. T. B. Dunn, H. W. Bainbridge, J. B. T. Chevallier, W. J. Anderson, H. C. Goodhart, R. H. Macaulay
Official Referee C. Crump
Goal Scorers BLACKBURN OLYMPIC Matthews, Crossley; OLD ETONIANS Goodhart
Attendance 8000
Guest of Honour Major Marindin
Copy The Sportsman 2 April 1883; The Accrington Times 7 April 1883

Blackburn Olympic's Cup-winning side of 1883

Free Wanderers at the Cottonopolis on Saturday. The home team were utterly unable to stop the scoring by the visitors, who were hailed the victors by three goals, six tries, four touch-downs, and one dead ball to the Wanderers' two tries, one touch-down, and one dead ball.

FOOTBALL NOTES.

As the Reds had nothing on last Saturday, owing to their date being taken by the county, it was arranged that Preston should visit Accrington. Friel, Eastham, and Whittaker stood out, and their places were filled by Hindle, Maudsley, and Deakin. The Accringtonians thought they had a cheap game on, but the visitors very quickly dispelled this idea by scoring two goals before the home team had a look in. At half-time the game was in favour of the Preston men by two to one.

During the second half the Reds played more unselfishly, and eventually pulled the match off by five to three. Had it not been for Howarth and Chippendale the Accrington team would have been beaten, and serve them right. The half-backs played a grand game, and saved the match. For a long time Hargreaves appeared to think he was the only forward player on the Accrington side, and played accordingly. Never was witnessed such selfish and foolish play, and it was fitting punishment for him that the visitors robbed him of the ball every time and made "small meat" of him. Yates, Clegg, and Wilkinson did well, as did Boyce. Deakin is too weak, and Maudsley far too slow.

Church were able to make a draw of it against Enfield.

Bolton Wanderers played St. Mirrens at Paisley. The Trotters won by four to three. In criticising the match Jonathan says, "The Scotch division of the English team played uncommonly well." Very neat that.

In the final for the Lancashire Cup the Rovers defeated Darwen by three to two though the latter had the best of the game. Suter makes a good goal keeper.

The Darwenians have protested and the matter was brought before the committee last night.

The Olympians also won the English Cup, beating the Old Etonians, after half-an-hour's extra play, by two goals to one. One has seen and heard so much of this victory that it is a relief to leave the subject, so I will content myself with saying that I am glad they have brought the cup out of London. No doubt it will have a good effect on the Southerners. Already one London correspondent writes :—" Now that the cup itself has gone out of London, the time has come for the great football centres of Lancashire, Sheffield, and Birmingham to be properly recognised by the Association authorities. The clique that has hitherto existed in all governing matters stands a chance of being successfully opposed, if not eventually broken up, and the ultimate out-come of this match will be seen in a more liberal dealing with the North and Midlands, whose players are excluded from international matches, and whose representation on the committee, and in general meetings, is nullified by the meetings themselves being always held in the metropolis."

The football season is drawing to the close, and but for unforeseen circumstances would have for the present been at an end as far as Accrington is concerned.

I believe Smallheath Alliance and the Rovers have yet to visit Accrington.

The Alliance visit us on the 14th and the Rovers probably on the 25th.

The cricket club committee, with their usual good sense and generosity, have kindly allowed the use of the ground on the occasions referred to, and as it is all "grist," I hope there will be full houses.

● Blackburn Olympic in 1883 were the first team to take the FA Cup north, and *The Accrington Times* in its Football Notes above rejoices in the fact, saying "No doubt it will have a good effect on the Southerners". It was 18 years before Spurs took the Cup back to the south.

THE ACCRINGTON TIMES, SATURDAY, APRIL 5, 1884.

THE FOOTBALL ASSOCIATION CUP: FINAL TIE.

At no previous Association match played in London has so large a crowd assembled as that which on Saturday witnessed the final struggle for the possession of the cup, between the Blackburn Rovers and the Queen's Park, Glasgow. Roughly estimated, there must have been from 12,000 to 15,000 spectators. But Londoners, who are as a rule devoted to Rugby football, care little for the Association game, and it was evident that a large portion of the crowd had come from Lancashire and Scotland. The broad Doric which one heard on all sides was proof enough of this. Very noteworthy was it that these excursionists were mostly of the artisan class, and equally noteworthy were their honest enthusiasm and their accurate knowledge of the different points of the game. Of course the greater distance of Glasgow caused the Lancashire excursionists, most of whom wore the Rovers' colours as favours, to preponderate, but Scotchmen were also present in surprising numbers. The arrangements for accommodating this huge crowd were ridiculously insufficient, and at each gate there was a dangerous and ugly rush to gain admittance. Moreover, it says much for the orderly behaviour of the crowd that the field of play was kept clear, for the absurdly weak barriers could have been broken through with the slightest pressure. The morning had been grimly cold and foggy, but just before the great battle began "the Sun of Austerlitz" broke forth, and for a time the afternoon was pleasantly warm. Soon after half-past three a tremendous cheer greeted the appearance of the combatants. The Glasgow men were attired in black and white striped jerseys, and the Rovers wore their well-known colours of light blue and white. The latter, in size and build, were by far the more even team, though their captain, H. M'Intyre, certainly towered over the rest. The Queen's Park team, on the other hand, was composed of some very tall and some very short men. The names and positions were as follow:—Queen's Park: G. Gillespie, goal; J. Macdonald and W. Arnott, backs; C. Campbell and J. J. Gow, half-backs; W. Anderson and J. Watt, right wing; W. Harrower and Dr. J. Smith, centres; and R. M. Christie and D. Allan, left wing. Blackburn Rovers: H. Arthur, goal; J. Beverley and F. Suter, backs; H. M'Intyre and J. Forrest, half-backs; J. Lofthouse and J. Douglas, right wing; J. Inglis and J. Sowerbutts, centres; and J. Hargreaves and J. Brown, left wing. M'Intyre and Campbell were the respective captains. The Queen's Park had the eastern goal till half-time, and the advantage (if it could be called so) of the very slight breeze. The ground was as hard as it would be in summer. The betting at starting was about six to four on Queen's Park.

Precisely at 3 32 Sowerbutts kicked off for the Rovers, but the ball was soon returned by the Glasgow backs, and then for about 20 minutes the game went all against the Lancashire men. The quick dribbling and clever passing of the Scotchmen completely puzzled the Rovers, whose forwards were never on the ball, and whose backs had the greatest difficulty in defending their citadel. Almost immediately there was a furious struggle right in front of the Blackburn goal, which was only just saved by some really clever work of the Lancashire backs. The ball went behind, and after the kick out some more beautiful passing of the Scotchmen ended in a shot which only just missed the Lancashire goal post. Again the Rovers were in peril, one of the Scotch forwards centring the ball to within a few yards of the goal by a marvellously agile heel kick behind him. "Hands" were now given against the Rovers, but nothing came of the free kick, and the ball went behind. Arthur's kick out being well followed by Forrest and the left wings, the Rovers now for the first time assumed the offensive. The ball was well returned by the Scotch backs, and being cleverly passed and centred a dangerous shot was made at the Rovers' goal, which again only just missed. Up to this time it looked any odds on the Glasgow men, and to say the truth, though some good football had here and there been shown by individuals, the Rovers had been all abroad as a team. But now the Lancashire men shook themselves together, and took the ball to the Glasgow territory. Hereabouts some funny head-butting of the ball backwards and forwards caused loud cheers and laughter. Soon afterwards the Rovers were again reduced to the defensive. The Scotchmen got a free kick for "hands," and the ball was finally kicked by Arnott right into the Blackburn goal. Within another minute or two a quick pass and centring from the Scotch right wing resulted in a shot which was only a little wide of the goal post. The Rovers then in their turn assailed their opponents' goal. Their left wing and one of their forwards got right past the Glasgow backs, and Gillespie with the utmost difficulty saved his goal. After some remarkably fast play on both sides the Rovers obtained a corner, but the ball went behind. Now for some time the play was very even, and M'Intyre for the Rovers and Arnott for the Queen's Park gained frequent applause for their fine and accurate kicking. Then out of some loose play Forrest and Brown got on the ball. The latter took it brilliantly round the Glasgow backs; Gillespie rushed out of his goal, and missing the ball badly Sowerbutts put it through at his leisure. It is unnecessary to say that this successful exploit roused the most tumultuous enthusiasm among the supporters of Lancashire. The play was now for a time of a give-and-take character, Arnott especially distinguishing himself with his skilful and forcible kicking. But it was not very long before the Rovers again pressed their opponents and got a corner. The ball was well placed, but the Scotchmen seemed to have got it away out of danger when it was brilliantly returned from the left wing Forrest made a splendid shot, and scored a second goal for Blackburn. In quick succession another corner was obtained by the Rovers, but this time the ball was taken away, and the Scotchmen in their turn gained a corner. This was badly placed, but directly afterwards out of some loose play Christie got possession, and sent the ball between the Rovers' posts too fast and too high for Arthur to stop. After a dangerous rush by the Rovers' forwards had been well eluded by Arnott half-time was called.

On resuming the game the ball was taken to the Scotch goal, but the defenders skilfully butted it away with their heads. The Scotchmen were now severely pressed, but nothing of importance occurred till one of the Glasgow backs, kicking the ball backwards over his own head, the Rovers obtained a corner. Shot after shot was now made at the Scotch goal, and once Gillespie had to use his hands. Brown here missed a capital chance, and the ball being taken to the Blackburn goal one of the Scotch forwards made a similar mistake. The play had been fast and furious, and it was now evident that the Scotchmen were tiring, and that their kicking was becoming wild and purposeless. However, they soon managed to press the Rovers again, and Arthur cleverly saved his goal from a perilous siege. Smith now distinguished himself by a long dribble, but Beverley smartly averted the danger. The same player immediately afterwards made a splendid long kick right into the jaws of the Scotch goal. Shortly afterwards Gillespie had to save his goal from a long but exceedingly fast shot. Most of the spectators, including some good judges, who were well placed for seeing what happened, declared that the ball was through the goal when the goalkeeper stopped it, but the umpire refused to allow the score. A minute or two before "time" Forrest sent the ball to Brown, who passed it easily under the tape, but the latter was obviously off side, and this goal was also disallowed. Then time was called, and the Rovers were declared victors by two goals to one. All the Lancashire men on the ground promptly went mad with delight, and those of the Rovers who could not escape were carried shoulder high (to their exceeding discomfort) back to the pavilion. All the Rovers played well. Beverly kicked with wonderful force and judgment; Forrest played most brilliantly throughout; and Brown, like the Knight o' Sheppey, "did not resemble a man asleep." M'Intyre never made a mistake in his kicking from first to last. Of the Queen's Park, Arnott, Christie, and Anderson may be singled out as the best players. The great disappointment was the Scotch "crack," Dr. Smith, and the Scotchmen on the ground declared themselves "clean wad" with his play. Indeed, he was out of all form, and never seemed able to get on the ball or keep possession of it. It should be added that the game was played all through with an entire absence of roughness or ill-temper.

A LONDON OPINION OF LANCASHIRE VISITORS.

The *Pall Mall Gazette*, in an article headed "A Northern Horde," says:—London witnessed an incursion of Northern barbarians on Saturday—hot-blooded Lancastrians, sharp of tongue, rough and ready, of uncouth garb and speech. A tribe of Soudanese Arabs let loose in the Strand would not excite more amusement and curiosity. This band of a thousand or more made the pilgrimage in order to witness their doughty companions contest the challenge cup of the Football Association, and of the 12,000 or so who formed the compact square at the Oval on Saturday, none shouted so wildly as this devoted body. It was a sight not to be forgotten. From more than one the excitement and the victory elicited tears. Strange oaths fell upon Southern ears, and curious words, curious but expressive, filled the air. Admirers of these gentlemen have numerous anecdotes of their quaint ways and racy sayings, which are as good as anything told of the pitman in his halcyon days of high wages and champagne. At the banquets held to celebrate their victories they have been heard to express surprise because the ice pudding was "cowd" (cold), and to declare with disgust their contempt for the custom of serving soup before joint. "It's nobbut fit to fill up wi," they say. Last year, on a similar occasion, the London and North-Western Railway ran a special train up to London. The thousand or so of passengers at every station where the train stopped descended upon the refreshment rooms and wrecked them. They ate, drank, and were merry, they broke the glasses and the windows, refused to pay, and struck horror into the usually complacent bosoms of the presiding goddesses. It was as an advancing army in an enemy's country. This year the railway company profited by experience. An order was given to close every refreshment room on the line. So the invading army had to carry supplies with it. It is said, and it redounds to the honour of these gentry, that Blackburn will turn out in its thousands to welcome back the conquering heroes, with bands of music and gay banners. For a few hours the loom will stand idle, and the sons of toil will drink much more liquor than is good for them. For whether it is eating, or (better still) drinking, or whether there is a little rioting to be done, or such a small matter as a house to be burned down—in fact, any ceremony that affords pleasant variation in their rather humdrum life, these Lancashire folk enjoy it with infinite zest. A word may be said for the excellent arrangements of the authorities at the Oval for the accommodation of this vast crowd—arrangements by which a few score of fortunate people narrowly escaped an untimely end in the crush. The turnstile at 3 p.m. was a sight to see and a place to avoid. We can only say a word to the wise: Keep away from the Oval on occasions of this sort.

ACCRINGTON SWIFTS *v.* WHITE ROSE.—This match was played on the Swifts' ground, and after a very pleasant game it ended in another victory for the Swifts by four goals to one.

STANLEY HEROES *v.* CASTLE ROVERS.—In the *Accrington Times* for last week it was reported that the Rovers won by three to two, but it was not true, as the whistle had blown for hands before the ball went through; thus the Heroes had their free kick, and the game ended in a draw two goals each.

CROSS RANGERS *v.* YOUNG ETONIANS.—The fourth match was played between these two teams on Saturday in splendid weather. The Etonians won the toss and chose to play with the wind and ground in their favour. Yates (captain) kicked off at 3 15, and a raid was made on the Rangers' goal, and from a scrimmage secured their first goal. Soon after this they scored another, and before the whistle blew for half-time number four was registered. On change of ends the Etonians played on the defensive, but the Rangers not to be denied went in with a dash, and soon put five to their credit, the game thus ending in a well-earned victory for the Rangers by five goals to four.

OSWALDTWISTLE NORTH END *v.* EWBANK ROVERS.—Played on the ground of the latter, at Accrington. The North End captain won the toss, and elected to play up hill with the wind in favour. The ball was started, and some give-and-take play was witnessed. At the call of half-time the game stood even, neither teams having scored. Scholes restarted the ball for the North End, who began to press their opponents. Five minutes before the call of time McGrath made a splendid run down the field, passed the ball to Duckworth, who by a splendid shot sent the leather flying through the home post amid great applause, thus winning the match for the North End by one goal to nil.

I ZINGARI *v.* CASTLE ROVERS.—The above match was played on Saturday on the ground of the former at Milnshaw. Play was commenced at 3 15. The Zingari at once pressed their opponents, and soon put two goals through, one of which was disputed. Not to be denied, however, the home team again ran up the field in grand style and scored another goal, which was disputed also. Half-time was now called, with the score one goal and two disputed in favour of the Zingari. The Rovers continued to be pressed, only breaking away occasionally, while the home team scored two more goals, thus winning a very easy game by three goals and two disputed to the Rovers' nil. Soon after half-time Kenyon (Zingari right wing) was badly kicked, and retired for the remainder of the game.

BLACKBURN OLYMPIC *v.* ACCRINGTON.—This game was played at the Hole-i'-th' Wall ground, Blackburn, on Saturday afternoon. The Olympic won the toss and elected to play downhill. The visitors were hard pressed during the first half, and the back play in one quarter was weak. The Olympians were in excellent form, and got four goals during the first-half, to one scored by their opponents. During the second-half Accrington played a better game, and pressed their opponents two or three times, Chippendale almost getting a goal by a good shot which barely went over the cross-bar. After a hard and exciting struggle close in the Accrington goal, the ball was got well away, and Bishop made a splendid run from one goal to the other, but he ended by kicking the off-side of the goal when he had no one to oppose him but the goalkeeper. Although they tried hard, the home team only managed to score another goal during the second-half, the game ending in a victory for the Olympians by five goals to one.

Date 29 March 1884
Place The Kennington Oval
Score BLACKBURN ROVERS 2
QUEENS PARK 1
Teams BLACKBURN ROVERS Arthur, Suter, Beverley, McIntyre (capt.), Forrest, Hargreaves, Brown, Inglis, Sowerbutts, Douglas, Lofthouse. QUEENS PARK Gillespie, Macdonald, Arnott, Gow, Campbell (capt.), Christie, Allan, Harrower, Dr Smith, Watt, Anderson
Goal Scorers BLACKBURN ROVERS Sowerbutts, Forrest; QUEENS PARK Gillespie
Attendance 14000
Copy *The Accrington Times* 5 April 1884

SUNDAY TIMES, APRIL 5, 1885.

YESTERDAY'S FOOTBALL.

THE ASSOCIATION CHALLENGE CUP.

Blackburn Rovers v. Queen's Park.—General interest in Association football reached a climax on Saturday last when, at Kennington Oval, London, over 12,000 people were present to watch Queen's Park, Glasgow, and the Blackburn Rovers do battle for possession of the Association Challenge Cup. Great preparations had been made for the occasion, and the weather proving of the most favourable description, the match was a great success. Whether the play came up to expectation may be doubted, but it can be stated without fear of contradiction, that the better side won. The Rovers were faster and better together, while there was no comparison in the play of the respective back divisions. Individually some of the Scotchmen were very good, but the clever passing by which they have gained so much renown was conspicuous by its absence. It may be stated, however, in excuse, that they had very bad luck in losing the services of Christie, Harrower, and Watt. Sellar was in good form in the centre, and both Arnott and Gillespie were good, but Campbell was not at his best, and McLeod was a distinct failure. General praise must be accorded the Rovers, but the main contributors to the result were Brown and the half-backs, McIntyre, Howarth, and Forrest; indeed, the defence and accuracy of these three constituted the feature of the game. The play is described in detail below so it may be merely prefaced by the remark that the victory of the Blackburn Rovers for the second year in succession was eminently popular.

Some exception had been taken to arranging the final tie for the Easter holidays, but any one who witnessed the scene at the Oval could not fail to acknowledge that the date was in every way judicious. Excursion trains from Scotland, the North, and the Midlands had brought up numerous football enthusiasts to witness the great match, and Kennington Oval presented an appearance never before witnessed on the occasion of a football match. The gates were opened early, and very soon troops of people were seen making their way to the scene of the encounter. At 15 o'clock the field of play was surrounded by rows of spectators, ten, fifteen, and even twenty deep. As if the means of transit were not sufficient to make the fixture a success, the day turned out one of the most charming that we have experienced this spring. The sun shone out brightly, the sky was clear, and, although there was a good deal of wind blowing end on, it served the purpose of rendering the ground firm in the extreme. At 15.30 the hour was fixed for the commencement, and during the long wait the crowd amused themselves by singing refrains of well-known songs, and otherwise putting in the wait to the best of their ability. Just about the appointed time a loud cheer announced the appearance of the Blackburn Rovers, Lofthouse and Brown coming in for a special recognition. They were speedily followed by Queen's Park, who were even more readily welcomed. Campbell beat Brown in the toss, and took the gas works end. Campbell kicked off, but the ball was brought back because Allen was off side. A charge by McWhannel and Hamilton was well put away by McIntyre, and then Lofthouse got beyond McLeod, but Arnott came to the rescue of his side. Some scrimmaging before the Blackburn goal was ended by Campbell kicking into touch. From the throw in to the Rovers Lofthouse got possession, and, dodging McLeod, sent in a very clever centre, which dropped over the bar. Queen's Park dashed away, and a fine shot by Hamilton was only just put away by Turner. Some desultory play followed about the centre of the ground, the ball going into touch three or four times, until at last Sellars obtained the ball, but, having Turner in front of him, made a wild shot at goal. Then after a lofty kick by Arnott both he and Campbell fell and the Rovers dashed on to the goal, Gillespie almost miraculously saving his side from a shot by Sourbutts, and two or three times, in a very short space of time, the ball was in immediate danger of going through the posts. Indeed, the Rovers appealed for a goal, but it was very properly not allowed. Within a minute afterwards the ball was again back, and for a straight kick by Sourbutts Gillespie had again to use his hands. Anderson then made a clever dribble down the right wing and McWhannel looking dangerous McIntyre gave away a corner. Nothing resulted and Lofthouse got right away and scored a corner off Arnott. This also had no result, but the Rovers got a couple of throws in on the Queen's Park left. Some clever passing between Anderson and Hamilton was stopped by McIntyre, and immediately afterwards Allen and McDonald again looked very dangerous. The ball, however, was got away and Brown, very cleverly passing Arnott, sent in a shot which hit the bar. Some head play between the Scotch backs and Brown and Sourbutts ensued, until at length Forrest put the ball through the posts, amid tremendous cheering. This occurred fourteen minutes from the start. Just after the ball had been re-started the Rovers secured a corner—very well taken by Brown—but Campbell headed it away. The ball, however, was returned, and went behind. Then Anderson and Sellar worked their way back, and on two or three occasions the defence of Suter, Turner, and Howarth was seriously tried. A clever run by Sellars, Hamilton and Anderson, looked dangerous until "hands" was given against the Scotchmen. Yet again Sellar broke away and though Anderson and Hamilton backed him up well the finish was a tame one. Another corner to the Rovers was taken by Brown, and Sourbutts sent in a shot which Gillespie just got against his chest and kicked out. It now came the turn of the Scotch lefts, Allen and Gray working their way down, and, passing Turner, and going right on until Suter came to the rescue of the Englishmen. Again some pretty play followed, Sellar, Campbell, Anderson, and Hamilton taking the ball to the other end of the field. Arnott, who had received the ball, sent in a splendid shot, but just when Queen's Park looked like scoring, one of the forwards touched the ball with his hands—a piece of very bad luck. A fine long shot at Sellar brought out loud cheers, and only missed the goal by a yard. Just afterwards Douglas and Brown, breaking away, the ball was headed over the Scotch goal by Arnott. From the corners, Rich, the Queen's Park goal, was in some jeopardy, Howarth, in particular, using his feet with great effect. At length the Scotch got a throw in, taken by M'Donald, and Sellar made his way along grandly—a very fine piece of play, being rendered unproductive through poor support. From some 30 yards from the goal Fecitt sent in a splendid shot to Gillespie, which the goal keep with one hand just managed to put over the bar. For some time the Scotchmen were very hard pressed, and their ill-success was still further increased when a cry of "hands" was allowed close to the Queen's Park posts. After a long period of defensive play Queen's Park got away, Allan, Gray, and Sellar being all conspicuous. Half-time arrived with the score, one goal to none, in favour of the Blackburn Rovers. On the resumption McIntyre kicked off, and Brown, passing to Lofthouse, Queen's Park had to act on the defensive. Anderson dashed away, but was stopped by McIntyre, and in another second McLeod had to put forth his best effort. Hands given against McLeod, dangerously near his own goal, followed, and a shot was sent in which gave the Blackburn Rovers a real opportunity. For a good minute a fierce attack was made on the Queen's Park goal. The ball went dangerously near the posts, and a goal was appealed for by the Blackburn men, but disallowed, Gillespie, who caught the ball, being apparently across the goal one. After some give-and-take play a foul was given against the Blackburn men. Arnott took the free kick, and some shots at the Blackburn goal wanted a lot of stopping, until Sellar kicked just over the bar. Other runs down the Queen's Park left, in which Sellar showed conspicuous, followed, the famous centre playing up to his highest form. Since the resumption, Queen's Park had had a decided advantage, but the back play of Turner and Howarth had been too much for the Scotch forwards. A fine run by Brown provoked loud cheering, but Allen stopped him, and Arnott returned the ball. Queen's Park were soon again acting on the offensive, Hamilton and Anderson playing into each other's hands very cleverly. Gray, too, showed up prominently, and Queen's Park secured a corner, but the ball fell behind the Blackburn line. For a few minutes the players seemed to flag in their efforts, and neither side could get the ball far away from the centre. At length Sellar worked his way down and passed to Allen, but McIntyre came to the rescue of his side, and then the ball was kicked by Grey over the Blackburn line. From a throw in Lofthouse passed to Brown, but after the latter had been once stopped, Fecitt and Forrest worked the ball back, and the Scotch goal being unaccountably exposed, Brown, who was just in front of the goal, had no difficulty whatever in just kicking the ball through, the Blackburn Rovers obtaining their second goal at 16.43. The enthusiasm of the English club supporters now knew no bounds—hats and sticks flying in the air in the wildest confusion. On re-starting the game the ball went over the Blackburn line, and just afterward Howarth gave away a corner. It was well taken by Gray, but Howarth immediately atoned for his mistake by kicking the ball well into the centre of the field. Shots by Gray, Sellar, and Anderson all failed to score, but the Scotch were having a distinct advantage for ten minutes. They were playing with plenty of dash, but a rearrangement among the forwards seriously affected the chances of Queen's Park, their famous combination being strangely absent. Lofthouse got away, and crossed to Fecitt. The latter shot into Gillespie, but the Scotch goal-keeper was equal to the occasion. Gray and Allen returned the ball, and McIntyre nearly gave away a goal Brown put in some very clever dribbles, but Campbell several times finished by getting the ball away from him. Queen's Park were frequently within an ace of scoring, first Sellar, then Gray, and next Anderson sending in shots, but they were for the most part rather wide ones, and Gillespie's defence was not seriously taxed. Later on Howarth relieved his side, and Lofthouse worked the ball right down the other end and got a throw in close to the Scotch goal. Some Scrimmaging in front of the Scotch goal ensued and McIntyre kicked right into the hands of Gillespie. With only a few minutes to play Queen's Park gained a corner, but like several taken by Gray, it fell the wrong side of the line. The ball was returned to the centre of the field, where neither side could get the ball away. Certainly Arthur had once to handle the ball, but there was really nobody near him to in any way impede his defence. Back-play by Suter, Forrest, and Howarth was admirable; but just at the close Gray sent in a grand shot, which Arthur only just put behind, the ball hitting his hand within a foot of the post. Queen's Park never seemed to give up hope, and played with plenty of dash, their forwards doing a lot of work, while the front division of the Blackburn team fell away at the close, and confining their energies mainly to defence. At last the whistle was blown, and the Blackburn Rovers left the field winners of a fine match by two goals to none, and thereby securing possession of the national trophy for another season.

THE FIFTY MILES BICYCLE CHAMPIONSHIP.

An excellent race for the Fifty Miles Bicycle Championship took place yesterday, at the Aylestone Road Ground, Leicester, in the presence of close upon seven thousand spectators. The prizes were a cup value £20 and £35 added money, and the following men went to the post:—F. Wood, of Leicester; F. de Civry, of France; H. O. Duncan, of Montpellier, France; R. James, of Birmingham; T. Battensby, of Newcastle; F. Lees, of Sheffield; T. Cleminson, of Newcastle; A. Hawker, of Leicester; J. Parkes, of Newcastle; T. Birt, of Northampton; J. Mace, of Birmingham; and J. Grose, of Northampton. For the first five miles the men kept very close together, but at the end of the tenth mile Battensby was in front, followed by Wood, Lees, Duncan, and Jones. Here Duncan went ahead, and the pace became a little slower. James retired at 25 miles, and a little later De Civry and Wood had to give way. Little of importance occurred until four laps from home, when Birt took the lead. On entering the last lap Birt rushed forward, hard pressed by Duncan, Lees, Cleminson, and Battensby. Coming down the hill Duncan made his effort, and won a splendid race by four yards; Birt was second, a yard in front of Cleminson, Lees was fourth, and Battensby fifth. Time, 3hrs. 17min. 14⅕sec. The winner was loudly cheered.

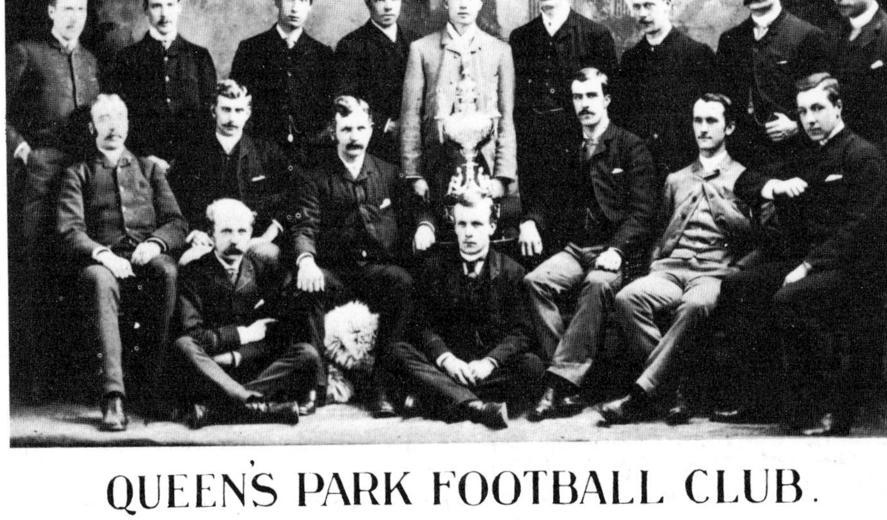

QUEEN'S PARK FOOTBALL CLUB.

Date 4 April 1885
Place The Kennington Oval
Score BLACKBURN ROVERS 2
QUEENS PARK 0
Teams BLACKBURN ROVERS Arthur, Turner, Suter, Haworth, McIntyre, Forrest, Sowerbutts, Lofthouse, Douglas, Brown (capt.), Fecitt.
QUEENS PARK Gillespie, Arnott, MacLeod, McDonald, Campbell (capt.), Sellar, Anderson, McWhannel, Hamilton, Allan, Gray
Official Referee Major Marindin
Goal Scorers Forrest 14, Brown 58
Attendance 12500
Gate Receipts £442
Copy *The Sunday Times* 5 April 1885

THE BLACKBURN STANDARD, SATURDAY, APRIL 10, 1886.

THE ENGLISH CUP COMPETITION.—FINAL TIE.

BLACKBURN ROVERS v. WEST BROMWICH ALBION.

This match was played on the Kennington Oval, London, on Saturday, in the presence of 12,000 spectators, two thirds of whom were visitors to the metropolis. Blackburn and North-East Lancashire furnished a strong contingent, by means of an excursion promoted by Messrs. Sharples and Aspden, Northgate, Blackburn. The Midlands were also numerously represented. The match was attended by leading football men from all parts of the country, and additional interest centred in the game, from a Lancashire point of view, in that it was witnessed by Mr. W. Coddington, M.P., and Mrs. Coddington, Sir Robert Peel, Bart., M.P., Lieut.-Gen. Feilden, M.P., and other well-known Lancashire figures. Prior to the match Mr. Coddington stepped into the enclosure, and offered a few words of encouragement to the captain of the Rovers. West Bromwich Albion having been photographed, the Rovers declining the honour, the teams entered the enclosure, the cupholders coming in last. Albion won the toss, and Brown had no alternative but to kick off with the sun in his face and against a strong wind. The game ended unsatisfactorily, since neither side scored, and there was some disappointment that the Rovers declined to play an extra half hour, although none of their real friends would have wished it, considering they were so unaccountably out of form, and that Turner received a nasty kick on the ankle. The kick-off was delayed until four o'clock, in order that any who had witnessed the boat race might also, if they cared, be in time for the football match. The Brums at once assumed the offensive and invaded the Rovers' lines, but the ball went out. After the throw in the Midlanders secured a free kick for hands, which Horton essayed, but McIntyre cleared the ball away, and Sourbutts ran it speedily down the left wing. The Albion half-backs were, however, on the alert, and after some clever play by Perry, Loach and Bell made a brilliant run, and a corner kick accrued to the Midlanders, but though well placed the ball was eventually sent over the goal-line. Few opportunities were given the Rovers of getting away, and with the sun in their faces Brown evidently thought it best to devote attention to keeping the goal intact. Both Suter and Turner kept well back, and the former had a very busy time of it, Loach and Bayliss keeping up a "running fire" on the Rovers' citadel. Several prolonged scrimmages ensued near that goal, but Arthur managed to stave off disaster, and after a time the forwards were enabled to cross over, Fecitt and Sourbutts putting in a couple of shots, which Roberts, however, saved. A free kick near goal and a corner followed, but the Albion half-backs partially cleared, and after a second unproductive corner kick to the holders the Brums replied with vigour. On one occasion Bayliss all but succeeded in rushing the ball through, Suter just kicking away in time, while a minute or two later Green put in a warm shot, which just passed over the cross-bar. Play then became a trifle slower and more even, though the Albion forwards appeared to play better together than their rivals. Woodhall and Green endeavoured to rush the ball through, but the former kicked over, while a little later the same player caused Arthur great anxiety, but he succeeded in sending the ball away just in the nick of time. Timmins also shot over the Rovers' cross-bar, but after a long kick by Horton, which Arthur saved, the Rovers' left wing dribbled the ball back, and some exciting play ensued near the West Bromwich goal line. The Brums, however, speedily relieved, and their left wings retaliated. Hands near the Rovers' uprights followed, but Brown got the ball away. Perry returned, and a united effort by Bayliss, Woodhall, and Green very nearly ended in a score, M'Intyre on this occasion proving the saviour of his side. The Albions still held the upper hand, and though Fecitt and Sourbutts made dashing runs, in each instance they were but poorly supported, and the ball was quickly returned to the vicinity of the Rovers' goal, where Arthur, assisted by the backs, proved proof against all the onslaughts of Bayliss, Green, and Horton, and when half-time arrived no goals had been scored. With the wind in their favour (the sun had by this time lost much of its brilliancy) the Rovers' supporters confidently anticipated that they would be able to make a better show, and for the first few minutes such seemed likely to be the case. Bayliss having restarted for West Bromwich, the former crossed over and a corner was obtained, but Douglas's efforts proved unsuccessful. A pretty run up the field by Bayliss, Green, and Woodhall evoked loud applause from the Brums, which speedily died away when Brown and Fecitt replied with vigour, and kept the ball in the Midlanders' territory for several minutes. A long shot by Sourbutts was saved by Roberts, and then the Albion made a determined effort to score, but Turner and Arthur stayed off danger, and the leather eventually went behind. After this play for a while continued very even, Green, Woodhall, G. Bell, Fecitt, and Forrest in turn attacking without result. Heyes was then ordered off the field in consequence of having spikes on his boots contrary to the rules, but having changed, reappeared. Towards the close, amid intense excitement, both sides made final bids for victory. Twice Arthur cleared prolonged scrimmages from which the Albion appeared certain to score, while Bayliss and Green also put in warm shots. A few minutes before the finish nearly everybody thought that Fecitt had put the ball between the Albion posts, and several of the Rovers jumped with excitement, but the leather, however, really passed a foot outside the posts. Several other attacks were made by either side, but at the close nothing had been scored, and the result was therefore a draw. With the chance of being in better form on another occasion, the Rovers very naturally declined to play the extra half-hour which the Albion, who had certainly had the better of the game, were willing to play. A committee meeting of the Association was accordingly held, and it was decided by a narrow majority that the pair should meet again at Derby on Saturday next, April 10th, or, in case that ground should not be available, at Kennington Oval.

SPORTS AND PASTIMES.

Once more the Rovers have astonished the football world with their prowess in the winter game, for on Saturday they won the English Cup in magnificent style for the third year in succession. After the poor display they made at the Oval the week previous, Blackburnians were not so confident as to the match at Derby resulting in a victory for the Rovers; but the team made ample amends on Saturday for their shortcomings at London, and played a game of as high a class as the other was poor. The result must, of course, be a source of the highest gratification to the inhabitants of the borough, with whom the Rovers will become more popular than ever, as they have by their skill on Saturday last rivalled the great feat of the Wanderers' Club, who won the cup three times. But it must be even more pleasing that the cup has once more found its way to Blackburn, for this makes it the fourth year in succession when it has been brought here, the Olympic having carried it off the first time. The sight on the Derby County Ground on Saturday was a most imposing one, there being about 15,000 spectators present. The Rovers were the first to appear and were received with slight applause, but the reception accorded "the Throstles" was a marked contrast to that shown the Rovers, and was ample evidence of the fact that the Rovers had nothing like so many supporters or sympathisers present as had the Albion. The latter looked exceedingly fit and well, and were a much heavier team than the Rovers, and opinion generally was in their favour. At 3 35, about five minutes after the advertised time, the kick off was made and immediately the Albions went off with a dash and stormed the Rovers' goal for fully five minutes, but their shooting was erratic, and the defence of the Rovers, in addition, was perfect, so that try as they would, "the Throstles" had to give over singing, whilst the Rovers played them a tune up the field. Sourbutts broke through their defence and scored the first goal amidst loud cheers. After this the Blackburn team seemed to have more sympathy from the spectators, and they were frequently urged on to victory, but this was unnecessary, as the men were fully determined that there should be no repetition of the previous week and the issue left in doubt any longer. Again Sourbutts scored, but this time the goal was not allowed, that player being ruled off-side, and half-time was called with the same result—one goal to love in favour of the Rovers. In the second half the finest run of the day was made by Jimmy Brown, who raced down the field with the ball at his toes twenty yards or so from his own goal, and although he was hotly pursued by his opponents they could never get up to him until he had by a grand shot notched the second legitimate point for his side. The run, it is needless to add, was highly appreciated by the spectators, who cheered the Rovers' captain most heartily. The score was unchanged when the whistle blew, and thus the Rovers retired the conquerors by two goals to none. In speaking of the play exhibited by each team we must say that everyone admitted that the best team had won, which is a fact that could not possibly be disputed for one moment. The Rovers were superior at every point, but more especially in the back division. As a team playing in the English Cup final "the Throstles" were a disappointing lot, and to our mind played very nervously all through the game. We most certainly give them credit for the dash they displayed for the first few minutes of the encounter, but after that they fell all to pieces, and yet they had been in training for three or four weeks. Roberts played a good game, but the backs and half-backs were a very poor lot. Woodhall and Loach were the best of the forwards, and would have shone to more advantage if they had been better fed by the half-backs, as it was they had too much work and consequently were the sooner "done up." For the Rovers Arthur was in splendid form, and the way in which he fisted out shot after shot delighted the spectators very much, and they were compelled to admit that the Association Committee were fully justified in their selection of Arthur over Roberts to play in the International match against Scotland. Suter played magnificently, his heading being most effective, and his coolness and judgment superb. The shots that he stopped were many of them most dangerous ones, and the ease with which he staved them off was most aggravating to the Albion supporters who nevertheless gave Suter the credit for his good play. Turner worked hard, but was not so sure as Suter, McIntyre showed up well, and played a really good game from beginning to end. He wanted a lot of passing, and several times sent in some good shots, one of which almost scored. Forrest was the best half back on the field, his tackling being sure. He fed his forwards well and throughout played brilliantly; and Douglas, although he did not shine in any particular manner, was energetic and useful as the partner of McIntyre and Forrest. Of the forward division Fecitt, although he did not score was certainly the best, his dodging being immense. The way he ran round those Albion men was superb, and gave the utmost gratification to unprejudiced spectators, who voted him the best forward on the ground. We endorse this opinion ourselves, but are bound to say, and we think, Fecitt might have scored at least two goals in the earlier part of the game had he shot instead of centred so much in front of goal. Sourbutts passed well, and along with Fecitt gave the Midland half backs lots of work. Brown in the centre was in his old form, and reminded us of times gone by when he gained such renown as a dribbler. His powers on Saturday in dribbling completely astonished the Albions, who we think had not seen anything of the kind before, and were not quite prepared to be outrun in such a manner as Brown did them on Saturday. Strachan played well, but was at a disadvantage in having Walton as his partner, who although he did his best could not be said to be as good as the other forwards. Taking the team as a whole, however, they proved themselves a grand lot, and should easily knock out of time the Bolton Wanderers to-day in the final of the Lancashire Cup Competition. At the conclusion of the match, Major Marindin in

The West Bromwich team and officials

Date 3 April 1886
Place The Kennington Oval
Score BLACKBURN ROVERS 0 WEST BROMWICH ALBION 0
Teams BLACKBURN ROVERS Arthur, Turner, Suter, Heyes, Forrest, McIntyre, Douglas, Strachan, Sowerbutts, Fecitt, Brown (capt.); WEST BROMWICH ALBION Roberts, H. Green, H. Bell, Horton, Perry, Timmins, Woodhall, T. Green, Bayliss (capt.), Loach, G. Bell
Official Referee Major Marindin
Attendance 12000
Copy *The Blackburn Standard* 10 April 1886

Replay
Date 10 April 1886
Place Derby County
Score BLACKBURN ROVERS 2 WEST BROMWICH ALBION 0
Team Changes BLACKBURN ROVERS Arthur, Turner, Suter, Douglas, Forrest, McIntyre, Walton, Strachan, Brown, Fecitt, Sowerbutts. WEST BROMWICH ALBION Unchanged
Official Referee Major Marindin
Goal Scorers Sowerbutts, Brown
Attendance 15000
Copy *The Blackburn Standard* 17 April 1886

THE BLACKBURN STANDARD, SATURDAY, APRIL 17, 1886.

presenting the cup to the winners expressed the great pleasure it gave him to do so, more especially as they had rivalled the great feat of the Wanderers in 1878. He thought the Rovers should have some distinctive trophy to commemorate their great performance, and he felt sure the association would fall in with his views. Mr. Brown in receiving possession of the cup said that football had very much improved since the Wanderers won in 1878, but his team would do their utmost to eclipse the performance of the London club and win the final a fourth time. It is to be hoped that Major Marindin's promise may be fulfilled, and that the association will confer some special mark of distinction upon the Rovers' club for their excellent performance, which if done, will not only be duly appreciated by the players but by the residents in the town generally.

THE ENGLISH CHALLENGE CUP.—FINAL TIE.
BLACKBURN ROVERS v. WEST BROMWICH ALBION.
VICTORY OF THE ROVERS.

Having played a drawn game at the Oval on the 3rd inst. in the final tie of the most important cup competition of the year, the Blackburn Rovers journeyed to Derby on Saturday to fight the battle over again with the West Bromwich club. The composition of the team was slightly different from that which did duty at the Oval Heyes having stood out from half-back position. His place was taken by Douglas, and Walton played on the wing in the place of Douglas. Arriving at Derby about a quarter-past one, the team at once proceeded to take lunch at the Midland Hotel. Their rivals had somewhat of an advantage over them in this respect, for they were in the town early in the morning, and after taking exercise, were kept quiet until 2 30 by order of their trainer. For more than an hour snow had been falling extremely heavily, and the country was completely enveloped in a mantle of white, and the prospects were not at all prepossessing for a good display of football; but, fortunately, the sun broke out before two o'clock, and under its influence the snow disappeared. As early as half-past one people began to wend their way to the ground at Nottingham-road, and although the match was not advertised to commence until 3 30, there would be about 7,000 or 8,000 persons present fully an hour before that time. There were a great lot of people from Birmingham and Staffordshire way, a number of trips having been run, and the majority of these—the Albion supporters—had in their hats a large blue card, upon which was a throstle and the words, "Play up, throstles." Before the termination of the match, however, the spirits of these ardent enthusiasts were damped to such an extent that they were glad to put the cards out of sight, their appearance being a subject more of ridicule than anything else. As the time drew close for a start to be made the number present on the ground at the very least must have been 15,000, and on all hands the customary "small talk" was going on as to who would and who would not be the conquerors. If anything opinion seemed to be in favour of the "Throstles," though it must be remembered that

they had by far the largest number of supporters present. Yet even the most confident of the Birmingham people had doubts on their minds which they could by no means rid themselves of. At 3 25 the Rovers, headed by their captain, Jimmy Brown stepped on the field, which was very soft in consequence of the downfall of snow. The Lancashire lads were cheered on appearing, but still more hearty was the applause that greeted the Albion men a minute or two afterwards. After the first five minutes it was palpable as to which side victory would reign, for after that time the "Throsties," who had played with a dash scarcely to be seen in a whole season's play, went to pieces, and the result of the game, which gave victory to the Rovers by two goals to none, was only surprising to the unprejudiced spectators in so far that the score was not large enough considering the play shown by the two teams. The Rovers therefore won the national and much coveted trophy for the third time in succession, and thus equalled the record of the Wanderers club, who were possessors of the cup in the years 1876, 1877, and 1878. At the conclusion of the match Major Marindin, in presenting the cup to the winners, promised to confer a distinctive medal on the Rovers to commemorate the event of their having won in three successive years, a promise which it is greatly hoped will be fulfilled and which will be most highly appreciated by the Rovers' team. The latter returned to Blackburn in the evening, and on leaving the Midland station were heartily cheered on leaving the Midland station which was repeated at Nottingham-road, and again at Bolton and Darwen, the team being recognised at each station. At Blackburn, however, their reception was of a most enthusiastic character, several hundreds of persons witnessing their arrival home, and, as the conveyance, drawn by four grey horses, conveying the men to their captain's house, drove off, cheers were raised again and again, and thus ended the last chapter in this year's English Cup competition.

Exactly at 3 32, the Albionites having won the toss, Douglas kicked off from the town goal, with the wind and sun against them, and immediately Brown and Sourbutts rushed up the field, but Woodhall, securing possession, made an excursion up the Albion right which was, however, well saved by the back. Not to be denied "the Throstles came on with much dash," said Woodhall, after a neat dribble, crossed to Loach, who lost the ball altogether, thereby missing an almost certain chance. Excellent defence was displayed by McIntyre and Forrest, but notwithstanding this the Rovers had to concede a corner, and Arthur had to handle twice over, which he did in grand style. For a few minutes the Rovers continued to be pressed, shots being rapidly sent in by Baylis and Green. Brown, Fecitt, and Sourbutts relieved the pressure by taking the ball to the Albion goal line, where Green just missed sending the ball through his own goal posts. The Albions once more rushed up the field and, getting near the Rovers' goal, T. Green shot, but the ball went over the bar. At length Suter cleared, and Brown and Walton dribbled smartly to the other end. The ball was returned, however, but Forrest, whose play all through the game was of a very high order, warded off danger. His tackling was sure, and the manner in which he fed his forwards repeatedly evoked a round of cheers. Fecitt now came in

for some notice, his dodging being superb; and for a grand run along the field, which terminated in his centring to Brown, he was loudly applauded. A scrimmage in front of the Albion posts resulted, out of which a fast shot by Sourbutts gave Roberts some trouble, but he managed to turn the ball just over the bar—a very lucky piece of work. From the corner kick nothing was gained, while from a second directly after Baylis headed the ball away at a critical juncture. Brown again got possession, and dribbling back in fine style sent the ball into Robert's hands. The attack was kept up with right down earnestness, and "the Throstles," although cheered on again and again by their supporters, could not get away from their goal line. Fecitt shot just over the bar, but from the kick out Walton worked the ball back and, amidst tremendous cheering, Sourbutts scored the first goal for the Rovers 26 minutes from the start

This seemed to rouse the Albions a little, and they tried hard to relieve the pressure which followed from the re start, but their efforts were not crowned with success, and the Rovers almost scored again. They were playing much the better game, and several times had very hard lines in not scoring, Brown just kicking over the bar. Fecitt then executed a capital bit of dodging, which was much admired, and he passed to Brown, who slipped just as he was about to take the final shot. The Albion goal continued to be seriously jeopardised for a time, and Roberts had to save several times. At last Sourbutts put the ball through for the second time, but it was disallowed on the ground of off-side, and although the Rovers kept up the attack nothing further was done up to half-time, which was announced with the score at Rovers one goal, Albion none. The second half of the game was well contested, the Albions striving hard to equalise matters, but try as they would they could not get over the splendid defence shown by Suter, Arthur, and the half-backs. Loach made an excellent run which elicited applause, but this bit of play was eclipsed by a rattling combined run by Sourbutts and Fecitt, the latter putting a hot shot straight in the hands of Roberts, to be coolly thrown out. The Albion then had a look in, and a shot by Perry caused Arthur to fist away, and shortly afterwards Suter saved a stinging shot, heading the ball and then kicking it to mid-field. Then the Albion secured a corner, but their attempt was futile, and Brown securing the ball, astonished the spectators with one of his famous runs, he taking the ball right up to the Albion goal, and shooting into the hands of the West Bromwich goalkeeper. The ball having been returned, Brown again was to the fore, and after a brilliant single-handed run, in which he fairly outpaced his pursuers, he sent the ball through amidst loud applause. After this the play became somewhat uninteresting. The Rovers being apparently satisfied with the advantage they had secured contented themselves with acting on the defensive They were always equal to any dangerous occasion, and the West Bromwich men, although keeping up a pretty stiff fusillade, could not score a point, Arthur and Suter always averting their shots. The Rovers broke away twice before the conclusion of the game, but Strachan shot wide of the posts, and just as the whistle sounded Brown put in a hot shot, which Roberts just saved, and the game ended in a victory for the Rovers by two goals to none.

The players who won the FA Cup for Blackburn Rovers in 1884, 1885 and 1886. Team picture, from left: Lofthouse, McIntyre, Beverley, Arthur, Suter, Forrest, Mr Birtwistle. Sitting: Douglas, Sowerbutts, Brown, Avery, Hargreaves. On left: Walton, Turner, Strachan. On right: Howarth, Inglis, Fecitt

THE BIRMINGHAM DAILY TIMES. MONDAY, APRIL 4, 1887.

THE ENGLISH FOOTBALL CUP.
OPINIONS OF THE PLAYERS.

A representative of the *Daily Times* this morning called upon Archie Hunter, the captain of the Villa, to elicit his opinion respecting the proceedings at the Oval on Saturday. In reply to a question as to what he thought of the result, the famous captain, in that unostentatious manner which characterises him, observed "Doubtless you have noticed the reports in the papers about the ideas entertained by Bayliss and myself prior to the match. We were both confident of winning up to the time of going upon the field, and in fact until the first goal was scored. After that, however, the confidence appeared to be altogether confined to our side, for we considered that we had as good as won, whilst from my own knowledge the West Bromwich men were very downhearted. I know the prevailing idea was that whoever scored the first goal would ultimately prove victorious, and that anticipation was justified by the result. As much as 20 to 1 was offered on the side which obtained the first goal." Our representative remarked that the supporters of the Albion were almost unanimous in their declarations that the initial goal was off side. "Nothing of the kind," remarked Archie; "a fairer or more deserving goal never was scored. The ball was taken up to the Albion goal, and getting possession I passed it across to Davies. He sent it swiftly over to Hodgetts, who with a well directed swift shot got it past Roberts. The movements leading up to the goal were not particularly brilliant, but they were so quick, and it was so uncertain in which direction the ball would be driven, that I am not surprised at Roberts missing it." "Then the suggestions respecting the offside have really no substantial basis?" "Certainly they have not. The quickness with which the umpires on both sides declared in our favour should be sufficient to dispel any doubts on that point which may have arisen in the minds either of our supporters or the admirers of the Albion." "Your tactics throughout the second half were superior to those which marked the first portion of the game," our representative observed. "Oh," said Hunter, "we simply ran away from them subsequent to half time. With the wind in our favour of course we had somewhat of an advantage, but I hardly expected that the change of ends would have had such a discouraging effect on the Albion. They are not a body of men who are 'knocked back' at a little, but on this occasion, with the exception of Green, they almost all appeared to have lost their heads." "Perhaps you would consider it invidious to single out any of the men who worked under you for special remark?" "Well, where all did so well it would perhaps appear ungracious to do so, but I cannot withhold offering a word of praise to Warner. During the first half, of course, his services were for the greater part brought into requisition. Some of the shots which he stopped were the most difficult imaginable, but Warner was always ready to hand out the ball, or by other dexterous movements frustrate the efforts of the Throstles. You ask me my opinion about Warner scooping up the ball and throwing it backwards over the bar to get out of the tremendous rush of a couple of the Albion men. Well, I consider it a magnificent bit of play. It evinced great presence of mind and a coolness which cannot be too highly spoken of. Had it not been for this movement it is highly probable that the Albion would have scored, and this perhaps might have had such an effect on our men as to have prevented us having the honour of bringing the cup to Birmingham." Upon being interrogated as to his opinion respecting the other players in his team, Hunter said that for sound and judicious play Coulton and Simmonds could not be surpassed. The latter player, he added, seemed to thoroughly frighten Green. But there was little to choose between the two, Coulton's coolness and Simmonds's dashing both being equally effective. Howard Vaughton played a harder game than usual, and Yates made a splendid half back. Just before leaving our representative, Archie remarked that perhaps he ought to say a word for their opponents. There was no doubt, he remarked, that Roberts exhibited skill and dexterity which it would be almost impossible to excel, but in the last half the quickness of the Villa men thoroughly overcame him. He, however, played a "stunning" game. It may be mentioned that the Villa, subsequent to the match, dined at the Manchester Hotel in company with the committee of the club. Mr. George Kynoch, M.P., presided, and subsequent to the repast some complimentary speeches were delivered. The association cup is now on view at the Bell Inn, Lozells Road.

Various opinions are entertained by the members of the Albion team, and also of the committee of the club, relative to the defeat of their side. A representative of the *Daily Times* sought an interview with W. Bayliss, the Albion captain, this morning, but Mr. Smith, the secretary of the club, informed him that Bayliss had not yet returned from London. Mr. Smith said, in answer to the inquiry of our reporter that he considered that the defeat of the Albion may be attributed to the fact of the team leaving home to train for the match. "Had they stayed at home," remarked Mr. Smith, "the men would have entered the field in much better condition." "But," said our representative, "the whole of the men appeared to me when I saw them at Ascot on Friday to be in excellent trim." "They were, that's true," answered Mr. Smith, "but I cannot get over the fact that the training they received at home before playing Notts County and Preston North End did them infinitely more good. I offered a strenuous objection to their leaving home on the present occasion, and Bayliss, too, concurred with me in my opinion that they would do better by remaining at home." "Why did they go to Ascot, then?" "Because the committee gave way to one or two of the players, who thought that they ought to have

a special preparation away from home. Had they not gone away there would undoubtedly have been a great deal of dissatisfaction, especially after the defeat." "Your are of opinion then that the committee made a mistake in sending them to Ascot?" "Yes, decidedly; we have discovered since the match that the air at Ascot was not bracing enough. It was what might be termed 'softening.' It tended to reduce the stamina of the men. My contention is that the defeat was solely caused by the fact of their leaving home." At this point Horton, who had just returned from London, came up. In answer to a question from our representative as to his opinion of the defeat, Horton said it was mainly owing to the bad play of the forwards. "They were," said Horton, "with the exception of Bayliss and T. Green, all at sea. I never saw Woodhall play a worse game. He was "fed" admirably by T. Green, his wing companion, but he failed entirely to take advantage of the opportunities offered to him to centre the ball. "What about the left wing?" "The remark that the men were 'at sea' applies more so to Paddock and Pearson. They played very randomly, and shot at goal seemingly without taking a survey of the surroundings. That was the cause of the ball going outside so much in the first twenty minutes." "You don't think T. Green was to blame in any respect for the bad play of Woodhall?" "Not in the least. He did as he always does, fed Woodhall at every possible opportunity. Green had little opportunity of getting away, as he was too well looked after by the Villa men." "Can you give any reason why your forwards should have played so badly?" "None; except that they were afraid of the rushes of Simmonds. The latter, I consider, played a rough game, and our forwards were in fear every moment of being kicked by him." "What's your opinion of the first goal scored by the Villa?" "I think it was offside. Both Davis and Hodgetts were offside. Roberts seldom makes a mistake in this respect, and he appealed against both men. So far as I could see both Davis and Hodgetts were offside. The shot for goal, however, was a peculiar one, and could not have been observed by Roberts."—It might be mentioned that the Albion team and committee dined with Mr. Spencer, M.P., on Saturday evening, and be sympathised with them in their defeat, and uttered some encouraging remarks.

● Aston Villa's proud FA Cup tradition really began in 1887 when they inflicted the second successive final defeat on West Bromwich Albion. At the centre of their success was Archie Hunter, reputedly the most respected captain in their history; so commanding did his presence become that on one celebrated occasion Villa chartered a special train to transport him to an away match when his work prevented him leaving with the rest of the team. It's Hunter's comments that comprise much of the post-match comments (left) in the *Birmingham Daily Times*. Hunter decries the criticism that the game's decisive opening goal, scored by Hodgetts, was

offside. "A fairer or more deserving goal never was scored." Hunter himself put the result beyond doubt with Villa's second goal two minutes from time.

In the early rounds Villa had enjoyed rasping successes over Wednesbury Old Alliance, 13–0, and Derby Midland by six goals to one; but the third round against Wolves occupied two replays spread over almost two months. In the semi-final at Crewe, perhaps chosen for easy rail access, Villa beat Rangers 3–1.

The *Birmingham Daily Times* also records an interesting and still topical post-match bleat from the Albion secretary that his team would have done better had they not broken their normal pattern of training by going away to a special headquarters for the final.

Date 2 April 1887
Place The Kennington Oval
Score ASTON VILLA 2
WEST BROMWICH ALBION 0
Teams ASTON VILLA Warner, Coulton, Simmonds, Yates, Dawson, Burton, Davis, Brown, Hunter, Vaughton, Hodgetts.
WEST BROMWICH ALBION Roberts, H. Green, Aldridge, Horton, Perry, Timmins, Woodhall, T. Green, Bayliss, Paddock, Pearson
Team Colours ASTON VILLA Claret and Blue.
WEST BROMWICH ALBION Blue and White
Official Referee Major Marindin
Goal Scorers Hodgetts, Hunter 88
Attendance 15500
Copy The Birmingham Daily Times 4 April 1887

Bayliss of West Brom heads towards the Villa goal

THE BIRMINGHAM DAILY POST, MONDAY, MARCH 26, 1888.

FINAL TIE FOR THE ENGLISH CUP

VICTORY OF WEST BROMWICH ALBION.

The English Cup is to remain in the Midlands after all. On Saturday afternoon, at Kennington Oval, in the presence of an enormous crowd, the West Bromwich Albion snatched a narrow victory over the Preston North End, and secured what it is the habit to call the coveted trophy to the Black Country borough. And a coveted trophy this shabby little cup is indeed, conferring as it does upon its holders the championship for the year of English football. We doubt if there is now any distinction to be won in sporting or athletics which is the subject of such keen rivalry, and the struggle for which evokes such deep and widespread feeling, as the English Football Cup. The enthusiasm in Birmingham and the neighbourhood over Saturday's result will be proportionately great. For until the last few weeks it had appeared to be almost a certainty that the cup would return to Lancashire, whence, after an unbroken stay of four years, the Aston Villa wrested it last season.

The Prestonians came on the field first, and were well received, but the West Bromwich men had the heartiest reception, it being evident that they had the greatest number of well-wishers. Both teams looked fit and well, and whilst the splendid physique of the North End players was much admired, the wiry look of the Albion men gave hope to the hearts of many of the team's supporters. No time was lost in getting ready, and the men were soon in position the North Enders playing towards the Gasworks end, with the sun behind them, Ross senior having won the choice of ends. The game once started, the Preston left wing players at once displayed their dribbling powers, and Horton only after a great deal of trouble took the ball from them. He gave it to his own forwards, and they with beautiful combination worked their way into the North End's goal. Dangerous was the attack, and Ross senior gave a corner-kick which was well taken, and Pearson shot hard and straight. So difficult was it to save that Mills-Roberts was forced to go down on his knees to stop the ball. The Albion forwards rushed for him, but Ross senior and Howarth covered him whilst he threw it clear. The forwards of the North End now began to dribble and pass beautifully, and went towards the Albion goal ; but harassed by the backs and half-backs they could not seize an opportunity to shoot. But they were soon back again, and a long shot was tried, which Roberts easily stopped. With a persistence that boded ill for the West Bromwich men the North End forwards, supported by the half-backs, again came up to the Albion's goal, and Aldridge, heavily pressed, kicked out. The ball was taken to the corner flag and kicked across goal by Gordon. Goodhall, who was close in, tried to shoot past Roberts, but his aim was untrue, the ball passing harmlessly out. Had the two Preston left-wingers been in their proper places they might have scored : in fact, the probability is that they would have done so, for the ball passed obliquely across the front of the goal, and it would have been the easiest thing in the world for Dewhurst to have touched it past Roberts. But the left-wing men, fortunately for the Albion, were not there, and so a splendid chance—which, as it proved, cost the Prestonians the match—was lost. A few moments later the North End forwards were swarming around the Albion's goal, and Roberts saved a splendid shot sent in by Goodhall. Dewhurst was now guilty of foul play, he using his hands in the endeavour to keep Horton from the ball. A long kick enabled the Albion to make a headlong rush towards the North End goal, but the backs repulsed the attack, and the Albion goal again became the scene of the fight. The North End forwards made no use of their splendid mid-field play, being, to our minds, not ready enough to shoot. A sudden breakaway by the Albion left-wing forwards relieved Aldridge and Green, and gave them a much-needed rest. The run came to nothing, for Ross senior let the ball roll inside. Bassett now did some pretty dodging, and ran well into goal. He passed to Bayliss, who, seeing that he had not an opening, tried to give Bassett the ball again, but Ross ran between them, and kicked clear. An attack on the West Bromwich goal followed, but Aldridge spoiled the North End forwards' efforts. One or two of the latter players exhibited a desire to play roughly, and two fouls were given against them. Gordon and "Nick" Ross were the transgressors, and the offence might have cost North End dear, for from the free kick Woodhall sent in a shot which Mills-Roberts, good goalkeeper as he is, had hard work to prevent taking effect. He threw the ball clear, but Bassett obtained it, and, dodging splendidly, kicked across the goal. Bayliss rushed in, and with a low shot scored for the Albion amidst tremendous cheering. The North End—who scarcely realised that the goal had been carried, so quick was the act achieved—appealed, but without success. Now the North End to a man began to play. The forwards worked magnificently together in the field, but so harassed were they by the Albion's half-backs that they got few opportunities to score, and when openings presented themselves they were either not utilised or the shots were wide or so slow and weak that Roberts had no trouble whatever in stopping them. Dewhurst had some beautiful chances, but threw them all away; whilst Ross jun. made some miserable shots, utterly unworthy of his usual form. These remarks do not lessen the credit due to the defensive players of the Albion, who played grandly. No matter whether high or low, straight or oblique, Roberts stopped all shots. His play, in fact, was perfect, and the spectators repeatedly cheered him. The Albion goal was continually besieged, except for short intervals occupied by their forwards' occasional rushes. So the game went on, the North End attacking and the Albion defending, and half-time drew closer and closer, and North End were not equal. Fiercer grew the attack, for the North End cared not to commence the second half a goal to the bad. And their efforts were all but successful, for Goodhall made a grand shot a moment before the whistle blew, but Roberts saved it.

So the Preston North End had to commence the second half behind, having had much the best of the game during the first. Their failure to score is attributable to two causes—the fine play of the Albion backs, half-backs, and goalkeeper, and the weak play before goal of their own forwards. The latter like to display their cleverness in dodging when they ought to shoot, and on Saturday this fault was very noticeable in their play. Times out of number the men dodged when they should [have shot, and Ross sen. (the captain) said at half-time, "If our forwards don't play better they'll lose us the match." For a time they did play better, but afterwards relapsed into their old faults, and as a consequence were beaten. At the commencement of the second half the Preston forwards again attacked, and the cleverness of Roberts alone saved his side, Goodhall sending in a shot which was exceedingly swift, and nine goal-keepers out of ten would have missed it. A moment later Dewhurst had the Albion goal at his mercy, but in his excitement he kicked the ball wide. Attack followed attack in quick succession, and at length the score was equalised by Dewhurst. The Albion appealed against the goal, but after the officials had consulted together they decided that it was a legitimate point. The Albion had one dangerous rush on the right, Woodhall shooting, and Mills-Roberts having to turn the ball outside. But the corner was of no use, and the grand combination of the North End forwards again asserted itself. They were now playing better than at any time during the match, and hard pressed were the Albion backs. But Aldridge played a dashing game, whilst Green's cool and clear judgment was often the saving of his side.

Time after time did the Northern men seem certain to score, but time after time were the hopes of their supporters dashed to the ground. Now and again the Albion made a brief rush into the North End's territory, but Ross, sen., excelled himself as a back. Some fine play by Bassett and Woodhall gave the former a difficult chance, but before he could reach the ball Howarth was there, and, of course, made use of his weight. This was a feature of the North End's play which would have been better absent. After two unsuccessful tries to score, Woodhall and Bennett, playing together beautifully, carried the ball into the corner, and Woodhall centred. Bayliss tried to head the latter through, but it went just too high. Roberts had again to save his goal from a shot by Drummond, and just afterwards the North End had hard luck in not scoring, a splendid shot made by Goodhall striking the upright and rebounding out of goal. Had the ball been directed a few inches further to the one side the North End would have been in front. The Albion forwards, who seemed fresher than their opponents, with the exception of Wilson, who played very indifferently throughout, were now seen to greater advantage than in any part of the game. They continually dribbled past the North End half-backs, who appeared fatigued, and only the grand defence of Ross senior prevented them scoring. He had much trouble with Bassett, who played as well as any forward on the field, working with unflagging spirit from start to finish. Ross, seeing that his forwards could not score, ran the ball into the Albion goal and passed to Dewhurst, who made an accurate shot, but Roberts punched out the ball. A rush by the Albion's forwards all but scored, Woodhall fouling the ball just at the critical moment. The free kick was taken, and again the West Bromwich goal was jeopardised, but the backs prevented its downfall. A sudden rush, a centre, and a sharp, quick shot by Woodhall, were made, and tremendous cheering announced that the North End's goal had fallen. This success, occurring as it did within ten minutes of time, thoroughly disorganised the North End, and the Albion forwards singly carried the ball to their opponents' goal, which would have fallen again but for Ross sen., the only man who kept his head clear at this juncture. He exhorted his men to keep cool, for ten minutes yet remained to play, and cheered by his words the North End forwards did their best to equalise.

The West Bromwich team of 1888

Date 24 March 1888
Place The Kennington Oval
Score WEST BROMWICH ALBION 2
PRESTON NORTH END 1
Teams WEST BROMWICH ALBION
Roberts, Aldridge, Green, Horton, Perry, Timmins, Woodhall, Bassett, Bayliss, Wilson, Pearson. PRESTON NORTH END Dr R. M. Mills-Roberts, Howarth, Holmes, N. J. Ross, Russell, Gordon, J. Ross, Goodall, Dewhurst, Drummond, Graham
Officials Referee Major Marindin. Linesmen M. P. Betts, J. C. Clegg
Goal Scorers WEST BROMWICH ALBION Bayliss 8, Woodhall 77; PRESTON NORTH END Dewhurst 52
Attendance 19000
Copy *The Birmingham Daily Post* 26 March 1888

1889

THE SPORTSMAN, MONDAY, APRIL 1, 1889.

TO-DAY'S MATCHES.

SUSSEX v. PRESTON NORTH END.

THE following are the probable players in this match, in Preston Park, Brighton, to-day (April 1):

Sussex: C. J. Richards (Lancing College) (goal), C. H. Holland (Sussex Martlets) and E. Jackson (Sussex Martlets) (backs), H. E. D. Hammond (Sussex Martlets), F. M. Ingram (Sussex Martlets), and T. W. Cook (Oxford University) (half-backs), G. Brann (Sussex Martlets) and C. H. R. Gresson (Worthing) (right wing), G. H. Cotterill (Cambridge University) (centre), and C. F. Ingram (Sussex Martlets) and G. L. Wilson (Sussex Martlets) (left wing) (forwards).

Preston North End: R. H. Mills-Roberts (goal), R. Haworth and R. Holmes (backs), G. Drummond, D. Russell, and J. Graham (half-backs), J. Gordon and J. Ross (right wing), J. Goodall (centre), and F. Dewhurst and S. Thomson (left wing) (forwards).

A smoking concert will be held in the evening at the Imperial Hotel, Queen's-road.

†STAFFORDSHIRE ASSOCIATION JUNIOR CUP.

THE final tie in this competition is to be re-played at Port Vale to-day at 4.30 p.m., the clubs left in being Hanley Town and Smallthorne. Umpires: Messrs Johnson and Bettoney. Referee: Mr H. Mitchell, jun.

†Bootle, Bootle v. Accrington

†Sheffield, Sheffield Wednesday v. Blackburn Rovers

†FOOTBALL ASSOCIATION CHALLENGE CUP.

FINAL TIE.

PRESTON NORTH END v. WOLVERHAMPTON WANDERERS.

VICTORY OF THE LEAGUE CHAMPIONS.

AT last the greatest wishes of the celebrated North End team which takes its name from the town on the banks of the Ribble have been gratified, and Mr Sudell and those associated with him are able to look with feelings of pride upon the achievements of the club in the season of 1888-9. Not only has the League Championship fallen to them without a defeat to mar the string of twenty-two games in which they have taken part, but they have succeeded in obtaining possession of what has been the idol of their heart, viz., the "paltry pot" annually offered for competition by the Football Association. This has now been competed for for eighteen years, in the course of which the trophy has been held by the Wanderers and Blackburn Rovers for three years in succession, the former club on obtaining the Cup outright restoring it to the body on the condition that it should become a perpetual object of rivalry. The great change that has come over the Association game has caused the provincial clubs to monopolise the leading places, and for the last six years the final has been fought by Midland or Lancashire clubs. Nevertheless the venue has never been changed from the Oval, and if Saturday's crowd, and the general excellence of the arrangements, be borne in mind, we would add, "with very good sense, too." The career of the Prestonians, as far as the Cup is concerned, has not been altogether of an encouraging nature. At the very outset they were disqualified for professionalism (then not recognised) on the protest of Upton Park, and during the last two seasons they had found the Westbromwich Albion a stumbling-block, being defeated by the Throstles in 1886-7 at Nottingham in the semi-final by three goals to one, and last year in the final by two goals to one. The new basis on which the competition was this season carried out has worked well, and in the course of the second stage the North End have beaten in turn Bootle, Grimsby Town, Birmingham St. George's, and Westbromwich Albion, the last named in the semi-final at Bramall-lane, Sheffield, a fortnight back by a rather lucky goal to none. They had expected to have had to meet in the final that famous combination, the Blackburn Rovers, but the exholders fell victims on the 23rd ult. (after a drawn game) to the Wolverhampton Wanderers—a club which, if report is true, has not been too kindly supported in its locality, but which is a sterling body of players, with a defence second to none. Those, however, who witnessed the games at Crewe were of opinion that they would fail to prove a thorn in the side of the League Champions, their forward combination and goal-keeping being regarded as the weak points. That such was the case was amply borne out by Saturday's match. Betting was naturally in favour of the Lancastrians, 5 to 4 and 6 to 4 being laid on their chance, though in the Midlands persons could be found ready to snap up even money.

Owing to the decision of the Boat Race it was very wisely resolved not to make a start until four o'clock, which would enable visitors from the country to witness both events. The Prestonians arrived in London on Friday, making the Covent Garden Hotel their headquarters, but the "Wolves" delayed their departure till Saturday, reaching town shortly after noon. The difficulty of dealing with an enormous crowd was met by an excellent alteration of the arrangements, the game being played much nearer the cricket pavilion than usual, and the large ring preserved as at the big cricket matches. Two or three rows of seats were placed round the inclosure, which had the effect of keeping back those behind, though, be it said, that the utmost order prevailed. The gates were opened at an early hour, and long before three o'clock there was a dense fringe round the field of play. As the time drew near for the start the stream continued to pour through the turnstiles, while the chaos of cabs and vehicles outside baffles description. Soldiers in uniform, as usual, formed a goodly proportion of the crowd, but there were strong contingents from the Midlands and Lancashire, special trains having been run from those parts. Punctually to time the teams turned out, the Prestonians in white jerseys, quickly followed by their rivals in striped garments, of which pink was the predominant colour. They were both very warmly received by the company, which by this time had occupied every coign of vantage, including the roof of the cricket pavilion and neighbouring housetops, while even the gasometer was not free from the invasion of a few daring spirits. As usual in such cases, opinions differed greatly as to the attendance, but, having formed one of both crowds, we venture to assert that Saturday's "gate" exceeded that registered at Bramall-lane, and was consequently nearer thirty than twenty-five thousand. It is needless to add that both teams were accompanied by the "great guns" of their clubs, the Prestonians being well looked after by Mr Sudell and "Sir" John Woods.

THE GAME.

Dewhurst and Brodie tossed for choice of positions, which fell to the former, and he naturally took the Vauxhall goal, with the wind in his rear. The conditions were eminently favourable for the encounter, as there was not sufficient breeze to materially affect the play, while the sky was overcast without rain. No complaint, too, could be lodged on the state of the turf. "The Major" gave the signal, and a minute after four Brodie kicked off for the Wanderers, who wore black armlets as a token of respect for their captain, who has recently lost his father. The Prestonians at once worked the ball down, Russell and Dewhurst being conspicuous, and play settled in the Wanderers' quarters. A claim for a "foul" was given by Mr Clegg, but not allowed by the referee, and, play continuing, Preston sent over their opponents' goal-line. Restarting, the "Wolves" worked through, and playing strongly together, crossed into their rivals' territory, where Brodie was "fed" by the left wing, and put in a hot shot, which passed over the bar. North End directly after had a free kick in the centre, from which Thomson ran up and shot. Baynton fell on the ball, and just turned it outside the posts. Give-and-take play now followed for several minutes, Mason playing a good game at back, which enabled the "Wolves" to have rather the best of the exchanges. Knight from the left wing put in a rare shot, which struck the post and then rebounded—a piece of hard luck for the Midlanders. They kept up the pressure for awhile, till Gordon worked the ball down the right wing and, dodging Mason, passed to Ross. That player sent in a rare shot, the ball striking the cross-bar and rebounding, when Dewhurst, rushing in two or three yards, shot a splendid goal amid much excitement about fifteen minutes from the start. Upon resuming the Wanderers were compelled for the most part to act on the defensive, and their half-backs had plenty of work to do. Twenty-five minutes had elapsed when a further disaster befel the Wanderers, though that club has chiefly its goalkeeper to thank. Goodall and Ross made a sharp attack, and the latter put in a shot which Baynton badly muffed, and allowing the ball to slip between his legs Prestonians obtained their second goal. The Wolves continued to act on the defensive, though the pace did not slacken one whit. The Prestonians literally penned their rivals for awhile, making it very hot for them, though Dewhurst missed one good opening for adding a third point. Then the Wanderers retaliated until a foul gave Howarth an opportunity for clearing. Gordon came away in grand style, but left shooting till he was too near the goal line, and sent wide. A free kick for hands next fell to Preston in front of their opponents' goal; Drummond had the kick, and sent well in, the ball being shot out of the scrimmage into Baynton's hands, he only just succeeding in throwing out in time. Give-and-take play followed, Hunter and Knight making shots from the Midlanders' wing—the former's a fine piece of play. Mills Roberts, however, was equal to the occasion, and some brilliant passing by the North End forwards took the ball to the opposite end, where they secured a corner-kick. Nothing, however, came of it, and after some further play, chiefly in the "Wolves'" territory half-time arrived, with the score—

PRESTON NORTH END .... 2 goals.
WOLVERHAMPTON WANDERERS ... None.

So far the Prestonians had much the best of the game, their forwards showing superior combination, while their defence was excellent. Their opponents had done very well at times, but evidently suffered from the ground being strange to them. Their system of individual rushes and long kicks at times compared unfavourably with the short passes and combined attacks of the Prestonians, who were often enabled to get the ball before their opponents could reach it. Having now the advantage of the wind at their rear they played up better, and caused the Lancastrians great uneasiness. Goodall re-started at six minutes to five, the Midlanders at once returning and attacking in force. Getting to close quarters Mills-Roberts had a hard time of it, but defended grandly, being well supported by the back division, among whom Howarth and Russell were conspicuous, and at length the ball was returned to the centre. The latter player a little later headed away another dangerous shot, but the Wanderers were not to be denied, and Hunter sent over the bar. Continuing to press they secured a corner, and after an exciting period in front of goal a second was credited to them, and essayed by Fletcher. From the *melee* that ensued a foul fell to the "Wolves" which Fletcher placed splendidly, but the ball was sent just wide. Resuming, the state of affairs became less anxious for the favourites, though Knight put in a splendid shot from the left, which very nearly took effect. A run up field by North End was checked, and a dribble by Hunter again carried the fight into the Preston territory, where Fletcher had a further corner-kick, but Knight shot too high. Ross and Gordon here broke away, and the former sent in, but Baugh saved, while Baynton kicked away a long side shot by Gordon. That player, however, kept the ball in the Wolverhampton quarters, and centreing fine, Dewhurst, who was well up, shot in. Baynton relieved, but Thomson, who was in close company, ran in and sent through amid applause mid-way through the second half. An appeal for off-side was disallowed, and the game continued from the centre. Ross put in another shot, which Baynton repulsed, though not too cleverly, and directly afterwards Thomson put through, but as the off-side rule had palpably been infringed, he was practically unmolested, and the ball was whistled back. Dewhurst wound up a spirited attack by a bad shot, and then Howarth cleared in brilliant fashion from a kick for hands right in front of the North End goal. The rest of the play contained no very prominent features, being carried on for the most part in the Midlanders' territory, and when hostilities ceased the Prestonians had won with the score:

PRESTON NORTH END .... 3 goals.
WOLVERHAMPTON WANDERERS ... none

A very curious feature was provided by the crowd in the last three or four minutes gradually breaking into the inclosure and proceeding to line as in cricket the entrance to the pavilion, or to form up in almost military fashion round the field of play. As soon as the whistle sounded the ground became a surging mass of humanity, and it was with the greatest difficulty that the players, whose names were as under, and who were one and all received most cordially, retired to the dressing-rooms:

Preston North End: Dr. R. H. Mills-Roberts (goal), R. H. Haworth and R. Holmes (backs), G. Drummond, D. Russell, and J. Graham (half-backs), J. Gordon and J. Ross (right wing), J. Goodall (centre), F. Dewhurst (captain) and S. Thomson (left wing) (forwards).

Wolverhampton Wanderers: G. Baynton (goal), R. Baugh and C. Mason (backs), D. Fletcher, H. Allen, and A. Lowder (half-backs), T. Hunter and A. Wykes (right wing), J. Brodie (captain) (centre), and H. Wood and T. Knight (left wing) (forwards).

Umpires: Lord Kinnaird (Old Etonians) and Mr J. C. Clegg (Sheffield). Referee: Major Marindin, R.E., C.M.G. (president Football Association).

PRESENTATION OF THE TROPHY.

THE crowd quickly dispersed after the conclusion of play, nevertheless a goodly number remained to witness the interesting ceremony of transferring the Cup to the Preston North End representatives. This duty was undertaken by Major Marindin, the president of the Football Association, who, in the course of a few remarks, stated that he was glad to know that the Cup, although an exceedingly small one, was considered such a great honour to win. The Preston North End team, who had secured it for the first time, had an extraordinary record. They were Champions of the League combination, having won the whole of their contests, whilst in the Association competition they had not had a single point recorded against them. For some years they had been very near winning the trophy, and he now congratulated them on having attained their purpose. Their opponents were a much younger club, but had played a good game, and deserved better luck in the future. On behalf of the Association he handed over the Cup to Mr F. Dewhirst, the captain of the team. The president then presented gold medals to the individual members of the eleven amidst much enthusiasm.

WINNERS OF THE CUP.

1871- 2. Wanderers beat Royal Engineers, one goal to none.
1872- 3. Wanderers beat Oxford University, two goals to none.
1873- 4. Oxford University beat Royal Engineers, two goals to none.
1874- 5. Royal Engineers beat Old Etonians, two goals to none, after a drawn game.
1875- 6. Wanderers beat Old Etonians, three goals to none, after a draw.
1876- 7. Wanderers beat Oxford University, two goals to none, after an extra half-hour.
1877- 8.*Wanderers beat Royal Engineers, three goals to one.
1878- 9. Old Etonians beat Clapham Rovers, one goal to none.
1879-80. Clapham Rovers beat Oxford University, one goal to none.
1880- 1. Old Carthusians beat Old Etonians, three goals to none.
1881- 2. Old Etonians beat Blackburn Rovers, one goal to none.
1882- 3. Blackburn Olympic beat Old Etonians, two goals to one, after an extra half-hour.
1883- 4. Blackburn Rovers beat Queen's Park, Glasgow, two goals to one.
1884- 5. Blackburn Rovers beat Queen's Park, Glasgow, two goals to none.
1885- 6.†Blackburn Rovers beat Westbromwich Albion, two goals to none, after a drawn game.
1886- 7. Aston Villa beat Westbromwich Albion, two goals to none.
1887- 8. Westbromwich Albion beat Preston North End, two goals to one.
1888- 9. Preston North End beat Wolverhampton Wanderers, three goals to none.

* Won outright, but restored to the Association.
† A special trophy was awarded for the third consecutive win.

RECEPTION OF THE NEWS IN PRESTON.

BEFORE four o'clock a large concourse assembled in the principal street opposite the newspaper offices, eagerly awaiting any bit of information which might be posted. All seemed confident as to North End's victory, but when it was announced that two goals had been scored in the first twenty-five minutes the excitement materially increased. Several thousands had congregated when the half-time statement came with the score unaltered, and long odds were now offered on the issue. The third goal was made known in due time, and then the final result was patiently and comfortably awaited. At five minutes to six, one big cheer proclaimed the victory by three goals to none—a feat never surpassed in the final tie, and the vast multitude quietly dispersed.

†WEST HAM HOSPITAL CHARITY CUP.

FINAL TIE (REPLAYED).

ILFORD (HOLDERS) v. CLAPTON.—This final tie was replayed at the Spotted Dog Grounds, Upton, on Saturday in the presence of an enthusiastic company, numbering about two thousand people. The general anticipation of a close match was realised, and it was not until another extra half-hour's play that a definite result was gained. Although neither side played quite up to its best form, the game all through was stubbornly contested, and the play was fast. Clapton generally held the upper hand when playing with the wind, while Ilford did the pressing when they had its aid. After about thirty minutes' play Perkins scored for Ilford from a pass by A. Porter, and Connell equalised with a fine screw shot shortly afterwards. No point was scored in the second half, but just at the close of the first stage of the extra half-hour Connell again sent the ball home but the point was disallowed on the ground that the whistle sounded for ha'f-time before the ball passed through. This decision gave rise to dissatisfaction. After crossing over Watts scored the winning point for Ilford. The backs and half-backs played well on both sides, H. Porter and Read deserving special notice. Connell, Latreille, Perkins, and A. Porter showed well among the forwards. Hailey and Baker did good service in goal for their respective sides. The winning team met with an enthusiastic reception upon their return to Ilford. The Cup and medals will be presented at a concert at Stratford. Sides:

Ilford: H. Hailey (goal), W. King and F. King (backs), H. Porter (captain), F. Brand, and E. Markland (half-backs), W. J. Somerville and H. Watts (right wing), A. Porter (centre), N. Perkins and J. P. H. Soper (left wing) (forwards).

Clapton : W. Baker (goal), A. E. Casselton and E. J. Watts (backs), P. A. Read, A. B. Mayes, and G. W. Turk (half-backs), W. G. Connell and J. Ude (right wing), G. Pottinger (centre), W. Latreille and E. Wilkins (left wing) (forwards). Referee : Mr Laver.

SAXON R.C.—Special general meeting this evening for the election of committee. Entries also close for the Double-sculling Handicap. Roll-call ten o'clock sharp. The speedy steam launch Aerolite, coach to the Oxford crew, for sale or to let by the season.—Particulars, Woodhouse, New Thames Hotel, Maidenhead.—ADVT.

*SUFFOLK v. ESSEX.

THESE counties met on the Portman-road ground, Ipswich, on Saturday, when the Essex team, a very strong one, won by two goals and two tries to nil. In the first portion of the match the Suffolk forwards forced the game, and Essex had twice to touch down. The home team, however, were quickly forced back, and after some passing between the Essex three-quarters, Bate, the old Leeds St. John man, ran in. Johnstone took the place and failed, and he also could not improve upon a second try gained directly afterwards by himself. Half-time followed, and for the next ten minutes play was confined to the forwards. At length Garrett dribbled through and gained a try, which Johnstone converted. From this point to the end Essex had all the best of the game, and from a clever try by himself Johnstone placed another goal. For the winners Bate was in splendid form as centre three-quarter, and forward the Garretts were always on the ball. Reynolds was the pick of the Suffolk rear division, and all the forwards played a fine game, though they were greatly weakened by an accident which occasioned M'Donell's retirement just after half time.

*CHISWICK F.C.—Special meeting to-night at the George, at eight.

†MARLBOROUGH ROVERS F.C.—A smoking concert will be held at the Champion Hotel, Aldersgate-street, E.C., to-night, at half-past seven.

Date 30 March 1889
Place The Kennington Oval
Score PRESTON NORTH END 3
WOLVERHAMPTON WANDERERS 0
Teams PRESTON NORTH END Dr R. H.
Mills-Roberts, Howarth, Holmes,
Drummond, Russell, Graham,
Gordon, Ross, Goodall,
Dewhurst (capt.), Thomson.
WOLVERHAMPTON WANDERERS Baynton,
Baugh, Mason, Fletcher, Allen,
Lowder, Hunter, Wykes,
Brodie (capt.), Wood, Knight
Team Colours PRESTON NORTH
END White shirts;
WOLVERHAMPTON WANDERERS Pink
striped shirts
Officials Referee Major Marindin.
Linesmen Lord Kinnaird, J. C. Clegg
Goal Scorers Dewhurst 15, Ross 25,
Thomson 70
Attendance 22 000
Guest of Honour Major Marindin
made the presentation
Copy The Sportsman 1 April 1889

● Preston North End completed the first League and Cup double in 1889, in a style to delight statisticians. The League was won without a defeat in their 22 matches, and Preston lifted the Cup without conceding a goal. No nickname has been better earned than the "Invincibles".

Preston had already clinched the League championship when their presence in the final, against Wolverhampton Wanderers, ensured a record 22,000 crowd crammed into the Oval. Their victims along the way had been Bootle (3–0), Grimsby Town (2–0), Birmingham St. George (2–0) and West Bromwich Albion (1–0) in the semifinal – revenge for their defeat in the 1888 final when Preston had been so confident that they had wanted to be photographed with the Cup before the match!

This time the lesson had been learned. Preston, whose forward line of Gordon, Ross, John Goodall, Dewhurst and Thompson was unequalled, led two-nil at half-time and produced a thoroughly superior performance. *The Sportsman* report (left) confirms the importance of the win to North End: "...but they have succeeded in obtaining possession of what has been the idol of their heart, viz, 'the paltry pot', annually offered for competition by the Football Association."

The kick-off was delayed until four o'clock so that visitors to London could see the Boat Race earlier in the afternoon and then have time to reach the Oval. The massive crowd had only to wait fifteen minutes from the start before Dewhurst, the captain and a Corinthian, opened the scoring after the ball had dropped to his feet from the crossbar. Earlier Wolves had less luck when Knight's attempt hit a post.

Preston added to their lead 20 minutes before half-time with a goal from Ross with Baynton badly at fault as the shot slipped through his legs, and with the error went Wolves hopes. They had the advantage of the wind in the second half, but Preston settled the match when Baynton did well to push out a shot from Dewhurst, only for Thomson to tap in the third goal from the rebound.

The subsequent ceremony had an unusual touch when Major Marindin, who had refereed the final, also presented the Cup to the winners in his capacity as President of the Football Association. Clearly the presentation did not carry the stature of the present day... "The crowd quickly dispersed after the conclusion, nevertheless a goodly number remained to witness the interesting ceremony of transferring the Cup to Preston North End representatives." Those who did stay saw the formal completion of that remarkable double.

Preston North End, 1888–89, the first team to perform the "double". Note the dog under the bench

TH' ROVERS.

Ther's nowt else talked abeawt this week nobbut th' final tie for th' English Cup; iv yo' ax Breawn heaw his wife an' th' twins is gooin' on he says: "O' reight. Heaw's ta think they'll go on?" Yo' ax Jones for thad five bob he owes yo' an' he promises to pay id o' Satterda', becos he's put id on th' Rovers; then there's Smith as lost his mother-i'-law t' other day—he doesn'd seem a bit deawn abeawt id—at leeast id isn'd o' so mich impoortance as th' result to-morn. Aw think mysel' as iv th' Rovers should appen *nod* to win its we shall nod hev th' Technical Schoo' sterted on this year, or enough brass alleawed for Foxcroft to mek th' Corporation Perk look nice. But mi private opinion is as th' Blues 'll give th' Blades a Oval lickin', an' thad 'll mek 'em cut up rough, iv id doesn'd give 'em "th' heeadwerch;" *my* tip is a win bi two clear goals, an' iv this comes off aw dorn'd mind gooin' to meet 'em at th' station o' Monda' neet when they come hoosm wi' th' pot. Id'll look like owd times ageean.—From Tum o' Dick o' Bob's Letter in the *Blackburn Standard*.

UNDER ASSOCIATION RULES.

FOOTBALL ASSOCIATION CUP.

FINAL TIE.

BLACKBURN ROVERS v. SHEFFIELD WEDNESDAY.

THE ROVERS WIN EASILY.

SHEFFIELD WON THE TOSS.

The Powder Blues elected to play from the goal nearest the Crown Baths, so the Rovers defended that adjacent to the Gasometer. At half-past three o'clock John Southworth set the ball in motion with a smart kick. It was smartly returned, and then Townley sped it along near the touch-line in hot haste. Up to the rescue came Waller, and with a smart kick he relieved his lines. Amidst shouts of "Play up, Wednesday!" the Powder Blues made a gallant attack on the Rovers' territory, Bennett, in the centre, exhibiting a rare turn of speed. The latter passed the ball to Crawley, who kicked behind. Shortly after restarting a free kick accrued to the Rovers on a plea of hands. Dewar then sent the ball to the left, and Townley and Walton putting in their full strength, carried the ball right in front of the Rovers' outposts. Then up stepped Brayshaw, and with a grand tall kick sent the ball spinning into the Rovers' half. Both had now warmed to their work, and there was very little in it. Now came some fierce Wednesday onslaughts, and more than one on each side turned a Catherine wheel in true Poor Joe gutter fashion. Then the tide chopped round, and Sheffield returned the attack compliment with interest. Ultimately Dungworth handled the ball, and a free kick fell to the lot of the Rovers. Forrest passed to Townley, and the latter sending the ball against one of the Sheffielders it went between their uprights.

SIX MINUTES AND FATE.

A SOFT GOAL FOR BLACKBURN.

It was indeed a bit of hard luck for Sheffield. On restarting a combined run by Mumford and Crawley ensued. Barton opposed, and with a good kick passed the ball on to Lofthouse. Trouble was then experienced by the Sheffield goal-keeper, and it took him all his time to keep his colours flying; for Lofthouse ran clean away with the ball, and evading Waller by a piece of fine play crossed to Campbell. At this point the Rovers were playing a considerably better combined game than their opponents. Now Morley, whose defence was as true as steel, moved up, and stopping Campbell's little game, with a result that the ball went off the cross-bar. So soon as it had been restarted Betts sent the ball to the right. Then Ingram and Woolhouse gave us glimpses of passing which were a treat to gaze upon, and they ultimately succeeded in working the ball down to the Rovers' goal. Once again Forrest's timely kick stood Blackburn in good stead. With the assistance of the other F—Forbes—danger was averted. Subsequently a corner fell to the Rovers. It was deftly placed, and then Brayshaw, who was at his best cleared the lines. The Blades strove with desperation to score, and once headed by Crawley swept along like an irresistible avalanche. The leader essayed a shot at goal, but the well intended coup proved futile. Now for a smart run by the Rovers. It resulted in Townley infringing the off-side rule. Attack upon attack was then made by Sheffield. There was no combination, however, and the shooting became a wee bit erratic. Blackburn now played a sound defensive game, and two brilliant charges by the Sheffield were cleverly repulsed by Southworth and Forbes. At length the Rovers changed the scene of action, and their forwards got the ball well in hand. After a brilliant dash on the part of Townley and Walton, a smart low kick from the foot of the last-named placed goal No. 2 to the credit of Blackburn.

BLACKBURN A HARD NUT.

These two successive reverses in no way damped the ardour of Sheffield. So soon as the ball was set rolling they went after it like giants refreshed with wine. Still they could not get in clover. Ultimately Campbell pulled them up short, and took the ball away, but failed to pass Morley, who returned to mid-field twice in succession. A free kick subsequently fell to the Rovers for hands. Next Mumford got on the ball, but Forbes beat him at the finish, but it was at the expense of a corner. This proved of but little consequence, however, as Dewar comfortably headed the ball clear, and John Southworth, obtaining possession of it, rattled it along into Sheffield land. However, two dangerous backs were in support, and the enemy was driven back. Another plucky attack by the wearers of "the powder blue jackets" was again repulsed. Finally Barton returned the ball with a regular skier, and Campbell chevied it along with nimble toes, then cleverly passed to Lofthouse, who in turn middled to Southworth. Now the admirers of the Rovers were radiant in their happiness. But the last-named player shot wide. What a relief to the partisans of "Wednesday!" But it was of momentary duration. Again the Rovers returned to the charge. Once more Sheffield stood on guard. It was a case of fight on brave hearts? After a hot melee in front of their citadel from a long pass on the part of Townley from Southworth, the Rovers won their third goal by the aid of a veritable daisy cutter.

It now looked long odds on the Rovers running their opponents out pointless. Still, how gallantly Sheffield tried to run in a goal! All honour to the Blades, for they strove hard to turn the tide in their favour. Still, it was now evident to the veriest tyro that the team was a trifle shattered. They did not possess the polish of their opponents, but both possessed the same old pluck. The cry of "Play up both" stimulated the rival teams to renewed exertions. On resuming the game, Woolhouse and Ingram got clean away, but overran the ball, but again Forbes certified to be the stumbling block. Then, at top speed, off dashed Townley with the coveted sphere—fairly skimmed over the turf as a matter of fact. True to the last stood Morley. Twice in succession sent he back the ball. A weak bit of play, and then "Hands against Sheffield." Not to be denied, the Rovers broke through, and then, just in the nick of time, after an adroit pass by John Southworth, Townley fixed the fourth goal for the Rovers.

ROVERS THE BOSS KICKERS.

Shortly after this "half-time" was whistled, the score then standing as above. During the few minutes interval the players refreshed, and it was pleasing to note the kindly spirit that existed between the contending parties.

AFTER CHANGE,

Now the light mended, though the sun shone but feebly. Still, such brief rays were better than nothing at all. Following a brief interval, Bennett restarted the ball, amidst rounds of applause. It was immediately returned by Dewar, and it was a case of hurry-cum-up with the Rovers. Right into the Sheffield lines they dashed, but thrice in succession Townley was whistled off-side. Then both Crawley and Bennett had a fair go for Blackburn; but the pressure was relieved by Walton and Dewar. The latter essayed a long shot at the Sheffield goal, and Smith was bombarded in a manner that must have been far from pleasant. Twice in quick succession he punched out some red-hot bombshells. In excellent fashion Betts passed the ball to Ingram, who after a gallant sprint transferred it to Ingram. The latter centred sharply, and Mumford dashing up, headed the ball past Horne. Plaudits like thunder-peals rolling greeted the success of Sheffield Wednesday.

Stimulated to renewed energies by this success, Wednesday strove hard to turn the tide. But they lacked pace. Bennett effected a clipping run, which was cheered to the echo, but Dewar stopped him doing any damage. It was about this time that Smith, the Sheffield goal-keeper, evinced tip-top form. A light scrummage ensued bang in front of his citadel. Swift as a rocket Townley sent the ball into the mouth of it. Quick as lightning Smith punched it out, in fact had to put in a double punch. It was left to Lofthouse to get hold of the ball, and then from a ripping pass Townley, who was always on the *qui vive*, popped the ball past Smith, and chalked up the fifth goal for Blackburn.

From the centre kick Betts tried a run, but Forrest prevented him travelling very far. Then the Rovers worked the ball into the Sheffield lines, but both Morley and Brayshaw offered a game and stubborn resistance. Twice in succession the Sheffielders gained corners, and then Blackburn swarmed on their opponents' goal. Then Sheffield returned the compliment with compound interest. But the Rovers proved too good for their courageous opponents. Grandly Brayshaw relieved his lines from the attacks of Walton, and three times Smith handled the ball out. From this point the Rovers had it all their own way, and they ultimately placed a sixth goal to their credit, through the instrumentality of Lofthouse, after a well-judged place on the part of Forrest.

THE MAJOR STOPS PLAY.

It was now close upon the call of "Time!" So eager were the spectators to take a minute inspection of the heroes of the hour that a regular stampede took place, and the public swarmed like bees towards the Pavilion—the same old irresistible Surrey rush. Ultimately Major Marindin stopped the play for about four minutes, but it is only fair to state that no one attempted to get inside of the touch-line. Ultimately play was renewed, and a corner accruing to the Rovers it looked very much as if a seventh goal would fall to their lot. However, Morley was equal to the occasion, and when the whistle finally sounded the score stood—

Blackburn Rovers	6 goals
Sheffield Wednesday	1 goal.

REMARKS.

In regard to the game no one can deny but that the best team won. From the outset till the whistle sounded Sheffield Wednesday were outplayed. However, every one must admire their pluck, for they stayed like tops to the bitter end. Smith proved by no means a brilliant custodian. Some of his saves were very primitive. Both Brayshaw and Morley played splendidly from first to last, and never flagged. Bennett and Mumford did yeoman service, and Betts and Cawley now and again did first-class business. Of the winners Forbes and J. Southworth at back each shone by turns, and Townley carried nearly everything before him. A trifle less off-side tactics would be better, though no fault could be found with J. Horne at goal. Still, he had but little work to do. The combination all round left nothing to be desired, and Lancashire has good cause to be proud of her sons.

Date 29 March 1890
Place The Kennington Oval
Score BLACKBURN ROVERS 6
SHEFFIELD WEDNESDAY 1
Teams BLACKBURN ROVERS Horne, Forbes, Jas Southworth, Barton, Dewar, Forrest, Lofthouse, Campbell, John Southworth, Walton, Townley.
SHEFFIELD WEDNESDAY Smith, Morley, Brayshaw, Dungworth, Betts, Waller, Ingram, Woodhouse, Bennett, Mumford, Cawley
Officials Referee Major Marindin. Linesmen R. P. Smith, M. P. Betts
Goal Scorers BLACKBURN ROVERS Townley 3, Walton, John Southworth, Lofthouse.
SHEFFIELD WEDNESDAY Bennett
Attendance 20 000
Copy *The Blackburn Evening Express and Standard* 29 March 1890

Blackburn Rovers' victorious team of 1890

THE LAST STRUGGLE FOR THE ENGLISH CUP.

(BY WANDERER.)

The interest in the final tie between the Blackburn Rovers and Notts County is naturally very keen, and everything points to an immense "gate" assembling at the Oval to witness the "grate fight." The match between the two teams last Saturday ended, as is well known, in a very decisive victory for the County men; but the game to-morrow will be of a very much different character. The Rovers were very much out of condition, but they have been carefully training at home during the week, and have every appearance of being in good trim, with the exception of John Southworth. It is very hard lines for the Rovers centre that he was hurt in the International match at Sunderland. He has been under the doctor with his leg, and tried it for the first time on Thursday afternoon. Unfortunately he still feels the injury, and his confidence in his ability to play his usual game is very slight. Of course he may probably be fit to play by to-morrow, but the committee would take a wise course by playing Fecitt, unless Southworth feels thoroughly well. Then there is some uncertainty as regards the custodian. It is generally believed that Pennington will do duty for the "blue and whites" between the sticks, in consequence of Gow's exhibition last week end. Of course the committee know their reasons for the contemplated change better than anyone else, but it is difficult to see the improvement to be gained by playing the St. Helen's man. I do not wish to say one word in disparagement of Pennington's ability to keep goal. He has played

SEVERAL GOOD GAMES

with the Rovers, and he kept goal exceedingly well at Stoke. He has, however, not had the same amount of experience that Gow has had, and it is in this respect that the latter would be of great service to the Rovers in the match. It seems to be the general opinion, and it is one with which I thoroughly coincide, that the substitution of Walton for Hall is a very good change. Walton has got back to his old form, and can combine far better with Townley than Hall. The latter is a good player, but under the circumstances it is well that Walton should be played. It is therefore impossible to give with certainty the team which will represent the Rovers, but it may be put down as follows:—Pennington (or Gow), goal; Brandon and Forbes, backs; Barton, Dewar and Forrest, half-backs; Lofthouse and Campbell, right; Southworth (or Fecitt), centre; Walton and Townley, left forwards. With regard to Notts the team which represented them at Ewood last Saturday will probably do duty at Kennington Oval, for the latest accounts of McLean are hardly favourable, and it is almost certain that Ferguson will play in his place. They have been in training at Ashover, in Derbyshire. The Notts eleven may be put down as :— Thraves, goal; Ferguson (or McLean) and Hendry, backs; Osborne, Calderhead, and Shelton, half-backs; M'Gregor and M'Innes (right); Oswald (centre); Locker and Daft (left), forwards. The officials will be Mr. J. C. Clegg (Sheffield), referee; and Messrs. W. H. Jope and C. H. Hughes, umpires. The kick-off has been fixed for three o'clock.

THE ROVERS LEFT BLACKBURN

by the 11 20 London and North-Western trip. A large crowd had assembled at the station, and as the train steamed out they were heartily cheered. Southworth had his leg examined yesterday by a medical man, who pronounced the opinion that the crack centre-forward was in a fit condition to play. The leg, he said, might be painful for a time, but it was quite strong. Pennington will play in goal. The team will therefore be: Pennington, goal; Forbes and Brandon, backs; Forrest, Dewar, and Barton, half-backs; Townley and Walton, left wing; Southworth, centre; Campbell and Lofthouse, right wing. It will thus be seen that there are only two alterations from the team which did duty in the final last year:—Pennington in goal and Brandon at back. The men appear to be all in the pink of condition. If only Southworth's leg keeps firm the result may be safely predicted. Fecitt, Hall, and Gow were taken as reserve men.

A FOOTBALL WRITER

in a Nottingham contemporary says:—If the Rovers are to beat Notts on Saturday they will require Southworth, Barton, and all their men in the pink of condition. We are quite aware that the Rovers know the Oval well, and maybe they think no more of playing in the final than in the first round. It must not be imagined that Notts are composed of men who will tremble before the crowd at the Oval. Most of them have had experience of great games, and we have every ground for saying that Notts will not lack supporters beyond those who will travel by the numerous excursions which the Great Northern and Midland Companies will run. People in London, Stoke, Liverpool, and other centres are, if their newspapers are to be trusted, going to shout for Notts. In every nook and corner of the country sympathy is being extended to Notts. The *Cambridge Express* of last Saturday went so far as to say that "Notts deserve the position they have reached by reason of their perseverance and pluck, and they have the hearty good wishes of the Cambridge footballers." This seems to be the tone in many parts of the country, so that the right hand of sympathy is being extended to Notts. The team are training at Ashover, and if the bracing air of Derbyshire, the chilling baths of Ashover, and the greatest possible care and forethought by the directors can make a team fit to play for a kingdom Notts will be fit. The men themselves are thoroughly in earnest. During their preparation for the semi-final stage not one member of the team gave the slightest trouble or wished to act contrary to the ideas of their trainers, and the same good spirit animates them now.

● The Saturday before the final Notts County had beaten Blackburn Rovers 7–1 in a League match, at Blackburn! Although Rovers had fielded a weakened team Notts County were still favourites but the FA Cup again confounded the odds. Rovers only fitness doubt for the final was John Southworth, the centre-forward, injured playing for his country. But Southworth repaid the gamble on his condition by scoring one of the three Blackburn goals in the opening 31 minutes. Rovers fielded eight players from the previous year's successful side, and their experience of the big occasion proved too much for Notts County, who were unsettled by their nerves. Dewar gave Blackburn the lead after only eight minutes, and after Southworth's goal, Townley quickly added a third. In the second half County recovered some of their composure and reduced the deficit with a goal from Oswald. Rovers' victory was their fifth in the FA Cup, and they now equalled the number of victories by the Wanderers.

JAMES FORREST,

the left half-back, is the only member of the team who has taken part in all the three matches in which the Rovers have won the Cup. Though a veteran in experience he is young in years, his age being 27. He weighs 10st. 4lb., and is 5ft. 7in. in height, was born in Blackburn, and followed his occupation as a tape-sizer up to a few weeks ago, when he became the landlord of the Darwen and County Arms. Originally, he was a member of the King's Own Club, and then for two seasons he captained the Witton eleven, being drafted into the Rovers in January, 1883. His reputation grew so rapidly, that in the following season he secured his International cap, and played against Wales, and the same season also found him representing Lancashire. So greatly had Forrest proved his superiority in his own position as left half-back, that he played in all the three internationals in 1884-5. County engagements and North and South matches were incomplete without the presence of Forrest, and more than once he has captained the team representing the North. In all, Forrest has been selected to play in thirteen International matches, and has actually played in eleven. Four times he has played against Scotland, four times against Wales, and three times against Ireland. No other player in the North of England has been so often singled out for International honours. In his own position, Forrest, when in his best form, has no superiors, and few equals. His tackling is most determined, and the judgment with which he feeds his forwards is almost faultless.

Date 21 March 1891
Place The Kennington Oval
Score BLACKBURN ROVERS 3
NOTTS COUNTY 1
Teams BLACKBURN ROVERS
Pennington, Brandon, Forbes (capt.), Barton, Dewar, Forrest, Lofthouse, Walton, John Southworth, Hall, Townley. NOTTS COUNTY Thraves, Ferguson, Hendry, H. Osborne, Calderhead, Shelton, McGregor, McInnes, Oswald (capt.), Locker, H. B. Daft
Officials Referee C. J. Hughes (Cheshire). Linesmen W. H. Jope (Wednesbury), T. Gunning (London)
Goal Scorers BLACKBURN ROVERS Dewar 8, Southworth 30, Townley 35; NOTTS COUNTY Oswald 70
Attendance 23000
Gate Receipts £1454
Copy *The Lancashire Evening Express* 20 and 21 March 1891

JOHN SOUTHWORTH

for four seasons has been the Rovers' centre forward, and his brilliant runs have placed him in the foremost rank of players. Southworth is only 24 years of age, weighs 11st., is 5ft. 9in. in height, was born in Blackburn, and is a professional musician. His first efforts at club football were with the Brookhouse Rangers, and then he passed into the second team of the Blackburn Olympic. In a very short time his ability was recognised, and he was included in the first team of the Olympic, playing in goal when he was not included in the forward division. Then came a break in his football career so far as Blackburn is concerned, and removing to Chester, he was asked to join the principal team in that city. Returning to Blackburn at Christmas, 1886, he joined the Olympians again, and was in the team when the Rovers defeated them in the final for the Lancashire Cup in 1887. At the beginning of the following season his services were requisitioned by the Rovers, and since then he has always occupied the position of centre forward. Southworth is an International player, and has also played for Lancashire, and holds two gold and two silver medals. He captained the Rovers last season but one, and is now unsurpassed as a centre forward by any man in England. Providing his leg does not give way again he is almost certain to be chosen for England against Scotland at Blackburn on April 4th. He has played for England against Wales this season and has been chosen for the trial match next week.

1892

TURF

THE most recent and, it is to be hoped, the last edition of winter has seriously interfered with all kinds of sport, but with no form of it so much as with racing, which came to a deadlock last week. Postponed meetings were crowded in hopeless confusion on top of each other, and one after another had to be abandoned. The longed-for change in the weather has come at last, and there is now no reason to fear the necessity for the opening of the flat-racing season at Lincoln on Monday next being deferred. The Lincoln Handicap is at present occupying the attention of racing men, but so far no very prominent favourite has been established, and the difficulties of training have been so great that the race may fall to some unexpected animal who happens to be in better condition than his opponents.

ROWING

The Cambridge men have been at work at Cookham for some time, but it was only with the return of Mr. Fison a week ago that the crew was finally settled upon. On Saturday they move down to Putney, and when it is seen how they perform in tidal water, it will be easier to form an opinion of their chance of winning the race this year, but that they already have ardent admirers is evidenced by the fact that in what wagering there has been on the event they have been favourites. Mr. D. H. McLean has been indefatigable in his attentions to the Oxford boat. Excellent work has been done during the past week, the men swinging well together, with a clean decisive stroke.

FOOTBALL

The hard and slippery condition of the ground put a stop to most of the important matches fixed for Saturday last, especially those to be played under Rugby Rules. For instance, Manchester should have played Blackheath and on Monday the London Scottish, but both matches had to be abandoned. The final tie for the Scottish Association Challenge Cup created an unpleasant degree of interest. The clubs engaged, Queen's Park and Celtic, met at Govan, and some 30,000 people assembled to witness the result. Never, perhaps, did a football match create so much excitement, but the crowd, which was largely composed of men from the neighbouring ironworks, gradually pressed on to the field and narrowed the limits of play to such an extent that, though the Celtics obtained one goal, their adversaries not having scored, the Committee of the Association met in the evening and decided to declare the match null and void, and ordered it to be played again on the 9th of April. Of the League division most interest centred in the match between Sunderland and Preston North End, as the latter had held a very decided lead in this competition, having only lost four out of twenty-one games, but when they visited Sunderland on Saturday, another defeat was added to their score, they having lost by three goals, and their play was generally voted to be disappointing. Aston Villa beat Accrington in the most hollow manner, and, with an ordinary amount of luck in their favour they should go very near winning the Association Challenge Cup.

ATHLETICS

After several postponements the final day of the latter portion of the Cambridge University Sports was brought off on Monday. The path was in a very bad state, and in consequence the performances were nothing very remarkable. C. J. Moneypenny was beaten in the Hundred Yards by A. W. Charles, and H. L. Fleming, in addition to the High Jump, in which he cleared 5 ft. 8¼ in., won the Hurdle Race by six yards, in the good time of 16 4-5th sec.

Cross Country Competitions are becoming more popular every year, and on Saturday the teams entered for the South of the Thames Junior Inter-Club Race, which was decided in the Wandsworth district, and resulted in favour of the Tunbridge Wells Harriers, who won the event last year. The pace was not very excellent from the time test, but the state of the ground being taken into consideration, no serious fault can be found with those who finished in the first dozen.

WEATHER ON THE CONTINENT continues most unpleasant. Many parts of Germany and Austria suffer grievously from heavy snowfalls, the mountainous districts being completely blocked. Spain is again in misery from floods, and even Rome complains of unprecedented wet weather, rain having fallen continually for a fortnight, with rapid changes of temperature.

The telegram received by the West Brom secretary

The losing Aston Villa side of 1892

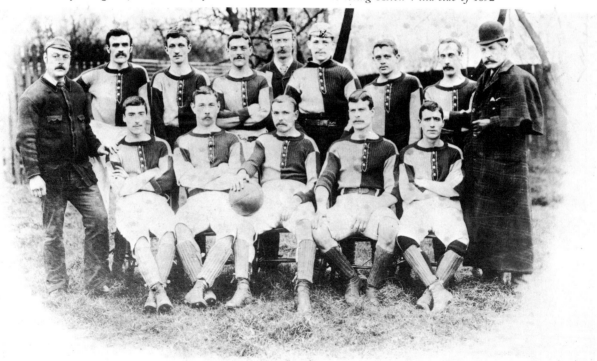

TURF

IT is many years since the flat racing season opened under as pleasant weather auspices as it did on Monday at Lincoln, a sharp frost during the early morning having been succeeded by a warm day, an unusual thing at this meeting, and to make things still pleasanter there were excellent fields for nearly every race, and though many of the horses would have been the better for a few more gallops, the sport was very much better than is usually the case on the first day of the season. The Batthyany Plate was the chief dish of the first day, and was won by Lord Dunraven's Simon Renard, and the Tathwell Stakes by a smart youngster of Mr. Hammond's called Gay Polly, a daughter of St. Gatien and Polaris. Thessalian took the Chaplin Stakes, and Nitrate Queen the Elsham Plate, so that Sherwood has early proved that his stable has not severely suffered by the recent frosts. On Tuesday the chief event was of course the Brocklesby Stakes, for which thirteen youngsters turned out. Mr. Maple's Minting Queen was made a strong favourite at 11 to 10, and she justified her position by winning most easily. The Brocklesby Trial Stakes fell to Springbeck, who beat Gold Crest by half a length, but the Sudbrook Selling Plate proved an upset to backers who had placed their faith in Obolus, who never looked like winning, and only came in fourth to Stanton, St. Isabella, and Little Tich.

ROWING

On Monday the Oxford and Cambridge Crews made their *début* on tidal waters at Putney, where their appearance excited a good deal of interest. The Dark Blues were the first to turn out. They seem to have plenty of material for a first class crew, but their training is not nearly as far advanced as was that of their predecessors at this time last year. However, they work well together, and came in for a fair share of approbation from the spectators on the bank. The Cambridge men show to much better advantage at Putney than in the dead water, and altogether created a very favourable impression. Mr. S. D. Muttlebury has worked wonders with the crew, but if Mr. Elin were a little steadier with his stroke the boat would be still more improved.

PASTIMES

FOOTBALL

All other matches sink into insignificance beside the final tie for the Association Challenge Cup, which was brought off on Saturday —Aston Villa and West Bromwich Albion being the contesting parties. Though both sides come from the same neighbourhood, the interest in the match was none the less keen, the number of spectators at the Oval (over 32,000) establishing a record for England. For more than a week before, every ticket was sold, and on Saturday there was not an available spot that was not occupied. Aston Villa were strong favourites, but they sadly disappointed their many admirers, as their play was far inferior to their usual form; while, on the other hand, West Bromwich Albion played in very good style and thoroughly deserved the victory which they gained by three goals to love. This success has been only once surpassed, when, in 1889-90, the Blackburn Rovers beat Sheffield Wednesday by six goals to one, and won the Cup—and it is a strange coincidence that West Bromwich Albion should win this year's contest, having beaten the Blackburn Rovers, and thus preventing them securing the Cup three years in succession, and establishing their claim to the special trophy.

MISCELLANEOUS

Lord Sheffield's cricket team is still pursuing its victorious career in Australia. The last match was that against Victoria, which the Englishmen won by nine wickets. The best scores were those of Bruce (of Victoria), who made 54 and 50. Dr. W. G. Grace made 44. The match was very poorly attended, but perhaps the almost invariable success of the visitors may have exhausted the interest taken in their contests.

● The 1892 final was the last to be staged at Kennington Oval. Some 25,000 watched West Bromwich Albion beat Aston Villa 3–0, and the increasing interest in the competition had stretched beyond the Oval's capabilities.

The result that was cabled (left) back to the Midlands left the area in astonishment. Villa already had the psychological advantage of the 1887 win over Albion, and now their side included James Cowan, a dominating personality at centre-half, and the clever right-wing pairing of Charlie Athersmith, then only nineteen but already an England international, and John Devey. But on the day Albion produced a talented forward of their own in Billy Bassett who had starred in their 1888 win over Preston. The underdogs benefited from a fourth minute goal, scored by Geddes, the 21-year-old outside-left who had won a regular place in the side only late in the season. Nicholls, a year younger, added a second. The third goal came from Reynolds whose wing-half displays along with Bill Groves prompted Villa to purchase both players. Reynolds, indeed, was to be a Cup winner in 1895 and 1897.

Warner, the unfortunate Villa goalkeeper, bore much of the blame for his team's defeat, particularly among the supporters who smashed the windows of his business, a public house.

West Bromwich Albion with the Cup won in 1892

Date 19 March 1892
Place The Kennington Oval
Score WEST BROMWICH ALBION 3
ASTON VILLA 0
Teams WEST BROMWICH ALBION
Reader, Nicholson, McCulloch, Reynolds, Perry (capt.), Groves, Bassett, McLeod, Nicholls, Pearson, Geddes. ASTON VILLA Warner, Evans, Cox, H. Devey, Cowan, Baird, Athersmith, J. Devey, Dickson (capt.), Hodgetts, Campbell
Officials Referee J. C. Clegg. Linesmen R. E. Lythgoe, R. P. Gregson

Goal Scorers Geddes 4, Nicholls 20, Reynolds
Attendance 32810
Gate Receipts £1757
Guest of Honour Lord Kinnaird
Copy The Graphic 19 and 26 March 1892

THE SPORTING CHRONICLE. MONDAY, MARCH 27, 1893.

THE ENGLISH CUP FINAL.

EVERTON v. WOLVERHAMPTON WANDERERS.

A TREMENDOUS CROWD.

WOLVERHAMPTON VICTORIOUS.

For the first occasion in the history of the English Association Cup—if we except the drawn game between Blackburn Rovers and West Bromwich Albion, which was replayed on the Derby County ground, in the season of 1885-6—the final tie of the English Association Cup was played out of London, and the Manchester Athletic Ground was the scene of the encounter on Saturday afternoon. The sun shone brilliantly, and the sight was one such as had never previously been seen at a football match in any part of the world. The only regret that can be expressed is that there was not a larger force of police to maintain order. As it was, there were several small encounters between individual policemen and the crowd, and some of the latter went home with cracked heads. The palisades were mounted and every point of vantage occupied, with the result that the little army of pressmen who were present were only able to give very poor accounts of the match. In fact, a large portion of it could not be seen from the Pavilion, where most of the reporters took refuge.

It was a very hard match, but not a particularly scientific one. The crowd behaved in admirable fashion, and kept clear of the lines all through. The spectators had every opportunity of breaking through, but they had evidently come to see the match, and behaved themselves accordingly. The first half was very much in favour of Everton, and they had hard lines on many occasions, but the "Wolves" reversed the order of things in the second half, and had just as much of the play and experienced similar luck. The game was won by sheer pluck and determination, and although the shot which scored was somewhat lucky itself, it was a grand effort on Allen's part. This occurred about half an hour from the finish, but it was palpably the deciding point, for Everton did not play up with anything like determination, and taken altogether it was a very quiet and not excited cup-tie. In the first half it seemed any odds on Everton winning, for during that period they played a very telling game; but immediately a re-start was made the "Wolves" went at it in a most vigorous fashion and fairly overplayed their opponents. Their defence was very prominent, and Baugh has hardly ever been seen to more advantage, whilst Swift was very useful. Rose had not a great deal to do, but he often showed great nerve, especially in the first half. The half-backs were very strong, and Allen was perhaps the best, but both Kinsey and Malpass did well. The forwards were not at all brilliant. Topham occasionally contributed some capital runs, but the biggest surprise was Wykes, who worked unceasingly, and was always about when required. As a whole, the forwards were more useful than brilliant, and this is a feature not to be despised in any team. Everton played a disappointing game in the second half. In the initial period they were all right, and in the play ought to have won before the interval, but they afterwards fell off a lot, and allowed Wolverhampton opportunities which they ought not to have had. Their forwards were good in the first half,

and wild in the second, and in the later stages of the game the "Wolves'" backs certainly bottled them up. Williams ought to have stopped the ball which scored, but otherwise kept goal well, and, taken all round, both backs were fair, but not up to form. The halves did well, but seemed nervous, and the forwards, after playing a really good game the first 45 minutes, fell off and scarcely showed any combination in the second portion of the game.

The result—a victory for the Wanderers by one goal to none—was disappointing to the Liverpool portion of the crowd, but there is no denying the fact that the "Wolves" played up in a most plucky fashion. We are not able to give the exact number of spectators present, but we should imagine the receipts will amount to £2,300. A large number of people were admitted without payment, and the police—192 in number—were singularly inactive in the performance of what might be supposed were their duties.

ENGLAND V. SCOTLAND.

The selection committee of the English Association met after the final tie and decided upon the following team to represent England against Scotland next Saturday, at Richmond:—

Gay (Old Brightonians), goal; Harrison (Old Westminsters) and Holmes (Preston North End), backs; Reynolds (West Bromwich Albion), Holt (Everton), and Kinsey (Wolverhampton Wanderers), half-backs; Bassett (West Bromwich Albion), Gosling (Cambridge University), Goodall (Derby County), Chadwick (Everton), and Spikesley (Sheffield Wednesday), forwards.

The Scottish Selecting Seven met in Glasgow on Saturday night, and chose the following team to represent Scotland:—

J Lindsay (Renton), goal; W Arnot (Queen's Park), and R Smellie (Queen's Park), backs; W Maley (Celtic), J Kelly (Celtic, captain), and D Mitchell (Glasgow Rangers), half-backs; W Sellars (Queen's Park), T Waddell (Queen's Park), J Hamilton (Queen's Park), A M'Mahon (Celtic), and J Campbell (Celtic), forwards.

The 1893 Wolverhampton Wanderers winning side

A FOOTBALL MATCH AT MANCHESTER.

The view here given represents a match between the Wolverhampton Wanderers and the Everton Club, at Fallowfield Ground, Manchester. The vast crowd therein shown is a good proof of the absorbing interest which a first-class football match now arouses in almost any of our great centres of population, but especially upon the northern and midland counties. Year by year this interest has grown, until now a match is often witnessed by tens of thousands. Even cricket does not in the north draw such crowds of spectators, or excite for weeks previously such animated discussion as an important match at football, and such a scene as here depicted well illustrates the innate love of the British people for manly sports.

Date 25 March 1893
Place Fallowfield (Manchester)
Score WOLVERHAMPTON WANDERERS 1 EVERTON 0
Teams WOLVERHAMPTON WANDERERS Rose, Baugh, Swift, Malpass, Allen, Kinsey, Topham, Wykes, Butcher, Griffin, Wood. EVERTON Williams, Kelso, Howarth, Boyle, Holt, Stewart, Latta, Gordon, Maxwell, Chadwick, Milward
Official Referee C. J. Hughes (Cheshire)
Goal Scorer Allen 60
Attendance 45 000
Gate Receipts £2559
Copy *The Sporting Chronicle* 27 March 1893

THE NOTTINGHAM EVENING POST, SATURDAY, MARCH 31, 1894.

THE CROWD BEGINS TO GATHER.

At three o'clock fully 15,000 persons had taken up their positions on the ground, and people were flocking in every minute by hundreds, still the accommodation proved quite ample. The tediousness of waiting was relieved to a great extent by the selection of music rendered by a band in the centre of the ground. The reserved seats on the grand stand were by no means filled, but the other parts were well occupied, and at a quarter to four there were 30,000 spectators waiting. Notts. colours were far more freely worn than those of Bolton; indeed few of the latter could be seen.

NOTTS. WERE IN GREAT EARNEST,

and Bruce got in a long shot, from which Sutcliffe had to throw away. Notts. still pressed, but were at length driven back. Cassidy sent well to Dickenson, who, however, was penalised for offside. Directly afterward Dickenson centred well, but Hendry was in the way, while Watson then sent out of touch. Hendry cleared well from Hughes, and Daft and Bruce sprinted down, but the ball was sent out. Harper frustrated a combined attack, and Notts. again hovered round the Bolton goal. Logan, however, failed to get up, and Tannahill and Wilson went away, and from a throw in Bolton made the game lively round the Notts. goal, but Hendry was again safe. The Wanderers relieved the attack and forced a corner, but Wilson shot behind. Notts. then took up the attack, and got well down.

Bruce had a chance at long range, and made a fine shot, which struck the cross-bar, the ball rebounding into play. This was the narrowest escape either goal had had so far, but Notts. had had by far the best of the game. Calderhead again dropped the ball just wide of the mark, while the determined manner in which Notts. maintained the attack evoked enthusiastic cheers. Bolton got down, and Toone saved marvellously from Wilson. Bruce and Daft again went to the front, but found an obstacle in Somerville. Notts., however, came again with a tremendous rush. Logan got possession and passed to Donnelley, who hit the upright, Watson catching the ball and rushing it through after twenty minutes' play, thus, amid tremendous plaudits, scoring

THE FIRST GOAL FOR NOTTS.

The Wanderers resumed with vigour, and Tannahill made a good run. Hendry tripped him within the penalty mark, and there were loud cries for a "penalty kick," but this was not allowed, and from the free kick Notts. broke away, and a pass from Watson gave Bruce a fine opening, but he shot wide. The Wanderers attacked, and Tannahill centring well Dickenson had a splendid opening, but he sent wide. At the other end Logan dashed in, and looked all like scoring, but he took the ball past. The Bolton right was again busy, and Harper had to stop a shot by Tannahill. Then Bentley troubled Toone, the Bolton men about this time being remarkably aggressive. Wilson shot in, and Toone had to clear. Daft made a run, and Logan sent so close that many

thought he had scored, but the ball went outside. A minute later all the Notts. forwards got in front, and Logan getting possession,

SCORED EASILY THE SECOND GOAL FOR NOTTS

after 30 minutes' play. This success was enthusiastically received, and Notts., as in all previous cup ties this season, were plainly playing the winning game. Play followed in Bolton quarters, and Daft sent over; then he was ruled off-side, but he was not a minute before he made another shot, and ere Sutcliffe could clear Watson was upon him, and there was a rare tussle on the ground. Sutcliffe, however, cleared. Watson made a grand shot over, and Donnelly sent close. Donnelly and Watson again circumvented Jones, the last named, however, just sending wide.

BRUCE WAS ROBBED BY PATON,

and Cassidy looked like getting through, when Harper came to the rescue. Calderhead also stemmed a threatening rush, and then Notts. were again pressing, forcing two corners in the same number of minutes. The ball was got away, but Hendry returned and the ball was then sent out of touch. Bramley kicked out to save, and Calderhead handling close up, the Notts. goal was besieged, Logan rushing away, and the Lancashire team being again put on the defensive. A free kick to Notts. was not improved upon. Bolton essayed to attack, but half-time arrived with the score:—

NOTTS.	2
BOLTON WANDERERS	0

The Wanderers were a long time before they appeared to commence the second half. Logan restarted, and Notts. at once went forward. In a minute, however, Cassidy was seen rushing away by himself, running round Harper, but Toone left his goal and luckily cleared. Bentley got in a shot, and the ball this time struck the posts, Hendry then clearing. Bolton continued to attack, and Tannahill sent near. Notts. got in front, and Logan shooting on the ground, Watson charged Sutcliffe, but he cleared, and then the ball was sent wide. Logan made a second wide shot, and Bolton relieved their lines. Jones stopped Watson, and just as he was becoming dangerous, and a second later he was ruled off-side. Notts. were completely out-playing their opponents at this point, and all play was in front of their goal. One or two shots were made, but all were stopped, and

BRAMLEY ENDED THE SCRIMMAGE

by sending past on the ground. Dickinson and Bentley got splendidly down, and Cassidy had an opening, but Shelton cleared grandly. Notts., in fact, were far too clever for their opponents, and again took up the running, Bruce getting in a shot which Sutcliffe had to deal with smartly. Sutcliffe next saved from Logan at the expense of a corner, and certainly did not know where the ball had gone to. The corner proved abortive, but Notts. came again, and Logan was responsible for a brilliant run, which he ended by scoring

A THIRD POINT FOR NOTTS.,

the cheers which greeted this admirable perform-

ance being loud and prolonged. Shelton was penalised for tripping Bentley, but Hughes shot wildly over the bar. Then Donnelly coming down passed to Logan who, sending the ball on, went in pursuit, and catching it on the run sent

INTO THE NET A FOURTH TIME

fifteen minutes from the recommencement. Notts. were displaying brilliant form and playing excellent football, while the Wanderers, it was evident, were getting disheartened, and gradually falling to pieces. Hendry, who played grandly with Harper and the half-backs, proved impassible obstacles to the Bolton forwards at almost every break away. Daft next sent wide, and then Watson forced a corner, Bramley heading over. Coming with a rush Donnelly all but regained another point, Sutcliffe giving a fruitless corner. Still another corner accrued, and after a little play Daft got a chance and he sent well in.

SUTCLIFFE HAVING TO FIST OUT.

Bolton made a run, but it was futile, and Notts. returning, Sutcliffe only just avoided Bruce as he was clearing. The Bolton goalkeeper had to save from Daft, and then he had to kick away from Donnelly. Notts. now seemed completely masters of the situation, and were continually pressing. Hughes handled, and Harper placed. A further attack on the Bolton goal followed, and the mid-field play ensued. Wilson made a dash, and a good shot, which just went across the goal and wide. Watson returned in splendid style, and passing into the centre, he gave Logan a grand chance. He took full advantage of it, for he shot hard on the ground, and

SUTCLIFFE EFFECTED A WONDERFUL SAVE,

falling in doing so. Open play again took place, but Donnelly, fouling an opponent, was penalised, was neutralised, and Notts. again went ahead. There was only eleven minutes left for play, and the game was practically in the hands of Notts. They had won the cup at last. They remained in front, but they were not putting forth very great efforts now. Yet they broke away and gained a corner, and a shot was just stopped. Logan made a splendid run, and Sutcliffe had to clear from Watson, and a corner to Notts. accrued, but this was not improved upon, and Bruce sent over. An expiring effort was made by Bolton, and getting in front Bentley shot. Toone fell, and Cassidy, rushing up, scored the

FIRST AND ONLY GOAL

for the Lancashire men. Almost before the game could be restarted the whistle went for time, and Notts. by brilliant play were left winners of the cup, the result being:—

NOTTS.	4
BOLTON WANDERERS	1

Notts County with Cup and trainer

Date 31 March 1894
Place Goodison Park (Everton)
Score NOTTS COUNTY 4
BOLTON WANDERERS 1
Teams NOTTS COUNTY Toone, Harper, Hendrey, Bramley, Calderhead (capt.), Shelton, Watson, Donnelly, Logan, Bruce, Daft.
BOLTON WANDERERS Sutcliffe, Somerville, Jones (capt.), Gardiner, Paton, Hughes, Tannahill, Wilson, Cassidy, Bentley, Dickenson
Official Referee C. J. Hughes (Cheshire)
Goal Scorers NOTTS COUNTY Watson 18, Logan 29, 67, 70; BOLTON WANDERERS Cassidy 87
Attendance 37 000
Gate Receipts £1 189
Copy *The Nottingham Evening Post* 31 March 1894

SUNDAY TIMES, APRIL 21, 1895.

THE ASSOCIATION CHALLENGE CUP.
FINAL TIE.
ASTON VILLA v. WEST BROMWICH ALBION.
A GIGANTIC CROWD AT THE PALACE.

(BY OUR SPECIAL REPORTER)

At length the much-talked-of game is over, and the Football Association Challenge Cup will during the ensuing months remain in possession of the far-famed Aston Villa club. They only beat West Bromwich Albion by a goal to love, and that point was obtained in the first minute of the game, but there could be no two opinions about the relative merits of the teams, the winners being far superior in combination to their rivals. To say that the game had been eagerly looked forward to but faintly expresses the immense enthusiasm it excited throughout England. Excursions were run by the various railway companies from the Midlands and the North, and the result was a gathering at the Crystal Palace the like of which had never before been witnessed in connection with a football match. There must have been over 40,000 watching the game, the turnstiles recording 42,560 persons as visiting the Palace. Not since 1892 had the Cup final been played in the Metropolis, and then, strangely enough, Aston Villa and West Bromwich Albion were the clubs to fight out the issue. This fact doubtless had a lot to do with the monster attendance. Although the crowd was such a vast one there was no hurry, no undue crowding, and no difficulty on the part of any of those present in seeing the play. The Crystal Palace authorities had made simply magnificent arrangements, and proved themselves capable of dealing most effectively with the vast concourse that flocked to their enclosure. As the ground is a new one, a few words may be spared perhaps for a brief description of it. In shape it is an ellipse, and when finished will measure seventeen acres. It is situated partly on the site of the old lake, which has been filled in and turfed over, whilst the cycle track has been taken in. Yesterday eight acres of the new space were utilised. The goals were pitched on the slant from east to west. At the southern side there was stand accommodation for 5,000 people, and provision for over one hundred reporters. Another three thousand reserved seats were placed inside the rails running round the scene of play, and beyond these the banked-up sides of the ground formed a natural grand stand for thousands upon thousands. The sea of faces that met one's gaze on all sides presented a sight far easier imagined than described, whilst the excitement and enthusiasm was pulse-stirring enough to be trying to weak nerves. And what of the game? Well, it was a good one. In the first half the exchanges were fast and furious, the passing neat and effective, the shooting hard, and the defence all that could be wished. The only point scored was obtained in the first minute, the Villans simply "rushing" a goal before the Albion seemed quite certain that hostilities had commenced. After the interval the pace fell off somewhat, and, compared with what had gone before, the play seemed moderate. Considering that the sun was shining with great force this was not surprising though. Although only defeated by such a narrow margin there could be no two opinions about the inferiority of the Albion. Their front rank was not so well balanced as that of their rivals, the left wing being yards slower than the right. The Albion backs, too, although they saved splendidly, were not too good in clearing, and it would not have been surprising had the Villa won by three goals to love. But enough in this strain; the game calls for detailed notice, and we will therefore proceed.

THE GAME.

Having won the toss West Bromwich started from the western goal with the sun at their backs, and a stiffish breeze in their favour. Devey set the ball in motion, and it was evident from the outset that forcing tactics would be adopted. The Villa forwards at once rushed forward, and the ball went out of play, thirty yards from the Throstles' goal. From the throw in Athersmith got past the rival half-backs, and then, cleverly eluding Horton, passed in beautiful fashion to Chatt. The latter seized the opportunity, and with the game only a minute old sent the ball flying past Reader. As soon as the crowd realised that a goal had been scored they cheered, waved hats, umbrellas, handkerchiefs, and sticks, the sight being a truly remarkable one as viewed from the Press tables. From the centre kick the Villa again rushed down, and finding he could not stop Athersmith, Horton fouled that player, whilst a trifle later the Albion back conceded a corner. This was well taken, and some pretty heading by the Villa men looked very dangerous. Williams got the ball away, and Higgins sending it on to Bassett, the famous right winger sprinted down head, but shot wide. A foul against the Villa gave the Throstles an opening, but Welford cleared beautifully, and Smith carried the war into the enemies' quarters, and a pass by Devey to Athersmith looked like upsetting Reader, but the Aston right winger's shot went wide of the mark. The Albion retaliated, but McLeod wound up with a weak kick, following which Bassett was dangerous, when pulled up for hands. Athersmith and Chatt once more attacked, and Horton fouling the Albion were severely pressed, and Reader was forced to concede a corner. For quite ten minutes the Villa men pressed very strongly, the forwards combining grandly, whilst Devey put in more than one shot which required a lot of stopping. One of these was only just kept out by Reader, and Hodgetts, running up, put the ball into the net, but the whistle had just sounded "off-side." After Banks had broken away the Villa returned to the charge, but a grand run by Bassett looked like bearing

Devey and Higgins clash heads

fruit. Just in front of goal, however, he was badly tripped by Welford. Following the free kick three corners in about five minutes fell to the share of the Albion. All were well taken, but the defence of the Villa was perfect, and the Aston attack culminated through one of their forwards transgressing the off-side rule. Honours were then easy for a while, but Athersmith then made an attack which all but beat Reader, the Albion goalkeeper only just getting out of the difficulty in the very nick of time. Another free kick was given against Horton, and Reader had to concede a corner, which was not at all well taken by Reynolds. Still, the Albion were penned in the neighbourhood of their own goal, but the defence never weakered, and at length Bassett raised the siege, and got well down field. He then centred to Hutchison, but the latter was off side, and the whistle promptly put an end to the Albion advance. However, the Throstles stuck to their task, Russell and Bassett being especially prominent. The latter had the ill-luck to see a fine shot hit the posts. Twice after the old International caused Wilkes to use his hands, and the crowd got terribly excited. Just before half-time Higgins and Devey came into collision, with the result that the first-named was stunned. He continued to play, however, after a few minutes, but nothing further had been scored up to the interval, when the record was

Aston Villa .... One goal
West Bromwich Albion... None

Nearly ten minutes elapsed ere the teams returned to the field. The Albion were then without Higgins, but he came on in a few more minutes, having stopped to have his head bandaged by members of the Palace Ambulance Corps. This was merely a precautionary measure, however, as the scalp wound he had sustained not being serious. By this time the wind had dropped considerably, whilst the sun was not as troublesome to the players as formerly Bassett was the first man prominent, but the Villa soon returned to the charge, and following a corner kick the Albion backs and goalkeeper had a bad time of it. Banks and Hutchison afforded relief, and Richards, having the ball sent to him had an open goal to shoot at, but made a mess of the opportunity, a feat he repeated shortly after. Bassett continued to show fine form, but he was not well backed up, the left wing men not having sufficient pace to keep up with him. From a pass by McLeod Richards made a fine screw shot at goal which only just missed, but the Villa forwards then dashed

away in a body, Devey and Chatt both causing Reader, at the other end, to use his hands. Still no fault could be found with the Albion defence, and although the Villa forced another couple of corners they could not get through, Bassett once more relieved his side, and following some exciting play in the neighbourhood of the Villa goal Wilkes allowed a corner, following which Higgins was applauded for some very clever work with his head. The minutes sped by, and it began to be apparent that the Throstles had met their masters. Their attacks were spasmodic and disjointed, whilst they were of infrequent occurrence compared with those they were called upon to repel. In the last five minutes the Villa men relaxed their efforts somewhat, and kicked out of play a good deal. The Albion persevered right up to the finish, but fortune would not smile on their efforts, and when the end came the score was still—

Aston Villa .... One goal.
West Bromwich Albion ...... None.

A scene of great excitement followed. The vast crowd swarming over the ground and cheering lustily for minutes. The Cup was presented to the winners by Lady Kinnaird.

REMARKS.

The first thing that struck one in connection with the game was the fact that in quality it was far above the average of final ties. This was especially the case in the first half, after which several of the men had palpably had enough of it. The result was strictly in accordance with public form, as during the season the Villa had won seventeen out of twenty-nine League matches, against the nine out of twenty-nine by the losers. Altogether with Cup matches and friendlies, the Villa had a total of fifty-three games, winning thirty-one and losing fourteen, against the fifty-two of the Albion, whose wins were twenty-five and losses nineteen. The goal average, however, did not show much difference in the capabilities of the rivals, the Villa record being 104 for and eighty-two against, and that of the Albion ninety-five for and ninety-eight against. It may be mentioned that this is the third occasion in which the final tie has been fought out by Midland teams. Comparing the teams is difficult, Wilkes did not have a fourth of the work that fell to Reader, but what he was called upon to do was well performed. The Villa backs were better at clearing (at saving they could not be) than their opponents. Bassett was the best forward on the field, and Higgins was about the best half for the losers. Richards was weak in the centre. Although several fouls occurred, it was not a rough game, and it will be long remembered by those fortunate enough to witness it.

Date	20 April 1895
Place	The Crystal Palace
Score	ASTON VILLA 1
	WEST BROMWICH ALBION 0
Teams	ASTON VILLA Wilkes, Spencer, Walford, Reynolds, Cowan, Russell, Athersmith, Chatt, Devey, Hodgetts, Smith. WEST BROMWICH ALBION Reader, Williams, Horton, Perry, Higgins, Taggart, Bassett, McLeod, Richards, Hutchinson, Banks
Official	Referee J. Lewis (Blackburn)
Goal Scorer	Devey
Attendance	42560
Gate Receipts	£1545
Guest of Honour	Lady Kinnaird
Copy	The Sunday Times 21 April 1895

Aston Villa with the Cup won in 1895

FOOTBALL.

THE HOME COMING OF THE ENGLISH CUP.

A TRIUMPHAL PROGRESS.

Yesterday afternoon the English Cup was brought to its twelve months' home amid a scene of enthusiasm never excelled since there was such a trophy. All along the route, within the confines of the Midland Station, and in many a part of the city which the procession never reached, the enthusiasm was unbounded and the cheering was tremendous. But it was evident—and we say it without any feeling that it should be otherwise—that the Wednesday Committee are not show-people. They have perhaps not yet got thoroughly imbued with the sense of what possession of the English Cup really means and what the public expect of them. Yesterday's programme would have been all the better for the guiding hand of a Barnum or the control of a Lord George Sanger. There was no method, no local knowledge of what was to be done, and the police were just as much in the dark as everybody else. All the members of the Wednesday Committee were up in London with the team; it was known that the whole party—together with the English Cup—was to come back to Sheffield per the 5.28 Midland train, but beyond this no details were forthcoming. And so the crowd began to gather, and the police had to take measures for its control as best they might. It is easy to see how all this could have been avoided. Clubs such as the gay and gallant Rovers from Blackburn, with all their Cup-holding experience, would never have made such an error, and when Wednesday have won the trophy a few times more perhaps we shall have a settled programme to work to, and enthusiastic supporters of the club have a better knowledge of where to go to see their favourites.

For a full hour before the train was due people were crowding down to the precincts of the Midland Station, and though the authorities did their best to keep them clear of the platforms, they were circumvented by the Sheffielders, who purchased tickets to Heeley, and became duly certified passengers. As time wore on these qualified travellers who did not intend to travel swamped the down platform to quite an uncomfortable degree, and when ex-Inspector Bestwick's Band filed in and took up a suitable position, where the saloon was expected to stop when the train came in, the holders of the instruments could scarce find room to square their elbows and get in proper order round their conductor. Telegraphic information from Chesterfield was to the effect that the expected train passed through there exact to time, and as 5.28 drew near the great crowd outside the doors of the station made a final frantic attempt to force their way within the sacred precincts. But they were once more foiled, and as the train steamed in with a rush and a roar as though aware of the burden it was bringing those outside had for the time being to take their pleasure in the roars of cheers which broke from the excited throng within. As the train—brought along as it had been by two powerful locomotives—drew up there was a concerted rush to the doors of the saloon in which the Wednesday men were, and the cheers burst out again and again till the players alighted and essayed to force their way through. Then one saw the difficulties of the task. Every man was forced to drag himself by sheer strength through the thick of his friends, more than one of whom tried to hoist especial favourites aloft and carry them thus to the "Old Times," which was waiting outside. Once outside the station the character of the crowd could be seen at once. Far as the eye could see was a mighty throng, a serried mass of faces, right away the length of the station approach, all along Station Road, on the roofs of the wooden sheds in hundreds, up the iron supports of the covered space in front of the station, and wherever standing room could be found. Through this it was speedily seen that progress on foot was practically impossible, and hansoms were called into requisition, which acted the part of tenders to ocean steamers, and piloted the players as well as might be through the stormy sea of spectators 'twixt the station and the four-in-hand. Favours were seen on every hand, women who had struggled down wore ribbons in extravagant profusion, and blue and white-washed hats, umbrellas of the same fearful pattern, and in fact ribbons and decorations of every character.

It was then in the midst of a crowd of thoroughly enthusiastic supporters that the Wednesday men emerged from the station. Of course there was a hitch—there often is in these impromptu processions—and the crowd in its simple joyfulness locked the break of the four-in-hand and prevented its pro-

THE ARRIVAL IN SHEFFIELD.

gress for a good twenty minutes until the break had been bodily detached. And then, amid ringing cheers and in an almost indescribable uproar of hand-clapping and hurrahs, the procession made a start, the band in front in as good order as could be contrived, and a dense mass of the crowd following close behind, after which came the "Old Times" with a company distinguished beyond its wont, and with a bodyguard of thousands—in front, behind, and on either hand. A few yards, and then came another stop; a few yards more, and again a stop, and so Station Road was negotiated, Captain Earp holding up the Cup to view now and then to the accompaniment of renewed enthusiasm. At the foot of Commercial Street the congestion was still greater, and it became a question of whether the four gallant horses would be able to drag their load up that steeply-inclined thoroughfare. But they did their work splendidly, though pulled up every few yards by the stoppage of the crowd to cheer. At the top an inspiring sight awaited those of us upon the drag. On every hand was a sea of faces—it was impossible to see anything else, and the antiquated phrase of being able to walk upon the people's heads was here no façon de parler. Right up into the High Street the crowd continued without sensible diminution, and with news to hand of a similar state of things prevalent all along the intended line of route, it became evident that part, if not the whole of the remainder, would have to be cut out. But true to his desire to give the supporters of his team a chance to cheer their favourites, the Wednesday President (Mr. John Holmes) called to Mr. Harry Thompson, who held the reins, to go "as well as he could down to Sheffield Moor, and then back to the Royal." But such instructions could not be carried out. It was impossible that the four in hand could keep on starting and pulling up on granite setts, and so, to the dismay and disappointment of the awaiting crowd, the "Old Times" was pulled sharply to the right, and made straight for the Royal Hotel, where dinner was taken, the players being the guests of Councillor George Senior and Mr. Arthur Nixon. But the crowd was not yet satisfied, and stayed outside, blocking up the Haymarket, surrounding the Royal, and cheering to their hearts' content all the time the dinner was in progress. It was in very truth a glorious home coming!

The 1896 final marked the first quarter-century of the competition, and the first presentation of the "new" trophy. In Sheffield Wednesday it produced appropriate winners, the first success for a city in which so much had been done to foster the game.

All three goals came in the first 18 minutes, one from Black of Wolverhampton Wanderers sandwiched between two from Spikesley for Wednesday.

The report from *The Sheffield Daily Telegraph*, apart from covering the great reception Wednesday received when they returned with the Cup, also records the following item concerning rowdyism at a football match.

Date 18 April 1896
Place The Crystal Palace
Score SHEFFIELD WEDNESDAY 2
WOLVERHAMPTON WANDERERS 1
Teams SHEFFIELD WEDNESDAY Massey, Earp, Langley, Brandon, Crawshaw, Petrie, Brash, Brady, Bell, Davis, Spikesley.
WOLVERHAMPTON WANDERERS Tennant, Baugh, Dunn, Owen, Malpass, Griffiths, Tanks, Henderson, Beats, Wood, Black
Officials Referee Lieut. Simpson (Hon. Sec. FA). Linesmen A. G. Hines (Notts.), J. Howcroft (Redcar)
Goal Scorers SHEFFIELD WEDNESDAY Spikesley 1, 18; WOLVERHAMPTON WANDERERS Black 8
Attendance 48836
Gate Receipts £1824
Guest of Honour Lord Kinnaird
Copy The Sheffield Daily Telegraph 21 April 1896

ROWDYISM AT A FOOTBALL MATCH.

On Saturday afternoon a disgraceful scene was witnessed in connection with the final tie of the Cheshire Junior Cup. The match was replayed at Nantwich by order of the Cheshire Association upon the report of the referee. The opposing team was Winnington Recreation. Ten minutes from time they led by a goal to nothing. The crowd, which was chiefly composed of the supporters of the Nantwich team, broke in at this point, and the referee (Mr. Peter Wright, of Macclesfield), was chased from the field. The Winnington players were severely used, and free fights were general, the small body of police being absolutely powerless. One of the members of the Association seized the cup, towards which the crowd rushed, and escaped across the fields. The referee left the field, strongly protected, after vainly endeavouring to restore order.

1897

● In 1897 Aston Villa emulated the achievement of Preston North End eight years earlier and became the second club to win the League and Cup double.

Villa had taken the Championship in 1896, and they powered their way to a second successive title, losing only four of their 30 league fixtures. Sheffield United, the runners-up, were left eleven points adrift. Villa had already secured the first half of the double when they travelled to Crystal Palace to meet Everton, their last obstacle in the FA Cup.

Howard Spencer, John Reynolds, James Cowan, Charlie Athersmith and John Devey remained from the Cup-winning eleven of 1895. Jimmy Whitehouse, signed from Grimsby Town for £200, a vast sum for the times, had taken over in goal. Albert Evans now partnered Spencer at full-back, and Jimmy Crabtree, already an England international with Burnley, was the new left-half. Freddy Wheldon cost £100 from Small Heath, and the attack was completed by two Scots, John Campbell, from Celtic, and John Cowan. An estimated 10,000 supporters left the Midlands on the morning of the final, swelling the crowd to a record 65,000.

Everton's credentials added to the occasion. Runners-up in the League in 1895 and third the following year, their class was emphasised in a smooth passage to their second final, leaving in their wake Bolton Wanderers, Bury, Blackburn Rovers and Derby Cunty. The contest fulfilled all its promise, and it was only at the end of a dramatic and highly skilled match that Villa confirmed their place in the annals of the game.

The exhilarating pace of the first quarter of an hour reflected the quality of both sides. Villa's right-wing pairing of Athersmith and Devey, a considerable force throughout the season, offered the greatest danger to Everton, but Villa themselves were threatened by an attack in which John Bell was outstanding. Near-misses at both ends were the preliminaries to a remarkable 25 minutes before half-time, which produced the game's five goals.

Villa's opener, after 18 minutes, arrived from a predictable source. Athersmith and Devey picked a route along the right; the final pass sent Campbell through to score

General scene of the 1897 Cup final

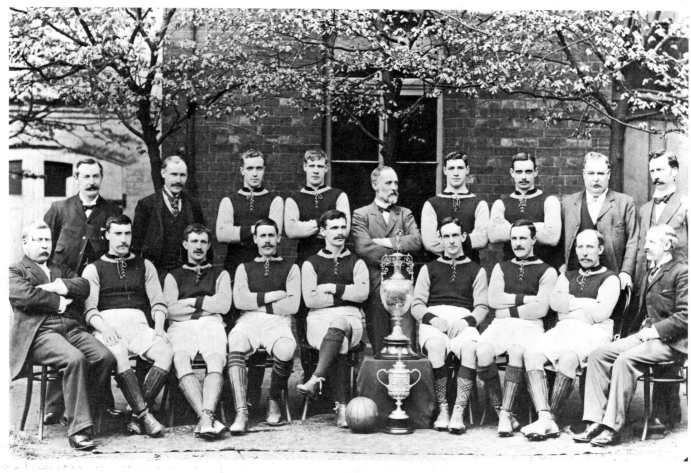

Aston Villa with the Cup and League trophies won in 1897

with a deceptive, swerving shot. The goal provoked a marvellous response from Everton who inside ten minutes not only equalised but then forged into the lead themselves.

Bell's individual skills levelled the score at 1–1; he broke clear, drawing White-house out of his goal before slipping the ball past him. The equaliser heralded more Everton pressure. From a free-kick in a dangerous position, Boyle, the right-half, put Everton in front. A lesser team than Villa would surely then have crumbled, but their reply, two goals of their own in equally quick tempo, provided a perfect testimony to the greatness of the side. It was Wheldon who claimed the equaliser, and Crabtree's fine header on the stroke of half time turned out to be the winner.

Villa dominated the second half for long spells without being able to add to their lead. Everton defended skilfully and still managed to muster enough forays to keep the result in doubt to the very last.

The key to Villa's remarkable season lay in their short-passing game with the emphasis on keeping the ball on the ground. Campbell's goal-scoring abilities were fully served by the creative talents of the wing-halves, the inside-forwards and the genuine pace of Athersmith. James Cowan, a renowned sprinter himself – he competed in the famous Powderhall event – remained a colossus at centre-half, a player of equal facility in defence or attack. Only Whitehouse, Evans and John Cowan never represented their country.

The historic season also marked the end of one era in the story of Aston Villa. It was the last in which their headquarters were at Wellington Road, Perry Barr. Later in 1897 the club moved to its present home at Villa Park.

The pictures from *Sporting Sketches* on the right show the switchback railway which was part of the Crystal Palace attractions.

Date 10 April 1897
Place The Crystal Palace
Score ASTON VILLA 3 EVERTON 2
Teams ASTON VILLA Whitehouse, Spencer, Evans, Reynolds, James Cowan, Crabtree, Athersmith, Devey, Campbell, Wheldon, John Cowan. EVERTON Menham, Meecham, Storrier, Boyle, Holt, Stewart, Taylor, Bell, Hartley, Chadwick, Millward
Official Referee J. Lewis (Blackburn)
Goal Scorers ASTON VILLA Campbell, Wheldon, Crabtree; EVERTON Bell, Boyle
Attendance 65891
Gate Receipts £2162
Guest of Honour Lord Rosebery
Copy *Sporting Sketches* 14 April 1897

A good bit of play by Storrier.

A throw in by Reynolds.

Everton claim a foul.

A pass to Athersmith.

The Football Season

THE spectacle of the huge crowd which lined the deep hollow of the Crystal Palace football ground, to watch the final tie of the Association Cup, was more impressive than the game itself. It is impossible to convey by the pen an adequate idea of the high banks of thousands of faces surrounding the green acres of the football ground, of the swelling volume of the shouts that went up from them as they followed the exciting moments of the game, of their not less impressive silences, and of their swaying movements, comparable to that of a cornfield shaken by the wind as they craned eagerly forward on the sloping ground to watch the players. Sixty thousand people, the population of a large town, followed the struggle between Derby County and Notts Forest for the possession of the most attractive prize of the football year. It cannot be said that they were rewarded either by seeing the popular side win, or by a very good game. Derby County's record in previous Cup Ties had been much more brilliant than that of their opponents, who, both on account of the comparative weakness of the clubs they had been drawn against, or of

Notts Forest winning their second goal: Fryer throws the ball at Benbow's feet
THE FINAL TIE FOR THE ASSOCIATION CUP AT THE CRYSTAL PALACE

Lord Rosebery showing the Cup
THE FINAL TIE FOR THE ASSOCIATION CUP AT THE CRYSTAL PALACE

the way in which they had beaten Southampton in the last two minutes of the semi-final game, were to be accounted as one of the luckiest clubs which ever figured in a final tie. The Notts Forest luck did not desert them in this match. With nothing to lose and everything to win, they played as many an inferior club has done before in such a match, with far more dash and vigour than their more talented opponents ; and in the end won a thoroughly well-deserved victory by three goals to one. Derby County's brilliant line of forward players never got thoroughly into swing, and their backs left a lot to be desired in their play, whereas the Notts defence was nearly perfect, and their forwards played like a winning side all through the match. The victory of Notts Forest makes the fifth time in the last decade when the winner of the Association Cup has been the club which was not the favourite. The other occasions were the victories of West Bromwich Albion over Preston North End in 1888, and over Aston Villa in 1892, of Wolverhampton Wanderers over Everton in 1893, and of Notts County over Bolton Wanderers in 1894. With this match the football season, both professional and amateur, comes practically to a close ; and the only remaining matches of importance are those which are played between

the least successful clubs belonging to the Football League for the privilege of remaining in the First Division of that body next year. There is some probability that the famous Blackburn Rovers may next year find themselves outside the pale of the best class Association Football. It has been in many respects a most successful year for Association Football, and its triumphs have to some extent compensated for the failure of English Rugby Football. England won all three matches against the other countries, beating Ireland by three goals to two, Wales by three goals to none, and Scotland easily by three goals to one. The last was an especially gratifying victory, and was the first game England has won since Scotland called upon Scotch professionals playing for English clubs to help her. The Championship of the English Football League, a distinction even more coveted in the North than that of winning the Association Cup, was won by Sheffield United, with Sunderland second, Wolverhampton Wanderers third, and Aston Villa, who last year won both the Cup and the League Championship, nowhere. In Amateur Association Football Cambridge University rather unexpectedly beat Oxford, and the famous Corinthians, by going through the season unbeaten by any English Club, well maintained amateur prestige. They drew twice with the best club in the League—Sheffield United—for the possession of the Dewar Cup, and won more games against the best professional teams than they drew. At the same time only three amateur players were considered good enough to represent England against Scotland—Mr. G. O. Smith, the best centre forward now playing, Mr. Oakley at back, and Mr. Wreford Brown a vigorous half-back. It is rather a curious fact that notwithstanding England's defeat of Scotland, yet in the professional inter-League match Scotland won.

All the World's Fighting Ships

IN "All the World's Fighting Ships" (Sampson Low, Marston and Co.), Mr. Fred T. Jane has set himself the task of supplying those details of warships which are not included in other naval annuals, and have hitherto been only obtainable in the confidential books of the different navies. The book is copiously illustrated with pen-and-ink drawings, in which the salient and characteristic features of some have been slightly accentuated. The book is admirably arranged. The indexes are especially well done. The first covers all the main division of the ship portraits, the order in which they are placed, and the pages on which they are to be found. The ships are primarily arranged by funnels, then by masts and military tops. Taking a picture of a warship any one may, by the aid of Mr. Jane's book, ascertain with tolerable accuracy to what navy and what type in that navy she belongs. Index II. gives the page on which each vessel is to be found. In the case of sister ships, one illustration is given, and any difference in construction is noted. Before the name of each vessel, or series of vessels, the class to which they belong is indicated by a figure or a letter, according to the system of classification adopted in the book. Mr. Jane has done his work with evident care, and the volume is of great interest and value now when there are war clouds on the horizon in more than one direction. As the book is printed in four languages—English, French, German, and Italian—the four texts being placed side by side, it will doubtless be valued on the Continent as a useful record as well as at home.

The 1898 final produced an East Midlands affair with Nottingham Forest winning for the first time over Derby County who, legend has it, were labouring under the handicap of a gipsy's curse – provoked by moving on gipsies camped on the area that was developed as County's ground. Forest are credited with being among the first teams to play in a 2–3–5 formation, and in Sam Widdowson they had already produced one of the game's pioneers. Widdowson's awareness of the need to protect players is still with us today; he developed the use of shin guards. Appropriately Forest beat Derby at Crystal Palace on the day that Widdowson celebrated his fiftieth birthday.

Derby County had reached the semi-final in the two previous years, and in Steve Bloomer possessed the greatest forward in the land. But Bloomer was to be defied by a Nottingham defence in which Adam Scott and Frank Forman gave superb individual performances.

Forest took the lead after only 19 minutes. Wragg, who had earlier been limping, took a free-kick after Somner had been fouled. The ball dropped perfectly for Capes who shot hard and low; Fryer was comprehensively beaten. Bloomer led Derby's retaliation, well supported by John Goodall; Forman had to throw his body in line with a Bloomer shot to keep Forest's goal intact.

It was only a temporary reprieve. Derby's pressure forced Forman into conceding a free-kick; from it Bloomer rose to head in the equaliser. Yet five minutes later Forest were back in front and this time it was a lead they would not lose.

The records show Capes once as the scorer, though *The Graphic* (left) indicates it was Benbow. The Forest players were benefiting perhaps from the studious preparations which would not be out of place today.

Forest went on to stretch their lead in the second half though they had to wait until four minutes from time until they made sure of victory. McPherson, the captain, produced a remarkable goal with a shot while he was flat out on the ground after he had robbed a defender. Derby County, like many a favourite before and since, were not able to impose their strengths on the match despite enjoying the predominance of the support of the crowd of more than 60,000. *The Graphic* (left) encapsulated the tone of the reporters of the day: "Derby County's record in previous Cup ties had been much more brilliant than their opponents, who, both on account of the comparative weakness of the clubs they had been drawn against, or of the way they had beaten Southampton in the last two minutes of the semi-final game, were to be accounted as one of the luckiest clubs which ever figured in a final tie. The Notts Forest luck did not desert them in this match. With nothing to lose and everything to win, they played as many an inferior club has done before in such a match, with far more dash and vigour than their more talented opponents; and in the end won a thoroughly well-deserved victory by three goals to one."

(Note: Whereas the present day abbreviation of the 1898 Cup winners is Nott'm Forest, Notts Forest was very much in use in the late nineteenth century.)

The result helped the discomfort of some of the East Midland journalists at Crystal Palace, one of whom wrote: "By the bye, a matter deserves mention which though it may not concern the public directly is still of importance to them in its results. This was the accommodation provided for the provincial Press. Influential papers of an old and high standard had their repeated applications ignored while some of the London journals of far less importance had secured and marked several seats – in one case five."

Below: Nottingham Forest's winning side of 1898 (players names): Left to right back row: McInnes, Ritchie, Allsop, Scott, Spouncer. Front row: Richards, Forman, McPherson, Wragg, Capes. In front: Benbow.

Date 16 April 1898
Place The Crystal Palace
Score NOTTINGHAM FOREST 3
DERBY COUNTY 1
Teams NOTTINGHAM FOREST Allsop, Ritchie, Scott, Forman, McPherson, Wragg, McInnes, Richards, Benbow, Capes, Spouncer.
DERBY COUNTY Fryer, Methven, Leiper, Cox, A. Goodall, Turner, J. Goodall, Bloomer, Boag, Stevenson, McQueen
Official Referee J. Lewis (Blackburn)
Goal Scorers NOTTINGHAM FOREST Capes 19 and 42, McPherson 86;
DERBY COUNTY Bloomer 31
Attendance 62017
Gate Receipts £2312
Guest of Honour Lord Rosebery
Copy The Graphic 23 April 1898

Notts. Forest Football Club 1897-8.

April 20, 1899.

SPORTING SKETCHES.

IT is but rarely one sees a really great game in the Association Cup final. All the conditions —especially that tremendous sea of faces surging all around—tend to create a nervous tension and over-eagerness in the players, and as a result the football is seldom scientific, and sometimes degenerates into a mere rough and tumble scramble. Saturday's game was no exception to the rule, for though it was a keen and in the first half very exciting encounter, the play was by no means of a high order. For this the state of the turf, soddened by the heavy rain of the previous days and of the morning, was largely responsible, for the players were constantly slipping down, and accurate passing and shooting were exceedingly difficult.

"Dogged does it," and the victory of Sheffield United was well deserved after the game and stubborn way in which they fought their way through the several stages of the competition. On Saturday last their game had the quality of stubbornness in an enhanced degree, for Derby were the first to score, and held their lead right up to the interval; but the United never lost heart, and when they did find their game were quite irresistible. In ten minutes—ten minutes of the most exciting football one can wish to witness —the fortunes of the game were completely reversed, for in that short space the United not only wiped out their disadvantage, but established a strong lead, which, at that period of the game, almost ensured success. The rushes of their forwards completely disorganised the Derby back division, and at one period it looked as if a much bigger score would have been run up against the County. The latter, however, bucked up somewhat after the third goal scored against them, and made a better defence; but just before the close a free kick from a foul was given against Derby, and from this Priest added a fourth goal for the winners. Thus the game ended in a triumph, far more easily gained than was anticipated, for Sheffield Wednesday by four goals to one.

As in the previous ties, Needham was the life and soul of his side. As usual he did not stick very closely to his own position, but he always seemed to be on the ball. He fed his forwards with great judgment, and found time to pay such attention to Bloomer that the famous crack was seldom able to get away. Morren and Johnson gave him splendid support; the backs, if not brilliant, were very steady, and tackled with determination; while Foulke, though severely tested, was only once beaten. The forwards were a long time in finding their game, but they made up for it when they did get going, and the way they swept down the ground in the second half is something to be remembered.

Derby gave a capital all-round display in the first half, and had undoubtedly the better of the game up to the interval. Fryer performed brilliantly in goal, meeting all attacks with fine coolness, and effecting some remarkable saves. The backs were a little slow, and of the half-backs Cox was by far the best. The forwards worked well, but their combination was spasmodic, and their kicks lacked accuracy. Whether Needham's attentions were the cause or not, it was certainly not Bloomer's day. He got going again and again, but he failed to avail himself of his chances, and once, at the opening of the second half, when he had the Sheffield goal at his mercy, he shot ridiculously wide.

Judging by the fact that 73,833 persons were checked to pass one or other of the turnstiles, it is safe to assume that the attendance was the largest ever seen at a football match, and the crowd was of such dimensions as to be almost awe-inspiring. The weather, after a dull and threatening morning, fortunately turned out fine, and with the exception that there were a few accidents to spectators—one poor fellow fell a distance of thirty feet from a tree, and apparently sustained concussion of the brain— everything passed off without a hitch.

Sheffield United with the Cup. Willie Foulke is centre, back row

Date 15 April 1899
Place The Crystal Palace
Score SHEFFIELD UNITED 4
DERBY COUNTY 1
Teams SHEFFIELD UNITED Foulke, Thickett, Boyle, Johnson, Morren, Needham, Bennett, Beers, Hedley, Almond, Priest. DERBY COUNTY Fryer, Methven, Staley, Cox, Paterson, May, Arkesden, Bloomer, Boag, McDonald, Allen
Official Referee A. Scragg (Crewe)
Goal Scorers SHEFFIELD UNITED Bennett, Beers, Almond, Priest. DERBY COUNTY Boag
Attendance 73833
Gate Receipts £2747
Guests of Honour The First Lord of the Treasury, A. J. Balfour, Lord Dalmeny
Copy *Sporting Sketches* 20 April 1899

ASSOCIATION FOOTBALL: THE FINAL CUP TIE AT THE CRYSTAL PALACE

SPORTING SKETCHES.

Football Association Cup: Final Tie.

(Illustrated with Instantaneous Photographs by the Standard Photo Co.)

FOR the first time since 1883 a Southern club this season reached the final stage of the above competition, but Southampton failed to outplay the survivors of the North—Bury—and were well beaten by 4 goals to nil, at the Crystal Palace on Saturday. Few finals have created more widespread interest than this year's, and many of the enormous crowd present on the ground were there in the hope of seeing the coveted Cup once more return to the South. These hopes were dashed to the ground, however, and, as the Mayor of Southampton said afterwards, his men were beaten by a superior side on the day's play. The terrible heat wave which has seemingly transported London from midwinter into a very fair imitation of the dog days, made even watching football a trial. A blazing hot sun poured down upon the greensward, and incidentally also upon the perspiring tens of thousands of excited partisans of the rival organisations who sat, stood, and sweltered long before the match was advertised to commence. An hour before the match there were fully 30,000 spectators present, and when the game started the attendance was quite up to that of the last few years—in fact, officials even declared greater than ever before.

Bury won the toss, and Southampton kicked off shortly before time. Southampton had the

A STOPPAGE OWING TO SLIGHT INJURY TO PRAY.

ROBINSON EFFECTS A SAVE.

disadvantage of the sun in their eyes, and in the first minute Wood tested Robinson, who punted away. In the first five minutes the combination was ragged, and the halves on both sides failed to feed their forwards. Robinson early on had to run out and fist away a lobbing centre from Richards. Turner, the Southampton outside right, was injured, and had to leave the field temporarily, but still there was little between the teams. Chadwick secured a great cheer for a fine long shot, which sailed a few feet wide of the bar. From the goal kick Wood got down and forced a corner for Bury, from which McLuckie scored the first goal after ten minutes' play. Bury, having established a lead, pressed hotly, tricky work by Sagar and Plant leading up to a regular bombardment of the Southampton goal, and Plant sent in a hot shot, which Robinson saved grandly, but could not clear, and Wood dashed up and scored a second goal just twenty minutes from the start.

This had a thoroughly demoralising effect on the Hampshire men, who were being outplayed. Ross gave McLuckie a magnificent pass a few minutes later. Taking the ball through beautifully, the Bury centre forward sent in a fast low shot which Robinson never even tried for, the ball beating him all the way. In the last few minutes before half-time Southampton improved a trifle, but there was a lifelessness about their methods, the team playing much under their usual form. The sun, which was blazing direct into

their faces, doubtless had a lot to do with it, but even allowing for this their play was feeble.

The second half was expected to be more in Southampton's favour, but the lead established by Bury seemed too big to wipe off. The opening stages certainly favoured them more, but they never seemed able to play the same sprightly football that Bury had done in the first half. Chadwick had several attempts with long shots, but the direction was almost invariably bad. Wood and Milward continued to peg away most pluckily, Milward making several attempts to score, but they were all futile. In saving a long shot from Pray, Robinson tipped the ball over the bar. Richards took the corner beautifully, and Plant, with a lightning shot, scored again for Bury. This was the climax of Southampton's misfortunes, and from that time forth the game fizzled out tamely, the final score being 4—0 in favour of the Northerners.

There can be no doubt at all that Bury deserved their victory, their work being better all round than that of the Sotonians, who seemed tired and stale. It was a great disappointment to the South and the Southern League's supporters, but Southampton never deserved to win, and another year must elapse at any rate before the South of England secures its ambition and "lifts the cup."

A BURY THROW IN.

Date 21 April 1900
Place The Crystal Palace
Score BURY 4 SOUTHAMPTON 0
Teams BURY Thompson, Darroch, Davidson, Pray, Leeming, Ross, Richards, Wood, McLuckie, Sagar, Plant. SOUTHAMPTON Robinson, Meehan, Durber, Meston, Chadwick, Petrie, Turner, Yates, Farrell, Wood, Milward
Official Referee A. Kingscott (Derby)
Goal Scorers McLuckie 9 and 23, Wood 16, Plant 80
Attendance 68945
Gate Receipts £2587
Guests of Honour Lord James of Hertford, Lord Rosebery, Lord Dalmeny
Copy Sporting Sketches 26 April 1900

THE DAILY GRAPHIC
ONE PENNY

LONDON : MONDAY, APRIL 22, 1901.

NO. 3536.—Vol. XLVI.

REGISTERED AS A NEWSPAPER.

THE WEATHER.

"FINE AND WARM GENERALLY."
(See page 3.)

Sun rises (at Greenwich), 4.53; sets 7.5.
Moon's age at noon, 3 days 14 hours.

THE ENGLISH CUP.

FINAL TIE AT THE PALACE.

A GOOD GAME AND A DRAW.

More than two army corps of the British public joined General Sir Redvers Buller at the Crystal Palace in watching a struggle that, for a day at least, obliterated the sterner interest of the fight which still harries South Africa. From Yorkshire, from the Midlands, from the great towns which make up the greater town of London, the army of footballers streamed along the lines of communication which led to Sydenham on Saturday, until 114,000 of them were gathered round the big green board of turf where Sheffield United and Tottenham Hotspur were to play their great Kriegspiel. Without exception, the days for final Cup ties at the Palace have been fine, but Saturday was the warmest and finest of them all, and this fact, added to the other that, for the first time in nearly twenty years, a London club's presence in the arena was giving ground for the hope that the Cup might come back South, made the numbers greater than have ever watched a final tie—or any football match—before. The nearest comparison to the numbers and the appearance of the crowd as it made its way through London would be the multitude that streams southwards on Derby day. No railway carriage that set out from Victoria or London Bridge or Holborn Viaduct held fewer than fifteen enthusiasts, and thousands of people—among them, no doubt, many who had suffered the tedious discomfort of the railways on previous occasions—went by the road. A long stream of brakes and 'buses, carriages, hansoms and coster-carts churned up the dust through Tulse Hill, Herne Hill and Dulwich; their progress making the resemblance to Derby day more marked than ever. Most of the brakes were gay with colours—blue

(Continued on page 3.)

FOULKES IS MARVELLOUSLY AGILE FOR HIS TWENTY STONE.

NEEDHAM FINDS TOM SMITH A GREAT HANDFUL

BROWN HEADS THROUGH AFTER A TUSSLE ROUND THE SHEFFIELD GOAL

GREAT SAVE BY CLAWLEY

TOTTENHAM'S SECOND GOAL

AN UNPOPULAR GOAL

LITTLE WILLIE'S LITTLE PUNCH WITH ALL HIS WEIGHT BEHIND IT

A DRAWN GAME: THE FINAL TIE FOR THE ASSOCIATION FOOTBALL CUP BETWEEN SHEFFIELD UNITED AND TOTTENHAM HOTSPUR AT THE CRYSTAL PALACE.

301

FOOTBALL ASSOCIATION CUP.

THE REPLAYED FINAL TIE.

TOTTENHAM HOTSPUR v. SHEFFIELD UNITED.

A KEEN AND EXCITING GAME.

UNITED RUN TO A STANDSTILL.

["SUNDAY TIMES" SPECIAL.]

When Bolton was selected for this replayed tie doubts were expressed as to the ground being large enough to accommodate the crowd. Whether it was the showery weather experienced in the morning, or that some important League matches in the Northern district kept spectators away, the fact remains that the attendance did not come up to expectations, barely 40,000 people being present. The teams took the field exactly as last week, when they played a draw of 2 goals each at the Crystal Palace. The Sheffielders had been staying at Lytham, while the 'Spurs spent the week at Southport, McNaught joining the party in case of emergency. The 'Spurs were reported fit and well, and felt confident of pulling through. The rest had worked wonders for United, and both Needham and Lipsham were reported to be fit, although the former's swollen toe joints were still troubling him. General Buller was unable to accept the invitation to present the cup to the winning team, and that pleasant duty fell to the lot of Lord Kinnaird, the president of the Association. Both teams met with hearty cheers on taking the field, but there was no mistaking the fact that the Northerners had the biggest following.

THE GAME.

Jones won the toss for the 'Spurs, and deputed Sheffield to kick off towards the railway goal. Immediately Copeland and Brown went through for Tottenham, but a fine clearance by Needham stopped a dangerous rush, and a concerted movement by Cameron and Brown was repulsed by Thickett. The 'Spurs were soon attacking again, off-side spoiling a fine pass out to Kirwan by Brown. The wind was slightly in favour of Tottenham, who had warned to their work much quicker than was the case at Sydenham last week. Copeland once had a capital chance at close quarters, but Johnson smartly knocked them off the ball. A free kick to the 'Spurs was nicely placed by Erentz, and a header by Copeland made a fine start, having all the better of the opening play. So far nothing had been seen of the Sheffield forwards. Needham at length gave Hedley an opening, but the latter's pass to Bennett went out of play. At the other end Smith passed across when close to goal, thereby losing a good chance of a score. Erentz cleverly stopped a break-away by Lipsham, and a further burst by the United was relieved by a free kick. Cameron next had the worse of a tussle with Foulke. A combined run by Priest, Hedley, Field, and Bennett forced a corner off Jones, after which Johnson sent a flying shot over the bar. A long drive by Kirwan was cleverly pushed out by Foulke, and following some midfield play the 'Spurs obtained two corners, both nicely placed by Smith, but nothing resulted therefrom. Sheffield gave one the impression that they had a little in reserve for the second half, when the wind would be more favourable to them. A determined attack by the United subsequently led to some excitement, Erentz upsetting Needham inside the twelve yards' line. A free kick was awarded, and Clawley gave a corner from Needham's kick. Thickett next ran right down, and shot into Clawley's hands. Three times did Needham, who was playing grandly, lead up to Sheffield attacks, and from the last of these Lipsham shot over. It was by no means Tottenham's game now, Sheffield improving greatly. A big effort by Hedley looked ominous, but the Sheffield centre wound up by sending wide, Smith doing likewise at the other end. Toward half-time Tottenham forwards became somewhat ragged, but Sheffield pressed heavily, Priest scoring five minutes before the interval, subsequent to some superb play by Needham. Tottenham then made a big effort, and twice tested Foulke, but at the interval the score still stood:—

| SHEFFIELD UNITED | .... | 1 |
| TOTTENHAM HOTSPUR | .... | 0 |

Sheffield pressed at the outset of the second half, but Jones promptly bowled over Field and let in Kirwan, who failed to keep the ball in play. Morren next transferred to Lipsham, and Tait stopped a dangerous rush just in time. Assiduous feeding kept the United forwards busy, while on one occasion, when Tottenham attacked, it was the ubiquitous Needham who cleared the Sheffield lines. Copeland once got clear of Thickett, who, however, managed to get in his kick, and after some exciting play Cameron equalised with a brilliant low shot. This was seven minutes after the resumption, and had the effect of making the exchanges more keen than ever. From a scrimmage in front of the Tottenham goal Clawley threw away in smart fashion. For once in a way Needham was beaten by Copeland, who gave Brown a pass, the latter shooting wide. For some time Sheffield were the more aggressive. In a collision, Needham was hurt, this causing a slight stoppage, after which a

downfall of rain made matters very uncomfortable for the reporters, who were without cover. Thickett once pulled up Brown close to goal, Clawley then stopping a shot from the Blades' left. Play became a trifle scrambling after the shower, but the Sheffielders had rather the better of matters. A corner off Tait was cleared, and then the 'Spurs rallied, and Smith gave them the lead with a low shot fourteen minutes from the close. This score led up to some more exciting play. The 'Spurs were showing great form and United were hard pressed. Following three corners, Brown scored again for them, and made the destination of the Cup a certainty, as time was shortly called with the final score:—

| TOTTENHAM HOTSPUR | .... | 3 |
| SHEFFIELD UNITED | .... | 1 |

THE TEAMS.

SHEFFIELD UNITED.

			Height.	Weight.	
			ft in	st lb	Born at
W. Foulke	..	goal	6 2½	.20 0	..Blackwell
H. Thickett	backs		5 8½	.14 7	..Doncaster
P. Boyle			5 9	.12 3	..Ireland
H. Johnson			5 9	.12 1	..Ecclesfield
T. Morren	half		5 6	.10 10	..Middlesbrough
E. Needham (capt.)	backs		5 6	.11 0	..Staveley
W. Bennett			5 7½	.13 0	..Mexborough
C. Field			5 6	.10 7	..Middlesex
G. A. Hedley	forwards		5 9½	.12 0	..South Bank
F. Priest			5 8	.12 12	..Darlington
B. Lipsham			5 9	.11 0	..Chester

TOTTENHAM HOTSPUR.

			Height.	Weight.	
			ft. in.	st lb	Born at
G. Clawley	..	goal	6 1	.12 7	..Scholar Gr..Ches.
H. Erentz	backs		5 11	.12 10	..Glenbuck (N.B.)
A. Tait			5 9½	.11 10	..Glenbuck (N.B.)
T. Morris	half-		5 9½	.11 0	..Grantham
E. Hughes	backs		5 8	.11 7	..Ruabon
J. L. Jones			5 10	.12 8	..Rhuddlan
T. Smith			5 7½	.11 4	..Maryport
J. Cameron			5 10	.11 6	..Ayr (N.B.)
A. Brown	forwards		5 10	.11 6	..Glenbuck (N.B.)
D. Copeland			5 7	.11 6	..Ayr (N.B.)
J. Kirwan			5 6½	.10 9	..Wicklow, Ireland

N.B.—Positions count from right to left.

● In 1901 Tottenham Hotspur became the first and only non-League club to win the FA Cup. As members of the Southern League, they had won that championship in 1900, and now they confirmed their quality against the best in the land.

The final at Crystal Palace, against Sheffield United, finished 2–2. Bennett's equaliser, a minute after Brown's second goal had put Spurs in front for the first time, was a disputed award by referee Kingscott because a linesman had indicated instead for a corner.

In the replay at Bolton, United had no reprieve even though they took the lead when Needham set up a goal for Priest five minutes before half-time. But once Cameron had equalised seven minutes into the second half Tottenham became the dominant force. With further goals from Smith and Brown, they ended the domination of the competition by the League clubs of the midlands and the north.

Date 20 April 1901
Place The Crystal Palace
Score TOTTENHAM HOTSPUR 2
SHEFFIELD UNITED 2
Teams TOTTENHAM HOTSPUR Clawley, Erentz, Tait, Morris, Hughes, James (capt.), Smith, Cameron, Brown, Copeland, Kirwan.
SHEFFIELD UNITED Foulke, Thickett, Boyle, Johnson, Morren, Needham (capt.), Bennett, Field, Hedley, Priest, Lipsham
Official Referee A. Kingscott (Derby)
Goal Scorers TOTTENHAM HOTSPUR Brown 23, 51; SHEFFIELD UNITED Priest 10, Bennett 52
Attendance 114815
Gate Receipts £3998
Guests of Honour General Sir Redvers Buller, Lord Kinnaird
Copy The Daily Graphic 22 April 1901

Replay
Date 27 April 1901
Place Burnden Park, Bolton
Score TOTTENHAM HOTSPUR 3
SHEFFIELD UNITED 1
Team Changes Both teams unchanged
Officials Unchanged
Goal Scorers TOTTENHAM HOTSPUR Cameron 52, Smith 76, Brown 87; SHEFFIELD UNITED Priest 40
Attendance 20470
Gate Receipts £1621
Guest of Honour Lord Kinnaird
Copy The Sunday Times 28 April 1901; Sporting Sketches 2 May 1901

[Photo by the Standard Photo Co.

Tottenham Hotspur v. Sheffield United at Burnden: Clawley effects a save.

THE CUP FINAL.

ARRANGEMENTS AT THE CRYSTAL PALACE.

Our London correspondent telegraphs that the arrangements made by the Crystal Palace authorities are much the same as those of last year. The polo park will again be utilised. The fence which usually encloses the ground has been removed, thus taking in the adjacent slopes for the accommodation of the crowd. In addition to the usual stands, a temporary erection has been built on the side next the cricket ground, to contain three long rows of seats. The Press seats are again in the open—two long lines on each side of the grand stand. Whilst a crowd of almost any size may witness the game from the slopes, seating accommodation has been provided for only 12,000 spectators, and all these seats have been secured already, so that the booking office will not be again opened. Dozens of extra turnstiles have been arranged, and the Palace people expect that practically instantaneous admission will be had, no matter how great the number. Visitors arriving at the Low Level Station will be admitted directly into the grounds, and thus saved the trouble of making their way through the main building. To prevent delay in checking, the railway companies will not this year issue tickets including admission. The entrance fee of one shilling must be paid at the turnstiles, and no change will be given, save at the change boxes. The shilling admission, of course, covers the match, as the removal of the enclosing fence has made the park part of the public grounds. It is almost unnecessary to say that everything has been done to secure the safety of the crowd and non-interference with play. The highest of the stands is not more than 7ft. above the ground. Barricades, whose props sink 3ft. into the ground, break the slopes, and, to further prevent any swaying forward on to the pitch, things have been so arranged that between the slopes and the playing ground there is sward of considerable extent, actually part of the level on which the match will be played, but separated from it by specially strengthened iron railings. Thus, in the event of a break in, the impetus will probably be expended on this grass, which, owing to its billiard table levelness, is unlikely to be occupied, and, in any case, the iron railings will prove an effective final barrier to any interference with play. Yesterday the ground was in excellent condition. A very great crowd is anticipated, and, should no rain fall, there must be witnessed one of the fastest finals for many years. The Post Office are granting special facilities to the Pressmen, a temporary office having been erected just outside the ground.

CONGRATULATIONS TO THE ENGLISH CUP WINNERS.

Congratulations have been showered upon the Sheffield team upon its fine victory, and shortly after the match a telegram was received from Lord Hawke to Ernest Needham, reading as follows:—" Heartiest congratulations to you all, Hawke."

Sir Howard Vincent, M.P., also sent a letter of congratulation, in which he says, writing from Grosvenor Square: " Dear Mr. Nicholson,—I was very sorry not to have had an opportunity at the Crystal Palace of personally congratulating you, Needham, Foulkes, and all our Sheffield eleven on the magnificent result of the final tie. To be in it three times in four years, to win it twice, and twice also to play an even game at the first trial, is, indeed, a record of which Sheffield United and all concerned in its management and interested in its welfare may, indeed, be proud. Lady Vincent and my daughter send their greetings to all, and especially to our giant goalkeeper, Foulkes, with his tremendous smite and prodigious kick, the best goalkeeper football has ever seen. May he live a thousand years. It was a splendid game to-day, and far less rough than last Saturday. The best team won by playing a real united game. I hope Bennett is not seriously hurt. I shall join in the welcome on Monday night which Sheffield will give to Needham, and the best football players in England, though not personally present. With best wishes, yours sincerely, C. E. Howard Vincent."

Date 19 April 1902
Place The Crystal Palace
Score SHEFFIELD UNITED 1
SOUTHAMPTON 1
Teams SHEFFIELD UNITED Foulke, Thickett, Boyle, Johnson, Wilkinson, Needham (capt.), Bennett, Common, Hedley, Priest, Lipsham.
SOUTHAMPTON Robinson, C. B. Fry, Molyneux, Meston, Bowman, Lee, A. Turner, Wood (capt.), Brown, Chadwick, J. Turner
Officials Referee T. Kirkham (Burslem). Linesmen J. Hawcroft (Bolton), A. Davis (Marlow)
Goal Scorers SHEFFIELD UNITED Common 55; SOUTHAMPTON Wood 88
Attendance 76914
Gate Receipts £2893
Guests of Honour Lord Kinnaird, Sir Thomas Lipton
Copy *Sporting Sketches* 17 April 1902; The *Sheffield Daily Telegraph* 18 April 1902

Replay
Date 26 April 1902
Place The Crystal Palace
Score SHEFFIELD UNITED 2
SOUTHAMPTON 1
Team Changes SHEFFIELD UNITED Barnes *for* Bennett.
SOUTHAMPTON Unchanged
Officials Unchanged
Goal Scorers SHEFFIELD UNITED Hedley 2, Barnes 79; SOUTHAMPTON Brown 70
Attendance 33068
Gate Receipts £1625
Guests of Honour Duc do Mandos (Spanish Ambassador), Sir Spencer Ponsonby Fane
Copy The *Sheffield Daily Telegraph* 28 April 1902

● Southampton, also of the Southern League, first eliminated Tottenham Hotspur, the holders, in the opening round of the 1902 tournament, and then set out to emulate their accomplishment.

As they had done two years earlier, Southampton again reached the final, but even though they took the powerful Sheffield United to two matches they again tasted defeat.

At right-back Southampton fielded C. B. Fry, a superb athlete who played cricket for England and also held the world record for the long jump. United included eight of the side that had beaten Derby County so convincingly three years earlier. One of the newcomers, Alf Common, who was later to be the first player transferred for a four-figure fee, gave United the lead in the first match at Crystal Palace; Robinson appeared to be distracted by Lipsham rushing in and the ball passed across the goalkeeper into the far corner. Southampton forced the replay two minutes from time. Wood looked offside when he put the ball past "Fatty Foulke", but the goal stood.

The replay took place a week later, again at Crystal Palace, and again Southampton showed tremendous resilience in their efforts to keep the Cup in the South and away from the grasp of the Football League. Sheffield United might have expected a less testing experience when they went in front after only two minutes with a goal from Hedley. In the second half, however, Brown equalised and this time there were no protests.

Eleven minutes from time, however, Sheffield United produced a killer goal. Barnes had replaced Billy Bennett, who had badly injured an ankle in the first game, and taking Common's pass he went on to score a goal from which Southampton could not recover.

After the hurly-burly of the first game, the replay produced a match of skill, with the football consistently of a high quality. This was little consolation for Southampton, who still had no prize to show for two seasons of defying the odds against the First Division.

WILKINSON. JOHNSON. THICKETT. FOULKE. BOYLE. HEDLEY.
BENNETT. COMMON. NEEDHAM. PRIEST. LIPSHAM.

SHEFFIELD UNITED.

[*Photo by J. Redfearn, Sheffield.*]

THE BURY GUARDIAN, SATURDAY, APRIL 25, 1903.

PRESS COMMENTS.

A few cuttings from the Press will serve to show the general opinion of the final tie:—

Never in the history of the final tie has the result been so one-sided as it was on Saturday at the Crystal Palace. Had both teams been at their best, there is no reason to doubt that the game would have proved a close one, but the Derby players, on their form of Saturday, had no chance whatever.—"Daily Telegraph."

Something like a debacle—that was the Cup final. As a Southampton director remarked after the game, "Our display was bad enough, but at least the four goals against us were good ones. This was more like opera Bouffe."—Morning Leader."

Briefly and candidly the Cup final was a fiasco. Nothing like it had ever been seen before. Bury defeated Derby County by six goals to none, and it might have been twenty. That it was not is testimony to the mercy exercised by the winners rather than to the defence of the losers, who have something to regret in the protraction of the season till players are stale and not sufficiently sound to do themselves full justice.—"Daily Chronicle."

Make every excuse you can possibly find, and you are bound to regard the final of 1903 as about the worst. All you can say is that Bury were decidedly the superior team, express your regret for unfortunate Derby, and wish them better luck another time.—Mr. J. J. Bentley.

Backers of Derby County knew after five minutes play that they were on the wrong horse. The best play for the losers was undoubtedly that of their captain, A. Goodall, who played a sound game for his side.—K. S. Ranjitsinhji.

Derby County never showed the slightest ability to either win the Cup or to hold their antagonists in check, although the Midlanders were sorely handicapped by being badly served in goal, for Fryer ought never to have played, owing to an accident on Easter Monday, from which he had not recovered.—"Athletic News."

I never saw Derby County play a poorer game than in this match, for they were weak all round and people wondered what they had come out to see and however they beat Millwall.—"Tityrus" in the "Athletic News."

No sane man who saw Saturday's match and who can remember the Preston North End team at its best would dream of instituting a comparison between the old and the new, simply because Bury have managed to establish a record score for the final. Had two amateur teams played such poor football as did the two presumably best clubs in the country on Saturday the ground would have been empty at half-time.—"Daily Mail."

How bitterly the Derby team disappointed its admirers can be best estimated at its headquarters. The side was below its form throughout, and though Fryer's breakdown obviously affected the score, it did not affect the result. The men seemed beaten by the pace of the ball, they adopted utterly wrong tactics forward, and the backs seemed to weaken under pressure.—"Sheffield Telegraph."

Without doubt it was the tamest and dullest final that has yet been played at the Crystal Palace—in fact, it would be impossible to recall a final that gave less satisfaction to the unbiassed spectator than that of last Saturday. True, plenty of goals were scored, but the work that led up to them, and the manner in which they were got was far from satisfactory from an enthusiast's point of view. In the first half the players on both sides showed a painful amount of anxiety—far more than is expected of seasoned players. The Derby forwards, however, were the biggest sinners in this respect. The anxiety of the Bury forwards was displayed in a far different manner. None of them appeared anxious to keep the ball any length of time, and very few indeed were the individual runs indulged in. However, by swinging the ball from one wing to the other they kept the Derby defenders always on the move; but at the same time their efforts at goal scoring were very poor indeed.—"Sheffield Independent."

Lord Kinnaird, on Friday night entertained at dinner the Council of the Football Association. He is best known nowadays (the "Westminster Gazette" remarks) in connection with his philanthropic work. He has, however, had a distinguished career as a footballer. Educated at Eton and Trinity College, Cambridge, he took a prominent part in the movement which resulted in the establishment of the Association game. He was then the Hon. A. F. Kinnaird, and in one of the Year-books of 1873 he was described as "without exception the best player of the day."

The Cup, like its predecessor, cost just £20. It was in 1888-9—the same reason that they won the League Championship without losing a

HOME-COMING OF THE BURY TEAM.

THE SCENE AT BOLTON ST STATION. WAITING FOR THE CONQUERORS

ARRIVAL OF THE CONQUERORS THE FIRST GRIP.

WORKING UNDER DIFFICULTIES

IN THE STREETS

MATT

(From the "Daily Dispatch.")

match—that Preston North End, the "team of all the talents," won the English Cup without having a goal scored against them throughout the competition.

Mr. McGregor, the Father of the League, is of opinion that the competition practically made the game what it has now become; that without it football would never have been a national game.

In that year (1872) the Football Association had a balance in hand of £1 13s. 6d., and were mightily pleased with the fact.

In the way of records, it is worth noting that Preston North End (1888-9) and Aston Villa (1896-7) are the only two clubs that have carried off the English Cup and the League championship in the same season.

Wanderers and Blackburn Rovers each won the trophy five times in all, and each secured it three times in succession.

Lord Kinnaird, the popular president of the Football Association, and J. Forrest, of the Blackburn Rovers, each possess five Cup final medals.

An excerpt from the first annual report of the Bury Club:—"The doing of our team and the enterprise of the committee in catering for the enjoyment of the public, besides popularly introducing the Association game into the town, have excited the wonder and the admiration of the neighbouring clubs. . . . We trust that no one will get into a panic when we tell you that we have an adverse balance of £8 0s. 1d."

A Bury Employer (to employee who has arrived late): Hullo, Jack, you are late this morning, how is it?

Employee: I had a dream, and overslept myself.

Employer: What has that to do with it?

Employee: Well, I dreamt I was at the Cup tie final. The game ended in a draw, and the referee ordered extra time. If it hadn't been for that extra time I should have been at work early.

● Bury's six-goal thrashing of Derby County still stands as a record margin of victory in an FA Cup final. Yet its one-sidedness was hailed at the time as a dull occasion. So out of touch were Derby that it was a surprise that Bury had to wait 20 minutes before George Ross, their captain, opened the scoring. Four goals in eleven minutes at the start of the second-half confirmed Bury's total superiority, and their final margin gave them a proud aggregate of ten–nil in their two FA Cup successes of 1900 and 1903. Of the Bury team only Hughie Monteith, the goalkeeper, was well known in the south of England; having been a popular player with West Ham United. The Bury party celebrated their triumph at a special dinner at the Trocadero restaurant, in Picadilly Circus.

Date 18 April 1903
Place The Crystal Palace
Score BURY 6 DERBY COUNTY 0
Teams BURY Monteith, Lindsey, McEwen, Johnstone, Thorpe, Ross (capt.), Richards, Wood, Sagar, Leeming, Plant. DERBY COUNTY Fryer, Methven, Morris, Warren, Goodall, May, Warrington, York, Boag, Richards, Davis
Team Colours BURY Blue; DERBY COUNTY Red
Officials Referee J. Adams (Birmingham). Linesmen F. Styles (Wellingborough and Northants FA); G. Wagstall Simmons (St Albans and Herts FA)
Goal Scorers Ross 20, Sagar 48, Leeming 56, 75, Wood 57, Plant 59
Attendance 63 102
Gate Receipts £2470
Guest of Honour Lord Kinnaird
Copy *The Bury Guardian* 25 April 1903

FOOTBALL.

NOTES ON SATURDAY'S GAMES.

The Cup Final.

IN MANCHESTER'S KEEPING.

The big match of the year is past and gone; those who make their annual trip to town for the occasion—Mr. Dick Birtwistle, the leading light of the Blackburn Rovers, has been in attendance at each final since 1882—are satisfied that they have done their duty; Manchester City are satisfied because they have accomplished their object; the railway companies are likewise on good terms with themselves; the Football Association were gratified at the attendance, which was much larger than was anticipated; the Crystal Palace ditto: indeed, it was a most successful day all round—save and except from a Bolton point of view.

THE ATTENDANCE.

Somehow the impression had got abroad that because there was no Southern club concerned, because both clubs came from one quarter, because one club was only a Second Leaguer, that the match would not be a success from a gate point of view; but if the figures registered at the turnstiles were less than since the second final at the Palace, an attendance of 61,374 is indeed most satisfactory, and the sharing of the spoils should afford some little consolation to the losers. The previous gates at the Palace have been:—1895, 42,560; 1896, 48,836; 1897, 65,891; 1898, 62,017; 1899, 73,833; 1900, 63,945; 1901, 110,020; 1902, 75,493; 1903, 63,100.

FORM BORNE OUT.

Many people were prepared for a surprise, but the saying "Class tells" was exemplified, for if the match was only won by the odd goal it was quite sufficient to cause the Cup to be handed over to Captain Meredith by the Colonial Secretary, himself an old international, as he jocularly reminded his hearers. There is no doubt that the City were rather the better side, and as both teams could not win it was only appropriate, as the natural fitness of things, that the result went as it did. The City players, if not at their best, all distinguished themselves.

WAS IT AN OFF-SIDE GOAL?

The validity of the only goal of the match, which was secured by William Meredith, has been seriously questioned by Boltonians, but expert judges avow that Meredith's position was a correct one when he received the ball from Livingstone and, after rounding Struthers, shot into the net. There is no doubt, however, that on several occasions the speedy Welshman was in an off-side position, but on the momentous occasion under notice it did not appear so, and what is to the point Mr. Barker, the referee, was of opinion not.

MEREDITH'S PERSONALITY.

It was indeed appropriate that City's captain should score the goal which brought the cup to Manchester. He is the oldest playing member of the club, its most brilliant exponent, and, without a doubt, the best outside-right in the kingdom. This is no mere gush because of the trend of events on Saturday, but an acknowledged fact throughout the land. On Saturday Freebairn was crossed over to hold him in hand, but he failed to do so, while Struthers, the left back, will remember the wily Willie for many a long day. The scoring of the goal was a case of one cunning Taffy outwitting another, though Davies could not at all be blamed for not securing the ball.

HIS ONLY CUP GOAL.

It is rather singular that the all-important goal was the only one which Meredith secured in the competition of the City's 12 goals. Turnbull has secured 5, Gillespie 3, Booth, Hynds, and Meredith one each, while Williamson, the Middlesbrough goal-keeper, helped the City to the remaining goal. Like the City, the

Wanderers had also secured eleven goals up to the final. Marsh, the crack shot, led the way with 5, Yenson 2, White 2, and Freebairn and Taylor one each.

A SECRETARIAL RECORD.

In connection with the match one unique record should be mentioned. On April 16 the Celtic Club, of which Mr. Willie Maley is secretary, won the Scottish Cup, and on April 23 his brother Tom's team carries off the English Cup. Again, Mr. Tom Maley, who did not reach the eminence of his brother—of playing against England—helped the Celtic to win the Scottish Cup in 1891-2. None of Saturday's contestants had had previous experience of the Final, but the Wanderers' secretary, Mr. John Somerville, played in the previous Final in which the Wanderers participated in 1894.

THE LEAGUE.

Bury should have wound up their games in the League tourney by a victory, but they didn't. They could not score a goal, but, on the other hand, neither could the "Wolves." Liverpool accomplished a capital result at Blackburn, which, however, will avail them nothing. The Rovers' position is none too creditable. In the Second Division Glossop's home defeat pinned them down in the last three, while on the other hand Blackpool, by a brilliant victory at Bradford, made themselves secure. Stockport County, like Glossop, failed to do themselves justice at home, though they did manage to secure one point from Burnley. Still they should have won to have had any chance of saving themselves. As with Glossop, they will now trust to the sympathy of the annual meeting. Manchester United, of course, defeated Burton United, and it must certainly be said of them that they are finishing the season in excellent fashion.

UP IN A BALLOON.

After Manchester City's Victory.

From Our London Correspondent.

It does not need much pluck to make a balloon ascent, but the man who calmly faces the banter of a huge Lancashire and London mob out for a holiday practically deserves the Victoria Cross. At least that is how I felt when seated in the car of the "Athletic News" balloon at the Crystal Palace on Saturday after waiting for the

close of the great game. Excited folk surged round our frail basket, grimy hands were thrust forth to secure mementoes in the shape of photographs of the teams, everyone yelled alleged witticisms and all about us was a tossing sea of eager faces. It was a nightmare to such a paragon of modesty as myself, and I was glad when the other multitude, that round the football field, began to rush towards the grand stand, for the moment to start had come. "All hands off," shouted the skipper, Mr. Percival Spencer, and instantly we lifted; the lieutenant, Mr. S. F. Cody, of kite fame, lightened our weight, and the burst of cheering from the crowd seemed to buoy us up. I bowed our acknowledgments and found that the car was right over the grand stand. People, who looked like ants, were jumping from the circle of seats and charging across the ground to where the English Cup was about to be presented, and as they ran they pointed to us, but all we could hear was one dull roar blended with the crash of musical instruments.

Date 23 April 1904
Place The Crystal Palace
Score MANCHESTER CITY 1
BOLTON WANDERERS 0
Teams MANCHESTER CITY Hillman, McMahon, Burgess, Frost, Hynds, Ashworth, Meredith, Livingstone, Gillespie, A. Turnbull, Booth.
BOLTON WANDERERS Davies, Brown, Struthers, Clifford, Greenhalgh, Freebairn, Stokes, Marsh, Yenson, White, Taylor
Official Referee A. J. Barker (Hanley)
Goal Scorer Meredith 23
Attendance 61374
Gate Receipts £3000
Guests of Honour Hon. Alfred Lyttelton (Colonial Minister), A. J. Balfour, Lord Stanley (Postmaster General)
Copy The Manchester Evening Chronicle 25 April 1904

Manchester City, winners of the English Cup, 1904

ASSOCIATION CHALLENGE CUP.

FINAL TIE.

NEWCASTLE UNITED v. ASTON VILLA.

THE VILLA'S FOURTH WIN.

The overnight forecast had been of a hopeful character, but few people could have been prepared for the gloriously fine weather that prevailed yesterday afternoon for the great match of the Association season—the final tie for the Association Cup between Aston Villa and Newcastle United. From an early hour the sun shone forth from an almost unclouded sky, and though the temperature was fairly high there was a delightful breeze that kept it pleasantly cool. Under these circumstances it was not at all surprising that a large crowd should have assembled. The early special trains from town were all well filled, and the crowd increased in numbers so quickly that by an hour before the time fixed for the start there must have been quite fifty thousand people on the ground. Apart from the fact that the day was fine, however, the result of the match was such an open question that there was bound to be an attendance above the average. So much has already been written about the performances of the teams that it is not necessary here to recapitulate their successes in the previous rounds. Suffice it to say that Newcastle United had never before reached the final stage, while the Villa were making their fifth appearance in the great match, they having won it on three out of the four other occasions. From a sentimental point of view the Villa were perhaps the more favoured, for their team was not only composed entirely of Englishmen, but the majority of them were local players. Newcastle, however, were regarded by sound judges as slightly the better eleven. There were six Scotsmen and five Englishmen—four of them forwards—in the side. The period of waiting before the match was relieved by the presence of the Crystal Palace Band, and this gave a section of the enthusiasts who wore the colours of both teams in the shape of black and white and claret and light blue top hats and caps and sunshades, in addition to large favours and impressive ties, to parade to the admiration of other enthusiasts. As the time drew on

THE CROWD BECAME ENORMOUS,

and must have approached very closely to 100,000. all the stands being packed. The Newcastle team played as selected, and Windmill occupied the left-hand position for Aston Villa. At twenty minutes past three the Newcastle team, in black and white-striped shirts and dark blue knickers, entered the field, and together with the officials of the club were photographed in front of the south goal. Two minutes later the Villa team came out in their claret and light blue jerseys and white knickers. They wore a black band on their left arm out of respect for the memory of the Lord Mayor of Birmingham, who died during the week. They were photographed under the north goal. There was a slight wind blowing obliquely across the ground from the south-east, and Newcastle, winning the toss, had it in their favour for the first half, while the Villa had to face the sun. The game opened in sensational style, for from the kick-off Brawn dashed down on the Villa right wing and centred. Hampton and Garratty both tried shots, but Carr cleared, and Gosnell got away, only to be pulled up by Spencer. The ball went across to the Villa left, and then two minutes after the start

THE VILLA SCORED.

Hall swung in a fine centre, and Bache tried a shot. The ball, however, only glanced off his foot, but Hampton was handy, and with a left-foot shot sent it wide of Lawrence into the corner of the net. Then Newcastle took up the pressure, and for some time the Villa were hard pressed. Spencer here put in a lot of fine work, but for the most part Newcastle controlled the game. Once, too, they came near scoring, Rutherford sending in a fine centre, which Spencer, in heading, sent straight up in front of goal. George, however, acted promptly, rushing out and fisting well away. Again shortly afterwards George fisted away a lovely centre by Gosnell, and then Gosnell headed over the line. From the goal kick Brawn, getting possession, tricked McWilliam and raced away down the line and centred. Hampton shot, but Lawrence just turned the ball behind. Nothing came of the corner kick, but a little later the Newcastle goal had a providential escape. Hall got in another centre, and Hampton had only Lawrence to beat. In trapping the ball, however, it bounced off straight to Lawrence, who cleared, Hampton falling in trying to reach it again. Then came another fine run by Brawn, who, after drawing the defence and making Lawrence run out, centred well. In some loose work Bache got in an overhead kick, but it was quite slow, and Lawrence, though dropping the ball, cleared easily. The Villa continued to force matters,

BRAWN BEING VERY PROMINENT;

but presently Newcastle were attacking again, and they missed a great chance of equalising. From near the centre Appleyard broke away and took the ball to the penalty line. Hampered by Spencer and Miles, he very cleverly passed to Howie, who was unmarked; but that player with a fine opening shot right over the bar. Again Brawn came away and put in a magnificent centre, but the danger was averted by the backs, and then Howie ran down, but Spencer cleared and Leake passed up to Garratty, who eventually sent in a fine dropping shot. Some clever work by Gosnell and McWilliam followed, the former nearly getting through, but again Villa broke away and Lawrence had to run out and clear, he and Bache being somewhat hurt in a fall. Try as they would, Newcastle could not get going properly, their passing near goal being faulty, while, with long sweeping passes, the Villa always looked dangerous. Again Brawn got away and, beating Carr, as usual, put in a lovely centre, Bache heading over. Just afterwards the Villa forced a corner, and the ball was sent up against the bar, dropping at Brawn's feet, close to the post. He kicked it against the post and Lawrence was enabled to clear. This was quite the luckiest escape that either goal had had. Newcastle came away, and Howie shot against the side of the net, while at the other end Bache just missed with a long shot. Some quiet mid-field play followed until Newcastle were awarded a free kick for a foul against Pearson. Nothing came of it, however, and Brawn got away again, but, for the first time, his centre was a bad one and went behind. It was close upon half-time now and the Villa nearly scored again, some pretty work by the left wing ending in Bache sending just wide of the net. Then the same player shot over, and the interval came soon afterwards, with the score standing:

Aston Villa	1
Newcastle United	0

The players were away about ten minutes. On the game being resumed play opened quietly, the first incident of note being a free kick against the Villa, but nothing came of it, however, and Hall getting away, the ball went over the Newcastle line. Villa, however, had the best of matters, and Bache, after tricking McCombie, shot just wide. Then Rutherford got away, and from the line shot straight at George, who cleared well. Then came another free kick against the Villa, but the ball went behind. A little later Gosnell broke away and centred. George with a crowd round him caught the ball, but fell. Still retaining it he got up again, but took more than the regulation number of steps with it, and a free-kick was given to Newcastle. Fortunately it was some little distance away from the goal and not directly in front, and after a rather anxious time of it the Villa cleared all right. The Villa then attacked, and Bache getting through put in a terrific shot which only just went wide of the post. Then Bache beat McCombie, but the ball went behind. There was another free kick to Newcastle, but after some neat passing and heading Gosnell took a long shot and sent the ball over. Shortly afterwards Gosnell beat Spencer and centred, but Miles cleared with a fine kick, and later on, after Aitken, Veitch, and Gosnell had taken the ball down,

LEAKE AVERTED DANGER CLEVERLY.

There was then a short stoppage owing to an injury to Leake, who had hurt his ankle. Again the Villa came away, and threatened danger on the right, but Brawn spoilt the movement by running off-side after he had previously made a nice pass. So far the play had not been so good as in the first half, the Villa men lacking for the time being that fine understanding that had characterised their movements in the first half, while the Newcastle players did not by any means come up to expectation. Once, however, Gosnell broke away and threatened danger. Spencer, although beaten in pace, stuck to his man and robbed Gosnell before he could centre. Then came an exciting incident, Brawn getting away and centring, McCombie mis-kicked, and Lawrence came out to catch the ball. Hampton, however, dashed up, and headed the ball, which just went over, Lawrence being charged over at the same time. He was hurt in the collision, and the game was stopped for a few moments. Then came a capital run by Aitken, who got through himself and made a fine opening for his forwards, but George cleared all right. The second half had now been in progress nearly half an hour, and immediately afterwards the Villa obtained their second point. There had been some pressure on the Newcastle left, and suddenly the ball was swung across to Hall, the Villa outside left. He ran in a little way, and then put in a magnificent shot with his left foot.

LAWRENCE SAVED IN GREAT STYLE,

but the ball went off his hands to Hampton, who with an open goal had no difficulty in scoring. This success, of course, placed the result beyond doubt, for the Newcastle men had not been playing in that form that suggested they would be able to pull the match out of the fire. Moreover, with the breeze and sun still behind them the Villa were not likely to throw away their advantage. They kept up the pressure well, and the Newcastle forwards could not break through the sound defence opposed to them. Lawrence had to handle once more, and after this the falling off in the pace of the play was very noticeable. Near the close Gosnell raced away and caused George to punch out, and then the Villa attacked again, Bache shooting wide. As the end was approached, the Villa defence controlled the game more and more.

No further goals were scored, however, and thus the Villa gained a great victory. The final score was:

Aston Villa	2
Newcastle United	0

At the conclusion of the game the Cup and medals were presented by Mrs. Kenneth Kinnaird. Lord Kinnaird, the president of the Football Association, after welcoming Newcastle United in their first appearance in a final tie, congratulated Aston Villa upon continuing their victorious progress in the Cup and upon their fourth triumph in carrying off the trophy, specially mentioning Howard Spencer, who had participated in the Villa's success eight years ago.

NOTES OF THE DAY.

THE CUP FINAL.

By A "SUNDAY SPECIALIST."

There are many ways of getting to the Crystal Palace, such as travelling sardine-like in a railway carriage, doing the luxurious in a hansom with a friend who sleeps all the way, forming one of a party to charter a coach and four with very mixed horses, leaders like Clydesdales and wheelers of the has-been division, knowing a man who is a fully-licensed chauffeur, or cycling as far as the turnpike on College-road and then pushing your machine to the top of the hill to save your heart. But on such a glorious afternoon as yesterday there was only one possible way of reaching Sydenham in anything like comfort, and that was by walking. From Camberwell-green the distance is well under four miles, and four more interesting miles could hardly be imagined. Load after load of humanity passed on coach, trap, 'bus, cycles, and motor, and, with but an occasional pause for lubricating or paying the toll, formed an endless panorama of all sorts and conditions with their favourites' colours in evidence in their button-holes, on their hats, and in several cases on the harness of the horses. Toy trumpets and rattles were the chosen instruments on which they vented their feelings, and the man who sold picture-postcards of the teams did a roaring business. Good humour abounded, and not a face in any conveyance looked anything but happy, with the solitary exception of the young man who had had rather a trying time at "nap."

While sightseers have this large selection, there is but one way to the final tie for a football team. It is hard work for four matches with a chance of replays, and when the sides form up at the Crystal Palace the spectator may rest assured that, whatever kind of game he witnesses, he is looking at two elevens that have done things. Of yesterday's combatants Aston Villa had had a fine run of luck in the choice of grounds in the earlier rounds, being drawn at home each time, but they had the harder nut to crack in the semi-final. Their recent form in the League had been rather disappointing, while the Novocastrians had won their games in most decisive fashion, and as a consequence the men from the North took the field with the odds slightly in their favour.

Date 15 April 1905
Place The Crystal Palace
Score ASTON VILLA 2
NEWCASTLE UNITED 0
Teams ASTON VILLA George, Spencer, Miles, Pearson, Leake, Windmill, Brown, Garratty, Hampton, Bache, Hall. NEWCASTLE UNITED Lawrence, McCombie, Carr, Gardner, Aitken, McWilliam, Rutherford, Howie, Appleyard, Veitch, Gosnell
Official Referee P. R. Harrower
Goal Scorer Hampton 2 and 76
Attendance 101 117
Gate Receipts £7785
Guests of Honour Mrs Kenneth Kinnaird, Lord Kinnaird, Sir Walter Plummer M.P.
Copy *Sunday Times* 16 April 1905; *The Aston and East Birmingham News* 22 April 1905

The invasion of London for "t' Coop Tie" is always a sight, an event, an experience. It is a wonder to those on the south side to see how the trains go steaming past with heavy loads the whole morning through till two o'clock in the direction of the Palace; it is a diversion to the Southerner to hear the Northman's dialect, and see his little ways; it is a thing to remember, having made one in the great crowd of 100,000 who saw the match; it was more novel still to walk through some familiar field, under the stars, in a Kent suburb and hear a roar come up from all sides like the tide retreating with a grind of pebbles down the Brighton beach. The songs of journeying brake-loads rose both east and west

END OF THE FOOTBALL FINAL.

in the lighted town, and behind a tree-tipped hill which was an outpost of the remoter country-side. Few people could have been prepared for the gloriously fine weather that prevailed for the great match of the Association season—the final tie for the Association Cup between Aston Villa and Newcastle United.

THE LIVERPOOL FOOTBALL ECHO, SATURDAY, APRIL 21, 1906.

ENGLISH CUP FINAL.

EVERTON v. NEWCASTLE UNITED.

CRYSTAL PALACE BESIEGED.

. AN IMMENSE CROWD OF SPECTATORS.

SANDY YOUNG SCORES THE WINNING GOAL.

CUP COMES TO LIVERPOOL AT LAST.

[From Our Own Reporters by Special Wire from the Crystal Palace.]

Date 21 April 1906
Place The Crystal Palace
Score EVERTON 1 NEWCASTLE UNITED 0
Teams EVERTON Scott, Crelley, Balmer (W), Makepeace, Taylor, Abbott, Sharp, Bolton, Young, Settle, H. P. Hardman. NEWCASTLE UNITED Lawrence, McCombie, Carr, Gardner, Aitken, McWilliam, Rutherford, Howie, Orr, Veitch, Gosnell
Official Referee F. Kirkham (Preston)
Goal Scorer Young 75
Attendance 75 609
Gate Receipts £6625
Guest of Honour Lord Kinnaird
Copy *The Liverpool Football Echo* 21 April 1906

"ECHO" CLOCK.

TIMED AND REGULATED.

BY JAY CEE.

3.29.—Veitch starts palpitation of the heart all round. One hundred and one kodaks fixed simultaneously, and the cinematograph man grinds away the film, which is almost as important as the match nowadays.

Off we go.

3.30.—Brave efforts on the part of both even that early.

3.31.—First danger comes from the Blues. Balmer lobs the ball in from a free kick, and the Newcastle goal is almost captured. Young's "header," however, is put over the bar by Lawrance. Corner proved useless.

3.32.—Everton giving the Geordies beans hereabouts.

3.33.—The much-vaunted Newcastle halves absolutely in Queer-street, but M'Combie and Carr defend like fury.

3.34.—The players show some heat already, and Mr. Kirkham called them together, and said a few words.

3.35.—Pressure all over the other people. Bolton shoots. His idea is good; his execution rotten.

3.36.—Play quieter, but still in favour of the Blues. United seem very much untried just now.

3.37.—Ditto.

3.38.—Everton forwards having a field-day, but they seldom shoot—the importance of the occasion too great, I suppose.

3.39.—Newcastle can't get out of their own half, and Lawrance is on tenter-hooks.

3.40.—Sandy Young gets in a lovely header, and it was worth a goal, but did not come off.

3.41.—Young is giving great satisfaction.

3.42.—John Rutherford at last changes the venue, and Newcastle get a corner.

3.43.—Poor play in midfield.

3.44.—The same.

3.45.—Worse.

3.46.—Sharp and Bolton scintillate and fairly walk round M'William.

3.47.—Jimmy Settle has half a chance, but fails to improve it. It was only half a chance, anyhow.

3.48.—Everton seem to be able to do anything but score. What a pity! Not half!

3.49.—Another minute without incident.

3.50.—At last Newcastle show the stuff they are made of. It was bound to come.

3.51.—Orr sails through and flashes a hurricane shot just past the post. Scott tiptoes to save and gets rid of impending trouble.

3.53.—Thousands of eyes are on him as he rubs his hands in dirt. Thousands of eyes are on him as he wipes them on his shirt.

3.54.—Newcastle bucking up wonderfully well, and Everton now seriously on the defence.

3.55.—High faluting play votoed by honest Jock.

3.56.—Everton redivides.

3.57.—Goals are mighty scarce.

3.58.—Exertions and alarms.

3.59.—Nothing between them just now.

4.0.—Crowd wants a goal badly, and fairly howled at every miss.

4.1.—Howie has a chance, but shoots too soon, and Balmer clears with plenty of room.

4.2.—Everton not nearly so cocky, but still on the job.

4.3.—Wonderful shot from Rutherford, but still more wonderful save b Scott.

4.4.—United busy as bees now, but the Everton defence holds them up.

4.5.—Pressure by the Blues hot and strong.

4.6.—More pressure.

4.7.—And still more.

4.8.—Yet no goal. Buck up Sandy.

4.9.—Newcastle press again, but no good. Balmer and Crelly on their best behaviour, likewise Scott.

4.10.—Mutual work in midfield.

4.11.—Ditto.

4.12.—Referee Kirkham a great success.

4.13.—Nil.

4.14.—Half-time, no score.

4.25.—Off again.

4.26.—Everton first away; John Sharp send bobby-dazzler over the bar.

4.27.—Corner to the Blues.

4.28.—Everton giving other people socks.

4.30.—Everton still top dog, and visions of the precious baubie loomed in my eye.

4.31.—Brave work by Newcastle spoilt by Everton halves.

4.32.—Makepeace glorious.

4.33.—Lawrence runs out 20 yards to save. Which he does—and well.

4.34.—Linesman Whittaker stops the game and examines the ball. He thinks it has gone soft, but it is all right.

4.35.—Everton press like demons.

4.36.—Young scores, but Kirkham declares him offside. Great snake! No matter. Only withers are unwrung.

4.37.—Takes the whole of this minute to recover from the shock.

4.38.—And the next.

4.39.—Only one team in it just now. The other team is Newcastle.

4.40.—Typical Cup-tie play. Either side attempting to settle down to their usual methods.

4.41.—Things quiet hereabouts, even the crowd.

4.42.—Nothing to enthuse over from either lot.

4.43.—Finest bit of play in the match from the Georgies' whole line participates and foot it right up to Scott, who saves grandly from Rutherford.

4.44.—Everton at it again, but Young offside.

4.45.—But Jack is as good as his master all the time.

4.47.—Further visions.

4.48.—Exciting attack on Scott's charge.

4.49.—Frantic efforts by Newcastle to settle the issue. They do not want to be bothered going to Sheffield.

4.50.—Promising play by the Blues right in front of Lawrence.

4.51.—Settle nearly does the trick, hooks the ball into the corner, but Lawrence just reaches it.

4.52.—Everton fairly racing round M'Combie and Coy.

4.53.—Nothing eventual.

4.54.—Newcastle still being pressed.

4.55.—At last a goal. Sandy Young a hero. Fireworks and minature earthquakes in galore—shades of San Francisco.

4.56.—The big glasshouse still shakes at its foundations.

4.57.—Everton still keeping up in good style.

4.59.—Newcastle somewhat disjointed.

5 o'clock—Game looks as good as finished, but Everton must be wary of a final rush.

5.6.—Everton declared winners.

5.11.—The Cup is ours. Hurro.'

SANDY YOUNG.

Young, the centre forward, is a variabe sort, who plays one good game in three matches on an average. He takes the bumps a centre forward must inevitably expect smilingly, and determination makes up for lack of skill at times.

● "The third time counts for all", the contemporary equivalent of third time lucky, was the most common phrase which greeted Everton's first FA Cup success after losing the finals of 1893 and 1897. Jack Sharp, a fine cricketer, set up the only goal for Sandy Young 15 minutes from time. The cuttings on the left imply that Young had been rewarded for his industry rather than skill, and the minute-by-minute match report, with its strange entries like "Referee Kirkham a great success", relates the goal to the famous San Francisco earthquake which had taken place in the week leading up to the final.

Cup final crowds outside St Pauls before the match

SHEFFIELD DAILY TELEGRAPH, SATURDAY, APRIL 20, 1907.

WEDNESDAY'S JOURNEY TO TOWN.

Although the time at which the Sheffield Wednesday players and party would commence their journey to town had not been made known to the public, there was an enthusiastic handful of people on the Midland Station yesterday afternoon when the 1.41 p.m. train departed. Those people happened to be in the vicinity of the station, or were passengers by other trains, but they were hearty in their wishes, and sent the party off to the accompaniment of a loud cheer. The players looked wonderfully fit, particularly Brittleton and Bartlett, the invalids, who had had to be nursed back to health in all too short a time. They have recovered quickly, and the former expressed himself fit and ready to go through to-day's hard game.

The saloon contained a large party, consisting of directors, friends, and players. Amongst the former were:—Alderman T. Nixon, J.P., Councillor W. F. Wardley, J.P., Councillor A. G. W. Dronfield, Messrs. H. Nixon, G. H. Lee, J. Cowley, W. Tasker, H. Newbould, C. Ellis, W. Fearnehough, and A. Mastin, together with Mr. A. J. Dickinson, the hon. secretary, and Dr. and Mrs. Bishop, of Buxton, whilst the players who went, and from whom the team will be selected were:—Lyall, goal; Layton and Burton, backs; Brittleton, Crawshaw, and Bartlett, half-backs; Maxwell, Chapman, Bradshaw, Wilson, Stewart, Simpson, and Lloyd, forwards. Messrs. T. Frith and Davis, the trainers, were also there.

The team arrived at St. Pancras shortly after 5 o'clock. Slavin followed by a later train. All the players are reported to be in the best of condition.

EVERTON'S REPORTED CRIPPLE.

A Liverpool correspondent understands on good authority that the report of the breakdown of one of Everton's players is not correct. It is reported that the only doubtful player is Abbott, who has not broken down, but has been suffering from a bad back, which is perhaps not so serious as to keep him out of the team. A decision will not be definitely made until shortly before the match, but if Abbott does not play Chadwick will appear at left half. In addition, Scott and William Balmer are reported to be suffering from colds, but both are certain to play. It has been rumoured that Settle and Makepeace were the doubtful ones, but both are very fit, and really the only doubt is with regard to Abbott. Chadwick is a capital half, and should he play the side will not suffer. News from Chingford states the players are confident, and, with the exceptions named, all are very fit. Thousands of people left Liverpool last night for London, and the exodus will, it is believed, be a record one. The local feeling is that if Taylor can circumvent Wilson, Everton will prove successful.

THE TRIPPERS AND THE TRAINS.

HOW SHEFFIELDERS WENT TO LONDON.

The smart young men employed on the London half-penny papers have a habit of describing the Yorkshireman as an uncouth individual with whiskers vicariously distributed, an ill-fitting cloth cap, with ear-flaps, and a suit of clothes of forked-lightning pattern. The ingenious gentlemen of the London ha'pennies will have to stretch a very fertile imagination if they would represent the Sheffielders who actually left Sheffield early this morning for London, as in any way exceptional from the ordinary traveller.

Theoretically, the Sheffielder en route for a Final at the Palace bears a white man's burden in the shape of a gallon jar of beer. Nobody, either at the Midland or the Great Central, saw anybody whose idea it was to overawe London by landing with such ammunition.

There were, of course, scenes of a sort at both stations, and outside both stations, also. Vendors of blue and white rosettes were as numerous as bees in a field of butter-cups, and no self-respecting excursionist left Sheffield until he had adorned himself with the badge of partisanship.

Up to 2.30 a.m. six trains had left the Great Central Station, all of which had been fairly well filled. Most of them, however, were stopping trains, with compartments or saloons reserved for other stations, and they would therefore pick up a great many more passengers before arriving at Marylebone or King's Cross.

The Midland early morning trains were more crowded, and enthusiasm, if it be represented by club colours, and expressed in noise, was more evident at the Midland Station. But the noise of enthusiasm never approached rowdyism, and the crowded trains destined for St. Pancras went away amid nothing worse than loudly-voiced inquiries, "Are we downhearted?"

LEAGUE MANAGEMENT COMMITTEE.

CUP FINAL REFEREE FINED.

(By Our Own Reporter.)

The Management Committee of the Football League met yesterday in London. Mr. J. J. Bentley was in the chair, and there was a full attendance.

SOUTHERN LEAGUE SECRETARY FINED.

Mr. Nat Whittaker, who is the referee appointed to officiate in the Final-tie to-morrow, was fined one guinea for being twelve minutes late at Leicester on March 30th. He wrote explaining that he was in the right train, but forgot to change at the right place.

Gainsborough Trinity were reported for playing with a man short at Clapton on April 1st, and were fined a guinea for the offence.

Burnley were similarly fined for playing the first fifteen minutes with a man short against Clapton Orient at Burnley on March 30th.

J. Carthy, on the Blackpool transfer list at £20, had the amount reduced to £5.

Graham, on the Bradford City list at £200, applied for a free transfer. The Committee fixed the amount at £25.

M Donagher, of Barnsley, applied for a free transfer, but the Committee refused to take any action.

The West Bromwich Albion v. Barnsley match, which was abandoned on January 19th through Barnsley arriving 30 minutes late owing to fog, was fixed to take place on April 25th.

The date of the annual meeting of the Football League was fixed for May 31st.

ENGLISH F.A. COUNCIL.

PROFESSIONALS AND THE WORKMEN'S COMPENSATION ACT.

The Football Association had consulted Mr. Charles A. Russell, K.C., as to how the compensation Act affects football clubs and players, and Mr. Russell's opinion is that a professional employed, whether by agreement in writing or by word of mouth, is a workman within the meaning of the Act, and in case of accident the club would be liable for compensation to him or his dependents. Mr. Russell thinks that arrangements should be made with an insurance company for a reasonable premium, so that clubs could insure their players.

● A last-minute goal by their 5ft 6in left winger Simpson brought Sheffield Wednesday the Cup, and revenge over the holders who had eliminated them in a classic third round tie in 1906. Stewart, an England international who later played for Newcastle in the 1911 final, gave Wednesday a first half lead. Jack Sharp equalised before half-time. Nat Whittaker, the referee, took charge of the game under something of a cloud (left) having been fined the previous day for holding up a league match that March.

Date 20 April 1907
Place The Crystal Palace
Score SHEFFIELD WEDNESDAY 2 EVERTON 1
Teams SHEFFIELD WEDNESDAY Lyall, Layton, Burton, Brittleton, Crawshaw, Bartlett, Chapman, Bradshaw, Wilson, Stewart, Simpson. EVERTON Scott, W. Balmer, R. Balmer, Makepeace, Taylor, Abbott, Sharp, Bolton, Young, Settle, H. P. Hardman
Official Referee N. Whittaker
Goal Scorers SHEFFIELD WEDNESDAY Stewart 21, Simpson 89. EVERTON Sharp 38
Attendance 84594
Gate Receipts £7053
Guest of Honour Lord Alverstone
Copy The *Sheffield Daily Telegraph* 20 April 1907

SHEFFIELD WEDNESDAY LIFTS THE CUP FROM THE HOLDERS, EVERTON, AT THE CRYSTAL PALACE.

THE FINAL CUP TIE AT THE PALACE—EVERTON VERSUS SHEFFIELD WEDNESDAY: DEFENSIVE BACK PLAY BY EVERTON.

Favoured by splendid weather the final tie for the Association Cup was played at the Crystal Palace on April 20. The crowd was, as usual, tremendous, and 84,000 spectators passed the gates. After a splendid game Sheffield Wednesday defeated Everton by two goals to one. The Teams are top row : SHEFFIELD WEDNESDAY 1 Chapman, 2 Layton, 3 Brittleton, 4 Burton, 5 Crawshaw Captain, 6 Lyall, 7 Bartlett, 8 Wilson, 9 Stewart, 10 Simpson, 11 Bradshaw. Bottom row : EVERTON 1 Makepeace, 2 W. Balmer, 3 Taylor Captain, 4 Scott, 5 Abbott, 6 Sharp, 7 Young, 8 Settle, 9 Hardman, 10 R. Balmer, 11 Bolton.

THE DAILY MIRROR.—APRIL 27. 1908.

WOLVERHAMPTON WANDERERS WIN THE ENGLISH CUP.

Wooldridge, captain of the Wolverhampton Wanderers, carrying the much-coveted Cup just after receiving it from Sir John Bell, the Lord Mayor.

The Lord Mayor of London, Sir John Bell (marked with a cross), presenting the English Cup to Wooldridge, the captain of the victorious Wolverhampton team.

Some of the spectators at Saturday's great match, who climbed into the leafless trees at the Crystal Palace to see the game.

A crowd estimated at between sixty and seventy thousand spectators visited the Crystal Palace on Saturday to witness Wolverhampton and Newcastle contest the Cup final. Above is a portion of the vast crowd watching play in front of Newcastle's goal. Wolverhampton won by 3 goals to 1.

An enthusiastic supporter of the Newcastle team, whose clothes, hat, stick, and even pipe bore the colours of the players he admires.

The actual scoring of the only goal gained by Newcastle. Lunn, the Wolverhampton goalkeeper, makes a gallant effort, but fails to stop the ball, which glanced into the net off one of the posts.

Lunn, the Wolverhampton goalkeeper, repels one of the fierce attacks made by the Newcastle forwards to reduce their two goals deficit.

● Newcastle United's formidable reputation foundered again on the Crystal Palace ground that proved such a hoodoo to them. An indication of the expectation of a Newcastle win is in the cutting above from *The Daily Mirror* who placed their photographer behind the goal that Wolverhampton were defending, and he captured Howie's goal in the second half. By then though Wolves were well on the way to winning the trophy for the second time after two goals in three minutes.

Date 25 April 1908
Place The Crystal Palace
Score WOLVERHAMPTON WANDERERS 3 NEWCASTLE UNITED 1
Teams WOLVERHAMPTON WANDERERS Lunn, Jones, Collins, Rev. K. R. G. Hunt, Wooldridge, Bishop, Harrison, Shelton, Hedley, Radford, Pedley. NEWCASTLE UNITED Lawrence, McCracken, Pudan, Gardner, Veitch, McWilliam, Rutherford, Howie, Appleyard, Speedie, Wilson
Official Referee T. P. Campbell
Goal Scorers WOLVERHAMPTON WANDERERS Hunt 40, Hedley 43, Harrison 85; NEWCASTLE UNITED Howie 73
Attendance 74697
Gate Receipts £5988
Guest of Honour Sir John Bell
Copy *The Daily Mirror* 27 April 1908

SCENES AND INCIDENTS OF SATURDAY'S GAME.

THE LOSS OF RIPPON AND MARR.

(BY "CENTRE FORWARD.")

It was a very orderly crowd that assembled at the Crystal Palace on Saturday last to witness the match of the season. The presence of many thousands of excursionists scarcely disturbed the pulse of the vast city of London. There was a little quicker business at the restaurants, the motor, horse, and electric 'buses were occasionally besieged with parties of football enthusiasts wearing their team's colours and strange hats, and all the trains to the Palace were busy; but the London business houses settled down without flurry, and the day passed off without untoward incident.

From which it will be gathered that London was pleased with the invasion and hoped for many more. Outside Paddington banners of welcome to Bristol City were flying, and Bristolians living in London paraded the fact to catch custom, while along the principal thoroughfares one could see the visitor filling up picture postcards to send home, or flocking across the roads in "droves" indicating the family or business party out for the day.

The party system of travel was in full force. Saloons were popular and conducted tours in demand, while the pleasant weather was all in favour of an enjoyable day's holiday irrespective of the match. And it is a fact that many of the excursionists did not see the game at all, but went about visiting.

The arrangements to convey the spectators to the Palace were excellent. The various companies had set about their task with resolution, and everything passed off well.

In the Palace itself the visitors amused themselves before the match at the side shows, while on the ground thousands upon thousands were quietly settling into their places, the band in the meantime playing selections. Very many of the crowd walked over the playing space, but to all intents and purposes it was a holiday crowd, content with their surroundings and the weather, and waiting for the game with open minds.

It was a happy augury for the future of football, and when Lord Charles Beresford made his appearance there was a roar of welcome which contained a note of joyousness.

The band continued playing, and when the group of boys in red assembled to wait round the touch lines and goal posts to prevent undue waste of time when the ball went out there was a furtive glancing at watches, and the cinematograph men stationed all round the touch line made their final preparations.

A few minutes before the time for kick-off Wedlock made his appearance, and there was a roar of welcome. Then Roberts led out the men of Manchester, and there was more cheering. The preliminaries were being fined down to nothingness, and the actual battle was awaited with anxiety and excitement.

The referee followed, and the rival captains were called together. They shook hands, and the spin of the coin was in favour of Roberts, though Wedlock was a little in doubt whether head or tail was uppermost.

Then the struggle commenced, and I must say at once that it was a hard vigorous game in which every man was a trier to the finish, and was fully determined on scoring methods, even though science went to the wind. That is exactly how the much vaunted superiority of Manchester United represented a goal to nil, and should have been whittled down to a draw.

Every man was thoroughly trained and determined, and the game was a strenuous one from start to finish.

To begin with, the City had a fierce breeze against them, and that meant that Manchester might adopt a wearing process with comparative ease. But there was no wavering of the City lines. The men plodded on; thrust back only to advance again. Clay, Annan, and Cottle, cool and determined, and the City wingers always ready for chances.

The great skill of the Manchester forwards, which on paper placed them far ahead of the City, went for little. They did not play as though they wanted to win in the first ten minutes. They were thrust back with ease, and even slips by the Bristol defence were comparatively safe.

The absence of Rippon and Marr was keenly felt in some of the movements, but the struggle was a typical one, with Manchester showing nothing of the brilliance which won for them the championship, and the City struggling gamely, but without parade, to get the lead.

It was here that Hilton began to show his paces, and some of his centres were really dangerous, one which was diverted to Hardy being propelled at a terrific rate towards the corner of the net. It was a magnificent and opportune shot by the little City man, but Moger's great height stood him in stead, and he effected a fine save.

Wall, in the meantime, had broken loose, and with a terrific cross shot had shaken up Clay, but these were the only really dangerous efforts apart from the actual goal, which had a great element of luck. The ball struck the bar and dropped to the feet of A. Turnbull, who had the leather all to himself and made the best use of it.

To say that it was a great goal is ridiculous. It was a soft goal for A. Turnbull, and Hilton might just as readily have put on the equaliser when similarly placed, but he shot outside, and Manchester's lead remained.

There were many chances missed by Manchester, and for a long time the City held the upper hand, but there was lacking just that element of dash which Rippon and Marr might have supplied, and sa Stacey, Hayes, and Moger remained unbeaten.

The second half was in favour of the City. The close and strenuous game continued, the City adapting their tactics to the varying phases. When it was found J. Turnbull and Meredith could not be stopped by "dandy tactics" heavy shoulder charging was indulged in, and there were cries from the spectators as though the two redoubtable internationals were of delicate china, and liable to be broken.

Unfortunately the referee confused shoulder charging with illegal tactics, and sometimes penalised accordingly, while the Northerners cheered Roberts for robbing the City forwards when he did not know the ball was coming his way. Presumably that is how reputations are made. Roberts did as badly as any of his colleagues. He kicked high over the bar in ridiculous fashion when he ought to have scored, and had to be supported by the backs in many a tussle in which Gilligan, Burton, and Hardy had mastered him.

Meredith played indifferently in the first half, and did better in the second, but was never in his best form, while Wall had one or two good tries and finished, while A. Turnbull was the best attacking unit, and he was considered unfit a few days ago!

I must say that Stacey, Hayes, and Moger played the best kind of football for the purpose they had in view, though they, too, made mistakes, one of which threatened the undoing of all their striving.

On the Bristol side the successes were with Burton, Hardy, Wedlock, Annan, and Cottle. Hardy was a fine little forward, a clever opportunist, and a terror to the halves. Burton was quick and clever, while Wedlock did not play his best game, but quite good enough to hold two out of the three outside men.

The third one (A. Turnbull) scored the goal. Gilligan and Burton had grand tries to equalise, and with a little luck might have done it, Burton being hacked down in unsportsmanlike fashion, and Gilligan being just beaten in the race for goal by inches only.

As the game approached the finish Manchester behaved like peevish schoolboys, and some of them had to be cautioned by the referee. They showed bad temper and kicked into touch to waste time. All this may be due to nerves, but it also showed that they feared the City would equalise, even at the last moment.

The game ended with a despairing rush by the City, and Manchester United hailed as winners of the Cup for the first time in their history.

"All's well, that ends well" may be the Manchester motto, and while it is clear that the City should have equalised, I firmly believe they would have lost the replay. The Manchester forwards were better as a line, and on that account deserved victory, but with the successfhl cup-tie quintette of the City, a different tale might have been told, At any rate the City live to fight another day.

MEREDITH'S TOOTHPICK.

FINAL INCIDENTS.

Perhaps the most discussed of the twenty-two players was Meredith, the Welsh international, who plays outside right for Manchester United. He is said to be the only footballer who plays with a toothpick in his mouth.

It has been hinted that he goes to bed with it. At any rate, it never left his mouth while the game was in progress. He cannot play football without that toothpick, and if Bristol City had been able to obtain possession of it they might have won the game, because Meredith was the most dangerous man against them.

Meredith met with several severe falls on Saturday, but he never relaxed his hold of that piece of quill. Once he was bundled over, and arose with a cut elbow.

Another time he was charged so heavily that it was thought he had broken his collar bone, but although he refused to leave the field, and played on in obvious pain, he retained possession of his toothpick.

He was rolling it with his tongue while his comrades were indulging in unrestrained delight at the scoring of the only goal, and when he went to the pavilion to receive his gold medal, he gave Lord Charles Beresford a closer view of it.

The streets of London were early taken possession of by the thousands of provincial visitors, who took the usual drive through the principal City and West End streets. But about one o'clock there was a marked decrease in the number of green caps that are the hall-mark of London's Cup-final visitors, for the exodus to the Crystal Palace was then in full swing.

More than a thousand spectators brought their own stands with them, and animated scenes took place on the outskirts of the crowd round the railings while the amateur carpenters hammered together their apparatus.—'Daily Express.'

Date 24 April 1909
Place The Crystal Palace
Score MANCHESTER UNITED 1 BRISTOL CITY 0
Teams MANCHESTER UNITED Moger, Stacey, Hayes, Duckworth, Roberts, Bell, Meredith, Halse, J. Turnbull, A. Turnbull, Wall. BRISTOL CITY Clay, Annan, Cottle, Hanlin, Wedlock, Spear, Staniforth, Hardy, Gilligan, Burton, Hilton
Team Colours MANCHESTER UNITED White
Official Referee J. Mason (Burslem)
Goal Scorer A. Turnbull 22
Attendance 71 401
Gate Receipts £6434
Guests of Honour Lord Charles Beresford, Lord Derby, Lord Carnarvon, Earl Howe
Copy *The Bristol Evening News* 24 and 26 April 1909

Charlie Roberts, United's captain

● Manchester United's first Cup final hung on a pre-match decision credited to their captain Charlie Roberts (right). Inside-left Sandy Turnbull, no relation to centre-forward James, was struggling with a severe knee injury to be fit for the final. Roberts opted for a gamble. "Let him play," he said. "He might get a goal and if he does we can afford to carry him." After 22 minutes Turnbull, who was killed in France in 1914, showed his opportunism, turning the ball over the line after it had rebounded from the bar. But if Turnbull was the matchwinner, Billy Meredith's presence was Manchester United's inspiration – just as it had been for Manchester City five years earlier. In a match which wracked the nerves of most of the players who were appearing in their first final, Meredith's class just gave United the edge despite a spirited performance from Bristol City's Billy Wedlock, the England international centre-half. City were also handicapped by the absence of two first choice players Rippon and Marr, but for United Vincent Hayes played for much of the match with a broken rib. It is not recorded whether or not Hayes took Dr Williams' Pink Pills (below), the manufacturers of which used the Cup final for their advertising campaign.

THE circumstances under which James Henry Farrow, of Manchester, will watch the Final Tie for the English Cup at the Palace, on Saturday, make a history more romantic than any mere dream of a novelist. Although greatly interested in his favourite team, Manchester United, Mr Farrow is sportsman enough to be satisfied to see the better team win the famous trophy. His happy, contented state of mind will be understood when it is explained that at one time he was regarded as

DOOMED TO GO UNDER.

just a frail, hopeless remnant of humanity, so affected by paralysis that his limbs were useless, and his spine was too weak to allow him even to sit up in bed.

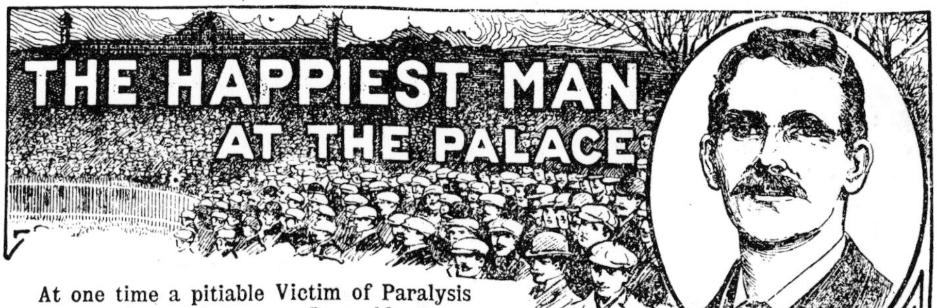

At one time a pitiable Victim of Paralysis and regarded as an Incurable.

Now he travels from Manchester to see the Final, as active as any man there.
A splendid tribute to Dr. Williams' Pink Pills.

NEWCASTLE AT LAST WIN THE CUP.

Crowd Indignant at Methods Adopted Against Barnsley in Replayed Final.

SHEPHERD SCORES TWICE.

LIVERPOOL, Thursday.—Newcastle United won the English Cup in the replayed final at Everton to-day, beating Barnsley by 2 to 0, but the manner in which they won did not commend itself to the crowd, and before the end cries of "Dirty Newcastle!" were heard on all hands, a state of affairs probably unique in the history of the club.

Newcastle have always been famed for their scrupulously fair play, but there were cases of deliberate kicking to-day. When Downs, who had been badly lamed in the first half, was lifted off his feet by a kick in the abdomen in the second half the foul play reached its climax, and the offender should without a moment's hesitation have been ordered off the field; but the penalty of a free kick was all that was given against Newcastle.

It really seemed as if some of the players had deliberately gone on the field to win at all costs. Had it been heavy charging it would have been another story, but kicking is inexcusable, and there were two or three glaring cases of it.

There was a tremendous crowd present, and if the ground holds 60,000, then that number were present. Half an hour before the crowd had broken in, and the mounted police and a strong posse of men on foot had been requisitioned to clear the playing arena, which was done before the time to start.

Rain had fallen heavily practically all the morning, and the ground was in a very sloppy state when the teams took the field. The sun broke through at the start, and but for the mud play was contested under fair conditions except that a high wind blew diagonally across the ground.

In the first half Barnsley, having won the toss, chose to play with the wind against them, and Newcastle were easily the more aggressive side for the opening exchanges. Quite early on Higgins laid out Mearns rather badly, and when the Barnsley goalkeeper recovered he broke from the players who were supporting him and ran with clenched fists at Higgins, but was forcibly held back by the referee and Downs, his clubmate.

McCracken made a couple of fine clearances from fierce dashes by the Barnsley forwards, in which Bartrop and Gadsby were conspicuous, but for the most part at this stage Newcastle were attacking, and Downs gave a corner once when Higgins and Shepherd looked certain to score. Carr was hurt by a heavy charge, but it was a fair shoulder charge, and the referee awarded no penalty.

McCRACKEN IN FORM.

Not so, however, when Downs, who had played such a sturdy, splendid game at the Palace, was kicked. Thereafter Downs, although he played as sturdily as ever, limped badly, and, although it lacked force, his kicking was wonderful.

It was quick, scrambling football, with Newcastle the cleverer side and Barnsley the more dashing. Bartrop and Gadsby made several dangerous incursions on the Barnsley right wing, and once, with Lawrence out of his goal, a shot by Gadsby was only turned aside by Carr at the expense of a corner. At the other end Boyle twice cleared from under the bar when Mearns was clean beaten. Wilson and Higgins kept making dangerous attacks on the Newcastle left wing, but they hung on the ball too long at times, and Downs and Ness, to say nothing of Boyle, were able to concentrate on defence.

By this time the field had churned up badly, and the lighter Barnsley men were simply covered with mud, whilst their heavier opponents were able to keep their feet. Veitch was the star artist of this half, and his play was simply delightful. He kept feeding both wings splendidly, and then he cleared after a corner when it looked certain that Barnsley would score.

Mearns once made a miraculous save from Rutherford after the latter had drawn the Barnsley goalkeeper out of his goal by diving at the ball and just turning it round the post. Half-time came with nothing scored.

Downs was going about with a limp and a jump in the second half, but he kicked as well as ever. Seven minutes after the interval a movement started by Veitch on the right, saw Higgins push the ball through for Shepherd to make one of his characteristic dashes. Downs could not catch him, and he went through the backs and, although Mearns came out, he was too late, and Shepherd scored for Newcastle with a fast ground shot.

DOWNS CARRIED OFF THE FIELD.

Just after this Downs was laid out, and after he had been attended to the other players held him up to see if he could stand, but he collapsed altogether and had to be carried off the field. He returned subsequently, but that did not minimise the offence, and it was noticeable during the stoppage that other members of the Newcastle team walked away or turned their backs on the offender when he spoke to them.

After this Bartrop had a glorious chance of equalising, but, with an open goal and close in, shot on the wrong side of the post. A minute or so later Higgins was tripped by Glendinning in the penalty area, and Shepherd scored the second, and what turned out to be the last, goal of the match. Higgins had just previously got through, but had pulled the ball down with his hands, and the point had been disallowed.

In the second half Newcastle made the same change as they did at the Palace, Wilson going inside to Higgins. With the exception that Carr played for Whitson, the sides were the same as on Saturday. That the better side won is unquestioned, and it is a pity that some of their players forgot themselves as they did. It would have been more excusable in the Barnsley men, for they had not the reputation or skill of the winners.

On the whole the football was better than on Saturday but, for all that, a lot of the exchanges were scrambling. Carr, the reserve back, came out of the ordeal well, but the best men on the Newcastle side were Veitch, McCracken, Wilson and Rutherford.

CITIZEN.

The toss, "wired from Manchester to London in nine minutes by the Thorne Baker telectograph"

● In 1910 Newcastle United finally achieved the Cup final victory that was beyond them in 1905, 1906, 1908 and 1911. In the first match Newcastle were on the verge of succumbing to their Crystal Palace jinx when Rutherford equalised Tuffnell's first half goal seven minutes from time.

Date 23 April 1910
Place The Crystal Palace
Score NEWCASTLE UNITED 1 BARNSLEY 1
Teams NEWCASTLE UNITED Lawrence, McCracken, Whitson, Veitch (capt.), Low, McWilliam, Rutherford, Howie, Higgins, Shepherd, Wilson. BARNSLEY Mearns, Downs, Ness, Glendinning, Boyle (capt.), Utley, Tuffnell, Lillycrop, Gadsby, Forman, Bartrop
Official Referee J. T. Ibbotson
Goal Scorers NEWCASTLE UNITED Rutherford 83; BARNSLEY Tuffnell 37
Attendance 77747
Gate Receipts £6898
Guests of Honour Lord and Lady Gladstone, Lord Rosebery

Replay
Date 28 April 1910
Place Goodison Park Everton
Score NEWCASTLE UNITED 2 BARNSLEY 0
Team Changes NEWCASTLE UNITED Lawrence, McCracken, Carr, Veitch (capt.), Low, McWilliam, Rutherford, Howie, Shepherd, Wilson, Higgins. BARNSLEY Unchanged
Goal Scorers Shepherd 2 (one penalty)
Attendance 69000
Gate Receipts £4166
Guest of Honour Earl of Derby
Copy The Daily Mirror 29 April 1910

Mearns saving for Barnsley at the Crystal Palace

ENGLISH FOOTBALL CUP FINAL FIASCO.

Wretchedly Poor Display by Both Teams in Drawn Game at Crystal Palace.

ONE REDEEMING FEATURE.

Newcastle's Forwards Held by Campbell and Taylor, Bradford's Splendid Backs.

Bradford were not expected to play very clever football, and, to be frank, with the exception of their backs, they did not. On the other hand, we have for years reckoned Newcastle the most scientific side in the country, and yet all their skill and artifice failed to pierce the rugged Bradford defence.

Truly the Palace is not a happy hunting-ground for the Magpies. Five times have they appeared there in the last round of the Cup, and three times have they been beaten and twice taken part in drawn games. Last year, after a draw they beat Barnsley at Everton, and this year, after a draw, they will probably defeat Bradford at Manchester on Wednesday.

It is true that Newcastle were handicapped by having Shepherd absent from their attack. He might have just supplied that touch of robustness which was so lacking in their play. Stewart, who filled the centre-forward berth, was clever in the way he distributed the work to his wings, but he never looked like breaking through the bustling Bradford backs to score himself.

NEWCASTLE FORWARDS BUMPED.

Wilson at outside left did a good many clever things, and once or twice tested Mellors in the Bradford goal. And Rutherford on the other wing was fast and clever, but he did not like the way in which the determined Bradford defenders bumped him over when he had the ball. He kept away from close quarters as much as possible, and his play suffered in consequence.

The other positions in the Newcastle side were filled fairly well by players who had little to do, for the Bradford forwards were helpless and hopeless as an attacking force. Under these circumstances it was not difficult for McCracken and Whitson at back to play well, and the half backs had such a hold over the Bradford forwards that Newcastle, had they cared, might have left this line to their own backs and played eight forwards in at least a laudable attempt to score.

But they did not. They were ultra-cautious, as if they were afraid that the Bradford men were playing a sort of possum game on them, and would jump when they least expected it. And so the feature was a dreary, aimless exposition of "footer" below mediocrity. As a Sheffield man sitting next to me said, "I have seen many a better Midland League match." Two Southern League sides in the final must have certainly put up a better match.

There is, however, nearly always a redeeming feature in the worst of bad games, and we had it on Saturday. I refer to the play of Campbell and Taylor, the Bradford backs. They were superb.

FAST, HEFTY BACKS.

Two great hefty giants, they bundled the Newcastle forwards about like ninepins. And their tackling was not cleverer than their kicking. Fast as any players on the field, they covered their goalkeeper so well that in the first half, when Newcastle were attacking continuously, Mellors, in goal, only had one difficult shot to stop, and that in my opinion came from a man who was yards offside.

Higgins sent in an oblique shot from this unmarked position, and Mellors just got his foot to the ball and turned it round the post for a corner kick. It was lucky that Mellors played to the whistle instead of appealing for offside because it would have been a goal.

Campbell was wonderful in all he did, and a better individual game has never been seen at the Palace in a final tie. He carried Bradford on his shoulders, so to speak, and never looked like letting them down. And Taylor, if somewhat overshadowed by Campbell, played fine, vigorous football. Rutherford will tell you that. And so cleanly did these two giants use their weight that scarcely a free kick was given against them in the match.

Newcastle had the wind behind them in the first half and played badly. Against the wind they did better, and their most dangerous attacks came in the second half, when they were facing it. Mellors then had difficult shots to save from Veitch, Rutherford, Wilson and Stewart.

Bradford but for their backs played very badly both with and against the wind, and Lawrence in the Newcastle goal had practically nothing to do. That's the match in a nutshell.

The crowd, too, was strangely unlike a final tie crowd. It was apathetic, sullen. There was no electricity in the air; no enthusiasm. And long before the finish thousands of them were streaming away to have a look at the preparations for the Festival of Empire.

Pronounced favours were difficult to discern. It is true thousands of supporters of both teams wore rosettes in their buttonholes, but I did not see a single spectator in a suit of clothes made up of Bradford's red and yellow, or one in Newcastle's black and white. I daresay there were some among the crowd, but they did not disport themselves on the ground in front of the stands, as they have done in previous years.

AN ESTIMATE OF THE CROWD.

And it was such a fine day, too. It seemed on the way to the Palace as if every vehicle in London must have been pressed into the service to take the people to Sydenham. And still the trains were packed. The exact figures of the crowd are not yet to hand, but the estimate is from 70,000 to 80,000. I should think that the latter figures are the more nearly correct.

At the conclusion of the match the Earl of Plymouth, who was to have presented the cup to the winning team, remarked that those present had witnessed a most excellent match, which, unfortunately, had had no result. He had no doubt that the same good football would be seen when the game was replayed elsewhere. Some people thought there was too much looking on at football nowadays and too little play, but that that was not the case was shown, he considered, by the fact that the Football Association had under their control half a million amateur players.

A vote of thanks to the Earl of Plymouth was proposed by Lord Portsmouth, who remarked that if the Festival of Empire at the Crystal Palace produced such a truly British scene as that witnessed that afternoon it was bound to be a great success. The vote was seconded by Lord Kinnaird, president of the Football Association, and carried with loud cheers.

An interested spectator of the game was Earl Rosebery, who sat next to the Earl of Plymouth.

In the evening the members of the Bradford City team dined at the Trocadero Restaurant, Piccadilly, W. Sir William Priestley, M.P., presided. After dinner the team witnessed the performance at the Alhambra, at which pictures of the Cup final were shown by the bioscope.

CITIZEN.

SATURDAY'S LEAGUE GAMES.

Aston Villa again took the leading place in the League table on Saturday by beating Manchester United at Villa Park by 4 goals to 2. A record crowd of 55,000 people saw an unpleasant game, in which Hunter and West were sent off the field just before the finish. The Villa meet Blackburn Rovers at Ewood Park this afternoon, and Liverpool at Anfield next Saturday, and at least one of these matches must be won for the Birmingham side to retain the championship.

Bristol City are making determined efforts to keep their place in the First Division, and it was a really fine performance to beat Manchester City at Hyde-road on Saturday by 2 to 1. Unfortunately for Bristol, however, Bury managed to draw at Oldham, so the Lancashire side have still the better chance of participating in First League football next season.

As matters stand now, Bury are a point in front with an inferior goal average, so if Bristol beat Everton next Saturday Bury must get both points from Sheffield United to keep their place.

All three leading sides in the Second Division won their matches on Saturday, so we shall have to wait until Wednesday, when Bolton and Chelsea meet at Bolton, to see who are to accompany West Bromwich into the First Division. The Throstles won at Lincoln on Saturday by 2 to 1, and as their remaining match is against Huddersfield Town at The Hawthorns, they should reach 53 points.

Chelsea, on the other hand, have to play at Bolton and Gainsborough, and those two matches are not likely to yield more than a couple of points, which would give them a total of 51. In that case Bolton would only need to draw at Birmingham to regain their place in the First Division.

With Swindon assured of the Southern League championship, the only interest remaining in that competition centres around the clubs struggling to avoid relegation. Portsmouth are doomed to a place in the Second Division next season, and it looks as if Southend will be their companions in misfortune.

● The trophy won for the first and only time by Bradford City was the third FA Cup, and is the Cup that is still fought for today. The first Cup was stolen in 1895, while held by Aston Villa. It was being displayed in a bootmaker's window when taken, and it was never recovered, despite huge publicity and the offer of a £10 reward. The second trophy was awarded to Lord Kinnaird in 1911 for services to the game. Lord Kinnaird played in no fewer than nine Cup finals and won five winner's medals.

It was appropriate that Bradford City should be the first winners of the new Cup, as it was manufactured in Bradford. Perhaps Yorkshire "closeness" had something to do with it.

Date 22 April 1911
Place The Crystal Palace
Score BRADFORD CITY 0
NEWCASTLE UNITED 0
Teams BRADFORD CITY Mellors, Campbell, Taylor, Robinson, Gildea, McDonald, Logan, Speirs, O'Rourke, Devine, Thompson. NEWCASTLE UNITED Lawrence, McCracken, Whitson, Veitch, Low, Willis, Rutherford, Jobey, Stewart, Higgins, Wilson
Official Referee J. H. Pearson (Crewe)
Attendance 69098
Gate Receipts £6512
Guests of Honour Earl of Plymouth, Earl Rosebery, Lord Kinnaird and Lord Portsmouth
Copy Daily Mirror 24 April 1911

Replay
Date 26 April 1911
Place Old Trafford, Manchester
Score BRADFORD CITY 1
NEWCASTLE UNITED 0
Team Changes BRADFORD CITY Torrance for Gildea. NEWCASTLE UNITED Unchanged
Goal Scorer Speirs 15
Attendance 58000
Gate Receipts £4478

BETWEEN 70,000 AND 80,000 PERSONS WATCH A COLOURLESS AND UNINTERESTING CUP FINAL WHICH ENDS IN A GOALLESS DRAW.

BLUEJACKET'S EXPERIENCE AT THE CRYSTAL PALACE.

A bluejacket who fell with a broken branch, but managed to cling to the branch beneath. Friends rescued him from the uncomfortable position in which he is seen in the photograph. He had climbed the tree to get a good view of the Cup final.—("Daily Mirror" photograph.)

NO WINNERS IN THE FOOTBALL CUP FINAL.

Barnsley and West Bromwich Albion Fail to Score at the Crystal Palace.

DULL, FEATURELESS GAME.

Only 59,000 People Present—Replay at Bramall Lane, Sheffield, on Wednesday.

Few final ties have been played which have aroused more diverse opinions than Saturday's game at the Crystal Palace, when West Bromwich Albion and Barnsley failed to score, and a further meeting at Bramall-lane, Sheffield, on Wednesday was rendered necessary.

Defence prevailed, and prevailed because it was brilliant. The Albion forwards were good, but they were never allowed to play their game, the pace of the opposing defenders ruthlessly breaking up all their schemes of attack almost before they were commenced.

Yet at times we saw flashes of really fine play from the Albion front line, and many times they nearly got through, but always found that, although one or two men of the Barnsley defence were beaten, the pace of the others enabled them to nip in and check the most dangerous onslaughts.

Barnsley, as expected, were poor in attack, and yet they on one or two occasions came much nearer scoring than the Albion, and twice or three times in the second half the Throstles' goal had the luckiest of escapes.

I have an idea that the lapses from fair play of some of the Barnsley team in the semi-final round and the consequent strictures upon their methods affected their play. They tried to play the Albion at their own game, especially in the first half. There were no heavy shoulder charges to speak of, and the forwards, instead of swinging the ball about, tried short passing, with the result that they as often as not sent the ball straight to an opponent's toes.

Twice in the first half the ball was robbed into the Albion goal mouth, and Pennington and Cook were allowed to clear when in the ordinary way at least three of the Barnsley forwards would have been on top of them, and although the ball might not have been forced through there would certainly have been a big scrimmage in the goal mouth.

BARNSLEY'S MISTAKEN TACTICS.

There is all the difference in the world between fair, honest, heavy charging and foul play. What is the good of men having all the attributes of weight, pace, courage and confidence, and then allowing smaller men to outplay them simply because they have been called over the coals quite rightly for using their physical advantages unfairly.

Had the Barnsley half-backs and forwards used their weight in the first half on Saturday as they were entitled to do, I do not think there would have been any necessity for a replay. Their stamina and pace would have worn out the defence of the other side. As it was they played a namby-pamby sort of game, and did not come into their own until well on in the second half.

In Mr. Schumacher there was a referee who would have put down any attempt at foul play. But the old amateur footballer would not have stopped honest charging, when it was fair and above-board.

Barnsley did throw themselves into the game wholeheartedly in the second half, and then we had some play well worth watching, fast and exciting, and a great contrast to the dull, drab stuff served up before the breather. That period reminded me more of two jaded League clubs

safely placed in the middle of the table, with no chance of championship honours, and no danger of relegation, playing the last match of the season, before a crowd thinking more of cricket and the summer, instead of a final tie for the most coveted of all football trophies.

The afternoon was delightfully fine, the sun blazing forth from a blue sky, flecked by the whitest of clouds, and a gentle breeze just tempering the fierceness of its rays. There were fewer incidents than usual before the start of the match, and fewer fanatics dressed in motley of the colours of the side for which they professed enthusiasm. Rosettes and a few flags were the only noticeable favours. And only about one half the usual number of special trains ran into London from the North. Yet there were 59,000 people present—a tribute to the popularity of the contest.

Both sides had their full available strength on the field, Bowser being able to turn out for the Albion. The Albion faced the sun in the first half and were quickly aggressive, a miss-kick by Glendenning nearly letting the left wing through. After Barnsley had forced a corner, which was well cleared by Pennington, the Barnsley goal was hotly assailed for a time, Cooper having to fist out a dangerous shot from Shearman, and catch a long, swerving ball from Jephcott, about the best shot of the whole match.

There was one curious incident, when Cooper, the Barnsley goalkeeper, appeared to protest to the referee about that official crossing him while a free kick was being taken. As the ball sailed over referee, Cooper, and the crossbar it did not matter much, but it might have been awkward had Buck's elevation been more accurate.

Cooper once dropped the ball from a long shot by Baddeley, and had an Albion forward been up a goal must have been scored. On another occasion Pailor headed just over the Barnsley goal, from a fine centre by Shearman.

As half-time drew on Barnsley improved in attack, but the only danger to the Albion goal came from a header by Travers, which was well saved by Pearson.

There is a different story to tell of the second half. Instead of the Albion doing most of the attacking, the Miners were frequently swarming round their goal with dangerous attacks, but all were badly finished.

ALBION'S LUCK.

Quite early on Tufnell had a great opening and overran the ball. Pearson just afterwards made a good clearance from a corner. Then Pearson missed the ball in running out, and Travers and Lillycrop overran it again, right in the goal mouth. After Cook had miss-kicked, Moore got in a good shot, and Pearson scrambled the ball away. Lillycrop hit the crossbar in another dash and Pearson kicked the ball away from Bartrop's toes.

Travers or Lillycrop was at fault when with an open goal one of the pair—it was impossible to distinguish which in the crowd—shot direct at Pearson. The ball seemed to hit the Albion goalkeeper on the knees and rebound to Tufnell, who with an open goal, and Pearson out, hit the upright about a foot from the top. This was the best chance of the match, the Albion goal having an absolutely miraculous escape.

The Albion's attacks were not so frequent during this half. Shearman in the first minute after the resumption hit the wing net when he should certainly have scored. Cooper once fisted out a fine shot from Jephcott with Wright challenging for possession of the ball, and it was some moments before Downs kicked clear. The Albion's other very dangerous attack came in the last minute, when Bowser, with only the goalkeeper to beat and the ball to himself, shot hard against the post supporting the wing net, inches only wide of the mark. That shot a foot the other way would have decided the destination of the Cup.

Beyond individual criticism of the players there is little to add. Downs, the Barnsley right back, was, as usual, the outstanding figure on the field, and, good as Pennington was, he was not so good as Downs, who, it must be remembered, had much better forwards to play against than Pennington.

Both Taylor (Barnsley) and Cook (Albion) were excellent, and it would, indeed, be difficult to recall a game this season in which the four backs have done so excellently. At half-back the Yorkshire side also had a slight pull, Utley, Bratley and Glendinning scarcely making a mistake, but Baddeley, Buck and McNeal, on the other side, held the Barnsley forwards quite easily until well on in the second half.

The Albion forward line was disappointing to those who know how cleverly they can play. Perhaps it was stage-fright, for they are mostly youngsters, but more likely most of them played just as well as the Barnsley defenders allowed them to do. Jephcott, however, their brilliant right winger, had an off day. He could not control the ball, and was generally a gift to Utley. Still, he managed to get in the two best shots for his side.

Bartrop, the Barnsley outside right, was nearly the best forward on the field. The others were about what I expected them to be—fast, but poor players for the most part. One real good inside forward in the Barnsley team and they would be a great side.

Mr. Schumacher refereed splendidly. He twice penalised what appeared to be fair charges from where we sat, a long way off in the Press-box, and made about one offside blunder. Except for offside, there was practically no whistle, and little need for it. With Pennington frequently playing the one-back game for long spells, we had a good deal of offside, and Mr. Schumacher's decisions were splendidly judged.

Among those present were the Lady Mayoress of London, who was to have presented the Cup and medals to the winners, Lord Portsmouth, Lord Dartmouth, Lord Lewisham, Lord Lucas, Sir Joseph Walton, M.P., and Mr. S. Hill-Wood, M.P.   P. J. M.

LEAGUE POSITIONS TO DATE.

LEAGUE I.	M. P.	LEAGUE II.	M. P.	SOUTHERN L.	M. P.
Blackburn R.	37 46	Derby County	37 52	Queen's Pk. R.	37 52
Everton	36 43	Burnley	37 48	Plymouth Arg.	37 50
Newcastle U.	37 43	Chelsea	35 48	Northampton	36 47
Bolton Wand.	37 42	Clapton O.	37 43	Swindon	35 46
Aston Villa	38 41	Hull City	37 41	Brighton & H.	37 45
Sheffield Wed.	37 39	Barnsley	34 40	Coventry City	37 43
Sunderland	38 39	Wolver. Wan.	37 40	Millwall Ath.	37 40
Middlesbro'	36 38	Grimsby	38 39	Crystal Palace	37 38
W. Bromwich	35 37	Fulham	37 38	Reading	37 36
Tottenham H.	37 37	Leicester F.	37 35	Watford	37 34
Woolwich A.	36 36	Bradford	36 34	Stoke	37 34
Sheffield U.	38 36	Blackpool	36 34	West Ham U.	36 33
Bradford City	36 35	Bristol City	37 33	Exeter City	37 33
Manchester C.	37 35	Notts Forest.	37 32	Norwich City	37 31
Oldham Ath.	36 35	Stockport C.	37 32	Brentford	36 31
Manchester U.	37 33	Birmingham	37 32	Bristol R.	37 31
Preston N. E.	37 33	Huddersfield	37 30	N. Brompton	37 31
Notts County	37 32	Glossom	37 29	Southampton	36 29
Liverpool	37 32	Leeds City	37 28	Luton	37 29
Bury	37 29	Gainsboro T.	36 21	Leyton	37 23

General view of the Crystal Palace ground while the Cup final was in progress on Saturday.—(" Daily Mirror " photograph.)

● During extra time in the replayed 1912 Cup final at Bramall Lane, Sheffield, Tufnell scored the only goal for "Battling" Barnsley. During a period of heavy Albion pressure, the ball was cleared to Tufnell near the half-way line. Only Pennington could get in a challenge, and a "professional foul" was required to stop Tufnell, but gentlemanly Pennington declined to make it and the goal was scored.

During this match, Glendinning of Barnsley, who was off the field being treated for a foot injury, suddenly ran on wearing only one boot to thump the ball away from the Barnsley goal. This incident led to the rule that a player off the field must receive the referee's permission before returning.

Barnsley's win over First Division West Bromwich, following Bradford City's win the year before, and Sheffield United's two years later, was a mini-boom for Yorkshire.

West Bromwich Albion, losing finalists in 1912

Barnsley, the 1912 Cup winners

Date 20 April 1912
Place The Crystal Palace
Score BARNSLEY 0
WEST BROMWICH ALBION 0
Teams BARNSLEY Copper, Downs, Taylor, Glendinning, Bratley, Utley, Bartrop, Tufnell, Lillycrop, Travers, Moore. WEST BROMWICH ALBION Pearson, Cook, Pennington, Baddeley, Buck, McNeal, Jephcott, Wright, Pailor, Bowser, Shearman
Official Referee J. R. Shumacher (London)
Attendance 54556
Gate Receipts £6057
Copy *Daily Mirror* 22 April 1912

Replay
Date 24 April 1912
Place Bramall Lane, Sheffield
Score BARNSLEY 1 WEST BROMWICH ALBION 0 (after extra time)
Teams BARNSLEY Unchanged. WEST BROMWICH ALBION Unchanged
Official Referee Unchanged
Goal Scorer Tufnell 118
Attendance 38555
Gate Receipts £2612
Guest of Honour Mr J. C. Clegg (Chairman, FA)

THE DAILY MIRROR, APRIL 21, 1913

121,919 AT THE ENGLISH CUP FINAL : RECORD CROWD SEES A THRILLING MATCH.

Panoramic view of the ground taken while the game was in progress. It gives a fine idea of the size of the crowd, which can be seen a great dark patch stretching away into the background.

The crowd clamber on the roof of a temporary refreshment building, though warned of the danger of doing so by the police.

The only goal of the match, which was scored by Barber, an Aston Villa half-back, about fifteen minutes before the finish.

Unable to bear the pressure, the roof collapses and several persons are injured. The photograph shows them being rescued.

Aston Villa fail to convert a penalty kick.

Watching the game from tree tops.

Low (Sunderland) gets the ball from Wallace.

Aston Villa scored the only goal of the match against Sunderland at the Crystal Palace on Saturday, and thus won the English Cup for the fifth time in their history. It was a thrilling game, in which there were many exciting incidents, and the general impression was that the better side had won. There was a record attendance, 121,919 persons witnessing the match.—(*Daily Mirror* photographs.)

● The renown of the two teams was responsible for the mammoth attendance; Sunderland at the time of the match led the First Division, Aston Villa, four times Cup winners already, were in second place. The game lived up to its billing. Wallace missed a penalty early in the match; Sam Hardy, Villa's international goalkeeper, was off injured for some ten minutes while Harrop took over in goal. A goal fifteen minutes from time settled the destiny of the Cup. Wallace's precise corner was headed in powerfully by Barber, just as Clem Stephenson, Villa's inside-forward, had dreamed it would happen the night before the final! The great Charlie Buchan

ended up a loser, but Sunderland had their revenge by winning the League championship, with Villa this time runners-up. Both sides had come within a whisker of the first double of the twentieth century. But in the Cup Aston Villa now equalled the record five wins of the Wanderers and Blackburn Rovers.

The first World War interrupted the progress of these two great teams. Sunderland had to wait until the 1930s before they became a power in the land again, and Aston Villa declined even more drastically. After a sixth Cup win in 1920, a fortuitous victory in 1957 is their only Cup or Championship victory since.

Date 19 April 1913
Place The Crystal Palace
Score ASTON VILLA 1 SUNDERLAND 0
Teams ASTON VILLA Hardy, Lyons, Weston, Barber, Harrop, Leach, Wallace, Halse, Hampton, Stephenson, Bache. SUNDERLAND Butler, Gladwin, Ness, Cuggy, Thomson, Low, Mordue, Buchan, Richardson, Holley, Martin
Official Referee A. Adams (Notts.)
Goal Scorer Barber 75
Attendance 121919
Gate Receipts £9 406
Copy The Daily Mirror 21 April 1913

THE ASSOCIATION CUP—FINAL TIE.

◆

BURNLEY BEAT LIVERPOOL.

◆

KING WITNESSES THE MATCH.

◆

LONDON INVADED.

◆

SCENES IN THE STREETS.

◆

Play started fast with Burnley aggressive. They early on were dangerous, and a fine shot by Lindley skimmed the bar. After this Liverpool, although playing against the wind, set up a steady attack, and Sewell was two or three times called upon and once had the ball knocked out of his hands. Nicholl was left with an open goal but ran the ball over the line. A few minutes later Nicholl put in a terrific shot. The ball looked like going through, but Taylor got his head to it and the force of the impact was so great that the Burnley back was knocked out for a minute or so. Liverpool continued on the aggressive, and Bamford had to concede a corner, and Lacey, after a brilliant effort in combination with Miller, put in a hard shot which

SEWELL SAVED SPLENDIDLY

on his knees. Burnley then broke away and Mosscrop put in a lofty shot which Campbell caught. In a trice the ball was at the other end, and Miller, bursting through the backs, had the goal almost at his mercy, but was slightly hampered in his shot, and hooked the ball just wide from a range of three yards. This was hard luck for Liverpool, for the work of the team had been steadier than that of the Burnley men, who were, however, dangerous in their breaks-away, and in one of them Boyle got in a shot which Campbell was lucky to turn round the bar from a corner kick. The sun was now blazing hot, and it was fortunate for the players that there was a stiffish breeze. McKinley, who was playing as substitute for Lowe, the Liverpool captain, made several

OPENINGS FOR LACEY AND NICHOLL,

but the Burnley backs were generally pretty steady and they were not often allowed to get too close to Sewell. After some time the pace, which had been pretty fierce, slackened down a lot and the Burnley forwards began to have more of the game. They kept the play for a long time in the vicinity of the Liverpool goal, but it cannot be said that Pursell and Longworth were very hard-pushed. A bad decision of the referee, who gave Miller offside when he was clearly yards inside, provoked derisive cheers from the crowd. From the free-kick the Burnley forwards went through, but again Longworth relieved the pressure with a clever kick. Another free-kick, this time just outside the penalty line, looked dangerous for Liverpool, but Ferguson, who shot hard, sent the ball many yards wide of the mark. Then came

AN EXCITING BURST

in the Burnley goal; Miller broke through and Nicholl, following up, got the ball from Bamford after the latter had deprived Miller of it. The ball bobbed about in front of goal for some few moments, but the defence prevailed. So far the play had been very bright if not particularly clever, and although Liverpool had certainly had a trifle the best of the exchanges it was anybody's game. There was, however, curiously little cheering from the crowd, but Liverpool were clearly the favourites, and when the pace of the vanguard made them dangerous there were cries of "Now Liverpool." Shortly before the interval a free-kick was awarded Liverpool, but nothing came of it. Half-time:

Burnley 0
Liverpool 0

Liverpool had the wind behind them in the second half and started attacking, but they were driven back and Nesbitt forced a corner kick, from which Boyle hooked the ball over the bar. Liverpool attacked and a long shot by Miller sailed over the Burnley goal. It looked as if he

could have done better by going on instead of shooting, for he was practically clear of the backs. Play was scrambling for a time, and then Liverpool took up the attack, and a blunder by Bamford nearly let Lacey through, but Taylor got in an effective kick into touch. Mosscrop had a nice chance of putting Burnley on the aggressive, but his centre was a bad one, and Liverpool were quickly at the other end. Sewell had to save from Nicholl with Miller and Metcalf bustling him. Liverpool were now playing towards the goal, which has usually produced the goals in final-tie football. After thirteen minutes

THE DECIDING GOAL

came. Burnley had a throw-in very near the flag, Freeman got the ball and, taking it on the full volley, drove it through with a terrific shot. It was so quick that many people did not see the shot, which was yards wide of Campbell and unstoppable. It was quite in keeping with Freeman's usual play, for he had not been seen much in the match up to this point, and this clever shot was quite characteristic of the man who is always an opportunist. Sewell had to save a long, dropping shot from Longworth, and a moment later he literally pulled the ball from under the bar from a great shot by Lacey. Both these saves were great efforts. Just afterwards Lindley missed a great chance of making the match a certainty. From a centre by Mosscrop he had almost an open goal to shoot at, but put the ball on the wrong side of the post from a range of three yards. Just after Sewell made another fine save from Metcalf. He was busy again a moment later and had a lot of trouble to keep a hard shot from Nicholl from going through.

LIVERPOOL KEPT PEGGING AWAY

and were decidedly unlucky in being a goal down, but goals are the accidents of the game and Freeman's lucky volley was determining the issue. Liverpool forced a corner and Lacey headed against the post. Another corner followed to the reds, but they could not break through a great defence, which made but few mistakes in the game. It had been a stubborn match, and Burnley were perhaps a lucky side to win by a goal to nothing. Final score:

Burnley 1
Liverpool 0

Date 25 April 1914
Place The Crystal Palace
Score BURNLEY 1 LIVERPOOL 0
Teams BURNLEY Sewell, Bamford, Taylor, Halley, Boyle, Watson, Nesbitt, Lindley, Freeman, Hodgson, Mosscrop. LIVERPOOL Campbell, Longworth, Pursell, Fairfoul, Ferguson, MacKinley, Sheldon, Metcalfe, Miller, Lacey, Nicholl
Official Referee H.S. Bamlett (Durham)
Goal Scorer Freeman 58
Attendance 72778
Gate Receipts £6687
Guests of Honour H.M. George V, Earl of Derby, Lord Kinnaird
Copy Sunday Times 26 April 1914

THE KING'S FIRST CUP FINAL: THE GREAT ASSOCIATION EVENT

WINNERS OF THE CHIEF TROPHY OF ASSOCIATION FOOTBALL FOR THE FIRST TIME
THE BURNLEY TEAM.

SOME OF THE 100,000 SPECTATORS: A SECTION OF THE VAST CROWD
AT THE CRYSTAL PALACE.

THE DECISIVE MOMENT: FREEMAN, THE BURNLEY CENTRE FORWARD, SCORES
THE ONLY GOAL OF THE MATCH.

DISCIPLES OF ST. SIMEON STYLITES: LIVING "STATUES" WATCHING THE FOOTBALL
ASSOCIATION CUP FINAL

SPORTS SPECIAL ("GREEN 'UN"), SATURDAY, APRIL 24, 1915.

LORD KINNAIRD, President of Football Association.

THE ENGLISH CUP.

PAST WINNERS OF THE CUP.

1871-2 Wanderers.	1891-2 W. Bromwich A.
1872-3 Wanderers.	1892-3 W'hampton W.
1873-4 Oxford 'Varsity.	1893-4 Notts County.
1874-5 Engineers.	1894-5 Aston Villa.
1875-6 Wanderers.	1895-6 Sheffield Wed.
1876-7 Wanderers.	1896-7 Aston Villa.
1877-8 Wanderers.	1897-8 Notts Forest.
1878-9 Old Etonians.	1898-9 Shef. United
1879-80 Clapham Rov.	1899-1900 Bury.
1880-1 Old Carthusians.	1900-1 Tottenham.
1881-2 Old Etonians.	1901-2 Shef. United.
1882-3 B'burn Olympic.	1902-3 Bury.
1883-4 Blackburn Rov.	1903-4 Manchester City
1884-5 Blackburn Rov.	1904-5 Aston Villa.
1885-6 Blackburn Rov.	1905-6 Everton.
1886-7 Aston Villa.	1906-7 Sheffield Wed.
1887-8 W. Bromwich A.	1907-8 W'hampton W.
1888-9 Preston N.E.	1908-9 Manchester Utd.
1889-90 Blackburn Rov.	1909-10 Newcastle.
1890-1 Blackburn Rov.	

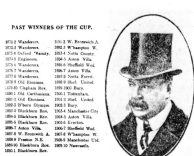

LORD DERBY,
who consented to present the Cup to the winning team in to-day's Final tie.

Mr. J. C. CLEGG, Vice-President of Football Association.

United's Players

H. Gough, Goalkeeper.

Manchester critics say that Gough is the greatest goalkeeper in the country, and what Manchester says to-day England thinks to-morrow. Gough is certainly the best custodian United have had since the days of big "Bill" Foulkes, which means that he is better than Joe Lievesley was. Consequently, "some goalkeeper," a Derbyshire man, of course, and was found by United at Castleford. Both brilliant and reliable, and has won many a game for his club.

W. Cook, Right Back.

Cook is one of the hardy men of the North, like English. He is small, like English, and one of the greatest backs anywhere, also like English. He can kick with either foot in any position, never knows when he's beaten, and has a thorough understanding with his partner. He is about as good now as Dicky Downs was three years ago, and that's saying something, and he expects to have a grip on his first Cup medal to-night.

J. English, Left Back.

English is one of the hardy men of the north, like Cook. He is small, like Cook, and one of the greatest backs anywhere, also like Cook. Being fair-haired and more jaunty in his style than his partner, he attracts more attention than Cook, but for effect if there is any difference between them they both have it, as the Irishman said.

Albert Sturgess, Right Half.

I have described Sturgess as a right-half, simply because he must have a label of some kind, but really he ought to be called "the one man football team"; Albert will play anywhere and will play well in any position. He was in the team against Scotland last year, but would rather you did not say too much about that. Has since had his revenge from Donnachie and hoped to square Croal's account to-day.

W. Brelsford, Centre Half.

A bit of real Sheffield is William, more commonly known as "Bill." When the Wednesday players looked at Croal a fortnight ago they said with one accord "Let's hope that Brelsford is kind to him in the Final." Bill has got some shoulders, and he uses them. If anyone gets in the way when he wants to use them, then so much the worse for the would-be trespasser.

George Utley, Left Half.

Utley is a specialist in Cup-ties and had played in two finals before to-day. He was on the losing side against Newcastle, on the winning side against West Bromwich, while he had no doubt about to-day's result. George is undoubtedly one of the greatest Cup-tie half-backs playing the game, and, as he did at Blackburn in the semi-final, is capable of turning the whole course of a game by his individual efforts. He thinks United's team very similar to the Barnsley one who won the Cup.

Fred Hawley, Centre Half.

Of Hawley it can be said, as has been said of the average husband, that he's a handy man to have about the place. If anything happens to any of the regular trio, Hawley can be brought in with the utmost confidence, because he is a fine man to have on the side.

J. Simmons, Outside Right.

Like most of United's players, Simmons can give a hand in most positions, and while some of his skill is lost when he is on the wing, there is no question about his worth as a winger. Small in stature, James has a heart almost as big as the body of his celebrated uncle, Bill Foulke.

S. Fazackerley, Inside Right.

This tall Lancastrian is the nearest approach to Buchan in football, and if not quite so clever as the Sunderland star, is good enough to be going on with. Dribbles beautifully, and has a host of tricks up his sleeve, while he passes well when he is in the mood. Was a fine shot when he was with Hull, but somehow or other doesn't shoot so well or so often nowadays.

J. Kitchen, Centre Forward.

Six years ago Kitchen, when quite a youth, came very near to playing centre-forward for England, and at that time was probably the best centre in the country., I think somebody must have told him how good he was, and it didn't improve him. Since then he has always been useful, but only recently has he recovered his 1909 brilliance. Makes a speciality of solo dashes, and once he gets a clear field it is odds on a goal.

W. Masterman, Inside Left.

The re-incarnation of some famous old Corinthian forward. Takes the ball with him as though it were tied to his foot, and has a positive genius for knowing the right moment at which to pass to a colleague. In addition he is the best shot United have.

R. Evans, Outside Left.

If this wily winger is thinking about arranging a family crest, might I suggest the Phœnix, with the motto, "Come again." Evans, who was once a Welsh Internationalist, and subsequently played for England, has certainly been renewing his youth this season.

SHEFFIELD UNITED, winners of English Cup, seasons 1898-99 and 1901-2.

Top row:—G. Waller (trainer), English, Brelsford, Hawley, Gough, Sturgess, Utley (captain), Cook, Gillespie.
Bottom row:—Simmons, Kitchen, Davis, Evans, Fazackerley, Masterman, Revill.
[Photo: Furniss. Block: Leng, Ltd.

CHELSEA, who made their first appearance in an English Cup Final [illegible]

Top row (left to right):—Taylor, J. W[illegible] (trainer), Bettridge, Molyneux, Logan, Walker, Harrow.
Bottom row:—Ford, Halse, Thomson, Croal, and McNeil.
[illegible]ock: Leng, Ltd.

Chelsea's Players

J. Molyneux, Goalkeeper.

Whatever may have happened in League matches the defence of Chelsea in the Cup has been A1, and in that defence Molyneux is certainly the leading ornament. The Chelsea warden has ideal physical qualifications for the job, and is assuredly in the first flight. High balls near the post seem to worry him, but then they bother most men. Used to be with Stockport, but has been five years at Stamford Bridge.

W. Bettridge, Right Back.

This young man is even lighter than Cook or English, but he is quite good, though not so accomplished as United's defenders. Chelsea, who got him from Burton United, have persevered splendidly with him, and are now reaping the reward.

J. Harrow, Left Back.

Harrow was born at Mitcham, where the lavender and the Surrey cricketers come from, so he is a real Southerner. Learned the game with Croydon, and has improved out of all knowledge this season. He is not tall, but is stocky and heavy, and can bump a bit. Was looking forward to his tussles with Simmons on that account.

F. Taylor, Right Half.

One of ours really, because he was born at Rotherham, learned his football in this district, and then went to Gainsborough, where he was contemporary with Harry Lowe, of Worksop and Liverpool. Splended half who knows every move on the board, and has practically nothing to learn. Some day will probably play for England, and so fill Ben Warren's place completely.

Tom Logan, Centre Half.

One of a great footballing family which has brought fame to the little town of Barrhead, near Glasgow. At one time it was thought that Tom would be the greatest of the Logans, but he has never played so well for Chelsea as he used to do for Falkirk. A big man physically, he prefers the scientific game to the "humpsti-bumpsti" business. In the semi-final he had Parker under his thumb, and that's not easily done.

A. Walker, Left Half.

A typical Scot, who was originally a centre-half, but got his place on the wing when Abrams got damaged, and has been keeping that place on his merits. Just a wee bit cumbersome, he can be bothered by fast light forwards, as for instance Capper, who did well against him a fortnight ago.

L. Abrams, Left Half.

Left Stockport a few years ago, and went to the Hearts as an outside left. They made him a half-back in Scotland, and what's more, made him a Scottish half-back with the touches of a McWilliam. He used to work the triangular business with Messrs. Croal and McNeil, but has been on the injured list for some time. When in form there isn't a better left half in England.

H. Ford, Outside Right.

The star of the Chelsea attack, and one of the two best right wingers in the country, the other being Chedzoy, of Everton. Ford is a match-winner, and represented a severe problem that Utley and English had to solve to-day. Not only fast, but clever, and eminently sensible in his placing of the ball.

H. Halse, Inside Right.

Collector of Cup medals. Like George Utley, was playing in his third Final to-day, but prior to this afternoon had never been on the losing side in a Final. Won his first medal with Manchester United, and his second with Aston Villa. A great snap shot, he is possibly the most dangerous man Chelsea have in that direction.

R. Thomson, Centre Forward.

Very, very useful. A stocky little man like McLean in build, but more energetic than Wednesday's David. Doesn't mind being bumped about, and is generally on the premises when there is half a chance of a goal. Is handicapped by the fact that his left eye is blind, but gets over that difficulty very well.

J. Croal, Inside Left.

This gentleman is cast for the "thinking parts" in Chelsea's performances. Represents the Scottish school of subtlety at its highest point, and is undoubtedly one of the craftiest forwards playing, but the bustling English game does not suit him too well. His greatest game of his life was in the International last year.

R. McNeil, Outside Left.

More Scotch. Burnley would have given tons of money to get this winger two years ago, but he thought London would suit his health better. Probably he was right. Can play the Scottish game, but is really more like an English winger, while one of his good points as a rule is his shooting.

Lieut. V. J. Woodward, Inside Right

The great amateur was hardly expected to play to-day, but none would have been more popular. Is not so great as when he first appeared for England at Bramall Lane, in 1903, but though his speed and shooting have left him somewhat, his subtle touches remain.

● This was the Khaki Cup final played at Old Trafford with much of the crowd composed of soldiers in uniform. Indeed there was some criticism about the continuation of football to the end of this season. Bradford City had played Norwich City in a third round second replay at Lincoln behind closed doors so that the war effort was not interrupted. Wet, gloomy conditions heightened the prevailing sense of concern, and Sheffield United won the Cup which was to stay in their possession for five years. Simmons gave United the lead after Fazackerley had miskicked, but the latter made no mistake seven minutes from the end after Masterman had struck the post. Kitchen's third goal sealed a comfortable victory.

Date 24 April 1915
Place Old Trafford, Manchester
Score SHEFFIELD UNITED 3 CHELSEA 0
Teams SHEFFIELD UNITED Gough, Cook, English, Sturgess, Brelsford, Utley, Simmons, Fazackerly, Kitchen, Masterman, Evans.
CHELSEA Molyneux, Bettridge, Harrow, Taylor, Logan, Walker, Ford, Halse, Thomson, Croal, McNeil
Goal Scorers Simmons 36, Fazackerly 83, Kitchen 88
Attendance 49 557
Gate Receipts £4557
Guest of Honour Earl of Derby
Copy *Sheffield Sports Special ("Green Un")* 24 April 1915

SPORT PICTURES, April 29, 1920.

WARNING TO CUP-ENTHUSIASTS. By J. HARROP (Aston Villa F.C.) EVERY WEEK £100 FOR SIX AWAY.

Sport Pictures 2d.
RACING, FOOTBALL & BOXING.

No. 56. [Registered at the G.P.O. as a Newspaper.] [For Week Ending] THURSDAY, APRIL 29, 1920. [Phone: CITY 5481.] [12 Pages.] Two Pence.

CUP FINALISTS' "STRONG" MEN.

C. SLADE. **T. WILSON.** **W. WATSON.**

The Huddersfield Town half-backs are typical of the whole team. There is no outstanding "star," but all three are players of great power and stamina and a high standard of skill. *(Exclusive.)*

● The first final after the ending of hostilities, and the first to take place at Stamford Bridge, brought Aston Villa their sixth FA Cup success.

Villa indeed saved the competition from an awkward situation by beating Chelsea in the semi-final, and thus averting the possibility of the West London side playing a final on their home ground.

In fact, Aston Villa had been extremely lucky to survive the quarter final round, where Tottenham Hotspur had very much the better of the game, and Villa were saved by an outstanding display by England's goalkeeper Sam Hardy. After Hardy had almost played Spurs on his own, Villa won when Tommy Clay, Spurs' immaculate and normally safe full back, sliced the ball into his own net.

Huddersfield Town's presence as Villa's opponents added to the catalogue of romance that characterises the FA Cup. By all the economic rights of the time Huddersfield should have been in liquidation and their forces amalgamated with the new Leeds United. That was the decree of the League Management committee when it was revealed that the club owed two directors a total of £40,000. By public appeal and by transferring players enough money was raised to satisfy the League and Huddersfield Town celebrated their reprieve with a glorious run in the FA Cup, and by winning promotion from the Second Division.

But in the very week of the final, controversy returned. W. H. Smith, a winger of high quality, was suspended for an incident in a League match several weeks earlier. Huddersfield would not be able to compensate fully for his absence, yet their determination was to stretch Villa to the very last.

Aston Villa's reputation as one of the game's elite was confirmed by the selection of a side in which only left-back Weston had not or would not represent his country. Goalkeeper Sam Hardy had first been capped in 1907, but was still good enough to be England's first choice in 1920. Young Billy Walker was to win the first of his 18 caps the following year, and he would still be playing for England in 1933. Andy Ducat, Frank Barson and Clem Stephenson were other revered names in the Villa line-up.

Huddersfield took into their dressing-room a lucky charm, a lamp from the local production of the pantomime Aladdin; all the players took their turn in rubbing it before the kick-off. If good luck, and some skilled defending from Tom Wilson, helped them overcome a tentative start, it did not help them in the long run.

And a long run it was too, because the final went to extra time; the more recent drawn games had been taken to a replay after the straight 90 minutes. The deciding goal came in the first period of extra time. A Villa corner was flicked into the Huddersfield goal via the head of Kirton, and the scorer himself was unsure as to what had actually happened. The after-match confirmation of the incident came from Mr. Howcroft, the referee.

Huddersfield's attack had shown little evidence of producing a goal in normal time, and now they could not produce an equaliser. Villa's sixth victory finally overtook the achievements of the Wanderers and Blackburn Rovers. But it was a season in which Huddersfield Town had turned a notable corner. Later in 1920 Herbert Chapman was appointed to mastermind their initial season in the First Division, and create a structure that saw the League Championship won three years in a row; Huddersfield would also be back for the third and last Stamford Bridge final in 1922, and would reach the final again three more times before the Second World War.

Date 24 April 1920
Place Stamford Bridge, Chelsea
Score ASTON VILLA 1
HUDDERSFIELD TOWN 0 (after extra time)
Teams ASTON VILLA Hardy, Smart, Weston, Ducat, Barson, Moss, Wallace, Kirton, Walker, Stephenson, Dorrell. HUDDERSFIELD TOWN Mutch, Wood, Bullock, Slade, Wilson, Watson, Richardson, Mann, Taylor, Swann, Islip
Official Referee J. T. Howcroft (Lancashire)
Goal Scorer Kirton 100
Attendance 50018
Gate Receipts £9722
Guest of Honour Prince Henry
Copy Sport Pictures 29 April 1920

1921

● In 1921 Tottenham Hotspur brought the Cup south for the first time since their own win 20 years earlier.

Over 70,000 spectators went in heavy rain to Stamford Bridge to see the match, and they gave a tremendous ovation to King George V who had come to meet the teams.

Spurs had scored readily in earlier rounds, principally through Cantrell and their inside forwards, Bliss and Seed, but on a muddy pitch against a rugged Wolves side could only score one. A beautiful goal from Dimmock (below) settled the issue. *The Sporting Life* described it thus: "Converging on goal he drove in a great low oblique shot and the ball entered the far corner of the net well out of reach of George." Dimmock is the player directly above the end photographer. An ambulance party in the foreground is attending to a spectator who fainted.

The Illustrated London News picture spread also showed a photograph of the Australian cricketers who were beginning their tour, including H. L. Hendry, the oldest Australian Test player present at the 1980 Centenary Test Match at Lord's. Of a

panoramic view it suggested "The mass of human heads looks, curiously enough, rather like a vast pile of coal!" This was a reference to the current coal crisis.

NOT A "FAIR WEATHER" KING! HIS MAJESTY AND THE DUKE OF YORK GREETING THE "WOLVES" TEAM IN POURING RAIN.

THE KING HANDING THE CUP TO GRIMSDELL, THE "SPURS" CAPTAIN, AMID TREMENDOUS ENTHUSIASM (THE DUKE OF YORK NEXT BUT ONE TO LEFT).

Date 23 April 1921
Place Stamford Bridge, Chelsea
Score TOTTENHAM HOTSPUR 1 WOLVERHAMPTON WANDERERS 0
Teams TOTTENHAM HOTSPUR Hunter, Clay, McDonald, Smith, Walters, Grimsdell, Banks, Seed, Cantrell, Bliss, Dimmock. WOLVERHAMPTON WANDERERS George, Woodward, Marshall, Gregory, Hodnett, Riley, Lea, Burrill, Edmonds, Potts, Brooks
Team Colours TOTTENHAM HOTSPUR White shirts; WOLVERHAMPTON WANDERERS Black and gold stripes
Official Referee S. Davies (Rainhill)
Goal Scorer Dimmock 53
Attendance 72805
Gate Receipts £13414
Guests of Honour H.M. King George V, The Duke of York
Copy *The Illustrated London News* 30 April 1921

THE DECISIVE MOMENT: THE SCORING OF THE ONLY GOAL IN THE MATCH, BY DIMMOCK, TOTTENHAM'S OUTSIDE LEFT (IN WHITE JERSEY, THIRD TO THE RIGHT FROM RIGHT-HAND GOAL-POST.)

Tom Wilson, captain of the Cup winners (on left), and Joe McCall, captain of Preston North End, with his lucky black cat, and the team's trainer. The Preston men left their cat behind in favour of sprigs of white heather—and lost the match   [*Delta and Johnson* Photos]

<table>
<tbody>
<tr><td>Date 29 April 1922</td></tr>
</tbody>
</table>

Date 29 April 1922
Place Stamford Bridge, Chelsea
Score HUDDERSFIELD TOWN 1
PRESTON NORTH END 0
Teams HUDDERSFIELD TOWN Mutch, Wood, Wadsworth, Slade, Wilson, Watson, Richardson, Mann, Islip, Stephenson, W. H. Smith.
PRESTON NORTH END J. F. Mitchell, Hamilton, Doolan, Duxbury, McCall (capt.), Williamson, Rawlings, Jefferis, Roberts, Woodhouse, Quinn
Official Referee J. W. P. Fowler (Sunderland)
Goal Scorer Smith 67 (penalty)
Attendance 53000
Gate Receipts £10551
Copy The Football Special and Sporting Pictorial 6 May 1922

THE CUP FINAL FIASCO

WAS IT A PENALTY?

(By Our Man on the Spot)

BY a great effort of the memory I can only think of one other Cup Final in addition to the last fiasco between Huddersfield and Preston North End that had a similarly depressing effect upon the crowd. The match to which I refer was that between Manchester City and Bolton Wanderers at the Crystal Palace, when the present Earl Balfour, then Prime Minister, presented the Cup. That particular match was a perfect nightmare, and, after careful consideration, I cannot find any better description for last Saturday's match at Stamford Bridge.

The men on either side were thinking too much of their opponents' strength than their own power to conquer, and such an attitude is ever detrimental to the best conception of Soccer football, or any other game, for that matter. I should say that Huddersfield well deserved their victory in the sense that the Yorkshire team represented the better of two bad horses; but such a conclusion merely amounts to condemnation with faint praise.

CONVICTION OF THE CROWD

How many years have passed since Cup winners secured the trophy by a penalty goal I am not prepared to say, but nothing like the incident of last Saturday occurs to me at the moment of writing. This 1922 Final sent the majority of people away from Stamford Bridge with a conviction that they had been badly used and badly entertained, too, for a three-shilling admission. We are accustomed to take the view that men who participate in the Cup Final are overcome by the importance of the occasion.

This is true up to a certain point—say, in the first half an hour—but it would be absurd to make such an excuse the main one for the puerile display at Stamford Bridge. No, the reason why this game proved so keen a disappointment was principally due to the fact that it was not played in the proper spirit.

AN UNUSUAL ATTITUDE

Certain men were obviously a little suspicious of each other, and where you find that attitude you must also look for a lower grade of mentality in sport. The action of the Preston fullback in bringing down Smith mid-way during the second half should not only have received the extreme penalty, but it should have been reported to the Football Association. Clubs, of course, are largely to blame in failing to make a gospel of clean, honest play.

As to the penalty goal scored by Smith—a goal that won the Cup for Huddersfield—I do not think that it came under the last dread punishment, but I am very glad that the referee thought otherwise. It was one of the best mistakes he ever made in his career, because it shows how difficult it is for the man in charge to interpret the real spirit of the game. You draw certain lines. You make an offence punishable to the extreme limit if it happens to be committed within such an area. Outside that area a man can do the same thing with a certain amount of impunity.

THE FILMS DO NOT LIE

Thus the rule is made to look nothing more nor less than a mere dalliance with unsporting conduct. For every trip I would give a goal without the risk of trying to get the goal from a penalty mark. As I have hinted, there can be little doubt that Smith was brought down outside the penalty area, and the films, which do not often lie, confirm it. Hence Huddersfield were lucky to win the Cup in one sense, but, under the circumstances, they would have been very unlucky to have lost it.

PRAISE FOR MANN

Huddersfield had the best of this dismal final, and what little constructive football was seen among the forwards belonged undoubtedly to the winning side. The best player in the Huddersfield attack was Mann, who played good football, and who gave Islip one of the finest chances to score in the opening half that any centre-forward could wish to have in a month of Sundays. Smith was also seen to advantage, and there were periods when Richardson and Stephenson endeavoured successfully to shake off the blight that fell upon this final. In the half-back line, Wilson, the captain, stuck to Roberts like a leech, but he might have set his comrades a better example in method.

The half-backs on either side were crude, and Joe McCall not only failed to reproduce his form in the semi-final, but he did not seem to be able to go the pace.

LIKE SCARED RABBITS

But at no period of the game did the Preston forwards work together. They rushed about for the most part like a pack of scared rabbits. Mitchell made one or two good saves, notably during the early stages, when he flung himself at full length to stop a magnificent grounder from Smith, but I have seen him keep goal much better. It was very comical to see him dancing about under the bar in the hope of putting off Smith when he took the penalty kick. West Ham had a goalkeeper many years ago who used to make a practice of this war dance, and his extraordinary antics when a penalty was taken were equal to those of a clown at a circus.

BRADFORD A CITY OF WOE

BRADFORD is the unluckiest football centre, and one cannot recall any city having such an experience as has befallen the clubs in the Yorkshire centre. Not only have Bradford City to go into the Second Division, but Bradford, their neighbours, seem doomed for descent into the Third Division next season. Only a miracle can save them. What a decline theirs has been! A little over twelve months ago they were in the First Division. It must be a sad blow to such a good judge of a footballer as Mr. Tom Maley, their manager. Thousands will sympathise with the Bradford enthusiasts, for the two clubs had to fight hard to establish Soccer in an old Rugby stronghold. They will both find it very difficult indeed to get back to top class.

HAPPY HUDDERSFIELD

IN happy contrast to their neighbours at Bradford, Huddersfield Town are rejoicing in the fact that the English Cup is in their possession. They played better football on the whole than North End in the Final, but a penalty goal victory was not so satisfactory as one would have desired. In some quarters the decision of the referee has been questioned, but Mr. Fowler had a better view than anyone else on the ground, and one must respect his decision, whatever else one thinks. No official would give such a verdict in so important a game if there was the slightest doubt in his mind.

PLAYERS AND THEIR WAGES

UNFORTUNATELY the season in England ends with the players dissatisfied over wages cuts, and, from what one hears, many of the professionals are doomed to disappointment, for many clubs intend not only to reduce wages, but to cut down their staffs. The Players' Union will put up a fight for the players, but they can only hope for sympathy from the rich clubs to pull them through. Developments will be awaited with interest; but it is foolish to talk of a footballers' strike. No such action was ever intended, for the players know that the start of the close season is the worst possible time for any such move. One wishes the players well, for the general view is that the wages cuts are too severe.

Action in the Preston goalmouth following a corner

1923

By "OLYMPIAN."

THE Challenge Cup of the Football Association, the most-coveted of all trophies offered for competition in connexion with the greatest of our national pastime, was won on Saturday by the players of the Bolton Wanderers' club, and won deservedly. They beat West Ham United pretty much as they pleased, on the new Wembley Stadium, which was invaded and stampeded by the greatest crowd that has ever assembled in the history of the game. It had been confidently stated that this new amphitheatre, the home of English sport, was structurally and scientifically perfect, offering comfortable accommodation and an unobstructed view to upwards of 125,000 spectators. Clearly the authorities were totally unprepared for what happened. It is computed that fully 250,000 people made their way to the imposing and spacious ground from all parts of the Empire, all anxious to see the blue riband of the football world decided. About 60,000 people had passed inside the turnstiles when pandemonium broke loose.

One of the main exits was broken down, and thousands of people surged inside the enclosure, and from that moment the situation showed signs of getting out of hand. People scaled high walls, and clambered into seats for which others had paid. Such was the pressure on the ring-side fences that they gave way. The crowd rushed across the large cinder track which encircles the playing pitch, and in an incredibly short time the beautiful greensward was occupied by a black, uncontrollable mass. The police, apparently taken by surprise, were for a time powerless to deal with the situation, and even after more officers, mounted and on foot, had been rushed to the ground, the task of clearing the playing pitch was

a tediously slow process. Indeed, when the players came into the arena, there seemed very little prospect of the game being started. Finally, however, when the players added their persuasion to the force resorted to by the constabulary, the crowd was gradually pressed back to the touch-line, and at 14 minutes to four the referee found it possible to make a start.

VISITORS WHO SAW NO PLAY.

The Bolton party made the Russell Hotel their headquarters for the week-end, the players with the manager, Mr. C. E. Foweraker, having spent the last few hours before the match at Harrow, and they made the short journey to the ground in excellent time. But the directors and their friends, who journeyed from London in charabancs, had an experience they will never forget. They certainly have no desire to see Wembley again. The road was packed with vehicular traffic, for long stretches trams, buses, charabancs, motors and horse conveyances were running four abreast, and frequently were held up for long periods at cross roads. The journey occupied two hours—and when the party had to alight, fully half a mile from the vast amphitheatre, many of us had abandoned hope of seeing any play in the first half. With scores of others, I made my way across a grass field, crossed a railway, scaled a high wall, and then found my way into the enclosure obstructed by corrugated iron hoardings with three rows of barbed wire above them. Some of the more daring spirits surmounted this formidable obstacle, whilst others less venturesome burrowed under the hoardings, only to find more difficulties ahead. Nobody seemed to know how to get inside the enclosure, and there were thousands of people shut out. It was my good fortune to reach the Press seats at the top of the north stand at 3-40, and then greatly to my relief I learned that the match had not started.

Dozens of Bolton people saw none of the game. None of the directors saw the first goal, and several of them did not

get as much as a glimpse of the game. Scores of people who had paid a guinea for a seat never got to it. Never in the history of the game has there been such a tragedy, and for the credit of those who are responsible for the good government of Soccer, the most popular of all pastimes, it is to be hoped it will never be repeated. The Football Association have since disclaimed any responsibility for what happened. They point out that all the arrangements were in the hands of the Wembley authorities. I venture to suggest the F.A. are merely begging the question by taking up such an attitude. The public look up to the F.A., and indeed to every football body, to keep faith with them, and such a debacle as this will do unquestionable harm to the game. The invasion of the playing field was due, it is alleged, to the snapping of the barriers when the inrush of spectators followed the breaking-in of the gates.

FEATURES OF THE GAME.

But to the game. Joe Smith won the toss from George Kay, and so West Ham to face the wind and sun, and before the crowd had settled down to the game, the Wanderers were well on their way to victory. It was a dramatic start, and the goal which [...] scored had its influence on the subsequent play. It is easier to play a game [...] with vital issues when you are a goal to the good, and it says much for the moral of the West Ham players that they made the contest interesting, and never ceased to try to discover a weakness in the Bolton rearguard. There was a ten minutes' stoppage early in the contest in consequence of the crowd again encroaching. The ball control, the method and the craftsmanship of the Wanderers' players were superior to that of their opponents, who had plenty of pace, swung the ball about with good judgment, and never spared themselves. Twice in the first half, the Wanderers, who kept the ball on the ground with rare discretion, might easily have lost the lead. From a corner placed nicely by Ruffell, Pym and one of his colleagues

both failed to get away a high ball, and Watson, in his eagerness to make the most of a gilt edged chance propelled the ball over the bar. The other attack which placed the Bolton goal in jeopardy emanated from the right wing, Richards, cutting in towards goal and smartly making his way past Jennings and Finney, shot obliquely when everybody expected him to centre; and Pym, who had advanced, pulled up just in time to thrust out his right foot, and so arrest a ball that would otherwise have gone into the net.

But as against these escapes must be set the goal which John Smith obtained from a centre by Butler after 38 minutes. Butler dribbled to within two yards of the line before he delivered a square centre, and racing in Smith just got his outstretched foot to the ball, which Hufton touched on its way into the net. The referee gave Smith offside, a palpably wrong decision for the simple reason that the scorer was always behind the ball. A Liverpool and a London pressman agreed with me that the Wanderers had been deprived of a perfectly legitimate goal. Happily, it did not affect the issue. In the early stages of the second half, West Ham certainly played well enough to inspire amongst their followers the hope that they would make a fight of it, but that hope vanished within nine minutes of the crossover, when J. R. Smith got a second goal for the Wanderers. From that moment, West Ham were a beaten team. Such method as they had shown in the early stages gradually died away, and playing well within themselves the Wanderers finished the game confident and comfortable winners.

THE ALL-IMPORTANT GOALS.

To David Jack fell the honour of scoring the first goal in the quick time of three minutes after the start. Thus he maintained his proud record of having scored in every Cup-tie since the first round. On Saturday he got his chance through Seddon cleverly changing the point of attack by smashing a long pass out to his right wing when the West Ham defenders obviously expected a pass to the left. Butler had a long race with Young for possession, and the back won by a foot, hooking the ball away, only to find himself challenged by Jack before he could clear. A quick flick of the foot gave the forward possession. Young went down with out-stretched leg in a last hope to spoil his opponent, but Jack was away in his full stride, and he shot a high ball on its oblique course into the net before anybody could touch him. Hufton had advanced when he realized that his goal was in peril, and in a last despairing jump to reach the ball, he came down heavily on to his shoulder and face, and had to be assisted to his feet again.

The second goal was engineered by four players. Jennings stopped his wing in clever fashion, and slipped a short pass to Joe Smith, who had been lying well behind his forwards as a sort of emergency half-back. The Bolton captain promptly pushed the ball up the centre, where John Smith, who was on his toes, held it until he deemed it prudent to send it out to Vizard. Henderson raced across to try and force the Welshman into touch, a policy he exploited fairly successfully in the first half, but this time Vizard evaded his rush, slipped round him, and raced inwards along the goal-line, with Henderson at his heels. Then we saw the value of two minds with but a single thought. Seeing John Smith coming towards him Vizard urged the ball gently towards his colleague, and Smith hooked it with his left foot so viciously that the ball rose sharply, went under the bar to hit the netting, which had been pulled tight, and then came out to be scrambled away. But Mr. Asson stood pointing to the centre; the ball had been in the net and out again. West Ham had lost the game irretrievably.

A GENERAL SUMMING UP.

Comments on the collective and individual merits of the players must be brief. By general consent, West Ham were conquered by a team which played with superb confidence, plainly conscious of its ability to win through. The Wan-

MEMORABLE SCENES AT THE OPENING OF THE STADIUM.

An aerial view of the crowd on the playing pitch

derers went about their work right from the outset in a manner which seemed to suggest: " We are bound to beat the best team in the Second Division if only we play our natural game." It was what is known as one of the most valuable assets any combination of footballers can develop—team spirit—that pulled the " Trotters" through. Here we had eleven men working with but a single purpose, dovetailing and blending perfectly, a mobile, virile force which operated in absolute unison and unity, whether concentrating on aggression or compelled to retreat. I cannot single out one player more than another for a special meed of praise. Where all did so well, it would be invidious to individualize. Suffice it to say that, in a comparatively quiet afternoon, Pym made one thrilling save, and displayed fine judgment and anticipation; that the two young backs, Howarth and Finney, never faltered; that Seddon, a giant in every phase of the game, had two polished wing halves as colleagues, and that the whole forward line worked together untiringly and with no little skill to lead and lure the " Hammers'" rear-guard into false positions.

There was nothing of the " hammer-your-way-through" policy about the Bolton attacks. The forwards achieved their object by much more subtle methods, by combination that was bound to create rifts in the West Ham line, and

by shooting of such a character that the wonder was the Wanderers did not win by a more convincing margin. That the correct score should have been three—nil I am convinced, but the referee is the official arbiter in these matters, and there I leave it. To those unfortunate enthusiasts who made the long trek to Wembley in vain, my sympathy; to Walter Rowley, whose lot it was to be the odd man out, a sincere assurance that every true Wanderer feels with him in his hour of disappointment; and to every player who has striven so heroically to bring fame to the town of Bolton, my hearty congratulations.

KING PRESENTS THE CUP.

It was found impossible to get the players through the dense crowds to present them before the match, as had been intended, to the King in the Royal box, and so this part of the ceremony had to be dispensed with. When the final whistle sounded Finney, the young Bolton defender, secured possession of the ball, and the spectators at once surged over the playing pitch like an irresistible wave. All one could see of the Wanderers' players for some time was a white shirt dotted here and there in the black mass of human beings.

The police helped them to reach the Royal box, where the King presented the Cup to the Wanderers' captain, Joe Smith. His Majesty said he was proud

to have the privilege of making the presentation, and expressed the opinion that the better side had won the game, which he feared, at one time, would not be completed. Smith briefly thanked the King, and introduced each of his colleagues, who shook hands with His Majesty, and received from him the handsome gold medal which goes only to the Cup winners, and which is the most coveted memento that can fall to the lot of a player. I know many great players who would willingly have sacrificed all their International honours for this medal.

OVERJOYED BOLTON PLAYERS.

At the close of the match, I succeeded in passing a number of police who had been posted outside the Wanderers' dressing room to keep off all intruders. Joe Smith and his colleagues were like a lot of happy schoolboys. Their joy was unbounded, and the skipper willingly responded to my invitation to send a message through the columns of the " Evening News" to the people of Bolton.

" Tell them," he promptly replied, " that this is the proudest day of our lives. We are pleased not only on our own account, but because we have gratified the wishes of our friends and supporters at Bolton. Our great ambition to bring the Cup for the first time to Bolton is realized. It was a good, hard game, and I was delighted with the way our boys played. We thoroughly de-

served to win because we were on top right from the start. The West Ham players came and congratulated us on our success, and most sportingly admitted that we were the better team, and quicker on the ball. We won because right from the kick-off we felt we were the superior team. But West Ham did well, especially in the first half, and I am sure they will improve if they get into the First Division for their style and play is more suited to the First Division than to the Second." In conclusion, Smith, in reply to a question, said it was a pleasantly contested game, not quite so hard as the semi-final game we played against Sheffield United. It had been said that in some of their Cup-ties their opponents had not played up to form. The natural answer to that was that their rivals had played quite as well as the Wanderers had allowed them.

Kay, the West Ham skipper, who looked a very disappointed man, in reply to a question, said he did not want to find any excuses. " West Ham on the day have been beaten by a better side. For some reason we hardly showed our real football. Bolton were the better side; further, they took their chances and everything they did came off."

Mr. White, the chairman of the losing club, and Mr. King, the manager, readily conceded Bolton were the better side.

One of the best pictures of the famous white horse that cleared the crowd

CUP CRUSH INQUIRY.

NOBODY COULD STOP THE TRAFFIC

There is to be an immediate inquiry into the causes which created the unprecedented situation at Wembley. This assurance has been given by Lieut.-General Sir Travers Clarke, who declares that the whole trouble was that the tap of traffic had been turned full on, and nobody could turn it off. " It was thought that at the most only about 100,000 people would come to the Stadium, and such a multitude as 200,000 was not bargained for. It was the biggest crowd ever seen at a Cup-tie. People poured in from all sides; there was no end to the crowd. We have learned our lesson and shall profit by it. There was a weakness somewhere. We must take steps that will make a recurrence of such a state of affairs impossible. We shall put everything right. The barriers over which the people climbed were only temporary barriers and were erected solely for the Cup-tie. When the next Cup-tie is held at the Stadium the defences will be very much strengthened. When the exhibition opens I conclude that there will be a ring of 'outer defences,' for the

barriers will then be skirting the road."

A SCENE OF WRECKAGE.

The Wembley Stadium after the match presented a remarkable spectacle. It was littered with waste paper, broken bottles, and twisted iron. It looked as though an army corps of tramps had passed the night there. Hundreds of pounds will have to be spent to put the great arena into its original condition, and the cost of clearing it of debris alone will run into a large bill. The beautiful stretch of turf, which, until two o'clock on Saturday was as green and level as a billiards table, is now a broken and uneven pitch, littered with almost every kind of rubbish and broken into holes by the boots of the horses of the mounted police.

It is a wonder that none of the players was seriously injured, for the game took place on a field sown thick with splinters of shattered glass. For two or three yards around the edges of the turf practically all the grass has disappeared. It has been trodden down by thousands of feet into wet and sticky mud. A number of Treasury notes were picked up from this confused mass by fortunate early-morning searchers.

Date 28 April 1923
Place Wembley
Score BOLTON WANDERERS 2
WEST HAM UNITED 0
Teams BOLTON WANDERERS Pym, Haworth, Finney, Nuttall, Seddon, Jennings, Butler, Jack, J. R. Smith, Joe Smith (capt.), Vizard. WEST HAM UNITED Hutton, Henderson, Young, Bishop, Kay (capt.), Tresadern, Richards, Brown, Watson, Moore, Ruffel
Official Referee D. H. Asson (West Bromwich)
Goal Scorers Jack 3, J. R. Smith 55
Attendance 126047
Gate Receipts £27776
Guests of Honour H.M. King George V, The Duke of Devonshire
Copy *The Bolton Evening News* 30 April 1923

THE SPORTS ARGUS, SATURDAY, 26 APRIL, 1924.

UGH!: SENSATIONAL FINISH TO THE CUP FINAL: TWO GOALS FOR "GEORDIES" IN FOUR MINUTES: UGH!

WEMBLEY—WOE, WET & WOBBLE.

Newcastle United Avenge 1905! Aston Villa Thrashed After Having Much the Better of the Play in the Wettest Final in History. Walker Injured: Newcastle's Individualism Prevails Over Villa's Combination. Cowan and Seymour the Marksmen.

OVER 100,000 SPECTATORS.

THE competition for the Football Association Cup—the "blue riband" of the football world—reached its climax this afternoon, when Aston Villa and Newcastle United contested the Final in the Stadium, at Wembley.

It was the game of games, and formed a fitting conclusion to a tournament which began with the qualifying rounds on 8 September last year, and in which nearly 7,000 players—professionals and amateurs—had competed.

Aston Villa and Newcastle United are two of the most wealthy clubs in the land, and the teams are the most famous. Truly it was a case of the survival of the fittest. They were the ideal Finalists, and it was the general opinion that the teams only needed to forget "the importance of the occasion" to provide the ideal Final.

It was a hectic day for football enthusiasts, and specially those of Birmingham, Newcastle and London. In all these three big centres of industry and sport enormous interest was engendered. The game was "the" talk of the football world ever since the semi-final ties were decided on 29 March. Both teams, backed by superb records in this season's tournament, were optimistic of victory, and the respective supporters were equally confident. In London Aston Villa are the most popular football visitors, and the "fans" of Cockaigne thought highly of Villa's chances of lifting the trophy.

Villa and United are renowned Cup fighters. This was the former's eighth appearance in the Final, and they held the record of winning the Cup on six occasions—in 1887, 1895, 1897, 1905, 1913 and 1920. Their failure in the Final was before West Bromwich Albion in 1892. United held a record of a different character. This was their sixth appearance in the Final, and only once in the previous five had they won, in 1910, when they needed a second match to beat Barnsley by two to nil.

This was the second Final clash between Villa and United. They crossed swords in the 1905 Final, when Villa won by two goals—both scored by Harry Hampton—to nil. On that occasion Villa started non-favourites. United were League champions that season, and they were regarded as the football crackerjacks.

Wembley, the scene of to-day's great match, was regarded as the ideal battle ground. In addition to the match there was another attraction in the shape of the British Empire Exhibition. Having regard to the fiasco on the occasion of the Final 12 months ago, to-day's was the first "all ticket" Final. Thus the attendance was limited.

Date 26 April 1924	Dorrell
Place Wembley	**Official** Referee W. E. Russell (Swindon)
Score NEWCASTLE UNITED 2	
ASTON VILLA 0	**Goal Scorers** Harris 83, Seymour 86
Teams NEWCASTLE UNITED Bradley, Hampson, Hudspeth, Mooney, Spencer, Gibson, Low, Cowan, Harris, McDonald, Seymour.	**Attendance** 91695
	Gate Receipts £14280
ASTON VILLA Jackson, Smart, Mort, Moss, Dr V. E. Milne, Blackburn, York, Kirton, Capewell, Walker,	**Guests of Honour** H.R.H. Duke of York, Prince Arthur of Connaught, Ramsay MacDonald
	Copy The Sports Argus, Birmingham 26 April 1924

● Although *The Sports Argus* gives Cowan as the scorer of the first goal, the handwritten account in Newcastle's archives says it was Harris.

COMMENTS OF A COCKNEY ON THE VILLA'S DEFEAT.

The first half was free from rain, and once or twice the sun came out. It was fine open footwork for the most part, and much faster than one might have expected.

The Villa wingers were in great form, Dorrell in particular playing a great game. Had the Villa inside men not found Bradley in an inspired mood they would have made the match safe at this point.

Jackson had little to do in the Villa goal, although the Midlanders' defence was not always too sound.

Harris did many fine things, but had

W. Cowan. **S. Seymour.**
the cracks who scored the goals which gave Newcastle the Cup for the second time in history.

little connection with Cowan, and McDonald, the Newcastle left winger, was strangely quiet.

Blackburn had a busy time with the fine Cowan and Low combination, and honours were about even.

Newcastle won almost entirely upon their magnificent work in the second half. They did not dominate the play during this period, but they were plainly the dangerous side.

Harris was a great forager, and never gave up his attempts to get through on his own. In fact, the first goal was practically his, for it was his shot which was beaten down by Jackson before Cowan got the ball into the net.

Seymour did comparatively little, but his second goal was a glorious effort, perfectly unstoppable.

Cowan was the brains of the Newcastle front line, and Gibson probably the best footballer on the field.

The Newcastle backs were steadier in the second half. Bradley greatly enhanced his reputation.

The Villa forwards fell away badly, possibly through H. Walker having sustained such a severe shock when colliding

A view of Wembley during the 1924 Cup final

Cup final programmes for (from top left), 1933, 1926, 1923, 1937 and 1935

Cup final programmes for (from left), 1925, 1928, 1927, 1932, 1929 and 1934. Inset is Sunderland's lap of honour, 1937

Cup final programme 1934

Cardiff City

BY CITIZEN.

There has been very little outside the Cup Final talked of or thought about at Ninian Park during the past week. The players have not been worrying unduly, but they have been quietly preparing and have done absolutely their best to get thoroughly fit. I don't suppose there ever was a club who have trained in the manner Cardiff have for this final. The players have been allowed to do pretty well as they liked. The Directors have a firm belief in their men and do not agree with any "policing". The average player's one ambition is to figure in a cup-final and secure a cup-medal, and if he cannot look after himself and get himself thoroughly fit then no one else can do it for him. The Citizens appreciate this attitude and have done everything possible could to get fit. Whatever has been the result of the game at Wembley to-day they have secured a wonderful triumph and have done more to strengthen the code than anything else possibly could have. The public have rather criticised the dropping of Len Davies, but the players themselves are quite satisfied that the directors have taken the best step. Len, of course, is bound to be disappointed, but he is sportsman enough to recognise that under the conditions he could hardly hope to play. His time will come again, and no one will wish the eleven players greater success than he, and no one will be more heartily pleased than he if they achieve success.

To-day is a general holiday at Ninian Park. All the staff are being taken to Wembley and the occasion is being made a special one by the management. Win or lose they will get a great reception on their return home and undoubtedly they have thoroughly earned it. Success has come in a season when it was least expected and the whole of Wales will be wishing Cardiff City good luck to-day.

95,000 There?

UNOFFICIAL ESTIMATE OF A RECORD CROWD

The official figures of the gate will not be published until some time next week. An unofficial estimate puts the crowd at 95,000.

This is the largest crowd that has ever seen a Welsh Rugby or Soccer team play.

CELTIC SYMPATHY.

The crowd cheered loudly when the band of the Irish Guards marched on to the field to relieve the Air Force Band, and in their scarlet coats they made a brave show, and immediately became popular with the Welsh crowd by playing one or two Welsh airs.

There was another cheer when the Royal car, which had just dropped the Duke and Duchess of York, appeared at the main entrance to the ground.

As the time of the kick-off drew near the packed arena presented a wonderful appearance. The outstanding feature was the predominance of the blue and white colour.

At 2.45 the two bands lined up in front of the Royal box to welcome the Duke and Duchess.

TEAMS TAKE THE FIELD.

There was a terrific cheer when Sheffield took the field at 2.50, but it was absolutely drowned by the wonderful outburst which greeted Blair when he led his men out, looking particularly smart in their new jerseys with the Cardiff coat of arms emblazoned on the left breast.

The 22 players, with their trainers, the referee and linesmen took up a position opposite the entrance, from where the Duke appeared. His Highness was greeted with tumultuous applause that rang through the Stadium as he shook hands with the players. He went to the Sheffield team first, and then returned to the end of the line, and, commencing with Blair, shook hands with every member of the Welsh team.

● The "international" nature of the 1925 final created notable interest, with Cardiff seen to be representing the whole of Wales. On the morning of the match countless cables and telegrams arrived at the Cardiff camp from Welsh emigrees from Canada, the United States and New Zealand, from the Welsh Regiment in India and from His Majesty's ship *Cardiff*. That those well-wishers did not have a victory to cheer hung on a mistake by Cardiff's right-half Wake. "Wake not Awake" was an obvious heading in the same edition of the *South Wales Football Express*.

Wake's moment of tragedy came after 30 minutes when Pantling pumped a crossfield pass that Wake should have cut out before it reached Fred Tunstall. However, Wake missed the ball and Tunstall's low shot gave Farquharson no chance (below). With Billy Gillespie a governing figure at inside-forward Sheffield United defended their lead with only a few moments of alarm, the most notable seven minutes from time when Beadles and Keenor both mis-hit attempted shots only for the ball to roll to Gill who hit the best chance of all tamely wide.

Date 25 April 1925
Place Wembley
Score SHEFFIELD UNITED 1
CARDIFF CITY 0
Teams SHEFFIELD UNITED Sutcliffe, Cook, Mitton, Pantling, King, Green, Mercer, Boyle, Johnson, Gillespie, Tunstall. CARDIFF CITY Farquharson, Nelson, Blair, Wake, Keenor, Hardy, W. Davies, Gill, Nicholson, Beadles, D. Evans
Goal Scorer Tunstall 30
Attendance 91763
Gate Receipts £15941
Guest of Honour Duke of York
Copy *The South Wales Football Express* 25 April 1925

PRESENTATION OF THE TROPHY

Great Ovations for the Victors and Vanquished

There was a scene of wild enthusiasm when the Sheffield players lined up in front of the Royal Box to be presented by the Duke of York with the coveted trophy.

Looking the picture of fitness after his recent tour, the Duke took evident pride in the duty allotted to him in his first public engagement since his return.

He has a thorough understanding of the Soccer code, and it was noticeable that throughout the game he was one of the first to applaud any particularly good bit of work by the players.

The Duchess of York, at all times vivacious, was equally interested, and indeed at times almost enthusiastic, and gave that touch of naturalness to the proceedings that those around the Royal couple felt quite at ease.

A MEMORABLE SCENE.

It was altogether a memorable scene when the players proceeded to the Royal box, where the Duke stepped forward to greet them.

Seldom has there been such cheering as one heard in honour of the Sheffield players as they passed in single file before the Duke of York, the latter standing to receive them in full view of a hundred thousand people who remained on the ground to give the victors the honours.

SPORTING WELSHMEN.

The Sheffield supporters naturally predominated in the crowd immediately in front of the Royal box, but there was a good deal of the blue and white about, and it was clear from the way Cardiff supporters joined in the tribute to the victorious team that the defeat was being accepted by the Welshmen in a good sporting spirit.

Mr. Ramsay MacDonald, who was next to the Duchess of York, joined her Royal Highness in congratulating Sheffield.

ROYAL CONGRATULATIONS.

Naturally, the greatest ovation was given to the Sheffield captain himself, and he looked a manly and inspiring figure as he received the cordial hand-shake of the Duke. His Royal Highness told him that he had never enjoyed a football match more in his life, and he was particularly satisfied with the magnificent spirit and keenness which had marked the game.

The Duchess of York added her congratulations.

It was to the winning captain, of course, that the Duke of York immediately handed over the emblem of victory, and Gillespie received it with natural grace and dignity. It was at this moment, too, that the greatest of all came.

Tunstall scores the only goal

1926
HOW THE GAME WAS WON AND LOST.

DAVID JACK'S CUP FINAL DISTINCTION.

WONDERFUL GOALKEEPING BY DICK PYM.

Butler takes his nerve powder

A great save by Pym, on his knees to deal with a shot from the Manchester City attack

"OLYMPIAN'S" COMMENTARY.

Bolton Wanderers set the seal on their fame as Cup fighters by winning the Football Association Challenge Cup for the second time in three years at Wembley Stadium on Saturday, David Jack, scoring the all-important goal when the game had only 13 minutes to run.

There was not a great deal between the teams in one of the hardest games and incidentally one of the best Finals I have ever witnessed, the quality of the football being a credit and worthy of two of the outstanding teams from the County which has a strong claim to be regarded as the hub of Soccer football.

His Majesty the King gave expression to the popular sentiment when, in handing the Cup to Joe Smith at the close of a thrilling struggle, he said he thought the Wanderers just deserved their success. Thus was avenged the defeat inflicted upon the Bolton team by the City in the Final tie of 1904, and that by a goal the legitimacy of which could not be questioned.

Jack's winning goal. David Jack is on the ground in front of the goal as the ball reaches the back of the net

● I'm not sure what today's stringent medical restrictions would have made of the "nerve" powder that the Bolton players happily took before beating Manchester City in the 1926 FA Cup final at Wembley. Two of its reported adherents, David Jack and Ted Vizard, combined to score the only goal of the game, which gave Bolton the second of their three Cup wins in the 1920s.

It was a highly competitive and enterprising final in which City were thwarted by Jack's opportunism and the splendid goalkeeping of Dick Pym, who had turned his back on a career as a fisherman in Devon to keep nets empty rather than full for Bolton Wanderers.

David Jack added to his record of having scored the first goal in a Wembley final three years earlier with the decisive touch just thirteen minutes from time. Vizard, the Welsh international, cut the ball back first time from the left, and Jack, who had timed his run to perfection, scored easily. The goal represented a triumph for Bolton's team selection because Jack had been restored to his preferred position of inside-right from the centre of that attack; a switch that had personally disappointing consequences for Bolton's match-winner because the player left out to facilitate the switch was Jack's brother Rollo.

For Bolton there was also a measure of revenge in the outcome. Manchester City had beaten them by the same score in the 1904 final at Crystal Palace.

Date 24 April 1926	McMullan, Austin, Browell, Roberts, Johnson, Hicks
Place Wembley	
Score BOLTON WANDERERS 1	**Officials** Referee Isaac Baker (Crewe)
MANCHESTER CITY 0	**Goal Scorer** Jack 77
Teams BOLTON WANDERERS Pym,	**Attendance** 91447
Haworth, Greenhalgh, Nuttall,	**Gate Receipts** £23157
Seddon, Jennings, Butler, Jack,	**Guest of Honour** H.M. King George V
J. R. Smith, J. Smith, Vizard.	**Copy** The Daily Sketch 22 April 1926;
MANCHESTER CITY Goodchild,	The Bolton Evening News 26 April
Cookson, McCloy, Pringle, Cowan,	1926

SOUTH WALES FOOTBALL ECHO. SATURDAY, APRIL 23, 1927.

CITY BRING THE ENGLISH CUP TO WALES.

WELSH PLAYER'SCOSTLY MISTAKE
GIVES THE BLUEBIRDS VICTORY.

FERGUSON, LEN DAVIES AND THE GOALKEEPER HAVE A HAND IN THE WINNING GOAL.

The F.A. Cup, never before wrested from English football since the competition started in 1871, has come to Wales. Cardiff City, thwarted in their hopes two years ago, renewed this challenge to-day against the Arsenal with the glorious result—a 1—0 victory for Wales.

It was an amazing goal credited to Ferguson that decided the great issue.

Ferguson shot at Lewis, the Arsenal goalie, who fumbled the ball, and Len Davies is believed to have helped it over the line.

It will ever be a debatable point as to who actually scored the goal, but obviously it came about primarily through Lewis's costly blunder.

It is an irony of fate that Lewis, who is a Mardy boy, should thus unwittingly helped the City to their great triumph.

CITY SCORE.

After 30 minutes Ferguson, at close range drew Lewis to his knees as the Arsenal goalie failed to hold the ball, Len Davies darted in and helped it on its way over the line. It will ever be a debatable point as to whether the goal will be credited to one of the Cardiff players or to Lewis, whose faulty work had proved so costly.

The Arsenal must have appreciated the need for increased effort, and they were quickly advancing towards the City's goal. Blyth was exceptionally elusive, for in manœuvring for an opening and from Hulme'scentre, Farquharson was deceived when rushing out with the hope of fisting clear. It was a moment of tense excitement, but Nelson and Watson, coupled with Sloan and Keenor, at the moment held a tight grip on the Arsenal forwards and prevented a shot.

Truly had the City concentrated on defence, in a crucial moment, but that they were not content to fill the role of defenders was evident a moment later, when they carried play to the other end, and Ferguson had a terrific drive charged down by Lewis, who had run opt from the goal-mouth.

Two Minutes to Go.

Curtis had another chance to win the game, and after tapping in from the wing, cleverly and confronted by a practically open goal, he was wide of the mark.

The game was near its close. There were just two minutes more to play when the Arsenal made an advance along the right wing, and from Hume's centre Brain might have done some damage if he had not wildly overrun the ball.

Keenor headed out of danger, and Sloan placed out to Curtis. The length of the repass to Ferguson was accurately ade, but Butler transferred play to midfield, and when play centred in the Cardiff half for a minute.

Again were the Gunners' right wing brought into evidence, Nelson who had been a hero, rushed across and kicked into touch.

It was a sporting action that was shown by Buchan when the teams walked across to the Royal Box for the presentation of the cup. He ran up to the City captain and warmly grasped him by the hand. Other Arsenal players followed suit of shaking the nearest City man by the hand.

Immediately the final whistle went hundreds of spectators swarmed across the ground, and it was with difficulty that the police could keep a clear space for the players to line up and walk to the Royal box. Naturally, the City, as winners, were first to appear before his Majesty, and there was loud and continuous applause as the Kin ghanded over the trophy to the Welsh captain, this sending it away out of England into Wales for the first time in its history.

Lost Ticket Incident.

Among the excursionists from Wales was a party which declined to enter the Stadium, although presenting tickets, unless their foreman, as they called him, could be admitted also, and he had lost his ticket. The officials, with great good humour, stretched a point and passed the whole detachment en masse,

The costly fumble which lost the Cup

Date 23 April 1927
Place Wembley
Score CARDIFF CITY 1 ARSENAL 0
Teams CARDIFF CITY Farquharson, Nelson, Watson, Keenor (capt.), Sloan, Hardy, Curtis, Irving, Ferguson, L. Davies, McLachlan.
ARSENAL Lewis, Parker, Kennedy, Baker, Butler, John, Hulme, Buchan (capt.), Brain, Blythe, Hoar
Official Referee W. F. Bunnell (Preston)
Goal Scorer Ferguson 75

Attendance 91 206
Gate Receipts £23 113
Guest of Honour H.M. King George V
Copy The South Wales Football Echo 23 April 1927

THE SUNDAY TIMES, APRIL 22, 1928.

BLACKBURN'S DIRECT METHODS WIN THE CUP.

◆

FIRST MINUTE GOAL UPSETS THE FAVOURITES.

◆

RELENTLESS HALF-BACK PLAY.

◆

From Our Own Correspondent.

Blackburn Rovers 3   Huddersfield Town 1

Blackburn Rovers won the Cup Final at Wembley yesterday by 3—1 after a game which Huddersfield were always fighting to save, for the Lancashire team scored within the first minute, and thereafter they kept their heads well in front by more direct methods

Huddersfield won the toss, and although they crossed the halfway line, barely thirty seconds had ticked off when the Rovers were a goal up. In the excitement of the moment it was difficult to say precisely what happened, but when the ball came across from the right—Healless swung it into the goal—Puddefoot bundled Mercer into the net, whilst Roscamp touched the ball through. Thus was recorded the most sensational start seen in a Cup final for very many years. So unexpected, indeed, was the goal that, strange as it may seem, people had no time to cheer.

There was a really shocking blunder by the Huddersfield defence almost as soon as the game recommenced, for Barkas, when bustled, tried to pass back to his partner, Goodall, who missed the ball. Very fortunately for Huddersfield Mercer had advanced almost to the edge of the penalty line, but Roscamp was on him in a flash, and the goalkeeper, with no time to gather the ball, tried to kick it clear. He made a very poor attempt, but Goodall recovered to remove the danger with a huge kick.

Yorkshire in Earnest.

But Huddersfield were settling down, and at the end of twenty minutes sparkling forward work from one wing to the other gave the Blackburn defence a rare fright. It seemed that Brown should have shot when Smith lifted the ball into the jaws of the goal instead of passing back, for it meant that Redfern in the end shot outside. Steele was playing good football, but Wilson, as he did against Scotland, hung too far back. McLean, with a great effort, beat two Huddersfield men before putting Roscamp through; but the centre-forward could not beat Goodall. Kelly and Brown were stopped in dashing style by Jones, and so fast did the game become that in the next moment Thornewell was round Barkas. He centred nicely, but Mercer caught Roscamp's header.

Back came the Rovers with a run that looked like real business from the start. All the forwards saw the ball, but Mercer did not, for McLean finished with a drive from just inside the penalty area which sent the ball at a great rate right into the centre of the net. This was a beautiful goal, and even if it came at a time when all Yorkshire had decided that Huddersfied were determined to show their power, none could gainsay that football merit earned due reward.

If Kelly had not dallied when Stephenson and Steele between them had worked out an opening, there might have been more than a crumb of comfort for Huddersfield. But first Kelly tried jugglery instead of shooting, and when he did elect to shoot it was with the wrong foot, and the ball went very wide. Jackson made a great run at long last. With the ball at his toe, he went half the length of the field and passed at least four men. Ultimately he parted with the ball to Smith, who won a corner from Hutton. Smith's cross from the flag was too powerful, and Jones easily cleared.

It was Blackburn's first half. Perhaps, on the whole, Crawford had had as many anxious moments as Mercer; but, even if it be conceded that the Rovers took full advantage of two "open doors," the fact remains that they pushed their advantages to a finality, whilst their opponents were more nonchalant. Blackburn's scheming, too, had been well repaid. Campbell stuck to Jackson as if it were his only mission in life.

There was some more good defence work by Blackburn as rain began to fall and Huddersfield, just as they had at times in the first half, were playing with a seriousness and purpose which suggested a goal. Kelly shot hopelessly over the goal in a hot attack, and

hurt himself in the effort. He was carried to the touch-line for attention, and just as he came back, Wilson fouled McLean, and from the free-kick Rankin fired hard into Mercer. The Blackburn goal had an escape when Crawford came out, but lost the ball. Jones only just beat Brown in what was virtually a race for an open goal.

Jackson's Goal.

Thornewell, who had had a very good first half, could make very little of Barkas this half; and it was just after the Huddersfield back had made a rousing clearance, when Thornewell was in possession, that Huddersfield scored. Kelly had returned to change places with Jackson. Smith, Brown, and Stephenson dovetailed delightfully, and the ball was worked between both backs. Jackson fastened on to it in a flash, and, although Crawford threw himself desperately at the forward's feet, it did not prevent the ball twisting into the net. Thus at long last Huddersfield had their reward, and they took new heart.

Stephenson went very close to an equaliser when he headed in from Smith's centre. Jackson was knocked out in a charge, but after the trainer had attended to him he went back to his rightful position on the wing. The Huddersfield halves did not spare themselves, and their efforts to keep their vanguard on the move was the feature. In stopping Kelly Campbell was kicked on the chin, and play was suspended until he had recovered. Hutton had a free-kick nearly turned through by Roscamp, and Goodall had to give a corner, which yielded nothing tangible. The shower ended soon after Huddersfield scored.

In one Blackburn attack Roscamp, who all through had been a live wire, nearly scored. He shot on the turn when Puddefoot passed to him, and the ball flashed only just wide of the net. Soon afterwards Roscamp actually got the ball past Mercer, but he was offside —only just, but still offside. Of course, the Blackburn players protested loudly, but the referee, who had an excellent view of what happened, was quite right in deciding Roscamp ran too far forward after he and Puddefoot had worked a way to goal by excellent passing.

With the end in sight, Huddersfield made a great effort. Jackson was limping, but Smith literally walked round Hutton and centred. Crawford fisted the ball away, Rankin helped it upfield, and Roscamp, profiting by the fact that Wilson was too far forward, went through splendidly and shot hard and true into the corner of the net as Mercer advanced.

It was a grand finale for Lancashire, and Huddersfield could not complain.

Date 21 April 1928
Place Wembley
Score BLACKBURN ROVERS 3 HUDDERSFIELD TOWN 1
Teams BLACKBURN ROVERS Crawford, Hutton, Jones, Healless (capt.), Rankin, Campbell, Thornewell, Puddefoot, Roscamp, McLean, Rigby. HUDDERSFIELD TOWN Mercer, Goodall, Barkas, Redfern, Wilson, Steele, A. Jackson, Kelly, Brown, Stephenson (capt.), W. H. Smith
Official Referee T. G. Bryan (Willenhall)
Goal Scorers BLACKBURN ROVERS Roscamp (2), McLean; HUDDERSFIELD TOWN Jackson
Attendance 92041
Gate Receipts £23238
Guests of Honour H.M. King George V, H.M. Queen, Duke and Duchess of York
Copy Sunday Times 22 April 1928

A scrimmage in the Blackburn goal area

THE BOLTON EVENING NEWS, MONDAY, APRIL 29, 1929.

"WE WON BECAUSE WE KEPT OUR HEADS," says Seddon.

HOW THE WANDERERS WON THE CUP.

PORTSMOUTH SPEND THEIR ENERGY IN A GREAT FIRST HALF.

BY "OLYMPIAN."

Bolton Wanderers' team, captained by a Bolton man, James Seddon, will bring the Cup to Bolton on Tuesday night for the third time in six years, and a great civic reception is being prepared in their honour. "I never had any doubts about our success," declared Seddon. "We played well within ourselves, and the great thing was that we kept our heads."

Both the Wanderers' goals were obtained at the same end where David Jack scored in the finals of 1923 and 1926, and in a match which produced plenty of good and interesting football, the Wanderers, after a disappointing first half, left no doubt in the minds of 92,576 spectators, who paid approximately £23,400 for admission, as to which was the better side.

The ground seemed firm and all in favour of a fast game, and I understand that the ball had been soaked in water for a time to prevent it being too lively. It was appropriate that at the finish the ball should be "won" by "Billy" Butler, who played a great part in the scoring of both goals. When the players went up to the Royal box for the presentation, the Prince of Wales, in handing the Cup to Seddon, congratulated the Wanderers "on having again won the Cup so soon."

The Wanderers have now joined the select circle of clubs who have won the Cup thrice or more, the others being Aston Villa and Blackburn Rovers, each with six successes to their credit, the defunct amateur club, the Wanderers, who won it five times, and Sheffield United, whose name has been inscribed on the trophy four times. Prior to Saturday 17 players had won three Cup medals. To the list must be added the names of Pym, Haworth, Seddon, Nuttall, and Butler.

A HAPPY BANQUET.

PLAIN SPEAKING TO F.A. ABOUT WEMBLEY TICKETS.

A CRITICAL NOTE.

An atmosphere of extreme happiness naturally prevailed (the champagne flowed freely), but a critical note was introduced when Mr. Nicholls, having proposed the toast to H.M. the King, and read a congratulatory wire from Lord Derby, rose to toast the Football Association. He expressed pleasure that the governing body was so well represented, although the President, Sir Charles Clegg, was not among the guests. The F.A., as they were all well aware, had for many years stood for all that is best in the football world. It had been said that football was the best governed sport in the world, and he agreed.

Sometimes the Association seemed to be inclined to adopt a somewhat autocratic and rather harsh attitude, as they in Bolton knew to their cost re a certain incident this season, but generally their decisions were effective, reasonable, and equitable. Whatever in the way of criticism may from time to time be levelled at the F.A. he was quite sure it was nearly always in the spirit of friendliness and goodwill, and whatever discussions or disagreements might arise from them they could always rely upon the Association eventually arriving at a wise decision in the interests of football generally.

A PLEA FOR MORE TICKETS.

"But I am afraid that remark does not apply to Cup Final tickets," Mr. Nichols remarked amidst applause. "This is the one great blot on the work of the F.A. Each year the trouble is becoming more acute, and it is rapidly developing into a public scandal, and will undoubtedly have to be seriously considered.

"I have no intention or desire to criticize what has been done this year, beyond saying our supply was totally inadequate, and caused us considerable difficulty, as well as disappointing our supporters, but I would most respectfully suggest that next year a much more generous allotment should be reserved for the Finalists."

"Why not 8,000 or 10,000 each," Mr. Nichols suggested, adding "You have 95,000 tickets to dispose of, and I understand from people quite competent to judge that Wembley will hold considerably more than 95,000. If it won't, then all I can say is that it was a terrific waste of money even to build it.

"The clubs who provide the entertainment at Wembley should certainly have first consideration." (Hear, hear). "This suggestion was made in the interests of the clubs who would be fortunate enough to go to Wembley next year, so that they might be saved the troublesome and trying experience which Bolton and Portsmouth have had to go through this year."

WIDER VISION NECESSARY.

Mr. Nichols continued: "I understand the Association say they are not responsible and that the distribution of these tickets is in the hands of the Wembley authorities, but surely such a powerful organization as the F.A. have some influence? All we ask is that they should exercise that influence. I hope the F.A. will give this matter their reasonable consideration if only to keep up their reputation for careful judgment and fair play and wide wisdom." (Applause).

● Bolton Wanderers' splendid achievement in the 1920s was completed by a third FA Cup success in 1929. Billy Butler, who along with Pym, Haworth, Nuttall and Seddon, played in all three finals, was the centre of the 2–0 win over Portsmouth, breaking the deadlock eleven minutes from time with a fine shot and in the last seconds setting up the second for Blackmore. Dick Pym, the goalkeeper, had the distinction of not conceding a single goal on his three appearances in a Wembley Cup final in the 1920s.

The contemporary reports on the left highlight two interesting observations. First is the soaking of the match ball in water to prevent it being too lively on a fast, firm surface; the footballs of the day would have absorbed the water and subsequently became noticeably heavier. The other eye-catching subject that 50 years later would still remain an unsolved problem is the reference to the "plea for more tickets". The plea in fact was for eight or ten thousand tickets to each finalist, indicating that the actual number received in 1929 was considerably less, a supply described as "totally inadequate". Wembley Stadium itself does not escape criticism: "If it won't (hold more than 95,000), then all I can say is that it was a terrific waste of money even to build it."

Date 24 April 1929
Place Wembley
Score BOLTON WANDERERS 2 PORTSMOUTH 0
Teams BOLTON WANDERERS Pym, Haworth, Finney, Kean, Seddon (capt.), Nuttall, Butler, McClelland, Blackmore, Gibson, W. Cook. PORTSMOUTH Gilfillan, Mackie, Bell, Nichol, McIlwaine, Thackeray, Forward, Smith, Weddle, Watson, F. Cook
Official Referee Mr. A. Josephs (South Shields)
Goal Scorers Butler 79, Blackmore 90
Attendance 92576
Gate Receipts £23,400
Guest of Honour H.R.H. The Prince of Wales
Copy The Bolton Evening News 29 April 1929

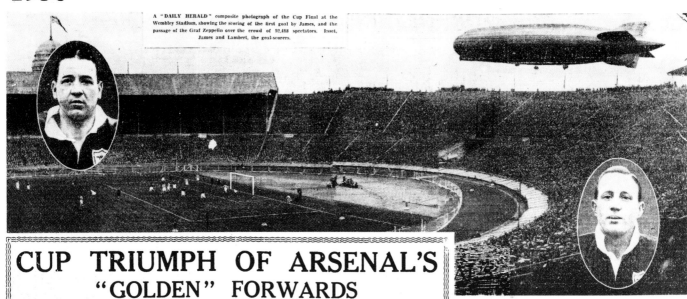

A "DAILY HERALD" composite photograph of the Cup Final at the Wembley Stadium, showing the scoring of the first goal by James, and the passage of the Graf Zeppelin over the crowd of 92,488 spectators. Inset, James and Lambert, the goal-scorers.

CUP TRIUMPH OF ARSENAL'S "GOLDEN" FORWARDS

Brilliant Huddersfield Rally Just Fails: Thrilling Final

Great Day for James and An Amazingly Lucky One For Preedy

By Harold Kendrick ("Syrian")

ARSENAL (James, Lambert) . . 2   HUDDERSFIELD 0

YES. It is all over. Arsenal have won the Cup. The final at Wembley was one of the best I have seen and Huddersfield Town were gallant—I might even say unfortunate—losers.

Not the most biassed follower of the Arsenal will deny that the Londoners were flattered by the score of 2 goals to 0 in their favour.

Arsenal were slightly the better team in the first half, and their interval lead of a goal was a fair reflection of the play. The second half was almost entirely Huddersfield's.

The fact remains, however, that Huddersfield, despite their many beautifully executed movements, failed to get the ball into the Arsenal net, and that Arsenal secured another goal from one of their few second-half raids.

SUCCESS DESERVED

Goals decide the destination of the Cup, and thus Arsenal were entitled to their success. Huddersfield lost because of the inability of their inside-forwards to take advantage of many scoring chances.

It was a fine game, and might have been even better had not Arsenal taken the lead so early. The Arsenal attack in the opening stage. was positively brilliant. The Huddersfield defence was pierced after 15 minutes' play.

More goals might have fallen to the Londoner. If they had played a five-forward game. Instead, they adopted a safety-first policy. Fortunately for them, this policy enabled them to keep Huddersfield out.

I maintain that an aggressive attack is the best defence. If Arsenal had kept their brilliant forwards in the positions they are expected to occupy, I am confident that Huddersfield would not have taken charg of the game as they did after ends were changed.

Jack and James, after the opening goal, were seldom up with their colleagues. They fell back to reinforce the defence. Consequently the Huddersfield halves and backs, opposed by only a skeleton attack, had little difficulty in holding the few Arsenal raids, and at the same time were able to forage for their own forwards.

DARING 'KEEPER

Thus we found that Huddersfield, by no means dismayed by their early reverse, were nearly always swarming round Preedy, the Arsenal goalkeeper.

I have seen numerous finals in which a single mistake by a player has cost his side a goal and the Cup. But in no final that I can remember, nor in any kind of match, for that matter, have I seen more blunders by a goalkeeper prove so profitless to the opposing side.

The supporters of the Arsenal must have held their breath on numerous occasions when Preedy dropped the ball in the goal-mouth through poor anticipation he left his goal, missed the ball only to see an opponent also miss it; and when Huddersfield men were right through only to place the ball anywhere but between the posts.

While giving Preedy credit for numerous fine clearances when surrounded by opponents, one can say that his unsteadiness in goal might have proved fatal. Flukes have frequently won the Cup.

Here was an opportunity for Huddersfield to have obtained numerous fluke goals, yet not one did they get.

The most brilliant player on the field—and I should say the most disheartened

at the end of it all—was Smith, Huddersfield's veteran left-winger. He did not always get the better of his duels with Tom Parker, the Arsenal captain, but he put across so many perfect centres that it must have been heartrending to the followers of Huddersfield to see them wasted.

Huddersfield's policy of playing Davies in the centre did not prove successful. Davies, although well watched by Seddon, had chances to go through, but always at the critical moment he failed.

Raw and Kelly, on each side of him, did much clever work in initiating attacks.

SOME FINAL FACTS

The official attendance was returned at 92,488 and the receipts £23,265 13s. 6d.

By winning the trophy for the first time in their history, Arsenal join the select band of 29 clubs which have monopolised Soccer's highest honour since its inauguration.

The Cup comes South after nine years, for it has remained in the North since 1921, when Tottenham won the trophy.

This is the third time the Cup has been won by a London club. The first occasion was the Spurs' initial success in 1901.

Arsenal have only reached the final on one other occasion—in 1927, when Cardiff City took the Cup out of England for the first time.

Huddersfield reached the final in 1920, when Aston Villa beat them, in 1922, when they defeated Preston North End, and in 1928 when they lost to Blackburn Rovers.

but they, like Davies, had not a single scoring shot in their locker.

Jackson, I thought, played well in the first half, when he had John, the Arsenal left-half, "in his pocket," but subsequently the Huddersfield flyer, although always fighting to make an opening, was hemmed in by the reinforced Arsenal defence.

Wilson, the Huddersfield captain, at centre-half, played manfully throughout. Campbell, however, I thought the best half-back on the field, and Naylor, on the opposite flank, after a shaky start did really well.

The men behind—Goodall and Spence—were as sound a pair of backs as one could wish to see, while Turner, in goal, completed a really fine defensive trio.

THE FIRST GOAL

Bastin and James were the stars of the Arsenal side, and, incidentally, they were responsible for the first goal. After 15 minutes' play Goodall was adjudged to have fouled James. Quick as lightning—I did not hear the referee's signal for the free-kick to be taken—James pushed the ball forward to Bastin.

The wing man ran nearly to the corner flag, and when challenged by Goodall, doubled back, and centred to James, who had run forward. James received the pass in his stride and shot a great goal.

Previously, Parker had shot over from a free kick just outside the penalty area, while a fine piece of headwork by Bastin and Lambert resulted in the former heading just over the bar. Lambert, on

another occasion, got right through, but Turner advanced to rob the Arsenal centre of what looked a certain goal.

Smith made a brilliant run and centre which Jackson received on his head, the ball going a little wide of the upright.

Subsequent play in the first half was fairly even. Hulme missed by inches with a left-foot drive when the ball came to him unexpectedly, and at the other end Preedy dropped the ball after Smith had centred. Hapgood managed to scramble it away.

A great shot by Naylor curled over the right angle of the bar and upright.

Arsenal's goal had another lucky escape when, following a free-kick, Smith sent in a high dropping shot which Preedy caught and dropped. Preedy, however, managed to clutch at the ball and fall on it. He was surrounded by Huddersfield men, and relief only came when the referee awarded a free-kick for an infringement.

SMITH'S EFFORTS

A moment later Smith shot into the side of the net, and followed with another fine centre. Preedy dashed out, but could only slightly deflect the ball. Fortunately for him, it rolled away harmlessly.

Thus at the interval Arsenal hung on to their 1—0 lead. Huddersfield began a terrific onslaught on the Arsenal goal immediately the game was resumed. Several shots were fired in, but all rebounded off Arsenal men who packed their goal.

At this period the Arsenal's forward line was missing, although Hulme, Lambert and Bastin, when they secured possession, lost little time in racing away with the ball. Three forwards, however, could not make much headway, and the fight was almost continually in the vicinity of the Arsenal goal. James was here, there and everywhere. Jack also had a roving commission.

It seemed almost impossible for the Arsenal goal to escape downfall. Yet it did. Wilson shot over from a corner, and immediately afterwards placed a free kick in a similar place. Raw once headed into Preedy's hands, while Smith saw another of his perfect centres sail right across the goal-mouth with no one able to deflect it into the net.

A CRUEL BLOW

Then while the Huddersfield assault looked like succeeding, James kicked down the field to Lambert. The Arsenal centre raced between the spread-eagled Huddersfield backs and Turner had no alternative but to run out. Just as he was on the point of challenging Lambert, however, the Arsenal forward shot out his foot and glided the ball into the net.

This second goal must have been a cruel blow to Huddersfield. They must have kept the Arsenal penned in their own half for nearly 40 minutes of the second half, yet the finishing touch that meant a goal was always lacking.

On the other hand, the Arsenal, in one of certainly not more than four raids to the other end, had been able to consolidate their position.

Parker and Hapgood played magnificently in the Arsenal defence. Seddon always had the measure of Davies, while Baker and John concentrating in the efforts to keep Huddersfield out proved rare stoppers.

It is difficult to estimate what Arsenal owed to James. He was magnificent throughout, and when the final whistle sounded he revealed a little more of his cleverness by pouncing on the ball and carrying it off as a souvenir of a great occasion.

Date 26 April 1930
Place Wembley
Score ARSENAL 2
HUDDERSFIELD TOWN 0
Teams ARSENAL Preedy, Parker, Hapgood, Baker, Seddon, John, Hulme, Jack, Lambert, James, Bastin.
HUDDERSFIELD TOWN Turner, Goodall, Spence, Naylor, Wilson, Campbell, Jackson, Kelly, Davies, Raw, Smith
Official Referee T. Crewe (Leicester)
Goal Scorers James 16, Lambert 88
Attendance 92 488
Gate Receipts £23 265
Guest of Honour H.M. King George V
Copy The Daily Herald 28 April 1930

The Gunners with the Cup

● The 1930 final was the tale of the two teams built by the greatest innovator of his time, Herbert Chapman. Chapman had revitalised Huddersfield in the early 1920s before moving south to have the same invigorating effect on Arsenal. The day belonged to Chapman's present team and to Alex James who scored the first goal, a rarity in itself, after a brilliantly quick free-kick. As Huddersfield pressed for an equaliser throughout the second half it was James' ball out of defence that sent Lambert through for Arsenal's second goal. The final is also remembered for the appearance of the German Zeppelin which cast a shadow over the stadium and the rest of the decade.

WETTEST CUP FINAL FOR YEARS.

92,000 RAIN-SOAKED PEOPLE AT WEMBLEY.

THRILLING MOMENT IN THE COMMUNITY SINGING.

SCORES of thousands of tired and worn-out people arrived home in the various large towns of England, early yesterday morning, still wet.

They had spent the whole of Saturday in rain-soaked London. They had wandered about the streets all the morning, staring at the rainy sights.

They had stood or sat in the vast Stadium at Wembley during the wettest Cup Final known for many years.

Then they had wandered about the rainy streets again for hours before catching their midnight trains.

The luckiest people were those who, like the King, who was at Windsor, listened to Mr. George Allison's broadcast description of the match. They, at least, were under cover, although many of them were in hospital, in blind homes, in almshouses.

Even on the grandstand I got very wet. Indeed, for the second half of the game, I stood right at the back of the stand, trying to hide from the cold, and sheltered by several portly forms, substantial enough to keep the wind away.

The rest of the 92,000 people at Wembley were braver than I. They revelled in the rain.

It began with the community singing organised by the "Daily Express," as in previous years, and the community concert ended with three verses of "Abide With Me," sung with a reverence that must amaze any person who encounters for the first time this paradox of England's greatest football event being preceded by the singing of the Church's most moving hymn.

When the West Bromwich Albion team lined up in front of the Duke of Gloucester, at the end, to receive the Cup, facing the Prime Minister, Mr.

The crowd looked more like a Boat-race crowd than a mass of football enthusiasts, because both teams were blue, and so all the favours worn were blue and white. The Albion fans had more white than the Birmingham supporters.

Experts, I am told, could sort them out, but they were all the same to me. They looked still more alike because they were all wet through. In front of me were scores of thousands of people whose hats and caps were soaked through. Yet no one noticed the rain, apparently. . . .

Stanley Baldwin, Mr. J. H. Thomas, and other statesmen, they presented the sorriest sight. They were all wet through; they were covered with mud.

They were dog-tired, for they had won one of the hardest-played games in the history of modern football. Fighting every inch of the way on a slippery ground, they had slid their way to victory.

The dirtiest of them all was Magee, the right half-back. Magee's dirt was the blackest of blacks. It covered his shorts and concealed half his jersey. In fact, he was the blackest-looking footballer I have ever seen.

NO TICKET RAMP.

There was not so much noise as usual, I thought, but no one moved, and, on the grandstand, only about a dozen people, I should think, left before the end. In the vast arena, no one seemed to move. They stood all through the rain.

Touts had a bad time, for, in spite of all the precautions, people usually succeed in getting hold of tickets and hawking them at Wembley.

You could have bought dozens of seats last Saturday without paying any premium.

A two-shilling ticket was two

shillings, but, even then, they were not sold, because nobody went to Wembley this year unless he had a ticket.

When Birmingham scored what many thought was their first goal, it was offside. The rain was never off-side. It fell first on one side and then on the other, . . . and it fell all the time.

There seemed less kicking out than usual. The ball, indeed, moved slowly along the rain-soaked ground. Every now and then you thought it was going over the line, but it stopped dead. Now and then Birmingham's superior

craft and combination came into action, but the more dashing methods of the youthful Albion team were better suited to the wet and mud. That was why they won.

No wonder the teams were tired at the end—much more tired than usual. Every step they took must have seemed a labour, so rain-soaked was the ground. It was like running on sand.

You saw no puddles. The turf had soaked up the rain and made the ground sponge-like. Every time a man put down his foot it sank in.

Manchester United should have been in the Final this year. They could have beaten any team—in rain like that.

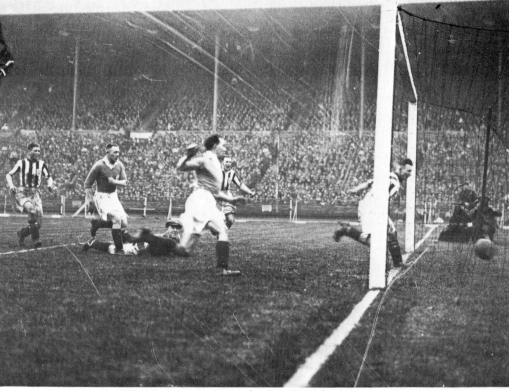

West Brom's winning goal – W. G. Richardson's second

Date 25 April 1931
Place Wembley
Score WEST BROMWICH ALBION 2 BIRMINGHAM CITY 1
Teams WEST BROMWICH ALBION Pearson, Shaw, Trentham, Magee, W. Richardson, Edwards, Glidden, Carter, W. G. Richardson, Sandford, Wood. BIRMINGHAM CITY Hibbs, Liddell, Barkas, Cringan, Morrall, Leslie, Briggs, Crosbie, Bradford, Gregg, Curtis

Official Referee A. H. Kingscott (Derby)
Goal Scorers WEST BROMWICH ALBION W. G. Richardson 26 and 58. BIRMINGHAM CITY Bradford 57
Attendance 92 406
Gate Receipts £23 366
Guest of Honour Duke of Gloucester
Copy The Daily Express 27 April 1931

● The 1931 final produced evidence from the highest levels that a team can be at its most vulnerable when it has just scored. Birmingham's Bradford, the England international, had equalised the goal from W. G. Richardson by which West Bromwich Albion led at half-time. But straight from the kick-off Albion interpassed their way through a Birmingham defence that for a crucial second had lost its concentration; Richardson slid his second goal past Harry Hibbs. Albion also won promotion from the Second Division.

Daily H

No. 5052   *   MONDAY, APRIL 25, 19

HITLER SWEEPS AHEAD

DOUBLE VOTE OF ANY OTHER PARTY

ADOLF HITLER

Ex-Kaiser's Son as a Nazi Member

HITLER swept ahead yesterday in the elections to decide the new Governments of Prussia—the key to all Germany—Bavaria, Anhalt, Wurtemberg and Hamburg.

Late last night, with four-fifths of the votes cast accounted for, Hitler's party, the Nazis, had scored almost twice as many as any other single party.

Of the 20½ million votes counted, the Nazis had obtained 7,450,000, the Socialists 4,500,000, the Centre Party 3,250,000, and the Communists 2,620,000. The indications are that neither Hitlerites nor anti-Hitlerites will have a majority in the new Parliament, and the Communists will hold the balance:

Prince August Wilhelm, the 45-year-old fourth son of the ex-Kaiser, is among the deputies elected to the Prussian Diet on the Nazi ticket.

SEVEN SEATS TO 160

From Our Own Correspondent

BERLIN, Sunday.

FOR the third time within a few weeks, millions of German voters went to the poll in the Prussian Parliament elections to-day. Voting also took place in Bavaria, Anhalt, Wurtemburg and Hamburg.

A Coalition Government of Socialists, Centre Party and Democrats in the last Prussian Parliament had a slender majority of

dead, while a Nazi was stabbed to death at Hamborn.

Berlin was heavily patrolled by police, many of them armed with carbines, and 350 arrests were made in the course of the day.

The chairman of the Socialist Party himself, Otto Wels, was attacked and injured by a group of Hitlerites, led by a Nazi M.P., at Cologne last night.

HIT WITH BOTTLE

Herr Wels was sitting in the restaurant of his hotel with Herr Bauknecht, the Socialist chief of the

PRESIDENT HINDENBURG leaving a polling station after recording his vote yesterday in the Prussian Diet election.

PROPOSED BEER STRIKE

CINEMA OWNERS CONSIDER CLOSING

BRITISH cinema-owners and publicans are discussing plans for protesting against taxation.

One idea considered by licensed victuallers and certain brewers is that when present supplies are exhausted, the publicans will refuse to order any more beer. They hope to make customers indignant.

The Cinematograph Exhibitors' Association has discussed making its protest against the reimposition of the Entertainments Tax on 6d. seats by closing cinemas.

Mr. W. R. Fuller, secretary of the association, and several colleagues, are to visit Paris to investigate the result of the recent showmen's tax strike there. Paris entertainments ceased for 24 hours.

ANXIOUS WHIPS

Government Whips are becoming alarmed at the proportions of the back-bench revolt against Mr. Neville Chamberlain's failure to reduce the beer duty, wrotes our Political Correspondent.

Behind the scenes Captain Margesson and his fellow Whips are exercising the utmost pressure to prevent Conservative M.P.s from suporting Sir William Wayland's amendment on the Finance Bill to decrease the duty by the full 31s. a

CUP FINA
GOAL WAS
NOT A GOAL

FILM PROVES IT YET IT MUST STAND

NO, IT WAS NOT A GOAL!

Newcastle United defe the Arsenal by two goals to or the F.A. Cup Final at Wembley Saturday—but the camera pr beyond doubt that their first was not a legitimate one.

The referee's word is law, howe and there the matter must end.

"Whatever the film may appea show will not make me alter my cision," the referee, Mr. W. Harper, yesterday.

To Hannen Swaffer on Saturday, Harper said:

"**It was a goal. As God is my ju the man was in play. I was e yards away. I do not mind what o people say.**"

The film record of the mat shown privately yesterday—makes it clear that Allen secured his goal after the ball had gone a foot over the dead-line.

It was mode clear, too, late last night, that it was Richardson, the United's inside-right, and not Boyd, outside right, who sent the decisive pass to Allen.

Allen himself said yesterday: "I didn't see whether the ball had gone out or not. The referee is the best judge."

Sir S. Hill-Woo

Mr. Harper was obviously clear in own mind that a legitimate goad been scored, and no signals were n by either of the linesmen—though were badly placed.

Sir Samuel Hill-Wood, chairman o Arsenal, said to the "Daily Herald" terday:—

"If the film demonstrates the

Will Alex James play for Arsenal next season?

It was revealed yesterday t neither he nor any other mem of the team has yet been asked re-sign.

ONE PENNY

PRUSSIA

RICHARDSON   REFEREE

ALLEN

…ECORD made by British Movietone News of the incident that led …stle's first goal. Richardson's right foot and the ball are clearly …d ball line. It was at first thought that it was Boyd who centred the ball.

…ly as you say, then we have luck.
…, we can take no further … matter. The referee has …ision, and that is the end

Sir J. Simon Comes Home Suddenly

SIR JOHN SIMON, the Foreign Secretary, unexpectedly flew back to London from Geneva yesterday, and left by car for Fritwell Manor, his home, near Banbury.

" There is no special reason for my return," he said to a " Daily Herald " representative.

BACK TO GENEVA

" I have routine work at the Foreign Office which will absorb my time for a few days. Then I shall rejoin the Prime Minister at Geneva."

Mr. MacDonald's health has already benefited from his few days' sta… …n Switzerland.

Sir Thomas Horder, his medical adviser, is returning to London, states Reuter, as Mr. Duke-Elder, his oculist, has arrived in Geneva, and will remain for the present.

CHANCELLOR ILL

Mr. Neville Chamberlain, Chancellor of the Exchequer, who has been suffering from lumbago, is now confined to the house with gout, which may prevent him from attending the House of Commons to-day.

Disarmament Conference—Page Two.

…VICE …LAZING …RCH

…COLLAPSED: …'S 5-MILE …GALLOP

…he roof of his church …into flames, a vicar …continued with the …n service, afterwards …onscious in an attempt …luable religious orna-

…ma was er…acted when …ar-old Hafod Churcl… …s Bridge, and 15 miles …stwyth, was destroyed

…e vicar, the Rev. Noah …nconscious, his son gal… …iles to summon the fire

…res, including the famous …tuary, valued at £60,000, …evably damaged.

…as first noticed during the

WHOLESALE ARREST OF CONGRESS DELEGATES

HIDE AND SEEK IN DELHI STREETS

From Our Own Correspondent
NEW DELHI, Sunday.

AFTER a day of hide-and-seek through all the streets and bazaars in New Delhi to-day the police rounded up and arrested 630 Congress members, who had gathered there to attempt to hold their forbidden annual meeting.

Pandit Madan Mohan Malaviya, the 70-year-old president-elect of Congress, who intended to lead the meeting in the absence of Mrs. Naidu, who was arrested on Friday, was himself arrested yesterday.

Those delegates who had avoided arrest on the way to New Delhi sprang a surprise on the police by gathering at 9 o'clock this morning in the Chandni Chowk, a main street in the heart of the city.

Amritlal Ranchodas, an Ahmedbad mill-owner, presided over the gathering, which lasted ten minutes.

Printed resolutions, reaffirming complete independence for India as the aim of the Nationalist Congress and pledging confidence in Gandhi's leadership, were circulated.

These resolutions also called for an intensification of the civil disobedience campaign.

As soon as the police realised they had been outwitted, reinforcements were rushed to the spot, the meeting was broken up, and 150 delegates, including the president, were arrested.

Pandit Malaviya

Then (adds the British United Press) began the game of hide and seek

(Continued on Page Three)

● The success of Adolf Hitler in the German elections produced the lead story on Monday 25 April 1932, but it could not keep off the front page one of the most controversial incidents in the history of the FA Cup.

Arsenal, even without the injured Alex James, led Newcastle United one-nil; indeed Bob John who had replaced James with Cliff Bastin switching to inside-left, had justified his selection by opening the scoring after a quarter of an hour. But the destiny of the Cup then swung on a decision by referee W. Harper to allow play to go on as Richardson crossed from the Newcastle right. Clearly the Arsenal defenders checked convinced the ball had gone over the goal-line. Allen, the Newcastle centre-forward, did not hesitate and made the most of the chance as the ball was swept into the middle.

Just how much Arsenal were affected by the award of the goal remains impossible to quantify but both photographic and film evidence later appeared to support their grievance. Nevertheless Newcastle seized the stroke of good fortune – if that's what it was. Allen was equally diligent with a second chance that came his way, and about this goal there was no dispute. It took the Cup to Tyneside. The *Daily Herald*'s quotes from referee Harper are revealing: "As God is my judge, the *man* was in play" (the ball is not referred to). Harper is also reported as saying he was eight yards away when the *Herald* photograph shows him outside the penalty area. But as always, of course, the referee's decision was irrevocable.

It is a pleasure to record Arsenal's reaction to what must have been a great disappointment. Captain Parker, known as "Gentleman Tom", would not allow his players to hold up the game by protesting, and Sir Samuel Hill-Wood's comment afterwards that it was "very bad luck" contrasts with today's usual reaction.

Date 23 April 1932
Place Wembley
Score NEWCASTLE UNITED 2 ARSENAL 1
Teams NEWCASTLE UNITED McInroy, Nelson, Fairhurst, McKenzie, Davidson, Weaver, Boyd, Richardson, Allen, McMenemy, Lang.
ARSENAL Moss, Parker, Hapgood, Jones, Roberts, Male, Hulme, Jack, Lambert, Bastin, John
Official Referee W. P. Harper (Worcs.)
Goal Scorers NEWCASTLE UNITED Allen 2; ARSENAL John
Attendance 92 298
Gate Receipts £24 688
Guests of Honour H.M. King George V and Queen Mary
Copy *Daily Herald* 25 April 1932

1933
HUSH-HUSH HEROES OF THE CUP FINAL

The Daily Sketch described the above picture of Manchester City as "in everyday drapery from an unaccustomed angle" and the Everton player on the left as "believed to be Dixie Dean". Below: Langford punches clear from a corner

ances for the club. Warney Cresswell remained a masterful defender even though he had won his first England cap eleven years earlier. Cliff Britton showed all the shrewdness on the field that he would later exhibit as an outstanding manager.

The 1933 final was the first in which the players were numbered – Everton in conventional style 1 to 11; Manchester City from goalkeeper Langford who wore number 22 through to 12. City included in their ranks their sturdy centre-half and captain, Sam Cowan, Matt Busby, to his right, Jimmy McMullen, who had captained the Wembley Wizards, the Scotland side of 1928, and Alec Herd, father of David, who led the attack.

Legend points at a too early arrival at Wembley that undermined City's performance; a long wait in the dressing-room only served to build the tension. Everton withstood some early pressure and then punctuated the match with three goals from Stein, Dean and Dunn.

Our research revealed the reluctance, unusual at the time surely, but not so in the 1980s, of players from both sides to allow access to photographers on the eve of the final. The Manchester City players are photographed in the top picture, backs turned, while on the left, Dixie Dean covers his face to avoid the camera. Whether an exclusive arrangement with another photographer or simple shyness was the case is not recorded.

● The 1933 FA Cup final success completed a remarkable treble for Everton, following their Second Division Championship in 1931 and their League Championship in 1932. At the core of their triumphs remained the marvellous goal-getting capabilities of William Ralph "Dixie" Dean who scored at Wembley and uncomplainingly shrugged off all Manchester City's physical attempts to unsettle him. But Everton were no one-man team; indeed Dean was the striking

force at the front end of a very sophisticated machine. Ted Sagar, in goal was on the way to more than 450 League appear-

Date 29 April 1933
Place Wembley
Score EVERTON 3 MANCHESTER CITY 0
Teams EVERTON Sagar, Cook, Cresswell, Britton, White, Thomson, Geldard, Dunn, Dean (capt.), Johnson, Stein. MANCHESTER CITY Langford;

Cann, Dale, Busby, Cowan (capt.), Bray, Toseland, Marshall, Herd, McMullen, Brook
Team Colours EVERTON White
Official Referee E. Wood (Sheffield)
Goal Scorers Stein, Dean, Dunn
Attendance 92950
Gate Receipts £24831
Guest of Honour The Duke of York
Copy *The Daily Sketch* 28 April 1933

THE DAILY EXPRESS.

He Became A Referee By Accident

Perfect Ambassador Of British Football

"Daily Express" Special Correspondent.

I SAT in the games master's room at Watford Grammar School. On the table I noticed a whistle. And somehow it fascinated me.

That whistle, I thought, will probably set in motion the greatest struggle, the biggest thrill, the most famous of Soccer's clashes—the Cup Final.

Its shrill blast will sound across the pitch at Wembley, yet, throughout all the frenzy of the struggle, it will be calm, assured, and unemotional.

In the midst of strong partisanship it will sound clearly and without fear or favour.

For the whistle belonged to Mr. S. F. Rous, games master at Watford Grammar School, the man with whom the F.A. have entrusted the task of ruling this year's Cup Final.

What manner of man was it to whom such power had been given? I had come to find out.

* * *

Looks An Athlete

AT that moment Mr. Rous entered the room. Tall, well-built, public school type. Pleasant smile beneath a small moustache. He looks an athlete himself. The sort of man who could hold his own in any place where athletes are gathered.

"You know," he said, "I'm very bucked about being appointed Cup Final referee, but I'm not at all sure that I want to talk about it. My work here is very important to me, and at the moment the boys are well satisfied that their games master has got such a distinguished job.

"But they won't stand for stuff and nonsense. So if you're going to start the 'From Cradle to Wembley' stuff I'm afraid I can't discuss the matter."

I assured him, however, that he could referee our conversation as well as the match. If I asked a question he didn't like he could rule it offside, or send me off the field altogether. And as football is the Englishman's most socialising influence, I soon persuaded him to betray some of the enthusiasm which lies behind his rather restrained manner.

"I'm afraid," said Mr. Rous, "that I'm a bit of a mountaineer. I like to climb up to the pinnacle of whatever I undertake, be it work, semi-work, or play.

"As this year's Cup Final referee, I feel I have reached the pinnacle of the semi-work section of my life. That is very satisfactory but I'm really glad, because—well"—he paused a moment—"I love the game."

* * *

The Shadow

THEN came the rather sad little story of how he became a referee. The story lies like a shadow behind the glow of his present success.

Years ago he was a player—a goalkeeper of such promise that professional clubs sought his services as an amateur. At Exeter College, a student and captain of the eleven, he gave many great displays of goalkeeping. Then, in one disastrous college game, he badly injured a wrist.

It was good-bye to playing. The injury never properly healed; the damaged wrist was about as much use to a goalkeeper as a wooden leg would be to a centre forward. Exeter College had to look for another captain.

"It was a great disappointment," he continued. "Much as I love football, I have never cared just to watch it—or any other game for that matter. Even if I lived next door to the Arsenal I should probably never go to watch a match. I simply must play some part in a game."

* * *

Services Volunteered

SO, for a time, football and Mr. Rous were parted. Then, one morning, while staying at Norwich, he heard a referee was wanted for local match in the afternoon. Original official had cried off.

Then the idea dawned. Where there was football there had to be referees. Where there was football Mr. Rous decided that he had to be too. Dashed off and volunteered his services.

So a referee arose from the ashes of a player, and Association football received into its service one of the most competent and popular officials the game has ever known.

* * *

Rich In Experience

ALTHOUGH his refereeing career is comparatively short (entered the lists proper in 1926, after graduating in amateur circles), it is rich in experience. All sorts and conditions of football.

His whistle has blown for a foul in Cairo; has set games in motion in Holland; granted goals in Belgium and France; ruled offside in Germany; sounded time in Hungary. Always has he been the perfect ambassador of British football. On one occasion, in Italy, was presented to Mussolini.

* * *

'Varsity Match

BACK to the English scene. Mr. Rous behind the whistle in the Oxford and Cambridge matches. Making a name for himself through the clever way in which he blended his discretion with undergrads' somewhat rugged valour.

And at Wembley—1926. Bolton Wanderers and Manchester City, then Cup losers, took their throw-ins at the decision of Mr. Rous, then linesman, now referee.

Perhaps it is superfluous to add that never once, on English fields, has today's referee had a decision criticised —that he is always in demand for this, that and the other football function.

Once refereed a League match on the Saturday, attended a dinner in the evening, refereed a Continental international on the Sunday, travelled overnight to resume duties at Watford Grammar School on the Monday morning.

And after the Cup Final he will referee the Holland v Belgium match. If that isn't love of football—what is? May to-day add to his laurels

---

● Stanley Rous, at the outset of his distinguished period of involvement in the world of football, refereed the 1934 final in which Manchester City fulfilled their claim of 1933 that they would return as winners to Wembley.

City's side included the 19-year-old goalkeeper Frank Swift.

Swift was so nervous that the night before the game Sam Cowan, the captain, paid him special attention by keeping the young goalkeeper's mind full of tales of the previous final. Swift would also later recall that as the junior player in the side it was his Saturday morning task to go out and buy the day's supply of chewing gum.

Jack Tinn, the Portsmouth manager, a planner ahead of his time, had invited the comedian Bud Flanagan into his team's dressing-room to help lessen the tension. Certainly Portsmouth gave a good account of themselves in the first half, during which Rutherford's cross-shot – the ball brushing Swift's fingers on the way in – gave them the lead. At half-time Tilson's promise that he would score twice in the second half was designed to calm Swift who felt that the goal was his responsibility. Tilson, though, was as good as his boast. While the Portsmouth centre-half Allen was off the field for treatment, Tilson grabbed the equaliser, and four

minutes from time he shot with equal accuracy after a clever pass from Alec Herd.

The relief at the final whistle proved too much for Swift who passed out as he set off to join in the celebrations. Cowan, ever mindful of his responsibilities, helped retrieve the youngster who was at the start of an illustrious career, before leading him up to the Royal Box to collect their medals.

Date 28 April 1934
Place Wembley
Score MANCHESTER CITY 2 PORTSMOUTH 1
Teams MANCHESTER CITY Swift, Barnett, Dale, Busby, Cowan, Bray, Toseland, Marshall, Tilson, Herd, Brook. PORTSMOUTH Gilfillan, Mackie, W. Smith, Nichol, Allen, Thackeray, Worrall, J. Smith, Weddle, Easson, Rutherford
Team Colours MANCHESTER CITY Maroon shirts, white shorts; PORTSMOUTH White shirts, black shorts
Officials Referee S. F. Rous (Herts.). Linesmen F. C. Wells, G. W. Ward
Goal Scorers MANCHESTER CITY Tilson 74, 86; PORTSMOUTH Rutherford 27
Managers MANCHESTER CITY Wilf Wild PORTSMOUTH Jack Tinn
Attendance 93 258
Gate Receipts £24 950
Guest of Honour H.M. King George V
Copy The Daily Express 28 April 1934

87

'SPORTS SPECIAL ("GREEN 'UN"), SATURDAY, APRIL 27, 1935.

What a Wednesday Jubilee! — Great and Glorious Cup Triumph.

Ellis Rimmer's Late Winning Goals.

SENSATIONAL START AND FINISH BY WEDNESDAY AT WEMBLEY.

Albion Miss Their Chances.

"THROSTLES" DRAW LEVEL AFTER TWICE BEHIND, BUT STAMINA TELLS IN THE END.

SHEFFIELD WEDNESDAY started the F.A. Cup Final in sensational fashion, Palethorpe scoring in two minutes. The Albion fought back with spirit and after Boyes had equalised — 21 minutes — they were the more dangerous side, their attack, particularly on the left, always threatening the Wednesday goal. Glidden missed a good opening, the teams crossing over on level terms.

Early in the second half, with Wednesday doing all the attacking, Rimmer missed a fine opportunity. Hooper, however, put Wednesday ahead half way through the second half, but Sandford levelled the scores almost immediately.

Then came Rimmer's winning goals three minutes and one minute from the end, and the Cup was Wednesday's.

Wednesday's outside-left, Ellis Rimmer, has scored in every stage of the season's Cup competition—a remarkable record.

● Ellis Rimmer, the Sheffield Wednesday left-winger, became the hero of a thrilling final with two goals inside the last three minutes. In truth Rimmer had not enjoyed a spectacular match to that point, but his intervention took the Cup to Yorkshire and maintained his personal record of scoring in every round.

The match which had such a tantalising finish also began with a considerable flourish; Palethorpe's scoring effort sent Wednesday into a third-minute lead. West Bromwich Albion included nine of the side that had beaten Birmingham four years earlier, but it was one of the newcomers, left-winger Boyes, who produced the equaliser half way through the first half, regarded as the best goal of the six.

It was in the second half when Ronnie Starling, Wednesday's gifted inside-left, began to impose himself on the match. Starling, capped just once with Wednesday in 1933 and only once more four years later after his transfer to Aston Villa, was a creative player of the highest calibre, and

now he began to free himself from the special attentions that Albion had planned for him.

Hooper confirmed Wednesday's increasing stature in the match by putting them back in front midway through the second half. But again Albion added to the drama with a spirited response; five minutes later Sandford brought the score back level again at two goals each; another

fine effort from the edge of the penalty area.

It seemed that the crowd were destined to see another half hour of superb entertainment when Rimmer struck to remove the possibility of extra time. Five years after they had won the League Championship by the enormous margin of ten points, Wednesday re-affirmed their power in the game with this, their third triumph in the FA Cup.

Date 27 April 1935
Place Wembley
Score SHEFFIELD WEDNESDAY 4 WEST BROMWICH ALBION 2
Teams SHEFFIELD WEDNESDAY Brown, Nibloe, Catlin, Sharp, Millership, Burrows, Hooper, Surtees, Palethorpe, Starling, Rimmer. WEST BROMWICH ALBION Pearson, Shaw, Trentham, Murphy, W. Richardson, Edwards, Glidden, Carter, W. G. Richardson, Sandford, Boyes
Team Colours SHEFFIELD WEDNESDAY

White shirts, blue shorts; WEST BROMWICH ALBION Blue shirts, white shorts
Official Referee A. E. Fogg (Bolton)
Goal Scorers SHEFFIELD WEDNESDAY Palethorpe 2, Hooper 67, Rimmer 88, 89; WEST BROMWICH ALBION Boyes 21, Sandford 72
Attendance 93 204
Gate Receipts £24 856
Guest of Honour H.R.H. Prince of Wales
Copy Sheffield Sports Special ("Green 'Un") 27 April 1935

THE SUNDAY TIMES, APRIL 26, 1936

ARSENAL SCRAMBLE THROUGH

◆

GLORIOUS DEFENCE — DRAKE'S FINE EFFORT

◆

SHEFFIELD MISS MANY CHANCES

◆

By A SPECIAL CORRESPONDENT

Arsenal 1   Sheffield United 0

Date 25 April 1936
Place Wembley
Score ARSENAL 1 SHEFFIELD UNITED 0
Teams ARSENAL Wilson, Male, Hapgood, Crayston, Roberts, Copping, Hulme, Bowden, Drake, James (capt.), Bastin. SHEFFIELD UNITED Smith, Hooper (capt.), Wilkinson, Jackson, Johnson, McPherson, Barton, Barclay, Dodds, Pickering, Williams
Official Referee H. Nattrass (Durham)
Goal Scorer Drake 74
Managers ARSENAL Tom Whittaker; SHEFFIELD UNITED "Teddy" Davison
Attendance 93384
Gate Receipts £24857
Copy Sunday Times 26 April 1936

For the second time in their history Arsenal have won the F.A. Cup, and I am sure that all the victorious players who took part in yesterday's great battle at the Empire Stadium, Wembley, will agree that this was one of the fiercest cup-ties in which they have ever played. The Arsenal deserved their victory, I have no doubt, but they also came nearer to losing the greatest of all football trophies, I am certain. The League champions of 1933-4-5 won because in Male, Hapgood and Roberts they had a trio who, as many times in the past, proved good enough to withstand all the furious attacks of their opponents.

It is these three that Arsenal have most to thank for their triumph. I have never seen Male play better. He was the outstanding man of the match. Time and again when the Arsenal goal seemed certain to fall, and when some of his colleagues had lost their usual brilliant sense of balance and positioning, Male would drop into the breach and save the situation.

Superb

At the moment there is no better full back in the four countries. Not once did he make a mistake, and when either Roberts or Hapgood erred—which was very rarely—Male's powers of recovery were wonderful.

For a Cup Final it must be written down as a good match. Usually on these occasions players are upset by the big occasion, the crowd and atmosphere, but only in the first few minutes was this noticeable.

It was Sheffield United who played the real football in the first half and, as I say, only great defensive work kept their clever forwards out. Arsenal had their chances, but if they had taken the lead at the time it would have been all against the run of the play.

United's defence was very sound in every way. Smith, in goal, must have made at least a dozen wonder saves during the period when Arsenal were on the top note, and after he had brought off two spectacular clearances from Hulme midway through the second half, the Arsenal players must have wondered if it was at all possible to get the ball past him.

One Chance But—

Hooper was the better of the full-backs, while in the half-back line McPherson and Johnson caught the eye. Johnson only allowed Drake one chance, and on that occasion the Arsenal centre scored the all-important goal.

Dodds had few clear-cut openings, because of the attention he received from Roberts, but he showed what a great centre-forward he could be by his determined dashes for goal. Williams found his master in Male, but Barton gave Hapgood a few anxious moments.

Crayston and Copping were masters in the art of tackling and distributing the ball to their forwards. Crayston played right up to international form, and nearly scored one of the most spectacular goals ever seen at Wembley just after the interval, when he went past opponent after opponent and finished with a great left foot shot which brought the best out of Smith.

Of the Arsenal forwards, Hulme, perhaps, took most of the honours. This was his fourth Cup Final since 1927 and probably his last, and he played as though he meant it to be a triumphant swan song. During the match he must have sent in at least a dozen shots, and most of them looked likely to score.

Bastin was not quite at his best, but he had a hand in most of the Arsenal's most dangerous raids, and it was his coolness which gave Drake the opportunity to score.

The Play

Sheffield United came near to scoring in the very first minute, when, after clever work by Pickering, Barton, and Barclay, Dodds headed the ball towards the Arsenal goal. It looked an easy save for Wilson, but the Arsenal goalkeeper, obviously suffering from nerves on this big occasion, allowed the ball to drop out of his hands.

The ball trickled across the goal, and just when Barclay was about to send it into the back of the net Wilson managed to get his hands to it and put it behind for a fruitless corner. Inspired by this early attack, the Sheffield forwards waltzed round the Arsenal goal, but the defence stood firm.

Time after time the Sheffield forwards swooped down, and it was then we saw the greatness of Male and Roberts. The last-named was always the master of Dodds in the air, and Male, probably the coolest player on the field, refused to be upset by the United shock tactics.

The best scoring effort in the first half-hour came from Hulme, when he worked his way across the field to finish with a terrific left foot drive, which Smith managed to just punch over the bar.

Just before the interval, Hulme again sent in a great shot, this time with his right foot, and Smith did well to get to the ball and save at the expense of a corner.

On the whole, it had been anybody's first half. Arsenal certainly had the more chances of scoring, but the better football had come from Sheffield United, and actually, on the run of play, they seemed more at home before the huge crowd than did Arsenal with their team of 10 internationals, most of whom had had previous experience of the Empire Stadium.

In the very first minute of the second half Crayston nearly gave Arsenal the lead. Put through by Drake on the right, he worked over to the left, beating man after man to finish with a terrific drive, which took Smith right across the goal. This was the fourth occasion in the match so far that Arsenal had looked certain to score.

Big Thrill

James then caused a big thrill by taking the ball to the edge of the penalty area from a pass by Hapgood, and sending in a great shot, which Smith just managed to save. The United were by no means out of it, and one run of Pickering's raised great hopes, but Roberts came to Arsenal's rescue by robbing Dodds just as the centre-forward was about to shoot.

A few minutes later the ball was passed right across the Arsenal goalmouth by one Sheffield forward after another, but no one man could apply the finishing touch.

Drake was still getting few chances, so well held was he by Johnson. Once the Arsenal centre did get through, but was shouldered off the ball by the United's pivot when he was about to get in his shot.

The Decisive Goal

Three Arsenal corners in three minutes gave us a spell of excitement. On the second occasion Smith, the United goalkeeper, dropped the ball right on the line from Drake's header. The Arsenal players claimed for a goal, but the referee refused to listen. Meanwhile, Smith had thrown the ball behind goal for another corner. This time James tried a shot, but Smith brought off another wonder save.

Arsenal had been pressing so continuously that it came as no real surprise when they did score. The goal came in the 29th minute. James started the movement by swinging the ball out to Bastin. The outside-left cleverly took the ball past Hooper before passing to Drake, and the Arsenal centre-forward, when challenged, side-stepped Johnson to send in a fine left-foot drive from ten yards out, high into the net.

In spite of this set-back, United rallied in great style, and a minute later Dodds had the bad luck to head against the bar when Wilson was out of position, and from the rebound Barclay lobbed the ball just over the goal.

Arsenal were inclined to concentrate on defence, and this nearly led to their downfall, for Dodds only just failed to work his way through after a great run by Pickering.

The end came with Sheffield United attacking desperately, but so anxious were they to score that chance after chance was missed. Just before the finish, when a corner was given to United, ten of their players went up into the Arsenal goalmouth in an attempt to force an equaliser. Johnson managed to get his head to the ball, and in doing so was injured.

SUNDERLAND WIN F.A. CUP FOR THE FIRST TIME

BRILLIANT WORK BY FORWARDS

By C. W. BALE

SUNDERLAND 3, PRESTON NORTH END 1

SUNDERLAND, for the first time in their long history, won the F.A. Cup at Wembley Stadium yesterday when they defeated Preston North End in clear-cut fashion after being a goal down at the interval. Not many teams win a Cup Final in such circumstances. The first goal means so much, but Sunderland fought back in wonderful fashion in the second half. They equalised seven minutes after the interval, took the lead after twenty-eight minutes and five minutes later, made certain of victory with a perfect goal.

Horatio Carter, bred and born in Sunderland, was indeed a proud man when he had the honour of receiving the Cup from the Queen. This was Sunderland's second appearance in the Final. In 1913 they were defeated 1-0 by Aston Villa. Preston's only Cup triumph dates as far back as 1889, when they were known as "The Invincibles." Yesterday's final by no means came up to expectations. From two such teams as Preston and Sunderland, both of whom are steeped in football traditions, we had hoped for a classic display, but the game fell far short of that. There were far too many free kicks to make the match a pleasant one, and it was not until Sunderland had equalised soon after the interval that we saw anything like the football both teams can play.

By the way they took their chances, Sunderland deserved their victory. Their forwards, with Carter and Gallacher creating most of the openings, were faster than the Preston attack. The Sunderland half-backs, too, were more impressive than their opposite numbers, and no player had a bigger part in their victory than Thomson. Thomson was ever helping in the defence and had a share in most of the moves which led to the goals. He was one of the few players who kept cool at the start—the greatest of all assets in the Cup Final.

Another Sunderland star was Gorman He put in a great amount of work, tackled cleanly and quickly, and cleared his lines time after time when danger threatened.

As expected, it was a great duel between F. O'Donnell, Preston's centre, and Johnston. On the whole I should say Johnston came out the master.

• The early play in the 1937 final was quiet, with rather too many free kicks and the need for the referee to speak to players. Preston began to get the upper hand and scored a fine goal after 38 minutes. Dougal passed to F. O'Donnell, who rounded Johnston and gave Mapson no chance. In the next minute Mapson dropped a header and conceded a corner, from which Preston netted again, but the referee had blown for a foul on the goalkeeper.

Sunderland improved after the interval and equalised after seven minutes. From a Burgess corner, Gallacher headed on to Gurney who flick-headed into goal. Gurney missed an open goal in the next minute. Sunderland eventually went into the lead after 73 minutes, Gurney coolly placing the ball in the path of Carter, who blasted past Burns. Preston fought back but five minutes later a free kick just outside the area was played to Burbanks who scored. Sunderland took command to the end.

The *Daily Sketch* story below refers to the imminent Coronation of King George VI and of Carter's meeting with the present Queen Mother.

Bride of Football Cup Hero Sees London
Decorations Only Fair, But It Was a Honeymoon Day to Dream About

WIFE of Sunderland's hero captain, Mrs. Rose Carter, spent the first day of her real honeymoon visiting the sights of London.

She saw her husband for only three hours after their wedding. He was too busy training.

Mrs. Carter was the guest of the DAILY SKETCH and, while appreciative of many things, she thought London's Coronation decorations were "skimpy."

"We in Sunderland must be far more loyal than you down here." she said. "There is hardly a house in Sunderland that has not put out its flags already."

Mrs. Carter was accompanied on her tour by her husband, idol of the crowd at Wembley on Saturday.

Whitehall and the Horse Guards she voted dull, but Westminster Hospital, surrounded by seats and stands, excited the wonder of the little party.

PITY FOR THE PATIENTS

"How do the patients get light and fresh air?" Mrs. Carter asked. "With the noise, they must have a real bad time, though I suppose they will have a real thrill listening to the cheering as the King and Queen ride to the Abbey."

She was told that some of the patients had been moved, and the rest did not mind because the sale of seats was helping to build a new hospital.

Appeased a little, Mrs. Carter turned in amazement to the Abbey annexe. She felt the bars outside the windows, and wanted to cut a little bit off "just to make sure" when her husband told her they were only made of wood.

At Buckingham Palace Carter wanted "just another glimpse" of the Queen who had shaken his hand on Saturday and told him the Cup was a fine wedding present.

MUST SEE THE QUEEN

The Palace policeman said Queen Elizabeth was at Windsor, and after lunch Carter and his bride "just had to go to Windsor." They saw both the King and Queen again, and thought them "fine."

Rotten Row made Carter laugh.

The Chamber of Horrors thrilled Mrs. Carter, but her greatest moment was when Jackie the chimpanzee put his arm round her neck in the Zoo.

Soon it was time to say good-bye.

"I am sure we are going to be very happy, and it is just the start for a honeymoon a girl could dream about. I have been to the Continent half a dozen times, but I had not seen London," said the happy bride.

Date 1 May 1937
Place Wembley
Score SUNDERLAND 3
PRESTON NORTH END 1
Teams SUNDERLAND Mapson, Gorman, Hall, Thomson, Johnson, McNab, Duns, Carter (capt.), Gurney, Gallacher, Burbanks. PRESTON NORTH END Burns, Gallimore, A. Beattie, Shankly, Tremelling (capt.), Milne, Dougal, Beresford, F. O'Donnell, Fagan, H. O'Donnell
Official Referee G. Rudd (London)
Goal Scorers SUNDERLAND Gurney 52, Carter 73, Burbanks 78; PRESTON NORTH END F. O'Donnell 38
Attendance 93495
Gate Receipts £24831
Guests of Honour H.M. King George VI and H.M. The Queen
Copy *Sunday Times* 2 May 1937; *Daily Sketch* 3 May 1937

Mr. and Mrs. Carter examining the Abbey annexe. Right: At the Zoo, with their new-found friend Jackie, a chimpanzee. Judging by the picture it seems that Jackie is congratulating him for being captain of the winning team at the Cup Final.

Cup penalty a mistake, says Henry Rose

"FOUL WAS OUTSIDE PENALTY AREA"

THE picture above is an enlargement of part of a film shot (on left) of the sensational tackle which won the Cup for Preston at Wembley on Saturday.

It shows Mutch, on left in dark knickers, being brought down by Young, the Huddersfield captain, whose left foot is in the penalty area.

For this foul Preston were awarded a penalty kick, from which Mutch scored thirty seconds from the end of extra time.

Henry Rose, in his Daily Sportlight on Page Sixteen, declares:

"In the split second that Mutch was fouled he was just outside the line of the penalty area. . . . I have seen the pictures (of the incident). . . . I think Mr. Jewell, the referee, made an honest mistake."

Henry Rose in Saturday's Daily Express prophesied that the match would be drawn after extra time. Half a minute robbed him of success in one of the most sensational Cup forecasts ever made.

He forecast accurately the result of the Harvey-McAvoy fight at Harringay on April 7. He did the same before the England-Scotland match at Wembley on April 9.

Mutch took kick in a daze

This is the story told by Mutch to the Daily Express yesterday:—

"Half a minute before the end of extra time I was tripped, and went down to Young's tackle in the penalty area.

"When I came round I was only conscious that my body was one mass of aches. I was dazed

"I did not even understand that a penalty had been awarded. They handed me the ball. I placed it automatically, thinking it was funny they had given it to me, an injured man.

"As I took my run I wondered what I was doing and why. I don't remember aiming at goal."

Below: George Mutch's penalty kick hits the net from the underside of the bar

Date 30 April 1938
Place Wembley
Score PRESTON NORTH END 1
HUDDERSFIELD TOWN 0
(after extra time)
Teams PRESTON NORTH END Holdcroft, Gallimore, A. Beattie, Shankly, Smith, Batey, Watmough, Mutch, Maxwell, R. Beattie, H. O'Donnell.
HUDDERSFIELD TOWN Hesford, Craig, Mountford, Willingham, Young, Boot, Hulme, Isaac, MacFadyen, Barclay, Beasley
Team Colours PRESTON NORTH END White shirts, blue shorts; HUDDERSFIELD TOWN Blue and white stripes, white shorts
Official Referee A. J. Jewell (London)
Goal Scorer Mutch 119 (penalty)
Attendance 93 357
Gate Receipts £25 723
Guest of Honour H. M. King George VI
Copy The Daily Express 2 May 1938

that occasion in Huddersfield's favour. Mutch's goal, however, enabled Preston to supersede their achievements of 1937 when they tasted the disappointment of beaten finalists.

The penalty was a cruel injustice to Young's superb performance throughout the rest of the match in which he had played a predominant role in frustrating Preston. Preston included Bill Shankly at right-half and contemporary reports confirm that if Mutch had not recovered sufficiently Shankly would have taken the penalty. Ironically Shankly later gave notice of his managerial potential at Huddersfield where he succeeded Andy Beattie, who also played for Preston in the 1938 final. The network of that year stretched even further, into the 1970s, when Iain Hesford, the son of Bob, who was beaten by Mutch's hit-and-hope penalty, began a promising league career of his own in goal for Blackpool.

Preston's victory was their first Cup success for 49 years, since the days of the "Invincibles" and the first double. It had taken Wembley 15 years to produce the first final in the Empire Stadium to be decided by a penalty. For Huddersfield Town it represented the end of their between-the-wars era of competitiveness of five FA Cup finals and three League championships, though they would reach the semi-finals of the Cup in 1939.

Defeat by Portsmouth robbed Huddersfield of the chance of matching Preston's achievement and of revenging the penalty that Alf Young disputed long after his playing days were over. And by then one of the competition's heroes had retired. Appropriately the last game of Joe Hulme's career, in his fifth final, was the 1938 contest against Preston.

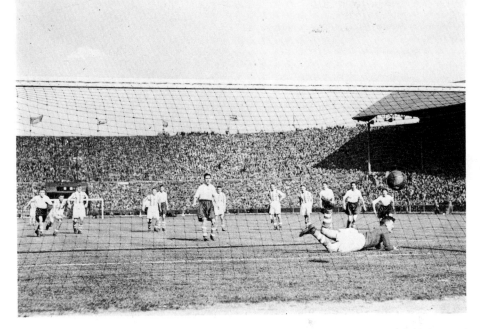

● The 1938 Cup final produced a remarkable and controversial finale. In the last minute of extra time George Mutch, Preston North End's inside-right, was tripped by Huddersfield Town's Alf Young, the captain and centre-half. Henry Rose, who was to lose his life in the Manchester United air tragedy, and the photographic evidence of the *Daily*

Express illustrate the contentious nature of the award by referee Jewell.

The report also records the bewilderment of Mutch himself who was entrusted with the penalty and whose shot only crossed the line via the underside of the crossbar. By a strange coincidence the two teams were repeating the 1922 final, which was also settled by a disputed penalty, on

ASSOCIATION FOOTBALL

CUP-FINAL SURPRISE

EASY WIN FOR PORTSMOUTH

FOUR GOALS FROM SKILFUL PLAY

WOLVERHAMPTON OVER-RUN

BARLOW INSPIRES THE WINNERS

BY J. T. BOLTON

PORTSMOUTH (2) 4   WOLVERHAMPTON WAN. (0) 1

Once again the germ of truth, bred in tradition, which lays it down that the favourites never win the Football Association Challenge Cup, has exerted itself. At Wembley yesterday before a crowd of 99,370, which included the King and Queen, Portsmouth beat Wolverhampton Wanderers by four goals to one, and take the Cup south of London for the first time in the history of the competition. Not for eleven years at least has any team been so strongly fancied to win the trophy as were Wolverhampton Wanderers, but they were more thoroughly outplayed, as far as the real art and craft of the game are concerned, than has any side been since final ties were first played at Wembley. Portsmouth played with less suggestion of nerves, more calm and collected football than any

team before in a final tie at Wembley. It cannot possibly be said of this game —as of so many other final ties—that the better team did not win.

Let it be admitted, quite frankly, that as a team, Wolverhampton Wanderers gave a most disappointing display. So much had been expected of them: they achieved so little. Indeed, it is not much exaggeration to say that the Wolverhampton men gave the poorest exhibition of football in a Cup final of our time. They scarcely ever settled down to play what their supporters have come to regard as their normal game. The real mystery of the match is how a team which is capable of playing so well could descend to such a mediocre level. It was not a case of a side merely playing as well as their opponents would allow them to do, although Portsmouth must be given full credit for the persistence and grit which they brought to bear, and

which prevented the Wolverhampton men from settling down. The Midlanders, however, contributed to their own downfall by bad tactics, and by individual errors, both of omission and commission.

COMMANDING LEAD AT HALF-TIME

In one respect the biggest attendance at Wembley since 1923 must have been disappointed. The game was over, to all intents and purposes, at half-time, when Portsmouth led by two goals to nothing, and it was certainly finished, as a contest of possibilities, immediately after the re-start. It was not third time lucky for Portsmouth, but the third time paid for all, for they have been twice to Wembley on previous occasions to finish as losers. The touch of tragedy from the Wolverhampton point of view lies in the fact that, so far as it can be said that one Portsmouth man did more than any other to bring about this result, Barlow, the inside-left, was that player. Yet two months ago Barlow was a Wolverhampton player, being then transferred to Portsmouth.

For the greater part of the game it almost seemed as if the Wolverhampton players were so convinced of their own superiority that it was scarcely necessary for them to put forth their most strenuous efforts. Time after time a player of the Midland side, safely in possession of the ball, would lose it to an opponent whose presence in a position to tackle was not even suspected. That, of course, is one way of saying that Portsmouth were more on their toes, and revealed greater pace. While the Wolverhampton players adopted the policy of waiting for the ball, those of Portsmouth ran to it, and, having done the running to secure possession, kept both the ball and their own feet. The men of the winning side on their toes; the men of the losing side on their heels. That, granting the writer a little licence, is as near a correct summary of the game, and conveying the secret of Portsmouth's success, as it is possible to get.

INSIDE MEN PLAY TOO CLOSELY TOGETHER

When any member of the Ports-

mouth forward line was on the move there was a colleague racing into position for the pass—to give him actual as well as moral support in beating an opponent, or, at any rate, making him doubt the wisdom of a full-blooded tackle. By way of contrast the forwards of Wolverhampton Wanderers did not give the open spaces. Rather did the inside men play so closely together that they were often in the way of one another, losing chances of making headway, and possibly even scoring, in consequence. This inability of Wolverhampton to make room in which to work the ball rendered the task of the Portsmouth defenders much easier than it otherwise would have been.

Rain fell as the spectators assembled in that orderly way which has become typical of all-ticket Cup Finals, and also at intervals during the match, rendering the turf slippery, but not slow. The wind, gustily strong, was blowing too much across the pitch to be of real help to either side. What advantage was to be gained was in Portsmouth's favour during the first half, but the players of the Midland side made the running in the early stages. Indeed, it would not have been surprising if they had taken the lead, as the Portsmouth full-backs were not particularly impressive during the first few minutes.

Rowe, the Portsmouth centre-half, was hurt as the result of one desperate but successful effort to save a situation made difficult by the mistake of a colleague. Later it was also necessary for Maguire to receive the attentions of his trainer, but in neither case did the injury prove serious. Wolverhampton had four corner-kicks before one fell to Portsmouth. All the same, even during the period of Wolverhampton ascendancy, there was confidence in Portsmouth. Whenever the forwards did make headway, they found each other with the ball. All too often the passes of Wolverhampton merely found an opponent, and once an indifferent back pass by Cullis meant difficulty for his goalkeeper in clearing. Westcott had one chance to give Wolverhampton the lead, and Dorsett raised hopes with a shot which Walker pushed round the post.

DOING THE WORK OF TWO MEN

All the time Barlow was doing the work of two men, both in attack and de-

Barlow beats Scott to give Portsmouth the lead

fence, to help Portsmouth to take over the initiative. As the clock pointed to three-thirty Barlow scored a grand goal for Portsmouth. He started a movement which carried the ball over to the right, and Barlow himself was actually in the inside right position when Worrall gave him a short pass. From fifteen yards Barlow sent in a shot which went high into the net, completely out of the reach of Scott.

From that moment the Wolverhampton backs began to flounder, as well they might, with the inside forwards of Portsmouth holding the ball, turning this way and that to get the opposition on the wrong foot. Barlow might have scored a second goal, but this time his shot sailed over the bar. In a Wolverhampton rally Walker made a thrilling save, going down and holding a hard drive from Burton. With one minute of the first half remaining, Anderson shot Portsmouth's second goal to finish off another movement started by Barlow. The Wolverhampton defenders were in a terrible tangle over this goal, and Scott, making a great effort to get back after leaving his goal, touched the ball with the tips of his fingers as Anderson shot, but could not prevent it travelling into the net.

Reflecting, during the interval, on the first-half play, many still considered it possible that if Wolverhampton could find their form they might still win. Nobody, however, could recall the day when a team two goals down in the final came through victorious. And before the second half was one minute old, Wolverhampton were placed in the well-nigh hopeless position of requiring four goals to win. Once more Portsmouth's left-wing pair schemed with such cleverness that the English international full-back, Morris, was almost bewildered. Certainly he was helpless to prevent Barlow getting in a low shot—this time with the left foot. Scott saved this shot. The ball eluded his grasp, but he recovered it dead on the goal-line. As the goalkeeper lay there, struggling to get the ball clear, Parker raced in to put it over the line.

SPEED OF THOUGHT AND OF MOVEMENT

That effort of Parker's was just typical of the speed of thought and of movement characteristic of the Portsmouth side as a whole. Ten minutes later a hint was given of what a thrilling match this game would have been if Wolverhampton had countered throughout with the best of which they are capable. Cullis, almost entirely a defender previously, carried the ball forward and pushed it to Westcott. A short pass from the centre-forward to Dorsett, and a low shot brought Wolverhampton's goal. That was the one move in the whole match typical of the Midland side, and it received its due reward.

Some more pressure was brought to

bear on the Portsmouth goal, but for the most part the defence of the Southern side held the mastery, and always there was that crowding of the middle by the Wolverhampton forwards plus the failure to run into a favourable position to receive a pass. Most of the danger to the Wolverhampton goal had come from the left wing, but the captain's effort to strengthen the defence on that side was readily accepted by Portsmouth as an opportunity to bring Worrall more into the game. Eighteen minutes from the end another movement worthy of the game's highest traditions had the Wolverhampton defence completely beaten. Worrall sent the ball high over from the right, and Parker was on the spot to nod a fourth goal.

A fourth goal over-emphasised the Portsmouth superiority, if the balance of play as a whole is taken into account, but there is no doubt that the trophy went to the deserving side. The part which Barlow played—the inspiration of the Portsmouth attack—has been commented upon. He did much to make the team, but it must be added that there was no failure anywhere in the winner's eleven. With Barlow to draw the opponent and make the ideal pass, often inside the opposing full-back, and always along the ground, Parker had a most successful day.

SOUND AND RELIABLE FULL-BACKS

The outstanding player in defence was Rowe, with a stranglehold on Westcott, who has scored in every previous round, almost complete. When the ball had to be headed—and the Midlanders tried the air route to goal to a much greater extent than did Portsmouth—Rowe was usually the man to get to it first. After a somewhat hesitant start the Portsmouth full-backs became sound and reliable, better than the Wolverhampton pair, who disappointed. The genius of Cullis was notable at times, but he has played more convincingly, and the wing half-backs of Wolverhampton were not nearly so persistent as those of Portsmouth.

Scott should have prevented the third goal, and seemed less calm than Walker, but the blame for the defeat cannot be laid at his door. Consider, for instance, the shortcomings of the outside wing forwards of Wolverhampton, Burton and Maguire, who dallied when they should have gone ahead. Beaten for pace, for cleverness, and even in the ability to make quick decisions; that was the experience of Wolverhampton Wanderers.

Portsmouth.—Walker; Morgan, Rochford; Guthrie (captain). Rowe. Wharton; Worrall, McAlinden, Anderson, Barlow, Parker.

Wolverhampton Wanderers.—Scott; Morris, Taylor; Galley, Cullis (captain), Gardiner; Burton, McIntosh, Westcott, Dorsett, Maguire.

Referee.—T. Thompson (Northumberland).

Freddie Worrall helps Jack Tinn to put on his famous lucky spats

Date 29 April 1939
Place Wembley
Score PORTSMOUTH 4
WOLVERHAMPTON WANDERERS 1
Teams PORTSMOUTH Walker, Morgan, Rochford, Guthrie (capt.), Rowe, Wharton, Worrall, McAlinden, Anderson, Barlow, Parker.
WOLVERHAMPTON WANDERERS Scott, Morris, Taylor, Galley, Cullis (capt.), Gardiner, Burton, McIntosh, Westcott, Dorsett, Maguire
Official Referee T. Thompson (Northumberland)
Goal Scorers PORTSMOUTH Barlow 30, 46, Anderson 43, Parker 72; WOLVERHAMPTON WANDERERS Dorsett 65
Managers PORTSMOUTH Jack Tinn; WOLVERHAMPTON WANDERERS Major Frank Buckley
Attendance 99 370
Gate Receipts £29 116
Guest of Honour H.M. King George VI
Copy The Sunday Times 30 April 1939

Two minutes before half-time Anderson makes it 2–0

1946

FREAKISH GOALS IN BEST-EVER FINAL

Stamps Sticks Derby's Name at Last on the Cup

By ALEX JAMES, Scotland and Arsenal Star, and HARRY DITTON, Our Special Commissioner

CHARLTON ATHLETIC 1, DERBY COUNTY 4

In a whirlwind, never-to-be-forgotten finish, Derby County, by virtue of one of the most classic exhibitions of football Wembley has ever staged, defeated Charlton by four goals to one during extra time in the F.A. Cup Final yesterday.

In doing so they won the trophy for the first time and avenged three previous Cup defeats. Incidentally, they destroyed Charlton's chance of winning the "double."

It was a remarkable and thrilling game which could have produced a hatful of goals. Indeed one lost count of the number of breath-taking escapes which both goals, especially Charlton's, experienced.

It also produced two freakish goals which came within a minute of one another with less than ten minutes of ordinary time to go.

The remarkable thing about the "freaks" was that Bert Turner, the Charlton half-back, was directly concerned in both. First he put the ball into his own net in a frantic effort to clear, and then in the next minute he took a free-kick and cannoned the ball off Doherty into the net.

But there was nothing freakish about Derby's three goals during the period of extra time. The form of this side of alleged veterans was a revelation and, just as in the semi-final against Birmingham, Derby ran Charlton to a standstill.

Derby's victory was complete and magnificent.

Looking back over the game, the wonder is that it ever went to extra time so much were Derby the superior side.

Getting an immediate grip on the game from the kick-off, Derby literally ran rings round Charlton's defence. With luck favouring Doherty and Carter, plus a little quicker thinking on the part of Duncan, Derby might have had the game well won by half-time.

During this phase the ball must have seemed like a capricious will-o'-the-wisp to the dazed and bewildered Charlton players.

It was the rapid thinking and twinkling feet of Carter and Doherty that caused Charlton most of their troubles—and the obvious psychological effect which these two great players had on their opponents.

But make no mistake, this Derby side was not just a "twin affair." The whole team had beautiful poise and balance. Leuty was magnificent at centre-half, the nearest approach to Cullis at his best Wembley has seen for years.

The way Leuty used the ball in a small space, in spite of the constant harrying of Arthur Turner, stamped Leuty as a truly great player.

The wing half-backs, Bullion and Musson, were not far behind. They tackled tenaciously and used the ball with fine judgment. Indeed, such was Derby's unquestioned superiority that even the full-backs, Nicholas and Howe, had time to look up and place the ball just where they wished.

On the other hand, Charlton, although they had also obviously built their scheme for victory on their two inside men, Welsh and Brown, found both were almost completely shut out of the game.

Occasionally Fell ran boldly, and almost made for himself one scoring chance by his surprising burst of speed, and Welsh, taking up one of the few through-passes which Brown had to offer, should have scored early in the second half.

It seemed that Charlton must have had a beneficial pep-talk during the interval. At all events, they shook off a good deal of the lethargy and confusion which previously marked their play. The wing half-backs, Turner and Johnson, came more into the game and found those extra split-seconds in which to work and use the ball.

Brown, too, laid his insidious through-passes with more frequency and menace, the wingers came into greater prominence, and the whole side played with much more bite.

For a time it looked as though the revived Charlton would get on top, and quite a few thrills took place inside Derby's penalty area, but their period of actual supremacy was short-lived. They merely brought the game to a more level keel and made Derby hurry rather more than they had done previously.

Then, with the sands of ordinary time fast running out, came the two freak goals.

After heavy pressure on the left flank Duncan shot and, in a desperate attempt to clear, Bert Turner put through his own goal. The frantic cheering had hardly died away when Turner, with a shot that came like a bolt from the blue, handsomely retrieved himself.

Charlton were awarded a free-kick and Turner shot against a human barrier lined up in front of Woodley. The ball touched Doherty on the way into the net well wide of Woodley.

Extra time produced a sensational goal for Derby within a minute. Stamps made all the running down the left flank and when he crossed the ball Bartram could only partially save. While he was on the ground Doherty cut in and slammed the ball into the net.

Just before half-time Stamps came right into his own with a brilliant solo effort and scored Derby's third goal, and in the second half, picking up a Doherty pass, Stamps scored again.

It was a glorious finish to a memorable game worth going miles to see

● The resumpton of the FA Cup after the Second World War produced an unusual final when Bert Turner scored for both sides within a minute! Later the ball burst after referee Smith had said on radio the previous evening that the odds were a million to one against such an occurrence.

Date 27 April 1946
Place Wembley
Score DERBY COUNTY 4
CHARLTON ATHLETIC 1 (after extra time)
Teams DERBY COUNTY Woodley, Nicholas (capt.), Howe, Bullions, Leuty, Musson, Harrison, Carter, Stamps, Doherty, Duncan.
CHARLTON ATHLETIC Bartram, Phipps, Shreeve, Bert Turner, Oakes, Johnson, Fell, Brown, A. A. Turner, Welsh, Duffy
Team Colours DERBY COUNTY White shirts, black shorts; CHARLTON ATHLETIC Red shirts, white shorts
Official Referee E. D. Smith (Sunderland)
Goal Scorers DERBY COUNTY Bert Turner 85 (o.g.), Doherty 91, Stamps 97, 106;
CHARLTON ATHLETIC Bert Turner 86
Managers DERBY COUNTY Stuart McMillan. CHARLTON ATHLETIC Jimmy Seed
Attendance 98 215
Gate Receipts £45 000
Guests of Honour H.M. King George VI, H.M. Queen Elizabeth, Princess Elizabeth
Copy *The News of the World* 28 April 1946; *The Sunday Times* 28 April 1946

Above: Derby take the lead: Turner's own goal
Below: Doherty restores Derby's lead

DERBY'S CUP TRIUMPH DURING EXTRA TIME

By CHRIS BALE

Derby County 4   Charlton Athletic 1

DERBY COUNTY for the first time in their 62 years' history, won the F.A. Cup at Wembley Stadium yesterday, when they defeated Charlton Athletic after one of the most dramatic finals I have ever seen, which included 30 minutes of exciting extra time. Five minutes before the end of full-time Derby took the lead through Turner, the Charlton half-back, kicking into his own goal. But a minute later the same player saved his side with a free kick which went in off one of the Derby defenders.

So we went into extra time with the honours even, but within a minute Derby got a goal through Doherty and, from then until the end, it was always Derby's Cup. Stamps scored two more goals and Charlton, hard as they tried, were a well-beaten team. Derby owe most to those two great inside forwards, Doherty and Carter, for their triumph, though young Stamps at centre-forward had a grand match. Best of the defenders was Leuty, the centre-half, who completely blotted out Arthur Turner, Charlton's amateur centre.

Both Welsh and Brown did many great things for Charlton, but it was not Charlton's day and I have seen them play much better. Young Phipps did well at right-back, but the veteran John Oakes stood out in defence and was indeed the best back on the field. Though Derby had never before won the trophy, their Cup record is a good one. It was their fourth appearance in the Final, and before this season they had reached the semi-finals on 10 occasions.

Derby made the first move, but Welsh robbed Doherty, and Charlton were quickly on the attack. Fell took the ball off Musson's foot and from his centre Welsh back-heeled to Arthur Turner, who miskicked. The first big thrill came after some beautiful approach work by Carter and Doherty. The former sent a shot across goal, and Charlton supporters were pleased to see Shreeve head behind for a corner. The Charlton defence was rather shaky for a time and had great difficulty in stopping the clever Doherty-Carter moves.

DOHERTY MISSES GOAL

There was far more spirit in Derby's attacks, and many moves were of high standard. Once Charlton had a narrow escape when Doherty popped up on the right to head a free kick from Musson just over the bar. Doherty then started a grand movement which Carter ended by sending a great left-foot shot just over the bar. It was all Derby up to this point, and Charlton's defenders, helped by Welsh, had some anxious moments. Doherty should have given Derby the lead after 22 minutes when, following a brilliant move by Duncan, the Irishman was left with an open goal. He shot wildly and Bartram was able to effect a clearance. Charlton's raids were few and far between and they rarely looked dangerous. Both Duffy and Brown kept the ball too long, allowing the Derby defenders to fall back into position when danger threatened.

Carter got the ball into the net after 35 minutes, but he was yards offside, and a few minutes later Doherty put Duncan right through. Bartram, however, beat his shot down and Phipps was able to kick clear. Derby were clearly the better team up to this stage.

Derby were on the attack as soon as the second half started and, from a terrific drive from Carter, Doherty nearly knocked himself out in trying to head a goal. The ball went well wide. Two minutes later Charlton had their chance of scoring when Fell and Brown put Welsh through, but the Charlton captain, harassed by the defenders and the goalkeeper, tamely shot wide. Charlton were now getting more of the game, and Brown and Welsh were finding each other with well-placed passes. It was after one of their smart moves that Duffy should have scored, but he shot over the bar. Hard knocks were given and taken without the play being too violent.

The boot was on the other foot now and it was all Charlton, with Welsh and Brown making gallant efforts to force a goal. Welsh went through again and hit the side of the net. Two minutes later Derby were back at the other end and Harrison tested Bartram with a grand left-foot drive, the best shot of the match.

After a fierce Charlton attack Carter sent Duncan away, but Bartram came out of goal and made a brilliant one-handed save. Brown set the crowd roaring with a long run, beating five men on the way, but his final pass to Welsh went astray. Five minutes from the end Derby scored Duncan slipped the ball into the goal-mouth and H. Turner, in trying to clear, hooked the ball into the net with Bartram helpless. But a minute later Turner made amends by putting Charlton on level terms. Taking a free kick 25 yards out he sent in a terrific shot The ball looked to be going harmlessly wide but hit a Derby defender and shot off into the far corner of the net. An exciting finish to the first 90 minutes, especially when the ball burst a moment later.

STAMPS THE HERO

Within two minutes of the start of extra time Derby were ahead again and most of the credit must go to Stamps, their young centre-forward. Taking the ball down the left wing he dribbled past Phipps and sent in a shot which Bartram could not hold. The ball fell at the feet of Doherty, who promptly hit it into the back of the net. With Welsh as their spearhead Charlton fought back but Derby went further ahead and once again Stamps was the hero. A pass from Howe found Doherty, who promptly slipped the ball down the middle for Stamps to go past Phipps and shoot into the net.

A few seconds after the start of the second half of extra time Stamps scored Derby's fourth goal, Doherty again giving the final pass. Derby did very much as they liked, but Charlton refused to be beaten, and the end came with them making a last-minute desperate rally to score. But Derby had well and truly won the Cup.

Above: Leuty and A. Turner in a heading duel
Below: Jack Nicholas with the Cup

SUNDAY GRAPHIC, April 27, 1947

RAYMOND GLENDENNING'S

" THE BURNLEY FORWARDS are crowding in . . . Morris shoots . . . Bartram leaps . . . but the ball sails over the bar in this assault on Charlton's goal in the sixth minute of the match . . .

" . . . AND HERE is Bartram going up . . . fingers stretching out . . . every muscle straining . . . but he doesn't get near it . . . it rises over his head . . . and over the bar. The crowd—particularly the Lancashire lads, cheer, but it's just another hope that failed.

" HERE COME these Burnley men again. . . . They crowd the penalty area . . . Harrison shoots . . . Bartram saves . . . That was a stinger . . . but he gathered it in.

" IT'S CHARLTON'S turn now . . . they're swarming in . . . Brown (No. 5) is back with Strong blocking the Burnley goal.

● Raymond Glendenning's renown as a radio broadcaster produced an interesting variation on the traditional match report for the *Sunday Graphic* on the day after Charlton Athletic had beaten Burnley in the 1947 FA Cup final. Photographic coverage of the game was captioned by the actual words transcribed from Glendending's commentary.

For the reporters it was a dreary match with a thrilling conclusion. Charlton's bid to cast aside the disappointment of the previous year was severely threatened by Burnley's defensive tactics that took the final again into extra time. Allan Brown, Burnley's captain, stood at the centre of Charlton's frustration with a commanding performance at centre-half.

But with a replay just six minutes away, Wembley unearthed another hero. Chris Duffy, a Scot who would later become a publican in trouble-torn Belfast, produced

SUNDAY GRAPHIC, April 27, 1947

CUP-FINAL CAMERA COMMENTARY

The game's big thrill

THE moment I shall never forget in this year's Cup Final was the one following Chris Duffy's half volley of Robinson's centre into the net when only six minutes of extra time remained.

The ball was pushed forward by Hurst, was chased by the agile Charlton centre-forward to the corner flag, and off the line he centred. Up went Don Welsh, but the ball only grazed his head, and as it dropped to Duffy's feet he let fly a perfectly timed half volley from 10 yards that gave Strong no chance.

Then, and this is the moment that will always thrill. Duffy, for three or four seconds stood stock still looking at the ball in the net as if he refused to believe it. Then as the other Charlton players rushed towards him he realised that he really had won the Cup for Charlton and raced round in circles.

On the whole it was a fair reflection of the game. Charlton were far the better of two dour struggling teams in which the defences took the honours.

" HARRISON has the ball . . . he's tearing in . . . he's going to shoot . . . but Bartram comes out to meet him . . . he crouches low . . . He judges it nicely . . . stoops, snatches . . . sweeps the ball off Harrison's feet.

" EXCITEMENT here is terrific . . . Duffy tries to get through . . . Woodruff, Burnley right-back, is there . . . slides the ball off his feet . . . is up in a flash . . . dancing away with it . . . and so it goes on . . . players trying desperately for those elusive goals.

THE GOAL THAT WON THE CUP

" CHARLTON ARE MOVING down . . . Hurst has the ball on the right wing . . . he passes to Robinson . . . The centre-forward is going through . . . He's right down at the Burnley goal . . . He centres . . . a beauty . . . just over Don Welsh . . . Duffy is on it . . . he half-volleys it into the net . . . It's a goal . . . Charlton have scored . . . Duffy (No. 11) throws his hands up . . . jumps for joy . . . This is it . . . Charlton players are crowding around . . . shaking his hand . . . and the hands of Johnson and Phipps, those magnificent defenders."

a stunning shot that flashed past the left-hand of Strong, the Burnley goalkeeper. For an instant Duffy stood like the proverbial pillar of salt before, in realisation of what he had achieved, he set off on a bolting run round the field. He defied the attempts of his team-mates to catch him until he jumped into the arms of full-back Peter Croker, the elder brother of the subsequent secretary of the Football Association. Charlton had survived all the gloomy forecasts about their ability to reach a second final and also defied the dreadful winter of 1947. Until Duffy's goal, however, it had been a less than grand occasion, made memorable only by the remarkable coincidence of the match ball bursting for the second successive year. The post-war lack of quality materials was the most likely cause.

Date 26 April 1947
Place Wembley
Score CHARLTON ATHLETIC 1 BURNLEY 0 (after extra time)
Teams CHARLTON ATHLETIC Bartram, Croker, Shreeve, Johnson, Phipps, Whittaker, Hurst, Dawson, W. Robinson, Welsh (capt.), Duffy. BURNLEY Strong, Woodruff, Mather, Attwell, Brown (capt.), Bray, Chew, Morris, Harrison, Potts, Kippax

Team Colours CHARLTON ATHLETIC White shirts, black shorts; BURNLEY Blue shirts, white shorts
Official Referee J. M. Wiltshire (Dorset)
Goal Scorer Duffy 114
Managers CHARLTON ATHLETIC Jimmy Seed; BURNLEY Cliff Britton
Attendance 99 000
Gate Receipts £39 500
Copy Sunday Graphic 27 April 1947

NEWS OF THE WORLD, April 25, 1948

THIS WAS WEMBLEY'S FINEST FINAL

Six-Goal Thriller

By HARRY J. DITTON

MANCHESTER UNITED 4, BLACKPOOL 2

What a magnificent Cup Final! It really was terrific. It had everything—intense drama, including six thrilling goals and some of the most delightful ball play Wembley has ever seen.

Above all, it was contested in a grand sporting spirit in spite of the fact that fouls preceded both of Blackpool's goals.

Yes, this was a game that will leave an imperishable memory with all who saw it—a classic exhibition which reflected nothing but the highest credit on every one of the 22 players.

There could be no possible doubt about the merit of Manchester United's triumph. After a slow start, in which they found themselves twice in arrears, they hit back bravely and finally developed form which was so irresistible that no side in England could have held them.

In the moment of Blackpool's defeat it is pleasant to be able to record that there need be no recriminations about Manager Joe Smith's decision in omitting centre-forward McIntosh and playing Mortenson at centre-forward with Munro at inside-right. Indeed, Munro was one of the heroes of this match.

He was a veritable will-o'-the-wisp, always to be found where the fight was thickest. He took many bold tilts at the United defence and in addition put in some magnificent defensive work. No one in this game gave more in sheer industry than this veteran Scot.

What made this game such a fascinating spectacle was the way both sides went all out from the first kick to scheme and score goals. There was none of the negative safety-first tactics which have characterised so many Wembley finals. Here we saw craft matched with craft and more true Soccer science than we normally see in half-a-dozen games.

Manchester were always the greater artists, for whereas Blackpool depended largely on the skill and initiative of Matthews, plus the industry of Munro, United's attack was definitely five-pronged and decidedly pointed.

Some of the attacking moves of Delaney, Morris, Rowley, Pearson and Mitten were brilliant in the extreme, and, as the score suggests, carried tremendous goal-scoring possibilities.

Blackpool have no reason to be critical of themselves, particularly their defence. Young Crosland, suddenly finding himself pitchforked into such a momentous struggle, stood up to his task with great courage and no small degree of efficiency.

The only goal that Blackpool might have saved was the equaliser obtained by Rowley after half an hour.

The ball could easily have been cleared by Hayward, but Robinson rushed out of his goal, called for the ball, and then failed to "make it," with the result Rowley was left with a sitter, which he accepted with avidity.

The goal scoring began 15 minutes earlier when Blackpool were awarded a penalty. They had set a cracking pace with Matthews dazzling at outside-right and Mortensen thrusting up boldly through the centre.

Chilton, United's centre-half, was clearly unnerved by Mortensen, and in a despairing effort to stop him lunged out his foot and brought the Blackpool flier down.

There was only one punishment to fit this crime, and Shimwell, taking the kick with the coolness he might show at shooting in practice on a Tuesday morning, scored easily.

United, instead of wilting under this blow, hit back with tremendous verve and Rowley equalised in the manner I have indicated.

Having tasted blood, each side seemed to like it and became more and more venturesome in attack and Blackpool regained the lead five minutes later.

From a free kick Kelly pushed the ball through and Mortensen, bearing down on it in a flash, delivered one of his "specials" and that was that.

The second half, however, was definitely United's. They found the means of cutting Matthews almost completely out of the game, while their own half-backs gave such a grand service to the forwards that the Blackpool defence was under almost perpetual pressure.

It withstood it for 25 minutes and then came three quick goals which meant curtains for Joe Smith's boys.

The first was the result of a quickly taken free-kick by Morris which gave Rowley the chance to head through.

Ten minutes later Pearson tore through the defence and scored United's third goal with a great shot which entered the net via the inside of the upright.

Five minutes later, following a clearance by Robinson, Anderson, United's right-half, gained possession and with a snap shot from quite 25 yards range scored the fourth.

A grand finish to a grand final.

Blackpool. — Robinson; Shimwell, Crosland; Johnston, Hayward, Kelly, Matthews, Munro, Mortensen, Dick, Rickett.

Manchester United. — Crompton; Carey, Aston; Anderson, Chilton Cockburn; Delaney, Morris, Rowley, Pearson, Mitten.

BOY OF SEVENTEEN WAS STAR

John Woodward, 17-year-old pupil at Royal Grammar School, High Wycombe, was the hero of Wasps' win from 138 clubs in the Middlesex seven-a-side Rugby tournament at Twickenham (writes **Vivian Jenkins**).

He used his 14-st. to knock his elders about like ninepins in scoring three brilliant tries in the 14—5 final against the Harlequins.

This was the first time Wasps had won the tournament, which began in 1926.

RECORD BY ROMAIN

Roy Romain, European champion, smashed his own English 100 yards breast stroke swimming record by .8sec when returning 62.8sec at Marshall-street Baths, London.

Rowley scoring Manchester United's curious first goal, as keeper Robinson and centre-half Hayward look on. The goal is described in Harry Ditton's report.

Rowley (on knees) nods in Manchester United's second goal

ROY PESKETT'S WEMBLEY REVIEW

Cup was won by a save at the other end

IT is midnight. The Blackpool team's Cup Final dinner at a London hotel is near its end. The losers have been congratulated; the players have forgotten their first sharp disappointment; memories of the greatest-ever Wembley come crowding back.

Stanley Mortensen, whose dynamic display did so much towards nearly winning the Cup, suddenly turned to me and said:

STANLEY MATTHEWS SAYS "WE WERE NOT DISGRACED"

NATURALLY, I am terribly disappointed. A Cup medal means so much. But I do feel that we were not disgraced. It was a great game, and must have been a fine match to watch.

We were not nervous, and tackled the game just like any other match.

Manchester United played really well, and they were terrific in the last 20 minutes.

We played our best, and I do think we contributed to one of the best Wembley finals yet.

When we were leading 2—1 I really thought it was our day, but Manchester United were inspired after their second goal.

We were beaten by a great team, and to them I offer my heartiest congratulations.

We did what we set out to do, played our best in the true sporting traditions of Soccer, and cannot grumble because we were beaten.

"If I had shot the ball into the crowd instead of to the goalkeeper, the score would still have been 2—2—and we might not have lost!"

Mortensen was recalling the dramatic moment when, with only 11 minutes to go, he impudently stole the ball from Chilton, streaked on, and crashed a shot wide to the right of Crompton. A magnificent save by the United goalkeeper, a quick clearance to Anderson, a short pass to Pearson—and United had won the Cup.

It all happened so quickly that when Pearson's shot entered the Blackpool net Mortensen was still walking out of the United penalty area!

SECRET OF DELANEY

That was the turning point of one of the finest football matches I have ever seen. And the reason for this magnificence? Both teams went on to the Wembley turf with the same instructions: *"Play football, take your chances but if you lose, then lose by playing football."*

How well the men obeyed will long remain in the memories of the 99,000 privileged to watch this Soccer feast.

There was special significance in the fact that the first player to be congratulated at the end by Manchester United's manager, Matt Busby, was Jimmy Delaney. Here's why:

"We kept quiet all week that Jimmy was a very doubtful starter for Wembley," said Mr. Busby. "The ankle injury he suffered against Chelsea the previous week was slow to heal . . . and although we passed him as fit, there was always a risk he would break down.

"We had an anxious moment 20 minutes after the start when Delaney got up limping after a tackle. He limped for the rest of the game."

Men in the middle said—

So much happened in this Final of the Century that it is difficult to set down all the highlights. Perhaps the drama of the goals made it outstanding, so here is the story of them, told by the central figures:

1. (12 minutes.) Referee C. J. Barrick unhesitatingly whistled for a penalty as Stanley Mortensen was brought down by Chilton. Said the official: "I was behind the play, but was certain that Mortensen was in the area when he was tackled. I did not consult my linesman, but looked to him for confirmation. His flag pointed to the spot." **Shimwell** scored, and **Blackpool led 1—0.**

2. (28 minutes.) Blackpool's centre half, Eric Hayward, describing it: "Delaney's lob floated over my head as my goalkeeper, Joe Robinson, called 'Right.' I felt **Rowley** flash past me, he hooked the ball out of Joe's hands, and dribbled into the empty net." **Score 1—1.**

3. (35 minutes.) Hugh Kelly's version: "I headed forward Matthews' quickly-taken free kick.

Mortensen, like a flash, picked up the pass, turned in his stride and hit the ball to the opposite corner." **Blackpool ahead 2—1.**

4. (69 minutes.) **Jackie Rowley**, scorer of a great goal, said this: "I saw Johnny Morris's free kick soaring between two Blackpool defenders, thought 'This is it,' and dived forward to head the ball into the net by the far post." **Score 2—2.**

5. (79 minutes.) **Pearson**, the scorer: "John Anderson's through pass was a beauty. All I had to do was to run on and score, but I placed the ball so far away from the 'keeper that for a second I thought it was going outside. But it hit the inside of the post and rolled across to the opposite corner of the goal." **Manchester in front for the first time, 3—2.**

6. (83 minutes.) Blackpool skipper Harry Johnston saw the last goal like this: "Anderson's 30-yard lob appeared to be covered by our goalkeeper, but the ball struck Hugh Kelly's head and was deflected away from the 'keeper." **Result, 4—2.**

'We've had it'

BLACKPOOL must consider themselves unlucky not to have won after leading twice. After a breathless first half, during which the ball flashed backwards and forwards in table-tennis fashion, Blackpool were definitely the better side for the first 20 minutes of the second half.

So much so that United's captain, Johnny Carey, as he told me, thought, "We've had it." But United never gave up, seized their chances, and swung the game full circle.

They nearly had another goal in that storming last ten minutes. Robinson brought off a terrific save when Morris was right through on his own.

It was a match without a failure. None played below normal club form. Several rose above it.

Date 24 April 1948
Place Wembley
Score MANCHESTER UNITED 4
BLACKPOOL 2
Teams MANCHESTER UNITED
Crompton, Carey, Aston, Anderson, Chilton, Cockburn, Delaney, Morris, Rowley, Pearson, Mitten.
BLACKPOOL Robinson, Shimwell, Crosland, Johnston, Hayward, Kelly, Matthews, Munro, Mortensen, Dick, Rickett
Team Colours MANCHESTER UNITED Blue shirts, white shorts; BLACKPOOL White shirts, black shorts

Official Referee C. J. Barrick (Northampton)
Goal Scorers MANCHESTER UNITED Rowley 28, 69, Pearson 80, Anderson 83; BLACKPOOL Shimwell (penalty) 12, Mortensen 43
Managers MANCHESTER UNITED Matt Busby; BLACKPOOL Joe Smith
Attendance 99 000
Gate Receipts £39 500
Guest of Honour H.M. King George VI
Copy The News of the World 25 April 1948; Sunday Express 25 April 1948; The Daily Mail 26 April 1948

Was it a penalty?
CAMERA AGREES
Trip was outside

By **GEOFFREY SIMPSON**, Sports Editor

AS it happened, it had no vital effect on the Cup Final result, but they were all talking at Wembley about Blackpool's first goal, whether the tripping of Mortensen merited a penalty, or if, technically, it was a penalty at all.

The referee, C. J. Barrick, had not a doubt in his mind as he came chasing up, finger pointing to the 12-yards spot. Later he emphasised his conviction (see Roy Peskett's column) that the trip was, indeed, inside the penalty-box.

From my position at Wembley I was equally sure Chilton's out-thrust leg tripped Mortensen *outside* the penalty line and that Mortensen went stumbling on to fall inside the area.

Well, alongside is the photographic proof of how close, but for Manchester United's second-half rally, we might have come to another "over-the-line" Final. The pictures are from Movietone's newsreel of the match.

Not much doubt, is there, that Mortensen was fouled before he reached the penalty area?

As to the merits of the case, no one, of course, will dispute that the foul denied Mortensen a wonderful scoring chance. He was clean through, with only the goalkeeper to beat.

'WE ARE LEVEL,' cried LEICESTER . . . 'OFFSIDE,' said REFEREE

Men in the middle tell Cup crisis story

LEICESTER CITY lost the chance of possible Cup victory by a yard. That was the distance Ken Chisholm was offside when he scored what would have been an equalising goal against Wolverhampton Wanderers in the 22nd minute of the second half at Wembley.

Recapture the moment as I saw it. Leicester, two down at half-time, and apparently well beaten, pulled a goal back immediately after the restart, and not only regained a firm grip on the game everybody thought all over, but got on top.

The determination and fire restored by Griffiths' goal shook Wolves out of their calm, cool demolition of the City defence.

* * *

THEN, with the Wolves' defence completely entangled—Williams was out of his goal, and even Billy Wright was caught out of position—Leicester right-winger Griffiths lifted a beautiful ball over the head of a Wolves defender.

Chisholm was there, and on the instant smacked the ball from an acute angle across and into the net to raise the biggest cheer of the day.

The Leicester players excitedly pounded their congratulations on Chisholm's broad back. But they could not see the drama being enacted behind them.

Referee R. A. Mortimer, who was bang up with the play, was pointing not for a goal but for an offside kick to the Wolves.

It was the correct, and instantly made decision. Chisholm was offside . . but only just.

Referee's view

LET Mr. Mortimer's comment to me after the game give the official view:

"It was my decision. I was told afterwards that a linesman had flagged simultaneously with my blowing the whistle.

"The ball was hooked over a full-back's head by one of the Leicester players, but it did not touch the defender. Chisholm was a yard offside. I blew the whistle before he kicked the ball."

Realise the meaning of this hairline decision. If the burly young Scot had been one stride farther away from the Wolves goal, Leicester would have been level, and with every chance of winning.

* * *

THE usually smiling Chisholm was terribly disappointed when I spoke to him.

"You can imagine how I felt when I scored, and then when the goal was disallowed," he said.

"Naturally, I accept the referee's decision. But I feel that when Mal hooked the ball to me it must have been slightly deflected when a Wolves player tried to head it, because, as I saw the ball coming, I shaped to 'kill' it with my left foot. Instead, it changed direction slightly, and I had to drag it for-

WEMBLEY AND AFTER

By Roy Peskett

ward with my right foot before I could shoot."

Upset though the Leicester players were, there was no protest to the referee—striking commentary on the magnificent sportsmanship of both sides throughout the match.

* * *

THE final blow to Leicester came a minute later, when the flame-haired Irishman Sammy Smyth weaved his way through to score perhaps the finest goal ever seen at Wembley. This made the score 3—1, and finished the game as a contest.

Picking up the ball after it had been partially cleared, Smyth coolly dribbled 50 yards upfield, evaded three tackles, touched the ball only three times, and leisurely cracked the ball into the net past the oncoming Bradley.

Still a little bewildered by the many congratulations he had received, when I spoke to him at the Wolves' banquet, Sammy Smyth confessed to me: "I just went on and on, and they [the Leicester defenders] fell away from me."

Leicester battled on pluckily, but most of their regained punch and confidence had been knocked out of them. Indeed, Wolves nearly scored another when Pye hooked over a great cross from Hancocks.

Early lead

IT was one of the quietest of Cup Final crowds, but there was plenty of good football, and much by Leicester. But they never showed the punch of Wolves, who set about the task of building up a half-time lead in cool, competent fashion.

As it happened, Wolves needed the two goals Pye scored in the 12th and 42nd minutes—the first a classic headed from Hancocks' magnificent centre. Later they cracked badly against the swarming Leicester forwards, and for 25 minutes in the second half were almost outplayed.

During this period we saw the true value of the brilliant Billy Wright, who rallied his ranks and whose blond head seemed to be everywhere.

England's captain had a magnificent game, and it was appropriate that as the star of the match it was his right to take the Cup

from the hands of Princess Elizabeth.

Second to him was the opposing left half, Johnny King, who only the previous day was not sure he would play!

King got through a terrific amount of work, constantly opening up moves down the left wing. So much so that Billy Wright often had to come over to help try to subdue Adam and Chisholm.

* * *

JUST as much as Wright helped to win the Cup for Wolves, so did the absence of Don Revie help to unsettle the Leicester forward line. Griffiths badly missed the inspiration of his partner, and was rarely given a chance to show his speed; Lee was handicapped by having to play out of position, while the experiment of playing Jim Harrison in the centre was not a success.

During the period Leicester were on top Harrison did well out on the right wing, with Griffiths inside and Lee back in his rightful place at centre forward. It was Griffiths who scored their goal two minutes after the interval, after Williams had punched out Chisholm's shot.

Wolverhampton Wanderers. — Williams; Pritchard, Springthorpe; Crook (W.), Shorthouse, Wright; Hancocks, Smyth, Pye, Dunn, Mullen.

Leicester City.—Bradley; Jelly; Scott; Harrison (W.), Plummer, King; Griffiths, Lee, Harrison (J.), Chisholm, Adam.

Referee : Mr. R. A. Mortimer (Huddersfield).

Now for safety

AT the Leicester team celebrations on Saturday night Chairman Len Shipman, after paying tribute to his players, said: "Enjoy your celebrations tonight, then look after yourselves for the next three matches. Then you've got 14 weeks' holiday you've earned it!"

Mr. Shipman's remark about three matches this week was a reference to Leicester's grim position in last place but one in the Second Division. The issue is now whether they or Nottingham Forest accompany Lincoln City to the Third Division next season.

Forest's terrific 5—0 win at West Ham saves them a chance, but Leicester need three points from their matches this week at Bury on Wednesday; at home to West Bromwich on Thursday; and away to Cardiff on Saturday.

Forest's last game is at home to Bury next Saturday. This is how the two teams stand in the table above doomed Lincoln:

	P.	W.	D.	L.	Goals	Pts.
Forest	41	13	7	21	49 54	33
Leicester	39	9	15	15	59 74	33

Hartnett's hat-trick from the left wing eased Middlesbrough's position near the foot of the First Division, but Preston, who dropped a home point, and Huddersfield, beaten by the League champions at Portsmouth, are deeply in trouble.

The Leicester mascot gives the skipper white heather for luck, and Don Revie, out of the game with a haemorrhage, hears his team lose over the radio at Leicester Royal Infirmary

PRINCESS GIVES CUP—IN LOSERS' COLOURS!

Princess Elizabeth hands the Cup to Wolves' captain Billy Wright—the first time she has performed the Wembley ceremony. The Princess wore a royal blue hat and coat . . . Leicester's colours.

The Duke of Edinburgh (above) greets the Wolves players before the kick-off. Below: The wine of victory is champagne! Pouring it into the Cup at celebration at London's Café Royal are (left to right) Pye, captain Billy Wright, Smyth and Stan Cullis.

Jesse Pye beats Leicester City goalkeeper Bradley to score Wolves' first goal

Date 30 April 1949
Place Wembley
Score WOLVERHAMPTON WANDERERS 3 LEICESTER CITY 1
Teams WOLVERHAMPTON WANDERERS Williams, Pritchard, Springthorpe, Crook, Shorthouse, Wright, Hancocks, Smyth, Pye, Dunn, Mullen. LEICESTER CITY Bradley, Jelly, Scott, W. Harrison, Plummer, King, Griffiths, Lee, J. Harrison, Chisholm, Adam
Team Colours WOLVERHAMPTON WANDERERS Old gold and black shirts, black shorts; LEICESTER CITY Blue shirts, white shorts
Official Referee R. A. Mortimer (West Riding)
Goal Scorers WOLVERHAMPTON WANDERERS Pye 12, 42, Smyth 68; LEICESTER CITY Griffiths 47
Managers WOLVERHAMPTON WANDERERS Stan Cullis; LEICESTER CITY Johnny Duncan
Attendance 99 500
Gate Receipts £39 300
Guest of Honour H.R.H. Princess Elizabeth
Copy *Sunday Graphic* 1 May 1949; *Daily Mail* 2 May 1949

8 THE DAILY MAIL, Monday, May 1, 1950.

DENIS HAD HIS FINAL FLING

And it was memorable

By ROY PESKETT

ARSENAL, holding a 1—0 interval lead, are filing out of the dressing-room at Wembley to resume the battle with Liverpool in the 1950 F.A. Cup final. Manager Tom Whittaker pulls aside the last player, Denis Compton, and says:

"*You've probably got only 45 minutes left in first-class football. Give all you've got, even if it means falling flat on your face at the end.*"

Away went Denis for his swansong in the April showers to play in the second half as well as he has ever played in his life, after being comparatively unnoticed in the first.

That was the behind-the-scenes drama of Wembley. On the field the Arsenal plan to win the Cup from the first kick-off was plain to see. Liverpool, worthy finalists, were never quite good enough to beat the Arsenal, whose players followed the Highbury script so well that only Denis Compton needed the prompter.

Tonight Denis plays in the Will Mather Cup match against Hendon, which club, as Hampstead Town, was the first the Compton brothers played for.

It is not strictly true that Denis ended his first-class Soccer career at Wembley, for Mr. Whittaker has asked the M.C.C. that Denis should be allowed to make his farewell appearance in the full Arsenal Cup side, against Portsmouth, at Highbury on Wednesday evening.

That may really end Denis's big Soccer. All being well he will be on the cricket tour of Australia next winter—and he will be 32 this month.

Wife's tears of joy

IT was sad that the person Denis most wanted as spectator at Wembley, his wife Doris, could not be there. She stayed at home with their eight-year-old son Brian, who had been suddenly taken ill with influenza. Together they listened to the match broadcast.

Mrs. Compton told me that only when she heard the commentator say that the Arsenal players were hoisting skipper Joe Mercer, with the Cup, on to their shoulders, did she really realise that her famous husband's team had won the Cup. The tears started to roll down her face.

Young Brian said: "*Mummy, why are you crying?*" Doris said: "*I always cry when I'm happy.*"

The closing memory of Denis's "last game" is a peep at the brotherly comradeship existing between him and the elder Leslie (38 next September). As the Arsenal players moved into position to go to receive the trophy and medals from the Royal Family, Leslie pushed Denis forward, leaving himself last in the line.

"*Did your brother say anything?*" I asked. And Denis replied: "*No, he was there behind me, as he has been all my life!*" What a tribute each paid the other.

THE PERFECT

Cause and effect . . . the flick of a foot and a second goal to Arsenal and Lewis. Right-winger Freddy Cox looks over his shoulder after flicking a pin-point pass from centre-forward Goring inside Liverpool left-back Spicer. As these pictures from the British Movietone newsreel of the Wembley final show, the ball goes to an open space, with Arsenal inside-left Reg Lewis speeding in to complete the move. Below: Lewis at home yesterday with his wife and twin daughters, Ann (left) and Caro

● The first Arsenal goal, described in the two articles on the opposite page, has acquired over the years the reputation of a classic, although Roland Allen's report suggests a deficiency in defence. Certainly the ball travelled from deep in the Arsenal defence to a tap into the Liverpool net with three passes and some effective dummy runs.

Sir Stanley Rous, a veteran at FA Cup finals, has been reported as saying that this one contained the best football.

Date 29 April 1950
Place Wembley
Score ARSENAL 2 LIVERPOOL 0
Teams ARSENAL Swindin, Scott, Barnes, Forbes, L. Compton, Mercer (capt.), Cox, Logie, Goring, Lewis, D. Compton.
LIVERPOOL Sidlow, Lambert, Spicer, Taylor (capt.), Hughes, Jones, Payne, Baron, Stubbins, Fagan, Liddell
Team Colours ARSENAL Old gold shirts, white shorts; LIVERPOOL White shirts, black shorts
Official Referee H. Pearce (Luton)
Goal Scorer Lewis 17, 63
Managers ARSENAL Tom Whittaker; LIVERPOOL George Kay
Attendance 100000
Gate Receipts £39 296
Copy *Sunday Times* 30 April 1950; *Daily Mail* 1 May 1950

VEMENT—AND IT'S ARSENAL'S CUP

Classic from the past

THAT Iron Curtain defence slipped once or twice, but I always had the feeling that, even if Liverpool did score, Arsenal would always score one more.

As it was, both their goals to which Liverpool could make no reply, were brilliantly taken, with the first, all-important effort ranking among the Wembley classics. Here's the flashback to that electric moment when the ice-cool Reg Lewis nonchalantly wrote Arsenal's name on the trophy in the 1950 space.

Eighteen minutes had gone, Liverpool having had the bulk of play, but with Arsenal showing signs of settling down to a steady rhythm. Hughes cleared upfield—a long, inconsequential kick which Leslie Compton's head effortlessly flicked sideways to Barnes, as Stubbins came boring in.

The back neatly placed the ball upfield to Logie, then occupying the inside-left position. As the wee man diddled the ball between his feet, in the James manner, to kill the spin, Goring moved away from the middle taking Hughes with him. Then, like a flash, the ball sped through the defence, at the instant Lewis strode forward. Taking the perfect pass, and two more strides, Lewis slipped the ball smoothly past the helpless Sidlow's left hand and wheeled away on the other side.

This goal bore all the hallmarks of being schemed in the Highbury back room. Moves earnestly planned and carried out, plus fighting team spirit, won the Cup.

The straight-from-the-kick-off move, with Forbes streaking through as Logie lobbed the ball towards the Liverpool goal, was blue-printed in the 1936 final. Substitute James for Logie, Drake for Goring, and Crayston for Forbes, and the move was the same. But unlike Crayston's effort, which forced Sheffield United goalkeeper Smith to make the save of the 1936 game, this one ended abruptly as Logie's lob was headed away by Hughes.

Beaten back

WHAT went wrong with Liverpool? The unexpected speed of the Arsenal forwards and their accuracy in passing; the ability of every Arsenal player to make the ball do the work; the magnificent covering by an often overrun Arsenal defence; a sterling halfback line in which Alec Forbes played a starring role—it was all too much for Liverpool.

The Liverpool inside forwards at times played so far back that their partners needed binoculars to spot them.

Laurie Hughes, under review as England's newly elected centre half, created a favourable impression against the vastly improved, intelligent, and quick-moving Goring. The youngster played a great game and ranked high, with Logie, behind Alex Forbes—the first perpetual-motion machine I have seen with red hair.

Forbes is out of the Wilf Copping mould.

Copping was heard to mutter, after the match: "That fellow can't get enough of it. They should give him two footballs to chase."

* * *

A WORD to George Swindin for his magnificent courage and anticipation, to Barnes, Scott, and Leslie Compton for rarely losing their positions; to Cox and Denis Compton for their contribution to the general triumph.

To Reg Lewis deservedly went the honour of scoring both goals. Each was taken coolly and well, and Sidlow had no possible chance. The second, 27 minutes from time, followed a long oblique pass by Goring, out on the left wing.

Cox, with his back to goal, flicked the ball past Spicer, and Lewis, shooting from the right of the penalty spot and about the same distance out, cracked low and hard into the near corner.

Taylor's pluck

SECOND to Hughes on the Liverpool side I made Skipper Phil Taylor, who all through played the polished, cultured football we expect from him. And what a magnificent gesture when he returned to the field ten minutes from time after being completely knocked out!

Still clutching a sponge to dab away the blood from his battered nose, Taylor refused the signalled suggestion of a colleague that he should go on to the wing to recover.

Instead, he led his troops forward in one of those desperate sorties on the Arsenal goal which supplied such a thrilling close to Arsenal's third Cup triumph at Wembley.

The 100,000 crowd, many of them braving the rain long before the kick-off, produced £39,296.

Arsenal.—Swindin; Scott, Barnes; Forbes, Compton (L.) Mercer (capt.); Cox, Logie, Goring, Lewis, Compton (D.)

Liverpool.—Sidlow; Lambert, Spicer; Taylor (capt.), Hughes, Jones; Payne, Baron, Stubbins, Fagan, Liddell.

Referee.—Mr. H. Pearce (Luton).

SOUTHAMPTON GO UP IF—

BY a terrific rally after being 1—0 down at half time at Derby, **Charlton** made sure of 3—0 or better (complications, there), which would be enough for promotion.

* * *

NO QUESTION OF 'LUCKY' ARSENAL

From ROLAND ALLEN—Wembley, Saturday

Arsenal .... 2 Liverpool 0

ARSENAL won the F.A. Cup here for the third time today. Liverpool were gallant losers and, if all their near misses were added together, they might be said to have been worth a goal. But in defence, at wing half-back, and especially in rhythm in attack, they were outmatched by a better all-round team.

And that, really, was the simple story of the 1950 F.A. Cup Final. No question of lucky Arsenal.

It could be called the battle of the gaps. There were many of them, out there on the slippery green pitch, left by the footballers from Liverpool. They were not fast enough over the ground, nor did they think as quickly as the Arsenal forwards and wing-half backs, who raced and skipped into and through those wide open spaces.

When Arsenal got the ball they kept it among themselves because their passes were made the more accurately, and their men were quicker at moving in to take them. On the rare occasions on which Liverpool had the ball they handed it back again through bad placing, or allowed it to be taken from them too easily.

One of the minor mysteries of a moderate match was why, after 17 minutes, Arsenal were allowed to keep the ball so long and take it in so close that Lewis, their inside left, merely had to roll it over the line to score. It looked as if Goring, their young centre-forward, or Logie, the small and clever inside-right who did the building up for this goal, should have been challenged sooner and more vigorously.

Copy-Book Goal

It was the smooth accuracy of the quick passing between Goring, Denis Compton and Cox which made it possible for Lewis to take steady aim when the ball came to him, after 18 minutes in the second half. And so Lewis scored the second goal for Arsenal, a goal which came from the old-fashioned Soccer copy-book.

Liverpool had their chances and squandered them. They won three corners in the first 10 minutes, and had two free kicks from favourable positions. In the early minutes of the second half Swindin, the Arsenal's red-jerseyed goalkeeper, missed a centre from Liddell but turned and dived to get the ball again and kick it desperately away.

In the last 10 minutes Liverpool played desperately—too desperately perhaps. A header from Taylor hit the bar and Fagan, their experienced Scottish inside-left, crashed his shot wide and high from a yard or two out.

In this interlude Swindin dived and leapt to keep his goal intact. And before the end Arsenal were back again with Denis Compton taking one or two potshots just to emphasise that it was Arsenal's match—and Cup.

Brilliance of Mercer

From the winners a young man and an old one are picked out for special mention. Joseph Mercer, the Arsenal left half-back and captain, has played many important games, but none, surely, greater than this. He was the corner stone in the Arsenal four-back defensive system. He was the master tactician in his inspiration of an efficient and straightforward attack, in which men kept positions and did not try any tricks.

Peter Goring, the young Arsenal centre-forward, was imperturbable and skilful in his first big game. It is, of course, his first season in top-class football. If Mercer is, without doubt, the footballer of the year, this young man is a footballer of the future. It has been a pleasure to have noted his steady progress.

Red-headed Alex Forbes, the other Arsenal wing half-back, played the bold and adventurous football of his recent match against England at Hampden, and still found time to help in subduing Liddell, who even then was Liverpool's most dangerous forward.

ARSENAL.—Swindin; Scott, Barnes; Forbes, Compton (L.), Mercer (capt.); Cox, Logie, Goring, Lewis, Compton (D.).

LIVERPOOL.—Sidlow; Lambert, Spicer; Taylor (capt.), Hughes, Jones; Payne, Baron, Stubbins, Fagan, Liddell.

Referee.—Mr. H. Pearce (Luton).

Langley's Epic Victory

From HENRY LONGHURST—Deal, Saturday

J. D. A. LANGLEY (Stoke Poges) beat I. R. Patey (Sandiway) by one hole in the 36-hole final of the English Golf Championship here today, the course on which fourteen years ago, at the age of seventeen, he had been runner-up. He was one down at lunch, and a more stirring struggle than the afternoon round in which he reversed the position it is difficult to

BLACKPOOL helped to beat themselves at W

WONDER GOAL—

IF ONLY
WE HAD
GOT THAT
GOAL!
by Stanley
Matthews

I AM disappointed. Who would not be in my shoes? At times that Cup-Final medal seemed almost there. But that first dramatic Newcastle goal made all the difference.

One minute we were on top attacking and 20 seconds later Newcastle had scored. That gave them the confidence they needed.

But I still think it's better to have lost at Wembley than anywhere else. I enjoyed the game, every minute of it.

I am really sorry for the thousands of Blackpool supporters. They must be more disappointed even than our boys. No team could have had greater encouragement.

There were hundreds of telegrams for us before the match. We knew that, win or lose, our town was with us all the way.

CONSOLATION

WE did our best. Maybe we didn't quite hit it off as in earlier matches. But then again, that's football. You can never be sure of anything.

At least I have the consolation of two Wembley medals. I've not finished, we're a good team—and there's always next year.

I would have liked to have taken that medal for young Stanley, but if he's going to follow me and be a footballer, he, too, has got to learn to be a good loser.

THE BEST LOSER

JOE SMITH, our manager, must be the best loser in the game. When we came into the dressing-room at the close he didn't show his emotion, he just said, "Come on, boys. Hurry up and get into the bath. You need it."

Newcastle deserved to win on the day. It might easily have gone the other way.

In the first half Mortensen's header seemed as good as in the back of the net, but Bobbie Cowell leapt up and headed it right off the line. If we had got that goal I think we would have won.

That second goal of Jackie Milburn's finished things. It was the sort of goal you dream about. After Newcastle's first I knew we needed to pull out something extra, but after the second I knew we would have to be superhuman to win.

MY FRIENDS . . .

THE crowd were wonderful. As I struggled down the steps at the end with a runners-up medal clutched in my hand there were cries of "Bad luck, Stan, better

One of the best I've ever seen—*says ALAN HOBY*

Newcastle United 2 (Milburn 2)   Blackpool 0

AT precisely 4.5 yesterday afternoon a tremendous roar rose from the great bowl of Wembley Stadium. It swelled and dinned in the ears as the Newcastle centre forward, Jackie Milburn, scorched down the Blackpool middle and then, with almost disdainful ease, slammed the ball into the net with his left foot.

In that moment a dream perished. Newcastle were one up five minutes after half-time and Blackpool never recovered from the heart blow.

It was the Seasiders' own fault. From the opening whistle they decided, for some peculiar reason, to play the offside game—a stupid stratagem which long before the end of any match invariably boomerangs on the team that employs it.

It was particularly senseless when you consider that Milburn seems to have two jet engines in place of feet.

★ LIKE A GROUP OF STATUES

ERIC HAYWARD, the Blackpool centre half, was as uncomfortable as a man with chapped hands against the tall, slim Geordie leader.

Thus it was that when Newcastle's dark raider, Chilean George Robledo, hit the ball down the middle, Hayward and the rest of the Blackpool defence stood like a group of statuary.

But to their consternation the linesman flagged Milburn on, and a gap as huge as the Sahara Desert opened up before his scudding feet. Frankly, it was the correct decision.

Five minutes later Milburn scored one of the greatest goals I have ever seen.

It was fitting that the player who helped to carve this fleeting chance from practically nothing was that tiny tornado in the size-four boots Ernie Taylor.

Throughout the game Taylor must have covered practically every blade of the manicured Wembley turf.

It was natural, therefore, that when Tommy Walker, Newcastle's outside right, showed the ball to left-back Tom Garrett, and then cut inside, Taylor should be there with him.

Walker slipped the ball to Newcastle's pocket Napoleon, and then followed three seconds of sheer Soccer genius.

★ TREMENDOUS

TAYLOR, as if he had all the time from then until next Saturday, semi-stopped the ball with his right foot before coolly back-heeling it to Milburn.

He hit it with his left foot from approximately 28 yards outside the goalmouth.

The ball, blurred by the speed of its flight, streaked into the top left-hand corner of the net with Farm, the Blackpool goalkeeper, groping like a blind man.

A tremendous goal capping a tremendous display by the man who surely MUST be England's centre forward against the Argentine next week.

To be honest, this match which had been so over-ballyhooed beforehand into the Cup Final of the century, never remotely measured up to this label. Indeed, it was not until the second half that the 100,000 spectators began to be treated to

Newcastle

● Below-par Blackpool forgot football's first commandment : " Play to the whistle." Milburn caught them flat-footed. Never use the offside trap. It is clear evidence of weakness.

● Best Blackpool player never played : The tragedy of £28,000 Allan Brown hung like a dark cloud over the Blackpool team. The losers desperately needed Brown's guile and craft at inside forward to draw Mortensen away from Mortensen. Both Mudie and Slater were "lost."

● Ernie Taylor was always the boss—cock of the north. He kept on picking up the loose ball and spraying it around with beautiful square passes.

● Matthews is the wizard without a shot. Last date he scored a goal was January 1, 1949, at Villa Park. Yesterday he was forced to "have a bang" because of the finishing futilities of his insides. He tried five times — without success.

● I was sorry for Harry Johnston, the only Blackpool half who measured up. Kelly was uninspired, while Hayward could never quell the fiery, tearaway Milburn.

the rhythmic brilliant flow of football they had come to see.

★ OFF THE LINE

IN that dull first half I counted three real chances. The first came in 21 minutes. From Perry's corner Mortensen, football's india-rubber man, leaped into the air, and as both Fairbrother and Brennan missed the ball, headed what seemed a certain goal.

luck next time " from all sides. I dared not look into their faces in case I saw some of my disappointed friends from home.

y with stupid offside tactics

Y MILBURN

Date 28 April 1951
Place Wembley
Score NEWCASTLE UNITED 2
BLACKPOOL 0
Teams NEWCASTLE UNITED
Fairbrother, Cowell, Corbett, Harvey (capt.), Brennan, Crowe, Walker, Taylor, Milburn, Robledo, Mitchell. BLACKPOOL Farm, Shimwell, Garrett, Johnston (capt.), Hayward, Kelly, Matthews, Mudie, Mortensen, Slater, Perry
Team Colours NEWCASTLE UNITED Black and white striped shirts, black shorts; BLACKPOOL Tangerine shirts, white shorts
Official Referee W. Ling
Goal Scorer Milburn 50, 54
Managers NEWCASTLE UNITED Stan Seymour; BLACKPOOL Joe Smith
Attendance 100 000
Gate Receipts £39 336
Guests of Honour H.M. King George VI and H.M. The Queen, Duke of Gloucester, H.R.H. Prince William, H.R.H. Princess Mary
Copy *Sunday Express* 29 April 1951; *News of the World* 29 April 1951

But Bobby Cowell, the Newcastle right back, had anticipated Morty's header and himself headed off the line.

The next goalworthy chance emerged from this first-half welter of nervy spasmodic Soccer when Milburn suddenly gave us a glimpse of what was to come.

He drew Hayward to him like a magnet, changed feet and shot off like crack sprinter McDonald Bailey, only for Farm, Blackpool's Scottish goalkeeper, to fist his firebrand of a drive over the bar.

Blackpool should certainly have scored when Stanley Matthews suddenly sent three Newcastle men the wrong way with his own brand of black magic.

The Wizard pushed the ball across goal to the left, where Billy Slater, Blackpool's amateur, hooked it a hairpin's width the wrong side of the post with the goal gaping like a paneless window

★ BEWILDERING

IN such moments, of course, there is no mortal team and no left-back living who can stop Matthews.

No set of human muscles, no reflexes on earth can anticipate the moves of this touchline professor with the intellectual feet.

But in sport the most two-faced enemy of all is Chance. Matthews must have been thinking this when Milburn scored Newcastle's first goal.

All through the game Blackpool's tragedy was that their four other forwards were as much in town as strangers on a street crossing. They were wastrels when it came to squandering chances.

One kick from Duquemin was the decider

Spurs 1, Sheffield Wed. 0

SPURS have duly won the First Division championship for the first time, to follow on the Second Division honour.

They made sure by beating Sheffield Wednesday by the only goal in one of the hardest matches of the season for the top-notchers.

Wednesday wanted the points, too, and put everything into their play in the effort to get them. But they found the 'Spurs defenders hadn't the jumpe to anything like the same degree as the forwards.

The spectators added their quota to the excitement of it all, and many of them were hit by shots which the 'Spurs forwards should have aimed at goal till Duquemin slipped one into the net just before the interval.

Afterwards, the 'Spurs forwards kept their heads much better, though goalkeeper McIntosh, ofttimes excellent and sometimes lucky, kept them out.

There's a young winger with a good name—Finney—in the Wednesday side about whom a lot may be heard in the future. And the team in general was not a bad one.

Whatever their status next season they can learn from this match that defenders don't really help their side by kicking the ball anywhere.

The Tottenham backs started attacks. The Wednesday backs merely stopped them.

Harvey, Walker and Milburn with the Cup

The Seven Men From Birtley

" News of the World " Reporter

SEVEN happy heroes were helped yesterday by this newspaper to do what tens of thousands of other folk were wanting to do. They were the seven men of Birtley colliery, Co. Durham, who were rescued on March 14 after being trapped underground for 32 hours.

From their mining village the "News of the World" brought them up for the Cup—all expenses paid for the week-end. It was intended as a tribute not only to their own courage, but to all that multitude which works underground, digging the coal on which our national existence so largely depends.

It began on Friday, this adventure for heroes, of whom only one had ever before seen a Cup Final (that was in 1913 when Aston Villa beat Sunderland 1—0 at Crystal Palace) and only two others had been to London.

Imagine the excitement, then, for these seven — Mr. Ned McKenna, the 63-year-old veteran of the 1913 Cup Final, who lives at Durham-place, Birtley; Mr. Thomas Hook, aged 22, of Havana-road, Washington, Co. Durham; Mr. Jack Halliday, aged 58, of Rose-street, Gateshead; Mr. Joseph Arthur, aged 54, of Leybourne Hold, Birtley; Mr. John Little, aged 35, of Hutt-street, Gateshead; Mr. Henry Brown, aged 44, of Northside, Birtley; and Mr. George Armstrong, aged 40, of Lowreys-lane, Low Fell.

When I asked Joe Arthur if he was one of the three who had been to London before, he replied: "No, man. Why I've never been away from the plate ends "—meaning the end of the pit rails. Apart from McKenna, it transpired, the others were Halliday and Little.

That first night " In Town," after tea and dinner at their West-end hotel, they all went on a tour of theatreland and then to see the Crazy Gang show at the Victoria Palace.

During the interval they were invited backstage to meet Mr. Jack Hylton and the Crazy Gang.

We were up early yesterday. The morning we spent in a sight-seeing tour by car of London.

Early in the afternoon we set out on the real purpose of our week-end—to see the Cup Final.

Inside the huge stadium we found ourselves among tens of thousands of other Newcastle supporters who had invaded London for the match.

They cheered and we cheered. And how we cheered. No doubt there were some cheers elsewhere for Blackpool, too, but I, for one, never had a chance to hear them.

And George Armstrong, who back in 1931 played for a while with Lincoln, commented: " I've no desire to be trapped in a mine again, but this Cup Final, plus the week-end's entertainment, was well worth the inconvenience—as it turned out."

He added: " It was wonderful of Newcastle United to give us the Cup tickets, but without the ' News of the World ' invitation it might not have been possible for us to find the fare and the price of accommodation. We have all had three weeks out of work because the pit has had to be closed down."

Late last night seven pleasantly weary men—and one equally weary reporter who had accompanied them—toured the offices of the "News of the World" and watched the great modern presses turning out this newspaper at the rate of 750,000 copies an hour. It was an impressive close to the Big Day of a week-end fit for heroes.

NEWS OF THE WORLD May 4, 1952

NEWCASTLE BEAT TEN C

ARSENAL HEROES HOLD UNTIL LAST MINUTES

George Robledo Heads Winner

By HARRY DITTON
ARSENAL 0, NEWCASTLE UNITED 1

Wonderful Arsenal! Yes, they've lost the Cup, which goes back to Newcastle—the first time in 61 years a team has succeeded in winning it in successive seasons—but Arsenal were great, even glorious, in defeat. Never has Wembley seen a more memorable failure.

For more than an hour Arsenal struggled through this game with the overwhelming handicap of having only 10 men through an injury which befell Walley Barnes, their Welsh international full-back.

But such was the unconquerable spirit of the men from Highbury that they more than kept the game alive until five minutes from the end, when George Robledo, with a spec-

PATH TO THE FINAL

ARSENAL		NEWCASTLE	
Norwich C.	(a) 5—0	Aston V. .. (h)	4—2
Barnsley ..	(h) 4—0	Spurs .... (a)	3—0
Leyton O..	(a) 3—0	Swansea .. (a)	1—0
Luton T...	(h) 3—2	Portsmouth (a)	4—2
Chelsea	...... 1—1	Blackburn R.	
Chelsea	...... 3—0	(Hillsboro)	0—0
(Both at White		Blackburn R.	
Hart Lane)		(Leeds)	2—1

tacular header from Mitchell's centre, scored the only goal—the ball sneaking into the net off an upright.

So long as they were at full strength, Arsenal were the dominant force in this game. They played brilliantly to a lively and co-ordinated plan and had Newcastle defending frantically. Indeed, I feel confident that but for Barnes's injury Arsenal would have won.

Lishman, seeming to pull out that little extra to take the weight off wee Jimmy Logie, not 100 per cent. fit, was for ever in the picture with clever tactical moves and menacing dribbles.

Newcastle hearts must have missed several beats before five minutes had passed when, from a long throw in by Holton, Lishman made a glorious overhead flick which seemed to have goal written all over it. At the last fraction of a second, however, it dipped away just enough to miss the net. A really lucky escape for United.

Throughout there was an impressive challenge in Arsenal's football and they were well into their stride while United were still in the process of trying to find their Wembley legs.

Then it happened—stark tragedy for Arsenal. In warding off a thrust by Jackie Milburn, Barnes pulled a ligament of the knee and fell in agony. A few minutes in the trainer's hands and then Barnes, with that wonderful fighting spirit which is so typically Arsenal, tried to continue at outside-right. Roper moved to full-back and Cox to outside-left, until the second half when he took over at centre-forward.

Willing as Barnes's spirit was, the effort was too great, and for more than an hour Arsenal struggled through with 10 men. But what a courageous 10. Inspired by the grand example of skipper Joe Mercer, who has never played better, they remained immaculate as ever in defence, and sufficiently bold and threatening in attack to keep Newcastle at full stretch all the time.

Newcastle, while they are to be congratulated on achieving such a rare feat as that of retaining the Cup, were disappointing, except for their rousing display in the last 20 minutes. They should have done very much better.

Here was a chance for them to exploit, in the grand manner they have, the misfortune of their opponents, but they seldom did.

Mitchell, at outside-left, always showed us the sparkle of a football genius, and when Milburn was in possession there was every threat that the centre-forward's phenomenal turn of speed and quick-fire shooting might be decisive.

However, with Robledo, in spite of his goal, Foulkes and Walker rarely touching the heights, the chances that came to Milburn were few and far between.

One would like to individualise in the case of every one of the Arsenal players, so well did they perform, but suffice it to say they were 10 heroes.

Outstanding for Newcastle were Cowell and McMichael at full-back; Harvey, who played a captain's part at right-half; Brennan and Mitchell.

Arsenal.—Swindin; Barnes, Smith (L.); Forbes, Daniel, Mercer; Cox, Logie, Holton, Lishman, Roper.

Newcastle United.—Simpson; Cowell, McMichael; Harvey, Brennan, Robledo (E.); Walker, Foulkes, Milburn, Robledo (G.), Mitchell.

Referee: Mr. A. E. Ellis (Halifax).

The winning goal, with Swindin beaten and watching the ball glide into the net.

JOE'S SECOND CUP

AND WINNIE'S FIRST

100% at the man with the proudest prize in soccer—and the look to match . . he's Newcastle United captain, Joe Harvey—holding up the F.A. Cup for the 100,000 crowd to see, after victory at Wembley yesterday. Newcastle beat Arsenal by a single goal scored five minutes from time, and became the first team of this century to take the Cup in successive years. Yes, two years running for Joe Harvey—but it was the first-ever Final for Mr. Churchill, seen shaking hands with Logie of Arsenal, RIGHT. Altogether, cups were in the news for the Prime Minister yesterday . . . his horse Loving Cup won the third race at Newbury.

THE GOAL...AND OTHER PICTURE HIGHLIGHTS...SEE BACK PAGE

Date 3 May 1952
Place Wembley
Score NEWCASTLE UNITED 1 ARSENAL 0
Teams NEWCASTLE UNITED Simpson, Cowell, McMichael, Harvey, Brennan, E. Robledo, Walker, Foulkes, Milburn, G. Robledo, Mitchell. ARSENAL Swindin, Barnes, L. Smith, Forbes, Daniel, Mercer, Cox, Logie, Holton, Lishman, Roper
Team Colours NEWCASTLE UNITED Black and white striped shirts, black

shorts; ARSENAL Red and white shirts, white shorts
Official Referee A. E. Ellis (Halifax)
Goal Scorer G. Robledo 84
Managers NEWCASTLE UNITED Stan Seymour; ARSENAL Tom Whittaker
Attendance 100 000
Gate Receipts £39 351
Guest of Honour Winston Churchill
Copy *Sunday Graphic* 4 May 1952; *News of the World* 4 May 1952; *Sunday Express* 4 May 1952

The caption above reads: look at the man with the proudest prize in soccer – and the look to match . . . he's Newcastle United captain, Joe Harvey – holding up the F.A. Cup for the 100,000 crowd to see, after victory at Wembley yesterday. Newcastle beat Arsenal by a single goal scored five minutes from time, and became the first team of this century to take the Cup in successive years. Yes, two years running for Joe Harvey – but it was the first-ever final for Mr Churchill, seen shaking hands with Logie of Arsenal, RIGHT. Altogether, cups were in the news for the Prime Minister yesterday . . . his horse Loving Cup won the third race at Newbury.

LLANT MEN TO KEEP CUP

HEY used to call them Lucky Arsenal. But 100,000 witnesses at W e m b l e y will in future think of them as Unlucky Arsenal. The Cup goes back to Newcastle for another year, but this Final will be remembered for the guts and courage of the Ten Red Devils, who hammered r rivals after Walley Barnes had limped off for good with torn ligaments in his right knee 10 utes before half-time.

rsenal were on top when the year-old Walley was accident- an, kicked by a back-heeler from kie Milburn after 19 minutes. y remained the better team till final whistle—even though all r efforts were wasted when rge Robledo headed the winner minutes from time.

Stan Seymour, always a sports- an, summed the game up in a tshell when he hurried into rsenal's dressing-room, shook m Whittaker by the hand and, rning to the team, said: "New- stle won the Cup, but Arsenal on the honours. On the day you ere the better team."

here was not one murmur nst the continuation of bad luck has dogged the Londoners these few weeks, when one player r another has been injured.

★ ★ ★
Proud In Defeat

TOM WHITTAKER thanked each individual player and said: "Boys, I have never been so proud of you in victory as I am of you in defeat."

★ ★ ★

Joe Mercer, Arsenal's 38-year-old skipper, who had one of his greatest games, did not show his disappointment. "We fought the best we could with heavy odds against us," was his comment.

★ ★ ★

Newcastle players realised this was one of their poorest displays of the season. George Robledo, who scored the only goal, said: "Arsenal were great, but sometimes the team with 10 men become more inspired than their opponents at full strength. That's what happened in this game."

★ ★ ★

George then explained how he

scored the goal. "Bobby Mitchell was dribbling in and the Arsenal defence thought he was going to go through on his own, but he looked up, saw me and centred. I intended to head the ball back to the far post, but Lionel Smith blocked my vision and so I aimed for the near post instead. The ball struck the post on its way in.

★ ★ ★

The Newcastle team hardly caught the eye, apart from the fine dribbling of Mitchell and the speedbursts of Milburn. Yet every one of the Ten Red Devils deserved a special medal for endeavour.

Arsenal lost the Cup, but they have made thousands of new friends. Remember, they used to boo Jack Dempsey until he lost his title to Tunney, and then he became everybody's hero. Now they have lost the Cup as well as the League Championship there is a new and warm affection for Unlucky Arsenal.

Another view of Newcastle's winning goal. Swindin turns to pick the ball from the net after Robledo's header had gone in off the post. Mitchell, who made the centre, is on his knees in the background, and Milburn of Newcastle and Daniel of Arsenal watch

1953

SUNDAY PICTORIAL, May 3, 1953

THE HAPPIEST MAN IN THE LAND

UP in the air for joy, on the shoulders of two of his team-mates, goes the happiest man in the land, after yesterday's Cup Final.

Yes—he is Stanley Matthews, and Stan has got THAT MEDAL. In the last half minute of the most exciting Cup Final ever seen at Wembley, Blackpool beat Bolton 4—3, after being 1—3 down in the second half.

Thrill followed thrill as the Blackpool men flung in attack after attack. Then Mortensen scored.

A couple of minutes before the end, Mortensen smashed home a third.

Forty-five seconds to go, and there began a movement that made the game the final of Wembley finals. Stan Matthews, playing superb footba.l, raced forward, and Perry crowned his magnificent efforts.

Blackpool—and Stan—had made it.

Date 2 May 1953
Place Wembley
Score BLACKPOOL 4
BOLTON WANDERERS 3
Teams BLACKPOOL Farm, Shimwell, Garrett, Fenton, Johnston (capt.), Robinson, Matthews, Taylor, Mortensen, Mudie, Perry. BOLTON WANDERERS Hanson, Ball, Banks, Wheeler, Barrass, Bell, Holden, Moir (capt.), Lofthouse, Hassall, Langton
Team Colours BLACKPOOL Tangerine shirts, white shorts; BOLTON WANDERERS White shirts, black shorts

Official Referee B. M. Griffiths (Newport)
Goal Scorers BLACKPOOL Mortensen 35, 68, 89, Perry 92; BOLTON WANDERERS Lofthouse 2, Moir 40, Bell 55
Managers BLACKPOOL Joe Smith; BOLTON WANDERERS Bill Ridding
Attendance 100 000
Gate Receipts £49 900
Guests of Honour H.M. Queen Elizabeth, Duchess of Kent, Princess Mary
Copy The Sunday Pictorial 3 May 1953; The Daily Express 4 May 1953

Matthews is in the 90-minute mood, and with wee Ernie Taylor laying on the passes I see the Coronation Cup Final being the crowning success for the Kingpin of football.

Here's how Desmond Hackett forecast the menace of Matthews in Saturday's Daily Express.

MANAGER PLAYS A 'BLINDER'

Blackpool 4 Bolton Wanderers 3

STANLEY MATTHEWS is scribbling with his fantastic feet the greatest Cup Final story of all time, filling the sun - goldened Wembley bowl with excitement that was for many unendurable, writes DESMOND HACKETT.

What, then, is in the mind of the maestro as the fading seconds are ebbing agonisingly away?

Matthews tells me: "My mind was cleared of all thoughts of Cup medals, scores, or minutes.

"I just kept on playing . . . on and on. It was only when it was all over that I spoke aloud to myself, 'I've done it at last.'"

When Blackpool manager, sturdy Joe Smith, dashed on to the pitch, where he helped to win the first Wembley Final 30 years before, Matthews told him: "You played a blinder, Joe."

He was recalling the times near the end when manager Smith was doing the ball boys out of a job racing along the touchline to get the ball back into play, saving

seconds that were to mean so much to Blackpool.

WEEPING WIVES LEAVE MATCH

When the game restarted for the last time there were only 35 seconds left.

It had been a game of unforgettable excitement, yes, of high drama. Wives of the players were weeping, several had left their seats unable to watch as their husbands collapsed under the strain.

But the man who shrugged aside the burden of leaden legs and crazed bewildered nerves was Matthews. Somehow the score had swung from a 3–1 lead for Bolton to Blackpool tying 3–3.

Two minutes of this ordeal to go and Matthews is gliding down the wing with all the menace and smoothness of a snake.

There is about him a cold, implacable purpose. There is the brave music of cheers rising, rising in salute to this slight, balding man with the ball.

There is the sudden shock of hushed silence as Matthews smooths over his pass, leaning widely over on his left ankle before he falls.

And he is still leaning on his elbow on the ground when Perry sweeps the ball past the frantically reaching foot of John Ball.

BELL CRIPPLED AFTER 20 MINS.

Inside a minute it is all over, Blackpool crazily happy, unlucky Bolton trying bravely to congratulate the winners.

Unlucky Bolton? Yes. Left-half Eric Bell was crippled by a torn muscle after 20 minutes.

Bolton were unlucky because they were the better team up to that point.

Blackpool, for all the gay trimmings of Matthews and energy man Ernie Taylor, were a poorish side in the first half. Guiltily they

passed on their scoring chances, afraid to shoot.

No wonder manager Joe Smith gave them this half-time blistering: "You are all scared to shoot. Get out and fight for goals."

Each side in turn had been shattered by body blows of ill-luck that looked complete Cup knock-outs. Inside 100 seconds Farm let a 25-yard Lofthouse power drive spin from his arms into goal. . . . Bell collapsed.

HIT SHOT INTO HIS OWN GOAL

Harold Hassall, playing tremendously as emergency half-back, tore in to check a Mortensen shot and hit it straight into his own goal. . . . Farm again blundered disastrously, failed to cover a Langton 20-yard shot which drifted in off Moir's shoulder.

Blackpool seemed right out of the Cup after ten minutes of the second half when the crippled Bell courageously went up to head a goal. Straight away Mortensen and Perry missed gaping chances as Matthews wrenched the Bolton defence wide open.

Tiredly the Bolton defence sags, crumples. Mortensen darts on to a Matthews centre and stabs the ball in as he crashes into the post.

Mortensen again—gambling on being able to crack a free kick into the slight gap as Bolton players barrier the goal. The gamble comes off.

And so to that magnificent flourish of a finish and the magnificent Matthews story moving indelibly into the history of football greatness.

F.A. invite Stan to join tour

By DESMOND HACKETT

STANLEY MATTHEWS . . . wonderful, wonderful Stanley Matthews . . . has only to say "Yes" today and he will be flying off to South America on Thursday aboard Flight No. BA353 with the England tour team.

Praise the Football Association for having the courage to admit they were wrong in not including this incomparable performer as their No. 1 selection.

DON'T WORRY, SAYS THE PRINCESS

● Bolton were leading 3—1 . . . Blackpool chairman MR. HARRY EVANS buried his head in his hands. . . .

A small voice consoled him: "Don't worry, you will win." It was his near neighbour in the Royal Box — PRINCESS MARGARET.

● MRS. LOFTHOUSE watched her son Nat, leading Bolton . . . until half an hour from the end. Then, her eyes blinded by tears, she stumbled away from the area. "I just can't stand another minute," she said.

● MR. ROWLAND ROBINSON, M.P. for Blackpool, on the Matthews omission, asked : " Why do England send their second team on tour ? "

● England goalkeeper GIL MERRICK to GEORGE FARM of Blackpool and Scotland : "Those two first goals were tough breaks." Farm : "Nothing of the sort—I just made a mess of them."

● The huge scoreboard at Wembley Stadium showed the score 4—4 just before the end. Said a Blackpool official, "afraid" to keep his eyes on the game : "How did Bolton get that one ?"

● Morning-of-the-match present for Blackpool was a silver cup from Arsenal supporters with the note : "Any team that can beat us must win the Cup."

The F.A. opinion that Matthews was too old at 38 to stand the pace was whisked away in that Cup Final which will be forever Matthews'.

When men years younger were collapsing with the cramp of fatigue Matthews was weaving in his magic way that touch of Soccer sorcery that will never be equalled.

He was the relentless, tortuous matador, coming in with probing, tormenting raids to further wrack a Bolton defence wearied almost beyond the point of any further resistance.

This, then, was the Matthews answer to those selectors who said he was not fit to play for England.

Matthews will make the decision after he has had a medical check-up. He has been having treatment for a damaged thigh muscle since the Christmas Holiday games.

Before he went out to floodlight the Final against Bolton he had an injection.

ECKERSLEY

Tour change No. 2 is Bill Eckersley, of Blackburn, in place of Lionel Smith, of Arsenal, as left back. Smith has sciatica in his right leg, and it has not responded to treatment.

I always rated Eckersley as ill-done by for not being picked in the original party. His record in internationals abroad all bear the same stamp—he was a fighting footballer.

Bustling Eckersley will be hustling Eckersley in the next four days.

Yesterday he was vaccinated. Today he flies to Copenhagen with the Football League team to play the Danish Combination tomorrow.

The F.A. have phoned Mrs. Eckersley to send on his clothes for the South American trip.

Today officials will be getting visas for Matthews and Eckersley from the American, Argentinian, Chilean, and Uruguayan embassies.

Eckersley returns from Copenhagen on Wednesday with England manager Walter Winterbottom and fellow tour men Billy Wright, Alf Ramsey, and Ray Barlow, who are also in the League team.

Mortensen scores Blackpool's second

● Blackpool's remarkable comeback from 3–1 down to beat Bolton Wanderers 4–3 puts 1953 high on the list of memorable finals. The romance, of course, was heightened by the contribution in those last, bewildering minutes of Stanley Matthews, who at 38 finally carried off a winner's medal after being thwarted in 1948 and 1951.

In retrospect the match is remarkable for the number of goalkeeping errors, the performance of Stan Mortensen, credited with a hat-trick, though clearly his first goal went in via the leg of Harold Hassall, and for the naivety of Bolton's approach.

The left-hand side of Bolton's defence was handicapped by an injury to Eric Bell after only 20 minutes, though he defied the pain to head Bolton into that 3–1 lead. Ralph Banks, at left-back, was left unprotected and increasingly lame himself, and totally vulnerable when Matthews dribbled to the goal-line to set up Billy Perry's winning goal in injury time.

JOHN GRAYDON spotlights West Brom's hero

GRIFFIN'S WONDER WINNER

I say Wayman's goal was well offside

WEST BROM. ALBION 3	PRESTON N.E. 2
Allen 2 (1 pen), Griffin	Morrison, Wayman

"MY heart stopped beating when I realised I'd scored the goal to win us the Cup," said West Bromwich Albion's right-winger, Frank Griffin, when I spoke to him in the Wembley dressing room after this rather disappointing Cup Final.

He should also have added it was a happy ending to a worrying week. For last Monday there was a big question mark behind Griffin playing in the final at all. His right ankle, injured in the semi-final, had shown little signs of improvement and last Monday Griffin underwent—with success he proved—a manipulation operation.

With the right foot, which had caused him all the worry, Griffin, with only two minutes left, cut into the middle. Showing commendable coolness, he rammed the ball across the chest of goalkeeper Thompson, into the far corner of the Preston net.

Victory-worthy

It was a goal worthy to win a Cup Final. It was a wonder goal which earned for Griffin a winners golden medal.

For so long it seemed that fate had decreed West Bromwich were not to win any football honour, after being in the running for the elusive double.

In a Wembley setting where football of the highest quality is expected, this final was a little disappointing.

Both teams spent so much time sizing up each other like boxers that for long periods there was little real action and little good football to go with it.

Finney, of course, would shine in any company, and his twinkling feet and baffling body-swerve several times had the Albion captain, Len Millard, running about like a scalded cat.

Fortunately for West Bromwich left half-back Barlow frequently dropped back to become a second left-back and always worried Finney.

And so Finney, who has dictated in most of the Preston Cup-ties, was not allowed to take command in the Wembley Final.

That hoodoo

Albion's method was to cut down the flow of passes to the "footballer of the year," and to some extent this was the basis of Albion's victory plan.

Albion also deserve great credit for the manner in which they

fought against the hoodoo which has been hanging over them ever since the Semi-Final. To win through, as they did, makes their victory all the more commendable.

It appeared that Albion had recovered all their old smoothness of movement and poise when, after 21 minutes, they coasted into the lead. For this goal Willie Cunningham, the Preston right-back, was entirely to blame.

With all the time in the world to clear he waited until Lee was

First blood in the 1954 F.A. Cup Final is drawn by West Bromwich Albion. Centre-forward Allen coolly puts the ball into the Preston net while the helpless goalkeeper lies flat on the ground, despairingly watching the ball enter the goal.

virtually on top of him, took a wild kick, and the ball rebounded off the winger. Lee pounced on it, and a hard cross found Allen sliding into an open space, and giving Thompson no chance.

The gaiety of the West Bromwich players was short-lived. A minute later Docherty crossed the ball to Morrison, who smartly headed the equaliser and Preston were once more in the hunt.

Near tragedy

Two minutes afterwards West Bromwich hearts took another jump when a Wayman hit crashed over the crossbar with Sanders beaten to the wide.

Then came what could have been a tragedy for West Bromwich. After 51 minutes a Marston-Docherty then Finney-Foster move saw the ball streak through to Wayman.

To me Wayman looked three yards offside. While the Albion defence hesitated, Wayman went on to place the ball past Sanders, and West Bromwich must have felt the world was against them.

Then fate, so long an enemy, turned in their favour after 63 minutes. Barlow, who had defended so resolutely, now tried to storm his way through the Albion defence. Docherty and he collided, and referee Luty, as Barlow was sent sprawling, pointed to the penalty spot.

Allen, as in the semi-final with Port Vale, took the kick. Goalkeeper Thompson managed to get both hands to the ball, but the pace beat him and it was 2—2.

Then with only two minutes left, Reg Ryan sent out to Griffin a delightful pass and the West Bromwich winger, cutting into the middle, put the finishing touch to the movement with his wonder shot.

This was a cup final which could have gone either way.

Date 1 May 1954
Place Wembley
Score WEST BROMWICH ALBION 3
PRESTON NORTH END 2
Teams WEST BROMWICH ALBION
Sanders, Kennedy, Millard (capt.),
Dudley, Dugdale, Barlow, Griffin,
Ryan, Allen, Nicholls, Lee. PRESTON
NORTH END Thompson, Cunningham,
Walton, Docherty, Marston, Forbes,
Finney (capt.), Foster, Wayman,
Baxter, Morrison
Team Colours WEST BROMWICH
ALBION Blue and white striped shirts,
white shorts; PRESTON NORTH
END White shirts, blue shorts
Official Referee A. W. Luty (West
Riding)
Goal Scorers WEST BROMWICH
ALBION Allen 21, 63 (penalty),
Griffin 88; PRESTON NORTH
END Morrison 22, Wayman 51
Managers WEST BROMWICH
ALBION Vic Buckingham;
PRESTON NORTH END Scot Symon
Attendance 100000
Gate Receipts £49 883
Guests of Honour H.R.H. The Queen
Mother, H.R.H. Princess Margaret
Copy The Evening News 1 May 1954;
Sunday Graphic 2 May 1954

Opposite below: *1954 was the year in
which the public hoped that Tom Finney,
seen getting in a cross, would emulate the
performance the year before of that other
great winger, Stan Matthews, and win a
Cup winners' medal. The miracle did not
happen again, and below Griffin's goal
finally denied Finney his medal*

Rosettes, a trumpet, long ties and happy faces—Preston supporters in London to-day.

Watch for Forged and Stolen Tickets at Wembley

"EVENING NEWS" REPORTER

A WATCH FOR FORGED AND STOLEN CUP FINAL TICKETS WAS MADE BY SCOTLAND YARD DETECTIVES AND TURNSTILE OFFICIALS AMONG THE 100,000 SPECTATORS WHO CRAMMED INTO WEMBLEY STADIUM THIS AFTERNOON.

Each and every ticket presented at the turnstiles was scrutinised by security officials.

"Although the possibility of forged tickets is rather remote, we are, nevertheless, making a thorough check," said an official.

He added: "We do know, however, that several Cup Final tickets have been stolen, and we are using special methods, in collaboration with the C.I.D., to trace them and the thieves."

THE TOUTS
And The 'Pirates'

Extra police were drafted to Wembley to clear ticket touts and pirate programme sellers from the stadium area.

The majority of touts had no tickets to sell when they first invaded Wembley several hours before the match between Preston North End and West Bromwich Albion began.

They asked passers-by for "any spare tickets, chum?" Touts who managed to buy 3s. 6d. standing tickets for 10s. each re-sold them within a few minutes at up to £3 a time. Several half-guinea seats changed hands for £10.

But generally the touts reported poor business. "We blame television," said one.

Bright sunshine broke through an overcast Wembley sky before the arrival of the Queen Mother and Princess Margaret.

The two teams were to have been presented to the Duke of Gloucester before the match, but he has laryngitis and could not attend the Cup Final.

His place was being taken by the Queen Mother.

Coaches, cars and motor-cycles began filling the stadium car parks hours before the kick-off. Families who had travelled south during the night claimed their places in the car parks at 7 a.m. to-day and, after a breakfast of sandwiches and tea from flasks, slept in their cars.

First arrivals at Wembley were a coachload of villagers from Dolphinholme, in the hills near Lancaster. Hours later they joined the huge crowds thronging to the stadium, waving rattles and sporting rosettes and comic hats.

MITCHELL THE MAESTRO LANDS CUP K.O. ON TEN WEARY MANCHESTER PLAYERS

"Better team won"—Revie

NEWCASTLE U. 3 MANCHESTER C. 1
Half-time 1-1
Attendance: 100,000 — Receipts £49,881.
BY KEN McKENZIE

Milburn's shocker

"THE better team won," Don Revie told me after yesterday's 23rd F.A. Cup Final played at Wembley.

That is, I feel, a comment both true and generous on a game in which City, losing right-back Meadows in the 18th minute, rallied magnificently to wipe out Jackie Milburn's sensational 50 seconds headed goal but could only battle on to avert rout after maestro Bobby Mitchell's knock-out goal in 53 minutes.

Five minutes later Mitchell, who had done very nearly a Stan Matthews' act in response to delightful service from Scoular and Hannah, said "Thank you" by laying on the final score for his inside partner.

LATER, I thought Newcastle, in casual control at practice-match pace, were themselves generous to unfortunate but sporting foes.

I am glad City got that equaliser. My half-time thought, in fact, was good for City; they had earned this encouragement of setting Newcastle's full strength team the job of getting the extra goal which should mean victory.

MILBURN PULLED MUSCLE

On these wide open and tiring Wembley spaces, however, it was really only a matter of how long it would take to land the vital blow.

All the Newcastle players expressed great regret at Meadows' injury. Yet, Newcastle, too, were labouring under handicap. White severely damaged his left ankle late in the first half and Milburn, from soon after the interval, could scarcely raise a real gallop owing to pulling a stomach muscle.

We saw sufficient of Manchester City's neatly patterned construction based on Don Revie's neat leadership to realise that, but for their crippling handicap, they might have gained a big victory despite their early setback.

Revie had not a great day, though working tremendously hard, and I thought City's chance might have been better if, after the interval at least, he had played in normal centre-forward manner.

Right-half Barnes played very well and the craft of Revie and Johnstone might have caused Newcastle additional headaches if Fagan, who was switched to outside-left due to Roy Clarke's recent withdrawal, had been more alert to some very fine openings.

SCOULAR IN CONTROL

But Newcastle's completion of a wonderful record was well earned.

Bob Stokoe played with fine confidence and Jimmy Scoular gave a delightful display, always having a controlling influence on the game and serving up football artistry worthy of the occasion, along with Mitchell, and, in the second half, Hannah.

Some of the long balls from Scoular and Hannah, often just an inch over the heads of defenders across to Mitchell, were perfection of strength and timing.

UNQUESTIONABLY THE GOAL WHICH JACKIE MILBURN SCORED IN THE SECOND ATTACK OF THE GAME WILL BE RECALLED AS THE GOLDEN MOMENT OF A RECORD WHICH MAKES NEWCASTLE THE GLAMOUR CLUB OF THE YEAR AND STILL MORE OF POST-WAR YEARS.

Three Wembley wins in five seasons makes wondrous soccer history. Manchester City kicked off, but were pressed back immediately. One Milburn thrust was checked in turn.

FORCED A CORNER

Then Scoular, whose captaincy and play made him fitting successor of that iron man of Wembley, Joe Harvey, started attack number two.

Through to Jackie, out to White, forward to the bye-line and Jackie forced a corner.

White placed the ball opposite the near post and some 15 yards deep.

Only one player was there—Milburn, in splendid isolation. Even "marker" Roy Paul had moved over to give extra cover against United's airborne specialist, Vic Keeble. Milburn rose to make a great header.

Trautmann, widely rated the world's greatest 'keeper, got nowhere near the ball as it whipped just under the bar near the post on his left.

I thought Newcastle tended to fiddle instead of pressing home their advantage to burn up the City goal after that flying start.

SHOULD HAVE BEEN 1-1

Mitchell declined the chance of two shots, electing to work the ball, and he placed some balls rather too close to Trautmann who, nevertheless, looked a bundle of nerves for some time after the opening shot.

It should have been 1-1 in seven minutes. A quickly-taken free-kick by Paul from just outside the "box" was cleverly squared back by Fagan, moved by Revie, and Hayes sliced wide at eight yards.

A swinging corner by Mitchell came back off the bar and in 17 minutes a shot by Hannah flicking off Paul's head led to Trautmann making the first of his three great saves in the game.

Already Newcastle were looking confident in defence and most potent forward.

The beginning of the end came when in 18 minutes City's right-back, Meadows, fell awkwardly in a bid to recover after a vain tackle against Mitchell's dummy. He badly wrenched ligaments of the knee and lower leg.

THIS HAPPENED WITHIN A YARD OR TWO OF WHERE WALLY BARNES, OF ARSENAL, SUSTAINED THE 18th MINUTE INJURY WHICH CAUSED HIS RETIREMENT IN THE FINAL AGAINST NEWCASTLE IN 1952.

Meadows was worked on by the City trainers behind goal for five minutes before being helped to the dressing room, and ten minutes later we learned in the Press Box that he would not resume. For the rest of the game outside-right Spurdle was at right-back, City playing with four forwards.

SIMPSON SAVES UNITED

Ewing headed off the goal-line from Scoular and Hayes failed again in 25 minutes when Cowell, on the far side, left the inside-right onside and well through. He shot too hurriedly and sent over. At this stage City were giving us good samples of their quick-blended passing moves on the ground.

White closed in after Hannah-Milburn service to hit a stinging left-footer from which Trautmann made his second brilliant save.

Save number three in 36 minutes when, from a diagonal hit by Mitchell, Keeble headed firmly at four yards and Trautmann, nearly falling into the net in taking the ball, managed to swing back and drop around in possession.

But City produced another spell of fine team moves, and five minutes from the interval Simpson saved United by darting well out and falling forward on to the ball as Johnstone nipping past Stokoe and Batty, seemed certain to jab a ten-yarder past the 'keeper into the net.

A ball from Cowell picked up by Barnes led to the equaliser. A pass to Revie, Barnes again, out to Hayes and a short air ball to Johnstone produced a hard-hit ten-yard header which had Simpson well beaten on his left.

BEAUTIFULLY PLACED

Newcastle's No. 2—the virtual winner—came just after Revie had pounced on a Trautmann clearance and almost put Hayes through.

White made a fine cross to Mitchell, who beat close marking Spurdle "on a sixpence," deceived Trautmann into expecting a cross, and from within a foot of the bye line rammed in an eight-yarder between the 'keeper and the near post.

Trautmann then saved a Mitchell right-footer, but had no chance when Scoular, cutting out a City pass, "left" Johnstone and hit a perfect 40-yarder over Spurdle's head for Mitchell to move in and square back for Hannah to score from 12 yards in the inside-right position.

IT WAS A DELIBERATE. BEAUTIFULLY PLACED SHOT.

After that Newcastle knew they had won and City, though persistent and never desperate, clearly had no great hope.

Scoular typically portrayed the situation when he made a beautiful cart wheel on to the grass behind the bye line after being charged over in a cut through.

Yet City could also have added goals. Fagan was "asleep" to a through ball by Revie to the six yards area.

Trautmann saved a Mitchell stinger from inside right. Keeble headed just over from White and three Newcastle men virtually drew aside for Spurdle to make a vain but defiant 50 yards dribble from right back.

THE QUEEN KNEW IT WAS CUP RECORD

"YOU have broken a record." That was The Queen's remark to Mr. Stan Seymour, chairman of Newcastle United, as the final whistle blew in Wembley Stadium yesterday afternoon.

The Queen and the Duke of Edinburgh — who must have supported United, for he once commanded the frigate Magpie—knew that United, conquerors of Manchester City, now hold every Wembley Cup Final record.

United is the only team ever to win at Wembley on every occasion they have been there; the first team to be in 10 F.A. Cup Finals; and this win equals the record of Blackburn Rovers and Aston Villa's six wins.

Again they are the first team to win the Cup three times in five seasons and once again Newcastle took over the Empire's Capital last night—for it was "Blaydon Races" all over the West End.

Another record was the quickest goal ever scored at Wembley, by "Wor Jackie" Milburn in 45 seconds — and from then on United were the masters.

The champagne flows for, left to right, chairman Stan Seymour, Cowell, Batty, Casey, Scoular, Stokoe, White, manager Livingstone, trainer Smith and Milburn

---

Date 7 May 1955
Place Wembley
Score NEWCASTLE UNITED 3 MANCHESTER CITY 1
Teams NEWCASTLE UNITED Simpson, Cowell, Batty, Scoular (capt.), Stokoe, Casey, White, Milburn, Keeble, Hannah, Mitchell.
MANCHESTER CITY Trautmann, Meadows, Little, Barnes, Ewing, Paul (capt.), Spurdle, Hayes, Revie, Johnstone, Fagan

Team Colours NEWCASTLE UNITED Black and white striped shirts, black shorts; MANCHESTER UNITED Blue shirts, white shorts
Official Referee R. J. Leafe (Nottingham)
Goal Scorers NEWCASTLE UNITED Milburn 1, Mitchell 53, Hannah 60;

MANCHESTER CITY Johnstone 44
Managers NEWCASTLE UNITED Duggie Livingstone; MANCHESTER CITY Les McDowall
Attendance 100000
Gate Receipts £49881
Guests of Honour H.R.H. Princess Mary, H.R.H. Prince Philip
Copy *Sunday Sun* 8 May 1955

14 THE SUNDAY SUN, MAY 8

United do it Again!

GOAL OF THE CENTURY and scoring it is Jackie Milburn. Forty-five seconds had ticked away after the start of yesterday's great Cup battle at Wembley, and United were one up. Here he is jumping to head the ball over the heads of the Manchester defence and into the net.

CHAIRED and cheered. A great moment for Jimmy Scoular, Newcastle United's captain, at the end of yesterday's Cup Final at Wembley. He had just received the F.A. Cup from the Queen, and was being carried triumphantly by his team mates from the field.

DARING Trautmann again! The crowd gasped as the City 'keeper went down to snatch the ball from the feet of Vic Keeble, the Newcastle leader.

AHEAD AGAIN At the interval the score was level, but six minutes later Mitchell had the City goalie on his knees and the ball into the net.

No. 3 Six minutes later Hannah (partially obscured) increased the Magpies' lead. And how the United supporters (below right) cheered!

THE ONLY shot which beat United's 'keeper Simpson, was one from the City's inside-left, Johnstone — a picture goal.

Suspense stays till Cup Final day after amazing week

REVIE PLAYS AT WEMBLEY: UNLUCKY SPURDLE WATCHES

★ To-night's Photo-News ★

11th-hr. drama—Johnstone switched to wing

BY ERIC THORNTON   WEMBLEY, The Day.

DRAMA mounted upon drama before Manchester City were able to announce their Cup Final team to-day. Then came the shock news that set the football world buzzing: "Forgotten man" Don Revie was to turn out in the game of the year at this famous stadium.

This is how this dramatic end to City's week of Cup worries came about:

● **BOBBY JOHNSTONE,** one of the problem men, was declared fit.

● **BILLY SPURDLE,** also a doubtful man, was ruled out.

Manager Les McDowall went into a telephone huddle from the team's Surrey H.Q. with the directors in London.

Then the line-up was announced at last: Johnstone on the right wing, with Revie in the centre.

● **BILL LEIVERS,** the injured full back, was also passed fit, so the defence is unchanged.

Tension high

What a problem faced Mr McDowall after the village doctor at Weybridge, two miles away, had given his verdicts.

He paced up and down—then finally decided it might be best to plump for experience.

Tension increased among officials and players as we padded up and down the carpeted lounge, turning to see if there was any sign of him leaving the telephone-box.

Finally he emerged, and, wiping perspiration from his forehead, said: "Well, here's the team."

IT MEANT Revie, hero of last year's side, was in the Cup team for only the second time this year

IT MEANT Johnny Hart, "robbed" of a Wembley appearance last year by injury, had missed his chance again after a fighting come-back

Good-luck calls

How did the players react to the team news?

Johnstone said: "I am prepared to play anywhere Only the result matters."

Revie was glad to be at Wembley again, though sorry that Spurdle's boils have cost him a team place.

Hart took the news in the spirit this great-hearted player always shows.

DON REVIE

A Titanic Struggle That Had Everything

By HARRY DITTON

LONG after the glory of the pageantry which makes Wembley such a wonderful spectacle has been forgotten, they will recall the 1956 Cup Final. It was the sort of game that will live—and deserve to live—in the memory for months, possibly years, to come. This was a titanic struggle which had almost everything—high drama, tension which at times was almost electrical, an abundance of brilliant footcraft, and four goals. Manchester City were not only thoroughly worthy winners, but they maintained the great Wembley tradition of a side never losing the second time when they have appeared there in successive seasons.

Until three hours before the match Manchester City kept their forward line a secret. Finally they decided to play Don Revie in the centre and Bobby Johnstone at outside-right. Manager Leslie McDowall's judgment was handsomely vindicated. No other Manchester City formation could have improved on that of Revie and Co. in the smooth and punchy nature of their football.

On the other hand it's doubtful if Manchester gained any real tactical advantage over Birmingham by withholding their team to the eleventh hour.

THREE MINUTES—ONE UP

True, Manchester got away to a much more convincing start and gained the tremendous inspiration of a goal within three minutes. But my own summing-up of the position was that Birmingham brought most of the trouble on their own shoulders through an attack of Wembley jitters which sometimes bordered on panic.

Not only did the Birmingham full-backs, Hall and Green, play too close to deal adequately with the raiding and clever footwork of Johnstone and Clarke, but it took young Trevor Smith a considerable time to find his touch at centre-half.

Manchester's defence, on the other hand, while often bamboozled by the clever control of the Birmingham forwards, made fewer mistakes and behind them Trautmann did everything one would expect from a goalkeeper elected the Footballer of the Year.

To suggest that Trautmann swayed the match in Manchester's favour would clearly be an exaggeration. However, by his courage on at least two occasions in diving at the feet of oncoming forwards, he took the danger out of situations which might well have kept Birmingham in the game with a chance. On each occasion Trautmann was painfully injured.

Other Manchester players who more than earned their medals were Roy Paul, the captain, for his fine generalship and centre-half Dave Ewing, whose uncompromising effectiveness meant an extremely quiet match for Eddie Brown, Birmingham's roving centre-forward.

DREAM GOAL

The goal by which Manchester went into the lead after only three minutes was of the type that every team playing at Wembley dreams—beautifully controlled passing, perfect positioning, and rapier-like finishing to which there is no real answer. This is what happened:

Revie, from near the half-way line, swung a perfectly judged pass across field to Roy Clarke, who had the ball back in the Birmingham penalty area before Len Boyd and his colleagues could even begin to position for a clearance.

The pass found Revie who, in much quicker time than it takes to write, had moved forward

From his neatly judged back heeler, Joe Hayes, with time to spare to take stock of the situation drove firmly and accurately past Gil Merrick.

It was a tremendous jolt to Birmingham, and the quick, confident incisive tackling of Ewing and his colleagues kept them on their heels to such a degree that Manchester appeared to be running away with the match.

Gradually, however, Birmingham—inspired by the example of skipper Boyd—came more into the game. After 15 minutes, a quick bout of passing between Astall and Brown made an opening for Kinsey to crash the ball past Trautmann, via an upright, for an equaliser.

From that moment Birmingham were revitalised. Their half-backs moved the ball with new-found confidence to bring their forwards strongly into the game and a battle royal developed between two fine attacking sides. Indeed Wembley has rarely looked upon a more pleasing spectacle of cultured footcraft by two opposing attacks.

THRILLING SOCCER

It was cut and thrust all the time with first Birmingham scheming to find a chink in Manchester's defensive armour and Revie and his colleagues exerting all their wiles to find a gap in Birmingham's defence.

It was thrilling and enthralling with goalkeepers Merrick and Trautmann never allowed to remain disinterested spectators for more than a few minutes.

Then with 25 minutes to go Manchester recaptured the lead with another great goal.

Johnstone and Ken Barnes did the scheming and Jack Dyson ran the ball past Merrick with a great shot.

If there were still any lingering Birmingham hopes that the game might yet be snatched out of the fire, the real awakening came five minutes later.

Trautmann made a long clearance to Dyson who pushed the ball through the middle.

Here, that will o' the wisp of an outside-right Johnstone was waiting for such a chance.

So, too, was Smith, the Birmingham centre-half. But Johnstone, thinking the more quickly, was through like a flash and again Merrick was powerless to save a rollicking drive.

Hard-pressed touts get £7 for seats

WHAT of the fans? The week of jitters had left them unaffected as they poured from Manchester into London throughout the night and morning.

Unlike yesterday, there were no pessimists A CITY WIN was the confident forecast—and 3-1 the popular score

This was the scene in two cities.

MANCHESTER.—It was noisy, raucous, bright and colourful long before 7 a.m. as the happy thousands set out.

London Road and Victoria Stations were a blaze of blue, white, and maroon.

Thousands of other fans travelled by road and air 'oor visibility at London Airport delayed the first of the nine planes for half an hour.

LONDON woke early to the rattles the handbells, and the shouts of thousands of Northerners

Blue top hats and bowlers false noses and gaily-coloured jackets brought a touch of fantasy to the City and the West End

The Queen and the Duke of Edinburgh were in the 97,000 crowd And it was a fine day again—every post-war Wembley has had sun.

For the first time at a Cup Final a helicopter hovered over the packed roads to the stadium to spot traffic blocks.

What of the rackets?

The official programmes were for the first time, on sale from

early morning in a move to defeat "pirate" sellers Police repeatedly moved on the touts

CHANGEOVER. — Five of the Australian cricket team went to the final instead of remaining with their colleagues at Leicester.

They were Colin McDonald Davidson Lindwall Maddocks and Benaud

LOOKING-IN. — The Russian delegation from Sverdlovsk which is visiting Birmingham saw the game on a set at the Central fire station

And 90 minutes before the kick-off there was evidence that the inquiry into the ticket black market held after last year's final had had some effect, for the touts had far fewer than usual to offer

Some tickets at 3s 6d changed hands for £3 or £2 10s and 10s. 6d tickets were going for £6 and £7.

Another Wembley novelty was a selection from the massed bands of the Royal Marines

Conducting community singing at his tenth Cup Final was the familiar white-suited figure of Mr Arthur Caiger a retired headmaster

He agreed to Manchester requests to put in his programme "Lassie from Lancashire"

Date 5 May 1956	Brown, Murphy, Govan	**Managers** MANCHESTER CITY Les McDonald; BIRMINGHAM CITY Arthur Turner
Place Wembley	**Team Colours** MANCHESTER CITY Maroon and white stripes; BIRMINGHAM CITY White shirts, blue shorts	**Attendance** 100000
Score MANCHESTER CITY 3 BIRMINGHAM CITY 1		**Gate Receipts** £49856
Teams MANCHESTER CITY Trautmann, Leivers, Little, Barnes, Ewing, Paul (capt.), Johnstone, Hayes, Revie, Dyson, Clarke. BIRMINGHAM CITY Merrick, Hall, Green, Newman, Smith, Boyd (capt.), Astall, Kinsey,	**Official** Referee A. Bond (Middlesex) **Goal Scorers** MANCHESTER CITY Hayes 3, Dyson 65, Johnstone 70; BIRMINGHAM CITY Kinsey 15	**Guest of Honour** H.M. Queen Elizabeth II **Copy** Manchester Evening News 5 and 9 May 1956; News of the World 6 May 1956

REVIE & CO. PAY A FINAL DIVIDEND!

The Toast Is : Manchester And The Double

By FRANK SWIFT

Manchester City Goalkeeper in the Cup Final of 1934

Teams:

BIRMINGHAM

Merrick

Hall   Green

Newman Smith Boyd

Kinsey Murphy

Astall Brown Govan

●

Clarke Revie Johnstone

Dyson Hayes

Paul Ewing Barnes

Little Leivers

Trautmann

MANCHESTER CITY

Referee : Mr. A. Bond
(Fulham).

PATH TO THE FINAL

Birmingham

Torquay (A) 7—1, Murphy 2, Astall, Kinsey, Brown 3.
Leyton Orient (A) 4—0, Brown 2, Murphy, Finney.
West Bromwich (A) 1—0, Murphy.
Arsenal (A) 3—1, Astall, Murphy, Brown
Sunderland (Hillsborough) 3—0, Kinsey, Astall, Brown.

Manchester City

Blackpool (H) 2—1, Johnstone, Dyson.
Southend (A) 1—0, Hayes.
Liverpool (H) 0—0, (A) 2—1, Dyson, Hayes.
Everton (H) 2—1, Hayes, Johnstone.
Tottenham Hotspur (Villa Park) 1—0, Johnstone.

MANCHESTER CITY (1) 3   BIRMINGHAM (1) 1

(HAYES, DYSON, JOHNSTONE)   (KINSEY)

Attendance : 100,000   Receipts : £49,856

THE boil that kept Bill Spurdle out of the Cup Final turned out to be a blessing in disguise for Manchester City. It allowed Manager Les McDowall to field both Bobby Johnstone and Don Revie in his Wembley attack—and these were the two who, more than any others, upset the form book that had made Birmingham the hottest favourites in years.

Only three minutes had ticked by when Revie, in his old deep-centre-forward role, gave red faces to half Manchester—the half who were against his playing in the Final. He laid the foundation of his side's convincing win when he swept out a lovely pass to left-winger Roy Clarke, raced in to collect the return, and cutely back-heeled a gilt-edged chance for Joe Hayes. And Joey put the ball in the proper place—Birmingham's net!

Johnstone was later to produce more red faces in the Press Box, where his first-half performance—with his left knee strapped up and limping—made us doubt the wisdom of Mr. McDowall's gamble in playing a half-fit man on the right-wing.

Five Brilliant Minutes

But you can never write off this little Scot with the sharp football brain. In a five-minute flash of second-half brilliance, he had won the game for the Manchester men.

He started the move that led to Jack Dyson's 65th-minute goal (via Ken Barnes). Three minutes later, he scored a wonderful goal—Manchester's third. And he would have had another just afterwards if Merrick's legs had not been luckily in the way.

I judged Revie and Johnstone the best ball-players on view in a match packed with entertaining football, especially in the first half before the Birmingham challenge faded. Some of the midfield moves were sheer poetry, and it was only near goal that the game fell short of a classic.

There was high drama, too, involving Bert Trautmann. The blond German goalkeeper showed something more than the acrobatic skill that has earned him his Footballer of the Year award. He showed courage beyond measure.

Saving By Instinct

When Trautmann flung himself at the feet of Peter Murphy he received sickening blows on the head and neck. He was knocked cold—but incredibly he stopped the ball. It must have been by instinct.

As he lay on the turf, Manchester fans took up a surging cry which grew in power until it rocked Wembley. "We want Bert," was the chant. It was almost a prayer—even though City were winning 3—1.

Then, when Trautmann staggered to his feet, dazed and hardly knowing what was going on, the theme changed to "For he's a Jolly Good Fellow."

Five minutes later. Bert collapsed again when he collided with his own centre-half, Dave Ewing, but again he got up to finish a game he was unable to remember for several hours.

That could have been Birming-ham's great chance, but they never looked like taking it. In fact, Birmingham were a sad dis-appointment. Only for about 20 minutes after Noel Kinsey's equalising rocket did Arthur Turner's tigers show their stripes.

Birmingham's all-out attacking policy was a tactical mistake. In my opinion. Skipper Len Boyd was a veritable driving-force as he sprayed slide-rule passes to the men in front. But Birmingham paid dearly for the gaps he and Newman left behind them.

The middle of the field was left like a prairie for Don Revie to launch a notebookful of dangerous moves that would have paid bigger dividends had the Manchester men been quicker to make the final pass.

Every Manchester man played his part in landing the second leg of the soccer double for the Northern Capital—the League Championship and The Cup.

Trautmann once again showed that he reserves his best displays for Wembley. Bill Leivers, at right-back, put on a wonderful show, blotting out the Murphy-Govan wing on his own and allowing right-half Ken Barnes to star as an attacking wing-half.

They Tied It Up

Dave Ewing and Roy Paul drew a zip-fastener across the middle of the field, so that the roaming tactics of centre-forward Eddie Brown seldom created the gaps we had expected.

And I thought that Hayes and Dyson rose magnificently to the occasion. They may have missed a few chances between them—but they were always in the right position. Never before have I seen 'hem use the open space so intelligently.

And on the left-wing. Roy Clarke gave a characteristic swashbuckling display—though Jeff Hall made it easy for him. At times Clarke looked as if he had half of Wembley Stadium to himself.

It was obvious from the start that the team with the jitters was Birmingham.

Even so, they had plenty of time to settle before Manchester turned on the heat that made the second half a one-horse race and a football exhibition.

Well done, Manchester. You are worthy Cup-holders !

A dive typical of the spectacular goalkeeping of Footballer of the Year Bert Trautmann. Wembley reserved a special ovation for him. He played the last 20 minutes in a daze after injury. Here he flings himself at the feet of Birmingham's Peter Murphy.

TRAUTMANN: NECK BROKEN

Detained in hospital after X-ray

The Wednesday after the game

GREAT PAIN

BERT TRAUTMANN, Manchester City's goalkeeper, was detained in Manchester Royal Infirmary this afternoon with a broken neck.

The injury was caused when he dived at the feet of Murphy, the Birmingham forward during the last minutes of Saturday's Cup Final at Wembley.

After seeing colleagues off to-day on their foreign tour at Manchester Airport (picture—Page 5) friends persuaded him to go to the infirmary, where several X-rays were taken.

Trautmann was said to be in great pain.

A colleague of Trautmann's father-in-law said to-day : " Bert has been feeling pretty miserable and was suffering from headaches.

" As we drove to Manchester from Ringway I advised him to come with me for a check-up.

" He was unwilling at first, but was delighted he had gone when he realised how serious his condition was.

" He had ricked his neck before Saturday's game."

Saw osteopath

" The club took him to see an osteopath, and he was due to go again to-morrow.

" He didn't go with his colleagues to-day because he was not fit enough, but was expected to join them to-morrow or on Friday. He's so disappointed he can't go on this tour."

His friend said Trautmann was put to bed after having about five X-rays to find out in which places his neck was broken.

Mrs. Trautmann said: " Bert has been in terrible agony."

Hayes scores for Manchester City

McPARLAND PUTS TH

Injury To Goalkeeper Wood Dashes Hopes Of Double

By HARRY DITTON

ASTON VILLA carved an imperishable niche in soccer history, by proving the most successful Cup fighters of all time. They have now won the F.A. Cup SEVEN times—more often than any other club.

But spare a thought for the misfortune of Manchester United which made such a difference to the game. The turning point came within six minutes of the start when Manchester were deprived of the services of goalkeeper Ray Wood.

Wood and Peter McParland, the Villa outside-left, came into violent collision and, while the Irishman made a quick recovery and eventually proved Villa's match-winner, Wood had to be taken to the dressing-room with a suspected fracture of the jaw.

Wood returned half an hour later for 10 minutes, but it was merely to have a nuisance value as an outside-right.

And he missed nearly 40 minutes of the second half by which time United were facing a two-goal deficit. Then he returned to see Taylor head through a brilliant consolation goal.

Jackie Blanchflower was pulled out of the centre-half position to take Wood's place in goal and Duncan Edwards took over at centre-half with Billy Whelan dropping back to wing-half.

All three, Blanchflower and Edwards especially, played creditably in their unusual positions. Blanchflower making a series of quite expert clearances. But it was not to be expected United would entirely succeed in overcoming such a severe handicap.

Nevertheless United more than held their own and what little forward play of real class was provided came mainly from them.

But the Villa defence held out and survived a confident appeal for a penalty when Charlton was floored in the 15th minute.

It was in the second half that Manchester produced the best football of the match in the attacking sense, yet it was Villa, on their less frequent excursions, who were the more dangerous.

Following one right-wing attack McParland headed against an upright and a minute later the Irishman provided a glorious opening for Myerscough, only to see the young centre-forward shoot wildly wide.

In the 62nd minute when the intrepid McParland had better fortune and came more into the game again with the first of his two goals. And what a magnificent effort it was.

Dixon schemed the opening but it still required exceptional judgment on the part of McParland to head through. His timing and placing were superb and Blanchflower was given no chance to save.

McParland Again

One could never see United winning after this, and in the 73rd minute McParland was on the spot once more to meet a rebound from Myerscough which had struck the crossbar and again the ball nestled in the back of the net.

Still United persevered and just before the end Duncan Edwards took a corner from which Taylor headed through his great goal.

In the fading moments of the game in a desperate effort to force a replay Wood came back and United pressed frantically.

Indeed the whole Villa team became defenders, but the day was saved.

For most of those who saw it the game will always be remembered for the Villa's successful defence of the 60-year-old record of being the last team to win the League and Cup in the same season.

From their point of view McParland, of course, was the man of the match. But one must not overlook the great work done by skipper Johnny Dixon at inside-left. He probably covered more ground than any other player.

Villa were also excellently served in defence in which I made wing-half back Crowther, right-back Lynn and left-back Aldis the outstanding players.

Their covering of one another was magnificent, though they were greatly aided by Whelan having to be pulled out of United's attack.

Disappointed as United must be at not achieving their goal—the Cup and League double—they can have no recriminations about their own form.

Considering their handicap they put up a remarkable show which left no doubt in anyone's mind of their all-round strength as a team.

Their heroes were Blanchflower, Edwards and left-back Roger Byrne.

ASTON VILLA.—Sims; Lynn, Aldis; Crowther, Dugdale, Saward; Smith, Sewell, Myerscough, Dixon, McParland. **MANCHESTER UNITED.**—Wood, Foulkes, Byrne; Colman, Blanchflower, Edwards; Berry, Whelan, Taylor, Charlton, Pegg.

'Goalkeeper' Blanch Is United's Hero

By FRANK SWIFT

THE most glamorous soccer challenge of our time ended at six minutes past three yesterday afternoon, when Manchester United goalkeeper, Ray Wood, was, tragically, carried off Wembley's lush turf by a St. John stretcher party.

The loss of Wood, who had a cheek bone broken in a collision with Aston Villa's Irish international left-winger, Peter McParland, was a crippling handicap which even the pride of England's soccer were unable to overcome.

So perished a magnificent bid for the first Cup and League Double of the century.

Centre-half Jackie Blanchflower was a magnificent deputy in the Manchester goal, Duncan Edwards a towering figure as emergency centre-half. But the depleted Manchester attack, denied the driving force of Edwards and the craft of Whelan —pulled back to left-half— showed few signs of its famous rhythm and balance.

The odds were stacked too high, and a rugged Villa side stepped in to snatch the Cup from as gallant a set of losers as ever Wembley has seen.

It was a cruel stroke that fate dealt United—and one which inevitably resurrects the old argument about show - game substitutes.

I am still wondering whether United would have lost had they taken a second half gamble with Wood—in goal! Wood's plucky performance as a right-winger passenger after resuming in the 33rd minute suggested that his early blackout had cleared, and that United had more to win than to lose by restoring him to the green jersey which had been adorned so magnificently by Blanchflower.

Skipper Roger Byrne, in a desperate bid to save the game, did just this after Tommy Taylor's header had made the score 2—1 —but by then it was too late. Villa, sensing their first Cup win in 37 years, packed their goal and beat off United's last thrill-

ing attempt to keep the Cup away from Birmingham.

Not that Wood would have had any chance with the goals that beat Blanchflower. The inspired Irishman was the main reason why Villa did not take the champions to the cleaners properly.

Jackie's performance was one of which I should have been proud, though it was no surprise to me that Blanchflower, one of Britain's finest centre-halves, had the ability to make the goalkeeping grade in top soccer.

In the goal-less first-half, when Villa did most of the attacking, I thought they made too little use of their extra man. They preferred to build up their attacks from the right and spoon feed McParland with long lobs to the far post.

But it certainly paid them dividends in the end. The bustling Irishman, who had been his side's match winner so often on the road to Wembley, struck the two lethal blows which ended the Manchester soccer dream. At the same time his goals preserved Villa's 60-year-old record as the last club to win the seemingly impossible double.

Even if United won the sympathy of neutrals, Villa deserve credit for their hard, tireless magnificent performance.

McParland, of course, was their hero of the hour, but most of Villa's big men were in defence.

Nigel Sims never put a hand wrong in Villa's goal, Stan Lynn took the sting out of David Pegg's left-wing sorties, and centre-half Jimmy Dugdale blotted out Tommy Taylor so completely that the England centre-forward's contribution was one missed chance, a scoring header and another that shaved past the post.

● Aston Villa's seven wins still represent the most of any team since the FA Cup competition began. Blackburn Rovers and Newcastle United have each recorded six wins, whilst the clubs on five are the first Cup winners The Wanderers, north London rivals Tottenham Hotspur (five times finalists and five times victorious), Arsenal, and West Bromwich Albion.

VILLA IN *7th* HEAVEN

Matt Busby leads out United at Wembley

Above left and below: McParland's clash with Wood, who (bottom) was carried off

● What the newspaper reports of the 1957 final cannot convey is that the desperately bad luck that Manchester United suffered in this match became insignificant when real tragedy struck them the following February. The team were returning from a European Cup game with Red Star in Belgrade when the plane crashed on take-off after a stop at Munich. Eight players, together with club staff and journalists, were killed.

The picture above, of the United side taking the pitch at Wembley, shows from the front: manager Matt Busby, who was badly injured in the crash, captain Roger Byrne, who was killed, John Berry, who received an eye injury, Jackie Blanchflower, badly injured, Ray Wood, seriously injured, Bill Foulkes, slightly injured, Bobby Charlton, head injuries, Tommy Taylor, killed, Eddie Colman, killed, Duncan Edwards, killed and David Pegg, killed. Behind Edwards is Bill Whelan who was also killed.

Date 4 May 1957
Place Wembley
Score ASTON VILLA 2
MANCHESTER UNITED 1
Teams ASTON VILLA Sims, Lynn, Aldis, Crowther, Dugdale, Saward, Smith, Sewell, Myerscough, Dixon (capt.), McParland.
MANCHESTER UNITED Wood, Foulkes, Byrne (capt.), Colman, Blanchflower, Edwards, Berry, Whelan, Taylor, Charlton, Pegg
Team Colours ASTON VILLA Light blue and claret striped shirts, white shorts; MANCHESTER UNITED All white
Official Referee F. Coultas (East Riding)
Goal Scorers ASTON VILLA McParland 65, 71; MANCHESTER UNITED Taylor 83
Managers ASTON VILLA Eric Houghton; MANCHESTER UNITED Matt Busby
Attendance 100 000
Gate Receipts £48 816
Guests of Honour H.M. Queen Elizabeth, H.R.H. Duke of Edinburgh
Copy *The Sunday Pictorial* 5 May 1957; *News of the World* 5 May 1957

PAGE 22   DAILY MIRROR Monday May 5, 1953

Mirror Sport

CUP FINAL SPECIAL

They call it the match that Manchester lost...

WHAT AN INSULT TO BOLTON!

By BILL HOLDEN

Bolton Wanderers 2, Manchester United 0

NEVER in history has any Cup-winning team been so unpopular as Bolton. Never has a team played so well for so little acclaim.

No bands play, no bells ring—except in Bolton, home of the £110 team that ruined the dewy-eyed dream of Manchester United ending their gallant fight back from tragedy by walking off with the Cup.

If United had won at Wembley, it would not have mattered how they did it. They would have been hailed as twice the heroes they already are even for getting there.

Because Bolton won—and won handsomely, outplaying United for most of the game—this sunlit final is being called drab dreary, dismal.

It is an insult to Bolton. A shocking disregard of the magnificent way each Bolton player performed.

Yes, the terraces were quiet. It was because the Wanderers just didn't allow the intensely pro-United crowd to be given anything to shout about

Handsome

And no one knows that better than United. They were more handsome than the fans in their tributes to the men who WON.

United's boss Matt Busby limped from his centre-stand seat to the Bolton dressing-room before he went in to console his own beaten Babes.

And he said to Bill Ridding, Bolton manager: "Congratulations. I want you to know I think the better team won. There's no doubt about it."

Then he asked: "Where's Nat?"

He wanted to congratulate Nat Lofthouse, lion of forward-line leaders, whose two goals had shattered United and earned the England international the Cup

Lofthouse's first

Never has a team played so well for so little acclaim

winner's medal he so richly deserves

"Well done, Nat," said Matt. "A great game"

And that came from the man to whom the Munich disaster was most real—the man who most wanted to see United win, yet thought first about congratulating the players who had proved themselves the masters

His assistant, Jimmy Murphy, who worked the miracle of rebuilding a team capable of getting to the final, said:

"Bolton may have had luck, but they were the better team, and deserved the Cup."

Set Pace

And Ernie Taylor, the little general of United's attack, told me:

"Bolton's covering was good and they made us play at their pace. They dictated the way things went. Jolly good luck to them."

Tommy Banks, Bolton left back, who never made a mistake in the entire ninety minutes couldn't contain his joy

Two of his missions were accomplished He had won his medal and avenged his

brother—and I believe his display will put him in the England party for the World Cup in Sweden.

Towelling his barrel-chest, he roared at me: "Never in doubt, were it? I thought we played well."

In came brother Ralph, the left back who got the run-around from Stan Matthews in Bolton's 1953 Cup Final defeat. Tommy's first question was: "Did Mom see the game?"

"Yes, she's right proud," said Ralph. "You stopped them playing and played well yourselves."

No one could have bettered the pin-point pass that left half Bryan Edwards swung across for Lofthouse to hammer the first, all-important goal in the third minute.

Tommy Banks had begun the move. Stan Crowther, United left half, conceded a corner. That wasn't cleared, and Edwards got possession.

"I saw a white shirt by the far post and sent a cross over to whoever it was," he said.

"I didn't even know it was Nat Lofthouse until he had hit the ball and I realised we had scored."

Harry Gregg, United's

goalkeeper, was guilty of mishandling and allowing that move to build up.

It was a fatal mistake. Yet he made two brilliant amends, saving from Lofthouse and outside right Brian Birch before United came into the game.

Screamer

Then Bolton goalkeeper Eddie Hopkinson, who had smeared his hands with resin to help clutch the ball more firmly, made two superlative saves.

He turned a Taylor header over the bar, and a screaming shot from centre forward Bobby Charlton round a post.

Showing his roughened, reddened hands afterwards, he said:

"The resin does this to them, but it's worth it. Helps you get your hands stuck round the ball."

In the other dressing room, Gregg was still lying on the treatment table, face down in agony.

He was hurt ten minutes after the interval, when Lofthouse clinched the game with a second goal.

Only two minutes before, Charlton had lifted the heart and hopes of millions

with a shot that all but equalised. That shot was the only one in the game that beat Hopkinson.

It whistled past him, crashed against an upright—and amazingly rocketed into his arms as he turned.

Eddie happily sent the ball upfield, and Bolton's attack built up again for Lofthouse to challenge Gregg in the air and score.

This incident was the only shadow on a great day for Lofthouse, captain and star of Bolton.

Won Bet

He won not only a medal, but a £1 bet with manager Ridding. Bill told me:

"When I saw him in hospital after he had hurt his shoulder in March I bet him he would never be fit for Wembley. He swore he would."

Nat grinned as he took the £1 and said: "I was worth it, wasn't I?"

You were, Nat, and worth the medal, the bonus, and the glory.

Worth it all—even though this match seems doomed to go down in history not as Bolton's success, but as "The Match that Manchester Lost."

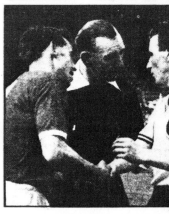

WHY THE R[EF] SAID 'SHAK[E]

● *Referee Jack Sherlock makes Colin W[ebster] (left) and Denis Stevens shake h[ands]*

● The happiest Wanderer of them all ... two-goal Nat Lofthouse is chaired off [with] the F.A. Cup after Bolton's great Wembley win.

EVEN the inquiring eyes of the TV newsreel and Press cameras missed the incident which became one of Wembley's big talking points, writes Bill Holden.

Eight minutes before the final whistle, United's Colin Webster was moving with the ball up the left wing. Bolton right back Ron Hartle tackled him and cleared out of play.

As the ball was retrieved from over the touchline, Bolton inside right Denis Stevens fell, and lay motionless on the turf

Players from all parts of the pitch, including both goalkeepers, massed and milled around.

Referee Jack Sherlock, of

Sheffield, called [Hartle] and Webster tog[ether] asked them to [shake] hands.

They did, and th[ey] went on.

Stevens told me:

"Hartle cleared something to m[e] something to Webster came were standing and I are stan[ding] And the next [I] found myself ground."

Webster denies [he was at] fault.

Referee Sherlock

"I didn't see w[hat hap]pened, so I c[ouldn't punish] two players tog[ether and] told them to sh[ake hands] and forget abou[t it]."

UNITED LOS[T]

FAIR ENOUGH
—says gallant Gregg about that controversial charge

PETER WILSON says—Alas!

BABES IN THE WOOD

The moment of impact—Nat Lofthouse charges into goalkeeper Harry Gregg

ALAS, fairy-stories belong only in the children's books. Although the grey stone and the famous twin towers of Wembley could have been the scene of one of *see* " once upon a time " tales, the Cup Final never looked as though it would end with **"** and the Babes lived happily ever after."

stead they were " Babes in the Wood " with a vengeance from the moment that an unbelievably uncertain Harry Gregg came out wrongly after a couple of minutes.

The Manchester goalkeeper got caught with the ball on the half-volley and United conceded a corner.

Nat Lofthouse—the Dragon of the tale, breathing fire and slaughter—made no mistake with Bryan Edwards's pass.

6 The better team won 9

And, as it turned out, the match was virtually over with less than three of the ninety minutes expired.

What a blinder Lofthouse played from whistle to whistle! There was never a time that he got the ball when Manchester were really comfortable.

And, thirty-two or not, how I should like to see him included in the England World Cup team.

Despite the pin in the shoulder he injured two months ago, Lofthouse looked fit enough for another ninety minutes, when he led Bolton up for the greatest reward any professional footballer can receive—THE CUP.

I thought Manchester were in it only twice—and then only for the briefest spells.

SMASHING SHOT

The first time was exactly half-way through the first half. A move between Bobby Charlton, Dennis Viollet and Ernie Taylor swept the ball along with shuttle-smoothness, and then half-a-minute later Charlton smashed in one of the few memorable shots of the whole game.

But it was not good enough to score—for goalkeeper Eddie Hopkinson made an amazing save.

The second time was seven minutes after the restart. Another Charlton shot—which with a two-inch variation would have gone down as one of the great Wembley goals—rebounded from the upright into the supremely competent Hopkinson's arms.

THAT WAS MANCHESTER'S LAST CHANCE.

There was no particularly jewelled or sculpted artistry about Bolton. Nor is there about a fireproof, burglar-defying safe. And that's what the Bolton defence was.

Lofthouse's disputed second goal did not really change anything—except to remove all hope from " The Babes."

About that goal . . . I should just like to say that from my seat it appeared perfectly fair.

But how glad I was to see Gregg finally get to his feet.

Under our rules Nat had done nothing wrong—but I still wish we would adopt a rule more in line with Continental practice concerning goalkeepers.

Frankly, sad though it is to write it, this was one of the dullest of the twenty-odd Finals I have watched.

CARPET ON FIRE

They say that £50 was paid for 50s. tickets before the match. At half-time I doubt whether anyone would have paid **fifty pence** for them.

Indeed, the only touch of excitement in the last half-hour came when the red carpet leading out to the pitch caught fire and an attendant had to fetch a bucket of water to put it out.

Today, sympathy must go out to United. But let there be no mistake about it—THE BETTER TEAM WON.

UNHAPPY FOOTNOTE: For the past seven years Joe Mears, chairman of the F.A. Selection Committee and chairman of Chelsea, has been invited to both the banquets held by the finalists.

On Saturday he had accepted United's invitation—the seventh year he has picked the losers' " do " !

Presumably if Chelsea ever got to the Final he would plump for the opposition's banquet.

WELL, AFTER ALL, INSURANCE NEVER HURTS.

Bolton lways in control

FRANK McGHEE

IPPED Manchester nited to win by a ker. And that shot by y Charlton, their only effective forward, n hit the inside of a could have put them in the picture.

, frankly, they didn't ve it. And the Man-er players admit it. ton never slackened eins of control. Left Bryan Edwards ed Ernie Taylor out of ame to cut the supply to the forwards.

Easy

l backs Roy Hartle Tommy Banks con-d both wings without .ding a teaspoonful of on a hot day. side right Brian Birch lways top man in his with left back Ian ves.

d with United right Freddie Goodwin hav-s worst game since ch, centre half Ronnie had to carry a burden for two.

ere was, of course, one reason for Bolton's A guy called Loft-

---

IN NAT'S PLACE I'D HAVE DONE SAME

FAIR enough ! — that's goalkeeper Harry Gregg's comment on Nat Lofthouse's goal which put Bolton two up and, inci-dentally, K.O.'d Harry.

"It's the first time in my life I've been hurt," Gregg said. "I don't mind.

"If I'd been in Nat's place I would have done the same."

Lofthouse gave this version of the incident.

"I went up for the ball with me nut and headed it. It was over the line before my shoulder, follow-ing through, hit Harry.

"I don't know where I hit him. All I knew was that the ball was in the back of the net."

After the game, Man-chester United trainer Jack Crompton began to massage the lower ribs at the right side of Gregg's back, where he felt pain.

As Crompton did so, Gregg was violently sick. A doctor gave him two pain-killing injections, and he recovered enough to attend the United banquet after-wards.

Town turns out for United

MANCHESTER United's homecoming last night was fit for a king—even though they hadn't got the Cup.

Thousands of wildly cheering fans lined the team's route from London-road Station to Manchester Town Hall. Red-and-white bedecked rattles crackled a welcome as United's coach went by.

Several times the coach was brought to a standstill by the swarm of people.

"We want Matt," was the chant from a huge crowd outside the Town Hall.

But Matt Busby didn't feel up to a speech in such an emotional, electrifying atmosphere.

He sat quietly on a chair

while the Lord Mayor of Manchester, Alderman Leslie Leven, led the sing-ing of "For they are jolly good fellows."

CHARLES LEADS 'EM TO THE TOP

JUVENTUS, the club that paid £75,000 for Welsh international star John Charles, won the Italian First Division championship yesterday when they held Fiorentina to a goalless draw.

Charles, who leads the Juventus attack, is top goalscorer in Italian Soccer this season.

---

the Munich tragedy. Four survivors, supplemented by new Busby Babes and the hastily acquired talents of Ernie Taylor from Blackpool and Stan Crowther from Aston Villa, had swept to Wembley on a crescendo of emotion. Bolton Wanderers, how-ever, gave a disciplined performance to deny United the ultimate come-back – a deserved victory marred only by the nature of Lofthouse's second goal in which he charged goalkeeper Gregg into the net.

● Manchester United's appearance in the 1958 final captured public sym-pathy like no other. Three months earlier the club had been decimated by

---

Date	3 May 1958
Place	Wembley
Score	BOLTON WANDERERS 2 MANCHESTER UNITED 0
Teams	BOLTON WANDERERS Hopkinson, Hartle, Banks, Hennin, Higgins, Edwards, Birch, Stevens, Lofthouse, Parry, Holden. MANCHESTER UNITED Gregg, Foulkes, Greaves, Goodwin, Cope, Crowther, Dawson, Taylor, Charlton, Viollet, Webster
Team Colours	BOLTON WANDERERS White shirts, dark blue shorts; MANCHESTER UNITED Red shirts, white shorts
Official	Referee J. U. Sherlock (Sheffield)
Goal Scorer	Lofthouse 3, 55
Managers	BOLTON WANDERERS Bill Ridding; MANCHESTER UNITED Matt Busby
Attendance	100000
Gate Receipts	£49706
Copy	*The Daily Mirror* 5 May 1958

AIN

11 Daily Sketch, Monday, May 4, 1959

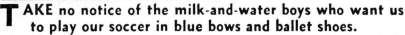

Substitutes! YES, IT'S THAT OLD WEMBLEY WAIL AGAIN...

I won't have them, says LAURIE PIGNON

DON'T MAKE OUR SOCCER CISSY!

TAKE no notice of the milk-and-water boys who want us to play our soccer in blue bows and ballet shoes.

All over the country you can hear them whining their annual Cup final anthem: *"WE WANT SUBSTITUTES."*

They are soccer's fifth column, and they are doing the rounds trying to kid you that you don't get your money's worth at Wembley, that it isn't right for a team like Nottingham Forest to play a man short for an hour.

They will tell you that Roy Dwight, with a broken right leg, is the sixth man at Wembley in the last seven years to be badly hurt. Some of them will even remember the other casualties—Wood (Manchester Utd.), Trautmann (Manchester City), Meadows (Manchester City), Bell (Bolton) and Barnes (Arsenal).

AND IN DOING SO THEY WILL ROB NOTTINGHAM FOREST OF THEIR FINEST HOUR.

If ever there was a soccer Dunkirk we saw it on Saturday, with ten men running themselves into treacherous turf while covering up for one of their star players, who was sweating it out in hospital.

THIS WAS ONE OF SPORTS MOST GLORIOUS MOMENTS, AND I FEEL HONOURED TO HAVE BEEN THERE WHEN THESE TEN MEN, WITH NOTHING LEFT BUT THEIR HEARTS, CONTINUED TO PLAY FOOTBALL TO THE FINAL WHISTLE.

THAT'S THE GAME...

Many teams haven't been able to do a Nottingham and hold on when they were a man short, and victory may have gone to the wrong side.

But that's soccer as we know it . . . as we invented it—and as I hope we continue to play it.

● In almost every country where substitutes are allowed there is abuse. I have known this for a long time. Even so, I was shaken yesterday when England team manager Walter Winterbottom told me:

"In my experience when players have been substituted it is not always for injury. In nine out of ten cases it is a tactical measure."

No Wigan double now

IT'S the red rose versus the white for the Rugby League climax, writes EDEN REYNOLDS.

Lancashire representatives are St. Helens for the League and Wigan for Wembley.

Yorkshire's teams are Hunslet for the League and Hull for the Cup.

By defeating Oldham 42-4, after Oldham had beaten them only five days previously. St. Helens, the League leaders, gain their reward for consistent good work over the season.

Wigan's hopes of a Wembley and League double faded in their 11-22 defeat at the hands of Hunslet.

St. Helens and Hunslet will meet a week later after the Wembley final, at the Wembley of the North, Bradford Northern's ground.

I want to see fight, not fakes

That's a very high percentage—but there is no man in this country who knows overseas football better than Walter Winterbottom.

● Then there is the old and unanswerable problem : When is a man injured enough not to carry on, and who will make the decision?

In Saturday's final there were eight minutes extra injury time for seven players who got knocks. And if Forest were to be allowed a substitute for Dwight, why not Luton a replacement for McNally, who had to leave the field for a minute and was never properly fit again?

TWO CLASSIC GOALS

It doesn't only happen in soccer. In all the Olympic sports, at Wimbledon, at cricket, injury can decide the result.

That's sport as I know it. THAT'S SPORT AS I WANT TO KEEP IT.

I give the last word to Dwight, who was still in Wembley hospital yesterday while the rest of the boys—and their wives—were at Brighton. "I would say that goalkeepers should be substituted—but I'm not sure it would be a good thing for other players."

If he had stayed on Wembley's sunny field I am sure Forest would have won the final with at least half a dozen goals to spare. Never have I seen a side settle in so quickly or so confidently.

Billy Walker has built the game's prettiest picture out of a jig-saw of misfits. The Dwight and Wilson goals were Wembley classics . . . and the ten men's courage is something I don't want to forget.

THERE IS NO SUBSTITUTE FOR COURAGE.

Roy Dwight (arms raised) puts Forest ahead

Date 2 May 1959
Place Wembley
Score NOTTINGHAM FOREST 2
LUTON TOWN 1
Teams NOTTINGHAM FOREST Thomson, Whare, McDonald, Whitefoot, McKinlay, Burkitt, Dwight, Quigley, Wilson, Gray, Imlach.
LUTON TOWN Baynham, McNally, Hawkes, Groves, Owen, Pacey, Bingham, Brown, Morton, Cummins, Gregory
Team Colours NOTTINGHAM FOREST Red shirts, white shorts; LUTON TOWN White shirts, black shorts
Official Referee J. H. Clough (Bolton)
Goal Scorers NOTTINGHAM FOREST Dwight 10, Wilson 14; LUTON TOWN Pacey 62
Managers NOTTINGHAM FOREST Billy Walker; LUTON TOWN No manager at the time – Thomas Hodgson, the club

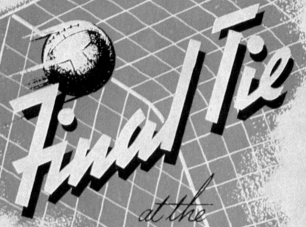

OFFICIAL PROGRAMME · *SIXPENCE* ·

THE FOOTBALL ASSOCIATION CHALLENGE CUP COMPETITION

Final Tie

at the

EMPIRE STADIUM
WEMBLEY
Managing Director A. J. ELVIN

CHARLTON ATHLETIC
v
DERBY COUNTY

SATURDAY APRIL 27TH 1946

Cup final programme 1946

Cup final programmes for (from left), 1969, 1978, 1972, 1980, 1973 and 1971. Inset are Stuart Pearson and Gordon Hill with the Cup, 1977

FOOTBALL ASSOCIATION CHALLENGE CUP COMPETITION
CENTENARY YEAR
1872 FINAL 1972
SATURDAY 6th MAY 1972 .... KICK-OFF 3 p.m.

ARSENAL v LEEDS UNITED

EMPIRE WEMBLEY STADIUM
Official Souvenir Programme 15p

FOOTBALL ASSOCIATION CHALLENGE CU
CUP FI
50th

ARSENAL v IPSWICH TOWN
Saturday 6th May 1978 Kick off 3pm
Wembley
Stadium
Official Souvenir Programme 50p

FOOTBALL ASSOCIA
CUP COMP
FINA
Leices
Manch
SATURDAY 26th

EMPIRE STADIUM WEMBLEY Official Programme 2/-

FOOTBALL ASSOCIATION CHALLENGE CUP COMPETITION

FINAL

ARSENAL · WEST HAM UNITED

Saturday
10th May 1980
Kick off 3pm

**Wembley
Stadium**

OFFICIAL
SOUVENIR PROGRAMME
80p

...IATION CHALLENGE CUP COMPETITION

...INAL

LEEDS UNITED
v
SUNDERLAND
WEMBLEY STADIUM
JUBILEE 1923-1973
SATURDAY, 5th MAY, 1973...Kick-off 3pm
Official Programme . . . 15 pence

...ck-off 3 p.m.
Official Programme . . . 10p

...VERPOOL
...n CHALLENGE
...ION

...L
...Y 1971

FA CUP FINAL REPLAY
OLD TRAFFORD · MANCHESTER

2'-

Chelsea

Leeds
UNITED

April 7

THE FOOTBALL ASSOCIATION CHALLENGE CUP COMPETITION

FINAL TIE
ARSENAL v NEWCASTLE UNITED
SATURDAY, MAY 3rd, 1952 KICK OFF 3pm

THE FOOTBALL ASSOCIATION CHALLENGE CUP COMPETITION

FINAL TIE
SATURDAY, APRIL 24th
1948
KICK-OFF 3 pm
ONE SHILLING

BLAC... ... MANCHESTER UNITED

THE FOOTBALL ASSOCIATION CHALLENGE CUP COMPETITION

Official
Programme
One Shilling

FINAL
SATURDAY MAY 20th 1967
Kick-off 3 pm

CHELSEA
v
TOTTE...
HO...

EMPIRE
STADIUM

THE FOOTBALL ASSOCIATION CHALLENGE CUP COMPETITION

FINAL

EVERTON
v
SHEFFIELD
WEDNESDAY

SATURDAY, MAY 14th 1966

Kick-Off 3p.m.

WEMBLEY
EMPIRE STADIUM
Official Programme
One Shilling

Cup final programmes for (from top), 1970 (replay), 1952,
1948, 1967 and 1966

And now the moment that could have turned the Final against Manchester United—reported by KEN JONES

CUP TRIUMPH SO NEAR TRAGEDY

Manchester Utd 3, Leicester City 1

The agony of skipper Cantwell

IN the delirium of the Wembley dressing room, United skipper Noel Cantwell revealed to me the moment that so nearly brought him tragedy instead of F A Cup triumph.

The moment when United, on their way back to the big-time again, could so easily have crumbled into the ragged rabble they have been all season

The moment when left back Cantwell, in a rare flash of panic, dived to head a ball so desperately close to his own far post that he thought he had given away a goal.

It happened in the fourteenth minute. In his quiet but commanding Irish brogue, he told me:

" Mike Stringfellow had come in on the near post and I could see that his shot had beaten our keeper Dave Gaskell.

Touch

" There was a Leicester player closing in quickly and as the ball flashed through I flung myself at it.

" I only got a touch. If I had missed it altogether, it would have gone right through. No danger.

"All I did was to turn it nearer our own goal. If I had turned it a little more, it must have gone in. For one awful moment I thought it had.

" It was the one moment when we were in real trouble. The one time when things looked bad for us."

Noel Cantwell's moment of agony. . . . As he went sprawling, he feared he had headed the ball into his own net.

" If Leicester had snatched a goal then it could have gone the other way.

" But the little men must have been smiling After that so were we. It was never in doubt from then on."

Tense

For me it was the moment on which the game turned. The one time when Leicester's much-vaunted strike out of a deep defensive position looked like paying off. A slice of Irish luck for United and their skipper.

Before the match I had suspicions that Leicester's tactics would get tangled up in the tenseness of a big Wembley game.

That they would tire on the turf And that it would be individuals who would turn the match

Those suspicions were confirmed as Leicester struggled to raise their game to meet the demands United made on them.

Above all, Leicester lacked character in vital positions.

A team plan that tends to subdue the individual for the team's sake blew up in their faces.

Blazing

And it was United and the blazing skill of Denis Law and Pat Crerand who dominated the game. Law

was Law at his best . . . virtually unmarkable.

Crerand revelled in the room and time he was given to make his telling passes.

And Leicester's defence a line without a leak in so many games this season, sprung a dozen and more as United's quick passing on the edge of the area made a mockery of their retreating tactics.

Dummy

Law selling a dummy and shooting as he turned, belted a pass from Crerand past Banks in the thirty-first minute.

After a spell of Leicester pressure at the start of the second half, United struck again.

Johnny Giles, on the right wing, found Bobby Charlton free on the other flank as right back John Sjoberg funnelled frantically into the defensive formation.

Charlton crashed in the ball. As Banks half saved, centre forward David Herd helped it home.

After a twice-taken, half scrambled free-kick, United's lead was cut when Ken Keyworth dived to deflect a header past David Gaskell.

Suddenly there was hope in the Leicester camp. But it lasted only long enough for Law to hit a post with a header, and for Herd to clinch the game after Banks had dropped a Giles cross at his feet.

Noel Cantwell with the cup

Gordon Banks lies helpless as David Herd (centre) scored United's second

Date 25 May 1963
Place Wembley
Score MANCHESTER UNITED 3 LEICESTER CITY 1
Teams MANCHESTER UNITED Gaskell, Dunne, Cantwell (capt.), Crerand, Foulkes, Setters, Giles, Quixall, Herd, Law, Charlton. LEICESTER CITY Banks, Sjoberg, Norman, McLintock, King, Appleton (capt.), Riley, Cross, Keyworth, Gibson, Stringfellow
Team Colours MANCHESTER UNITED Red shirts, white shorts; LEICESTER CITY All white
Official Referee K. G. Aston (Essex)
Goal Scorers MANCHESTER UNITED Law 29, Herd 57, 85; LEICESTER CITY Keyworth 80
Managers MANCHESTER UNITED Matt Busby; LEICESTER CITY Matt Gillies
Attendance 100000
Gate Receipts £88882
Guests of Honour H.M. The Queen, H.R.H. Prince Philip
Copy *The Daily Mirror* 27 May 1963

HERE IT IS—THE CUP WINNER

• Goal! The joy of West Ham and the despair of Preston are mirrored in this dramatic scene as inside right Ron Boyce's winner nestles in the net. Boyce runs behind the goal while Johnny Byrne and John Sissons (11) acclaim a great victory

West Ham grab it in injury time

by ALAN HOBY

WEST HAM 3 (Sissons, Hurst, Boyce) PRESTON 2 (Holden, Dawson)

H.T. 1—2 Attendance 100,000 Receipts £89,000

IT is the second minute of injury time in the most dramatic Cup Final I have seen since Stanley Matthews won the match for Blackpool against Bolton in 1953. West Ham, twice behind, their nerves jumping like crickets in that electrifying first half when classic Preston had them rocking and reeling, are sweeping into the counter-attack.

The ball swings to their thrusting inside left, Geo.f Hurst, as the 100,000 spectators gaze down in fascination on the green pile carpet of the Wembley pitch.

Hurst stumbles, recovers, thrusts aside a lunging tackle, and dribbles on.

Back fall the tired Preston defenders like so many scurrying black and white ants.

On runs the lonely claret and light blue figure as he slants to the right in a beautifully controlled bid for victory.

Hovering on the right wing is Hammers' Peter Brabrook. The crowd crane forward as Hurst slips the ball to Brabrook who moves inside.

And this is it. The few crucial moments of nerve and skill when the destiny of this blood-stirring and glorious Cup Final will be decided, are upon us.

• Goal! Left winger John Sissons (dark shirt) whips West Ham's first past Alan Kelly

LINE-UP

PRESTON NORTH END

Kelly

Ross   Smith

Lawton   Singleton   Kendall

Ashworth   Spavin

Wilson   Dawson   Holden

Sissons   Byrne   Brabrook

Hurst   Boyce

Moore   Brown   Bovington

Burkett   Bond

Standen

WEST HAM UNITED

Referee: A. Holland (Barnsley)

In the first half West Ham, usually so inventive and unorthodox with their unexpected angles and subtle variations, found the burden of being such uncompromising favourites almost too hard to bear

From the opening whistle Preston, sparked by Lawton and his splendidly tireless colleague inside left Alan Spavin, were faster on the ball.

In the first minute Spavin set the mood when he beautifully beat Boyce to cross the ball which Moore cleared with difficulty

Then the 17-year-old Kendall, defying the label of "youngest-ever Cup Final player," hit another long one—not a trace of nerves in this boy—and again the blond Moore headed edgily away.

It was Preston practically all the way, with their wingers, Dave Wilson and Doug Holden, bringing the West Ham supporters to the verge of a heart attack every time they attacked.

A tide of white shirts was beating against the West Ham defensive system like water rising against a dam.

Unmarked

Brabrook fights a floating, cunning cross from right to left. The ball soars over the entire Preston defence — and there, galloping in unmarked, with the goal roar rising up from the stands and terraces, is the Hammers' hard-working inside-right Ron Boyce.

Hurling himself at the ball, Boyce heads into the Preston net and all Wembley is ablaze with claret and light blue scarves and favours.

West Ham have won for the first time in the club's history in only their second F.A. Cup appearance at Wembley and for the second time in 10 years Preston have been beaten in the dying minutes by the same score—West Bromwich Albion did it in 1954.

But what a desperately narrow escape the London favourites had as Preston, the underdogs from the Second Division, shocked the Londoners and surprised the whole world of football with the quality and splendour of their play.

After Boyce snatched the winning goal in what looked like one of the clearest cases of football burglary in Cup Final history, Preston staged one last frantic sortie on the West Ham goal.

Alec Ashworth, a rugged and dynamic inside-right, who, for most of the match, had with his centre forward Alec Dawson given the West Ham defence a hellish time, was brought down a yard outside the West Ham penalty box.

From the free kick Dawson, a muscular and menacing figure,

fired wide. The ball spun away. The last few seconds of this wonderful game flashed by and then referee Arthur Holland blew "time."

And there, jumping high into the air, was centre-forward Johnny Byrne.

Behind him an even more moving scene was being enacted. Hugging one another were the two youngest players in the match, 17 - year - old Howard Kendall, the Sunday school organist who came into the Preston team at the last moment at left half, and John Sissons, the West Ham left winger.

An unhappy man, however, was Preston's heroic captain Nobby Lawton, whose first half play as an attacking right half and extra forward in North End's 4-2-4 system had fired his team to unprecedented heights.

As West Ham skipper and Footballer of the Year Bobby Moore led his team up the steps to the royal enclosure, where he was presented with the Cup by the Earl of Harewood, Lawton stood with tears in his eyes.

Great game

I understood only too well how he felt. He had played the game of his life.

He had sprayed cultured passes to his forwards. He had roamed over the green turf in an exquisite display of ball skill. He had run, prompted and nudged his side towards greatness.

He had seen Preston take the lead with magnificent goals by that other outstanding half artist, left-winger Doug Holden, and the dynamic Alec Dawson.

But in the end his dreams had collapsed when young Boyce burgled the winner.

Terrific

Then, in the ninth minute, Preston went ahead. Kendall started the movement and Dawson brought his foot down on the ball with the full meat of his instep.

West Ham goalkeeper Jim Standen could only parry this terrific shot. The ball hovered about the line but the wily Holden, who has played in two previous Cup Finals, had moved into the goalmouth and coolly prodded it home. This was a sensation.

The Cockney favourites were jittery. Their rhythm was missing. Yet despite their uncertainty the Hammers equalised in the very next minute.

It was Ashworth's error of judgment—he dallied too long with the ball—which allowed Moore to take it away from him and dribble forward towards the left.

Side-stepping a Preston tackle, Moore loped on before pushing the perfect pass to 18-year-old left winger Sissons.

Sissons flicked the ball inside to the thoroughbred Byrne and cut inside for the return pass.

There was a gasp, a mass suspension of breath, and then the ball was through from Byrne to Sissons, who raced past two defenders before hitting the ball into the near hand side of the net with his left foot. 1—1.

West Ham were level—and their supporters were breathing easily again. Indeed, the cockney rallying song "We're For Ever Blowing Bubbles" could be heard on the terraces—but not for long.

Although Byrne volleyed a good chance high and wide from Brabrook's header after Preston's efficient stopper centre half, Tony Singleton, had headed away another Sissons centre—it

was Preston who were making this Final one of the most enjoyable shows this famous old stadium has staged.

Cool Moore

They were playing wonderful stuff—the old Scottish style of football—with the 20-yard ground pass moving sweetly from man to man.

Lawton—and I simply cannot keep him out of this report—thrust the ball through to Dawson as Moore, who was once or twice drawn out of position, challenged.

Moore, indeed, was being given no time to settle.

But he kept his head—as did every Hammer.

The ball went to Ashworth. It looked a certain goal but West Ham's No. 1 defender, centre half Ken Brown, who had a superb tactical match, came over and charged down Ashworth's shot to the vast relief of Standen.

Then, from a Lawton free-kick, the stylish Kendall belted the ball so hard that it could easily have been a goal if it had not unluckily hit the burly Dawson.

This was in the 40th minute when once again drama seized the spectators and held them enthralled.

From the flag kick taken by Wilson, Dawson rose above everyone to head the match straight into the West Ham net. That Dawson header was really travelling but he might not have scored if the West Ham goalkeeper Jim Standen had not slipped as he was coming out and if centre-half Brown had not also stumbled going to cover.

Preston were not only leading, they looked as if they were heading for a most deserved and astonishing victory over the

Dynamite

True, the West Ham attacks were breaking down because their final pass was often inaccurate and also because Boyce, their midfield workhorse, simply could not get into the game.

The duel between Brown and Dawson was pure dynamite and

both will have a few bruises to show this morning.

Despite Preston's fluent midfield superiority and the calm way their defence was containing the West Ham attack it was the Londoners who should have taken the lead in the 34th minute

Byrne, who was picking up the midfield balls and doing a lot of unspectacular work, slung a lovely diagonal pass which clipped the Preston defence.

The ball found Hurst dead centre in front of goal. The West Ham inside left crashed it to the right but Preston's goalkeeper Alan Kelly brought off an equally brilliant save, hurting his left hand in the process.

The ball went for a corner which Brabrook wasted.

This effort apart, West Ham were too stereotyped and too predictable. They were prisoners of their own pattern whereas Preston were improvising freely and joyously in a fine display of Soccer show business.

Holden deceived the entire West Ham defence when he pulled back an unorthodox centre to Kendall whose shot was luckily deflected for a corner by Moore.

Yes, Preston were making the match-transforming it into a tremendous contest and we were being given a feast of thrills and plenty of physical contact and hard knocks.

Key man

But in the second-half West Ham changed their tactics. Manager Ron Greenwood, one of the shrewdest tacticians in football, had spotted the trouble.

He ordered Boyce to mark the penetrative Lawton, Preston's key player.

That other Preston keyman, the industrious Spavin, was padlocked by right-half Eddie Bovington closing for the tackle whenever the Preston inside-left received the ball.

And with a far more composed Moore watching Ashworth, West Ham began to command—even if they never dominated—and in the seventh minute a howl of joy rose from the Cockney thousands as Brown, who had moved up, beat Dawson in the air from a Brabrook header.

Goalkeeper Kelly got his hand to Brown's header but could only parry it out to Hurst who nodded it back into goal.

Somehow Kelly, stretching in a desperate dive, got his hands to the Hurst header as it ricocheted off the underside of the bar. But the Preston goalkeeper could only help the ball across the line and West Ham were level again. 2—2.

The match was in the balance but much of the Preston fire and finesse had gone.

West Ham, while never playing their characteristic game with success—the sudden break-out from the citadel of their own goal—nevertheless had recovered from their former fumblings.

Fighters

Even so brave Preston never capitulated.

They fought to the end and almost

• Goal! A Geoff Hurst header is on its way for Hammers' second

Dramatic Wembley moments

Preston 'keeper Alan Kelly lets the ball slip through his arms and Geoff Hurst has scored for West Ham.

Preston's proud young star, Howard Kendall, looks at his medal . . . if only it was a winner's.

until their tongues were hanging out.

It looked like stalemate—although Johnny Byrne could have remedied this when he hesitated with a perfect chance after right-back John Bond had placed a long ball right to the centre-forward's foot.

Indeed, West Ham had fallen back on speculative long balls from Moore, Bond, and the rest. Holden was still a wriggling, dribbling menace. Only a late Bond tackle stopped him going through in the closing minutes of the match.

But the excitement, the spectacle —if not always the football—was still being presented by these two tired teams.

Hurst missed a good chance as Byrne centred low from the left from Bovington's pass. The bubbling Sissons shot across goal, missing the right post by a whisker again from a Byrne centre.

Preston's Wilson corkscrewed through on the left but from his final pass Ashworth failed to clobber the ball and Standen saved easily.

And so it went. But in the end West Ham snatched the game from the embers.

Lucky

They were a little lucky even though the second half went to them on points. I particularly remember a stupendous Kelly save from Hurst who played with courage and conviction. The goalkeeper was hurt but continued after treatment.

Boyce also volleyed what looked like a winner but it hit young Kendall. And so this robust entertainment ended on the highest of notes when Ron Boyce, who also scored twice in the semi-final, came out of nowhere to head the winner.

FOOTNOTE : As the Preston players were getting into their coach inside-left Alan Spavin left them and walked out on to the track round the pitch. "I am just having a last look—I hope we'll be back next year," he said whimsically.

HOWARD KENDALL, 17-year-old hero of Preston's Cup Final team, got a pop star's welcome home yesterday.

He stood in the centre of the team party on the steps of the Harris Library while shrieking girls among the thousands packing the market square chanted: " We want Kendall."

Altogether about 80,000 people turned out at Preston to cheer the team beaten 3-2 by West Ham at Wembley on Saturday.

As the team coach crawled through the packed streets from the station to the market square the crowds sang: " We love you, yeah, yeah."

● We've won! Bobby Moore's Hammers parade the Cup

QUOTES :

What they said to JAMES CONNOLLY

● BOBBY MOORE: They dominated the first half, but we felt that we were on top in the second. Although that vital goal seemed a long time coming I always believed we would get it.

● RON GREENWOOD (manager) : To fight back twice means you are always in with a chance and I thought we were. We changed our tactics in the second half, with Bobby Moore watching Ashworth and Ken Brown taking Alex Dawson—they had had too much room to work in. Afterwards we cut out the flow from Spavin and Lawton.

● RON BOYCE: Johnny Byrne was in front of me when I moved in, but I knew that Peter Brabrook's cross was for me. It was a fantastic feeling to see the ball in the net.

● JOHN SISSONS: Honestly, I have never been as nervy during a match—even after I had scored that first equaliser. But I was glad to see my pal, Howard Kendall, have a fine game.

● NORBERT LAWTON : It's nice to know you have played well. I reckoned we could have had a couple of penalties, but that's how it goes in football. Twice it looked very much like a case of hands—especially when Brown stopped a shot from Spavin. I would like to see a film of these incidents.

● JIMMY MILNE (manager) : We don't grumble. You can only do your best. I am pleased the lads put on a good show.

● HOWARD KENDALL: I was a bit edgy before the game but once I got out there I relaxed. My job was to cover the West Ham strikers—sometimes I was stuck with Byrne, sometimes Hurst.

● ALAN KELLY : I had some pain from my left hip during the last 10 minutes, but I am not making any excuses. I collided with another player—I don't even know who it was—after a corner kick. But it didn't affect the last goal at all. It was such a good header.

● In 1964 17-year-old Howard Kendall played for second division Preston against West Ham, and became the youngest ever FA Cup finalist. His record lasted until 1980 when Paul Allen beat it.

Date 2 May 1964
Place Wembley
Score WEST HAM UNITED 3 PRESTON NORTH END 2
Teams WEST HAM UNITED Standen, Bond, Burkett, Bovington, Brown, Moore (capt.), Brabrook, Boyce, Byrne, Hurst, Sissons. PRESTON NORTH END Kelly, Ross, Lawton (capt.), Smith, Singleton, Kendall, Wilson, Ashworth, Dawson, Spavin, Holden
Team Colours WEST HAM UNITED Claret and blue shirts, white shorts; PRESTON NORTH END White shirts, dark blue shorts
Official Referee Arthur Holland (Barnsley)
Goal Scorers WEST HAM UNITED Sissons 11, Hurst 52, Boyce 92; PRESTON NORTH END Holden 10, Dawson 40
Managers WEST HAM UNITED Ron Greenwood; PRESTON NORTH END Jimmy Milne
Attendance 100 000
Gate Receipts £89 289
Guest of Honour Sir Alec Douglas Home
Copy *Sunday Express* 3 May 1964; *Daily Sketch* 4 May 1964

NO. 26,557   SATURDAY, MAY 1, 1965   FOURPENCE

LIVERPOOL 2   LEEDS UNITED 1

EE - AYE - ADDIO, THE REDS HAVE WON THE CUP!

By LESLIE EDWARDS

When Ronnie Yeats led his team out onto the lush Wembley pitch, Liverpool fans almost brought down the Wembley roof with their enthusiasm. With the sun failing to come through, it was not a spectacularly colourful Wembley, but the humour of Liverpool contingent more than enlightened the gloom. After the arranged community singing ended the chant "Ee-aye-addio we're going to see the Queen." The receipts were £89,000, and what they cost in aggregate including black market transactions, is anyone's guess.

The Duke of Edinburgh spent a few minutes in conversation with Ron Yeats and Manager Shankly and seemed to have particular attention also for the three match officials.

The side which defended the dressing room end would have the advantage of playing with the wind in the first half. Yeats won this advantage for Liverpool. Strong certainly started up in the right half position, Bremner left the field immediately before the kick-off to hand a ring to Revie at the touch-line.

Stevenson was soon seen to be calming his colleagues in the first minutes, in which no side produced anything definite. The first foul was by Collins on St. John, and Stevenson took it but a big clearance by left half Hunter removed all the danger.

Foul By Collins

Lawrence picked up a good length centre from Reaney after Collins had found the full back going down the right wing, like an express train.

Then Thompson came into the centre circle to start Liverpool's first real attack, which Collins ended with a heavy foul against Byrne who needed trainer's attention.

At teh same time, Hunter was having attention for a left leg injury he had received a moment or two before Byrne went down. Thus within the space of a few minutes both trainers had been on, and both sides had players suffering fairly severe knocks.

Bremner was now sandwiched by Byrne and Smith and was brought down heavily just outside the penalty box. Johanneson and Bell having initiated this first Leeds attack of any importance.

Bremner also needed attention. Leeds' free kick ruse with Bremner feinting to take the award, and in fact Collins doing so, came unstuck, and the game continued in its tentative vein.

Sharp Tackling

Charlton was dominant in the air but now he misheaded a big clearance kick by Lawrence, and yet the mistake cost his side nothing.

Charlton did well to nod for a corner a big right foot shot by Strong, and although Liverpool were inclined to play the ball across the field too much it was clear that they were prepared to shoot whenever opportunity offered.

Stevenson was unlucky not to be able to hold and control a very fine pass by St. John, and then Lawrence came to the edge of his box to kick away direct, rather than chance fielding the ball with Johanneson around. Collins won a brave tackle against St. John, then dug the ball up in a cheeky reverse pass for Sprake.

Hunt made the best run of the game so far with an interchange of passes with St. John, and the pity was that his right foot shot at the end of it all should pass over the bar.

Leeds were rather pedestrian in their play and so far at least, there was no doubt that Liverpool had the edge on them.

Glorious Run

St. John made a glorious individual run and dribble with a final pass to Callaghan that invited him to score, and he most certainly would have I think, if Charlton had not taken the shot full amidships to turn it for a corner.

Not unexpectedly he was yet once more to need the trainer's attention. A bad foul by St. John on Johanneson, who was streaking away after the corner kick had been cleared, led to referee Clements having a very stern word of caution with the Liverpool player.

Leeds covered up well in defence, and now started to play good constructive stuff for the first time, but Byrne and Stevenson between them ended their good right wing attack. Neither Leeds back was slow to come up into the attack, and Bell now won a corner on the left.

Collins floated this one in splendidly, but when Peacock got his head to it he got too far under the ball which sailed innocuously over the bar. A fine cross field pass by Bremner just beat the head of Peacock by inches and went in for a goal kick.

Bremner was now in the wars, and Leeds United trainer came on yet again—surely the greatest spate of stoppages ever to afflict the continuity of a showpiece match like this. And now with the sky getting darker and darker, rain began to fall.

The Liverpool attack was playing with much greater fluency than Leeds, but a good number of their shots were crowded out by a defence which gave very little away.

Giles now came to the left wing to initiate with Collins one of Leeds best attacks, and after a rather shaky beginning, the Yorkshire side were now settling down to play some good closely linked stuff.

Sprake failed to grasp a fine centre from Callaghan, who had been found by St. John, but happily for Leeds, right winger Giles dropped back and was there to pick up the loose ball and take it away.

St. John was much too bold with an attempt at a through pass, having brought the ball out of defence, and though Liverpool were having the better of it, they still had to make their superiority count.

Playing It Cool

Leeds made pretty poor use of the several freekicks they had been given so far. Lawler extricated himself from difficulty near the corner flag with Johanneson in attendance and the possibility of a reverse pass to Lawrence to dangerous to contemplate.

Sprake was able to pick up with time to spare, a tentative back header by Reaney.

How They Lined Up

LIVERPOOL

Right   Lawrence   Left
Lawler   Byrne
Strong   Yeats   Stevenson
Callaghan   Hunt   St. John   Smith   Thompson

Referee: Mr. W. Clements (West Bromwich)

Johanneson   Collins   Peacock   Storrie   Giles
Hunter   Charlton   Bremner
Bell   Reaney
Left   Sprake   Right

LEEDS UNITED

attack. Neither Leeds back was slow to come up into the attack, and Bell now won a corner on the left.

Liverpool were playing it coolly and safe in defence, and so far Leeds had shown little indication that they had got the ability to find a shot, much less achieve a lethal position.

Collins found Peacock with a peach of a pass, and it took Yeats's long-leg tackle to get the ball away at the expense of a corner.

Liverpool got a free kick out of this right wing corner, in which Strong and Charlton had been involved in a bodily duel inside the box.

St. John was playing well, and all but put Hunt clean through at this stage, and Leeds must have been relieved indeed to take possession, at the crucial moment when, if Hunt had obtained the ball, he must have been well nigh clean through.

Hunt On Target

The best shot so far came from a standing start from Smith, who hammered the ball just wide from a square pass by Strong. Bell hereabouts made an all too nonchalant reverse pass to Sprake.

Collins now had his best moment winning two tremendous clinches for possession against the odds, and starting a Leeds attack which might well have brought Hunt if Johanneson had not been tackled so incisively.

Hunt was now showing all his determination and brought cheers from the Liverpool fans with a great long range shot that Sprake did exceptionally well to flick over the top. He made an excellent catch from the corner kick also.

Peacock made one good downwards header, but Lawrence had the situation nicely covered. A pass from St. John to Hunt nearly undid the Leeds defence completely, but they escaped luckily at the expense of a corner, and another one followed on the same wing when a shot by Strong was deflected. This came right on the interval.

Half-time.—Leeds Utd. nil. Liverpool nil.

The rain now fell heavier than ever. Liverpool started this half with a move in which the ball was passed some half a dozen times, and yet finished up little nearer from the Leeds goal than it had been from the start.

Sprake and Bell were glad to give away a corner to escape from St. John, and then Lawler, with a right wing centre landed the ball squarely to the head of Hunt, whose nod for goal was wide of target.

All-out Attack

Bremner with a despairing left foot now cut out for a corner Thompson's centre, and it took the combined efforts of the Leeds defence to keep out Hunt, and a moment later to keep out Callaghan whose fierce close-in shot struck Charlton and passed for a corner.

This was Liverpool at their best and most dangerous and the Leeds fans certainly had their most anxious few minutes of the entire match so far.

It was Bremner who more often took the eye. Smith was having a good match and Liverpool were so much on top they were now playing it almost nonchalantly and at walking pace.

The Leeds defence always stayed back in depth to put a spoke in any movement which promised to reach finality.

Date 1 May 1965
Place Wembley
Score LIVERPOOL 2 LEEDS UNITED 1 (after extra time)
Teams LIVERPOOL Lawrence, Lawler, Byrne, Strong, Yeats (capt.), Stevenson, Callaghan, Hunt, St. John, Smith, Thompson. LEEDS UNITED Sprake, Reaney, Bell, Bremner, Charlton, Hunter, Giles, Storrie, Peacock, Collins (capt.), Johanneson
Team Colours LIVERPOOL All red; LEEDS UNITED All white
Official Referee W. Clements (West Bromwich)
Goal Scorers LIVERPOOL Hunt 93, St. John 111; LEEDS UNITED Bremner 101
Managers LIVERPOOL Bill Shankly; LEEDS UNITED Don Revie
Attendance 100000
Gate Receipts £89103
Guests of Honour H.M. Queen Elizabeth II, H.R.H. Duke of Edinburgh, George Brown
Copy The Liverpool Echo and Evening Express 1 and 3 May 1965

Ian St. John falls as he tries a shot on the turn. Sprake, the Leeds goalkeeper, is on the left.

Liverpool's tremendous welcome to the Cup winners

Hunt and Charlton in a heading duel with Reaney close at hand.

Hunt falls as he is dispossessed by Reaney

Strong's Effort

In most cases of a physical battle for the ball it was Liverpool who came out in possession. It was far from being a great final by any standards, but so far at least there was no doubt that Liverpool were far the better side.

Bremner was spoken to for kicking the ball from hand into the crowd when Liverpool had been given a throw-in, and the Liverpool crowd were not slow to let him know what they thought about it, nor was referee Clements.

Johanneson had done nothing of note so far, nor had Giles, so Leeds' vaunted wing strength had been negligable.

Callaghan struck the side netting with a left foot shot which seemed booked for the back of the net in its initial stages.

Storrie slipped when an unexpected through ball from right back Reaney might well have put him through down the inside left position.

The Leeds wingers were having an extraordinarily thin time against the excellent defence of both Byrne and Lawler. Smith made one glorious tackle on Hunter to turn defence into attack in a twinkling, but Callaghan's centre was cut off.

Then St. John did not get enough forehead on the ball and glanced it very wide from an astute crossfield pass by Lawler.

It was incredible that Liverpool could have the game so much in their grasp without being in the lead, yet their propensity for too many crossfield passes left many of their moves without much penetration, and that was the crux of the matter and the reason why they were still goalless.

Liverpool were luckless at the moment when a right foot shot by Thompson speeding just inside the far post all but caught Sprake napping.

He got down to the ball at the last moment and appeared to turn it for a corner by the use of his forearms.

Feeling The Strain

Bremner, not Collins, seemed to be taking most of Leeds free kicks. The experience of Liverpool's long cup run, plus the European success they have had, had clearly given them a wealth of tactical experience and knowledge.

Charlton collided with a photographer just off the pitch when allowing the ball to pass out of play and got to his feet rubbing his thigh. While this semi-stoppage took place Thompson got attention from Paisley at the touchline.

A moment later a wide shot by Storrie on the right wing hit a photographer seated at the other end of the pitch.

Liverpool were almost strolling through the match at times, and Leeds psychologically must have been at their wits end to know just where to start to attempt to break down the Liverpool defence.

Sprake now produced his most thrilling save, one at full stretch from a shot by Thompson to turn the ball for a corner.

Two Corners Passes

The Leeds goalkeeper made a wonderful catch to beat the head of Yeats following the corner kick.

Collins seemed a tired little man and incapable of raising much more than a gentle gallop. And the outlook so far as Leeds were concerned with six minutes to go, could not have been more grim.

Rarely has a Liverpool defence had such an easy afternoon and seemed so unlikely to be beaten. A fine shot by Byrne cannoned out to Strong and he returned it hard and true to goal, but Sprake who has had a great day was perfectly positioned to take it almost on the goal line.

90 MINUTES—NO SCORE

It's Extra Time Now

This is the first time it has happened at Wembley since 1947 when Charlton and Burnley finished level after 90 minutes.

Wembley erupted three minutes after the restart when Hunt scored from a pass by Byrne. Thompson had slipped the ball out to the full back near the left wing corner flag in such an expert way Byrne might have been tempted to try a shot, but sensibly he turned the ball into the goalmouth where Hunt stooped low to nod it over the line for a first-rate scoring point.

Amazing Scene

Liverpool's contingent went wild. One interloper climbed the barrier and appeared on the pitch trying to congratulate the scorer and was removed from the scene carried by five policemen, but still waving his red and white scarf to acclaim the goal which it seemed would never come.

The shock of an equaliser when it came at 11 minutes jolted us all. It came from a Leeds right wing move with Charlton nodding the ball across to Bremner just inside the penalty box and the sandy-haired half back crashed the ball full on the volley to ram it into the top corner of the net.

That Leeds should have scored off this one difficult chance was incredible. This must have been one of the most shaking goals Liverpool ever endured. It meant that they had got to start out all over again to do what it had taken them more than a complete 90 minutes to achieve.

Both teams were playing almost as if they were in a have been denuded of their strength to the last ounce. Storrie was still virtually a passenger on the left wing.

Half-time of extra time.— Liverpool 1, Leeds 1.

Bremner's stamina was remarkable. He was going like a rearing lion when most of the others had clearly had as much as they could take. Bremner controlling the ball quickly and shooting it on the half turn from a pass by Reaney was on target without having sufficient force in his drive to bother Lawrence.

Strong five yards outside the box, now found his best right foot shot but Sprake with a full length save to put the ball away for a corner. From this St. John hooked the ball on to the top netting.

Nine minutes from the end Callaghan crossed the ball magnificently and fast and St. John nodded the ball in like a bullet. Again a Liverpool fan found his way onto the pitch and again he was removed unceremoniously by the police.

Thus Liverpool had reprieved a situation which seemed beyond their recapture with so little time remaining and all the portents shaping towards a replay.

Bremner was picked up narrowly offside, a minute after Liverpool had scored otherwise he might have snatched the game out of the fire for the second time. Thompson dispossessed Charlton in full cry, and forced Sprake to his final glorious full length save.

SCOTTISH SUMMER CUP			
Dundee ...	1	Dundee Utd	4
Falkirk ...	O	Dunfermline	O
Hibernian	3	Hearts......	O
Kilmarnock	3	Airdrieon'ns	1
Motherwell	3	Th. Lanark	1
Partick Th.	2	Morton......	1
St Johnst'ne	2	Aberdeen...	O
St. Mirren	1	Clyde	3

Peacock, the Leeds centre forward, and Ron Yeats leap for a corner kick, watched by Charlton.

Everton, two down in 57 minutes, make wonder recovery

SALUTE TREBILCOCK

EVERTON (Trebilcock 2. Temple 1) **3**, **SHEFFIELD WED** (Wilson o g, Ford) **2**

Attendance : 100.000.   Receipts £109,600.

CORNISHMAN Mike Trebilcock, socks jammed down to his ankles, sweat-drenched Everton jersey flapping outside his shorts, took the Cup to Merseyside after one of Wembley's most sensational smash-and-grab performances.

Unsung Sheffield Wednesday led 2—0 with little more than half an hour to go and the blue banners of Everton sulked low on the terraces.

Enter Trebilcock, last-minute Cup Final choice, his name not even on the Wembley programme, with two acts of devilish opportunism in six minutes.

And to complete a quarter of an hour of woe for Wednesday, their left half Gerry Young made a calamitous error of judgment to present left winger Derek Temple with a massive gift of a matchwinner.

MIKE'S MAGIC

Trebilcock was the obvious hero of an entertaining and dramatic Cup Final, though I was delighted to see Sheffield Wednesday become the first Wembley losers ever to make a lap of honour at the finish.

The 21-year-old Cornishman joined Everton from Plymouth on New Year's Eve for £18,000, chicken-feed by today's huge transfer prices.

After a frustrating first half when Everton just could not get going when their forward line made not one concerted advance on the goal of England 'keeper

By SAM LEITCH

Ron Springett, it was Trebilcock who changed the whole course of the Final.

He had only three shots at goal, scoring with the first two — dynamic first timers — and fluffing the third, the easiest chance of all, in the seventy-seventh minute.

But it was definitely Mike's magic day.

Wednesday opened with eye-catching confidence: their football, hard, simple, direct, and telling.

Within four minutes they had forced Everton to do what they had not done in 660 Cup minutes this season —surrender a goal.

Wednesday right half Peter Eustace took a quick throw-in on the left, found unmarked David Ford, whose low drive across the Everton goal was gobbled up by young Jim McCalliog.

His left-foot drive struck the leg of England left back Ray Wilson and goalkeeper Gordon West, committed to McCalliog's shot, had no chance with the sudden deflection.

A GOAL TONIC

It was just what this Cup Final needed, the powerful tonic of an early goal, a wonderful gift for manager Alan Brown and his young Yorkshire side.

Everton flopped so badly in attack that it began to look as if manager Harry Catterick's decision to drop Fred Pickering was going to prove a costly error of judgment.

Still, Everton should have had a penalty in the 19th minute when I thought Springett brought down Everton leader Alex Young

in a dive which would do justice to next week's Rugby League Final.

Eustace was all over the place for Wednesday. But Jimmy Gabriel the Everton midfield link man, was making no impact on his forwards.

The excessive Wednesday energy was to prove an error of pace. It was noticeable immediately after the interval that Everton had much more running power.

GREEDY FEET

Four minutes after half-time only a remarkable England-class leap and one-handed save by Springett thwarted the unlucky Young.

Wednesday's luck stuck grimly to their boots for their second goal in the 57th minute.

John Fantham's deadly dribble into the guts of the Merseyside rearguard left four trailing Everton defenders.

His drive rebounded from the chest of goalkeeper West to the greedy feet of Ford, who had a simple goal at his mercy.

So Wednesday were two up and few people in the 100,000 crowd could have given Everton any chance.

But within one minute Trebilcock lashed a right foot half-volley past Springett after left half Brian Harris and left winger Temple had set up the goal.

By now Wednesday were missing the experience of injured centre half Vic Mobley, and six minutes later hesitancy in the Wednesday goal area let in Trebilcock for his second unstoppable shot.

An Alex Scott free kick sailed into the Wednesday goal area, the ball was headed hesitatingly down by

The Prime Minister, Mr. Harold Wilson, is greeted by Cup final fans as he steps out of No. 10, Downing Street.

Mobley's young deputy, Sam Ellis, and the ball spun away to Trebilcock's eager and lethal right foot.

The squat Trebilcock may not be the classiest ball player Wembley has seen, but his rapid-fire, trigger-happy shooting in front of goal pinched the Cup from Sheffield Wednesday.

AMAZING SCENES

There was an amazing scene after the equaliser when Trebilcock was thrown to the ground by two over-joyed Everton fans who had invaded the pitch.

One London copper dashed on to the field, dived at one fan, missed him. A second policeman then sprinted after the fan and crash-tackled him to allow six policemen to lift him struggling from the ground.

All this in front of Princess Margaret and all soccer's V I Ps.

Those two Everton "invaders" must have wished they had stayed to see the winner ten minutes later, the result of that deadly error by Gerry Young.

A harmless punt upfield from Everton goalkeeper West should have been trapped by Young, but the ball flew from his boot— "Ninety-nine times out of a hundred I would have tamed that ball, but the hundredth had to be in the Final," said the sadly dis-

appointed Young at the finish.

Temple collared yet another Wembley gift ball.

PERFECT SHOT

He had plenty of time and space to advance on goal. Springett came out to narrow the angle, spat on his hands, then saw a perfect shot flash past

The Cup had been lost in a quarter of an hour.

Sheffield Wednesday deserve a lot of sympathy. Their first-half football was excellent and they had the Cup in the palms of their Yorkshire hands.

But Everton refused to panic when all seemed lost, a reflection of the experience and determination of their star performers.

The sweet taste of success. Everton hero Mike Trebilcock gratefully accepts champagne from the FA Cup he helped to win. Temple gives him an extra up-lift.

I'VE NEVER SEEN THIS BEFORE

● A pick-me-up for the boss—Everton manager Harry Catterick is chaired off by his delighted players, the first time I have seen such a tribute, says Edgar Turner in his story

HAPPY, BUT HE DIDN'T PLAY

● Between Jimmy Gabriel and Alex Young—Fred Pickering the man who was left out of Everton's Wembley team. Now Pickering is thinking over his future, but he has not asked for a transfer

Gerry Young's blunder shatters the Wednesday dream

WEMBLEY CUP HERO

OH, IT'S SO IMPOSSIBLE TO BEAR

- Oh the shame of it! Gerry Young, flat out, dejected, wishes the Wembley turf would swallow him up after his mistake gave Temple the vital third goal.

- Not even the consolatory tap from goalkeeper Springett could help Young disguise his grief. Nothing could.

- Young had to suffer alone for the error probably he'll remember all his life.

TRIBUTE TO THE BOSS

AT last it seems manager Harry Catterick is appreciated at Everton. The man brutally attacked by some Everton supporters earlier this season—ironically a day or two after signing yesterday's hero Mike Trebilcock—was surrounded by delighted back-slapping fans and asked for his autograph.

The players showed their appreciation by lifting him shoulder high—the first time I have ever seen a team pay such a compliment to their boss after a Cup Final.

The action spoke far more than words.

It showed their faith in a man who has had to endure not only kicks but ill health, bad luck and intense pressure.

It was also an expression of faith in the fact that he'd chosen the right team.

Said the delighted Catterick: "It was a great match. I wasn't panicking when we were two down, but no-one feels on top of the world when they are trailing against a fast and competent team in the Cup Final.

"But the lads clicked and I was delighted with all eleven of them."

GLORIOUS!

Two-goal Mike Trebilcock who came in for Fred Pickering in a controversial Catterick move, said: "It was a glorious day for me, but I felt so sorry afterwards for Fred. He deserved a Cup Final more than I did."

Said winning goal scorer Derek Temple: "I hadn't time to feel sorry for Gerry Young when he did not control the ball.

"I knew the instant the shot left my foot that it was a goal."

Wednesday boss Alan Brown was not too downhearted. "I was pleased as punch with the boys," he said. "I'm sure they will be back. It is tough on them. I am used to defeat.

"Everton deserved their success after being two down."

Last word from Gerry Young, the man who slipped up: "I am inconsolable."

Jim McCalliog (left) beats Gordon West to put Wednesday one up

Date 14 May 1966
Place Wembley
Score EVERTON 3 SHEFFIELD WEDNESDAY 2
Teams EVERTON West, Wright, Wilson, Gabriel, Labone, Harris, Scott, Trebilcock, A. Young, Harvey, Temple. SHEFFIELD WEDNESDAY Springett, Smith, Megson, Eustace, Ellis, G. Young, Pugh, Fantham, McCalliog, Ford, Quinn
Team Colours EVERTON Blue shirts, white shorts; SHEFFIELD WEDNESDAY All white
Official Referee J. F. Taylor (Wolverhampton)
Goal Scorers EVERTON Trebilcock 58, 63, Temple 80; SHEFFIELD WEDNESDAY McCalliog 4, Ford 57
Managers EVERTON Harry Catterick; SHEFFIELD WEDNESDAY Alan Brown
Attendance 100000
Gate Receipts £109691
Guest of Honour H.R.H. Princess Margaret
Copy *The Star Green 'Un* 14 May 1966; *The Sunday Mirror* 15 May 1966

THE SUNDAY TELEGRAPH   MAY 21, 1967   M, R & S   Page 25

F.A. Cup

By David Miller

Arrogant and disdainful... Spurs saunter to victory

NEVER sprinting where they could canter, never cantering where they could saunter, Spurs won their fifth F.A. Cup victory in five finals, their third of the sixties, in a slightly one-sided, yet always entertaining, match.

If not quite playing as they pleased, they dictated the game for all but a few sporadic anxious moments. Chelsea were, in a word, outwitted.

Half-an-hour before the start a heavy shower swept down the stadium on to the Chelsea bank of supporters at the East end. It was perhaps symbolic, for Spurs proceeded to tame and finally demoralise Tommy Docherty's vibrant youngsters. If it was the result nearly everyone had predicted, they could not have expected it to be so conclusive.

It was only when Spurs slowed the game almost to a walk with 10 minutes to go that Chelsea scored the goal that might have meant hope, an impetuous rush by Jennings out of his goal and mistimed punch allowing Tambling to head a soft one from Boyle's centre. Yet such was Tottenham's confidence by now that they continued to play out time with insolent, arrogant disdain.

Elusive prize

Docherty had asserted that Spurs would play only as well as Chelsea allowed them, but on the day it proved to be exactly the other way about, and after three seasons of near success Chelsea have still to claim a prize.

London's first final had beforehand been seen as one of clearly defined patterns and personal duels, and in almost every one on this sunny, showery afternoon, Spurs came out top, none more than the elegant, imperious Gilzean with his total domination of Hinton in the air.

Not only were Spurs transparently the better balanced and co-ordinated side, but they had this edge, too, in the individual clashes. This team may not have the flamboyance of the one it succeeded, but it has every prospect of an outstanding season in Europe if it sustains its combination of tactical clarity and physical discipline.

Spurs in fact, have become hard of late. We knew however, that Chelsea were even harder, but Wembley's open spaces and the velvet turf—which gives men like Greaves, Gilzean and Robertson with refined touch another yard to spare over defenders—never permitted Chelsea to get to close quarters and ruffle the poise of their technically superior adversaries. Mr. Dagnall, the referee, was also unmistakably in favour of confining physical challenge within the laws.

Basic error

Wembley is a place where the first 10 mins of the Cup Final, following the tremendous emotional strain on the players in the preceding days, are all important, and to my mind Chelsea made a fundamental error in starting with only two forwards Hateley and Baldwin, consistently lying upfield, employing in preference a central quartet of Hollins, Cooke, Tambling and Boyle. The initiative instantly fell to Spurs.

In the first quarter of an hour Chelsea had hardly a smell of Spurs' goal. Hateley and Baldwin were smothered by England, as steady as a rock bar a couple of errors, and Mullery, once more playing with an invincible dependability that marks him down for the national team. Though Chelsea may have had numerical superiority in midfield their build-up was of necessity slow because there was no one to play the ball through too.

From the 15th to the 25th minute Chelsea briefly prospered. Already it was clear that Mackay is not quite the man he was, several times having to resort to obstruction when beaten for pace. Yet Chelsea never gained enough rhythm to put pressure on any weakness and by the half hour Spurs had stroked their way back into command and scored the first goal, a lucky one by Robertson, at a vital psychological moment just before half-time.

There were many factors in Chelsea's failure—and it would be idle to pretend it was not as much their failure as a triumph by Spurs.

Dave Mackay said a few weeks ago that there's nothing like having two wingers playing out wide and now the value of this to Tottenham was there for all to see. From the very first minute when Robertson outpaced McCreadie onto a flick from Gilzean, the Scottish winger put the screw on McCreadie to achieve the double effect of creating danger at one end and preventing McCreadie making his overlapping runs which are an integral feature of the Chelsea plan.

So there it was—Gilzean's wonderful heading, Robertson's exhilarating speed, Greaves's darting in and out and only just failing to unhinge Ron Harris: a trio to remember.

If there was one man who threatened to save the game for Chelsea it was, excepting some fortuitous heading by Hateley, Cooke with his nimble, exciting and erratic dribbling. Again and again he set off full tilt towards the Tottenham defence. But he had neither the response nor the luck and it was a vain effort.

Fine future

In the fourth minute Greaves and Gilzean combined and suddenly there was Kinnear, a little full-back with a tremendous future, streaking clear on the right, but his centre was pulled back too deep. With 10 minutes gone, Gilzean headed a centre by Mullery square over two defenders and the ball fell free to a waiting Saul, but he was so surprised and/or slow to see the opening that his eventual lunging half-volley was blocked by Allan Harris. A few minutes later Bonetti made an incredible save from a left-footed hook by Robertson and then Saul headed past a post.

Now came Chelsea's first response and Jennings had to save low at the feet of two forwards as Hollins put in a cross-shot from 25 yards. At the other end Greaves sidled past Ron Harris and sent the ball dangerously close to the angle of the posts. But back came Chelsea and Jennings needed to be at his best to turn away a cross by Cooke.

Quietly taking their time Spurs seemed to know even now the game was theirs. When Cooke fouled Mullery Greaves "bent" the free-kick round the wall and inches over the bar.

With his forwards failing, it was Hollins again who forced Jennings to save in the 41st minute and Cooke, twice beating Mackay, brought a great save out of Jennings. Almost immediately there was a free-kick against Boyle, Mullery broke down the middle, came on and on at last let fly and his shot rebounded off Allan Harris straight to Robertson who swept it low into the corner past a helpless Bonetti.

Near miss

It was going to need a lot of improvement for Chelsea to pull out of this one, and rarely in the second half did it look even remotely possible. The better openings were nearly all Tottenham's, though in the 58th minute a bad pass by Knowles created a scare and Spurs were thankful that Hateley's header crept over the bar.

Now Greaves and Gilzean began to move considerably at their leisure, and Greaves made a snap shot which nearly caught Bonetti off guard. With 22 minutes left a throw by Mackay was pushed by Robertson across the back of the penalty area and Saul with a quite remarkable hooked shot from his blind side pulling the ball through 230 degrees, tucked it just inside a post past a startled and dismayed Bonetti.

That surely was the end. There should have been a third when Kinnear broke on the right to the goal line, but misdirected his pass back to Saul. With seven minutes to go Hateley again headed just over the bar and finally came Tambling's goal. You had to be a Chelsea fanatic to believe that they could still save the day.

THE TEAMS

Tottenham.—Jennings; Kinnear, Mullery, England, Knowles; Venables, Mackay; Robertson, Greaves, Gilzean, Saul.

Chelsea.—Bonetti; Harris (A.), Hinton, Harris (R.), McCreadie; Hollins, Cooke, Boyle; Baldwin, Hateley, Tambling.

Referee: K. Dagnall (Bolton).

TOTTENHAM (1) 2	CHELSEA (0) 1
Robertson	Tambling
Saul	
100,000	£109,649

Spurs captain Mackay being crowned with the lid of the F.A. Cup by Robertson (right), who scored the first goal, while Mullery lends a hand to carry the coveted prize during the lap of honour.

Greaves becomes airborne as he tries to crack the ball into the net but a late tackle from R. Harris averts the danger.

Spurs take the lead through Robertson

Date 20 May 1967

Place Wembley

Score TOTTENHAM HOTSPUR 2 CHELSEA 1

Teams TOTTENHAM HOTSPUR Jennings, Kinnear, Knowles, Mullery, England, Mackay, Robertson, Greaves, Gilzean, Venables, Saul. Sub. Jones.
CHELSEA Bonetti, A. Harris, McCreadie, Hollins, Hinton, R. Harris, Cooke, Baldwin, Hateley, Tambling, Boyle. Sub. Kirkup

Team Colours TOTTENHAM HOTSPUR All white; CHELSEA All blue

Official Referee K. Dagnall (Lancashire)

Goal Scorers TOTTENHAM HOTSPUR Robertson 45, Saul 67; CHELSEA Tambling 86

Managers TOTTENHAM HOTSPUR Bill Nicholson; CHELSEA Tommy Docherty

Attendance 100000

Gate Receipts £109649

Guest of Honour Sunday Telegraph 21 May 1967; *The Sun* 22 May 1967

Mike England and Tony Hateley go up together and England gets the ball away for Spurs. Tambling watches in the background

FINAL INSULT FOR CHELSEA
£50 BONUS RILES LOSERS

By STEVE RICHARDS

CHELSEA players fly off to America this morning, leaving behind them a season of bickering within the club and still choked by the bitterness of what they call "the great Cup Final let-down."

Beneath the uneasy atmosphere of the banquet for the Wembley runners-up, at which manager Tommy Docherty reprimanded speakers for virtually snubbing his team, ran an undercurrent stoked up by players who felt like returning the meagre £50 they receive for finishing second to Spurs.

PROMISE

A team spokesman told me: "We were promised £12,000 for our pool of 19 players if we won the Final. We weren't told about it until the eve of the match.

"What an encouragement for us to take into such a match! To know that, if we won, it would be £12,000, and, if we lost, under £1,000.

"And to be told at that time, too. No wonder relations are strained."

The spokesman added: "We think the board have been stingy and unfair.

"We are not money-grabbers. We are professionals and we believe that, for getting to Wembley, we deserve more.

"We have confirmed that Spurs were on a substantial reward for reaching the Final. People imagine we got a lot of Wembley tickets. We got 12.

"We think we have been shabbily treated and we are disgusted with the way the board have handled the situation."

Charlie Pratt, the Chelsea chairman, said yesterday that the figure of £50 was a legacy of agreements made before he took over the club's helm. If Chelsea had beaten Spurs, the £12,000 would have been paid as talent money on future contracts.

It is still open to Mr. Pratt and his directors, of course, to express their appreciation of their team's achievement in the next agreement they draw up. Perhaps they will.

Chelsea's major banquet was held in one room of a Knightsbridge hotel. Manager Docherty's "mini banquet" for 14 of his friends who didn't get official invitations was in another.

CIGARETTE BOXES

The players, who did receive silver cigarette boxes from the club, heard manager Docherty tell the official function: "I am glad of this opportunity of speaking because I was beginning to think that the players responsible for getting us to Wembley weren't going to be mentioned.

"We've heard a lot of past Chelsea players and I believe a little more credit should be given to the present bunch. No manager could be more proud of them than I am."

Despite all the speculation about Docherty's future at Chelsea and the cat-and-mouse politics between board and management, my most interesting encounter of the banquet was with centre-forward Peter Osgood, who hasn't played since he broke a leg last October.

The presence of Osgood, a talented if sometimes emotional and hot-headed young man, would surely have bridged the gap between Chelsea and Spurs at Wembley.

Chelsea waved farewell to him today, hoping that, whatever they do on the American Soccer scene without him, he will win the final lap back to complete fitness in England and be ready to join their assault on next season's honours.

SINGING SPURS took the FA Cup back to Tottenham yesterday and for the 120,000 fans who turned out to welcome their heroes—more than the Wembley crowd who saw them beat Chelsea 2-1 on Saturday—it was music all the way.

Spurs, who have won the Cup three times since 1961, made the three-mile drive along Tottenham High Road aboard an open-topped double-decker bus.

Mounted police, part of the 200 on crowd duty, had to force a path for the coach through the cheering hordes, while an estimated 30,000 fans walked, skipped and sang their way from Edmonton Town Hall to Tottenham Town Hall behind the coach.

Everyone, but everyone roared: "Glory, glory, Halle-

SINGING.. SWINGING CUP-STYLE

lujah, the Spurs go marching on." The Enfield Silver Band played it and the team sang, too.

And all the time Spurs' scorers, Scot Jimmy Robertson and fair-haired Frank Saul (above), were repeatedly called on to hold up the cup their goals had won.

Captain Dave Mackay—only one of the team to play in all three winning finals—said: "We were flabbergasted by the numbers."

Manager of the decade

BILL NICHOLSON is tied for life to Tottenham Hotspur, but not by the small print of any contract. He hasn't got one (writes PETER LORENZO).

He could be fired tomorrow, and it would all be perfectly legal!

Somehow I do not think that is likely to happen . . not to the No. 1 candidate for the accolade, Manager of the Decade.

Bill Nicholson, who joined the Spurs' ground staff from his native Scarborough in 1936, was appointed manager on October 11, 1958. Football should have been warned, for Spurs celebrated the occasion by beating Everton 10-4.

Now, three FA Cups, one League championship, one European Cup-winners' Cup and the illustrious "double" stand to his credit.

Tried and failed

Sheffield Wednesday were one of several clubs who tried and failed to lure Nick from White Hart Lane. Even England couldn't do that.

"I am a one club man," he said simply and honestly during the banquet on Saturday night that celebrated his and Tottenham's third Wembley triumph in seven seasons.

"I am well paid here," he told me quietly. "Very well paid. I have all I want. What is the use of a contract? Your only security is your ability."

Now England's top two footballing clubs, Spurs and Manchester United, will next season challenge for European honours, in the same way as Scotland's top two, Celtic and Rangers, have challenged so magnificently this.

Regrettably, perhaps, but unavoidably in the world swing to defensive football, Nicholson and Matt Busby go back with changed tactical concepts.

United triumphed as much through their rearguard resolution as their attacking inventiveness: the goal Bobby Tambling scored four minutes from time on Saturday was only the fifth conceded by Spurs in their last 16 games.

Unlike the 1963 Spurs side that became the first British team to win a major European competition, their 1967 successors have not yet reached their peak.

Kinnear, Saul, Robertson, Knowles and Jennings have their best days ahead of them.

But in the same way that Busby is building an 18-man first-team pool to launch his attacks on European and domestic targets, so Nick is determined to strengthen his cover squad.

Complete player

No man hopes more than he that Dave Mackay has at least one more season of top-class competition left in him. Nicholson unashamedly rates him the complete professional, the complete player.

"He can do anything," says Nick. "His brain, his skills, his knowledge and reading of the game, his enthusiasm, his driving force make him the magnificent player he is.

"How can you replace Dave Mackay?"

Mackay, although having one of his rare, moderate, surprisingly inconspicuous games on Saturday, has no doubts about next season.

"I am still full of running," he said within minutes of picking up the Cup. "I could go out there and play another game.

"I will want to finish when I cannot hold my first-team place. I am confident that day is not here yet."

Danny Blanchflower didn't last long after steering Spurs to the European Cup-winners' Cup triumph.

I am sure skipper Mackay will not go so quickly.

P.S. By far the happiest thing at Wembley was the gesture of Dave Mackay, the Spurs skipper, who instead of claiming the ball they had played with, had it autographed by all the players, then presented it to that splendid referee, Ken Dagnall.

Pat Jennings clears from the feet of Tommy Baldwin

Easy, Spurs.. all according to plan

IF THE Wembley occasion did not turn out as expected, the tactical contest certainly did. Spurs were as accurate in their plotting of the game as they were convincing in winning it. No one can dispute that victory went to the better-equipped, more enterprising and adaptable team.

Spurs' No. 1 plan worked like a dream—to exploit the uncertainty in the air of Chelsea centre-half Marvin Hinton.

As a sweeper, Hinton has few superiors. When he has to mark tightly, he is distinctly vulnerable.

Spurs schemed accordingly. The uninterrupted superiority in the air that Alan Gilzean commanded over Hinton, particularly in the opening 30 minutes, gave Spurs an attacking edge they seldom lost.

Power attempts

Gilzean's flicks constantly brought his fellow forwards

SPURS 2, CHELSEA 1

into action. Hateley's headers were more often than not power attempts at goal.

Spurs played to Gilzean to unsettle the Chelsea defence and to make him a springboard for their raids. Chelsea played to Hateley as a striker alone.

The feeling was ever that Spurs were the more organised side and the likely winners.

Their goals by Jimmy Robertson and Frank Saul were the results of clever anticipation.

With Joe Kinnear cleverly and skilfully exploiting his freedom down the right flank—who did he have to mark?—Spurs had three wingers on the field.

Here was further evidence of the mastery and accomplishment of the Spurs' tactics.

Chelsea were solidly served by skipper Ron Harris but his subduing of Greaves left him little scope to offer anything else.

John Hollins, now even more of a certainty to win his first full England cap on Wednesday, was as brilliant as Bobby Tambling was disappointing. Thanks to Alan Mullery.

Charlie Cooke? Take away his superb run and shot a few minutes before Robertson scored, and you struggle to add to his productivity.

No, this was the day when the Chelsea style spluttered against opposition that knew what was coming and countered convincingly.

Now it's back to Europe . . but before they get there they have a couple of little matches in pre-season . . against Celtic in Glasgow on August 5 and against Manchester United a week later!

1968

Astle delivers knock-out to Everton in extra time

Brian Glanville

WEST BROMWICH ALBION (0) 1
Astle (after extra time)

EVERTON .... (0) 0
Receipts £110,000 Attendance 100,000

IF IT WAS not the Final we had hoped for and expected, if tempers were bad and much of the football worse, if two generals as able as Ball and Hope deserved a better response, at least it was won by an excellent goal.

Astle scored it for West Bromwich, just as he had scored in every previous round. Defeat was the more bitter for Everton in that Husband, five minutes from the end of normal time, had missed a ludicrously easy chance.

If he'd headed in instead of over the top, one would not have grudged the Cup to Everton, who had generally been the more aggressive. But if they were still then ahead on points, Astle's goal came as the irrevocable knock-out, giving Albion their third victory at Wembley.

There were, alas, some dreadful, cynical fouls by both sides and Mr Callaghan was altogether too passive and indulgent a referee. He might well have sent Ball off for a fearful kick at Fraser late in the game, rather than simply admonish him.

We came to see attacks and we saw . . . defences.

Albion's forward line is a curious affair, one in which Astle lacks the comfort and support of a second spearhead, in which Lovett, the outside-right, looked the half-back that he is; and missed an ultimate chance as easy as Husband's.

The excellent Hope dribbled subtly, held the ball judiciously, and shot occasionally with surprising power, while the industrious Collard came forward when he could. But with Clark so ineffectual on the left, it wasn't much to pit against a defence as robustly well organised as Everton's.

Astle, finding little profit in challenging Labone in the middle, tended to drift out of the centre to the wings. The rangy Hurst was a mobile deputy sheriff to Labone, but against that, Talbut and Kaye (though sorely injured) were just as solid a defensive couple for Albion; the admirable Talbut almost casually taking care of Royle—and so much else besides.

What surprised one about Everton's attack was the rigid way they kept Husband out on the right wing for the first hour, when he's essentially a striker rather than a winger. Predictably, he looked cold and unhappy till he came into the middle; though when he did, he missed that vital and essential chance.

Ball was the untiring motor of Everton's attack, brave, intelligent and quick, with enough energy to spare to scold Royle for one mistake, like a Neopolitan mother. Behind him and in front of the back four, Kendall and Harvey were full of running and intelligent distribution. Morrissey overcame his technical limitations with persistence and steady efficiency.

The opening minutes were hard and nervous bodies lying around in profusion. Astle inadvertently put Morrissey through his own defence, but Kaye raced across to block. More appositely, Astle, moving out to the left, sent Collard away with a glorious pass. Collard found Lovett but the winger had his back to goal and couldn't turn before being tackled.

Everton retaliated quickly when Morrissey beat Brown with some ease, to cross an excellent ball which Osborne reached but could not hold. When it ran loose, Husband got it, but as Albion's defenders crouched anxiously on the line he shot wastefully wide.

For a while, Osborne looked shaky with the high crosses, though in time he was to play himself out of this uneasiness. He dropped a free kick from Wright, though without ill consequence, and it was a long time before Everton looked menacing again. Kendall, served by Ball, hit a dipping shot not far over the top, with five minutes left to the interval.

Then Ball found his other winger, Morrissey, with a square pass and this time the right foot shot flew high and true. Osborne leapt to turn it over. It was some small consolation for a dreary first half; some small token of hope for the second.

Astle was the first to strike, after the break, moving far enough away from Labone at last to head powerfully for goal from Hope's cross. The ball passed just outside the left-hand post. But after 59 minutes Everton came still closer. Morrissey fouled by Fraser, took a free kick on the left of the box, while two Albion defenders confronted him, clutching each other's hands like frightened children. The kick went wide of both of them, Royle got his head to it, Osborne was beaten, but Kaye shepherded the ball off the line.

Everton now briefly took wing, Husband racing electrically through the middle. Albion responded through the busy little Hope, whose high cross shot West punched uncomfortably away. Then Husband, receiving, inevitably, from Ball, was probing the middle again, rounding Talbut, only to have his shot blocked by Fraser. Albion again swiftly responded when Collard rose to Hope's corner, and the ball flew just above the bar.

Though Kaye was hobbling with a bandaged foot, Albion's defence had plainly survived Everton's sudden spell of pressure, and were off the ropes; another fine shot by Hope just cleared the bar. Ball responded with a curving right footer which Osborne capably took, then Morrissey beat two defenders, crossed and Ball headed past a centre which should have been left for Royle.

Now came Husband's dramatic error. When Kendall crossed, the ball was deflected out to Morrissey, who lobbed neatly back into a naked, vulnerable goalmouth. Husband, quite unmarked had infinitive time to contemplate, direct and convert his header but instead, he put it over the top.

Shades of Dean and Lawton !

So it went on to extra time, the gallant Kaye limping slowly off to give way to Clarke, a right-back, Fraser moving into the middle.

We were two and a half minutes into the first period when Astle won the match. Shaking off and stumbling through a foul tackle by Kendall, he went on, had his first, right-footed shot blocked, then sent a beautiful left-footer high and wide of West, into the far, right-hand corner.

Royle, inspired to emulation, hit a fine left-footer of his own, but Osborne knocked it down. Desperately, Everton pushed Hurst up for the second period, and he beat Osborne to a right-wing centre, heading just past the post.

Yet it was Albion who should have scored again. When Osborne threw the ball out after Wilson's free kick, they broke away in a three against one situation, Brown on the ball, Clark in the centre and Lovett on the right, the man who eventually received; and blazed prodigally high.

But the history of the game was written by now. If you miss chances like Husband's you must expect to give away goals like Astle's.

Everton: West, Wright, Wilson; Kendall, Labone (capt.), Harvey; Husband, Ball, Royle, Hurst, Morrissey. Sub: Kenyon.

West Bromwich Albion: Osborne; Fraser, Williams (capt.); Brown, Talbut, Kaye; Lovett, Collard, Astle, Hope, Clark. Sub: Clarke.

Referee: L. Callaghan (Merthyr Tydfil)

What it feels like to be on the winning side in a Cup Final—just great. Ian Collard stoops to receive touchline congratulations from West Bromwich fans

SPORT MIRROR 7

IT was no classic Cup Final and a run of injuries did not help the game. By the thirty-fourth minute eleven players had needed attention from the trainers. Albion right back Doug Fraser was the first to be injured and he needed touchline attention for a damaged left knee. At half-time it needed three stitches.

WEST BROM'S John Kaye, who missed the extra time because of a leg injury, was given a place of honour when the players climbed the stairs to the Royal Box to receive their medals. Kaye, wearing a track suit, followed skipper Graham Williams up the steps and took the Cup stand. The Midland men then did a lap of honour.

IT'S EXTRA SPECIAL FROM ASTLE

I'LL NEVER FORGET MY GOAL, HE SAYS

● After their hard-fought Wembley victory this is what West Bromwich Albion's goal-scoring hero Jeff Astle had to say . . .

● I've made the usual cracks about wanting to jump over the stand. I told somebody I felt ten feet tall, but these are other people's expressions.

● How can I truly describe the tremendous emotion surging inside me? Instead, let me tell you about the goal, the moment I'll keep razor-sharp for the rest of my days.

● The ball came to my right foot at the edge of the box. I had a bash and duffed it. But this was my lucky, lovely day. Back it bounced from

Colin Harvey's knees and I met it with my left.

● I saw this huge gap, the white net and the yellow ball streaking for the corner. Nothing else will ever be the same. Nothing to match that moment.

● Seconds later I was laughing at the idea of doing it with my left. That's the dummy leg—the one that's just for standing on.

● My mates make a joke of it. Yet that's the

third goal in a row it has brought me.

● What a perfect end to a hectic week. It was my birthday on Monday, but everybody forgot in the excitement. All I got was a big kiss from my wife Loraine.

● My legs are sore and gashed, but tonight I feel nothing. Since that ball hit the net I've wanted to run . . . run . . . run.

● Yet I was so worried and nervous before the off. We walked into

that Wembley dressing room and all I could think of was our hammering last year from Queen's Park Rangers.

● I couldn't bear to hang my clothes on the same peg. I persuaded Clive Clark to swop. He scored twice at Wembley last time, so he wasn't bothered.

● Big Brian Labone only gave me two chances in the whole match. The other one was a header that just missed the post

● Frankly, apart from scoring, I did very little. But that's the last thing bothering me right now.

● An exclusive story by Jeff Astle appears on Page 36.

Cheers ! Jeff Astle, the West Bromwich Albion Wembley goal hero, takes a dip and a drink. It's a cool, cool way to celebrate a great day.

Astle, fourth from left, scores the only goal with his dummy left, as he describes above

---

Date 18 May 1968
Place Wembley
Score WEST BROMWICH ALBION 1 EVERTON 0 (after extra time)
Teams WEST BROMWICH ALBION Osborne, Fraser, Williams (capt.), Brown, Talbot, Kaye, Lovett, Collard, Astle, Hope, Clark. Sub: Clarke. EVERTON West, Wright, Wilson, Kendall, Labone (capt.), Harvey, Husband, Ball, Royle, Hurst, Morrissey. Sub: Kenyon
Team Colours WEST BROMWICH ALBION White shirts, white shorts; EVERTON Amber shirts, blue shorts
Official Referee L. Callaghan (Merthyr Tydfil)
Goal Scorer Astle 93
Managers WEST BROMWICH ALBION Alan Ashman; EVERTON Harry Catterick
Attendance 100000
Gate Receipts £110064
Guest of Honour H.R.H. Princess Alexandra
Copy *The Sunday Times* 19 May 1968; *Sunday Mirror* 19 May 1968

As happy Joe says: 'It's nice to get my hands on the old tin pot again'

BEST IS YET TO COME—MERCER

F.A. CUP
Joe Mercer
1969

Boy Booth the find of any season

IT was great to get my hands on the FA Cup once again, but I believe our Wembley victory is only the start of a truly great future for Manchester City.

We go back into Europe still reflecting on our bitter experiences of earlier this season and determined not to make the same mistakes again.

Europe is where the lolly is, so instead of being idealistic we have to be more financially minded. Our defeat by Fenerbahce in Istanbul in October taught us a firm lesson in that we should never underestimate the opposition—any opposition.

WE MUST GET DOWN TO BASICS ALL THE TIME AND I SINCERELY BELIEVE THAT WE HAVE STILL TO SEE THE BEST OF THIS CITY TEAM.

I don't really like talking about potential but we have here a bunch of players who are going to become a really great side.

Things didn't go so well for us earlier this season and, quite naturally, I was disappointed at our results because I knew, Malcolm knew, that the entire team was capable of so much more.

Thanks for Heslop

There is absolutely no substitute for experience and this latest experience of a Wembley Cup Final victory will help to make these boys more mature for next season.

And one player in particular who must be watched out for is Tommy Booth. What a fabulous young centre half he is—he's the find of this or any other season.

And he didn't cost us a penny. We found him on our own doorstep.

At this point let me say a word of praise for one of our "forgotten men" at Maine Road. George Heslop, the man Tommy Booth took over from last October after that European Cup defeat in Turkey, has done a magnificent job with the reserves, helping them, coaxing them, driving them to third place in the Central League.

Remember too, our young reserves made a dreadful start to the season so the job George has done in getting them up there with the leaders is really tremendous.

It's fair comment to say, however, that but for the injury to Tony Book, George might today still be in the first team with young Tommy continuing to wait for his big chance. But that's football.

It was electric

I thought Tommy had a great game, but then who had a bad one? It was a magnificent performance. Sure I was worried. You've got to be worried with only one goal tucked under your belt. But the boys really did us proud.

And how superbly they overcame the electric atmosphere that always charges Wembley on Cup Final day. We told them before the game that though there would be plenty of emotion, they should leave it to the fans to get worked up.

The way they played in the first half took the breath away and the goal was a storybook affair with Mike Summerbee brilliantly pulling the ball back for Neil Young. IT WAS PERFECT FOR NEIL AND HE RARELY MISSES THOSE SORT OF CHANCES.

Like I say, it's nice to have hold of that old tin pot again. It's 19 years since I last took it when captaining Arsenal.

Now I hope we can build from here.

FOR THE LOVE OF MIKE...

SALUTE to Mike Summerbee. Mercer joyously embraces City's international winger Mike Summerbee, right, soon after the end of the Cup Final. Summerbee was one of City's stars and laid on the goal for Neil Young

SALUTE by Mercer in the article above goes to Tommy Booth, whom he describes as the "find of any season." And there is Booth in the centre of the action below as Leicester right-back Peter Rodrigues is just wide with a flying kick. City left back Glyn Pardoe watches his goalkeeper Harry Dowd make a flying dive to cover the ball while also in the scene, extreme right, is Leicester winger Len Glover

SALUTE to the fans. Manager Joe Mercer shows the Cup to the Manchester City supporters whose backing has been so important to their League championship success last year and FA Cup this weekend. Worth recording that there was praise, too, for the fans for their behaviour from the police. Among those with the boss are Francis Lee and Colin Bell, on the left, and Harry Dowd, right

SALUTE to his assistant. Joe Mercer in a madcap moment at Wembley raises his hat to Malcolm Allison, his right-hand man whom he brought back into the game when no one else wanted him. It was certainly a shrewd move as all the soccer world now knows

Wembley special—and it's Manchester's Cup

THE YOUNG CONQUEROR

THE YOUNG touch wins the Cup. Neil Young's shot has Peter Shilton diving in vain, leaving the net bulging

Neil's winner sets up the double for Joe

IT was celebrations all the way from Wembley to Manchester when Joe Mercer's conquerors took the FA Cup for the fourth time in the club's history. Celebrations, too, for Joe Mercer, who last picked up the Cup at Wembley 19 years ago when he skippered Arsenal to victory over Liverpool.

And celebrations also for Malcolm Allison, the controversial coach, who was banned from the trainer's bench by the FA.

For he had the last word by sitting on a second row bench in front of the stand—at least one yard nearer to the field than the trainer's bench.

There was no Cup of kindness for Leicester. This was their fourth visit to Wembley in 20 years, and it was fourth time unlucky for a side who have spent their time between the First and Second Divisions since 1954.

Battle

Now they have to fight again for First Division existence needing to grab seven points in their five remaining League games to avoid the drop once more.

I won't dispute that Manchester deserved to win. They were a more methodical side with steam-engine power in the forward line from the very lively Colin Bell, Francis Lee and Mike Summerbee. Yet Leicester had the chances to win.

Allan Clarke, the most stylish forward at Wembley for my money, had put in the best shot of the game outside of Neil Young's one and only goal.

This was in the 30th minute when the tall Leicester forward put in a terrific shot. Dowd, the Manchester goal-

By FRANK BUTLER

Man City (1) 1 Leicester (0) 0
Young (24 mins)

keeper, who had a quiet afternoon, earned his Cup-winner's medal, making a great leap to push the ball round for a corner.

And after this, Leicester's right-back Peter Rodrigues made the miss of the game when, only a few yards out of Manchester's goal, he failed to connect. It looked easier to score than to miss.

So Leicester could have had two goals in the first half. Then in the second half Lochhead, who had a lively, bustling game, missed a sitter after Clarke had headed down perfectly a centre from Fern.

And the energetic Scot had another chance 15 minutes from time when he burst through, but allowed himself to be hustled off the ball.

So while Shilton had little more work to do than Dowd, what can you say about a team that misses easy chances?

This surely explains why Leicester are fighting so desperately for their First Division lives.

Power

It was not the greatest Cup Final, but it was always good entertainment — especially in the first half. The game later deteriorated, but it was always a game worth watching.

It was the power of Manchester's forwards plus the

efficiency of the half-backs Doyle, Booth and Oakes that made the difference.

Clarke looked worth every penny of that £150,000 Leicester paid for him. His rough passes were an education but he never had too much support. Many of the delightful cross-field passes went unrewarded.

Gibson, Glover and Fern never really got going and Lochhead, while giving Booth a busy afternoon, failed when the chips were down.

Glover had not played like a man 100 per cent fit and he was limping when Leicester manager Frank O'Farrell called him off 20 minutes from the end and sent on 18-year-old Malcolm Manley as substitute with Cross moving forward.

LEICESTER 'keeper Peter Shilton saved this one from Neil Young

and sportsmanship and entertainment.

Special praise for Tony Book, Manchester's 34-year-old captain, who spent so much of his career playing for Bath City, in the Southern League. He played extremely coolly throughout and produced a burst of surprising speed when necessary.

Shaky

The Leicester defence stood up well after a slightly shaky start when Dave Nish, their 21-year-old captain, found Summerbee a handful and Lee gave Woollett a hard time.

Lee, always, was tremendously supported by the strong and fast-moving Bell, who came next to Clarke in my table of merit.

Manchester's goal in the 24th minute looked a winner all the way.

Summerbee rounded Woollett as he cut in along the goal-line to put the perfect ball back to the unmarked Young.

The inside-left just gave it everything with his left foot, and the ball was in the back of the net with goalkeeper Shilton sprawled on the ground looking a little disgusted at the hopelessness of his effort. He had no chance.

It was a game that I am delighted to say was void of any vicious fouls. Both teams produced a good standard of skill

TEAMS

MANCHESTER CITY	LEICESTER CITY
Dowd, Book, Pardoe, Doyle, Booth, Oakes, Summerbee, Bell, Lee, Young, Coleman. **Sub:** Connor.	Shilton, Rodrigues, Nish, Roberts, Woollett, Cross, Fern, Gibson, Lochhead, Clarke, Glover. **Sub:** Manley.

Referee: George McCabe (Sheffield).
Linesmen: Ken Burns (Worcester), Fred Lane (Sussex).
Attendance: 100,000. **Receipts:** £128,000.

ROAD TO WEMBLEY

LEICESTER

3rd Round v Barnsley (away) (Glover)	1—1
Replay (home) (Fern, Glover)	2—1
4th Round v Millwall (away) (Glover)	1—0
5th Round v Liverpool (home)	0—0
Replay (away) (Lochhead)	1—0
6th Round v Mansfield (away) (Fern)	1—0
Semi-Final v WBA (at Hillsborough) (Clarke)	1—0
Goals —For 7: Against 2	

MANCHESTER CITY

3rd Round v Luton (home) (Lee, pen)	1—0
4th Round v Newcastle (away)	0—0
Replay (home) (Young, Owen)	2—0
5th Round v Blackburn (away) (Lee 2, Coleman 2)	4—1
6th Round v Tottenham (home) (Lee)	1—0
Semi-Final v Everton (at Villa Park) (Booth)	1—0
Goals —For 9; Against 1	

Date 26 April 1969
Place Wembley
Score MANCHESTER CITY 1
LEICESTER CITY 0
Teams MANCHESTER CITY Dowd, Book, Pardoe, Doyle, Booth, Oakes, Summerbee, Bell, Lee, Young, Coleman. Sub. Connor.
LEICESTER CITY Shilton, Rodrigues, Nish, Roberts, Woollett, Cross, Fern, Gibson, Lochhead, Clarke, Glover. Sub. Manley
Team Colours MANCHESTER CITY Red and black shirts, black shorts;
LEICESTER CITY Blue shirts, white shorts
Official Referee George McCabe (Sheffield)
Goal Scorer Young 24
Managers MANCHESTER CITY Joe Mercer; LEICESTER CITY Frank O'Farrell
Attendance 100 000
Gate Receipts £128 238
Copy News of the World 27 April 1969; Manchester Evening News 28 April 1969

What a heavy hangover

LEICESTER players wined and dined and danced with their wives at a plush London hotel last night.

This morning they awake from their Cup celebrations with a League hangover—the sobering thought of relegation.

Leicester need seven points from five games to avoid relegation—and three of those fixtures, Ipswich (away), Everton (home) and Manchester United (away), are full of hazards.

Ipswich would delight in pushing Leicester down. Their pride was hurt when Frank O'Farrell declined to become their manager.

Everton players could need a couple of points for a final third spot and bigger bonuses.

And Leicester will find it tough in their last game with Manchester United. Riva's-in-distress Coventry are managed by Noel Cantwell, a former Old Trafford favourite.

Clarke's big secret

THE best-kept secret of the Final was that Leicester's **ALLAN CLARKE**—voted Football Monthly's Player of the match—went into action with an injury sustained

in training on Wednesday.

"I strained a leg muscle and wasn't able to kick a ball for a couple of days," said Allan. "We decided to keep it quiet, but fortunately it didn't affect me until I tired in the closing 20 minutes.

THE SUNDAY TIMES, 12 APRIL 1970

'A GREAT DAY IN THE ENGLISH WAY OF LIFE'

Chelsea (1) 2   Leeds United (1) 2

Houseman, Hutchinson   Charlton, Jones

After extra time—score 90 mins. 2-2.   Att. 100,000.   Rec. £128,000.

(Replay at Old Trafford, April 29)

Brian Glanville

WHETHER or not, to use the words of Chelsea's manager, David Sexton, this Final was "a great day in the English way of life," it was certainly vibrantly exciting; and as certainly unique. After the thousand natural shocks of an extraordinary game, Chelsea and Leeds became the first two teams to fail to achieve a result since the final first came to Wembley, in 1923. They will meet again at Old Trafford on Wednesday, April 29.

The surprise of the game, played on a thickly sanded pitch which must, in time, have made the players feel like travellers lost in the Sahara, was that it should be so pre-eminently a forwards' affair. The era, as we all know, is a stonily defensive one, but yesterday, defenders floundered and blundered and continually fell from grace, redeeming their mistakes (though not all of them) at the last gasp.

Leeds' defence, the rock on which their success was initially built, was sorely and frequently embarrassed by a Chelsea attack which would doubtless have worried them still more had young Hudson been there, with his energy, his thoughtful passes and his ability to beat his man.

As for Leeds, they found out early in the match that Gray, the absolute master of Webb, could cut vast swathes on Chelsea's right flank. Bremner, however, after a splendid beginning, in which he twisted and turned on the ball with insolent aplomb, using it beautifully, faded notably after half an hour, so that the midfield no longer belonged to his team; though Giles was inventive to the end. A pity he should spoil his performance, early in extra time, with a nasty foul on Hollins. A better and stronger referee than Mr Jennings would surely have dealt with him severely.

For Chelsea, Houseman was no Hudson, but he scored an important if fortuitous goal, very nearly made another, and was

always capable of creating dangerous situations. His team's threat was always sporadic rather than consistent, with Hutchinson more incisive than Osgood. His goal was a proper reward, while Clarke for Leeds, emphasised the value of a player who does good by stealth, and can never be left unattended. He struck the woodwork of the Chelsea goal with frustrating consistency.

Cooke, one felt, with his control and speed, might have had almost as much sport with the statuesque Madeley as Gray had with Webb; but he never established dominance over him.

As for the two goalkeepers, it would perhaps be kindest to say that they have both had better games, even if Bonetti may have a valid case over the scoring of Leeds's first goal.

The first indication that Gray could pass Webb as he pleased came after 11 minutes. Hurdling the right back with no great difficulty, the winger set up a cross for Giles, which Bonetti clutched with difficulty from the head of the jumping Lorimer.

Leeds, after Chelsea's lively beginning, were coming more forcefully into the game, and Bonetti's next save was a more difficult one, a soaring tipover from Lorimer's fine shot, after Cooke had slackly lost the ball to Madeley. Chelsea retorted at once with a lively movement up the left, Hollins finding Houseman, whose calm cross was swept from the thundering feet of Baldwin by Madeley's desperate sliding tackle.

After 21 minutes, however, it was Leeds who went ahead with a rather banal goal. Dempsey gave away a corner on the right, that Gray took; an in-swinger which seemed destined for Bonetti's hands. The goalkeeper, however, lost it in the heavy traffic as he came out, Charlton got his head to it, and it trickled over the line. McCreadie's foot kicked desperately over the top of it like a lead footballer on a seaside machine; perhaps he was protesting too much. It was a moment of crystalised horror for Chelsea, of dawning joy for Leeds.

Had Hollins's long, accurate cross come to the head of Hutchinson or Osgood, rather than Houseman, Chelsea might have equalised, but the inside-right put it unemphatically wide. Gray proceeded to rub in his superiority over Webb by beating him first on the outside, then the inside, before shooting wastefully over the bar.

Six minutes from half-time, a Chelsea team, which appeared to be faltering slightly, returned to life with a splendid move which almost brought and would have deserved a goal. Hollins and Hutchinson worked the ball cleverly up the left with a smooth exchange of passes. Hollins crossed, Osgood beat the defence to the ball, and his shot was flying into goal as Charlton lunged in to kick it for a corner.

Two minutes later, such are the perversities of football, Chelsea were level with a gift of a goal. McCreadie lobbed into the middle,

Hutchinson headed the ball on, Houseman controlled it and shot with his left foot. There seemed to be little to it—a straightforward cross shot which Sprake could pick up in his own time. But the malign spirit which has afflicted so many a Wembley goalkeeper settled on Sprake's shoulder as he mistimed his dive for the ball, which spun through his arms and in, by the far post.

There was vastly more venom behind the left-footed drive which Gray released after once more beating Webb but Bonetti dramatically turned it over the bar. So half-time came with the score even at one unsatisfactory goal each and a displeasing brawl between Hunter and Hutchinson raising questions about the character of the second half.

This was still very young when Madeley, showing great composure gave Gray the chance for still another shot, which Bonetti was obliged to knock down.

But Leeds had quite lost their early command in midfield, and Chelsea's attack was becoming an increasing problem to their heavy men. A move cleverly initiated on the left by Baldwin and Hollins suddenly grew teeth thanks to Houseman's perception and control. Hutchinson, on the right of goal, forced his way past his man, and Sprake could only block his drive. Osgood shot again, and this time, Hunter kicked shrewdly off the line.

Back came Leeds at once, Giles finding Lorimer, whose neat pass should have meant a goal for Jones; but the centre-forward shot straight at Bonetti from point-blank range. Next, the busy Jones crossed from the right, the ball cleared Harris, and Clarke, the man he dogged throughout the game, got in a header which Bonetti saved.

With a quarter of an hour left, Leeds' increasingly uncertain defence ignored Houseman's in-swinging cross from the right, and Sprake fell on the ball only in the nick of time; the kind of incident which might almost sum

up this curious game. Leeds retaliated when Giles, picking up a weak header, served Gray, whose shot flew over Bonetti's desperate hands and struck the bar.

There were six minutes left when Chelsea's citadel fell. Clarke flung himself at a low cross by Giles, for a daring header. It beat Harris, rebounded from the inside of the post, but this time, Chelsea were not to escape. Jones, retrieving the ball, drove his left-footed ground shot into the left hand corner.

But Chelsea were still not beaten. Two minutes more, and Harris had touched a free kick on the left to the inextinguishable Hollins. The right-half curled in one of his familiar right footed crosses, and Hutchinson plunged boldly to head just wide of Sprake, into the near corner of goal.

So there was extra time, with Chelsea bringing Hinton on, in place of Harris. With five minutes of it gone, Dempsey wheeled himself up like some giant cannon, for a shot which Sprake tipped over. Leeds surged to the other end, and Clarke found Gray, whose cross Giles volleyed superbly, only for Webb to hook the ball over the top. Just on the quarter hour, Leeds struck wood yet a third time when Clarke, receiving from Lorimer, volleyed beautifully against the bar.

There were two more dramatic incidents to come. Madeley, casually beating his man early in the second period, crossed to Jones, but Bonetti took the header. Then Lorimer beat McCreadie on the left, and Bonetti kept the shot out with his legs.

So the teams must try again. Poor, put upon Leeds.

Chelsea: Bonetti; Webb, McCreadie; Hollins, Dempsey, Harris (sub. Hinton); Baldwin, Houseman, Osgood, Hutchinson, Cooke.

Leeds United: Sprake; Madeley, Cooper; Bremner, Charlton, Hunter; Lorimer, Clark, Jones, Giles, Gray.

Referee: E. Jennings (Stourbridge).

A battle at goalmouth. Allan Clarke and Jackie Charlton of Leeds go up in the air after a ball with Bonetti of Chelsea

The ball enters the net under Sprake's body for Chelsea's first goal from Houseman (second left)

Stop-start Final

THE pattern set by two hours at Wembley was re-established in the first minutes of this FA Cup Final replay with Leeds pounding through on attack and Chelsea living breathlessly from escape to escape at Old Trafford.

Webb, who had seen too much of Gray in the first match, was relieved to be shifted into the centre. But Gray came booming through the middle unexpectedly and Webb renewed their acquaintance with the first great lunging foul of the night.

Hutchinson, boring in from the right, swung Chelsea's first shot wide of goal. Then Osgood brilliantly beat Bremner and Hunter on the edge of the penalty area to make room for their second. This, too, was wide.

Laid out

Players from both sides were cut down by awful tackles and referee Jennings, seeking peace in his final important match, was content to wa the odd reproving finger.

Leeds were storming ahead between the stoppages and Jones moved on to meet a cross from the quick and

Chelsea...........2

Leeds 1

agile Gray to scrape the outside of a post with a shot.

Then Bonetti was lured from his goal and beaten to the ball by Lorimer on the right of the area. It took the insight of McCreadie to get back on the line and clear a certain goal.

The match was halted for nearly three minutes when Bonetti was laid out by a late and pointless charge from Jones. The incident brought a mass protest from the Chelsea team and an angry mass attack when the game was restarted.

This reaction can be said to have cost Chelsea a goal. For they were all up pushing desperately when Leeds played their way coolly out of trouble to where Clarke picked up the running on the halfway line.

He beat three men before sending Jones on a long run at the Chelsea goal. And, despite having to squeeze between Dempsey and McCreadie, Jones' persistence and strength earned him the room to shoot a brilliant goal.

Cooke and Clarke were involved in a brisk kicking match soon after the restart and, like all the other earlier nastiness, it went unpunished.

But, finally, there came an incident which could not be ignored. Charlton and Osgood

were involved in a scramble near the touchline and the floored Charlton got up and ran three paces before knocking Osgood flat.

This time Mr Jennings did have a long chat with the two concerned.

Jennings finally decided on sterner action in the 65th minute. Osgood and Bremner had tangled and when Bremner appeared to be hacking at the fallen Chelsea man the referee thought it worth only another cool glance. So Hutchinson rushed up impetuously to knock Bremner flat and was booked.

Leeds' grip on the game had seemed unshakable when Chelsea again displayed their capacity to save themselves with an equaliser 12 minutes from time.

Cooke made the goal. From an inside right position halfway to the line, he produced a magnificent pass over the Leeds defence. And Osgood, sprinting free at last, dived to head a magnificent goal.

Bremner was constantly in trouble in the last few minutes. First he was kicked unconscious by a wild and dangerous clearance from Baldwin.

Then he appeared to have been booked after a skirmish with Hutchinson and, finally, he was brought crashing to the ground as he charged in on goal and lay screaming his protest at the refusal of a penalty.

Just before the end of the first period of extra time came the seventh goal of this saga—and for the first time Chelsea were ahead.

A long throw from Hutchinson on the left brought the tall Chelsea defenders up in support. Centre half Dempsey got to the ball to back-head it under the bar and it was there the lunging Webb forced the ball home.

The last 15 minutes of this incredible final were almost unreal. With Hinton on to reinforce Chelsea's defence almost the entire period was spent with Leeds pounding away in and around the Chelsea area.

Chelsea. — Bonetti; Harris, McCreadie, Hollins, Dempsey, Webb, Baldwin, Cooke, Osgood, Hutchinson, Houseman. Sub.: Hinton.

Leeds. — Harvey; Madeley, Cooper, Bremner, Charlton, Hunter, Lorimer, Clarke, Jones, Giles, Gray. Sub.: Bates.

BRIAN JAMES

THANKS, CHIPPER

PETER OSGOOD, scorer of the second-half goal which took the replay to extra time: We often practise the move from which I scored. Charlie Cooke chips in this beautiful pass and I run in on the blind side to head it in. Whoosh.

I came off just before the end of extra time because I was feeling a calf injury I got against Liverpool on Saturday. It also let on our substitute, Mr Unflappable Marvin Hinton.

JOHN DEMPSEY: We wanted to win. We're happy that we did, but we feel sorry

for Leeds. I hope they can soon accept that there is another season starting next August.

RON HARRIS: We play better coming from behind. We deserved it on the run of the game although we didn't play well in the first half.

PETER BONETTI, who had a badly swollen left knee after his first-half clash with Jones: I think, but for the injury, I would have got the Leeds goal. It was not long after the clash and I just could not spring to it.

Date 11 April 1970

Place Wembley

Score CHELSEA 2 LEEDS UNITED 2

Teams CHELSEA Bonetti, Webb, McCreadie, Hollins, Dempsey, Harris (Hinton), Baldwin, Houseman, Osgood, Hutchinson, Cooke.
LEEDS UNITED Sprake, Madeley, Cooper, Bremner, Charlton, Hunter, Lorimer, Clarke, Jones, Giles, Gray

Team Colours CHELSEA All blue; LEEDS UNITED All white

Official Referee E. Jennings (Stourbridge)

Goal Scorers CHELSEA Houseman 41, Hutchinson 86; LEEDS UNITED Charlton 21, Jones 84

Managers CHELSEA Dave Sexton; LEEDS UNITED Don Revie

Attendance 100 000

Gate Receipts £128 272

Copy *The Sunday Times* 12 April 1970

Replay

Date 29 April 1970

Place Old Trafford, Manchester

Score CHELSEA 2 LEEDS UNITED 1 (after extra time)

Teams CHELSEA Bonetti, Harris, McCreadie, Hollins, Dempsey, Webb, Baldwin, Cooke, Osgood (Hinton), Hutchinson, Houseman. LEEDS UNITED Harvey *for* Sprake

Team Colours CHELSEA All blue; LEEDS UNITED All white

Official Referee Unchanged

Goal Scorers CHELSEA Osgood 78, Webb 104; LEEDS UNITED Jones 35

Managers UNCHANGED

Attendance 62 078

Gate Receipts £88 495

Copy *Daily Mail* 30 April 1970

DOUBLE UP!

ARMSTRONG GEORGE GRAHAM KELLY KENNEDY McLINTOCK McNAB RADFORD RICE ROBERTS SAMMELS SIMPSON STOREY WILSON

Charlie's king of London

ARSENAL 2,   LIVERPOOL 1
After extra time: 90-min. score 0-0

HE'S BEEN called conceited, peevish and arrogant. But Charlie George, a cockney boy of 20, won the Cup, clinched the double and launched North London last night on the biggest booze-up since the Coronation.

An extra-time pass by Radford just outside the penalty area set up string-haired George for his historic shot.

Liverpool's defenders, their stockings down on aching legs, their minds on a Tuesday replay at Sheffield, watched him wearily.

Maybe they forgot that George could strike a deadlier, faster, straighter ball than anyone in this deadlocked slog.

Or maybe they remembered, yet could do nothing about it.

For George's right foot became a rocket launcher, streaking the ball into the net. A deflection off Lloyd made it impossible for Clemence to anticipate.

MIKE LANGLEY REPORTS

Six days

So all in six days Arsenal have cleared the shelf—League championship, F.A. Youth Cup, Footballer of the Year for skipper Frank McLintock, and now the F.A. Cup.

And this is the side that finished last season in the wrong half of the First Division and were heaved out of the Cup in the third round by Blackpool.

It's a side managed by a physiotherapist whose footballing career was ended by injury before he could play even one League game.

A side with men who feared they were doomed never to be first up the steps at Wembley. Six of them had lost there twice, McLintock had been defeated there four times.

And when Heighway scored in the second minute that jinx fell on Arsenal like a sack of wet cement. Heads hung, bodies sagged.

Yet from the memories of a nearly invincible League season they dredged up the spirit to hurl themselves forward once more.

Forward towards a goal defended not only by the apparently impregnable Smith, Lloyd and Clemence but the banner-flaunting choirs of the Kop singing with heartless derision: "Poor old Arsenal, ain't it a bleeding shame."

No song

For Heighway, the Kop sing: "On him we look with great elation"—but they didn't sing it this time.

Heighway had been a touchline spectator, draped on the turf by a deplorably late tackle from Storey in the opening seconds and ever after given only a work house ration of the ball.

Then suddenly Heighway struck. A headed clearance by Lloyd, a pass by Thompson was the sequence he crowned with a swift, deceptive shot from a sharp angle.

After 90 minutes of deadlock, this seemed surely the goal to win the Cup.

But Arsenal, even though they couldn't recapture the thundering aggression that won the title at Tottenham last Monday, hadn't completely lost the confidence that made victory possible.

Don Howe, their assistant manager, slung young George up among the front-line troops. "He was wilting," said Howe, "but we thought he might just snatch a goal."

Graham was pulled back again into midfield to let George free but it was Graham, aided by an instant of unusual confusion in the Liverpool defence, who equalised.

An overhead kick by Radford bounced into the box and was forced goalwards by Kelly. Hughes and Smith missed it, Graham slid it in.

Swagger

A messy goal, not in keeping with the swaggering skill that made Graham an unquestioned winner of the Press-box "Man of the Match" vote.

But Arsenal at that stage weren't worried about the artistic value — if indeed they ever had been.

They came to win. Liverpool came not to lose. The result was a spectacle not unlike a six-day cycle race.

Many Wembley observers groaned that it was the worst final since the war, although in a text-book way it was always interesting.

For me, the historic value saved it from being a flop — Arsenal in search of the double, Liverpool wanting to be Cup-holders as well as the first team to conquer the new champions.

Liverpool's trouble was that they couldn't rewrite the form book. They've been short of goal-power all season

Search

Only a most thorough search through a crowded

notebook can unearth information about Liverpool's chances—a Lindsay free kick saved at the end of the first half and a Hall header saved at the finish of normal time.

Yet for Liverpool there is the consolation that they got so far with a young, transitional team.

They were beaten, but go into the Cup winners Cup next season. Arsenal, winners of the Fairs Cup last year, will be battling for the European Cup for the first time.

No-one will recall this Arsenal side with starry-eyed affection. They're too serious, too intently professional, too defensive.

But they do win matches and next season Ajax, Inter Milan, Barcelona and Red Star will learn to tremble at their name.

STOREY OUT?

ARSENAL'S Peter Storey is doubtful for England's games against Malta and Ireland this week. His ankle injury forced him to limp off in the second-half at Wembley.

● "WE'VE done it"—Don Howe and Frank McLintock dance in their double delight.

ARSENAL

Bob Wilson 7;

Pat Rice 6,
Frank McLintock 7,
Peter Simpson 7,
Bob McNab 7;

Charlie George 6,
Peter Storey (injured) 5,
★GEORGE GRAHAM 9;

John Radford 6,
Ray Kennedy 6,
George Armstrong 7.

Sub: Eddie Kelly 6.

LIVERPOOL

Ray Clemence 6;

Chris Lawler 6,
Tommy Smith 7,
Larry Lloyd 7,
Alec Lindsay 6;

Ian Callaghan 7,
★BRIAN HALL 8,
Emlyn Hughes 7;

Alun Evans (w'drawn) 5,
John Toshack 5,
Steve Heighway 6.

Sub.: Peter Thompson 7.

Ref.: N. Burtenshaw 10.

● Both reports on this spread name George Graham as the scorer of Arsenal's first goal. In fact Graham did not touch the ball, as TV cameras behind the goal later proved. Subsequently the goal was correctly credited to Kelly.

● *CHARLIE GEORGE is flat on his back—but has just stood Wembley on its head by scoring the Arsenal winner.*

Cup Final drama: 111 taut minutes, then George clinches it

Prone portrait of a cup-winner: Charlie George, flat out after scoring the winning goal, attended by Arsenal colleagues George Armstrong and Ray Kennedy. Mournful portrait of a cup-loser: Ray Clemence, the Liverpool goalkeeper

Sorry, lads— you're bores

MAURICE

SMITH

COMMENTS

ARSENAL and Liverpool . . . Cup final of the decade, the clash of giants? The match worth £90 a black-market seat?

Not on your flippin' nelly !

If Soccer blurbs were liable under the Trades Descriptions Act, this one would surely have been referred to the Director of Public Prosecutions.

For in fact, it was the non-event of the century. One hundred and twenty minutes of football that lived for only five.

At the end of the futile scoreless 90 minutes, Sam Bartram, who kept goal for Charlton in two finals here, turned to me and said: " They always say our final against Burnley was the worst in Wembley history. "This one must surely

have beaten it hands down for boredom."

I couldn't agree more with my old buddy.

The only tag I was applying to it all as they went into extra time was: never mind the quality, feel the width.

Arsenal fans will doubtless go overboard about

their team's performance in achieving the great double.

Well, let me congratulate them. But let me say that Arsenal won this one without ever looking like worthy winners.

The better side overall, perhaps, but never great Wembley champions to match even their own teams of the past.

True, to win it they had to come from behind, as they came from behind to win the League title.

Master stroke

Liverpool seemed to have achieved a master match-winning stroke when they pulled off Evans to replace him by the veteran Thompson 22 minutes from the scheduled end.

Thompson's arrival set Arsenal panicking. Liverpool, when they went into extra time, looked as if they had the game in their grasp.

And when Thompson set up the chance for Heighway to open the scoring it looked over.

Arsenal had awakened from their dream to stern reality.

It was appropriate, that Thompson - Heighway part-

nership. For it was Thompson, already an established England international, who first recommended that Liverpool should sign Heighway when he found him playing in a match for a university side.

Arsenal's goalkeeper Wilson seemed at fault with his positioning when Heighway beat him with an oblique shot that passed between Wilson and the near post.

But that mistake was nothing like the keeper's mistake that led to Graham's equaliser.

Fumbled

Hughes, Smith and Lawler were all there within touching distance of the ball as Kelly forced it through from Radford's overhead kick. Clemence came out to pick it up, but he, too, fumbled.

The winner from Charlie George was a redeemer. For George, of the long hair and slide-rule passes, had almost disappeared from the game at the interval until he cracked that thundering long shot past Clemence.

Of all the Arsenal performers, George Graham is the one who can look back on the day with the greatest pride. But like everyone else on this blunder-ridden afternoon, he made his mistakes.

But Graham, dour Scot that he is, never let one mistake stop him trying again. It was Graham's persistence that finally broke Liverpool's midfield grip, established for so long by bright young science graduate Hall.

So to sum it up: Congratulations, Arsenal. You were the better side—but that doesn't say much . . .

Date 8 May 1971

Place Wembley

Score ARSENAL 2 LIVERPOOL 1 (after extra time)

Teams ARSENAL Wilson, Rice, McNab, Storey (Kelly), McLintock, Simpson, Armstrong, Graham, Radford, Kennedy, George. LIVERPOOL Clemence, Lawler, Lindsay, Smith, Lloyd, Hughes, Callaghan, Evans (Thompson), Heighway, Toshack, Hall

Team Colours ARSENAL Yellow shirts, blue shorts; LIVERPOOL All red

Official Referee N. Burtenshaw (Great Yarmouth)

Goal Scorers ARSENAL Kelly 101, George111; LIVERPOOL Heighway 92

Managers ARSENAL Bertie Mee; LIVERPOOL Bill Shankly

Attendance 100000

Gate Receipts £187681

Guests of Honour H.R.H. Duke and Duchess of Kent

Copy *The People* 9 May 1971; *The Sunday Times* 9 May 1971

● *GEORGE GRAHAM stabs in Arsenal's equaliser and suddenly the threat of defeat starts to turn into the promise of success.*

'BARNETT NEVER HAD A CHANCE'

SEE that horror on goalkeeper Geoff Barnett's face. He's diving but he's too late. As Arsenal skipper Frank McLintock watches, Allan Clarke's header flies in for the goal that takes the Cup to Leeds for the first time.

Clarke, voted Wembley's man of the match, said: "The goalkeeper never had a chance. I picked my place and it was well out of his reach."

DOUBLE UP TOMORROW

But Mick will be missing....

AGONY FOR WEMBLEY HERO

MICK JONES, who dislocated his left elbow challenging Arsenal goalkeeper Geoff Barnett for a last-minute goal that Leeds didn't need, is out of tomorrow night's match at Wolverhampton—the match in which just a draw will give Leeds the double.

Team-mates Allan Clarke, man-of-the-match in this centenary final, and Johnny Giles will be pumped full of pain-killers tomorrow. They were yesterday before winning the Cup for Leeds with performances that leave Arsenal no arguments.

Said manager Don Revie: "Clarke will play even if he can only just walk."

And those are no idle words from Revie who said in the dressing-room: "I've waited and sweated years for this day."

The loss of Jones, who'll probably be replaced by young Joe Jordan, makes the presence of Clarke vital.

Their combination — a Jones cross and Clarke's stooping header swerving past Barnett's left-hand in the second half—lifted the Cup and what had seemed almost a curse on Leeds, the team destined always to be bridesmaids.

'Brilliant'

But Revie singled out Hunter, not Clarke. . . . "Every coach in the country will tell you he's brilliant. I think he's the best player who ever lived."

And, regrettably, it was the sort of match requiring the stern single-mindedness and unnerving tackling of players like Hunter. The chopping started in the first minute and four were booked — McNab, Hunter, Bremner and George in that order.

Ball, who crunched rival redhead Bremner into the damp turf, should feel thankful for not making history as the first sending-off case in a Wembley final. Referee David Smith didn't even book him. Perhaps by then, his pencil was worn to a stub.

A tyre-slashing attack on the Leeds bus, mass fights broken up by mounted police and obscene chanting from Arsenal fans did not build up an edifying spectacle for the Duke of Edinburgh, or the Duke and Duchess of Kent.

By MIKE LANGLEY

The first-half football was similarly unsporting. Violence was never far below the surface, as Arsenal manager Bertie Mee subconsciously admitted by likening the teams to boxers and saying : "We didn't allow each other to play. Our styles don't mix. It was a disappointing game."

If Arsenal's banquet last night was shrouded in gloom they can look back for the reason to an attack immediately before Leeds scored.

Giles had lost the ball, George and Radford were running through an under-manned defence, but George, instead of pressing forward, turned and stopped. Instantly, the way to goal was flooded by white shirts.

Against Leeds no-one gets two opportunities. They cleared, swept on to score and that was the death of Arsenal, even though George's right-footed hook smacked the bar a little later.

With this goal, a load was lifted from Leeds. They began to flow in welcome contrast to the tight, spoiling fragmented football of the first half.

Joyful

Through the last 10 minutes, Gray, Lorimer, Jones and Clarke surged joyfully towards a tunnel-end that was a vivid and audible panorama of scarves, banners and song.

At the other end, the few Arsenal flags still feebly waving looked like signals of distress.

At the finish Bremner, Charlton, Hunter and Giles, the old soldiers who've battled through two previous F.A. Cup finals without success, looked emotionally towards the royal box. Charlton hugged Revie, the others danced and cavorted in the circle.

For a time no one was aware of the crumpled Jones, writhing 50 yards away.

When everyone, Arsenal and Leeds both, had been up the steps, Jones lurched off a stretcher so heavily swathed in crepe bandage that he looked like Tutankhamun.

Painful

He tottered at the foot of the steps, weighed up the painful ascent and then, guided and assisted by Hunter, climbed to where the Duke of Edinburgh waited with his medal.

On the way he stopped to kiss a girl fan. On the way down, everyone left in Wembley gave him a cheer.

Later Jones explained: "It was a complete accident. I put out my hand to break my fall, but it gave way under me."

Arsenal fans might like to plead: "Accidental defeat"—but it wasn't so. Their strikers, Radford and George, hardly disturbed the Leeds centre backs.

George let himself drift out of the action, and Radford was replaced near the end by Kennedy although I felt these two should have started the game together.

Geoff Barnett	6
Pat Rice	7
Frank McLintock	7
PETER SIMPSON	8
Bob McNab	6
Alan Ball	6
Peter Storey	5
George Graham	6
John Radford (withdrawn)	5
Charlie George	5
George Armstrong	7
Sub.: Ray Kennedy	

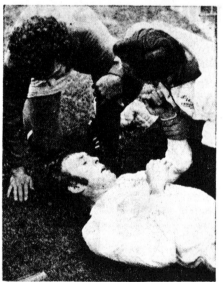

Mick Jones in agony. Arsenal's Barnett comforts him as Leeds trainer Cocker tests the injury.

David Harvey	7
Paul Reaney	8
Jackie Charlton	8
Norman Hunter	8
Paul Madeley	8
Billy Bremner	8
Johnny Giles	7
Eddie Gray	7
Peter Lorimer	7
Mick Jones	7
ALLAN CLARKE	9
Referee: David Smith (Gloucester)	8

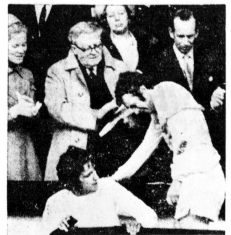

Jones at the end. Cheered by the Duke of Kent and assisted by team-mate Hunter.

THIS WAY OUT

NO joy on Cup Final day for two past heroes—Mike Trebilcock and Alex Dawson. They were both given free transfers.

Trebilcock, who scored twice in Everton's 1966 F.A. Cup victory, was shown the door by Portsmouth.

Ex-Busby Babe Dawson is no longer wanted even by Southern League side Corby Town.

You're worth it, Don

NOW I'm keeping my fingers crossed for Leeds. Manager Don Revie must be, too. For they need just one point from their last League game at Wolverhampton tomorrow to take over the complete double from Arsenal.

I'm no Yorkshireman but I'm wishing them luck all the way.

Leeds will be without their attack spearhead, the go-getting Mick Jones, one of yesterday's heroes.

But I'm still saying they can and will do it.

They were as impressive as any Cup-winning side since the Tottenham of Blanchflower's heyday.

Forget the fouls—most of them committed through over-enthusiasm.

Forget—though the F.A. won't — that four players were booked.

Ironically, the saddest man in this centenary Final must be the man who won last year's for Arsenal: that erratic wonder-boy Charlie George, no less.

CHECKED

There he was slipping past Bremner for once in

Maurice Smith comments

a while with two other Arsenal forwards close. All Leeds had left in defence were Reaney, Madeley and Harvey.

They were caught outnumbered, yet poor George, instead of moving forward to exploit the opening, inexplicably decided to back-pedal.

And it was only a minute later that Clarke popped up

at the other end to score the winning goal on a day when Arsenal's forwards were clearly check-mated.

Their one big moment came when George hit the bar with a tremendous first-time effort after a Ball free-kick.

But don't take that as evidence that Arsenal deserved to share the honours. Leeds twice did

the same thing.

Arsenal deserve every credit for fighting until they dropped to try to keep the trophy.

CLASSIC

When the inquest is held at Highbury the forwards will no doubt earn censure.

They had warned me that their intention was to prey on "Old Jackie" in the expectation that he would not last the pace. What a hope !

If those Arsenal forwards plead that they lacked support from behind then it is some mitigation. They did.

Graham, Ball and Storey were kept far too busy combating the wiles of such as Bremner and Giles to be able to bother much about the needs of the men in front of them.

Even McLintock and McNab were tiring for the last 15 minutes.

Yet two Arsenal men never cracked. One was the relatively inexperienced Barnett. One of his saves from Gray was a classic. He flung himself through the air to tip away a shot at the last moment.

Yet it was Simpson, tall, strong, always defiant, who was the keystone of the Arsenal defence.

● Leeds United in the late 1960s and early 1970s were the most powerful side in England, and with a little more luck might have collected an unprecedented amount of honours. From the mid-1960s on, however, it happened that for every trophy they won, they finished runners-up on another two or three occasions.

Always in with a chance of the "double", they had actually finished runners-up in both league and Cup in 1969-70. Two years later, in 1971-72, they had their best-ever opportunity, for after winning the Cup the championship appeared at their mercy, as *The People* headline "Double up Tomorrow" indicates.

On the Monday, in an extraordinary evening of football, Leeds lost at Wolverhampton 2–1, when a draw would have won the title. The result should have left Liverpool champions, but they could only draw 0–0 at Highbury, and Derby County, already on tour, were champions.

Next season Leeds lost the European Cup-winners Cup final.

Frank McLintock knows more than anyone the despair of a losing final. He's been to Wembley six times – and lost five.

Super Celtic lay Jock's jinx

CELTIC didn't only win their 22nd Scottish Cup final — and the Cup and League double—in a cold, clinical, sometimes cruel annihilation of Hibs at Hampden.

They also claim, and not for the first time, the title of the brightest and best Soccer entertainers in Britain.

They knocked six goals past former Birmingham 'keeper Jim Herriot—the biggest victory since 1888—to give them ample compensation for their dramatic penalty kick exit from the European Cup last month.

But for personal triumph there was nothing to excel the performance of striker Dixie Deans, who had a brilliant hat-trick — after missing the vital penalty that allowed Inter-Milan to slip through to the European Cup final.

His three great goals yesterday made amends for that, and the way Jock Stein hugged him at the end suggested that the Celtic boss agreed.

And it seems as if Jock's Jinx is laid. With final defeats in 1966, 1968 and 1970, it looked as if Celtic and Stein were fated on

CELTIC......6	HIBERNIAN......1
McNEILL 2	GORDON 12
DEANS 24, 55, 78	
MACARI 86, 89	Att.: 106,102

By JOHN BLAIR

the even years.

But 1972 now belongs to them—without any argument.

But Stein refused to name any of his heroes. He said: "I was absolutely delighted with every man in the team."

Celtic opened the massacre in two minutes when skipper McNeill whipped home a Callaghan free-kick. Gordon got one back for Hibs, but before half-time Deans put them ahead with a superb header.

Then, Deans made it 3-1 with a great individual effort, and 15 minutes from the end he added another. To add to the slaughter, Macari added two more before the final whistle.

Hibs never appeared capable of withstanding the tremendous pressure.

Apart from Deans, McNeil, Murdoch and Callaghan were in brilliant form, and captured the midfield from their struggling opponents.

Hibs had no excuses. They met Celtic on a day when no team in Britain would have stood up to them—Leeds included.

That's my opinion, and that of every man at Hampden yesterday. But please, please, please—let's get it sorted out with a Match of the Champions between Leeds and Celtic before next season starts.

CELTIC: Williams 6—Craig 6, Connolly 7, McNeill 7, Brogan 6—Dalglish 6, Murdoch 7, Callaghan 7—Johnstone 8, Macari 6, *DEANS 9.

HIBS.: Herriot 6—Brownlie 6, Blackley 7, Black 6, Schadler 6—Hazel 6, *STANTON 8, Edwards 6 —O'Rourke 6, Gordon 6, Duncan 7 (inj.). Sub.: Auld 6.

Ref.: A. Mackenzie (Larbert) 7.

Date 6 May 1972
Place Wembley
Score LEEDS UNITED 1 ARSENAL 0
Teams LEEDS UNITED Harvey, Reaney, Madeley, Bremner, Charlton, Hunter, Lorimer, Clarke, Jones, Giles, Gray. Sub: Bates. ARSENAL Barnett, Rice, McNab, Storey, McLintock, Simpson, Armstrong, Ball, George, Radford (Kennedy), Graham
Team Colours LEEDS UNITED All white; ARSENAL Red shirts with white

sleeves, white shorts
Official Referee D. Smith (Gloucester)
Goal Scorer Clarke 53
Managers LEEDS UNITED Don Revie; ARSENAL Bertie Mee
Attendance 100000
Gate Receipts £191917
Guests of Honour H.M. The Queen, H.R.H. The Duke of Edinburgh, The Duke and Duchess of Kent
Copy *The People* 7 May 1972

'WE WANT STOKOE, WE WANT STOKOE'

THE SUNDAY EXPRESS London May 6 1973

Leeds...........(0) 0 Sunderland...........(1) 1
(Porterfield, 31 min. 31 sec.)

(at Wembley. Attendance : 100,000. Receipts : £233,800.)

IT WAS not so much the Cup Final fall of the century as a shattering CRASH which could be heard throughout the whole world of football. Soccer has never known—or seen—anything like it.

It was the Sunderland miracle . . . the Roker explosion that destroyed Leeds, the overwhelming favourites, in the biggest Wembley upset of all time.

ALAN HOBY reports

The golden goal that sent Don Revie's white - faced men reeling to defeat, their faces choked with shock and disbelief, was scored—amid an hysterical hurricane of sound from the Second Division's side's supporters — in the 31st minute.

From Billy Hughes's corner out on the left the ball arched into the Leeds box. Man-of-the-match Dave Watson, a centre half extraordinary, challenged, but the ball dropped, bounced, and Ian Porterfield, normally a left-footed player, pivoted perfectly and hit a devastating right-foot volley.

The next few moments were unbelievable. A frenzied mass of red and white scarves and wildly waving hands splashed the terraces behind the Leeds goal in a blaze of colour and excitement.

Sunderland, with not a single full international in their line-up . . . Sunderland, the battling underdogs from the North-East were asked against a side of 10 international stars with another cap Welshman Terry Yorath on the substitute's bench.

And there they stayed—the better team — by sheer guts mingled with skill and a positively unnerving coolness for a side which, with one exception—defender Ritchie Pitt —had never before played at Wembley.

Triumph

It was a triumph for a written-off team who played with a refreshing innocence—a team who refused to be flurried by some shabby Leeds acts particularly in the first half.

And when referee Ken Burns, of Stourbridge, blew up for "time" at the climax of this astonishing game, Wembley went crazy.

The heroic Vic Halom, whose legs must have felt—like the rest of his team-mates—as if they had turned to lead with so much running, had tears streaming down his face as he embraced Micky Horswill.

They were like men who could not quite believe the miracle had happened. But as the ear-vibrating roar from the Sunderland thousands rang around this famous old stadium they knew that the "impossible dream" had come true.

As Sunderland's small Scottish skipper, Bobby Kerr, led his band of heroes up the steps to receive the Cup from the Duchess of Kent, he almost staggered from exhaustion.

"We want Stokoe . . . We want Stokoe," howled the Sunderland fans—all those amazing folk in their funny red and white hats, red and white bow ties, red and white jackets, and even red and white moustaches !

Then Bob Stokoe, the Messiah of Roker Park, holsting up his little skipper as if he were his own son.

Stokoe finally ran off with his bruised but ecstatic players.

But Leeds shattered and stunned, had slouched off miserably after their manager, Don Revie, had congratulated the winners.

For holders Leeds, despite enjoying large slices of play, did not deserve to win.

I had expected them to take the field and produce super football. But instead of silence their abrasive army of critics, including Wolves manager Bill McGarry, England captain Bobby Moore, and Stokoe himself—who accused them of over-professionalism—Leeds never produced the right answers.

They could not rid themselves of old bad habits. They marred their magnificent record by leaving their sportsmanship in the dressing-room and remembering it only at the bitter end.

Fouled

I am not suggesting that Sunderland who last won the Cup back in 1937 when they beat Preston 3—1, were all little angels with halos Pitt, who did a magnificent job at the heart of the Sunderland defence, fouled Allan Clarke three times in the first 10 minutes but they were not serious offences.

But always I come back to Watson, who on this form will soon be challenging Derby's Roy McFarland for an England place.

Three times in the first half Watson mastered the off-form Clarke as the England striker was about to shoot. One fabulous through pass from Paul Madeley deserved a better fate. But Watson, scything across the wet turf whipped the ball away from Clarke's feet to save a certain goal.

Then Clarke dragged down Billy Hughes, who was already limping, and was rightly booked. Norman Hunter, Leeds' superb defender, bowled over the tenacious Dennis Tueart. And the frustrated Bremner slung a punch at Porterfield.

True their top two, Giles and Hunter, surged forward in the second half and full-back Trevor Cherry was their best attacker. True they could have had a penalty when Bremner was brought down in the box but, ironically, they did not get one . . .

The Montgomery second-half double-save was sheer India-rubber magic. It defied every law of human anatomy. It equalled Gordon Banks's fabulous save from Pele in Mexico.

First, Monty dived to his right to clear Cherry's header. Then, in a pure reflex reaction he twisted like a cat to his left, flung out his arms and somehow punched a close-in Lorimer drive, which looked a certain winner—up on to the underside of the bar.

Leeds appealed that the ball had crossed the line, but they were wrong. The Montgomery save, which had Bob Stokoe drooling, was worthy of a Soccer Oscar.

LEEDS. — Harvey; Reaney, Cherry, Bremner (capt.), Madeley, Hunter, Lorimer, Clarke, Jones, Giles, Gray. **Sub :** Yorath.

SUNDERLAND.— Montgomery; Malone, Guthrie, Horswill, Watson, Pitt, Kerr (capt.), Hughes, Halom, Porterfield, Tueart. **Sub :** Young.

Ref : Ken Burns (Stourbridge).

● THAT'S MY BOY! Bob Stokoe, tears in his eyes, hugs *his* 'man of the match,' Jim Montgomery.

EVEN FINER THAN 'OUR' CUP WINS!

GIVE US an S. Give us a U. Give us an N. It's the SUN that shines in Sunderland, folks, on their brightest ever day. Raise your glasses to the greatest tonic English football has had for years. The toast is Sunderland — the finest team of heroes to carry off the F.A. Cup in my experience of Wembley.

DANNY BLANCHFLOWER comments

It was the most gripping, emotional final I have been to and that includes the two in which I carried off that Cup.

The Sunderland crowd were marvellous. They brought a breath of fresh air to Wembley from the North-East, full of warmth and humour and love for the game as well as their team. Their team were magnificent. When I saw these players earlier in the season I never thought they could play like this. They were great.

They beat more than Leeds out there on the damp, lush pitch They beat the majority of critics They beat the establishment's view of success. Some of us wanted them to win in our hearts but could not accept it in our minds. Well, they warmed our hearts and scattered our minds.

Leeds looked more dangerous at the start and had four successive shots blocked as evidence of this. But gradually it became more obvious that Watson, Sunderland had the

man of the match. He was a tower of strength all through the game, particularly in the most critical moments when he was needed.

Leeds played well enough to a point but never got on top of Sunderland in that first half as most people expected. On the contrary, Sunderland had the better of things in the first half and thoroughly deserved their narrow lead at the interval.

Leeds did most of the attacking in the second half. The Sunderland lads had run themselves crazy in that terrific first half and everyone had fears that they might crack under such pressure. But they did not. Every man jack of them stood the test.

What a fine young player Horswill is. What a great game Malone had. He stuffed Eddie Gray down the throats of those Leeds players and officials who claimed that Gray would be the match-winner. In the second half Revie subbed Yorath for Gray and that was Malone's tribute.

Bobby Kerr played his captain's part well. It was a tantalising lob from him into the Leeds goalmouth which forced Harvey to give away the corner from which Sunderland eventually scored. Nobody had a better right to collect that Cup.

SAVED

Guthrie was great too and so was Pitt. And Montgomery saved the Cup for Sunderland with two remarkable instant and instinctive saves in the second half.

Hughes was exciting and a bundle of energy. Tueart was tricky and had a heart like a lion. Porterfield was constantly in that long stride of his doing great work all over the field like his name suggests.

And Halom was a 90-minute handful for the Leeds defence. He deserved a goal in the last moments of the game for a great-hearted effort when his legs were buckling with fatigue and he summoned deep reserves to hammer a shot and then a rebound that Harvey turned for a corner. But what about Leeds? Well, they were Leeds. They performed with skill as they always do. They fought as hard as they could. They finished second as they often do. And they did not win any friends with some of their behaviour.

They will get little sympathy outside of Leeds this weekend because all the world loves a winner. And how refreshing it is to have a new one. The name is Sunderland. Sunderland, you were wonderland for football.

● THE WINNER! Ian Porterfield (right) turns to hail his Cup Final goal.

Sunderland's win was possibly the biggest Cup final shock of all. Leeds United were in the top three of the First Division six years running, and were champions the year after Sunderland beat them. Every player in the team played for his country. Sunderland, on the other hand, were the first Second Division Cup winners for 42 years, and at one time were in danger of dropping into the Third Division. Jim Montgomery's save from Lorimer has become legendary, remembered better than many a great goal.

Magnificent Monty

QUOTES

as told to
TONY HARDISTY

BOB STOKOE, Sunderland manager : "Jim Montgomery won the Cup for Sunderland — and Sunderland won it for the good of the game. I said all along we would win the Cup — and win it in an entertaining fashion.

"That was what I wanted to give the Wembley fans — a match to remember. We won it on merit and, naturally, I'm the proudest man in the world.

"I have said for years that there is no better goalkeeper than Montgomery and he proved it with those second-half saves. They even took my breath away — and I am used to seeing that kind of quality from him.

"I just could not stop myself sprinting across to hug him. All the players were magnificent, as they have been throughout this Cup run, but

there were times when Monty was out of this world.

"I don't want to talk much about Leeds. They played the way they wanted it and when you look at the result it obviously suited us.

"It's all over now and Leeds will feel dead sick. But Billy Bremner came into our dressing room to congratulate us and that can't be bad."

JIM MONTGOMERY : "I'm just floating — and it's not the champagne. I wasn't in the slightest bit nervous. I don't think any of us were really.

"We had all made up our minds that we were going to win and if for any reason we couldn't, then we were going to damn well enjoy ourselves.

"Well, we did win — and we had a ball doing it !

"When I saved that one from Peter Lorimer in the second half I knew the Cup was ours. I just couldn't see Leeds getting a better chance and failing to score."

IAN PORTERFIELD : "When Billy Hughes's corner came over and Dave Watson jumped for it, it dropped near me. I turned and whacked it and it flew in.

"I knew as soon as I connected that no 'keeper would stop it. Although, come to think of it, Monty probably would have done. What a game he had."

BILLY HUGHES : "Leeds tried all they knew but they couldn't hold us. The whole of Europe will have seen the way they approached it and the way we won it. That's good enough for me."

DAVID WATSON : "I didn't foul Bremner. He was just play-acting and it didn't work."

A grim Trevor Cherry charges for a half-chance

Half-way through the great double-save. Montgomery palms out Cherry's header; Lorimer (7) closes in to crack the rebound

Date 5 May 1973
Place Wembley
Score SUNDERLAND 1 LEEDS UNITED 0
Teams SUNDERLAND Montgomery, Malone, Watson, Pitt, Guthrie, Horswill, Kerr, Porterfield, Hughes, Halom, Tueart. Sub: Young. LEEDS UNITED Harvey, Reaney, Madeley, Hunter, Cherry, Bremner, Giles, Lorimer, Gray (Yorath), Jones, Clarke
Official Referee K. Burns (Stourbridge)
Goal Scorer Porterfield 32
Managers SUNDERLAND Bob Stokoe; LEEDS UNITED Don Revie
Attendance 100000
Gate Receipts £233800
Guest of Honour H.R.H. Duke of Kent
Copy The Sunday Express 6 May 1973

Rangers power sinks Celtic

by **HARRY ANDREW**

Rangers - - - - 3
Celtic - - - - - 2

THE FIRST and surely most important thing to say about this Royal Hampden occasion is that the real winner is Scottish football.

For this was a super show to set before Princess Alexandra, a dramatic battle that did more than justice to Britain's biggest crowd of the season – 122,714.

And the second point to emphasise is that Rangers did deserve to win the Scottish Cup in this, their centenary year.

Rangers had a tremendous star in young Derek Parlane, whose 20th birthday it was. His non-stop running and superb courage destroyed Celtic.

The League champions were never really allowed to settle and their prospects were not improved when Jim Brogan had

to limp off after 14 minutes of the second half.

Celtic's first on-target shot brought the opening goal. Dave Hay hit a hard pass at Dixie Deans who flicked the ball on first time and Kenny Dalglish moved in to net.

Ten minutes were needed to produce the equaliser - Parlane coming from nowhere to score.

Crossed

An Alex MacDonald cross just 17 seconds after the interval and Rangers were in front when Alfie Conn outstripped the Celtic defence to score.

Again the equaliser came quickly. A Deans' shot was a winner until John Greig dived across to punch the ball around

the post. George Connelly netted the spot-kick.

Everything was happening now. Johnstone had the ball in the net with a wonderful piece of football, but a linesman ruled him offside.

That bit of bad luck was balanced when Macdonald got his head to a Jardine cross, beat Hunter all ends up, but saw the ball rebound from a post. In this scramble Brogan was hurt and ultimately taken off.

And so to one of the most amazing goals ever to have won a cup. Rangers had Derek Johnstone and Tom Forsyth up for a Tommy McLean free-kick. Johnstone got his head to the ball.

It hit the inside of a post, ran slowly along the line to hit the other upright, bounced back and lay on the line — until the astounded Forsyth realised glory was there for the taking.

A gentle tap took the ball the few inches that were needed and the Cup was Rangers'.

HIS WORSHIP - BILL SHANKLY

Liverpool 3, Newcastle United 0

I'VE SEEN managers cheered off, chaired off and even knighted, but Bill Shankly is the first inspiring such heights of worship that Liverpool fans flung themselves prostrate on Wembley's pitch to kiss his feet.

And only Shanks could have handled this rather embarrassing devotion with a joke. . . . "While you're down there," he cracked, "give my shoes a quick polish."

The most one-sided final since 1960 was further evidence that Shanks never misses a trick.

At 60, he's about to delight us again with the greatest side even of his career.

"I made no predictions," he reminded us afterwards. "All I said was that we were the best team in England and probably in the world. Now you have all seen it.

SWEETEST

"If the League had started at Christmas we'd have walked that as well. A new Liverpool has emerged in the past three months and next year we'll win the League and the Cup."

Such a programme is

MIKE LANGLEY REPORTS

really beyond the compass of a team that's also playing in Europe. When next season starts, the siren song of Europe will sound sweetest to the Kop.

My advice is to plonk down some money now on Liverpool sweeping on from Wembley to capture the Cup-winners Cup for the first time.

Eight years ago they failed in an extra-time final against Borussia Dortmund but they didn't have Keegan then, or Clemence, or Thompson of the match-stick legs who will surely pay for England.

Thompson is so little known that security men didn't recognise him. Because he was wearing a

swapped Newcastle shirt, they tried to order him away from Liverpool's ascent to the Royal Box for their winners' medals.

Trainer Bob Paisley, who has been at Anfield even longer than Shanks, was also brushed aside by the guards. But no-one made any mistake over identifying The Boss.

Shankly, hair-cropped to his skull and wearing a shirt nearer pink than Anfield red, stationed himself at the start of the red carpet.

As Newcastle, a dejected assortment of black-and-white stripes, straggled up the steps towards Princess Anne, Shankly intercepted each man with a handshake and word of consolation.

MOCKING

A great gesture by a master showman.

But the only perfectly honest thing to say to Newcastle was: "You're lucky it wasn't six!"

The verdict on the running at the Blaydon Races is that there ought to be a stewards inquiry.

Supermac fired only two shots, the first not until the 77th minute. Both skewed yards wide towards the mocking Liverpool terraces who derided him as "Supermouth."

Macdonald needs the ball on a platter. He didn't get it. Hibbitt, his usual butler, seemed to have awarded himself a half-day off.

WEAKNESS

Smith could have been substituted an hour before Liverpool's second goal. Clark was a constant weakness on the right flank.

Except for 20 minutes of first-half sprightliness,

THEY'RE EVEN KISSING HIS FEET

IT'S the ultimate in fan-worship. Bill Shankly has his feet kissed by supporters after the final whistle.

McDermott and Hibbitt couldn't assert their vivacity on the midfield.

And when McFaul started slapping, punching and fumbling crosses, nerves infected a defence that relied on the steady Moncur.

Cormack, unusually sluggish through the first half, began moving up in the second. And the breaches that Keegan and Heighway made before the interval were further enlarged.

Lindsay thumped in a dis-

disallowed goal from the left, and a legal one quickly followed.

PENETRATING

Keegan, although standing between two defenders, created a private ocean of time as he checked Smith's penetrating cross and volleyed through the gap.

Toshack back-headed the second for Heighway, running in from the left and turning to shoot.

Keegan crowned an afternoon of personal perfection by side-footing the third goal. Smith crossed it low from the right flank, Keegan knocked it in on the left. And that was that.

LIVERPOOL: Clemence 8 — Smith 8, Thompson 9, Hughes 8, Lindsay 9 — Hall 9, Callaghan 8, Cormack 7 — *KEEGAN 10, Toshack 8, Heighway 8.

NEWCASTLE: McFaul 6 — Clark 5, Howard 7, *MONCUR 8, Kennedy 6, Smith (w'drawn) 5, McDermott 7, Cassidy 6, Hibbitt 6 — Tudor 7, Macdonald 5. Sub.: Gibb.

Ref: G. Kew (Amersham) 9.

F.A. CUP FINAL

LIVERPOOL (0) 3, NEWCASTLE (0) 0

Keegan 57, 88
Heighway 74

Att. 100,000
Receipts £233,600

SCOTTISH CUP FINAL

CELTIC (2) 3, DUNDEE U. (0) 0

Hood 20
Murray 26
Deans 89

75,959

Supermac is Final failure

MAURICE SMITH comments

BLACK AND WHITE emblems hung like mourners' drapes. Newcastle, the side that had never lost a Wembley final, surrendered at the sixth bid with hardly a fight.

"Don't worry, it's our second home," their manager Joe Harvey had counselled me before the game.

But Wembley yesterday was far from being any Geordie's London pad. Two facts underline the whole pathetic story.

Newcastle forced a corner in the 72nd minute. It was their first and only one of the game.

SuperMac — Macdon

the striker who went out like a light—had his first shot at goal with just 12

minutes left. It was yards wide.

Mac did manage a repeat performance. His second effort—again with his cherished left foot—ended up in the crowd.

So the Cup went back to Anfield. And even if Liverpool hadn't exactly burned while Newcastle fiddled, at least they proved their

class, certainly in the last half-hour.

Frankly, I can't recall another final in which I've seen possession surrendered so weakly in a team's own half.

Newcastle, sorry to say, were almost non-runners.

Their midfielders had an afternoon they'll want to forget. Their counterparts

—Cormack, Hall and player-of-the-year Callaghan — were the dictators.

Howard, Moncur and 19-year-old Kennedy, the youngest man afield, fought to turn the match.

But all the individual honours, like the medals and the Cup itself, were earned by Liverpool's braves.

Lindsay ran boldly and was always willing to chance a shot from depth. Young Thompson handled the Macdonald-Tudor threat with assurance. They looked it all up at the back.

It wasn't anything like the classic we'd been promised. But then, there was really only one team in it.

Brian James on the man of verve who provided Wembley with its fantasy

THERE are only two sorts of medals to be carried away from Wembley, but an infinite variety of memories. Playing in an FA Cup Final leaves something with a man, a moment or two he will always remember, or about which he will never want to be reminded and yet cannot quite forget.

This is one thing about the Cup Final that does not change. Each year the rituals surrounding the occasion become more exaggeratedly tilted towards show business, more grubbily tarnished by commercial in-fighting. But the match, the play, remain inviolate.

I have yet to meet a player so steeped in ambition, so immersed in the business of capitalising on achievement that he did not want to play at Wembley and there excel. Cynicism, happily, has not yet bitten so deeply into sport. So what of yesterday's men?

Yesterday's man was Kevin Keegan. He scored two goals, and what more could we ask of a man in a Final? We might hope that he would take those goals with a nerve that made nothing of the burden of the occasion. Keegan did. We might hope that he provide, too, touches of fantasy to liven the end of a game that had mostly been about the realities. Keegan did.

I once said of Liverpool that if they were a machine then Keegan was both sparking plug and mascot on the bonnet. Those words would have been better saved for yesterday.

Newcastle's belief had begun to drain away, Liverpool's easy superiority not yet begun to show itself, when Keegan created what seemed the perfect goal for Lindsay. It was offside, a fraction.

Lesser men would have crumpled beneath the disappointment; Keegan ran away from the free-kick gesticulating for more effort, for the concentration that would create another chance. And when Smith's cross produced that chance, Keegan's touch to kill the ball left Newcastle stranded.

Keegan will never need a cutting of a photograph to recapture *that* decisive split second.

What, this apart would be taken from the game by the two men we judged in advance to be most influential, Callaghan of Liverpool and Hibbitt of Newcastle? For these are the generals and at every level they establish the winning rhythms or encourage the triumphant mood. Yet they come from different moulds, and seldom more contrasting than these two.

Callaghan came clanking to this Final with the weight of recent honours, seemingly every man's choice as Footballer of the Year. Curious this at the close of his 13th full season with Liverpool: he is that cliché figure who toils a footballer's lifetime to become an instant success.

Callaghan is about involvement, the initial obstacle over which Newcastle often stumbled, the apex of every triangle in the advance, the willing shadow hovering hopefully at the elbow of each attack. So he was all through yesterday and his memory must be a mosaic, made up of dozens of passes neatly received and cleverly dispatched. No special moments perhaps, but the cement for victory.

Hibbitt, too, is a worker but in a less apparent way. He plays in space as a sort of left luggage office where the ball may be left in safe keeping while the defence redeploys, the attack waits for direction. His greatest ability we saw in the first half-hour with aim and range in the pass. But his marvellous value is in being able to operate unseen where he cannot fail to be noticed—yards of uncluttered grass about him often, yet he lies in ambush like a guerrilla in jungle.

Wembley's plains were made for a talent like that. Hibbitt surely will have vivid recall of those moments in the first 10 minutes when he sneaked in unseen behind the right flank of Liverpool's defence to deliver passes that on luckier days might

have decided the match before it was properly begun. Yet, inevitably, he will not forget the instant in the 40th minute when, turning acrobatically to clear, he horribly wrenched his knee and lay in pain on the pitch. When he got up to trudge on to the end he must have known already that he could never be so effective again.

Rob Hughes listens to socialist Shankly express the people's happiness

IN the beginning, as grown men wept and crumbled forged tickets in their fists, a Jehovah Witness beseeched the swirling masses at the turnstile: " Repent ye unto the Lord." The answer came back from amid the red scarves: " We do, every week. His name's Shankly."

And when it was over, a supporter threw himself at the Liverpool manager's feet and began to kiss his shoes. Shankly did not ask the man to rise, but said: ' I wish I'd got a duster so you could give them a rub while you're down there."

In the dressing room Shankly admitted: " I liked that. I hope my shoes were clean for the man." Kevin Keegan, who'd scored two of the goals, said: " It's unbelievable. Shanks is the only boss in the English league whom the fans think more of than they do the players."

Outside the dressing room, shaking hands with a crippled Liverpool man in a wheelchair and ushering a couple of youngsters towards the dressing room, Shankly added: " I'm happiest not for myself, the players or the staff but the multitudes. I'm a people's man, a socialist. I'm sorry I couldn't go amongst them and speak to them. I'm happy that we have worked religiously, that we didn't cheat them and that we have something to take back to them tomorrow."

Across the corridor, Newcastle's first thoughts were also for the fans. Malcolm Macdonald, who had boasted loudest and now seemed hardest hit by defeat, sat with a towel around his midriff and stared blankly into a cup of champagne. " I'm just sorry we let them down," he said. " We never even started to play. After half time we went haywire,

Liverpool turned it on and we turned it off. It's been an experience; you can make a fool of yourself."

This was to have been the Geordies' return after the locust years. Joe Harvey, who captained the side to two successive Cup victories in the 50s, stood upright in the centre of the room. " It's not defeat that upsets me. It's the fact that we didn't do the simple things properly," he said.

" Liverpool had eight men that's played here before; makes a difference does that. I've been here before, and Wembley has no terrors for me. But for the lads it was new."

Emlyn Hughes, the Liverpool captain, admitted: " Actually, I was very disappointed. They did all that talking, came to Wembley and what did they do? Nothing." Keegan saw things differently: " In the first half they matched us for everything and played it our way. But to do that for 90 minutes you've got to be a bit special. We paced it much better."

One Newcastle man prepared to enter into post-mortems was Terry Hibbett, the midfield player whose judicious passing had set up so many of Macdonald's goals which brought them to Wembley. " Liverpool are so good at closing up space," he began. " You beat one man and there's another, and then another niggling away at you.

" I thought in the first ten minutes I really had the beating of Tommy Smith. But after I got by him twice they put Hall out wide so that they closed up not only the path for me to get at Smith but also stopped our full-back from coming forward. This is Liverpool. They tighten absolutely everything up."

● Liverpool's emphatic win over Newcastle United, with two goals from the fast developing Kevin Keegan at the end of his third season in the First Division, saw the headlines again pay tribute to Bill Shankly. No hint that within weeks Shankly would relinquish his post as Liverpool's manager, leaving Bob Paisley – the trainer who, as Mike Langley reports (opposite page), was brushed aside unrecognised by security guards at Wembley – to develop Shankly's side of 1974 and then to build others of his own.

Keegan's exuberance was in stark contrast to the Wembley experience of Malcolm Macdonald, Newcastle's charismatic striker whose career was running along similar lines. Unlike Keegan, though, Macdonald would rarely taste success on the biggest of occasions, and in 1974 he never received the service he needed to bring Newcastle into the game.

Remarkably Newcastle held out until the second half, and even survived a legitimate-looking goal from Liverpool's Alec Lindsay which was ruled out by referee Gordon Kew. Liverpool, true to type, won the day by their exemplary team-work and Keegan – awarded the rare distinction of ten out of ten in the Sunday People – produced flair and finishing.

Shankly's post-match predictions about what his side would go on to achieve would be justified – though his boast about the double in 1975 did not materialise – but when further trophies arrived at Anfield he would no longer be there to share in the winning of them.

Date 4 May 1974
Place Wembley
Score LIVERPOOL 3 NEWCASTLE UNITED 0
Teams LIVERPOOL Clemence, Smith, Thompson, Hughes, Lindsay, Hall, Callaghan, Cormack, Keegan, Toshack, Heighway.
NEWCASTLE UNITED McFaul, Clark, Howard, Moncur, Kennedy, Smith (Gibb), McDermott, Cassidy, Macdonald, Tudor, Hibbitt
Team Colours LIVERPOOL All red

NEWCASTLE UNITED Black and white striped shirts, black shorts
Official Referee C. G. Kew (Amersham, Bucks)
Goal Scorers Keegan 58, 88, Heighway 75
Managers LIVERPOOL Bill Shankly; NEWCASTLE UNITED Joe Harvey
Attendance 100 000
Gate Receipts £212 650
Copy *The Sunday Times* 5 May 1974; *The Sunday People* 5 May 1974

WHEN A WEMBLEY DREAM COMES TRUE

FULFAM ....(0) 0   **WEST HAM** ....(0) 2

At Wembley. Attendance: 100,000.
Receipts : £303,000 (record).

Alan Taylor 2
(first was scored in 60 min. 55 sec.)

TWENTY-ONE-year-old Alan Taylor, who was playing Fourth Division football for Rochdale before Christmas, was the shining Soccer knight of Wembley in a Cockney Cup Final which will go down as the cleanest ever seen on this great, old ground. Two goals in four minutes (60 and 64) by West Ham's flash-fast striker—surely at £40,000 the best and cheapest buy of the season—destroyed Fulham's hopes.

A former Preston reject, the Lancaster-born Taylor is the first player for 18 years to score six goals in the last three rounds of the Cup. But his greatest triumph was Wembley. "*It's like a dream come true,*" he said.

In 1957 Irish international Peter McParland netted two for Aston Villa against Burnley in the sixth round, two against West Brom in the semi-final and two against Manchester United in the Final.

Cultured

Tragically for cool and cultured Fulham, whose football had been as smooth as oil in the first half, it was a sudden

ALAN HOBY reports

shattering medley of errors which wrote full stop to their hopes and those of their manager—Alec Stock—of winning Wembley glory.

It was West Ham's young, aggressive Pat Holland, brought in for the injured Keith Robson, who launched the vivid sequence of events which led up to both goals.

A horrifying slip by Fulham right-back John Cutbush gave the racy Holland his vital moment of freedom 15 minutes after half time.

After unluckily treading on the ball, Cutbush, temporarily unnerved, lost it to the challenging Holland. Cutting inside Holland passed to Billy Jennings who shot hard and low for the far post.

Peter Mellor, Fulham's big

blond 'keeper who had looked uneasy throughout, moved late and had to stretch full length, fingers straining, for the ball.

Amid a stony silence from the Fulham fans, poor Mellor could only push the ball away and you simply cannot do that with a centre forward of Taylor's speed.

Following up like a claret-and-blue bolt of lightning, Taylor cracked the loose ball past Mellor into the opposite side of the net.

The yellow-haired youngster from the North had done it yet again for West Ham and a swelling typhoon of sound burst from the Cockney thousands at the opposite end of the stadium.

Up to this paralysing first

goal Fulham had equalled and, at times, even outplayed their First Division opponents. Bobby Moore hit some immaculate long balls, but Fulham's finishing was blunted by the quick reactions of West Ham's young defensive master, Kevin Lock. Here is a second Bobby.

Four minutes later Holland struck again. He pushed a beautifully weighted pass into the stride of the bearded Graham Paddon. Graham shot ferociously straight at the unhappy Mellor.

The 'keeper, falling backwards, dropped the ball as if it was a red-hot coal and Taylor, with that built-in positional sense, pounced almost on the goal-line to crack home his second goal.

What a romantic storybook game for this modest yet brilliant striker. He has become both the mascot and the delight of every Hammers supporter.

Defiant

Fulham, brave, and defiant, now swung every man into attack and to hell with the gaps at the back. This is the Stock way and this was how they went out—not in cramped defensive fear but bravely with style.

It was, in one way, a strange victory in that Fulham never looked two goals inferior, although West Ham deserved to win in the end. It was just that Hammers had the man who, in four searing minutes, turned the game inside out and upside down.

It might all have been so different if Fulham's hungry goal-poacher John Mitchell had scored just after half-time. From Mullery's throw-in Mitchell, with his back to goal, dummied Lock, swivelled like a black and white top, swerved round the baffled Hammer and hit a "blinder" straight for the tiny gap between post and 'keeper Mervyn Day.

But young Day is England potential and he saved dazzl-

ingly to deny Fulham what would have been the so important opening goal.

Then, after Hammers decisive two-goal act, it was Mitchell again who broke through the enemy rearguard and shot only to be foiled once more by Day's acrobatic dive.

Yes. Fulham who had all their troops committed to total attack died bravely.

I wish I could say that West Ham for all their polished passing won the Cup for the first time for 11 years because of their immense First Division experience. But they did not. They won it on errors. That was all.

And although they had chances at the end a stranger would never have known which of the two teams operated in Division Two.

Cheek

Fulham — who began their Cup run as 500—1 outsiders — displayed enough cheek and desire to run at their opponents.

I admired Viv Busby, best dribbler on view, but Viv did not receive the support he needed.

Holland, Frank Lampard, John McDowell, Lock, Brooking and Alan Taylor were West Ham's heroes.

As Bonds was receiving the Cup from the Duke of Kent, the F.A. president, a multitude of teenage West Ham fans burst through the police barrier and swarmed ecstatically on to the pitch.

It was an astonishing sight for Wembley, but there was no nastiness—only the famous Hammers song—"We're forever blowing bubbles" ringing round Wembley.

FULHAM.—Mellor: Cutbush, Fraser, Mullery Lacy, Moore, Mitchell, Conway (Jim), Busby, Slough, Barrett. Sub : Lloyd.

WEST HAM. — Day: McDowell, Lampard, Bonds Taylor (T), Lock, Taylor (A). Paddon, Jennings, Brooking, Holland. Sub : Gould.

Ref : P Partridge (Durham).

Bargain of all time!

THE COCKNEYS made it a Cup Final carnival. With bells and hooters, tassels and ribbons, songs and dances, they came together in a glorious spirit of Mardi Gras.

The famous colours of the teams turned Wembley into a kaleidoscope of claret, blue, black and white. All around the stadium the Londoners—West Ham fans from the East End and Fulham supporters from their friendly Thames-side retreat — shared drinks and peanuts, and smiled through an afternoon that reflected the spirit of the good-natured play going on before them.

Rapturous

And long after they had disappeared on their merry-making way from Wembley, a young Lancastrian named Alan Taylor stood gazing into the F.A. Cup, a trophy he had won for his team by scoring two splendid goals.

A bobble-cap in claret-and-blue nestled on his copper-coloured head, placed there by a rapturous fan during West Ham's near delirious lap of honour.

"Tremendous," said Taylor. "Tremendous." His own per-

by JAMES MOSSOP

sonal story is one of the most romantic of all Cup tales.

Last November, this slim 21-year-old from the shores of Morecambe Bay was playing for Rochdale in the Fourth Division. He was due to take part in a first round tie against a non-League club.

Had he done so, he would have been ineligible for Hammers' Cup games. Intending to buy, West Ham asked Rochdale to pull Taylor out of the tie and he suddenly developed a convenient ankle injury.

West Ham then paid a £40,000 transfer fee, and the two goals Taylor scored at Wembley —which brought his total in the competition to six—made him one of the most stupendous bargains of all time.

"I've come a long way," he smiled. "Today I just seemed to be in the right place at the right time. I owe a lot to the lads at West Ham and Rochdale.

"Now we're going into Europe and I have only ever been abroad twice before in my life, That was to Spain on holiday."

While Taylor and his pals were quaffing champagne at the end of this friendly Final, there were deeply sympathetic thoughts for Fulham manager Alec Stock.

The 58-year-old son of Somerset with his asthma and his memories — he was the figure behind the greatest giant-killers of all Yeovil Town in 1948—had arrived at Wembley with a carefree band of Second Division players.

He sat on the touchline, dapper in his dark blue suit, with white handkerchief peeping from his breast pocket, mentally kicking every ball. But it would not go into the Hammers net for him.

And when it was all over, he would quietly reflect, as he has done so often before, and say : "Never mind, we have lived a little."

Last night, the carnival was back in the terraced streets and high-rise flats of the East End. There were street parties among the houses festooned with bunting.

Taylor and his mates were at a banquet in a Park Lane hotel with the Lancashire lad still sighing with disbelief.

He had some wonderful moments to retell, not least those incredible, emotional minutes after the final whistle sounded.

That was when the Hammers supporters, magnificent with their tuneful anthem, "I'm Forever Blowing Bubbles," vaulted the barriers with an unprecedented invasion. Everyone wanted to get at the new hero of West Ham — young Alan Taylor.

Scorer Taylor and substitute Gould

No regrets —Stock

● **Alec Stock**, Fulham's manager: "I thought my blokes were magnificent all the way through and there are no regrets in our camp. We lost it when they scored their first goal, but one of the best points about the game was the way it was played—that's how football should be."

● **John Lyall** : West Ham team manager : "I can only pay tribute to these lads for what they have done. Alan Taylor did a marvellous job, and, in the later stages, I felt we played some delightful football. It was a team thing and that is what it has got to be at Wembley. It has been a marvellous experience.

● **Alan Mullery** : Fulham's captain : "It was an enjoyable game—until they scored. It was disappointing to lose but I think we did ourselves credit. Fulham will be back."

● **Billy Bonds** : West Ham's captain : "I thought Fulham played very well in the first half but did not get very far with our back four closing up the game. Of course, the goal made all the difference, and we were able to play the ball about a little after that. We never reached the heights we are capable of, but in our second half we deserved to win. The younger players were superb."

The decisive goal. Alan Taylor scores from Mellor's dropped ball

Court battle over Cup boots

FULHAM'S footballers will have to wait until just before the kick-off today to find out what boots they c: wear in the FA Cup Fin:

A firm of bootmakers c: that the players broke an agreement to wear only their football boots this season.

The Yorkshire firm of Stylo Matchmakers International applied in the High Court yesterday for an injunction restraining Fulham skipper Alan Mullery and his team from wearing any other boots.

Mr Justice Walton adjourned the case to allow the players to be represented at an emergency hearing at 10.30 this morning.

Mr Alexander Irvine, representing Stylo, said that under a written agreement made last August, the players agreed to wear only Stylo boots for the 1974-75 season.

The agreement also provided that if Fulham reached the Cup

By JEFF POWELL and JAMES GILHEANY

Final Stylo would pay them £2,000. In fact, that sum was paid to the club secretary on April 12.'

It was at last Saturday's match between Bristol City and Fulham that Stylo first learned their boots were not being worn by the players.

Since then it had been stated that the players had no intention of wearing their Stylo boots for the Final, and the £2,000 had been returned.

Mr Irvine said his clients were driven to suspect that the footballers proposed to wear and advertise boots of another make for a greater reward.

It was known before the hearing that Stylo have been in competition with West Germany's Adidas to get both Final teams to use their equipment.

Stylo boots bear a distinctive trademark—a thick white horizontal line

Mr Justice Walton said : 'I watch a lot of football on television and I have never noticed any design on football boots. Next time Fulham appear on Match of the Day I will watch out for them.'

The 59-year-old judge said he did not want to wreck a sporting fixture 'on this evidence.'

He would have been more sympathetic if the application had not been made at the 'eleventh hour.'

Mr Irvine replied that there had been discussions until Thursday and it was not until 10.45 yesterday morning that it was learned negotiations had failed.

The judge gave leave for Fulham to be served by 7 p.m. last night for the court hearing today. Counsel remarked : 'Whoever serves Fulham with the notice will not be too

popular with supporters.'

Mr Justice Walton: 'I think that is the understatement of the year.'

Most of the Fulham players were practising body swerves as a small man in glasses tried to serve the writs at their Hertfordshire hotel last night.

Skipper Alan Mullery saw the solicitor with the 14 papers in his hand and swayed neatly round him on his way to a television interview.

Former England captain Bobby Moore was taking a phone call in the lobby as the solicitor placed the papers nearby.

Moore said later : 'We've just changed the formation. We've got an outside writ, an inside-writ and a writ-half.'

WEST HAM, Fulham's Final opponents, will be wearing Adidas boots. The firm clinched the deal at £3,500

Date 3 May 1975
Place Wembley
Score WEST HAM UNITED 2 FULHAM 0
Teams WEST HAM UNITED Day, McDowell, Lampard, T. Taylor, Lock, Bonds, Paddon, Brooking, A. Taylor, Jennings, Holland. Sub: Gould. FULHAM Mellor, Cutbush, Fraser, Lacy, Moore, Mullery, Conway, Slough, Mitchell, Busby, Barrett. Sub: Lloyd
Team Colours WEST HAM UNITED

Claret and blue shirts, white shorts; FULHAM White shirts, black shorts
Official Referee P. Patridge (Durham)
Goal Scorer A. Taylor 60, 65
Managers WEST HAM UNITED John Lyall; FULHAM Alec Stock
Attendance 100000
Gate Receipts £303000
Guests of Honour H.R.H. Duke and Duchess of Kent
Copy *Daily Mail* 3 May 1975; *Sunday Express* 4 May 1975

Old-timers Moore and Mullery

A word in your ear that says it must be United

AN UNPRECEDENTED insight into the psychology of England's premier sporting occasion is the exclusive privilege of Daily Mail readers this morning.

Tommy Docherty has given me permission to publish, in advance, the full text of the team-talk which will launch Manchester United into the 1976 FA Cup Final.

Not one syllable of information will be muttered about Mike Channon, Peter Osgood, or anyone else in the Southampton team. Not so much as a solitary phrase will escape the lips of United's manager about the way his own team should play the match of their young lives.

Condensed

Docherty's exhortation will be condensed into a single word: 'Sunderland.'

Docherty trusts that emotive reminder of what happened to Leeds at Wembley three years ago will suffice to insure his own overwhelming favourites against similar humiliation at Second Division hands.

The one-word team-talk over, Docherty will settle into his seat in chirpy expectation of the winning performance which will crown his remarkable achievements with United this season.

He explains : 'What Sunderland

JEFF POWELL

talks to the manager who provides a unique preparation for a Wembley Cup Final.

did to Leeds that day is now the perfect warning to my lads to take nothing for granted. Of course we're the favourites. Of course if we turn it on we ought to win well. But Cup Finals are one-off occasions and Sunderland showed Leeds there are no prizes for just turning up.

'Southampton won't give it to us. If our lads want to get their hands on that cup, they must play the way we know they can. The beauty of it is that we do know they're good enough.'

That succinct appraisal of the main problem confronting United is more impressive than any tortuous analysis of Southampton and the tactics which might be needed to defeat them.

Docherty has trusted his instinct with the introduction of every fresh young talent into his team. He has no reason to doubt his own conviction that United ought to win.

He says : 'We haven't watched Southampton and we won't talk about them. They're a lovely club full of good people like Lawrie McMenemy, Ted Bates and Micky Channon. But this Final is about an exciting performance by Manchester United.

'We've a message for 200 million people live or on TV that English Soccer isn't sick any more. And that a few of our clubs have pumped back the life blood of entertainment and adventure into the game.

Saviours

'I want the world to know teams like United, Queen's Park Rangers and Derby have brought an end to the drift that began in the 1960s. These teams are the modern saviours of a great game and it is even more vital than the Wembley result for us to go out as ambassadors and to get this message over to the rest of the world.

'All I hope is that we play as well as we did against Derby in the semi-final. If we do we shall show we are a great team again and the leading light of English football.'

In Macari, McIlroy, Coppell, Hill, Greenhoff, Pearson and the remarkable young Daly, United are equipped to pour down on Southampton in a torrent of breathtaking attacks. 'Win or bust and to hell with the opposition' has been Docherty's refreshing policy all season. He won't change now.

Tougher

Even so Southampton will make it a good deal tougher for them than most critics suggested when the two clubs first emerged from their semi-finals. Since they would be most unwise to fling men forward with the same abandon as United, exposing themselves to Pearson and Company, Southampton's best chance is to keep it tight and hope that the guile and experience of Peter Osgood will help them exploit Channon's talent as the best counter-attacker in the modern game.

Channon is at his most potent when making mighty runs into wide open spaces—just like those at Wembley. This thoroughbred England forward is the principle reason why United will have to give of their best in a tighter final than this likely result will suggest : Manchester United 3, Southampton 1.

Now the fans just love you, Lawrie

MY CUP — Osgood

LAWRIE McMENEMY, who went to Wembley without a hope and came away with a Cup, made his peace with Southampton's fans in one brief, emotional moment yesterday.

As he walked back into the Wembley tunnel, the fans chanted "Give us a wave, Lawrie," and the big fellow responded to a deafening ovation.

"Moving, that was," he said. "It's not so long ago that they were throwing things at me. Still, that's all forgotten now, and that little moment gave me my greatest thrill."

He might also be a little thrilled by the size of the contract which Southampton are now certain to offer him as a reward

By PATRICK COLLINS

for leading them into the riches of Europe's Cup-winners' Cup.

But he insisted that yesterday's victory was no surprise. "There could be no surprises at Wembley after Sunderland's defeat of Leeds," he said. "Nobody is going to underrate anybody. We won it on sheer ability today.

"They'll be singing and dancing in the streets of Southampton—and they deserve to be."

The beaten Tommy Docherty, thoroughly deflated, took defeat with dignity.

"No excuses," he said. "I thought that the first goal would decide it, and if Sammy McIlroy's effort had gone in, it

might have been our Cup. But that's the way it goes.

"I took off Gordon Hill because Peter Rodrigues was playing him so well. Hill is an honest lad, and when he came off he said to me: 'Sorry, boss, I've picked a great day to have a stinker, haven't I?'

"I'm so disappointed for our lads and our fans, but they're good people at Southampton and I'm glad for them."

And one of those good people, Lawrie McMenemy, had every excuse for indulging in a little crowing amid the hand-shakes and champagne of the winners' dressing room.

To those who once felt that the best thing about the Southampton club was the quality of the tea served in bone china cups by charming ladies in floral hats, he said :

"We were supposed to be country lads . . . we wouldn't find our way up the tunnel . . . we'd need a map to get to Wembley. That's what people said.

"Well, nobody's saying that now."

Stepney beaten for the only goal

Despair for Docherty, joy for Rodrigues

ALL SAINTS DAY!

WE'VE DONE IT—Ian Turner is all arms and legs as he celebrates Southampton's victory

Jim McCalliog takes the FA Cup

Stokes makes it hell for those Red Devils

MAY DAY became All-Saints Day at Wembley yesterday.

The Saints from Southampton came marching in to win the FA Cup for the first time. Docherty's Devils, the Red Army from Manchester, were sent retreating with their tails between their legs.

This Cup Final never really got off the ground until seven minutes from time when Bobby Stokes, a 25-year-old Portsmouth-born lad who you would sooner have on your side than against you, sent the ball quietly and gently past Alex Stepney.

Though Stokes has already made some 200 first - team appearances, bookmakers offered 25-1 against him getting the first goal.

This so-important goal was scored at half pace and at a time when everybody, including the United team, had given up hope of a goal and were looking wearily to extra time.

It caught the United defence with their pants down. Ex-United Jim McCalliog put the ball across.

Stokes thought he was offside, but as the whistle didn't sound, he moved forward and the whole Manchester defence did a hesitation Waltz. Buchan played Stokes-on-side.

Stepney, realising he was now on his own, made a brave bid to cut down the angle as he came out, but Stokes guided the ball well to the 'keeper's left into the net.

Southampton, 5-1 against underdogs, were the 1976 Cup winners. Manchester United, heralded as the fastest and fittest team in the League, had, like Leeds in the old days, fallen between the Cup and League and finished the season empty handed.

It was sad for United, having played sparkling football for eight months. But nobody from Manchester would deny that Southampton were the better side on the day.

United never wound themselves up. They lacked speed and flair and performed like a side that had tried too hard for too long

FRANK BUTLER reporting

Manchester United (0) 0
Southampton (0) 1

Stokes (83)

Attendance 100,000   Receipts £420,000

and Wembley was all too much for them.

STINKER

Where was the speed, the stamina and the wings that would make them fly so high into the sky?

Don't ask me. Ask the boys who left it all behind them.

Gordon Hill, the two-goal hero of the semi-final, only produced the form expected of him when a Third Division player with Millwall.

Tommy Docherty realised that Hill was having a poor game and, 24 minutes from time, pulled him off and sent on Dave McCreery. It was tough on the cocky Hill to save up his first stinker in months for Wembley.

The football was never actually bad. There were some very admirable touches, but it was all so dull because Docherty's Devils had no fire in their bellies and no speed in their legs.

They allowed Southampton to block them out and, at the same time, had not a clue how to stop the Saints playing an efficient but far from brilliant game.

A stranger would have been forgiven for inquiring which team came from the Second Division.

What class was shown came from two Southampton players Mick Channon and Peter Osgood, while the unpublicised Stokes looked far more dangerous than Hill or Steve Coppell, members of the England squad being carefully watched by Don Revie.

The Manchester failure was as big an upset for bookies' odds as the defeat of Leeds United against Sunderland and Wolves against Portsmouth yet I was not surprised by Southampton's win. Class tells at Wembley and the class of Channon and Osgood sorted the men from the boys.

Last week I urged readers not to put their shirts on the United certs.

United never started to play like a team with pride or the will to win.

Their defence was OK. Their mid-field play was

splendid.

Skipper Martin Buchan was their star. Gerry Daly worked like a Trojan, but with the wingers who were guarded by close marking by Rodrigues, Peach, Holmes and Steele, they couldn't limp home.

Lou Macari didn't rise above mediocrity. Pearson tried too hard despite an injury and Sammy McIlroy was unlucky when his header hit the top of the post from a corner in the 59th minute.

JUSTICE

Rodrigues, still dizzy after being knocked out, didn't challenge him.

In the end, justice was done.

IPSWICH MISS EUROPE

SOUTHAMPTON'S FA Cup victory leaves Manchester United to claim the remaining UEFA Cup place along with Manchester City, Derby and either Liverpool or QPR.

It so ends the Ipswich dream of playing in Europe.

It's a financial blow for the FA as well. Southampton won't pack 'em in like Manchester United for the Charity Shield on Aug 14.

Date 1 May 1976
Place Wembley
Score SOUTHAMPTON 1
MANCHESTER UNITED 0
Teams SOUTHAMPTON Turner, Rodrigues, Blyth, Steele, Peach, Holmes, Gilchrist, McCalliog, Channon, Osgood, Stokes. Sub: Fisher.
MANCHESTER UNITED Stepney, Forsyth, Greenhoff, Buchan, Houston, Daly, Macari, Coppell, McIlroy, Pearson, Hill (McCreery)
Team Colours SOUTHAMPTON Yellow shirts, blue shorts; MANCHESTER UNITED Red shirts, white shorts
Official Referee C. Thomas (Treorchy)
Goal Scorer Stokes 83
Managers SOUTHAMPTON Lawrie McMenemy; MANCHESTER UNITED Tommy Docherty
Attendance 100000
Gate Receipts £420000
Guests of Honour H.M. Queen Elizabeth, H.R.H. Prince Philip
Copy Daily Mail 1 May 1976; News of the World 2 May 1976

I thought Clemence would stop my goal

—STUART PEARSON

By PAUL HINCE

THE SCENE in the Manchester United dressing-room, moments after they had completed a memorable 2-1 victory over Liverpool, was one of elation and satisfaction.

And the conversation inevitably led to the goals which took the FA Cup back to Old Trafford.

Said STUART PEARSON, scorer of the first goal: "I struck the ball well, but I think it was the kind of shot Ray Clemence would save nine times out of ten.

"Even when they equalised I still felt we would win. When they came off at half-time they looked shattered, and I was convinced then in my own mind that we would win the Cup."

JIMMY GREENHOFF, credited with United's second goal, said "Lou Macari's shot was going wide when it struck my chest and went in If it hadn't, Lou would have been claiming the goal for himself.

Tired

"We were under a lot of pressure during the last 15 minutes, but somehow I was never seriously worried. I felt we finished the stronger.

"Liverpool have had a lot on their plate, and it showed today."

ALEX STEPNEY: "I have waited a long time to get my hands on an FA Cup-winners' medal. Now I am a happy man—I have got a full set.

"The only time I was

WHAT THEY SAID

worried was when they equalised. The whole team were fantastic-particulary full-backs Jimmy Nicholl and Arthur Albiston."

JIMMY NICHOL: "I made one or two good tackles on Steve Heighway in the first 15 minutes, and that really settled me down.

"Although they pressed forward in the last 25 minutes, I was never really worried because they were not creating chances.

"I don't know how the other lads felt, but I was really tired in the last 10 minutes."

ARTHUR ALBISTON: "I wanted to give my medal to Stewart Houston because I didn't really think it was mine, by rights."

"But he said I had earned it, so I suppose I will end up keeping it. I was surprised how relaxed I was.

"For me, it was just an enjoyable game, and I am flattered to know that so many people think I played well."

STEWART HOUSTON: "It was terrible to watch from the sidelines. I was kicking every ball with the lads.

"I felt the game needed a goal to get it going, but once we had scored it was a cracking match.

"And what about young Arthur? He must have been the man-of-the match."

Tremendous

SAMMY McILROY: "In the first half I found it difficult to get going. I just couldn't seem to get my breath.

"But things went better in the second half. Once we had scored I really felt that the Cup was ours. I thought both our full backs were tremendous."

BRIAN GREENHOFF: "I thought we did everything right throughout the game. Jimmy Nicholl was tremendous and Arthur Albiston played out of his skin.

"I knew that if Martin Buchan and I concentrated for the full 90 minutes we could do it. They didn't exploit us in the air very often, and when they threw any high balls over we always got them away."

MARTIN BUCHAN: "I would like to take this opportunity to pay tribute to Arthur Albiston.

"I have been one of his sternest critics in the past, but today he deserves all the praise which is flying around. He was superb.

"As for the result . . . well, it is a fairy tale come true, after coming to Wembley last year and losing to Southampton."

STEVE COPPELL: "After that know exactly how the Liverpool players must be feeling.

"I am completely drained, physically and mentally, and this is the kind of match they have had to play almost every week over the past month or so.

"But take no credit away from us. On the day we beat them at our own game."

LOU MACARI: "Despite what most people were saying, I knew we would be running stronger at the end than Liverpool.

"I was pleased that the game was played in a tremendous sporting spirit, though I must admit that I panicked for a few moments when they scored their equaliser."

GORDON HILL: "Absolutely fantastic. At last we have made up for last year's final.

"Our defence played so well that I was never worried. I don't think you could find a fault anywhere in the team."

Amends

DAVID McCREERY: "When Jimmy Case equalised I had visions of last year's final repeating itself.

"From the line I was slightly disappointed in Liverpool. It looked as if the season had finally caught up with them.

"I didn't expect to be brought on I was simply told to go and fill-in in midfield. This is the first major trophy I have won, and it is one I will alway treasure."

TOMMY DOCHERTY: "I am still waiting for it all to sink in. I thought I would be doing handstands and cartwheels if we won, but in fact I feel absolutely drained of emotion at the moment.

"But I am delighted for all my players, particularly after last season's disappointment.

"And I know just how Bob Paisley and his players must be feeling. Let's pray that they make amends by winning the European Cup."

TOMMY CAVANAGH: "The thing which delighted me the most was that we saw a game of football out there.

"By that I mean that both sides allowed each other to play. There was no ill-feeling on either side, and the match was an advertisement for English soccer.

"Most people thought that we would be in trouble at the back but we fooled them, didn't we?"

LAURIE BROWN (physio): "I am pessimistic by nature and, to be honest, I was as nervous as a kitten during the game. It was only when the final whistle went, and I realised we had won, that I began to enjoy myself.

"I was particularly pleased to see Martin Buchan come through the game. On Wednesday he virtually had no chance of playing, and it gave me great personal satisfaction to have got him fit in time.'

LEFT: Jimmy Greenhoff wears the crown, as the United players soak up the glory in the bath.

BELOW LEFT: Champagne time for the Reds "backroom boys" . . . (left to right) Tommy Cavanagh (coach), Tommy Docherty, Frank Blunstone (assistant manager) and Laurie Brown (physio). RIGHT: Such a happy fella . . . Gordon Hill won't let the Cup go . . . even though he's in the bath.

BELOW RIGHT: Hero Arthur Albiston (right) shares his dream day with Stewart Houston, the defender he replaced because of injury.

FA CUP FINAL

Ruins on the road to Rome

PETER CORRIGAN: Liverpool 1   Manchester United 2

Attendance : 100,000.   Receipts : £420,000.

LIVERPOOL'S beckoning vision of a treble faded as tantalisingly as a mirage at Wembley yesterday and not without leaving a mocking echo as Manchester United claimed the FA Cup. The winning goal cannot be described as other than drenched in good fortune, Macari's shot being deflected into the net off Jimmy Greenhoff's body. It was the third goal in a five-minute spell of frantic, fascinating activity which stood out in sharp relief from a game not otherwise memorable for stirring action.

On a sunny and sporting afternoon, Liverpool were the better side before and after that spell, but suffered defensive untidiness during it. At the end, when Liverpool's p l a y e r s slumped in dismal unison in the centre circle, their manager. Bob Paisley, rushed out to try to lift the spirits that must be restored before they meet Borussia München Gladbach in the European Cup Final in Rome on Wednesday.

For that match they hope to have Toshack available to lead the attack, a department, occupied ineffectively yesterday by Johnson, and the main reason

why their more composed and thoughtful football was not better rewarded. Hindsight suggests that manager Paisley would have been able to help his side more had he named Fairclough as substitute instead of Callaghan, for the young forward might have been more influential in assisting the finishing power which the excellent Case provided, Keegan being unable to follow up his promising first half. United took their chances with a familiar hunger, but the rest of their game was not as urgent and instinctively cohesive as we have grown to expect. At least they proved once more that in Pearson, who scored their first goal, they have the type of player who can win a match on half a chance.

Like the inhabitants of the control room of a rocket launching site, Cup Final crowds are all too familiar with that moment when, after the button

has been pressed and the first flames flicker, there is that awful feeling that the thing is not going to take off. There were several such moments early in the match which were quickly dismissed as premature, but gradually those occasions in which there was a sudden flurry of action gave way to the realisation that this was a game unlikely to satisfy our great expectations.

United had held the key in our minds. One of their bright, brisk beginnings would set the pace and style of an urgent and dramatic game. But although Coppell looked promising in his preliminary skirmishes with Jones down the right, and Macari found space to drill a shot into Liverpool's side netting, United's was a start which signified either a totally unexpected approach, or the sort of nervous paralysis which affected their game in last year's final.

LIVERPOOL'S opponents in the European Cup Final, Borussia Munchen Gladbach, won their third successive West German championship yesterday when they drew 2—2 with Bayern Munich, the European champions. Borussia learnt of Liverpool's defeat as they left the field in triumph.

For their part, Liverpool entered the game as if it were a darkened room, feeling their way until their senses were accustomed to distances and shapes. That is their way, and the lack of speed was to their liking.

Once Keegan had shown— and he did so quite early on— that this was likely to be one of those games to which he was perfectly attuned, United's battle looked all the harder. That impression remained until

Although Hill made one of his rare entries into the game a telling one with a viciously swerving cross-shot which Clemence had to tip hurriedly over the bar, the first half contained far more memories of Liverpool chances. Kennedy, arriving unannounced as usual, met Case's cross at the far post and headed it expertly downwards, Stepney having to rely on his legs to stop the ball. Then Jones hit a shot close enough to the top of the crossbar to send Liverpool into the interval with every hope of the game continuing to develop their way.

But the second half was only five minutes old when Pearson changed all that. He took a pass from Jimmy Greenhoff and, in that quick, instinctive manner of his, was into space and shooting the ball low under Clemence's body at the near post, when a shot to the far post might have been more predictable. Within two minutes Liverpool brought the voices of their supporters to join the ear-splitting row the United fans were making. Jones's cross found Case, and he turned crisply on the edge of the box to beat Stepney with a shot into the left-hand corner of the net.

Then the season's richest five minutes produced another goal which stunned us, not only by the speed of its arrival on the heels of the other two, but by the way in which it was scored. Smith had made a mistake in his penalty area which gave Jimmy Greenhoff the opportunity of a shot. The ball rebounded back off a defender into the range of Macari, who swung his foot immediately and haphazardly, the destination of the ball as it left him being anyone's guess. It struck Greenhoff's body and was bound for the net so abruptly that Clemence could do nothing but watch in dismay.

Liverpool brought Johnson off to allow Callaghan to leave the substitute's bench and contribute in midfield while Case moved into the main striking role. It was a change from which Liverpool seemed to benefit as they moved determinedly and with some attraction in search of an equaliser. Case ended one excellent movement by dragging the ball away from Brian Greenhoff and shooting strongly for the far corner, but Stepney pounced confidently on the ball.

United exchanged Hill for McCreery and massed in defence against Liverpool's attacks, which were being carefully constructed despite their fast escaping dream. Kennedy, who had had a good second half, almost brought the scores level when he took Keegan's pass at the edge of the box and aimed a huge shot at goal, which was close enough to strike the top of the stanchion, but not to alter the course of the match which went into United's possession with no further threat.

Liverpool—Clemence; Neal, Jones, Smith, Kennedy, Hughes, Keegan, Case, Heighway, Johnson, McDermott. Sub. Callaghan.

Manchester United—Stepney; Nicholl, Albiston, McIlroy, B. Greenhoff, Buchan, Coppell, J. Greenhoff, Pearson, Macari, Hill. Sub. McCreery.

Referee: R. Matthewson (Lancashire).

It's Wembley, not Twickenham. It's goalkeeper Clemence flying through like a scrum half.

Almost disaster for United as Ray Kennedy's header hits the post

Pearson suddenly brought breath and life to their supporters. That the lead lasted no more than two minutes was a numbing blow to them—but at least the games was electrified. That the batteries had been allowed to get so flat in the first half was due in the main to the fact that Liverpool lacked the certainty of finish which the rest of their game was collecting.

Johnson, chosen in preference to the red-haired Fairclough, was not able to contribute enough sharpness in thought or action to match the contributions made by Keegan and Case. Neither was Heighway—who appeared to have the beating of Nicholl—equipped with positive objectives when he was in possession. This allowed the United defence more chance to keep a grip on the strings of their composure, and in this they were not let down by young Albiston, who had taken the place of the injured Houston.

Date 21 May 1977

Place Wembley

Score MANCHESTER UNITED 2 LIVERPOOL 1

Teams MANCHESTER UNITED Stepney, Nicholl, B. Greenhoff, Buchan, Albiston, McIlroy, Macari, Coppell, Pearson, J. Greenhoff, Hill (McCreery). LIVERPOOL Clemence, Neal, Smith, Hughes, Jones, Kennedy, Case, McDermott, Keegan, Johnson (Callaghan), Heighway

Team Colours MANCHESTER UNITED Red whirts, white shorts; LIVERPOOL White shirts, black shorts

Official Referee R. Matthewson (Bolton)

Goal Scorers MANCHESTER

UNITED Pearson 50, J. Greenhoff 55; LIVERPOOL Case 52

Managers MANCHESTER UNITED Tommy Docherty; LIVERPOOL Bob Paisley

Attendance 100 000

Guest of Honour The Duchess of Kent

Copy *The Observer* 22 May 1977; *Manchester Evening News* 23 May 1977

WOODS THE WIZARD TORTURES ARSENAL

ARSENAL (0) 0   **IPSWICH TOWN (0) 1**

100,000   Osborne (scored in 76min 42sec)

Receipts: £500,000 (a record)

IT WAS the great East Anglia n miracle . . . the victory of the Ipswich crocks . . . the country cousins scoring the biggest Cup upset since Sunderland shocked L eeds five years ago. Arsenal were, clinically and almost contemptuou sly, played off the Wembley pitch in this dramatic and explosive 50th Wembley Final.

Three times Ipswich, written off by many, hit the woodwork through the waspish John Wark and the graceful Paul Mariner, surely the most complete centre forward in the country.

Twice, only world-class saves by Pat Jennings—centre-half David O'Leary was the only other Arsenal player I really noticed—foiled superb headers from Kevin Beattie and George Burley.

In midfield, as the leaderless Gunners sagged more and more, the dynamic Brian Talbot, socks round his boots, led the Ipswich cavalry charge which broke the favourites as if they were so many pale shadows.

And, at the back, the cool, authoritative Mick Mills, the indomitable Burley and those two damaged Titans Allan Hunter and the tremendous Beattie—both suffering from suspect knees — ruthless'y smashed Arsenal's few feeble raids with devastating tackling.

But standing head and shoulders above the others was

by ALAN HOBY

Ipswich's hero of heroes. Colin Woods—Woods the wizard. "It was a golden wing man's display," said Ipswich manager, Bobby Robson. It was. Magically, it evoked haunting memories of Stanley Matthews.

It was Woods and Roger Osborne, decisive scorer of the winning goal in the 77th minute — later Osborne, after running himself sick, staggered from the field — who supplied the most electrifying moments in this classic upset by a small-town team whose victory can do nothing but good for the game.

For, in the end, Ipswich overpowered the city slickers from North London with a stunning display of character, courage and sheer old-fashioned football to win the trophy on their first appearance in the Final.

Straight from the start Ipswich nerves were twanging like a banjo. In the first minute Hunter, passed fit only a few hours before the match, proved himself ready for the battle with a tremendous tackle on Frank Stapleton.

From the subsequent free kick Arsenal forced the first corner of the game and David O'Leary, from Alan Hudson's cross, cracked the ball menacingly close.

Already Talbot was complaining about the ball — apparently he thought it was not playing completely true on the greasy surface—but suddenly Ipswich burst into full flower.

JUGGLING

Mariner shot with devastating swiftness and the ball slashed like a razor thrust across the Arsenal goal but, alas, for Ipswich, it just rolled the wrong side of the far post.

And more Ipswich magic was on the way. Woods, coming more and more into the game with deft feints and dummies, proceeded to give Arsenal a series of frightening shocks.

In the 10th minute, after some mesmeric juggling, Woods broke clear and, from his square pass, Osborne just got a touch to the ball. It spun across the squelching turf and there was unmarked Mariner slamming the ball against the bar.

There was no holding Woods, who was giving a Stanley Matthews show on either wing. He terrified Pat Rice, the Arsenal right-back and skipper, and was a blue and white will-o-the wisp.

There was another desperate moment for the Gunners when,

following more Woods wizardry, Geddis chased the winger's cross towards the corner flag. So did the Gunners 'keeper Pat Jennings who flattened the post in his desperate, lunging clearance.

FINESS

So far nearly all the finess and football had been supplied by Ipswich.

Talbot and John Wark were everywhere and at the back, when Arsenal did break, the Ipswich tackling by Hunter, George Burley, Mick Mills and Beattie was devastating.

Arsenal broke and from Stapleton's overhead kick, Alan Sunderland headed wide. Then Sammy Nelson burst into an open space as wide as the M.1. If he had shot with Ipswich's 'keeper Paul Cooper well out of goal, Arsenal would have been ahead. but he passed not only the ball but the buck and Ipswich were safe.

In the 28th minute Geddis stunned Jennings with a blasting 22-yard drive which bounced off the 'keeper's body and shot over the angle of the bar.

Even Brady was forced to foul the rampaging Ipswich winger. At half-time Ipswich could reflect that they would have scored but for some ragged finishing. Their final cross was often off target.

Even so Arsenal could not produce their normal intricate and inventive patterns.

Arsenal's incredible luck stretched into the second half. They were shoddy, shaken and almost utterly outplayed. In the 52nd minute Mariner laid on the perfect ball for Wark who, to the collective collective horror of the Ipswich fans, hit the post. Then Mariner crashed the ball wide and the same player drove the ball over when clean through.

Sunderland broke for Arsenal, but Cooper, coming off his line, dived heroically at his feet. Then Woods started his wanders again. Dancing down the left he shot, the ball went square and loose but no Ipswich forward could connect.

Ipswich never stopped running, challenging, tackling, and fighting. From Talbot's cross, Woods headed down and Jennings only just beat Mariner in a frantic dive. Then Brady went off—limping as if he had pulled a muscle.

This was in the 65th minute and young Graham Rix came on. But Rix might have been a ghost for all the good he could do for Arsenal Again Woods came prancing down the line, beating everybody before crossing the ball only for the horrified Wark to drive it hercely against a post.

That was in the 71st minute and three minutes later came a world class reflex save by Jennings frustrated Burley as the Ipswich full-back's bullet of a header flew towards the corner of the net. And who crossed the ball? The unstoppable, devastating Woods.

The fear was growing among the tense Ipswich ranks that Arsenal might still steal it, when in the 77th minute, Robson's men scored.

APPLAUSE

Amazingly Woods had popped up on the right to flick the ball through to Geddis. Beating Nelson on the outside the Ipswich striker squared the ball. Big Willie Young tried to clear, but put the ball straight to Osborne who hammered it at last into the Arsenal net.

The goal that Ipswich had threatened to score for so long had finally arrived.

There was a hold-up after Osborne had scored. He had hurt himself in winning the match and eventually went off, amid deafening applause.

O'Leary was hurt, too, but in the end there was only one squad of braves who deserved the Cup and it was the rustic heroes of Ipswich Town.

ARSENAL — Jennings : Rice, Nelson, Price, O'Leary, Young, Brady, Sunderland, Macdonald, Stapleton, Hudson. Subst : Rix.
IPSWICH TOWN—Cooper : Burley, Mills, Talbot, Hunter, Beattie, Osborne, Wark, Mariner, Geddis, Woods. Subst : Lambert.
REFEREE—D Nippard (Bournemouth).

Here it comes! Roger Osborne hammers his left-foot winner

Country boys light up town

by JAMES MOSSOP
who said last Sunday:

DESPITE THE PRE-CUP FINAL NERVES...
I GO FOR IPSWICH

THEY CAME with a proud, white Suffolk Punch emblazoned on their royal blue shirts and never has Wembley seen a more fitting symbol

For effort, loyalty and total endeavour, Ipswich won the hearts of every neutral in the famous old stadium.

Now, for the first time in history, the F.A. Cup goes to the Constable country of East Anglia—the perfect reward for a footballing performance that was superb.

Anything less than victory would have been a sporting travesty. For this was the day Ipswich came to town and put on a show

They came with an army of fans all decked in blue and white, and their enormous gallery swaying with banners and flags, matched the London sky as the clouds rolled back and the sun smiled in.

This was the friendly final. The day without vandals The afternoon the fans stood and sang "Abide With Me" in a way we thought football crowds have long forgotten. The response from the men in the middle was perfect.

Arsenal had started as firm favourites. Ipswich manager Bobby Robson looked pale in the pre-match ceremonies. It was the biggest match many of his players had ever been involved in.

Responded

But they responded with the hearts and minds of giants. Arsenal's defenders were turned by the long striding David Geddis and the baffling trickery of the blond-haired Clive Woods.

Leading the attack Paul Mariner was just as heroic, while the Ipswich defenders reduced the Arsenal forward threat to nothing with Malcolm Macdonald wandering about like a hapless super ghost.

But singling out Ipswich heroes seems unfair. Victory was a credit to this marvellous little club with its sporting directors and spirit of togetherness.

Three times they bounced the ball off the Arsenal woodwork—one on the bar from Mariner and twice on the post from John Wark.

From Arsenal there could not be an excuse. They did not play. They were not allowed to. They were out-fought, out-thought, out-run and out-played. The skills that decorated an enthralling afternoon belonged to the lads in blue.

"A lot of people have called us country cousins so on that score we have a few mouths to shut," said Robson beforehand.

The man who closed them was that bandy-legged toiler in number seven Roger O'borne who hit the winner, collapsed, and limped off without getting another kick at the ball.

But long after the many stirring memories of the 50th Wembley Cup Final have faded, he will have his, and his medal, and deservedly so. Ipswich, you were beautiful, all of you.

Ref's lap of honour

Dorset referee Derek Nippard and his linesmen broke new ground at the final whistle when they did a lap of honour ahead of the Ipswich players. Mr Nippard, 47, is in his last season as a League referee.

Jubilant Ipswich players celebrate the golden goal

'We don't begrudge them, but...'—Rice

ARSENAL skipper PAT RICE summed up his team's bitter disappointment last night when he admitted : "Obviously we are all sick. On the day the better team won because we did not compete as hard as they did. I just feel sorry for all our supporters."

Rice added : "We knew right from the start that Bobby Robson would field his strongest team. He always plays this crying game.

"If Ipswich had lost they could have said they had done so with a patched-up team. Now they can say 'We won with a patched up team.'

"Still, I do not begrudge Ipswich anything. But we also had our injury problems. Liam Brady and I had ankle trouble. Pat Jennings had a foot injury and Willie Young was troubled with a sore knee.

"Saying this now may sound like an excuse, but it is not. We are the first to agree that Ipswich deserved their win."
ROGER OSBORNE, who scored

BOBBY ROBSON

the winning goal : The excitement of scoring was just too much for me. I was physically and mentally drained. I think the sun had got to me. I felt faint and asked to come off. The goal? It was an easy chance and it was great to get it with my left foot. My dad will be really pleased.
MICK MILLS, Ipswich skipper : We were a credit to the nation today. That was English football at its best. Clive Woods was absolutely magnificent and David Geddis also played an important part in our win.

JOHN WARK : I knew after I had hit the post the second time there was no way I was going to score, but I knew a goal just had to come.
GEORGE BURLEY : I thought I had scored with a header. I just couldn't believe it when Pat Jennings dived across to save it.

'Rubbish'

LIAM BRADY : I played rubbish. I came to Wembley expecting to win, but Ipswich were outstanding and fully deserved their victory.
BOBBY ROBSON, Ipswich manager : It's a great day for Ipswich and I thought we thoroughly deserved our win. After hitting the woodwork three times I felt it was going to be one of those days, but we were always in control and full of confidence. Clive Woods was almost untouchable on the skiddy surface.
TERRY NEILL, Arsenal boss : Ipswich deserved to win. I am pleased for Bobby Robson but I just wish they had done it against someone else. We have learned from this defeat and we will be back next season more determined than ever.

Mick Mills with Ipswich's first Cup

Date 6 May 1978
Place Wembley
Score IPSWICH TOWN 1 ARSENAL 0
Teams IPSWICH TOWN Cooper, Burley, Hunter, Beattie, Mills, Osborne (Lambert), Talbot, Wark, Mariner, Geddis, Woods.
ARSENAL Jennings, Rice, O'Leary, Young, Nelson, Price, Hudson, Brady (Rix), Sunderland, Macdonald, Stapleton
Team Colours IPSWICH TOWN Blue shirts, white shorts; ARSENAL Yellow shirts, blue shorts
Official Referee D. R. G. Nippard (Christchurch)

Goal Scorer Osborne 77
Managers IPSWICH TOWN Bobby Robson; ARSENAL Terry Neill
Attendance 100 000
Gate Receipts £500 000
Guest of Honour H.R.H. Princess Alexandra
Copy *Sunday Express* 7 May 1978

Wembley belongs to Brady

THE GOAL that ended a dream. Alan Sunderland lunges to stab home Arsenal's last-gasp winner. And United's hopes crash to the ground. Arthur Albiston and 'keeper Gary Bailey, both well beaten by Graham Rix's cross, can only watch as their side's fightback fizzles out.

YOUNG—delighted

SEXTON: IT'S SO CRUEL

DAVE SEXTON, United's manager, described it as "a cruel result."

Sexton went on: "It was a demanding game mentally and physically for us because it was uphill all the way.

"When we astonishingly got the two goals back we were thinking of the breather before extra time and lost concentration for a few vital seconds which ollowed Arsenal to snatch the winner.

"I though! we were the better side in the first half because we had more of the play."

DON HOWE, Arsenal coach: "It was a great game for supporters, but terrible for managers and coaches.

"I thought we'd thrown it away. Coming back as they did, United would have had the initiative in extra time."

LIAM BRADY, Arsenal midfield star: "When they pulled level, I was dreading extra time because I was knackered and our substitute was already on.

"I wasn't happy at the way we were sitting back on our lead. We deserved to get caught and lose it the way we were playing.

"You have to feel sorry for Manchester United."

TERRY NEILL, Arsenal manager: "What a finish! I just sat on the bench saying nothing when they pulled back.

"I hope this win is just the start for Arsenal."

WILLIE YOUNG, Arsenal's defender who had a nightmare final last y e a r, admitted: "I thought we had blown it. I was already looking forward to going up the steps for the Cup when their goals started going in.

"We have been accused of lacking character all season, but proved today that we have got it."

JIMMY GREENHOFF, United striker: "We've got to admire Arsenal for the way they beat us after we hit them with our recovery."

Arsenal's army taste victory

by ALAN HOBY

WHO OF the millions who watched will ever forget the scenes of hysteria and emotion which signalled the end of this fabulous head-on Final. As it all ended Arsenal manager Terry Neill and coach Don Howe embraced like long-lost brothers. On the field, substitue Steve Walford wiped away tears of pure joy with the hem of his sweat-streaked yellow shirt.

And as the losers sad manager Dave Sexton shook hands with the winners' "top brass", from every corner of the stadium the Arsenal clans celebrated in a vast explosion of sound.

Earlier, the fans had poured up Olympic Way—two rival, raucous, banner-waving, beer-swilling armies.

Before them as they chanted, jeered, and swore cheerfully at each other rolled a tinny, clattering cacophony of empty beer cans kicked hither and thither by a thousand careless feet.

THE SPIVS

Arsenal and Manchester United were on the last stage on the long march to Wembley. Flitting like shabby shadows amid that human mass were the ticket spivs. Since early morning they had the Cup Final killing of their tawdry lives.

A single seat had fetched a staggering £200 to £250. Even £2·50 standing tickets had changed hands for £40.

Year after year the bartering and the profiteering at what should be the country's finest

show window game goes on. It is a never-ending Wembley ritual. But the only people who benefit—apart from the touts—are the players who sell these precious briefs to the sharks.

Inside the stadium as skipper Pat Rice and Liam Brady inspired the Gunners to their nail-biting win, a red and yellow phalanx of Arsenal banners waved triumphantly.

As shirt-sleeved Dave Sexton fidgeted more and more unhappily down on the trainer's bench, a huge gold standard on the far side of the arena ironically underlined his anguish.

Terry's all-gold" ran the jubilant message in tribute to Arsenal's Neill.

At United's end, the flaming scarlet flags proclaiming " Sexton's Bionic Reds" were slowly lowered in grudging surrender although they waved ecstatically during those few deceptive moments when United dramatically drew level.

As the valiant Rice held the Cup aloft at the end, roar upon roar rose into the warm spring air The Highbury hordes were in full strident spate They were hailing with pride and gratitude an Arsenal team pledged to a man to avenge last year's Wembley defeat by Ipswich.

WHO DID SCORE?

by RAY BRADLEY

WHO SCORED Arsenal's first goal? This was the great talking point all over London last night.

Both Brian Talbot and Alan Sunderland a r e claiming the 12th minute goal that put the Gunners on the victory path.

Talbot, who won a Cup winner's medal with Ipswich last May—ironically against Arsenal—claimed after the game: "I thought I got a touch and so did Alan Sunderland.

"Both Alan and I went for David Price's cross and it is impossible to say exactly who got the final touch. But who cares." We won and there was no disputing Alan's winner. It was a beauty and finally killed United almost on the whistle."

UNCERTAIN

Arsenal manager Terry Neill was also uncertain who actually scored his side's first goal, and admitted : "We have not sorted out who will be credited with it, but Brian's claim was loudest and he was always in the thick of things."

From the Press box I thought Sunderland had scored and his name was the first to be flashed on the scoreboard. But I go along with Talbot, who deserved a special mention for his non-stop industry.

Added Talbot: "It was great

to pick up a winner's medal for the second year running. It was very emotional to win one with Ipswich last year, but this medal is just as precious to me."

Neill best summed up the mystery when he claimed : "The goal wasn't important —the final result was. This Final may not be remembered for flowing football, but it will live on in everyone's memory for its explosive finish."

'CRUEL'

United manager Dave Sexton described it all as "a cruel result. It was a demanding game mentally and physically for us because it was an uphill struggle all the way.

"After fighting back to cancel out Arsenal's two-goal lead, we were thinking of extra time and lost concentration. This allowed them to cash in and grab the winner."

Perhaps former England and United maestro Bobby Charlton best capsuled the ecstasy and the agony in those dramatic closing minutes.

Said a sad-faced Bobby : "I felt terrible for United. They had scored twice in the closing minutes and were then pipped right on the whistle. It shouldn't happen to a dog, but then Manchester United didn't have a bit of luck all day!"

● Man - of - the - match Liam Brady said : "I was dreading extra time. I was really tired."

Brady, Sunderland, Stapleton, Price (Walford), Rix.
MANCHESTER UNITED Bailey, Nicholl, Albiston, McIlroy, McQueen, Buchan, Coppell, J. Greenhoff, Jordan, Macari, Thomas. Sub: B. Greenhoff

Team Colours ARSENAL Yellow shirts, blue shorts; MANCHESTER UNITED Red shirts, white shorts

Official Referee R. Challis (Tonbridge)

Goal Scorers ARSENAL Talbot 12, Stapleton 43, Sunderland 89; MANCHESTER UNITED McQueen 86, McIlroy 88

Managers ARSENAL Terry Neill; MANCHESTER UNITED Dave Sexton

Attendance 100000

Gate Receipts £500000 .

Guest of Honour H.R.H. Prince of Wales

Copy News of the World 13 May 1979; Sunday Express 13 May 1979

Date 12 May 1979
Place Wembley
Score ARSENAL 3
MANCHESTER UNITED 2
Teams ARSENAL Jennings, Rice, Nelson, Talbot, O'Leary, Young,

THE SUNDAY EXPRESS May 13 1979

the Master Gunner

HAS THERE EVER BEEN A FINAL LIKE THIS !

ARSENAL (2) 3   MANCHESTER UTD (0) 2

Talbot (scored in 12 min 2 sec)   McQueen (86 min 20 sec)
Stapleton (43 min 28 sec)   McIlroy (88 min 15 sec)
Sunderland (89 min 10 sec)

Attendance : 100,000   Receipts : £500,000

SOCKS TUMBLING around his ankles, the sweat of effort darkening his shirt, Liam Brady stood in the centre of Wembley's vast stage and took his share of the applause at the end of a Cup Final that will be written into history because of its sensational climax.

Brady was the maestro of an afternoon that carried the thousands soaring into a world of Soccer make-believe.

He was behind all three Arsenal goals. A little chap with enormous heart. A leprechaun figure with a left foot that steered the ball around as though he had it completely bewitched.

But that is only half of the heart-stopping drama of the final minutes. Arsenal, were leading 2—0, were home and dry with just four minutes to go. It had not been a classic encounter, but the Arsenal

by JAMES MOSSOP

fans were singing in celebration as the scoreboard glittered with the names of Brian Talbot and Frank Stapleton.

Suddenly the amazing Manchester United, that team of fighting hearts, came plunging through with a final death-or-glory fling to score through Gordon McQueen and Sammy McIlroy. Extra time looked a certainty.

That belief lasted no more than a few fleeting seconds before Brady picked up his men for another attack and Alan Sunderland hurled himself forward to snatch the Cup for North London.

WE'VE WON . . . and skipper Rice clings to the Cup!

EMOTION

Has there ever been a Final like it? I doubt it! The emotion showed in every face as the team's went off on their laps of honour.

For Arsenal it was a mad-cap romp for United a proud, but painful walk. Jimmy Nicholl, their right back, was wearing Brady's yellow shirt—it will remind him for the rest of his life of the day the leprechaun lorded it.

Teams advance on Wembley with the conviction that the first 20 minutes are vital. This is when the break of the ball, the early touch, can bring a touch of confidence or a seizure of the nervous system and set the mood for the entire afternoon.

The perfect dream is a quick goal. Nothing lifts hearts and mind like the sight of the ball in the net. Supporters are dancing. The skills can flow. The road to victory lies ahead.

Arsenal shared that special feeling after only 12 minutes and two seconds. They had been testing each other. Some fierce tackling showed in the determination of both camps.

Then, suddenly, Brady pranced into centre stage and the Arsenal audience rose in the expectation of a master stroke. They were not disappointed.

With that aggressive wee terrier Lou Macari desperately trying to hold him back, Brady ran wide, refused to submit, and slipped the ball to his fellow Irishman, Frank Singleton.

A brilliant move was taking shape and developed delightfully as Stapleton pushed the ball through to David Price. The roar rose to a deafening howl of celebration as two Arsenal players hurtled into the area together and fired the Gunners in front.

But who scored? That was the great Wembley whodunit last night. Talbot and Sunderland both claimed to have got a touch. TV could not clear up the mystery and the official statisticians, after listening to all sides, finally put it down to Talbot.

He was on his way to history anyway. Never before has a

LINE-UP

ARSENAL.—Pat Jennings ; Pat Rice, David O'Leary, Willie Young, Sammy Nelson, David Price, Brian Talbot, Liam Brady, Alan Sunderland, Frank Stapleton, Graham Rix. Sub : Steve Walford.

MANCHESTER UNITED. — Gary Bailey ; Jimmy Nicholl, Gordon McQueen, Martin Buchan, Arthur Albiston, Sammy McIlroy, Lou Macari, Micky Thomas, Steve Coppell. Jimmy Greenhoff, Joe Jordan. Sub : Brian Greenhoff.

Referee. — Ron Challis (Tonbridge).

man a winners' medal with different teams in successive Finals Talbot, No. 4 with Ipswich last May, joined Arsenal for £450,000 in January.

United's response was energetic. They had chances. Micky Thomas, a defiant worker with the lung capacity of a long distance runner, turned the ball into Pat Jennings' arms. So did Macari.

Joe Jordan was winning a bruising battle with Willie Young and causing all kinds of concern among the Arsenal defenders. Their captain, Pat Rice, was booked for a blatant obstruction when McIlroy was bursting through like a man determined to create some kind of terrorism in the Arsenal half.

But United could not win the battle to subdue Brady. He has an incredible knack of appearing on the scene just when you think he is starting to fade.

His next intrusion brought him into the United white awards. In a run that took him left Arthur Albiston and Martin Buchan wavering in his slipstream. His right-footed centre was perfection and 20-year-old 'keeper Gary Bailey could get nowhere near the header that Stapleton battered down into goal.

United manager Dave Sexton, with his lucky blue suit, lucky red tie and St. Christopher medal that have been worn during United's Cup run, now needed more than the favours of talismen if his Reds were to rediscover their form.

GROAN

The omens were perverse. The United thousands, who had long lowered their flags and voices, could only muster a moan of groan as once hoisted the ball out of his own goalmouth when Thomas curled it away from Jennings.

They never ceased to slave at the monumental task of hauling themselves out of the long dark tunnel that had become the prison of all their dreams.

Big Gordon McQueen was the man who inspired their "No surrender" approach. There were some tired, aching muscles around him. The unusually high temperature sapped away at stamina. Fatigue showed for United were having to chase those swift yellow shadows as Arsenal used the flanks.

But United rallied. They charged up for a defiant surge that brought their supporters to life again. Jennings arched backwards to flick the ball over his bar from Macari and then stood firm to hold a stinger by Steve Coppell.

Down on the bench Sexton and his assistant Tommy Cavanagh shuffled and squirmed and looked at their watches. Surely the minutes seemed to be sprinting by.

Arsenal's fans were already celebrating. So it appeared, were the men on their bench because with five minutes to go, they called off David Price and sent on Steve Walford.

The next four minutes were sheer bedlam. An explosion of goals and incident that left every man in the ground utterly drained.

First there was McIlroy raking out a long, left leg to drive the ball past Jennings and within seconds the hope that goal engendered turned to unharnessed ecstasy.

MERRY

For there was McIlroy of the twinkling feet, dancing a merry path into the penalty area and then stroking the ball past the 'keeper.

Brady had no intention of going to a Thursday replay on the same pitch. He came looping out of midfield with the ball on his left foot. He pushed it forward and wide giving Graham Rix just enough time to get in a centre and Sunderland came thundering in to claim the winner.

The players, the fans and the commentators were not the only ones bowled over by the majesty of this great climax.

For as the people went slowly home I saw one of the 3,000 policemen on duty pick up a divot of the famous turf, and place it in his helmet, which he promptly placed back on his head.

The winning goal. Alan Sunderland (right) scores in the last minute

There's only one Liam Brady

Man-of-the-match Brady

Brooking with a nod and a wink

WEST HAM failed to make the third all-London FA Cup Final the thrilling show-piece they had intended, but they rewrote the script successfully enough to win it with something to spare and to make nonsense of the walk-on part they had been given by many.

To a very large extent the match was settled as early as the 13th minute when Trevor Brooking scored the goal which eventually gained West Ham the trophy and which rewarded the tall, elegant midfield player for a colossal personal contribution to the event.

From that moment on, Arsenal were compelled to play in a style totally alien to them. Instead of absorbing their opponents' pressure and catching them cold on the break, the North Londoners had to try to force the pace of the game in heat which did not encourage unremitting physical effort.

The scoreline shows how un-successful Arsenal were at making the adjustment from the cat-and-mouse tactics which had carried them past Juventus and Liverpool into the finals of two major competitions this season.

For all the urgent prompting of Brady, who broke loose in the second-half from the tenacious marking of Allen, the youngest player ever to appear in a Cup Final, Arsenal rarely looked capable of dismantling a reso-lute, well-organised and composed Wes Ham defence.

Bonds and Martin were particu-lary impressive at its heart. Only occasionally was Stapleton allowed to look the most im-proved striker in the business, while Sunderland, scorer of the winning goal against Manchester United here last year, was reduced to total untypical anony-mity.

Indeed, the enormous advant-age Arsenal enjoyed of having appeared at Wembley for three years running counted for little when set against West Ham's bristling determination to com-pensate themselves, and their supporters, for the failure to gain promotion from the Second Divi-sion.

COLIN MALAM reports from Wembley

Arsenal (0) 0   West Ham (1) 1
Brooking

Att: 100,000   Receipts: £700,000

If there was a 50-50 ball to be won it was usually West Ham who did the winning. That competitive-ness, which John Lyall, their young manager, has worked hard to instil, provided a solid founda-tion for the finesse of Brooking, Pearson and Devonshire and for the telling experience of the first two.

Brooking, watched by the Argentine players against whom he will probably pit his wiles here for England on Tuesday, was absolutely outstanding. The master craftsman one minute, he was tackling back like an old-fashioned wing half the next.

One tackle Brooking made in the second-half not only halted one of Brady's forceful, sinuous runs into the West Ham defence but was a classic example of how to win the ball from the side without fouling the man in possession.

For the most part the game resolved itself into a mildly in-teresting struggle between Arsenal's power and West Ham's capacity to resist opponents hell-bent- on becoming the first team since Spurs in 1961 and 1962, to win the Cup twice in succession.

Towards the end, however, it was West Ham who were looking the stronger and more dangerous team. Three minutes before the final whistle sent the claret and blue end of Wembley, and the whole of the East End of London into ecstasy, Young deliberately tripped Allen as the youngster collected a pass from Brooking and burst into the clear.

The speed with which Young emerged as a dominant figure in the Arsenal defence was a measure of how quickly West Ham settled down. Even during the usual nervous opening period they emerged as the more imaginative and resourceful team.

That impression was confirmed when Devonshire suddenly accel-erated past Talbot and Rice down the left as though the Arsenal men had lead in their boots. Devonshire's centre from the by-line was so finely judged that Jennings could only touch it on to where Cross and Pearson were waiting hungrily at the far post.

Cross had the first shot, but the ball was blocked and it seemed the chance had been wasted until Pearson had a go at the rebound. This time Brook-ing was stooping to deflect the ball into the net with his head from close range as the shot flew across the face of the Arsenal goal.

Before West Ham scored Jen-nings had had to get down quickly to stop a shot from the endlessly industrious Pike when Pearson, whose regular with-drawal into midfield often con-fused Arsenal tactically out-stripped everyone on the left and pulled the ball back invitingly.

Though Rix and Talbot forced diving saves from Parkes, and Brady shot into the side netting, Arsenal were no more successful in the second-half than they had been in the first at prising loose West Ham's iron grip.

Their football lacked verve and imagination to such an extent that one is bound to wonder not only how much of their form and energy they left in that marathon semi-final with Liverpool, but whether they can revitalise them-selves in time for Wednesday's European Cup Winners' Cup final against Valencia in Brussels.

ARSENAL: Jennings; Rice, Devine (Nelson, 61), Talbot, O'Leary, Young, Brady, Sunderland, Staple-ton, Price, Rix.
WEST HAM: Parkes; Stewart, Lampard, Bonds, Martin, Devon-shire, Allen, Pearson, Cross, Brook-ing, Pike.
Referee: G. Courtney (Spenny-moor).

Geoff Pike (left)

Knees-up on terraces

IF EVER there was an excuse for a jolly knees-up, this was it. Arsenal, the favourites, beaten, West Ham, the Second Division underdogs, victorious.

Two old dears bedecked in claret and blue duly obliged as they left the singing West Ham terraces. And manager John Lyall could not resist a beaming smile, either, down in the privacy of the dressing rooms.

West Ham's victory had pro-vided the club with "the best day in their history" he said. He praised Trevor Brooking, usually a reluctant nodder of the ball, but yesterday's hero with his goal, and young Paul Allen, at 17, the youngest ever player to appear in a Wembley final.

Story: JOHN MOYNIHAN

Pictures: PHIL SHELDON

"Allen," said his manager, "went from strength to strength. He filled in all sorts of holes and areas. He's not only a tackler, he is an interceptor. He's typical of the spirit of the club at the moment."

Meanwhile, Arsenal's manager, Terry Neill, was gracious in defeat. Now his main concern is to raise his beaten side (they looked so tired under the hot sun at the end) for Wednesday's European Cup Winners' Cup Final against Valencia, with Kempes, Bonhof and company.

"There are no excuses," Neill reflected over a beer in a paper cup. "West Ham did well and congratulations to them.

"We have another game on Wednesday and, personally, I'm very much looking forward to it. O'Leary has a right calf prob-lem. It has tightened up but he should be fit.

"I thought we were much better than we were two years ago against Ipswich."

"West Ham were the better side early on and we were obvi-ously unsettled by the early goal. Later, we were not opening anything up or doing any damage."

Lyall believes defeat will not affect Arsenal's performance in Brussels. "They've got the quali-ties of a great side. I think they should be spurred on after this."

Ironically, West Ham may be our sole representatives in the European Cup Winners Cup next season — if Arsenal lose to Valencia.

Lyall is very proud that the club has made it into Europe. "Once you're in Europe you know you are on the right road to success. To beat the Arsenal you've got to do it with collective performances.

"One of our positive moves was putting Allen on Brady. It was vital to score the first goal — and we got the break."

en parade with the Cup

Goal! Trevor Brooking (on floor) heads a hard cross in and (below) turns to celebrate

Date 10 May 1980
Place Wembley
Score WEST HAM UNITED 1 ARSENAL 0
Teams WEST HAM UNITED Parkes, Stewart, Lampard, Bonds, Martin, Devonshire, Pike, Brooking, Cross, Pearson, Allen. Sub: Brush. ARSENAL Jennings, Rice, Devine (Nelson), Talbot, O'Leary, Young, Price, Rix, Brady, Stapleton, Sunderland
Team Colours WEST HAM UNITED All white; ARSENAL Yellow shirts, blue shorts
Official Referee George Courtney (Spennymoor, Co. Durham)
Goal Scorer Brooking 14
Managers WEST HAM UNITED John Lyall; ARSENAL Terry Neill
Attendance 100000
Gate Receipts £729000
Guests of Honour H.R.H. Duke and Duchess of Kent
Copy *The Sunday Telegraph* 11 May 1980; *Sunday Express* 11 May 1980

Cockneys make it a Friendly Final

by ALAN HOBY

WEMBLEY on Cup Final Day is like a giant drum. The noise booms and reverberates round the stands and terraces in deafening waves.

It reaches its crescendo when the two teams, mouths dry, nerves jumping, emerge from the cool shadows of the tunnel into the blinding sunlight. Then the roar of the huge crowd greets and engulfs them.

SAME SCENE

This is the route trodden by past giants like Stanley Matthews, Tom Finney, Bobby Charlton, Jimmy Greaves, Bobby Moore and Denis Law.

The Soccer greats have all played in the year's most glamorous games in front of waving multi-coloured banners and swaying, screaming thousands. It was the same scene yesterday for West Ham and Arsenal and particularly for the Cup Final's youngest player, 17-year-old Paul Allen.

The emotions and butterflies bubbled and swarmed in the players' stomachs: but young Allen came through magnificently.

It was the greatest day of the season, too, for this raucous enthusiastic all-London crowd. There was a particularly special cockles-and-whelks flavour, especially at the West Ham end. The Cockney tumult grew even louder when that elegant England hero, Trevor Brooking fittingly headed the Hammers ahead.

Instantly, the West Ham fans chanted "Salt of the earth . . . salt of the earth." But, despite a few taunts, there was no vindictiveness shown either by players or supporters as Arsenal stuttered and spluttered in their third successive Wembley appearance.

STUNNED

It was the Friendly Final with, ironically, the Second Division side shutting down the game just as these jaded sub-par Gunners generally do.

At the end, as the Highbury clans stood silent and stunned, it was the West Ham anthem "I'm For Ever Blowing Bubbles" which rang out ecstatically as the indomitable Billy Bonds led his Cup underdogs on the ritual lap of honour.

SUMMARY OF RESULTS

A quick reference to the Cup final
results 1872–1980

1872 Wanderers 1 Royal Engineers 0
1873 Wanderers 2 Oxford University 0
1874 Oxford University 2 Royal Engineers 0
1875 Royal Engineers 2 Old Etonians 0
(after 1–1 draw)
1876 Wanderers 3 Old Etonians 0
(after 1–1 draw)
1877 Wanderers 2 Oxford University 1
(after extra time)
1878 Wanderers 3 Royal Engineers 1
1879 Old Etonians 1 Clapham Rovers 0
1880 Clapham Rovers 1 Oxford University 0
1881 Old Carthusians 3 Old Etonians 0
1882 Old Etonians 1 Blackburn Rovers 0
1883 Blackburn Olympic 2 Old Etonians 1
(after extra time)
1884 Blackburn Rovers 2 Queen's Park 1
1885 Blackburn Rovers 2 Queen's Park 0
1886 Blackburn Rovers 2 West Bromwich Albion 0
(after 0–0 draw)
1887 Aston Villa 2 West Bromwich Albion 0
1888 West Bromwich Albion 2 Preston North End 1
1889 Preston North End 3 Wolverhampton Wanderers 0
1890 Blackburn Rovers 6 Sheffield Wednesday 1
1891 Blackburn Rovers 3 Notts County 1
1892 West Bromwich Albion 3 Aston Villa 0
1893 Wolverhampton Wanderers 1 Everton 0
1894 Notts County 4 Bolton Wanderers 1
1895 Aston Villa 1 West Bromwich Albion 0
1896 Sheffield Wednesday 2 Wolverhampton Wanderers 1
1897 Aston Villa 3 Everton 2
1898 Nottingham Forest 3 Derby County 1
1899 Sheffield United 4 Derby County 1
1900 Bury 4 Southampton 0
1901 Tottenham Hotspur 3 Sheffield United 1
(after 2–2 draw)
1902 Sheffield United 2 Southampton 1
(after 1–1 draw)
1903 Bury 6 Derby County 0
1904 Manchester City 1 Bolton Wanderers 0
1905 Aston Villa 2 Newcastle United 0
1906 Everton 1 Newcastle United 0
1907 Sheffield Wednesday 2 Everton 1
1908 Wolverhampton Wanderers 3 Newcastle United 1
1909 Manchester United 1 Bristol City 0
1910 Newcastle United 2 Barnsley 0
(after 1–1 draw)
1911 Bradford City 1 Newcastle United 0
(after 0–0 draw)
1912 Barnsley 1 West Bromwich Albion 0
(after extra time, after 0–0 draw)
1913 Aston Villa 1 Sunderland 0
1914 Burnley 1 Liverpool 0
1915 Sheffield United 3 Chelsea 0
1920 Aston Villa 1 Huddersfield Town 0
(after extra time)
1921 Tottenham Hotspur 1 Wolverhampton Wanderers 0

1922 Huddersfield Town 1 Preston North End 0
1923 Bolton Wanderers 2 West Ham United 0
1924 Newcastle United 2 Aston Villa 0
1925 Sheffield United 1 Cardiff City 0
1926 Bolton Wanderers 1 Manchester City 0
1927 Cardiff City 1 Arsenal 0
1928 Blackburn Rovers 3 Huddersfield Town 1
1929 Bolton Wanderers 2 Portsmouth 0
1930 Arsenal 2 Huddersfield Town 0
1931 West Bromwich Albion 2 Birmingham 1
1932 Newcastle United 2 Arsenal 1
1933 Everton 3 Manchester City 0
1934 Manchester City 2 Portsmouth 1
1935 Sheffield Wednesday 4 West Bromwich Albion 2
1936 Arsenal 1 Sheffield United 0
1937 Sunderland 3 Preston North End 1
1938 Preston North End 1 Huddersfield Town 0
(after extra time)
1939 Portsmouth 4 Wolverhampton Wanderers 1
1946 Derby County 4 Charlton Athletic 1
(after extra time)
1947 Charlton Athletic 1 Burnley 0
(after extra time)
1948 Manchester United 4 Blackpool 2
1949 Wolverhampton Wanderers 3 Leicester City 1
1950 Arsenal 2 Liverpool 0
1951 Newcastle United 2 Blackpool 0
1952 Newcastle United 1 Arsenal 0
1953 Blackpool 4 Bolton Wanderers 3
1954 West Bromwich Albion 3 Preston North End 2
1955 Newcastle United 3 Manchester City 1
1956 Manchester City 3 Birmingham City 1
1957 Aston Villa 2 Manchester United 1
1958 Bolton Wanderers 2 Manchester United 0
1959 Nottingham Forest 2 Luton Town 1
1960 Wolverhampton Wanderers 3 Blackburn Rovers 0
1961 Tottenham Hotspur 2 Leicester City 0
1962 Tottenham Hotspur 3 Burnley 1
1963 Manchester United 3 Leicester City 1
1964 West Ham United 3 Preston North End 2
1965 Liverpool 2 Leeds United 1
(after extra time)
1966 Everton 3 Sheffield Wednesday 2
1967 Tottenham Hotspur 2 Chelsea 1
1968 West Bromwich Albion 1 Everton 0
(after extra time)
1969 Manchester City 1 Leicester City 0
1970 Chelsea 2 Leeds United 1
(after 2–2 draw, both games extra time)
1971 Arsenal 2 Liverpool 1
(after extra time)
1972 Leeds United 1 Arsenal 0
1973 Sunderland 1 Leeds United 0
1974 Liverpool 3 Newcastle United 0
1975 West Ham United 2 Fulham 0
1976 Southampton 1 Manchester United 0
1977 Manchester United 2 Liverpool 1
1978 Ipswich 1 Arsenal 0
1979 Arsenal 3 Manchester United 2
1980 West Ham United 1 Arsenal 0